D1605209

REFERENCE ENCYCLOPEDIA

OF THE
AMERICAN INDIAN
4TH EDITION

BARRY T. KLEIN

Published by:
Todd Publications
P.O. Box 92
Lenox Hill Station
New York, New York 10021

REFERENCE ENCYCLOPEDIA OF THE AMERICAN INDIAN

Fourth Edition, Volume II

Copyright © 1986

TODD PUBLICATIONS

Library of Congress Catalog Card Number 86-050046

Contents

Introduction

The following is an alphabetically arranged listing of American Indians prominent in Indian affairs, business, the arts and professions, as well as non-Indians active in Indian affairs, history, art, anthropology, archaeology, and the many fields to which the subject of the American Indian is related. Included are the biographical sketches of individuals named in Volume I—authors of books listed in the *Bibliography,* curators listed under *Museums,* tribal chiefs listed under *Tribal Councils,* etc. In this issue, for the first time, we have added a *Geographical Index.* This will allow the reader to see, at a glance, all listees in a particular state or city.

Format and style: The reader will note that these biographical sketches concentrate primarily on professional achievement; therefore, the usual personal data—name of spouse, date of marriage, and names of children, etc.—have not been included. The greater bulk of information has been culled from research questionnaires completed by the individuals themselves; however, in the case of a hastily written or otherwise incomplete questionnaire, I have consulted other reliable published sources. Whenever possible, direct quotations have been employed to give the reader greater insight into the life and work of each biographee than mere facts can supply. The length of each listing reflects the quantity of material received; no judgement is intended. Home and/or business addresses have been included when available.

The names and addresses of individuals who merit inclusion in future editions should be forwarded to The Editors, *Reference Encyclopedia of the American Indian,* Todd Publications, P.O. Box 92, Lenox Hill Station, New York, N.Y. 10021.

Barry T. Klein
Editor

REFERENCE ENCYCLOPEDIA OF THE AMERICAN INDIAN

AASBY, LEROY H. 1926-
(teacher, principal)

Born March 28, 1926, Hyde County, S.D.
Education: Dakota State College, B.S.,
1955; University of North Dakota, University of South Dakota, Augustana College,
1958-1972. *Principal occupation:* Teacher,
principal. *Affiliations:* Teacher, South
Dakota rural schools, 1947-1951; teacher
and principal, B.I.A., Bridger Day School,
Howes, S.D., 1955-. *Military service:* U.S.
Army, 1951-1953 (several decorations).
Community activities: TriCommunity
Development Association (advisor, 1966-;
Black Hills Girl Scout Council and Board,
1968-1975; president, 1972-1975); Boy Scout
Committeeman, 1971-; Operation Friendship, 1972. *Memberships:* Phi Delta Kappa.
Awards, honors: Outstanding Teacher
Award, 1972; Service Award, Girl Scouts.
Interests: Mr. Aasby is considered by others
to be an expert in Indian culture (Lakota).

ABERLE, DAVID FRIEND 1918-
(anthropologist, educator)

Born November 23, 1918, St. Paul, Minn.
Education: Harvard University, B.A., 1940;
University of New Mexico, 1938-1940;
Columbia University, Ph.D., 1950. *Principal occupation:* Professor of anthropology.
Affiliations: Instructor, Harvard University,
1947-1950; visiting associate professor,
Johns Hopkins University, 1950-1952; associate professor and professor, University of
Michigan, 1952-1960; visiting professor and
honorable research associate, Manchester
University, 1960-1961; professor, Brandeis
University, 1961-1963; professor of anthropology, University of Oregon, 1963-. *Military service:* U.S. Army, 1942-1946 (Army
Commendation Ribbon). *Community activities:* Faculty-Student Committee to Stop
the War in Vietnam, University of Oregon
(chairman, 1965). *Memberships:* American
Anthropological Association (Fellow);
American Sociological Association; Royal
Anthropological Institute of Great Britain
and Ireland; American Ethnological
Society; Society of Applied Anthropology.
Awards, honors: Sohier Prize for B.A. thesis, Center for Advanced Study in the
Behavioral Sciences, 1955-1956. *Interests:*
Navaho Indians; Native American Church

and other religious movements; Mongol culture. *Published works: Psychological Analysis of a Hopi Life-History* (Comp. Psych.
Monog. Series, 1951); *Kinship System of the
Kalmuk Mongols* (University of New Mexico Publications in Anthropology, 1953);
*Navaho and Ute Peyotism: A Chronological
and Distributional Study,* with Omer C. Stewart (University of Colorado Series in
Anthropology, 1957); *The Peyote Religion
Among the Navaho* (Aldine Press, 1966).

ABEYTA, NARCISO *(Ha-Sodeh)*
(Navajo) 1918-
(interpreter)

Born December 18, 1918, Canyoncito, N.M.
Education: Santa Fe Indian School, 1939;
University of New Mexico, B.A. (Fine Arts,
Economics). *Principal occupation:* Interviewer, interpreter, New Mexico State
Employment Commission, 1952-. *Military
service:* U.S. Army, 1941-1945. *Community
activities:* American Legion. *Memberships:*
International Association of Personnel in
Employment Security, 1953-1965. *Awards,
honors:* Second Prize, Advertising Poster,
San Francisco Exposition, 1939. *Published
works:* (as illustrator): *Aychee, Son of the
Desert* (Hoffman Birney Penn Publishing
Co., 1935).

ABRAMS, GEORGE H.J. (Seneca) 1939-
(museum director)

Born May 4, 1939, Allegany Indian Reservation, Salamanca, N.Y. *Education:* State
University of New York, Buffalo, B.A.,
1965, M.A., 1967; University of Arizona,
Ph.D. program, 1968-1971. *Principal occupation:* Museum director. *Home address:*
Salamanca, N.Y. 14779. *Affiliations:* Chairman, North American Indian Museums
Association, Salamanca, N.Y., 1978-. *Other
professional posts:* Trustee, Museum of the
American Indian-Heye Foundation, New
York, New York, 1977-; member, advisory
board, Center for the History of the American Indian, The Newberry Library, Chicago, 1980-; member, Commission on
Museums for a New Century, American
Association of Museums, Washington,
D.C., 1981-; member, National Advisory
and Coordinating Council on Bilingual

Education, Washington, D.C., 1984-. *Community activities:* Seneca Nation Library, N.Y. (member, board of trustees, 1978-); Mohawk-Caughnawaga Museum, Fonda, N.Y. (member, board of advisors, 1980-); Gannagaro Archaeological Site, New York State Division of Historic Preservation, Parks and Recreation (member, advisory group.) *Membership:* American Association of University Professors. *Awards, honors:* John Hay Whitney Fellow, 1968-1969; American Indian Graduate Scholarship Program Grant, School of Law, University of New Mexico, 1971. *Interests:* Contemporary American Indian anthropology; American Indian education; applied anthropology; ethnohistory, museology, Iroquois Indians. *Published works:* "The Cornplanter Cemetary" (*Pennsylvania Archaeologist,* 1965); "Moving of the Fire: A Case of Iroquois Ritual Innovation" (*Iroquois Culture, History and Prehistory,* 1967); "Red Jacket" (*The World Book Encyclopedia,* 1976); *The Seneca People* (Indian Tribal Series, Phoenix, 1976).

ACKERMAN, LILLIAN A. 1928-
(anthropologist)

Born April 14, 1928, Detroit, Mich. *Education:* University of Michigan, B.A., 1950, M.A., 1951; Washington State University, Ph.D., 1982. *Principal occupation:* Anthropologist. *Home address:* Route 2, Box 559, Pullman, Wash. 99163. *Affiliations:* Researcher (courtesy faculty), Washington State University, Pullman, Wash. *Other professional posts:* Ethnographic consultant. *Community activities:* Development Services Board (for developing and overseeing programs for the mentally retarded; served as chairperson several times); American Civil Liberties Union (board member). *Memberships:* American Anthropological Association, 1950-; American Ethnological Society, 1980-; Sigma Xi, 1982-. *Awards, honors:* Woodrow Wilson Fellowship; American Association of University Women - Dissertation Fellowship. *Interests:* "Primary areas of research interests are in the Indians of the Plateau Culture Area, and the Yupik Eskimos of Alaska. I studied sexual equality on the Colville Indian Reservation for six months and did a short study of Nez

Perce socialization of children. I have made several short visits to the Colville Reservation since 1982. Spent three seasons doing research in Alaska, and made several trips there for the purpose of contract research." *Published works:* "Sexual Equality in the Plateau Culture Area" (Ph.D. dissertation, Washington State University, 1982); several shorter articles.

ACKERMAN, ROBERT E. 1928-
(professor of anthropology)

Born May 21, 1928, Grand Rapids, Mich. *Education:* University of Michigan, A.B., 1950, M.A., 1951; University of Pennsylvania, Ph.D., 1961. *Principal occupation:* Professor of anthropology. *Home address:* Route 2, Box 559, Pullman, Wash. 99163. *Affiliations:* Instructor to professor in anthropology, Washington State University, Pullman, Wash., 1961-. *Military service:* Airman first class, U.S. Air Force, 1952-1956. *Memberships:* American Anthropological Association (Fellow), 1951-; Society for American Archaeology, 1951-; American Association for the Advancement of Science (Fellow), 1960-; Arctic Institute of North America (Fellow, 1969; American University of University Professors, 1962-; Sigma Xi, 1968-. *Awards, honors:* Research grants from the Arctic Institute of North America for archaeological studies in southwest and southeast Alaska, 1962; National Science Foundation, 1966, 1967, 1971. Fellowships in the American Anthropological Association, the American Association for the Advancement of Science, and the Arctic Institute of North America, for contributions to the discipline of anthropology and arctic research. *Interests:* Archaeological research and surveys throughout Alaska and Canada. *Biographical sources:* Who's Who in the West; American Men of Science; International Scholars Directory; Contemporary Authors. *Published works:* Various articles and reports.

ADAMS, MARGARET B. (Navajo) 1936-
(anthropologist-museologist, art historian)

Born April 29, 1936, Toronto, Ontario, Can.

Education: Monterey Peninsula College, A.A., 1969; San Jose State University, B.A. (Anthropology and Art History), 1971; University of Utah, M.A. (Anthropology), 1973. *Principal occupation:* Anthropologist, museologist, art historian. *Home address:* 363 Hillcrest Ave., Pacific Grove, Calif. 93950. *Affiliations:* Chief of Museum Branch, Fort Ord Military Complex; and, Head Curator of Fort Ord and Presidio of Monterey Museums, 1974-. *Other professional posts:* Panel member (Indians in Science) for American Association for the Advancement of Science, 1972-; reviewer, "Project Media" of American Indian Education Association. *Community activities:* American Indian Information Center of Monterey Peninsula (volunteer executive director); member of Monterey Speaker's Bureau. *Memberships:* National Indian Education Association; California Indian Education Association; American Anthropological Association; American Association of Museums; Monterey History & Art Association. *Interests:* "Higher education for Native Americans, particularly in the sciences; media presentations concerning Native Americans; review of media on Native Americans and advertising of bad publications; observations and reporting of improper excavation of Native American ceremonial and burial sites; preservation of Native American ceremonial, burial, and historical sites." *Biographical sources:* Who's Who in America; World's Who Who of Women; The Science Teacher (Journal); Women in the Social Sciences. *Published works: Indian Tribes of North America and a Brief Chronology of Ancient Pueblo Indian and Old World Events* (Monterey Museum of Art, 1975); *History of Navajo and Apache Painting* (Indian America, Tulsa, 1976); *Historic Old Monterey* (DeAnza College History Center, 1977); *Silver & Sheen—Southwestern Indian Jewelry* (Indian America, Tulsa, 1977).

ADAMS, RICHARD EDWARD WOOD (Osage) 1931-
(archaeologist)

Born July 17, 1931, Kansas City, Mo. *Education:* University of New Mexico, B.A., 1953; Harvard University, M.A., 1960, Ph.D., 1963. *Principal occupation:* Archaeologist. *Home address:* 208 Village Circle, San Antonio, Texas 78232. *Affiliations:* Professor of anthropology, University of Minnesota, 1963-1972; dean of humanities and social sciences, University of Texas, San Antonio, 1972-. *Other professional posts:* Professor of anthropology, U.T.S.A., Guerrero Project, Mexico. *Military service:* U.S. Marine Corps, 1954-1957. *Memberships:* American Anthropological Association; Society for American Archaeology; Seminario de Cultura Maya; Sociedad Mexicana de Antropologia; American Association for the Advancement of Science (Fellow); Royal Anthropological Society of Great Britain and Ireland (Fellow). *Interests:* Middle American anthropology, especially prehistory; world archaeology. *Travels, expeditions:* Archaeologist, Tikal Project, Guatemala, 1958; archaeologist, Altar de Sacrificios Project, Guatemala, 1961-1963; project director, Cotzal Project, Guatemala, 1965-1966; field director, National Geographic Society, Becan Project, 1970; director, Rio Bee Project, 1973. *Published works: The Ceramics of Altar de Sacrificios* (Peabody Museum, Harvard University, 1971); *Prehistoric Mesoamerica* (Little, Brown & Co., 1977); editor, *The Origins of Maya Civilization* (University of New Mexico Press, 1977); various papers.

ADAMS, VIVIAN M. (Yakima, Puyallup, Suquamish, Quinault) 1943-
(museum curator)

Born March 21, 1943, Toppenish, Wash. *Education:* Institute of American Indian Art, Santa Fe, N.M., AFA (Museology), 1981. Principal occupation: Museum curator. *Affiliation:* Yakima Nation Cultural Center, P.O. Box 151, Toppenish, Wash. 98948. *Community activities:* Yakima Agency Employees Club (secretary-treasurer); IAIA Student Senate Representative; Yakima Women's Investor's Club. *Memberships:* Washington State Folklife Council; American Association of State & Local History; Toppenish Chamber of Commerce; Yakima Chamber of Commerce; Washington Museum Association; Yakima Valley Visitors and Convention Bureau; National Trust for Historic Preservation; Native American Task Force, Washington State Centennial; Washington State Native American Task Force, Native American Consortium; Washington State Centennial Heritage Subcommittee of Lasting Legacy. *Awards, honors:* Outstanding Artistic and Academic Achievement, 1980-1981; Institute of American Indian Art President's Award; Who's Who Among Students, American Junior Colleges, 1981; Scholastic Achievement Award, Yakima Nation Education, 1982. *Interests:* "My main interest is two-dimensional art (sketching, pen and ink). I love to work with Indian artifacts—those items which are hand made of natural materials. Plus, it is a joy to design ways to display these items which teach a lesson in an aesthetic manner. It is important to present our cultural history and traditions from our (Native American) point of view to promote a better understanding by other cultures--and to learn from them. Oral history and elders input into telling our ways is extremely important to accomplishing those goals of the museum. Therefore, museology is my second interest, my financial base to a sporadic art career! But being a curator allows me the time to work with objects of art—my main love. My third interest is pursuing conservation techniques: recognizing and maintaining basket weaving, textile weaving, restoration techniques, time allowing I hope to accomplish conservator's training." *Biographical sources:* Yakima Herald Republic news article; Girl Scouts of America; *Who's Who Among Students in American Junior Colleges.*

AGOGINO, GEORGE A. 1920-
(distinguished professor of
anthropology, museum director)

Born November 18, 1920, West Palm Beach, Fla. *Education:* University of New Mexico, B.A., 1949, M.A., 1951; Syracuse University, Ph.D., 1958; Harvard University, Wenner-Gren Foundation Post Doctoral Fellowship in Anthropology, 1961-1962. *Principal occupation:* Distinguished professor of anthropology, museum director. *Home address:* 1600 S. Main, Portales, N.M. 88130. *Affiliations:* Instructor in anthropology, Syracuse University, 1956-1958; museum director and assistant profes-

sor, University of South Dakota, 1958-1959; assistant professor of anthropology, University of Wyoming, 1959-1962; associate professor of anthropology, Baylor University, 1962-1963; professor of anthropology and museum director, Eastern New Mexico University, 1963-; director of Paleo-Indian Institute, 1968-. *Other professional posts:* Founding director, Blackwater Draw, Miles Museum and Anthropology Museum of Eastern New Mexico University, Potales, N.M. *Military service:* U.S. Army Signal Corps, 1943-1946. *Community activities:* Eastern New Mexico University, Local National Educational Association (president and vice-president, 1976-). *Memberships:* American Anthropological Association (Fellow); American Association for the Advancement of Science (Fellow); Royal Anthropological Institute of Great Britain and Ireland (Fellow); Institute Inter-American (Fellow); Current Anthropology (Associate); Explorers' Club (Fellow); Senato Academico (regent) Accademmia Romania de Science ed Arti. *Awards, honors:* Ph.D. Rome (Italy) Institute of Arts and Sciences; multiple grants from Wenner-Gren Foundation for Anthropology, American Philosophical Society, Sigma Xi; twice Eastern New Mexico University Outstanding Educator, 1972, 1974-1975; fourth distinguished professor in 70-year history of Eastern New Mexico University. *Interests:* Indian religion and culture; North America and Mexico Paleo Indian; Indian physical anthropology, pictoglyphs. "Have worked with and published on Navajo, Kickapoo, Seminole, Seri, Yaqui, Sioux, Mayo, Maya, Huastica and Otomi Indians." *Travels, expeditions:* Anthropological research in Canada, Mexico, New Guinea and Australia. *Biographical sources: Who's Who Among Authors and Journalists; Directory of International Biography; Who's Who in the Southwest; Who's Who in the West; Who's Who in American Education; Dirctory of International Biography; Contemporary Authors; Outstanding Educators in America; American Men of Science.* *Published works:* Over 225 articles and monographs, including: *Sandia Cave,* 1973; and *Ceremonialism of the Tepecano,* 1972 (Eastern New Mexico University Press).

AHSHAPANEK, DON COLESTO
(Delaware-Nanticoke) 1932-
(professor of biological sciences)

Born April 29, 1932, Milton, Del. *Education:* Indiana University, 1949-1950; University of Kansas, 1951; Haskell Institute (Business Certificate), 1953; Central (Okla.) State University, B.S. (Biology), 1956; University of Oklahoma, M.S. (Botany), 1960, Ph.D. (Botany), 1962. *Home address:* 1845 W. 28th Terrace, Lawrence, Kansas 66044. *Affiliations:* Clerk, stenographer, Bureau of Indian Affairs, Anadarko, Okla., 1953-1954, 1957, 1959; assistant professor of biology, 1962-1967, associate professor of biology, 1967-1971, Kansas State Teachers College, Emporia, Kansas; instructor of biological sciences, 1971-1973, chairman, Native American Culture Division, 1973-1976, instructor of biological sciences and program director—Haskell Minority Biomedical Sciences Program (NIH), Haskell Indian Junior College, Lawrence, Kan. *Other professional posts:* Taught biology in the Indian Health Careers Program at Mackinaw City, Mich. (summers, 1975-1977); taught courses, "The Native American in Contemporary Society," for the Master of Liberal Arts Program, Baker University, Bladwin, Kan. (summer, 1975). *Memberships:* National Indian Education Association; National Congress of American Indians; The Ecological Society of America; Southwestern Association of Naturalists; Kansas Academy of Sciences.

AGUILAR, ALFRED *(Sa wa pin)*
(San Ildefonso Pueblo) 1933-
(artist, teacher)

Born July 1, 1933, San Ildefonso Pueblo, N.M. *Education:* Santa Fe Indian School; Pojoaque High School; University, Albuquerque, N.M. *Principal occupation:* Artist, teacher (Chapter I, 1967-). *Home address:* Route 5, Box 318C, Santa Fe, N.M. 87501. *Military service:* U.S. Air Force, 1952-1956 (Good Service Award). *Community activities:* Pueblo official council member. *Memberships:* Eight Northern Pueblo Art Council; The Indian Pueblo Cultural Center. *Awards, honors:* For painting, pottery, and sculptures from the New Mexico State Fair, Inter-Tribal Ceremonial, Jemez Pueblo, Heard Museum, and New Mexico Fine Arts Museum. *Interests:* Education, art-travel expeditions. Mr. Aguilar "specializes in black and red pottery, and is well known by many people around the world with his nativity set and story teller. He sculptures black on black buffalos, and animal and dancing figures on pottery. He has gained versatility in water color, and is adept in depicting Indian dances and in preserving ancient design and symbols on his work."

AGUILAR, JOSE V. *(Suwu-Peen)*
(Tewa Pueblo) 1924-
(technical graphic artist)

Born January 8, 1924, San Ildefonso, N.M. *Education:* Otis Art Institute, Certificate, 1949; Hill and Canyon School of Art, 1950. *Principal occupation:* Technical graphic artist. *Home address:* 9682 Mt. Darnard Dr., Buena Park, Calif. 90620. *Affiliation:* Project Coordinator, Rockwell International, Downey, Calif., 1954-. *Military service:* U.S. Army, 1944-1946 (European Theatre Medal; Purple Heart). *Memberships:* National Congress of American Indians, 1954-. *Awards, honors:* Certificate of Merit, Inter-Tribal Indian Ceremonial Association, 1949; First Purchase Award, Philbrook Art Center, 1953; Denver Art Museum Purchase Award; Mary Wartrous Award, 1954; Honorable Mention, Philbrook Art Center, 1959; Lippencott and Wellington Award; Museum of New Mexico Award for Collection of Museum of Contemporary Art; paintings in permanent collections of Philbrook Art Center, Museum of New Mexico, and Museum of the American Indian. *Private collections include:* Millard Sheet, artist and educator; Vincent Price, actor and art collector; and Darwin Goody, educator.

ALFONSI, JOHN 1961-
(archaeologist, cultural resources management)

Born January 16, 1961, New York, N.Y. *Education:* University of Alaska, Fairbanks (degree in progress). *Principal occupation:* Archaeologist, cultural resources management. *Home address:* Mile 1403.5 Alaska

Hiway, Delta Junction, Alaska 99737. *Affiliation:* Ahtna, Inc., Fairbanks, Alaska. *Membership:* Alaska Anthropological Association, 1984-. *Awards, honors:* Outstanding Senator and Outstanding Student—USUA, University of Alaska, Fairbanks Student Government, 1984 and 1985, respectively. *Interests:* Hunting, trapping, fishing, building; cultural resource assessments throughout Alaska. *Published works:* (In progress) Ahtna Cultural Resources throughout the region. Work includes mainly archaeological fieldwork and intensive investigation, e.g. on-the-ground archaeological survey of the Copper River Basin. "First of its kind."

ALLARD, L. DOUG (Flathead-Confederated Salish and Kootenai) 1931- (museum founder and owner)

Born August 30, 1931, St. Ignatius, Mont. *Education:* Montana State University, B.S., 1956. *Principal occupation: Founder and owner of the Flathead Indian Museum and Allard Auctions. Home address:* P.O. Box 460, St. Ignatius, Mont. 59865. *Military service:* U.S. Marine Corps, 1950-1953 (Korean War Ribbon, U.N. Medal, two Battle Stars, Good Conduct Medal). *Memberships:* Indian Arts and Crafts Association (charter member, board of directors); International Society of Appraisers; Big Brothers and Sisters (director). *Awards, honors:* Million Dollar Round Table — National Association of Life Underwriters. *Interests:* Tribal culture; avid collector of Indian artifacts. *Biographical source: Who's Who in the West.*

AMBLER, J. RICHARD 1934- (professor of anthropology, university archaeologist)

Born January 23, 1934, Denver, Colo. *Education:* University of Colorado, B.A., 1958, Ph.D. (Anthropology), 1966; University of Arizona, M.A. (Anthropology), 1961. *Principal occupation:* Professor of anthropology, university archaeologist. *Address:* Department of Anthropology, Box 15200, Northern Arizona University, Flagstaff, Arizona 86011. *Affiliations:* Field foreman and research assistant to director, University of Colorado Museum, 1956-1957; ranger, archaeologist, Mesa Verde National Park and Great Sand Dunes National Monument, 1957-1958; foreman, University of Colorado Field School, 1958; archaeology field assistant, University of Utah, 1958; museum assistant, Arizona State Museum, 1958-1959; field foreman and research archaeologist, University of Utah, 1959-1960; field foreman, archaeologist, Museum of New Mexico, 1960-1961; archaeologist, Glen Canyon Project, Museum of Northern Arizona, 1961-1963; teaching assistant, University of Colorado, 1963-1965; archaeologist, University of Utah, 1964-1965; instructor in anthropology, University of Colorado, Denver Center, 1965; executive director, Texas Archaeological Salvage Project, University of Texas, 1965-1967; assistant professor of anthropology, University of Texas, 1966-1967; associate professor of anthropology, 1967-1984, professor of anthropology, 1984-, and university archaeologist, 1968-, Northern Arizona University. *Memberships:* Society for American Archaeology, 1957-; Sigma Xi, 1965-. *Biographical source: American Men of Science. Published works:* Various articles, papers and reports on anthropology and archaeology.

AMES, MICHAEL M. 1933- (professor of anthropology, museum director)

Born June 19, 1933, Vancouver, Can. *Education:* University of British Columbia, B.A., 1956; Harvard University, Ph.D., 1961. *Principal occupation:* professor of anthropology, museum director. *Home address:* 6393 N.W. Marine Dr., Vancouver, B.C. V6T 1W5. *Affiliation:* Museum of Anthropology, University of British Columbia, Vancouver, B.C. *Memberships:* Canadian Ethnology Society; American Anthropological Association; Canadian Museum Association; American Association of Asian Studies. *Awards, honors:* Guggenheim Fellowship; Fellow of the Royal Society of Canada. *Interests:* Research in Northwest Coast of North America and South Asia. *Published works: Manlike Monsters on Trial,* co-edited with M. Halpin (UBC Press, 1980; *Museums, The Public and Anthropology* (Concept and UBC Press, 1985.)

AMIOTTE, ARTHUR DOUGLAS
(Oglala-Teton Sioux) 1942-
(artist, teacher)

Born March 25, 1942, Pine Ridge, S.D. *Education:* Northern State College, B.S. (Art Education), 1964. *Principal occupation:* Artist, teacher. *Affiliations:* Iowa State Education Association and Sioux City Education Association, 1964-. *Community activities:* Community speakers panel on promoting minority and ethnic group awareness; lecturer on American Indians. *Memberships:* Northern Art Education Association. *Awards, honors:* South Dakota Indian Scholarship, 1960-1964; inclusion in Who's Who in American Universities and Colleges, 1964; various awards in art education and sculpture from Gallery of American Indian Art, the Philbrook Art Center, the Institute of American Indian Art, 1963-; nominated for Outstanding Teacher of Year, Sioux City, 1966. *Interests:* Art education, Plains Indian culture.

AMYLEE (Iroquois) 1952-
(director of Indian organization)

Born January 3, 1952, Ohio. *Education:* State University of New York, 1976-1979; Kent State University, 1970-1980 (concurrent). *Principal occupation:* Director of Indian organization. *Home address:* Hawk Hollow Private Nature Preserve, Tippecanoe, Ohio 44699. *Affiliations:* Founder and director, American Indian Rights Association, Kent State University, 1970-1983; director, Native American Indian Resource Center, Inc.; Licensed Raptor (Bird of Prey) Rehabilitator (ongoing); Medicine Woman Initiate (ongoing). *Other professional posts:* Professional lecturer and artist for NAIRC, Inc. *Memberships:* National Wildlife Rehabilitators Association; Earthwalker Learning Lodge. *Awards, honors:* Numerous awards for artistic achievement. *Interests:* AmyLee has appeared with Native American leaders and dignitaries including Sakokwenonkwas of Akwesasne, Mad Bear, Rolling Thunder, Sun Bear, Grandfather Sky Eagle and Vernon Bellecourt. She has also had the opportunity to serve as a script consultant for the Smithsonian Institution and a character actress in the Public Broadcast System's film, *Americas Ethnic Symphony. Published works: The Pathfinder Directory: A Guide to Native Americans in the Ohiyo Country* (Indian House, 1982).

ANTIQUIA, CLARENCE (Tlingit) 1940-
(federal government administrator)

Born April 16, 1940, Sitka, Alaska. *Education:* Sheldon Jackson Junior College, Sitka, Alaska, 1958-1959. *Principal occupation:* Federal government administrator. *Home address:* Box 1111, Juneau, Alaska 99802. *Affiliations:* Area director, Bureau of Indian Affairs, Juneau, Alaska, 1965-1975. *Awards, honors:* Outstanding Performance Awards, B.I.A., 1965, 1967, 1970. *Interests:* Public administration, government, personnel management, race relations, Indian affairs.

APODACA, RAYMOND D. (Ysleta del Sur Pueblo) (Tigua Indian Tribe of Texas) 1946-
(administrator)

Born October 15, 1946, Las Cruces, N.M. *Education:* New Mexico State University, B.A., 1969, M.A. (Public Administration), 1976. *Principal occupation:* Administrator. *Home address:* 8220 Research, Apt. 116B, Austin, Texas 78758. *Affiliation:* Executive director, Texas Indian Commission (State of Texas), Austin, Texas, 1983-. *Military service:* U.S. Air Force, 1969-1972. *Memberships:* National Indian Education Association, 1973-1980; National Congress of American Indians, 1973-; Governors' Interstate Indian Council, 1977- (national president, 1985-1986); Texas American Indian Sesquicentennial Association (executive board member, 1985-); Texas State Agency Business Administrators Association, 1982-; North Amerian Indian Museums Association, 1977-1980; New Mexico State University All-Indian Adult Advisory Board, 1976-; Citizens' Advisory Board, ETCOM Public Radio (El Paso, Texas), 1980-1985; OPM—Intergovernmental Committee on Indian Affairs, Southwest Region, 1982-; University of Texas, Austin, El Paso, Master of Science in Social Work Program, Advisory Council, 1984-; Texas State Committee on the Protection of Human Remains and Sacred Objects (American Indian) (co-chairman, 1984-). *Awards, honors:* Colonel Aide-de-Camp, Governor, State of New Mexico, 1977. *Interests:* History, government, theology, education. *Biographical source: To Live in Two Worlds,* by Brent Ashabrenner (Dodd, Mead & Co., 1984.) *Published work: Directory of Information on Health Careers for American Indians* (ERIC/CRESS, National Education Laboratory Publishers, Inc., 1977.)

ARAGON, ARNOLD (Crow-Pueblo)
1953-
   (artist)

Born July 9, 1953, Crow Agency, Mont. *Education:* American Indian Art Institute, Santa Fe, N.M. (Art/Sculpture), 1979 graduate; University of Nevada, Reno, 1980-1984. *Principal occupation:* Professional artist. *Home address:* P.O. Box 64, Walker River Reservation, Schurz, Nev. 89427. *Affiliation:* Rites of Passage Wilderness Camp, Schurz, Nevada. *Other professional posts:* Art consultant, board member, Nevada Urban Indians—Earth Window. *Interests:* Sculpturing using hand tools. His art includes water colors, pastels and pencil drawings. Arnold's sculptures are in various galleries and museums throughout the West as well as private collections throughout the country. He enjoys travel and the outdoors.

ARMAGOST, JAMES GRAYHAWK
(Mohican) 1945-
   (silversmith and lapidary)

Born July 8, 1945, Johnstown, Penn. *Education:* Accredited G E D two year college. *Principal occupation:* Silversmith and lapidary. *Address:* c/o The Silver Phoenix, 2946-D Chain Bridge Rd., Oakton, Virginia 22124. *Affiliation:* Owner, The Silver Phoenix, Oakton, Virginia. The Silver Phoenix has been promoting Native American crafts for over ten years. *Military service:* U.S. Army Special Forces. *Community activities:* American Indian Inter-Tribal Cultural Organization (member, board of directors.) *Awards, honors:* Numerous first place and Best of Show Awards for his jewelry in assorted regional competitions (Native American and non-Native American). *Art*

form: "His Navajo leafwork and multi-level chizeled boarders are some of the cleanest to be found. The geometrics in his overlay styles are crisp and exact, and his animals, plants and people are nearly animated. He has also produced breathtaking pieces blending inlaid stone and highly polished metal with flawless skill. He has walked away with top prizes in every competition he has ever entered."

ARTICHOKER, JOHN HOBART, Jr.
(Sioux) 1930-
   (government administrator)

Born January 17, 1930, Pine Ridge, S.D. *Education:* State University of South Dakota, B.S. (Education), 1951, M.A., 1957. *Principal occupation: Government administrator. Home address:* 4722 W. State Ave., Glendale, Ariz. *Affiliations:* Director of Indian education, State of South Dakota, 1951-1961; tribal operations officer, B.I.A., Billings, Mont., 1961-1962; superintendent, Northern Cheyenne Reservation, 1963-1968; superintendent, Papago Agency, Sells, Ariz., 1968-1969; superintendent, Colorado River Agency, Parker, Ariz., 1969-1972; area director, B.I.A., Phoenix Area Office, 1972-. *Community activities:* Division of Indian Services, University of Montana (advisory council); Tongue River Jacees (board of directors); National Advisory Committee on Indian Work, National Council of Episcopal Church. *Awards, honors:* Ten Outstanding Young Men Award. U.S.J.C.'s, 1965; Indian Achievement Award, 1965. *Published works: Indians of South Dakota* (South Dakota Dept. of Public Instruction, 1956); *The Sioux Indian Goes to College,* master's thesis, with Neil Palmer (Institute of Indian Studies, Vermillion, S.D.)

ATKINSON, LA VERNE D. (Navajo)
1934-
   (teacher)

Born July 3, 1934, Ganado, Ariz. *Education:* University of Minnesota, B.S., 1960. *Principal occupation:* Teacher. *Home address:* 404 Shonto Blvd., Window Rock, Ariz. 86515. *Affiliation:* Program specialist, Cultural Awareness Center Trilingual Institute,

Albuquerque, N.M., 1976-. *Other professional posts:* Steering committee, Native American Bilingual Education Association. *Memberships:* New Mexico Association for Bilingual Education; Arizona Bilingual Association; Native American Bilingual Education Association. *Interests:* "Mainly interested in bilingual, bicultural education for the Native Americans."

AUSTIN, FRANK *(Bahah-Zhonie)* (Navajo) 1938-
(artist)

Born April 10, 1938, Tsegi Canyon, Ariz. *Education:* Phoenix Indian School; University of Arizona; Tempe College, 1959. *Principal occupation:* Textile artist and painter. *Home address:* 710 Memorial Dr., Cortez, Colo. 81321. *Affiliation:* President, Nizhonie, Inc., Cortez, Colo., 1970-. *Memberships:* American Craftsmen's Council, 1961-; American Institute of Interior Designers; Arizona Arts and Crafts. *Awards, honors:* American Institute of Interior Designers Award; Walter Brimson Grand Award; Catherine J. McWhirter Grand Award; Scottsdale National Exhibit Award. *Biographical source:* Contemporary Craftsmen of the Far West.

B

BAERREIS, DAVID A. 1916-
(professor of anthropology)

Born November 2, 1916, New York, N.Y. *Education:* University of Oklahoma, B.A., 1941, M.A., 1943; Columbia University, Ph.D., 1948. *Principal occupation:* Professor of anthropology. *Home address:* 4715 Sheboygan Ave., Apt. 106, Madison, Wis. 53705. *Affiliation:* Professor of anthropology, University of Wisconsin, 1947-; chairman, Department of Sociology and Anthropology, 1956-1958, 1959-1960; chairman, Department of Anthropology, 1971-1973. *Military service:* U.S. Army. *Memberships:* American Ethnohistoric Conference (president, 1957); American Folklore Society (vice-president, 1958, executive committee, 1959-1961); Society for American Archaeology (secretary, 1959-1965; president, 1962); American Associa-

tion for the Advancement of Science (chairman, secretary, vice-president, 1963); American Anthropological Association (Fellow); Royal Anthropological Institute. *Awards, honors:* Lapham Research Medal, Wisconsin Archaeological Society. *Interests:* Prehistory and ethnohistory of North and South American Indians; field trips to Wisconsin, Oklahoma, New Mexico, South Dakota, Iowa, Brazil. *Published works: The Preceramic Horizons of Northeastern Oklahoma* (Anthropological Paper, Museum of Michigan, No. 6, 1951); editor, *The Indian in Modern America* (State Historical Society of Wisconsin, 1956); articles in various journals.

BAHTI, MARK 1950-
(shop owner)

Born September 28, 1950, Tucson, Ariz. *Education:* Prescott College, 1968-1969; University of Arizona, 1969-1970. *Principal occupation:* Owner of Tom Bahti Indian Arts and Crafts, 1972-. *Home address:* 1708 East Speedway, Tucson, Ariz. 85719. *Affiliation:* Coordinator, 'Indian Advocacy Program,' 1976-. *Community activities:* Society of Professional Anthropologists, Tucson (senior advisor); Tucson Chapter of American Indian Affairs (charter member.) *Memberships:* Association of American Indian Affairs; Inter-Tribal Ceremonial Association; Indian Arts and Crafts Association (charter member, past president, board of directors). *Awards, honors:* Established award for Outstanding Indian Graduate Student at the University of Arizona, 1975; studied jewelry under Charles Loloma, 1965. *Published works: Consumer's Guide to Southwestern Indian Arts and Crafts,* 1975; *Navaho Sandpainting Art,* with Eugene Baatsolani Joe (Treasure Chest Publications, 1978).

BAINES, RAYMOND GEORGE (Tlingit-Tsimpshean) 1926-
(pastor)

Born September 26, 1926, Ketchikan, Alaska. *Education:* Phillips University, B.A., 1959; Pacific School of Religion, B.D., 1963. *Principal occupation:* Pastor. *Affiliations:* Executive director, United Church

Committee on Indian Work; pastor of churches, El Cerrito and Berkeley, California, Gardiner, Oregon, and Metlakatla and Sitka, Alaska. *Military service:* U.S. Army Infantry, 1944-1945. *Community activities:* School board, P.T.A., Metlakatla, Alaska (vice-president); Central Council, Tlingit and Haida Indians of Alaska (executive treasurer). *Memberships:* Minnesota, Minneapolis, St. Paul Councils of Churches; Governor's Advisory Committee on Children and the Young; Minnesota Fair Employment Practices Commission; Minnesota Council on Religion and Race.

BAKER, ANSON A. (Mandan-Hidatsa) 1927-
(government administrator)

Born May 26, 1927, Elbowoods, N.D. *Education:* North Dakota Agricultural College, 1946-1947; Minot Business College, 1947-1948, 1949-1950. *Principal occupation:* Government administrator. *Home address:* Box 237, Browning, Mont. 59417. *Affiliations:* Clerk, Aberdeen Area Office, B.I.A., Aberdeen, S.D., 1953-1955; credit officer, Rosebud Indian Reservation, Aberdeen, S.D., 1953-1954; property and supply assistant, loan examiner, Pine Ridge Indian Reservation, Pine Ridge, S.D., 1955-1960; supervisory finance specialist, Fort Belknap Indian Reservation, Harlem, Mont., 1960-1964; administrative manager, Blackfeet Indian Reservation, Browning, Mont., 1964-1967; superintendent, Fort Peck Indian Reservation, 1967-1971; superintendent, Crow Indian Reservation, Crow Agency, Mont., 1971-1973; superintendent, Fort Berthold Reservation, New Town, N.D., 1973-1976; superintendent, Blackfeet Indian Reservation, Browning, Mont., 1976-1979. *Military service:* Seaman First Class, U.S. Navy, 1945-1946. *Community activities:* American Legion, Pine Ridge, S.D. (Post Commander, 1958); American Legion Post 300, New Town, N.D. (Post Commander, 1976); Little Shell Pow-wow, New Town, N.D. (president, 1976.) *Awards, honors:* Certificate of Superior Performance, B.I.A., 1964; Boss of Year Award, Browning, Mont., 1966; Boss of Year Award, Poplar Jaycees, Poplar, Mont., 1968; Certificate of Appreciation, Fort Peck

Tribal Industries, 1969, 1970; Fort Berthold Person Award, Fort Berthold Reservation, N.D., 1974. *Interests:* "My interest is working with people, attempting to bring about a better understanding of Indian people and their tribal government." *Biographical source: Indians of Today,* Fourth Edition (Marion E. Gridley).

BAKER, ARLENE ROBERTA *(Cata)* (Seneca-Cayuga-Pueblo) 1938-
(English instructor)

Born April 13, 1938, Albuquerque, N.M. *Education:* Northeast Oklahoma A & M Jr. College, A.A., 1969; Missouri Southern State College, B.S. (Education), 1972. *Principal occupations:* English instructor (secondary). *Home address:* Route 2, Box 1C, Fairland, Okla 74343. *Affiliation:* Fairland, Okla, 1972-. *Memberships:* Oklahoma Council of Teachers of English, 1977-; Oklahoma Education Association.

BAKER, BETTY 1928-
(writer)

Born June 20, 1928, Bloomsburg, Penn. *Principal occupation:* Writer. *Memberships:* Western Writers of America, 1963-. *Awards, honors:* Western Heritage Awards for *Killer-of-Death,* 1963, and for *And One Was a Wooden Indian,* 1971. *Interests:* The American Indian. Miss Baker proposes that the non-Indian recognize the differing cultural traits of the many American tribes, instead of lumping them together in one mass. Miss Baker writes, "I detest authors who portray Indians as one's next-door ·neighbors in costume. Tribes differed as much as Indian and white-eye. The tribal beliefs, codes, and even the geography of their lands, formed thought, action and reaction. Apaches didn't think like Papagos, nor did Hopi react like Iroquois, but few authors take the trouble of slipping inside the Indian's mind. The view is entirely different from back of the eyes." *Published works: Little Runner of the Longhouse* (Harper, 1962); *The Shaman's Last Raid* (Harper, 1963); *Killer-of-Death* (Harper, 1963); *The Treasure of the Padres* (Harper, 1964); *Walk the World's Rim* (Harper, 1965); *Blood of the Brave* (Harper, 1966); *The Dunder Head War* (Harper, 1967); *Great Ghost Stories of the Old West* (Four Winds, 1968); *Do Not Annoy the Indians* (Macmillan, 1968); *Arizona* (Coward-McCann, 1969); *The Pig War* (Harper, 1969); *And One Was a Wooden Indian* (Macmillan, 1970); *The Big Push* (Coward-McCann, 1972); *A Stranger and Afraid* (Macmillan, 1972); *At the Center of the World* (Macmillan, 1973).

BAKER, ODRIC (RICK) (Lac Courte Oreilles Chippewa, Wisconsin) 1931-
   (tribal council chairman)

Born May 26, 1931, Lac Courte Oreilles Indian Reservation, Wisconsin. *Principal occupation:* Tribal council chairman. *Home address:* Route 5, Hayward, Wis. 54843. *Affiliations:* Tribal chairman, Lac Courte Oreilles Tribe, 1973-. *Other professional posts:* Past-president, Great Lakes Intertribal Council, Wisconsin; past-treasurer, National Tribal Chairman's Association, Washington, D.C.; consultant, O.M.B., Washington, D.C. *Membership:* Loyal Order of Moose (legionnaire degree.) *Interests:* "Indian affairs—advocate of Indian sovereignty, pursuit of recognition, dignity, and peace for Indian people; defense of Indian treaties and agreements with the U.S. Government.

BALES, JEAN ELAINE MYERS (Iowa Tribe) 1946-
   (artist)

Born December 25, 1946, Pawnee, Okla. *Education:* Oklahoma College of Liberal Arts, B.A. (Professional Art), 1969. *Principal occupation:* Artist. *Home address:* Box 274, Washita, Okla. 73094. *Community activities:* National Wildlife Federation (member). *Memberships:* Oklahoma Indian Art League, 1973-1974; Indian Arts and Crafts Association (member-board of directors, 1978-1981, 1976-.) *Awards, honors:* Governor's Oklahoma Cup for Outstanding Indian Artist of the Year, 1973; awards and exhibitions at the following shows: 1973 Annual Festival of Arts, Altus Air Force Base; Shepherd Mall Indian Show; American Indian Exhibition; Ward Mall Indian Art Show; Heard Museum Indian Art Exhi-

bition; works displayed at the Oklahoma Historical Society Museum. Red Cloud National Indian Art Show, 1974; Scottsdale National Indian Art Show, 1974; Philbrook Art Center Annual Indian Exhibition, 1974; 43rd Annual American Indian Exposition; one woman show at the Southern Plains Indian Museum, Anadarko, Oklahoma; one woman show at the Museum of the Western Prairie; works displayed at the Oklahoma Historical Society Museum; Eight Northern Pueblos Art Show, 1975; Gallup Intertribal Ceremonial, 1975; Gallup Intertribal Ceremonial, 1976; selected as one of the Oklahomans for Indian Opportunity (OIO) calendar artist for the painting "Oklahoma Open Drum." 33rd Annual American Indian Artists Exhibition, Philbrook Art Center, 1977; New Mexico State Fair, 1977; Comanche Cultural Center, Indian Art Exhibition, 1977. *Interests:* Mrs. Bales writes, "I have done and still do lectures and seminars for groups and colleges throughout the U.S. I am very active with school systems throughout Oklahoma. By taking the Indian art forms into the classroom we help students (whether they are Indian or non-Indian) to appreciate the rich American Indian culture we have in Oklahoma. I have worked with the schools planning counselors to plan curriculum to include Indian studies. My works are represented in many private and public collections throughout the U.S., Canada and Europe.

BALL, EVE
   (teacher, writer)

Born in Clarksville, Tenn. *Education:* Kansas State Teachers College, B.S.; Kansas State University, M.S. *Principal occupation:* Teacher (retired), writer. *Home address:* Box 3215, Ruidoso, N.M. *Affiliations:* Various teaching appointments until retirement; presently operates own business. *Memberships:* Pi Lamda Theta; Delta Kappa Gamma; Kappa Kappa Iota; New Mexico Folklore Society; New Mexico Historical Society; Western Writers of America. *Awards, honors:* Elected to Hall of Fame, New Mexico Folklore Society, 1970. *Interests:* Mrs. Ball writes, "My major interest is in the field of Southwestern history, and particularly that of the Apaches. I have done twenty years of intensive research from accounts given me by sons or grandsons of the famous Chiricahua and Warm Springs chiefs; but I have not neglected to do the conventional research through publications." *Published works: Ruidoso, the Last Frontier* (Naylor, 1963); *Bob Crosby, World Champion Cowboy,* with Thelma Crosby (Clarendon Press, 1966); *Ma'am Jones of the Pecos* (Arizona University Press, 1969); *In the Days of Victorio* (Arizona University Press, 1970); more than 50 magazine articles in *Arizona and the West, New Mexico Magazine, Frontier Heritage Press,* and *Western Publications.*

BALLARD, JOHN K. (Cherokee) 1920-
(teacher, principal)

Born September 20, 1920, Bernice, Okla. *Education:* Arizona State College, B.S., 1949; Northern State College, M.S., 1957. *Principal occupation:* Elementary school principal. *Affiliations:* Teacher, Santa Fe Indian School, 1949-1953; teacher, Mt. Edgecumbe Indian School, 1953-1956; teacher, Cheyenne River Boarding School, 1956-1960; Chemawa Indian School, 1960-1965; principal, Porcupine Day School, Porcupine, S.D. *Military service:* U.S. Navy, 1941-1945 (Purple Heart).

BALLARD, LOUIS WAYNE (Quapaw-Cherokee) 1931-
(composer, educator)

Born July 8, 1931, Miami, Okla. *Education:* Northeast Oklahoma A & M, A.A., 1951; University of Oklahoma, 1949-1950; University of Tulsa, B.A., B.M.E., 1954, M.M., 1962; College of Santa Fe, Doctor of Music, Honoris Causa. *Principal occupation:* Composer, educator. *Home address:* 3956 Old Santa Fe Trail, Santa Fe, N.M. 87501. *Affiliations:* Chairman, Music Department, Institute of American Indian Arts, Santa Fe, N.M., 1962-1964; chairman, Performing Arts Department, Institute of American Indian Arts, 1964-1969; music curriculum specialist, Central Office-Education, B.I.A., Washington, D.C., 1969-1979; chairman, Minority Awareness Committee for New Mexico Education Association; project director and composer, First National All

Indian Honor Band, Santa Fe, N.M., 1979-. *Other professional posts:* Music consultant and lecturer; president, First American Indian Films, Inc. *Memberships:* ASCAP; American Music Center; American Symphony Orchestra League; National Music Educator's Association; Minority Concerns Commission, MENC (member); Society for Ethnomusicology. *Awards, honors:* Composer's Assistance Grants, Select Composer's Bicentennial Grant, National Endowment for the Arts; New Mexico American Revolution Bicentennial Commission Grant, 1967-1976; First Marion Nevins MacDowell Award, Chamber Music, 1969; Ford Foundation Grant, American Indian Music and Music Education, 1970; Outstanding Indian of the Year, Tulsa Council of the American Indian, 1970; National Indian Achievement Award, Indian Council Fire, 1972; Distinguished Alumnus Award, Tulsa University, 1972; Outstanding Indian of the Year, American Indian Exposition, Anadarko, Oklahoma, 1973; Certificate of Special Achievement, Department of the Interior, 1974; Catlin Peace Pipe Award, National Indian Lore Association, 1976; Annual ASCAP Awards, 1966-1976. *Interests:* Mr. Ballard has traveled extensively throughout the U.S. as music consultant for Volt Technical Corp. headstart programs, to B.I.A. area offices and workshops establishing bicultural music programs from kindergarten to college level. He has lectured at U.C.L.A., Northern Arizona University, 1970, and at the M.E.N.C. Regional Music Conference, Albuquerque, N.M., on a variety of subjects relating to American Indian art and music; Mr. Ballard has been a guest composer and conductor at numerous events across the country. *Published works: The American Indian Sings,* Book 1, 1970; Composed: (ballets) *Ji-Jo Gweh, Koshare, The Four Moons;* (orchestral music) *Scenes From Indian Life, Why the Duck Has a Short Tail, Devil's Promenade, Incident at Wounded Knee, Fantasy Aborigine, Nos. I, II and III;* (chamber music) *Ritmo Indio, Desert Trilogy, Kacina Dances, Rio Grande Sonata, String Trio 1, Rhapsody for Four Bassoons;* (choral cantatas) *Portrait of Will Rogers, The Gods Will Hear, Thus Spake Abraham;* (band works) *Siouxiana, Scenes From Indian Life, Ocotillo Festival Overture, Nighthawk Kee-*

towa; (percussion) *Cecega Ayuwipi;* numerous others. Sheet music of Mr. Ballard's are available from the following publishers: Bourne Music Co., 1212 Ave. of the Americas, New York, N.Y. 10019; and Belwin-Mills Publishing Corp., 25 Deshon Dr., Melville, N.Y. 11747.

BALLARD, W.L. 1936-
(professor)

Born April 5, 1936, Fargo, N.D. *Education:* Tufts University, B.A. (summa cum laude), 1958; University of Calfiornia, Berkeley, Ph.D., 1969. *Principal occupation: University professor. Home address:* 132 Aidai Shukushya, 1375 Yokogaward, Shigenobo-Cho, Onsen-gun, Ehime, Japan 791-02. *Affiliations:* Professor, Georgia State University, Atlanta, 1969-1985; professor, Ehime University, Matsuyama, Japan, 1985-. *Military service:* U.S. Navy, 1958-1963. *Memberships:* Linguistic Society of America, 1969-; Society for the Study of the Indigenous Languages of the Americas; Chinese Linguistic Society of Japan, 1985-. *Awards, honors:* Sigma Xi, Phi Beta Kappa; Distinguished Alumni Professor, Georgia State University, 1985. *Interests:* Chinese dialects, dialectology, phonology theory; history of chinese; languages and cultures of the American Southeast, especially Yuchi. *Published works:* Monograph: *The Yuchi Green Corn Ceremonial: Form and Meaning,* (American Indian Studies Center, University of California, Los Angeles, 1978); articles: "Aspects of Yuchi Morphonology, Studies in Southeastern Indian Languages," edited by James Crawford (University of Georgia Press, 1975); "More on Yuchi Pronouns," (IJAL, 1978); "Lexical Borrowing Among Southeastern Native American Languages, Proceedings of the 17th MALC," (University of Kansas, 1982).

BANK, THEODORE P., III 1923-
(cultural anthropologist)

Born August 31, 1923, Patterson, La. *Education:* Harvard University, 1941-1943; University of Michigan, B.S., 1946, M.S., 1950, plus four years advanced research and study. *Principal occupation:* Cultural anthropolo-

gist. *Home address:* 1809 Nichols Rd., Kalamazoo, Michigan 49007. *Affiliations:* Associate professor of anthropology and chairman of the World Explorations Program, Western Michigan University, 1973-; assistant professor and director of the Aleutian-Bering Sea Institutes, Western Michigan University, 1967-. *Other professional post:* Executive director, American Institute for Exploration, Inc. *Military service:* U.S. Navy Air Corps, Aerology, 1944-1946, North Pacific campaign. *Community activities:* Subcommittee on ethnobotany, Pacific Science Association (chairman, 1954-1958). *Memberships:* American Anthropological Association (Fellow); Society for American Archaeology (Fellow); American Association for the Advancement of Science (Fellow); Polar Society; Current Anthropology; The Explorers Club (Fellow); contributing editor, *The Explorers Journal. Awards, honors:* Fulbright Research Fellow in Anthropology, Japan, 1955-1956; research grants from various organizations. *Travels, expeditions:* Leader, Interdisciplinary (anthropology, bio-ecology, archaeology—expeditions to Alaska and the Aleutian Isles, Bering Sea region (1948-1954, 1958, 1962, 1966, 1969-; leader, joint Japanese-American expeditions to the Aleutian Islands, 1975-; leader, joint British-American Expedition to Bering Sea, 1977-1978; leader, expeditions to Canadian Arctic, and elsewhere; filming expeditions in the Arctic, Aleutians, Japan and around the world. Major fieldwork among the Aleut-Eskimos. *Biographical sources: Who's Who in America; Who's Who in the Midwest; Who's Who in California; World Who's Who in Science and Industry; American Men of Science; The Blue Book* (England); *International Directory of Educational Specialists; Contemporary Authors; Who's Who Among Authors and Journalists;* and others. *Published works: Birthplace of the Winds* (Thomas Y. Crowell, 1956); *Student Manual for Cultural Anthropology* (Quest, 1966); *People of the Bering Sea* (MSS, 1971); *Aleut-Eskimo,* 1973; *Ethnobotany as an Adjunct to Archaeology,* 1977; (script and narration) *Canoeing Into the Past,* 1979; associate editor, *Current Field Reports* (Anthropology), 1968-; various articles.

**BARRETT, JOHN ADAMS (ROCKY),
Jr. (Citizen Band Potawatomi) 1944-
(corporate president)**

Born March 25, 1944, Shawnee, Okla. *Education:* Princeton University, 1962-1964; University of Oklahoma, 1964-1965; Oklahoma City University, B.S. (Business), 1968, M.S. (Business), 1986. *Principal occupation:* Corporate president. *Home address:* 4002 N. Market St., Shawnee, Okla. 74801. *Affiliations:* Warehouseman and salesman, U.S. Plywood Corp., Oklahoma City, Okla.,1966-1969; promotion and supervisor of construction, Greenbriar Development Co., Memphis, Tenn., 1969-1970; Barrett Construction Co., Southaven, Miss., 1970-1971; director, C.T.S.A. Enterprise, Shawnee, Okla., 1971-1974 (intertribal organization, under Indian Action Team Training Contract from B.I.A., whose objective was to trade hard-core unemployed adult Indians in construction trades); Barrett Drilling Co. (family owned business in contract drilling and oil production), 1974-1982; self employed, J. Barrett Co., 1982-1983; tribal administrator, Citizen Band Potawatomi Tribe, 1983-1985, chairman, 1985-; president, Barrett Refining, Shawnee, Okla., 1985-. In the Fall of 1985, Barrett Refining was awarded a $52 million jet fuel contract from the U.S. Department of Defense—the only Defense contract to go to an Indian. *Other Professional posts:* Paid lobbyist for Oklahoma Home Builders Association in the Oklahoma Legislature; Citizen Band Potawatomi Tribe (business committee member, tribal administrator (1983-1985), vice-chairman, and chairman (1985-). *Other tribal activities:* Member, board of directors, United Western Tribes (representing 32 tribes in Oklahoma and Kansas); chairman and director, Shawnee Service United Indian Health Service Advisory Board; director, Oklahoma Indian Health Service Advisory Board; president, National Indian Action Contractors Association; delegate to National Tribal Chairman's Association and National Congress of American Indians. *Community activities:* Member, Emanuel Episcopal Church (ordained lay reader); member, board of directors, Shawnee Quaterback Club; Elks (B.P.O.E.); member, Shawnee Citizens Advisory Council, Lions Club, and Boy Scouts of America as troop leader.

**BARSE, HAROLD G. (Kiowa,
Wichita, Sioux) 1947-
(readjustment counseling specialist)**

Born June 30, 1947, Riverside, Calif. *Education:* Black Hills State College, Spearfish, S.D., B.S. (Secondary Education), 1973; University of Oklahoma, Norman, Okla., M.Ed. (Guidance and Counseling), 1979. *Principal occupation:* Readjustment counseling specialist. *Home address:* 1814 Windsor Way, Norman, Oklahoma 73069. *Affiliations:* Director, Adult Education Program, Lake Traverse Sisseton-Wahpeton Sioux Tribe, Sisseton, S.D., 1973-1975; instructor, Sinte Gleska Community College, Rosebud Sioux Reservation, S.D., 1975; director, Inhalent Abuse Treatment Project, Oklahoma City Native American Center, 1977-1980; outreach specialist, Veterans Administration's Vietnam Veteran Outreach Program, 1980-; founder, Vietnam Era Veterans Inter-Tribal Association, 1981-; planned and organized first National Vietnam Veterans Pow-Wow, 1982. *Other professional post:* Co-chairman, Vet Center's American Indian Working Group. *Military service:* U.S. Army, 1969-1971 (secialist 4th class E-4). *Memberships:* Kiowa Blacklegging Society (Kiowa Veterans Association), 1983-; Native American Veterans Association. *Interests:* "Working with Vietnam veterans; primary program development specialist for video *Shadow of the Warrior: American Indian Counseling Perspectives.*

**BARZ, SANDRA 1930-
(editor, publisher)**

Born August 4, 1930, Chicago, Ill. *Education:* Skidmore College, B.A., 1952. *Principal occupation:* Editor, publisher. *Home address:* 162 East 80 St., New York, N.Y. 10021. *Affiliation:* Editor, publisher, *Arts and Culture of the North* (newsletter, journal), 1976-. *Community activities:* Yorkville Civic Council (member of board). *Interests:* "Eskimo art—circumpolar; traveled to Alaska, Canada (Arctic) and Greenland, and have lead tours to Arctic Canada and Greenland; run conferences at major museums in Canada and the U.S. since 1978, where Eskimo art-related activities are taking place." *Published works: Inuit Artists*

Print Workbook (Arts and Culture of the North, 1981); newsletter/journal *Arts and Culture of the North (seven volumes, 1976-1981; 1983-1984).*

BATAILLE, GRETCHEN M. 1944-
(professor)

Born September 28, 1944, Mishawaka, Ind. *Education:* Purdue University, 1962-1965; California State Polytechnic University, B.S., 1966, M.A., 1967; Drake University, D.A., 1977. *Principal occupation:* Professor. *Home address:* 1861 Rosemount Ave., Claremont, Calif. 91711. *Affiliation:* Iowa State University, Ames, Iowa, 1967-. *Community activities:* Iowa Civil Rights Commission, 1975-1979 (chairman, 1977-1979); Iowa Humanities Board, 1981- (president, 1984-1985.) *Memberships:* National Association for Ethnic Studies (executive council, 1980-; treasurer, 1982-); Association for the Study of American Indian Literature (executive board, 1978-1981; Modern Language Association. *Interests:* "I am interested in American Indian literature in the academic sense as well as the literature as a reflection of the culture, history, and world view of diverse peoples. As a collector of popular culture artifacts representing American Indians, I find the popular view in sharp contrast to the image presented in both the oral tradition and contemporary literary expressions." *Published works: The Worlds Between Two Rivers: Perspectives on American Indians in Iowa* (Iowa State University Press, 1978); *The Pretend Indians: Images of Native Americans in the Movies* (Iowa State University Press, 1980); *American Indian Literature: A Selected Bibliography for Schools and Libraries* (NAIES, Inc., 1981); *American Indian Women Telling Their Lives* (University of Nebraska Press, 1984); *Images of American Indians in Film: An Annotated Bibliography* (Garland Publishing, 1985).

BEALER, ALEX W., III 1921-
(writer)

Born March 6, 1921, Valdosta, Georgia. *Education:* Emory University, B.A., 1942; Northwestern University, 1946. *Principal occupation:* Writer. *Home address:* 5180 Riverview Rd., Atlanta, Ga. 30327. *Affiliation:* Alex W. Bealer & Associates, Atlanta, Ga. *Military service:* U.S. Marine Corps Reserves, 1942-1961. *Community activities:* Trustee, Atlanta Historical Society, Westville Handicrafts, Inc.; Georgia Republican Party (state, district and county executive committees; press secretary; assistant state chairman, 1960-1969); Pocket Theatre, Atlanta, Georgia (former president, board of directors, 1958-1962); Honorary Royal Swedish Consul, 1969-. *Memberships:* Commerce Club, Atlanta, 1960-; Artist Blacksmiths Associaiton of North America (president, 1973-1974; director.) *Awards, honors:* Eagle Scout, B.S.A. *Interests:* Advertising, writing (published articles in various journals since 1936); wrote and helped produce a 30 minute television documentary on the Cherokee Removal, shown on WSB TV, Atlanta in December, 1965; historical research; painting; study of the American Indian; blacksmithing; general crafts. Mr. Bealer has lived with the Teton Sioux, Rosebud Reservation, S.D. in 1941, and the Eastern Cherokees of North Carolina at different times between 1939 and 1942; and others. *Published works: The Picture-Skin Story* (Holiday House, 1957); *Only the Names Remain; The Cherokees and the Trail of Tears* (Little, Brown, 1972); and others.

BEAN, LOWELL JOHN 1931-
(anthropologist, ethnologist)

Born April 26, 1931, St. James, Minn. *Education:* Los Angeles City College, 1954-1955; University of California, Los Angeles, B.A., 1958, M.A., 1961, Ph.D., 1970. *Principal occupation:* Anthropologist, ethnologist. *Home address:* 1555 Lakeside Dr. #64, Oakland, Calif. 94612. *Affiliations:* Reading and teaching assistant, U.C.L.A., 1958-1960; instructor, Pasadena Junior College, 1962-1965; curator of ethnology, Palm Springs Desert Museum, 1962-1964; instructor and professor of anthropology (chairman, 1973-), Department of Anthropology, California State University at Hayward, 1965-; research fellow, R.H. Lowie Museum of Anthropology, University of California, Berkeley, 1971-1973; curator, Clarence E. Smith Museum of Anthropology, CSUH, 1974-1978. *Other professional*

16

posts: Consultant on ethnographic films, North American Films, 1963-1964; contributing editor, *American Indian Historian,* 1968-1972; consultant, American Indian Scholars Conference, American Historical Society, 1969; consultant, Rincon Reservation Water Case, 1971; member, California State Board of Education Task Force on Social Studies Textbooks, 1972. *Military service:* U.S. Marine Corps, 1951-1953. *Community activities:* American Friends Service, Southwest Indian Committee (member, advisory Indian committee, 1961-1963); Teaching Institute, American Indian Historical Society (participant, 1968); American Indian Studies Curriculum Committee, San Francisco State College (consultant); Planning Committee for Gabrileno Cultural Center, Rancho Los Alamitos, 1972; Malki Museum (member, board of trustees); *Journal of California Anthropology* (associate editor); editor, Ballena Press *Anthropolical Papers. Memberships:* American Anthropological Association (Fellow); Society for California Archaeology; Southwestern Anthropological Association (president, 1974-1975). *Awards, honors:* George Barker Memorial Grant-in-Aid for research among American Indian, 1960; National Science Foundation Faculty Research Grant-in-Aid, California State University, Hayward, 1967-1972; Postdoctoral Museum Fellowship, Wenner-Gren Foundation for Anthropological Research, 1971; Smithsonian Institute (Center for the Study of Man) Grant to research the history of economic development at Morongo Indian Reservation, Banning, California, 1972-1974; Grant-in-Aid, American Philosophical Society, 1972; Outstanding Educators of America Award, 1972; National Geographic Society (grantee, 1975; California State University at Hayward (mini-grantee, 1977). *Interests:* California Indians; Ethnographic research; directed field studies among Miwok, Wintun, Tubatulabal and Chemehuevi Indians of California. *Published works: The Romero Expeditions in California and Arizona, 1823-1826,* with William Mason (Palm Springs Desert Museum, 1962); *Cahuilla Indian Cultural Ecology,* Ph.D. dissertation (University Microfilms, 1970); *Temalpah: Cahuilla Knowledge and Uses of Plants* (Malki Museum, 1972); *Mukat's People: The*

Cahuilla Indians of Southern California (University of California, Berkeley Press, 1972); *Antap: California Indian Policy and Economic Organization,* with T. King (Ballena Press, 1974); *Native American California: Essays on Culture and History,* with T. Blackburn (Ballena Press, 1975); *California Indians: Primary Resources,* with Sylvia Vane (Ballena Press, 1976); *A Comparative Ethnobotany of Twelve Southern California Tribes,* with Charles Smith; *Ethnography and Culture History of the Southwestern Kashia Pomo Indians; The Native Californian: A Regional Ethnology;* and *Madman or Philosopher: Essays on Shamanism,* with Rex Jones.

**BEARTUSK, KEITH LOWELL
(Northern Cheyenne) 1947-
(forest manager)**

Born December 21, 1947, Crow Agency, Mont. Education: Eastern Montana College (two years); University of Montana, B.S. (Forestry), 1971. *Principal occupation:* Forest manager. *Home address:* P.O. Box 445, Lame Deer, Mont. 59043. Military service: Montana National Guard, 1971-1977 (American Spirit Honor Medal).

**BEATTY, JOHN J. (Mohawk) 1939-
(anthropologist)**

Born September 5, 1939, Brooklyn, N.Y. *Education:* Brooklyn College, B.A., 1964; University of Oklahoma, M.A., 1966; City Univerity of New York, Ph.D. (Anthropology), 1972. *Principal occupation:* Anthropologist. *Home address:* 2983 Bedford Ave., Brooklyn, N.Y. 11210. *Affiliations:* Teaching assistant, University of Oklahoma, 1964-1965; instructor, Long Island University, 1966-1967; professor of anthropology, Brooklyn College, CUNY, 1966-. *Other professional post:* Private investigator, Phoenix Investigative Associates, 1982-. *Military service:* New York Guard (captain.) *Major research work:* Ethnographic and linguistic: American Indians in Urban Areas (major U.S. cities) 1963-; Tlingit Language and Culture (in New York and Alaska) 1964-1967; Totonac Language and Culture (in New York and Mexico) 1964-1967; Kiowa-Apache Language and Culture (Anadarko,

Oklahoma) 1965-; Mohawk Language and Culture (New York City and various Mohawk Réserves) 1964-; Japanese and Japanese Americans: Language and Culture, 1973-; Scots and Scottish Americans, 1974-; Cross Cultural Perspectives on Police, 1978-. *Memberships:* American Anthropological Association (Fellow); New York Academy of Sciences (Fellow); American Indian Community House. *Awards, honors:* National Science Foundation Training Grant, University of Oklahoma, 1965 (for research with the Kiowa-Apache); City University of New York and National Science Foundation Dissertation Year Fellowships, 1971 (for research with Mohawk languages); National Science Foundation Grant (U.S. - Japanese Co-operative Program, 1973); Brooklyn College Faculty Award, 1973, for research with Japanese macaques; Faculty Research Award Program, CUNY, 1974 and 1975, for research with chimpanzees and for research on sexual behavior; Department of Health, Education and Welfare: Office of Native American Programs, 1975 grant to work with urban American Indians in New York State; National Endowment for the Arts, 1977, for filming Iroquois social dances; Rikkyoo University (Japan) Research Fellowship, 1986-1987, for research on solidarity; Certificate of Appreciation, New York Academy of Sciences; Sigma Xi. *Interests:* Anthropology; linguistics, symbolic anthropology - American Indians; Asia; theatre; forensics; lecture series on American Indians and Japanese culture, 1969-. *Published works: Kiowa-Apache Music and Dance* (Museum of Anthropology, University of Northern Colorado, 1974); *Mohawk Morphology* (Museum of Anthropology, University of Northern Colorado, 1974); *A Guide to New York for Japanese: An Ethnographic Approach* (Gloview Press, Tokyo, 1985); numerous articles. Recording: *Music of the Plains Apache* (Folkways Records). Films: *Iroquois Social Dances,* Two parts, with Nick Manning, 1979; and others. Videotapes: *The American Indian Art Center,* 1978; *American Indians at Brooklyn College,* 1978; Scottish Highland Dances, 1979; *Custer Revisited,* 1980. Books being developed: *Intercultural Communications; The Anthropology of Sexual Behavior; The Nature of Language and Culture;* and *Cross Cultural Perspectives on Police.*

BEATTY, PATRICIA 1922-
  (writer)

Born August 26, 1922, Portland, Oregon. *Education:* Reed College, B.A., 1944. *Principal occupation:* Writer. Home address: 5085 Rockledge Dr., Riverside, Calif. 92506. *Affiliations:* Teacher, Coeur D'Alene (Idaho) High School, 1947-1950; librarian, Riverside (Calif.) Public Library, 1953-1957; teacher, creative writing, University of Califorinia, Riverside, 1967-1968, U.C.L.A., 1968-1969. *Memberships:* Riverside Roundtable Women's Organization (secretary, president); Society of Children's Book Writers. *Awards, honors:* Honorary member, Quileute Tribe. *Interests:* Travel for book research. *Biographical sources: Contemporary Authors; Dictionary of International Biography; Third Book of Junior Authors; Who's Who in California. Published works: Indian Canoemaker* (Caxton); *Squaw Dog* (William Morrow); *The Lady from Black Hawk* (McGraw-Hill); *At the Seven Stars,* 1965; *Campion Towers,* 1966; *Hail Columbia,* 1970; *A Long Way to Whiskey Creek,* 1971; *Who Comes to King's Mountain,* 1975; *Lupita Manana,* 1981; among others.

BEAUDIN, JOHN A. (Lac Courte Oreilles Chippewa Band of Great Lakes Ojibwe) 1946-
  (attorney)

Born June 28, 1946, Chicoutimi, Quebec, Can. *Education:* University of Wisconsin, Green Bay, B.S.; University of Wisconsin, Madison, J.D. *Principal occupation:* Attorney. *Home address: 1317 Reetz Rd., Madison, Wisc. 53711. Affiliation:* Partner (four years), Dewa, Beaudin & Kelly, 217 S. Hamilton St., Madison, Wisc. *Other professional post:* President, Native Horizons, Inc. *Military service:* U.S. Army, 1966-1969 (rank SP/5-E5; Bronze Star with clusters, Army Commendation Medal, Viet Nam Combat and Campaign Medals). *Community activities:* Director, American Indian Peace & Justice League; board of directors, Madison Indian Parents, School Superintendent's Human Relations Advisory Committee; lobbying. *Membership:* American Indian Lawyer's League. *Interests:* Advocate of Indian rights, human rights and educational needs and issues, and general practice. *Published works: American Indian Rights* (Madison Metro School District, 1981); many articles dealing with Indian or legal affairs. "Major work in development for Wisconsin judges and attorneys dealing with Indian Child Welfare Act."

BEAUVAIS, ARCHIE BRYAN (Rosebud Sioux) 1948-
(education administrator and instructor)

Born December 30, 1948, Rosebud, S.D. *Education:* Northern Arizona University, Flagstaff, B.A., 1970, M.A. (Education), 1976; Harvard University, Ed.D., 1982. *Principal occupation:* Education administrator and instructor. *Home address:* P.O. Box 426, Mission, S.D. 57555. *Affiliation:* Department chair, Education Department, Sinte Gleska College, Rosebud, S.D., 1984-. *Military service:* U.S. Army, 1967-1970 (Vietnam, 1968-1969, Specialist Fifth Class, Army Commendation Medal.) *Community activities:* Doctoral student representative to Student Association Cabinet, Harvard Graduate School of Education. *Memberships:* School Administrators of S.D.; Ducks Unlimited; Harvard Chapter of Phi Delta Kappa; S.D. Indian Education Association. *Interests:* "Primary vocational interest is furthering the cause of education on the Rosebud Sioux Reservation by making some impact as a higher education administrator and instructor. Also, to act as a positive role-model for young people and convey the fact that with education comes the right to make the right choices that effect a person's destiny."

BEAVER, FRED (Creek) 1911-
(artist)

Born July 2, 1911, Eufaula, Okla. *Education:* Haskell Institute, 1933-1935; Bacone Junior College, 1931-1932. *Principal occupation:* Freelance artist. *Home address:* 437 Locust St., N.W., Ardmore, Okla. 73401. *Affiliations:* Clerk, Bureau of Indian Affairs, Okmulgee and Ardmore, Okla.,

1935-1960; freelance artist, 1960-. *Military service:* P.F.C., U.S. Army Air Force, 1942-1945. *Community activities:* Postal Employees Credit Union (supervisor); Federal Employees Union, B.I.A. (president). *Awards, honors:* Waite Phillips Trophy Award, Philbrook Art Center, Tulsa, Okla., 1963; Outstanding Contribution in Religious Activities, Bacone College; various art prizes in shows throughout the U.S. *Interests:* Painting and exhibiting professionally; has performed as baritone soloist; painting reproductions for books: *Songs from the Earth; Southeastern Indians;* also in Dorothy Dunn's *American Indian Arts,* exhibited personally in 36 states; illustrated book, *Creek-Seminole Legends,* by Strickland and Gregory.

BECENTI, FRANCIS D. (Navajo) 1952-
(higher education administrator)

Born May 18, 1952, Fort Defiance, Ariz. *Education:* Navajo Community College, A.A., 1973; University of California, Berkeley, B.A., 1975. *Principal occupation:* Higher education administrator. *Home address:* 1624 E. Pitkin, Fort Collins, Colo. 86504. *Affiliations:* Director of financial aid, Navajo Community College, 1975-1979; director of financial aid, University of Albuquerque, 1980-1981; director of student services, College of Ganado, 1981-1984; director, Native American Student Services, Colorado State University, Fort Collins, 1984-.

BECK, SAMUEL (Catawba) 1916-
(electrician, tribal secretary-treasurer)

Born February 12, 1916, Rock Hill, S.C. *Principal occupation:* Electrician. *Home address:* Route 3, Box 324, Rock Hill, S.C. 29730. Affiliation: Rock Hill Printing and Finishing Co., Rock Hill, S.C., 1946-. *Other professional post:* Secretary and treasurer, Catawba Nation. *Military service:* U.S. Army, 1943-1946 (T-4 Sergeant).

BEELER, SAMUEL W., Jr.
(Cherokee) 1950-
(tribal executive director, planner)

Born January 29, 1950, Paterson, N.J. *Education:* Passaic County School of Nursing, Wayne, N.J., Nursing Degree; American Indian School on Alcohol and Drug Abuse, Reno, Nev., Certified Counselor. *Principal occupation:* Executive director and tribal planner. *Home address:* Poospatuck Indian Reservation, Mastic, N.Y. 11950. *Affiliations:* Executive director, Paumanok Algonquian, Poospatuck Indian Reservation, Mastic, N.Y. *Other professional post:* Tribal planner, Poospatuck Tribal Council, Poospatuck Indian Reservation. *Military service:* U.S. Air Force, 1968-1970. *Community activities:* Executive director, New Jersey American Indian Center, Hillside, N.J. *Memberships:* American Indian Nurses Association; American Indian Medicine Society; National Congress of American Indians; Association of American Indian Social Workers, Vietnam Era Veterans Inter-Tribal Association; Cherokee National Historical Society.

BEGAY, D.Y. (Navajo) 1953-
(weaver, textile consultant)

Born September 3, 1953, Ganado, Ariz. *Education:* Rocky Mountain College, 1974; Arizona State University, B.A., 1978. *Principal occupation:* Weaver, textile consultant. *Home address:* 10 Fairview Ave., Woodcliff Lake, N.J. 07675. *Affiliation:* Owner, Navajo Textiles & Arts, Woodcliff Lake, N.J., 1984-. *Other professional posts:* Textile instructor, lecturer. *Memberships:* Palisades Guild; Indian Education; Museum of Natural History, Museum of the American Indian; Handweavers Guild of America. *Interests:* "Have done extensive traveling (Canada, Mexico, Europe and U.S.) All my interest is in the field of textiles (Navajo weaving). *Biographical sources:* "A Navajo Weaver" (*N.Y. Times*); "Navajo Weaving" (*Bergen Record*). *Published works:* Co-editor, *The Sheep* (documentary film), 1982.

BEGAY, EUGENE A., Sr. (Lac Courte Oreilles Chippewa, Wisc.) 1933-
(business administration, Indian affairs, mechanical engineer)

Born June 6, 1933, Hayward, Wis. *Education:* North Park College, 1952-1954 (Pre-Medicine); Illinois Institute of Technology, 1955-1959 (Mechanical Engineering). *Principal occupation:* Business administration, Indian affairs, mechanical engineer. *Home address:* 765 Hartwell St., Teaneck, N.J. 07666. *Affiliations:* Executive director, United Southeastern Tribes, Inc., Nashville, Tenn., 1972-1976; Associate Native American Ministry, United Presbyterian Church-USA, New York, N.Y., 1976-. *Other professional posts:* Consultant, B.I.A. and Indian Health Service, U.S. Government. *Military service:* Illinois National Guard, 1950-1952. *Community activities:* Chicago American Indian Center (board of directors); National Indian Review Board (NIAAA/HEW) (chairman); National Indian Board on Mental Health (chairman); National Indian Council Fire (member). *Memberships:* National Congress of Amerian Indians; Research Committee on Mental Health (NIMH/HEW). *Interests:* "Active originally in Indian affairs in the area of developing priority by the Federal Government in mental health and alcoholism programs and services. I have lobbied in Congress and advocated amongst tribes and tribal organizations in the area of economic development, education, nutrition, housing, and health services. I am currently active in Indian rights, treaty rights, jurisdiction, and land issues. I provided White House testimony on these issues at the request of the Vice President."

BEGAY, JIMMIE C. (Navajo) 1948-
(Indian educator)

Born September 4, 1948, Rough Rock, Ariz. *Education:* New Mexico Highlands University, A.S., 1969, B.A., 1972, M.A., 1974. *Principal occupation:* Indian educator. *Home address:* Box 656, Rough Rock, Ariz. 86503. *Affiliations:* Teacher, principal, executive director, Rough Rock Demonstration School. *Other professional posts:* Native American Studies teacher; coordinator,

Black Mesa Day School. *Community activities:* Navaho Culture Organization (chairman); originator of Navaho psychology classes; sponsor of Black Mesa five mile run. *Memberships:* National Association of Secondary School Principals; Smithsonian Institution; Harvard Education Review; Dine Biolta Association. *Award:* "*Outstanding Accomplishments,*" *Rough Rock School Board. Interests:* Betterment in education programs, especially for Indians; travel. "(I) would like to pursue higher educational goals." *Biographical sources:* "*Principals and Views About Indian Education,*" *(Rough Rock News);* "Candidate for NACIE" *(Navajo Times); History of Rough Rock,* by Robert Roessell. *Published works: Navajo Culture Outline,* and *Navajo Philosophy of Education.*

BEGAY, RUTH TRACY (Navajo) 1940-
(family nurse practitioner)

Born May 14, 1940, Ganado, Ariz. *Education:* Loretto Heights College, School of Nursing, Denver, Colo., B.S.N., 1978. *Principal occupation:* Family nurse practitioner, director, Navajo Community College Health Center, 1978-. *Address:* P.O. Box 193, Navajo Community College, Tsaile, Ariz. 86556. *Other professional posts:* Member, Navajo Health Authority, Office of Nursing Education Board; member, Navajo Community College Nursing Program Board. *Memberships:* Arizona Nurses Association (council on practice); Arizona Public Health Association; Pacific Coast College Health Association; *Awards, honors:* Two documentary films on Nurse Practitioner on Navajo Reservation by NBC and University of Arizona, School of Medicine, 1973; Navajo Community College 1978 Student Service Employee of the Year Award; Outstanding Young Woman of the Year, 1977. *Interests:* "Involvement in local community health-social work among the Navajo people. Travel locally, regionally in college health service and nurses association. Interested in continual growth and development in cross-cultural aspects of a different society integrated with our own Navajo Society." *Biographical sources:* Articles: Arizona Nurses Association *Newsletter,* 1973; *The Navajo Times,* 1973; *Gallup Independent,* 1977.

BELGARDE, HAROLD (Turtle Mountain Chippewa) 1939-
(teacher, media specialist)

Born October 1, 1939, Belcourt, N.D. *Education:* Utah State University, M.Ed., 1975. *Principal occupation:* Teacher, media specialist. *Home address:* 1408 Como St., #4, Carson City, Nev. 89701. *Affiliation:* Teacher (library usage), Bureau of Indian Affairs, Stewart, Nev., 1975-. *Community activities:* Stewart Booster Club (president). *Published works: Resource Materials on American Indians* (Harry Belgarde, 1975).

BELINDO, DENNIS WAYNE
(Aun-So-Te) (Kiowa-Navajo) 1938-
(artist)

Born December 12, 1938, Phoenix, Ariz. *Education:* Bacone College, Diploma, 1958; University of Oklahoma, B.F.A., 1962. *Principal occupation:* Art teacher. *Affiliation:* Central High, Oklahoma City, Okla., 1963-. *Other professional post:* Freelance commercial artist. *Military service:* U.S. National Guard, 1955-1957. *Memberships:* Artists of Oklahoma. *Awards, honors:* Honorable Mention, Philbrook Art Center Indian Annual, 1956, 1961; First Award, Poster Division and Plains Division, Gallup Inter-Tribal Ceremonials.

BELINDO, JOHN (Kiowa-Navajo) 1935-
(organization executive)

Born November 3, 1935, Phoenix, Ariz. *Education:* Central State College, Edmond, Okla., B.S., 1966. *Principal occupation:* Organization executive. *Affiliations:* Staff announcer, KOCY-AM and -FM, and KFNB-FM, radio stations, Oklahoma City, Okla; columnist, *Oklahoma Journal,* Oklahoma City, Okla., 1965-; director, Washington Office, National Congress of American Indians. *Military service:* U.S. Marine Corps Reserves, 1954-1960.

BELL, AMELIA RECTOR
(anthropologist)

Born in Oak Ridge, Tenn. *Education:* Georgia State University, Atlanta, B.A., 1977;

University of Chicago, M.A., 1979, Ph.D., 1984. *Principal occupation:* Anthropologist. *Home address:* 950 East Ave., Rochester, N.Y. 14607. *Affiliations:* Research assistant, Department of Anthropology, and Department of Linguistics, University of Chicago, 1977-1982; instructor, Field Museum of Natural History, Chicago, 1979; assistant professor, Department of Anthropology, University of Rochester, N.Y., 1983-. *Memberships:* American Anthropological Association; American Society for Ethnohistory; Central States Anthropological Society; Mid-America Linguistics Conference; Oklahoma Historical Society; Northeastern Anthropological Association; Rochester Academy of Sciences; Royal Anthropological Institute of Great Britain and Ireland; Society for Linguistic Anthropology; Society for the Study of the Indigenous Languages of the Americas; Southern Anthropological Society. *Research and teaching specialization:* Linguistic anthropology, sociocultural anthropology, Native North Americans, and West Africa. *Awards, honors:* Research grants from: Georgia State University (for B.A. thesis, 1977, *Instant Indians: An Analysis of Cultural Identity in the Southeastern U.S.);* Whatcom Museum of History and Art; American Philosophical Society, National Science Foundation, Wenner-Gren Foundation for Anthropological Research, University of Rochester, Archival Research Grant. *Dissertation and theses: M.A. thesis, 1979, Coming from the Sun: The Kashita Legend;* Ph.D. dissertation, 1984, *Creek Ritual: The Path to Peace. Interests:* Field research: Creek Indians, Oklahoma and Georgia; Seminole Indians, Oklahoma and Florida; Mississippi Band of Choctaw Indians; Cherokee Indians, North Carolina and Oklahoma; and Yuchi Indians of Oklahoma. Linguistics: Algonquian, Shawnee linguistic analysis, and Muskogean (Creek, Seminole and Choctaw); archival research. *Published works:* Numerous papers and articles on the Creek Indians, 1977-; forthcoming, *The White Path to Peace: Creek Ritual, Politics, and Language (book); Creek Women: The Ideology of Gender and Social Reproduction,* (paper); "Language and the Poetics of Politics: The Logic of Conflict and a Creek Stikinni" (article).

BELL, WILLIAM F. (Mississippi Choctaw) 1932-
(elementary principal)

Born December 27, 1932, Philadelphia, Miss. *Education:* Meridian Jr. College, A.A., 1955; Univerity of Southern Mississippi, B.S., 1957; University of Mississippi, M.Ed., 1964, Ed. Sp., 1976. *Principal occupation:* Elementary principal. *Home address:* P.O. Box 15, Carthage, Miss. 39051. *Affiliation:* School system, Carthage, Miss., 1976-. *Other professional posts:* Teacher, guidance counselor; administrative assistant, Governor's Office of Education and Training; director, Off-Reservation Indian Manpower Programs; planning specialist, National Indian Management Service, Inc. *Community activities:* Governor's Council on Manpower Planning, 1973-1975; Governor's Council on Adult Basic Education, 1973-1975. *Memberships:* Kappa Delta Pi, 1956-; Phi Delta Kappa, 1977. *Awards, honors:* Appointed by Governor of Miss. as liaison officer between State government and tribal government. *Interests:* "Research and writing are my primary interests. I have written several articles about Indian education for college classes."

BENEDICT, PATRICIA (Abenaki) 1956-
(executive director-Indian organization)

Born August 11, 1956, Waterbury, Conn. *Education:* Mattatuck Community College, Waterbury, Conn., A.S. (Alcohol and Drug Counseling), 1980. *Principal occupation:* Executive director, Indian organization. *Home address:* 53 Green St., Waterbury, Conn. 06708. *Affiliation:* American Indians for Development, Meriden, Conn. (social worker, 1975-1981; executive director, 1981-

Other professional post: Co-editor of American Indians for Development *Newsletter. Community activities:* American Indians for Development (past chairman, board of directors); member, Energy Assistance Program Policy Making Board, Meriden, Conn.; member, Federal Regional Support Center, American Indian Committee, New Haven, Conn.; organized Waterbury Indian community into an organization. *Membership:* Title IV Indian Education Committee, Waterbury, Conn.

(chairperson). *Interests:* "Personal interests include: furthering my education in the field of social work, attending and participating in Native American cultural activities, and with the assistance from my staff and Indians in Connecticut, American Indians for Development will once again become a multi-service agency."

BENHAM, WILLIAM JOSEPHUS, Jr.
(Creek) 1928-
(B.I.A. administrator)

Born June 4, 1928, Lamar, Okla. *Education:* East Central State University, Okla., B.A., 1950; Univerity of Oklahoma, Ed.M., 1956, Ed.D., 1965. *Principal occupation:* B.I.A. administrator. *Home address:* 8790 Lagrima De Oro, NE, Albuquerque, N.M. 87111. *Affiliations:* Junior management assistant, Dept. of the Interior, Management Training Program, 1950-1951; principal, teacher, Leupp School, B.I.A., Leupp, Ariz., 1951-1953; principal, Tuba City Boarding School, B.I.A., Ariz., 1953-1954; assistant to director of schools, B.I.A., Window Rock, Ariz., 1954-1955; education specialist, adult education, assistant area director, B.I.A., Gallup Area, N.M., 1957-1963; area director of schools, B.I.A., Gallup Area, N.M., 1963-1966; acting commissioner of education and programs, B.I.A., Washington, D.C., 1970; director of schools, Navajo Area Office, B.I.A., Window Rock, Ariz., 1966-1972; acting director, Office of Indian Education Programs, B.I.A., Washington, D.C., 1973-1974; administrator, Indian Education Resources, B.I.A., Albuquerque, N.M., 1974-. *Community activities:* National Council, Boy Scouts of America (member, Interrelationships Committee and executive board, 1957-); American Association of School Administrators (panel discussions, 1957-); Southern Baptist Churches (superintendent, teacher, 1957-); Annual National Tribal Leaders' Conference on Scouting (member, Steering Committee, 1958-); worked with Navajo Tribe in getting boards of education established for all Navajo schools operated by B.I.A., 1966-1970; *Journal of American Indian Education* (member, editorial board, 1966-1970); Southwest Cooperative Educational Laboratory, Albuquerque (member, board of directors, 1966-1970); Ganado Presbyterian Mission (member, advisory board to president, 1968-1969); *Indian Ed,* University of Alberta, Can. (member, editorial board.) *Memberships:* American Association of School Administrators; National Indian Education Association (charter member). *Awards, honors:* Silver Beaver Award, Boy Scouts of America, 1969; Distinguished Alumnus Award, East Central Oklahoma University, 1975; Meritorious Service Award, Department of the Interior, 1977. *Biographical sources: Who's Who in Government,* Second Edition, 1975-1976; *Indians of Today,* Fourth Edition, 1971; *Who's Who in American Education,* Volume XVIII, 1957-1958. *Published works:* Numerous articles in the *Journal of American Indian Education,* among others.

BENN, ROBERT C. (Choctaw) 1934-
(printer)

Born September 10, 1934, Philadelphia, Miss. *Education:* Clarke Memorial College; Mississippi College, B.A., 1956. *Principal occupation:* Printer. *Home address:* R.F.D., Box 9-A, Carthage, Miss. 39051. *Military service:* U.S. Navy, 1957-1962. *Interests:* "Promoting and encouraging younger Choctaws to prepare themselves and become better citizens of America."

BENNETT, KAY C. (Navajo) 1922-
(writer, doll maker)

Born July 15, 1922, Sheepsprings, N.M. *Education:* "Acquired, for the most part, as a teacher-interpreter at the Phoenix, Arizona Indian Boarding School." *Principal occupation:* Writer, doll maker. *Home address:* 6 Aida Ct., Gallup, N.M. 87301. *Community activities:* New Mexico Human Rights Commissioner, 1969-1971; Inter-Tribal Indian Ceremonial (director); McKinley County Hospital (advisory board). *Memberships:* Heard Museum, Gallup, N.M. (Navajo central committee); City of Gallup Citizens Committee. *Awards, honors:* Appointed Colonel-Aide-de Camp, staff of the Governor of New Mexico; elected New Mexico Mother of the Year, 1968; "have received many awards at state fairs and ceremonials for dolls and dresses I have created." *Interests:* Doll making, dress designing; entertaining as a singer; "have published two albums of Navajo songs. I'm especially interested in Navajo culture, and serve on a school advisory board as a lecturer at schools in New Mexico and Arizona;" travel. *Published works: Kaibah: Recollections of a Navajo Girlhood* (Westernlore Press, 1965; paperback, Kay Bennett, 1976); *A Navajo Saga* (Naylor Co., 1969).

BENNETT, NOEL KIRKISH 1939-
(organization director, author, artist, teacher)

Born December 23, 1939, San Jose, Calif. *Education:* Stanford University, B.A. (Art), 1961, M.A., 1962; Navajo Reservation Weaving Apprenticeship, 1968-1976. *Princpal occupation:* Organization director, author, artist, teacher. *Home address:* P.O. Box 1175. Corrales, N.M. 87048. *Affiliations:* Lecturer, College of Notre Dame, Belmont, Calif., 1963-1967; lecturer, University of New Mexico, 1971-1976; lecturer, International College, Los Angeles, 1979-1981; founder, Navajo Weaver Restoration Center, 1978-; Director, Shared Horizons, Corrales, N.M. (non-profit, educational, perpetuating the Navajo, Southwest textile art tradition. *Other professional post;* Navajo weaving workshops, lectures, demonstrations to museums, universities, and guilds across the nation, 1971-. *Awards, honors:* Cum Laude graduate and recipient of the Mortimer C. Levintritt Award for outstanding work in Departments of Art and Architecture, Stanford University, 1961; Weatherhead Foundation Grant, 1975; Communication Arts Award, "Three Looms, One Land: Shared Horizons" poster award for concept, copy, photo, 1982. *Interests:* Painting, tapestry weaving, restoration of Navajo rugs, philosophy. "Though intensely involved in my own painting, weaving and writing, the area of Navajo life and weaving continues to provide inspiration and satisfaction. With the nine years that I lived and wove on the Navajo Reservation as a basis, my core goals have been to seek out, internalize and share the beauty of traditional Navajo weaving in three main areas: the pure symetry and balance of designs,

refined through generations of use; the rhythm of effortless techniques, a oneness of self and loom evolving over time; and the underlying sustaining beliefs, legends and taboos that give meaning not only to the activity but beyond, to life itself." *Biographical sources: Contemporary Authors; World Who's Who of Authors; Dictionary of International Biography; World Who's Who of Women; The Directory of Distinguished Americans; International Book of Honor; Personalities of America; Personalities of the West and Midwest; 5,000 Personalities of the World; International Directory of Distinguished Leadership; International Authors' and Writers' Who's Who.* *Published works: Working With the Wool -- How to Weave a Navajo Rug,* with Tiana Bighorse (Northland Press, 1971); *Genuine Navajo Rug -- Are You Sure?* (Museum of Navajo Ceremonial Art - Wheelwright Museum - and the Navajo Tribe, 1973); *The Weaver's Pathway -- A Clarification of the "Spirit Trail" in Navajo Weaving* (Northland Press, 1974); "How to Tell a Genuine Navajo Rug" (final chapter) *Navajo Weaving Handbook* (Museum of New Mexico Press, 1974, 1977); *Designing With the Wool -- Advanced Navajo Weaving Techniques* (Northland Press, 1979); *Shared Horizons-/Navajo Textiles,* (catalog of exhibition) with Susan McGreevy and Mark Winter (Wheelwright Museum, 1981).

BENNETT, ROBERT L. (Oneida) 1912-
(former commissioner of Indian Affairs)

Born November 16, 1912, Oneida, Wisc. *Education:* Haskell Institute; Southeastern University, LL.B., 1941. *Home address: 604 Wagon Train, S.E., Albuquerque, N.M. 87123. Affiliations:* Former area director, Bureau of Indian Affairs; former commissioner of Indian Affairs, Bureau of Indian Affairs, Washington, D.C., 1965-1968. *Military service:* U.S. Marine Corps, 1944-1945. *Memberships:* American Society for Public Administration; Society for Applied Anthropology; American Academy of Political and Social Science, 1960-. *Awards, honors:* Indian Achievement Award, Indian Council Fire, 1962. *Biographical sources: Indians of Today* (Indian Council Fire, 1960).

BENNETT, RUTH (Shawnee) 1942-
(assistant director of
Indian organization)

Born December 12, 1942. *Education:* Indiana University, B.A., 1964; University of Washington, M.A. (English), 1968; California State University, San Francisco, Standard Secondary Teaching Credential (Multi-Cultural Education), 1973; University of California, Berkeley, Ph.D. (language and reading development with a specialization in bilingual education), 1979. *Principal occupation:* Assistant director of Indian organization. *Home address:* P.O. Box 883, Hoopa, Calif. 95546. *Affiliations:* Teaching assistant, University of Washington, 1964-1966; pre-school teacher, Inner Sunset Neighborhood Cooperative, San Francisco, 1971-1972; teaching assistant, University of California, Berkeley, 1973-1974; children's literature instructor, School of the Arts, Berkeley High School, Calif., 1973-1974; enrichment program instructor, Washington Laboratory School, Berkeley, 1975-1978; resource teacher, Hoopa Elementary School, 1976-; field director, Native Language and Culture Program, 1978-1979, assistant director, 1980-, Center for Community Development; director, Title VII, Institute of Higher Education Training Grant, Bilingual Emphasis Program, Center for Community Development, 1981-; teacher, Department of Education, Humboldt State University, 1981-. *Memberships:* Phi Delta Kappa, Phi Beta Kappa, Alpha Lambda Delta, Alpha Omicron Pi; University of California and Indiana University Alumni Associations. *Interests:* Dr. Ruth Bennett has conducted innovative curriculum work for 15 years, leading to computer uses for curriculum. *Published works:* Downriver Indians' Legends, 1983; Let's Go Now, 1983; *1983 Hupa Calendar,* 1982; *Karuk Fishing,* 1983; *Look Inside and Read,* 1982; *Unifon Update,* 1983; *1983-1984 Yurok Unifon Calendar,* 1983; *Origin of Fire; Songs of a Medicine Woman; Hupa Spelling Book; Legends and Personal Experiences; Ceremonial Dances; Yurok Spelling Book; What Is An Indian?; Karuk Vocabulary Book; Karuk Fishing; Basket Weaving Among the Karuk; Tolowa Legends; Tolowa/English Lesson Units; and others (all published by The Center for Community*

Development, Humboldt State University; numerous articles, including Ph.D. dissertation, "Hoopa Children's Storytelling," University of California, Berkeley.

BERRIGAN, TED (Choctaw) 1934-
(poet)

Born November 15, 1934, Providence, R.I. *Education:* University of Tulsa, B.A., M.A. (English Literature.) *Principal occupation:* Poet. *Affiliations:* Editor, *"C," A Journal of Poetry,* 1963-; New York editor, *Long Hair* magazine, London; editorial assistant, *Art News* magazine; instructor, Poetry Workshop, University of Iowa. *Military service:* U.S. Army, 1954-1957 (Good Conduct Medal; U.N. Service Medal; Korean Service Medal). *Published works: The Sonnets* (C Press, 1964, Grove Press); *Many Happy Returns* (Corinth); *In the Early Morning Rain* (Goliard, Grossman); *Bean Spasms,* with Ron Padgett Kulchur).

BERTHRONG, DONALD J. 1922-
(professor of history)

Born October 2, 1922, La Crosse, Wisc. *Education:* University of Wisconsin, B.S., 1947, M.S., 1948, Ph.D., 1952. *Principal occupation:* Professor of history. *Address:* Department of History, Purdue University, Lafayette, Ind. 49707. *Affiliations:* Instructor, University of Kansas City; assistant professor, associate professor, professor of history, University of Oklahoma; professor and head, Department of History, Purdue University. *Military service:* U.S. Army and Air Force, 1942-1946. *Memberships:* American Historical Association; Association of American History; Olahoma Historical Society; Western Historical Society. *Awards, honors:* Fellowship, Social Science Research Council; Fellowship, Americn Philosophical Society; Award of Merit, Society for State and Local History, for *The Southern Cheyennes. Interests:* Western U.S. history; expert witness before the Indian Claims Commission; Fulbright lecturer in American history at the University of Hong Kong and Chinese University (Hong Kong, B.C.C.) *Published works:* Co-editor, *Joseph Redford Walker and the Arizona Adventure* (University of Oklahoma Press, 1956); *The Southern Cheyennes* (University of Oklahoma Press, 1963); *A Confederate in the Colorado Gold Fields* (University of Oklahoma Press, 1970); *Indians of Northern Indiana and Southwestern Michigan* (Garland, 1974); *The Cheyenne and Arapaho Ordeal: Reservation and Agency Life in the Indian Territory, 1875-1907* (University of Oklahoma Press, 1976).

BETTELYOUN, LULU F. (JANIS)
(Oglala Sioux) 1947-
(teacher, social welfare/caseworker)

Born April 10, 1947, Pine Ridge, S.D. *Education:* Northern State College, Aberdeen, S.D., 1965-1968; Black Hills State College, Spearfish, S.D., B.S. (Education), 1972. *Principal occupation:* Teacher, social welfare/caseworker. *Home address:* P.O. Box 66, Pine Ridge, S.D. 57770.

BIGSPRING, WILLIAM F., Sr.
(Blackfeet) 1919-
(rancher, artist)

Born January 3, 1919, East Glacier Park, Mont. *Principal occupation:* Rancher, artist. *Home address:* Box 531, East Glacier Park, Mont. 59434. *Military service:* U.S. Army Infantry, 1944-1945. *Commuity activities:* Art Exhibition, Glacier Park, Mont. (chairman). *Memberships:* Blackfeet Artists Group (president, 1964); Montana Institute of Arts, 1962-.

BITSIE, OSCAR (Navajo) 1935-
(teacher)

Born October 30, 1935, Tohatchi, N.M. *Education:* Fort Lewis College, B.A., 1964; Northern Arizona University, M.A., 1973, Post Graduate work in School Administration, 1974-1975. *Principal occupation:* Teacher. *Home address:* P.O. Box 1496, Tohatchi, N.M. 87325-1496. *Affiliations:* Gallup-McKinley County Schools, Gallup, N.M.; teacher of social studies, Tohatchi Middle School, Tohatchi, N.M. (21 years).

Other professional posts: Coordinated Title 7 - Bilingual Education, Johnson-O'Malley Indian Education, Title IV - home/school liaison coordinator. *Military service:* U.S. Army 1958-1960 (Expert Rifle; Good Conduct Medal). *Community activities:* Tohatchi Chapter President, 1970-1974, Vice President, 1978-1982; Public Health Service, Gallup, N.M. (board member, 1970-1980); Public Health Service, Gallup Indian Medical Center (health board president, 1980-); Friendship Service for Alcoholic Recovery Center (board of directors, vice-president, 1982-1985).*Memberships:* Christian Reformed Church (delegate to Calvin College in Michigan, 1976); Navajo Tribe. *Awards, honors:* Community service award by Tohatchi Chapter for Community Leadership. *Interests:* Reading books in social studies; travel throughout the Rockies for historical information; political activities in Navajo Tribe, county and state.

BLUE SPRUCE, BERYL
(Laguna/San Juan Pueblo) 1934-
(obstetrician)

Born November 24, 1934, Santa Fe, N.M. *Education:* Stanford University, B.S., 1960; University of Southern California, M.D., 1964. *Principal occupation:* Obstetrician. *Community activities:* Indian Rights Association, American Friends Service Committee (board of directors); National Indian Youth Council. *Memberships:* American College of Obstetrics and Gynecology (Fellow); Phi Rho Sigma. *Awards, honors:* John Hay Whitney Fellow, 1961-1962.

BLUE SPRUCE, GEORGE, Jr.
(Laguna/San Juan Pueblo) 1931-
(health systems director)

Born January 16, 1931, Santa Fe, N.M. *Education:* Creighton University, D.D.S., 1956; University of California School of Public Health, M.P.H., 1967; Feeral Executive Institute, Certificate, 1973. *Principal occupation:* Health systems director. *Home address:* 3834 E. Yale, Phoenix, Ariz. 85008. *Affiliations:* Dental officer, U.S. Navy Dental Clinic, 1956-1958; dental officer, U.S.P.H.S. Indian Hospital, Fort Belknap,

Mont., 1958-1960; U.S.P.H.S. Outpatient Clinic, New York, N.Y. (resident, 1960-1961; deputy dental director, 1961-1963); resident in dental public health, Dental Health Center, San Francisco, Calif., 1967-1968; consultant in dental health (special assignment), Pan American Health Organization, World Health Organization, Washington, D.C., 1968-1970; Education Development Branch, Division of Dental Health, National Institutes of Health, Bethesda, Md. - chief, Auxiliary Utilization Section, 1971, special assistant to the director for American Indian Affairs, 1971, director, Office of Health Manpower Opportunity, 1971-1973; liaison officer for Indian concerns, Health Resources Administration, U.S.P.H.S., Department of HEW, 1973-1974; director, Office of Native American Programs, Office of Human Development, Dept. of HEW, 1976-1978; director, Indian Health Manpower Development, Indian Health Service, DHEW, 1978-1979; director, Phoenix Area Indian Health Service, DHEW, 1979-. *Other professional posts:* Chairman, Intra-Departmental Council on Indian Affairs (DHEW); chairman, Health Manpower Opportunity Advisory Committee; chairman, Feasibility Study Team for Project: Center for Health Professions Education (Navajo Reservation, Arizona); special consultant, Special Committee for the Socio-economically Disadvantaged, American Dental Hygienist's Association. *Memberships:* National Indian Education Association (board of directors); Health Education Media Association (board of directors, Minority Affairs); American Indian Bank (board of directors); American Fund for Dental Education (member, Selection Committee); Task Force for Medical Academic Achievement Program; Students American Veterinary Medicine Association (member, Selection Committee; Health Manpower Study for American Indians (member, Advisory Committee); Navajo Health Authority (member, board of commissioners, Kellog Scholarship Committee, Dean Selection Committee, Health Professions Education Committee); American Indian School of Medicine - Feasibility Study (member, Advisory Council); Health Professions Education System, Rockville, Md. (board of directors); U.S.P.H.S. Commissioned Officers' Association ; American Public Health Association; American Indian Physicians' Association; American Dental Association; American Association of Dental Schools; New Mexico State Dental Society; North Americn Indian Tennis Association; U.S. Lawn Tennis Association. *Awards, honors:* Outstanding American Indian for 1972, American Indian Exposition, Inc., Anadarko, Okla.; Outstanding American Indian Achievement Award, 1974, American Indian Council Fire, Inc., Washington, D.C.; "Award of Merit", presented by the Association of American Indian Physicians for: "Significant Contributions Towards Raising the Level of Health Care of the American Indian and Alaskan Native," August 1980; "Alumni of the Year," presented by Creighton University, Omaha, Neb. in May 1984, for "his distinguished service to his fellow man and his alma mater while keeping with the finest traditions of the University. *Biographical sources: American Indians of Today; Contemporary American Indian Leaders; Who's Who in the Federal Government,* Second Edition; *National Indian Directory* (National Congress of American Indians); *Dictionary of International Biography; Men of Achievement,* 1974. *Interests:* Recruitment of minority students into health professions; health manpower development for American Indians; American Indian education; public health administration. *Published works:* Articles: "Toward More Minorities in Health Professions" (National Medical Association Journal, Sept. 1972); "Needed: Indian Health Professionals" (Harvard Medical Alumni Bulletin, Jan.-Feb. 1972); "Health Manpower Grants Open New Opportunities for American Indians" (Official Newsletter of the Association of American Indian Physicians, Vol. 1, No. 1, Nov. 1972); "The American Indian as a Dental Patient" (Public Health Reports, Dec. 1961); *The Fabrication of Simplified Dental Equipment - A Manual* (Pan American Health Organization Publication, pending publication); *The Development and Testing of a Mobile Dental Care Unit* (Public Health Residency Report).

BLUMER, THOMAS J. 1937-
(senior editor, Library of Congress)

Born July 7, 1937, Freeport, N.Y. *Education:* University of Mississippi, B.A., 1967, M.A., 1968; University of South Carolina, Ph.D. (English Literature), 1976. *Principal occupation:* Senior editor, Library of Congress (Law Library). *Home address:* 642 A St., N.E., Washington, D.C. 20002. *Affiliations:* Assistant professor, Tidewater Community College, Portsmouth, Va., 1968-1972; Teaching assistant, University of South Carolina, Columbia, S.C., 1972-1976; lecturer in English, Winthrop College, Rock Hill, S.C., 1976-1977; Data Analyst, Planning Research Corp., McLean, Va., 1977-1978; senior editor, European Law Division, Law Library, Library of Congress, 1978-; consultant, Native American Rights Fund, Boulder, Colo., 1980-; consultant, McKissick Museums, University of South Carolina, 1984-; consultant, Pamunkey Indian Museum, King William, Va., 1985; editor, American Indian Libraries Newsletter, American Library Association, Chicago, Ill., 1984-. *Military service:* U.S. Navy, 1956-1960. *Memberships:* American Library Association; American Indian Library Association, 1982-; American Folklore Association; Mid-Atlantic Folklife Association, 1982-; Library of Congress Professional Association. *Interests:* Southeastern Indians, Catawba Indian history, Pamunkey Indian history, Southern Indian pottery traditions (Catawba, Cherokee, Pamunkey); lectures. *Published works: Catawba Indian Pottery: An Exhibition* (Winthrop College, 1977); *Catawba Indian Bibliography* (Scarecrow Press, 1985); numerous articles. *Works in Progress: Catawba Indian Folk History Project; Pamunkey Indian Folklife Project; "*The Pamunkey Indians in the War Between the States.*"

BOISSEVAIN, ETHEL 1913-
(professor of anthropology
and archaeology)

Born February 5, 1913, New York, N.Y. Education: Vassar College, B.A., 1934; University of Prague, Prague, Czechoslovakia, Ph.D., 1936. *Principal occupation:* Professor of anthropology and archaeology. *Home address:* 1350 - 15th St., Apt. 12-O, Fort Lee,

N.J. 07024. *Affiliations:* Professor of anthropology, Hunter College, 1937-1944, 1959-1967; professor of anthropology, Drew University, 1967-1968; professor of anthropology, Lehman College, CUNY, 1968-1979. *Community activities:* American Civil Liberties Union (member, American Indian committee, 1956-1959.) *Memberships:* Americn Anthropological Association (Fellow); American Society for Ethnohistory, 1954-; Society for Historical Archaeology, 1968-; Archaeological Society of New Jersey, 1943-. *Awards, honors:* Grants from the Rhode Island Historical Preservation Commission: For surveying and mapping the historic village of the Narragansett Indians in Charlestown, R.I., 1969; Lehman College Grant for Faculty Research (George N. Shuster Fellowship Fund); from the Research Center of C.U.N.Y., a grant in support of research on the ethnohistory of the Indians of Southern New England and Eastern Long Island, for writing a chapter on this subject for the Smithsonian Institution's, *Handbook of the North American Indians,* 1971. *Interests:* New England ethnohistory and ethnoarchaeology; travel to central and eastern Europe. Dr. Boissevain writes, "My major areas of vocational interest are teaching and researching American Indian cultures." *Published works: The Narragansett People* (Indian Tribal Series, Phoenix, Ariz., 1975); *Hidden Minorities* (University Press of America, 1981); numerous articles and papers published in journals and as chapters of professional anthropological texts.

BOISSIERE, ROBERT 1914-
(retired, writer)

Born December 23, 1914, France. *Education:* Law School, Paris (three years). *Principal occupation:* Retired, writer. *Home address:* Route 11, Box 6B, Santa Fe, N.M. 87501. Military service: World War II, Frnce (two decorations). Memberships: Western Writers of America. *Biographical sources: Contemporary Authors. Published works: Po-Pai-Mo - The Search for White Buffalo Woman* (Sunstone Press, 1983); *The Hopi Way - An Odyssey* (Sunstone Press, 1985); *Meditations With the Hopi* (Bear and Co., 1986).

BOMBERRY, DANIEL RICHARD (Cayuga) 1945-
(organizer, educational administrator)

Born March 24, 1945, North Vancouver, British Columbia, Can. *Education:* California State University, A.B. (Political Science), 1970. *Principal occupation:* Organizer, educational administrator. *Affiliations:* Coordinator, American Indian Center, California State University, Long Beach, 1969-1970; associate director, Educational Opportunity Program, California State University, 1970-1971; director, Owens Valley Indian Education Center, Bishop Reservation, California, 1971-. *Community activities:* American Indian Culture Program Board, U.C.L.A., 1969-1970; American Indian Education Council, California State Department of Education; Native American Alliance of California (organizer, 1969-1971); Coalition of Indian Controlled School Boards, Denver, Colorado (executive board, 1972-1973); D.Q. University, Davis, Calif. (board, 1972-1973). *Memberships:* California Indian Education Association (1969-; nominating committee, 1973); Nationl Indian Education Association, 1971-; Indian Fair Association, 1972-; Bishop Indian Athletic Association, 1972-. *Awards, honors:* Robert F. Kennedy Memorial Fellowship for 1973 to organize a statewide network of Indian controlled educational programs throughout rural California. *Interests:* "Organizing Indian communities or groups to assume control of their own educational programs."

BONNEY, RACHEL A. 1939-
(professor of anthropology)

Born March 28, 1939, St. Paul, Minn. *Education:* University of Minnesota, B.A., 1961, M.A., 1963; University of Arizona, Ph.D., 1975. *Principal occupation:* Professor of anthropology. *Home address:* Route 1, Box 395, Mooresville, N.C. 28115. *Affiliations:* Assistant professor, Tarkio College, Mo., 1965-1967; instructor, University of South Florida, 1967-1970; graduate teaching associate, University of Arizona, 1971-1973;

instructor and professor, University of North Carolina at Charlotte, 1973-. *Other professional posts:* Teacher, guidance, B.I.A., Teec Nos Pos Boarding School, Ariz. (Navajo), 1964. *Community activities:* Charlotte-Mecklenburg Title IV (Indian Education Act) Indian Parent Committee (ex-officio member, 1975-1977); Metrolina Native American Association, Charlotte, N.C.; UNCC Phoenix Society (American Indian Student Organization) and Phoenix Dancer (Indian dance team), (advisor). *Memberships:* American Anthropological Association (Fellow) 1963-; American Ethnological Society, 1967-1971, 1977-; Southern Anthropological Association, 1973-; National Congress of American Indians, 1972-1973; Anthropological Council on Education, 1977-; National Indian Education Association, 1977-; Southeastern Indian Cultural Association, 1977-. *Awards, honors:* HEW Title IX (ethnic heritage studies) Project Grant, 1977-1978. *Interests:* Indian studies; multi-ethnic studies; culture change (Catawba land claims case); Indian powwows; powwows with Phoenix Dancers; archaeological projects in Minnesota, New York, New Mexico, and Austria. *Biographical sources: Who's Who in America - The South* (Marquis). *Published works: "American Indian Studies in the Social Studies Curriculum"* (Proceedings, North Carolina Association for Research in Education, May, 1975); *"The Role of Women in Indian Activism"* (The Western Canadian Journal of Anthropology, Vol. VI, No. 3, 1976); *"The Role of AIM Leaders in Indian Nationalism"* (American Indian Quarterly, Vol. 3, No. 3, 1977); *"Indians of the Americas, Courtship Customs"* (Encyclopedia of Indians of the Americas, Scholarly Press, 1978); among others.

BORMAN, LEONARD D. 1927-
(anthropologist, research associate)

Born May 24, 1927, Toledo, Ohio. *Education:* University of Toledo, 1946-1948; University of Chicago, M.A. (Thesis: *Work Camp Among the Penobscot Indians*), 1952, Ph.D., 1965. *Principal occupation:* Anthropologist, research associate. *Home address:* 2405 Lawndale, Evanston, Ill. 60201. *Affiliations:* Director of program development, Stone Brandel Center, Chicago, 1966-1970; program director, W. Clement & Jessie V. Stone Foundation, Chicago, 1970-1974; research associate and director, Self-Help Institute, Center for Urban Affairs, Northwestern University, 1974-; research associate, Department of Behavioral Science (Human Development), University of Chicago, 1976-. *Other professional posts:* Chief, Anthropological Section, V.A. Hospital, Downey, Ill., 1958-1965; consultant, North American Indian Foundation, Norman, Okla., 1973-1975. *Field work:* Penobscot and Passamaquoddy Indians, Maine (financed by grant from the American Friends Service Committee, Philadelphia, Pa.). *Community activities:* American Indian Center, Chicago (member, board of directors, 1956-1968); Grand Council of the American Indian Center, Chicago (member, 1968-; chairman, 1968-1970); Self-Help Development Institute, Evanston (president, 1975); Council for the Study of Mankind (member, board of directors, 1977); *Memberships:* American Anthropological Association (Fellow); Society of Sigma Xi; Society for Applied Anthropology (Fellow); National Association of Social Workers; Current Anthropology (Associate, Fellow); Council on Anthropology and Education; Council on Medical Anthropology; American Association for the Advancement of Science; Royal Anthropological Institute of Great Britain and Ireland (Fellow). *Biographical sources: Who's Who in the Midwest; Dictionary of International Biography; Royal Blue Book; Two Thousand Men of Achievement; Roster of Prominent Americans; Community Leaders of America; International Who's Who in Community Service.* Published works: "Indian Citizenry: A Bridge or a Sawdust Trail" (*Down East* magazine, Nov., 1954); "An Indian Chief Retires" (*Down East* magazine, June 1957); "American Indian Tribal Support Systems and Economic Development" (*The Diverse Society: Implications for Social Policy,* National Association of Social Workers, 1976) "American Indian: The Reluctant Urbanites" (*The Center Magazine,* Center for the Study of Democratic Institutions, March-April, 1977); among others.

BOSIN, BLACKBEAR (Kiowa-Comanche) 1921-
(artist, muralist, designer)

Born June 15, 1921, Anadarko, Okla. *Principal occupation:* Artist, muralist, designer. *Affiliation:* Artist, president, Blackbear's Ltd., Great Plains Studio, Wichita, Kansas. *Other professional posts:* Advisor, Wichita Art Museum, Mobil Gallery; board, acquisitions committee, Mid-America All Indian Center, Kansas. *Military service:* U.S. Marines, 1943-1945. *Memberships:* Advertising Club of Wichita; Wichita Artists Guild, 1948-; International Arts & Letters, Switzerland. *Awards, honors:* Invited to the Festival of Arts, The White House, 1965; delivered a paper on "Traditional Indian Arts" at the Convocation of American Indian Scholars, Princeton University, 1970; commissioned to design a 44' Indian figure made of Corten steel given to the City of Wichita, Bicentennial Commission for Kansas; medallic designer for the Historical Indian series for the Franklin Mint; recipient of the National American Indian Achievements Award for Visual Arts, Traditional Painter; Kansas Art Commission appointed Governor's artist, 1977. *Biographical sources: Who's Who in American Art. Exhibits:* The Smithsonian Institute; Eisenhower Museum, Abilene, Kansas; Albany Institute of History and Art; Currier Gallery of Art; Miami Beach Art Center; Wichita Art Association; George Walter Vincent Smith Art Museum; Museum of the Great Plains; Los Angeles County Museum; Palace of the Legion of Honor; Denver Art Museum; Heard Museum; Philbrook Museum; Chicago Indian Center; Oklahoma City Art Center; The National Gallery; Whitney Museum; The White House. *Lectures:* Wichita State University; Princeton University; Mid-America All Indian Center, Wichita; and Philbrook Art Center, Tulsa, Okla.

BOURGEAU, DEAN (Colville) 1928-
(musician)

Born July 14, 1928, Inchelium, Wash. *Principal occupation:* Musician. *Home address:* Inchelium, Was. 99137. *Affiliations:* Colville Business Council; Indian police. *Mil-*

itary service: U.S. Army, 1950-1952, 1956-1957 (U.N. Service Medal, Combat Medal.) *Community activities:* American Legion; Eagles.

BOUWENS, WILLIAM CLAYTON, Jr. (Aleut, Tanaina-Kenaitze) 1947-
(president, Alaska Cultural Services)

Born November 23, 1947, Anchorage, Alaska. *Education:* Univerity of Alaska at Fairbanks, Anchorage, and Soldotna, 1966-1972. *Principal occupation:* President, Alaska Cultural Services, 1976-. *Home address:* Box 173, Ninilichik, Alaska. *Other professional posts:* Shareholder, Cook Inlet Region, Inc.; secretary-treasurer, Ninilichik Native Association. *Military service:* Air National Guard, 1971-1976. *Memberships:* American Legion; Cook Inlet Native Association; Alaska Federation of Natives; American Indian Education Association, Project Media Evaluation, 1977-1978.

BOVIS, PIERRE G. 1943-
(shop owner)

Born February 3, 1943, Nice, France. *Education:* Beaux Arts, France, B.A. equivalent. *Principal occupation:* Shop owner. *Home address:* P.O. Box 324, Santa Fe, N.M. 87501. *Affiliation:* Owner, Winona Trading Post, Santa Fe, N.M., 1968-. *Military service:* French Army (two years). *Community activities:* Loaned Indian artifacts for local and national traveling exhibits. *Memberships:* Appraisers Association of America; Indian Arts and Crafts Association; Genuine Indian Relic Society; English Westerners, London. *Awards, honors:* "Have won several first, second and third place cups and trophies for my displays of Indian artifacts at Indian shows." *Biographical sources: Who's Who in Indian Relics,* Vol. III: *International Who's Who in Art & Antiques,* Vol. XI. *Interests:* "Interests lie in anthropology and primitive art, and I travel through Europe and Far East, etc." *Published works: American Indian and Eskimo Basketry: A Key to Identification,* with Charles Miles, 1970; *Pine Ridge, 1890: Eye Witness Account of the Events Surrounding Wounded Knee,* 1972. Both published by Mr. Bovis.

BOWLAN, LORI A. 1964-
(tribal rolls director)

Born June 25, 1964, Danbury, Conn. *Education:* Oklahoma State University, Stillwater, (four years, degree pending). *Principal occupation:* Tribal rolls director. *Home address:* P.O. Box 746, Tecumseh, Oklahoma 74873. *Other professional posts:* Scholarship committee director.

BOY, CALVIN J. *(Warring Shield)* (Blackfoot) 1923-
(artist)

Born September 18, 1923, Browning, Mont. *Education:* High school. *Principal occupation:* Artist. *Home address:* General Delivery, Browning, Mont. 59417. *Affiliations:* Machine shop apprentice (three years); railroad foreman (ten years); worked with John C. Ewers as an illustrator.

BOYD, ROSE MARIE (Chippewa-Oneida) 1958-
(administrative assistant)

Born March 2, 1958, Detroit, Mich. *Education:* Schoolcraft College, Livonia, Mich., 1975-1978. *Home address:* 16739 Beaverland, Detroit, Mich. 48219. *Affiliations:* Administrative assistant, South Eastern Michigan Indians, Inc., Warren, Mich., 1985-.

BOYER, MOMMA QUAIL (United Lumbee-Cherokee) 1925-
(homemaker)

Born October 16, 1925, Oklahoma. *Education:* High school. *Principal occupation:* Homemaker. *Home address:* P.O. Box 512, Fall River Mills, Calif. 96028. *Other professional post:* National secretary, United Lumbee Nation of N.C. and America. *Affiliations:* United Lumbee Nation of N.C. and America (Grand Council, national secretary); Title IV and Johnson O'Malley Indian Education Program in Tulare, Kings Counties, Calif. (parent committee & chairperson, five years); *Memberships:* Native American Wolf Clan (1977-1982; chief, 1982-); Chapel of Our Lord Jesus (treasurer, vice-chief).

**BRADLEY, RUSSELL (Kickapoo) 1942-
(B.I.A. agency superintendent)**

Born July 25, 1942, St. Joseph, Mo. *Education:* Haskell Institute (Business), 1962; Metropolitan Junior College, Kansas City (Business Admininistration), 1966. *Principal occupation:* B.I.A. agency superintendent. *Home address:* Box 2075, Whiteriver, Arizona 85941. *Affiliations:* Assistant director, United Tribes of North Dakota Training Center, Bismarck, N.D., 1972; employment director, United Sioux Tribes, Pierre, S.D., 1973; superintendent, Winnebago Agency, Winnebago, Neb. (four years); superintendent, Turtle Mountain Agency, Belcourt, N.D. (two years); superintendent, Fort Apache Agency, Whiteriver, Ariz. (two years). *Military service:* U.S. Army, 1964-1966 (Specialist 5th Class, Good Conduct Medal.) *Community activities:* Requires alignment with most all community services and functions, such as: education, law enforcement, social services, economic development and planning, road and judicial services. *Memberships:* Younghawk/Bear American Legion Post (Albuquerque chapter, 11 years); Haskell Alumni Association; National Indian Contractors Association; National Intertribal Timber Council. *Awards, honors:* B.I.A. Outstanding Achievement Award, 1982; Community Service Award, 1984, Turtle Mountain Chippewa Tribe. *Interests:* Minority employment development; reservation economic development; Indian education; traditional preservation and enhancement of recreation and athletics on reservations. "Enhancing tribal governments in serving its members provides the greatest challenge and satisfaction." *Biographical sources: Who's Who in North Dakota, 1984.*

**BRANDON, WILLIAM 1914-
(writer)**

Born September 21, 1914, Kokomo, Ind. *Principal occupation:* Writer. *Affiliations:* Visiting lecturer, University of Massachusetts, 1967, California State College (Los Angeles, 1970, Long Beach, 1970). *Military service:* U.S. Air Force, 1944-1945. *Awards, honors:* Western Heritage Award for *The American Heritage Book of Indians,* 1961.

Interests: Mr. Brandon writes, "I have been interested in introducing experimental courses in American Indian literature, and in American Indians and American history, at various colleges and universities. My essay, 'American Indians and American History,' published in *The American West,* Journal of the Western History Association in 1965, has been used as the basis of these courses. Most of 1969 was spent traveling over the country, preparing a series of articles on current Indian matters, titles, 'American Indians: The Alien Americans,' published in *The Progressive* from December, 1969 to February, 1970 (and) reprinted in various publications, including the *Congressional Record.* I attended as an invited observer the First Convocation of Americn Indian Scholars, held at Princeton (University) in March, 1970." *Published works: The Men and the Mountain* (William Morrow, 1955); *The Amerian Heritage Book of Indians* (American Heritage Publishing Co., 1961; Dell, 1964); *The Magic World: American Indian Songs and Poems* (William Morrow, 1971).

**BRAUKER, SHIRLEY M. (Ottawa) 1950
(potter)**

Born August 11, 1950, Angola, Ind. *Education:* Mid-Michigan Community College, Harrison, A.A., 1980; Central Michigan University, Mt. Pleasant, B.A., 1982, M.A., 1983. *Principal occupation:* Potter. *Home address:* 1044 Silver Rd., Coldwater, Mich. 49036. *Affiliation:* Secretary, Central Michigan University, 1982-1984. *Memberships:* National Collegiate Education of Ceramics; National Honor Society. *Art Exhibitions:* Bachelor of Fine Arts, Central Michigan University, 1981; Great Lakes Traveling Indian Art Exhibition, Dept. of the Interior, Washington, D.C., 1983; Ethnic Art Show, Lansing Art Gallery, 1983; Sacred Circle Gallery, Seattle, Wash., "American Indian Ceramic Art; Yesterday, Today and Tomorrow" exhibit, 1984; Midland Christmas Arts Festival, 1984; Museum of the Plains Indian, Browning, Mont., "Contemporary Clay Indian Art" exhibit, 1985; Larson

Gallery, Grand Rapids, Mich. *Community activities:* Demonstrates pottery techniques aboard the Traveling Art Train, 1983; worked on a documentary film depicting Indian artists in Michigan, 1983; illustrates pamphlets and handouts for community service. *Awards, honors:* Outstanding Community College Student Scholarship Award, 1980; Mae Beck Indian Artist Scholarship Award, 1982; Potter of the Month, Lansing Art Gallery, 1983. *Interests:* Indian history, culture and art work; craft work, doll making, quilting, painting, beadwork, stained glass; travel and camping. *Biographical sources:* Documentary film: *Woodland Traditions: The Art of Three Native Americans; American Indian Index.*

BRENNAN, LOUIS ARTHUR 1911-
(writer, archaeologist)

Born February 5, 1911. *Education:* University of Notre Dame, A.B., 1932. *Principal occupation:* Writer, archaeologist. *Home address:* 39 Hamilton Ave., Ossining, N.Y. 10562. *Affiliations:* Assistant professor, Pace University; director, Museum and Laboratory for Archaeology at Muscoot Farm (Westchester County Parks Dept.) *Other professional posts:* Editor, *Archaeology of Eastern North America;* editor, New York State Archaeological Association journal of archaeology, *The Bulletin. Military service:* U.S. Naval Reserve, 1943-1945 (Bronze Star for gallantry). *Memberships:* Society for Professional Archaeologists; Society for American Archaeology. *Awards, honors:* Achievement Award, NYSAA: fellow, NYSAA. *Interests:* American archaeology and prehistory; field of specialty, historical and prehistoric archaeology of Lower Hudson Valley. *Published works: The Long Knife,* (Dell, 1957) and *Tree of Arrows,* (Macmillan, 1964) both historical novels; *No Stone Unturned: An Almanac of North American Prehistory* (Random House, 1959); *The Buried Treasure of Archaeology* (Random House, 1964); *American Dawn: A New Model of American Prehistory* (Macmillan, 1970); Beginner's Guide to Archaeology (Stackpole, 1974; Dell, 1975); *Artifacts of Prehistoric America* (Stackpole, 1975); numerous articles.

BRESCIA, WILLIAM, Jr.
(Mississippi Choctaw) 1947-
(director, research and curriculum development)

Born November 4, 1947, Chicago, Ill. *Education:* Wartburg College, Waverly, Iowa, B.A. (Drama), 1970; University of Wisconsin, Madison, M.S. (Curriculum and Instruction), 1973. *Principal occupation:* Director, research and curriculum development. *Home address:* Route 5, Box 364, Union, Miss. 39365. *Affiliation:* Editor, *Daybreak Star Magazine* (Daybreak Star Press, 1976-1981; Curriculum coordinator, 1976-1978, director, Community Educational Services, 1978-1981, United Indians of All Tribes Foundation, Seattle, Wash.; director, Curriculum Developer, Ethnic Heritage Program, 1981-1982, director, Division of Research and Curriculum Development, Mississippi Band of Choctaw Indians, Philadelphia, Miss., 1982-. *Other professional posts:* Computer education consultant, Mississippi State Department of Education, 1984-. *Community activities:* D'Arcy McNickle Center, Newberry Library, Chicago, Ill. (advisor, 1985-); ERIC/CRESS National Advisory Board (American Indian educational specialist, 1984-); *The Native American* (advisory committee member, 1984-); Indian representative, Washington Urban Rural Racial Disadvantaged Advisory Committee, 1979-1980; Indian representative, *New Voice* Advisory committee, WGBH-TV, Boston, Mass, 1977-1980; Scientists and Citizens Organized on Policy Issues, Seattle, Wash., 1980-1981; Seattle Museum of History and Industry, 1979-1981. *Memberships:* American Education Research Association; International Reading Association; National Indian Education Association; National Association for Bilingual Education; Mid-South Educational Research Association; Association for Supervision and Curriculum Development. *Awards, honors:* American Indian Heritage High School (special recognition for work in support of that school and Indian education); Northwest American Indian Womens Circle (special recognition for work in support of National Conference, 1979); Northwest Regional Folklife Festival (for administration of Seattle Pow-Wow, 1978); Ethnic Heritage

Employee of the Year, 1981; Choctaw Department of Education (Employee of the Year, 1982). *Interests:* Computers in education; curriculum development; learning styles and brain functions; economic education; organic gardening; Choctaw literacy. *Published works:* Co-author, *Reeves-Brescia, Developmental Checklist,* (Mississippi Band of Choctaw Indians, 1975); *script advisor, Yesterdays Children: Indian Elder Oral History,* 30 minute video (Daybreak Star Press, 1980); co-author, *Development of Native American Curriculum,* workbook (Daybreak Star Press, 1979); editor, *Ways of the Lushootseed People: Ceremonies and Traditions of the Northern Puget Sound Indians* (Daybreak Star Press, 1980); editor, *Sharing Our Worlds* (Daybreak Star Press, 1980); script advisor, *Voices from the Cradleboard,* 30 minute slide presentation (Daybreak Star Press, 1980); editor, *Indians in Careers* (Daybreak Star Press, 1980); editor, *Starting an Indian Teen Club* (Daybreak Star Press, 1980); co-author, *Fisherman on the Puyallup & Teachers Guide* (Daybreak Star Press, 1980); co-author, *Suquamish Today & Teachers Guide* (Daybreak Star Press, 1980); executive editor, *Tribal Sovereignty, Indian Tribes in U.S. History* (Daybreak Star Press, 1981); editor, *Free Range to Reservation: Social Change on Selected Washington Reservations* (Daybreak Star Press, 1981); editor, *Outdoor Education for Indian Youth* (Daybreak Star Press, 1981); *Getting Control of Your Money* (Daybreak Star Press, 1981); *Knowing Your Legal Rights* (Daybreak Star Press, 1981); editor, "Daybreak Star Pre-School Activities Book (Daybreak Star Press, 1979); editor, *Twana Games* (Daybreak Star Press, 1981); editor, *Our Mother Corn* (Daybreak Star Press, 1981); *A'una* (Daybreak Star Press, 1981); editor, *Washington State Indian History for Grades 4-6, A Techer's Guide* Daybreak Star Press, 1981); editor, *O'Wakaga* (Daybreak Star Press, 1981); editor, *By the Work of Our Hands,* co-editor, "Teacher's Guide (Choctaw Heritage Press, 1982); editor, *Choctaw Tribal Government* (Choctaw Heritage Press, 1982); co-author, *Looking Around, Na Yo Pisa* (Choctaw Heritage Press, 1982); editor, *Okla Apilachi* (Choctaw Heritage Press, 1982); editor, *How the Flowers Came to Be* (Choctaw Heritage

Press, 1982); executive editor, *Choctaw Anthology I, II, and III* (Choctaw Heritage Press, 1984); *Lowak Mosoli* (Choctaw Heritage Press, 1984); editor, *Little Pigs - Shokoshi Althiha* (Choctaw Heritage Press, 1984); editor, *The Tale of the Possum* (Choctaw Heritage Press, 1984); editor, *Welcome to the Choctaw Fair!* (Choctaw Heritage Press, 1984); *James at Work* (Choctaw Heritage Press, 1984); "The Choctaw Oral Traditions Relating to Their Origin," chapter from *The Choctaw Before Removal* (University of Mississippi Press, 1985).

BRESHEARS, GARY
(executive director)

Affiliation: Executive director, Creek Nation, P.O. Box 580, Okmulgee, Okla. 74447.

BRIGHT, WILLIAM 1928-
(professor)

Born August 13, 1928, Oxnard, Calif. *Education:* University of California at Berkeley, A.B., 1949, Ph.D., 1955. *Principal occupation:* Professor. *Affiliation:* Professor of linguistics and anthropology, University of California at Los Angeles, 1959-. *Military service:* U.S. Army, 1954-1955 (captain). *Memberships:* Linguistic Society of America (editor, *Language*); American Anthropological Association. *Awards, honors:* Fellowship, American Council of Learned Societies, 1964-1965: Guggenheim Fellowship, 1972. *Interests:* Field work in languages of California Indians, and languages of India. *Published works: The Karok Language* (University of California Press, 1957); editor, *Studies in California Linguistics* (University of California Press, 1964); editor, *Sociolinguistics* (Monton, 1966); *A Luiseno Dictionary* (University of California Press, 1968).

BROCKIE, LEO
(B.I.A. superintendent)

Affiliation: Superintendent, Fort Berthold Agency, Bureau of Indian Affairs, New Town, N.D. 58763.

BRODY, J.J. 1929-
(professor)

Born April 24, 1929, Brooklyn, N.Y. *Education:* The Cooper Union, New York, N.Y. (Certificate of Fine Arts), 1950; University of New Mexico, B.A., 1956, M.A., 1964, Ph.D., 1970. *Principal occupation:* Professor. *Home address:* 1824 Luthy Dr. N.E., Albuquerque, N.M. 87112. *Affiliations:* Curator of art, Everhart Museum, Scranton, Penna., 1957-1958; curator, Isaac Delago Museum of Art, New Orleans, 1958-1960; curator, Museum of International Folk Art, Santa Fe, 1960-1961; curator and director, Maxwell Museum of Anthropology, University of New Mexico, 1962-; professor of anthropology and art history, University of New Mexico, 1964-. *Other professional post:* Research curator, Maxwell Museum of Anthropology. *Military service:* U.S. Army, 1952-1954 (sergeant). *Community activities:* City of Albuquerque (art advisory board, 1970-1974); Seton Museum and Library, Ghost Ranch Museum, Mimbres Valley Museum (board member); Governor of New Mexico Task Force Paleontological Resources, 1978-1979. *Memberships:* American Association of Museums; International Commission on Museums; Society for American Archaeology; Mountain Plains Museum Conference; New Mexico Museum Association; New Mexico Cactus and Succulent Society. *Awards, honors:* Popejoy Prize, University of New Mexico best dissertation, 1971; nonfiction award for *Indian Painters and White Patrons,* Border Regional Library Conference, 1971; 1977 Art Book Award for *Mimbres Painted Pottery; Award of Honor, New Mexico Historic Preservation Commission, 1978; resident scholar, School of American Research, 1980-1981. Interests:* Indian art, especially of the Southwest; museology; rock art; education; museum exhibitions. *Biographical sources: Who's Who in America; Who's Who in the West; Who's Who in American Art. Published works: Indian Panters and White Patrons* (UNM Press, 1971); *Between Traditions* (UNM Press, 1976; *Mimbres Painted Pottery* (School of American Research and UNM Press, 1977); *Beatien Yazz: Indian Painter,* with Sallie Wagner and B. Yazz (School of American Research, 1983); *Mimbres Pottery,* with

Catherine Scott and Steve LeBlanc (Hudson Hills Press, 1983.)

BROSE, DAVID S. 1939-
(professor)

Born February 20, 1939, Detroit, Mich. *Education:* University of Michigan, B.A. (cum laude), 1960; University of Rome (Italy), graduate studies, 1960-1961; University of Michigan, M.A., 1966, Ph.D., 1968. *Principal occupation:* Professor. *Affiliations:* Director, Archaeological Field School, Ann Arbor, Mich., 1967; research assistant, University of Michigan, Museum of Anthropology, 1964-1968; assistant professor of anthropology, Case Western Reserve University, 1971-. *Other professional posts:* Docent, University of Michigan Exhibits Museum, 1950-1960; associate curator of anthropology, Cleveland Museum of Natural Science, 1969-; archaeologist, Western Reserve Historical Society, 1970-. *Military service:* U.S. Army, 1962-1964. *Memberships:* American Anthropological Association (Fellow); American Association for the Advancement of Science; Archaeological Institute of America; American Ethnological Society; Central States Anthropological Society; Council on Michigan Archaeology; Current Anthropology (Associate); Michigan Academy of Science, Arts and Letters; Michigan Archaeological Society; Michigan Historical Society; Ohio Academy of Science; Great Lake Prehistory Foundation (board member); Ohio Archaeological Society; Society for American Archaeology; Society for Pennsylvania Archaeology; The Wiliam Clements Library (Associate); The Society for Historical Archaeology. *Awards, honors:* National Science Foundation: U.S.E.P. participant, 1964; University of Michigan, Rackham Research Grant, 1966, Graduate Fellow, 1966; Kettering Foundation Grant, 1968-1969; National Science Foundation Grant, 1970-1971—for analysis of the late prehistoric period in northeast Ohio; N.E.H. grant for research on pioneer settlement in the Western Reserve, 1971-1972. *Interests:* Prehistoric archaeology, paleo-ecology, prehistoric social organization; prehistory and protohistory of the Great Lakes and Central Sub-Arctic; ethnohistory and acculturation of North American Indians; historic sites archaeology; problems and procedures in archaeological research. *Field work:* Michigan, Wisconsin, 1964-1966; Michigan, Ontario, 1967; Ohio, 1968-1970, 1970-1971; Florida, 1970. *Published works: The Archaeology of Summer Island: Changing Settlement Systems in Northern Lake Michigan* (Anthropological Papers, Museum of Anthropology, University of Michigan, No. 41, 1970) *Prehistoric Cultural Ecology and Social Organization in the Northern Lake Michigan Area* (CWRU Studies in Anthropology, No. 1, 1970); many articles and papers published in professional journals.

BROWMAN, DAVID L. 1941-
(professor, consultant)

Born December 9, 1941, Missoula, Mont. *Education:* University of Washington, A.M., 1966; Harvard University, Ph.D., 1970. *Principal occupation:* Professor, consultant. *Home address:* 429 Treetop Lane, St. Louis, Mo. 63122. *Affiliation:* Professor and consultant, Department of Anthropology, Washington University, St. Louis, Mo., 1970-. *Other professional posts:* Consulting survey archaeologist; pastoral development consultant for Andean arid lands. *Community activities:* Advisory Council on Historic Preservation (historic archaeologist). *Memberships:* American Anthropological Association; Society of Professional Archaeologists (assistant secretary treasurer, secretary treasurer, board of directors); Missouri Association of Professional Archaeologists (board of directors); Academia Nacional de Ciencas, Bolivia; Archaeological Institute of America; Society for American Archaeology; International Union of Anthropological and Ethnological Sciences (Commission on Nomadic Peoples; Association for Field Archaeology; Institute for Andean Studies. *Awards, honors:* National Science Foundation Fellowship and Research Grants; Latin American Studies Research Grant. *Interests:* "Special focus on Andes; worked several years in Peru and Bolivia; also worked/visited several other Latin American countries, conducting anthropological research; current interest focus on camelid and ovicaprid pastoralism in the semi-arid Andes; previous

work includes several archaeological excavation projects in Peru, Bolivia, and the U.S. states of New Mexico, Washington, Idaho, Montanma, Illinois, and Missouri." *Biographical source: Who's Who in the Midwest. Published works: The Central Peruvian Prehistoric Interaction Sphere* (R.S. Peabody, Andover, 1975); *Advances in Andean Archaeology* (Mouton, The Hague, 1978); *Cultural Continuity in Mesoamerica* (Mouton, The Hague, 1979); *Peasants, Primitives and Proeletariates* (Mouton, The Hague, 1979); *Spirits, Shamans and Stars* (Mouton, The Hague, 1979); *Early Native Americans* (Mouton, The Hague, 1980); *Social and Economic Organization in the Prehispanic Andes* (BAR International, Oxford, 1984.)

BROWN, CHARLES ASA *(Fus Elle Haco)*(Muskogee) *(Gos Quillen)*(Shawnee) *(Eagle Star)*(Cherokee) 1912-
(attorney, farm owner, lecturer)

Born October 17, 1912, Woodsfield, Ohio. *Education:* Virginia Military Institute, A.B., 1935; University of Michigan Law School, 1935-1937; Western Reserve University Law School, J.D., 1938. *Principal occupation:* Attorney, farm owner, lecturer. *Home address:* 721 Washington St., Portsmouth, Ohio 45662. *Affiliations:* Self-employed lawyer and farmer, Portsmouth, Ohio, 1938-; Municipal Prosecuting Attorney, Portsmouth, Ohio, 1946; Assistant Attorney General, State of Ohio, 1963. *Military service:* U.S. Army (active duty, 1941-1946; reserve service, 1931-1972) (Lt. Colonel; American Defense; European Theater Medal with three battle stars; Purple Heart; Bronz Star with oak leaf cluster; Victory Medal; German Occupation Medal; Distinguished Unit Presidential Citation; Army Reserve Longevity Medal). *Community activities:* Scioto Area Council (executive board); Boy Scouts of America, Portsmouth, Ohio (merit badge counselor, 1946-, commissioner); co-founder, Jaycees, Portsmouth, 1938; Chamber of Commerce, Portsmouth; Bentonville, Ohio, Anti-Horse Thief Society. *Indian activities:* Member, Cedar River Tulsa Band, Muskogee Indian Tribe, Holdinville, Okla.; honorary councilman, Creek Indian Nation, Tulsa, Okla., 1962-1969; councilman, Western Black Elk Keetowah, Cherokee Nation; councilman,

Feerated Indian Tribes. *Memberships:* Scioto County Bar Association (trustee); Ohio State Bar Association; American Indian Bar Association; Phi Delta Phi Legal Fraternity; American Legion; Retired Officers Association and Reserve Officers Association, Washington, D.C. (life member); U.S. Horse Cavalry Association (life member); Masonic Lodge. *Awards, honors:* Silver Beaver Award, Boy Scouts of America; Vigil Honor, Order of the Arrows; President's Award for Distinguished Service, 1982, Boy Scouts of America; Advisory Chief of Indian Tribes, 1961-1980); Master Mason, 1944-; Chief's liaison to visiting persons at ceremonials; "Tecumseh was my great-great grandfather." *Interests:* Lecturer on Indian lore throughout the U.S.; writer on many Indian subjects; writer on various Masonic subjects; speaker at many public gatherings of all kinds continually. *Biographical sources: Who's Who in Freemasonry; Who's Who in the Midwest; Who's Who in the World; Who's Who in Ohio; Distinguished Americans. Published works:* Numerous articles in various publications.

BROWN, DEE ALEXANDER 1908-
(librarian, educator, author)

Born in 1908, Louisiana. *Education:* George Washington University, B.S., 1937; University of Illinois, M.S., 1951. *Principal occupation:* Librarian, educator, author. *Home address:* 7 Overlook Dr., Little Rock, Ark. 72207. *Affiliations:* Librarian, Department of Agriculture, Washington, D.C. 1934-1942; librarian, Aberdeen Proving Ground, Md., 1945-1948; agricultural librarian, 1948-1972, professor, 1962-1975, University of Illinois, Urbana. *Military service:* U.S. Army, 1942-1945. *Memberships:* Authors Guild; Society of American Historians; Western Writers of America; Beta Phi Mu. *Published works: Wave High the Banner,* 1942; *Grierson's Raid,* 1954; *Yellowhorse,* 1956; *Cavalry Scout,* 1957; *The Gentle Tamers: Women of the Old Wild West,* 1958; *The Bold Cavaliers,* 1959; *They Went Thataway,* 1960; *Fighting Indian of the West,* with M.F. Schmitt, 1948; *Trail Driving Days,* with M.F. Schmitt; *The Setller's West,* with M.F. Schmitt; *Fort Phil Kearny,* 1962; *The Galvanized Yankees,* 1963; *Show-*

down at Little Bighorn, 1964; *The Girl From Fort Wicked,* 1964; *The Year of the Century,* 1966; *Bury of My Heart at Wounded Knee,* 1971; *The Westerners,* 1974; *Hear That Lonesome Whistle Blow,* 1977; *Tepee Tales,* 1979; *Creek Mary's Blood,* 1980; editor: *Agricultural History,* 1956-1958; *Pawnee, Blackfoot and Cheyenne,* 1961.

BROWN, DONALD NELSON 1937-
(professor, researcher)

Born February 1, 1937, Colorado Springs, Colo. *Education:* Harvard College, B.A., 1959; University of Arizona, M.A., 1967, Ph.D., 1973. *Principal occupation: Professor and researcher in anthropology. Affiliations:* Assistant professor of anthropology, Oklahoma State University, 1971-. *Other professional posts:* Editor of recordings of Indian music for the Taylor Museum, Colorado Springs Fine Arts Center and Taos Recordings and Publications, Taos, N.M. *Memberships:* American Anthropological Association; Society for Ethnomusicology; Society for Applied Anthropology; American Ethnological Society; Committee on Research in Dance (board). *Awards, honors:* Jaap Kunst Prize, Society for Ethnomusicology. *Interests:* Research on contemporary Native Americans; Native American music and dance; prehistoric music and dance in North America; ethnography of the Rio Grande Pueblos. *Published works: Masks, Mantas, and Moccasins: Dance Costumes of the Pueblo Indians* (Taylor Museum, 1962); *A Study of Heavy Drinking at Taos Pueblo, N.M.* (mimeographed for restricted distribution, 1965); *Archaeological investigations at the Hermitage* (Ladies Hermitage Association, 1972); *Inventory of Archaeological Sites* (Sargent and Lundy Engineers, 1973).

BROWN, JOHN (Seminole) 1914-
(tribal official)

Born February 20, 1914, Sasakwa, Okla. *Education:* Elementary school. *Principal occupation:* Tribal official. *Home address:* P.O. Box 24, Sasakwa, Okla. 74867. *Affiliation:* Past chairman, general council, Seminole Nation of Oklahoma. *Memberships:*

Five Civilized Tribes Inter-Tribal Council; S.E.E., Inc. (board of directors); Five Civilized Tribes Foundation, Inc.; Inter-Tribal Counci (secretary, treasurer); Five Tribes Museum (board of directors).

BROWN, JOSEPH (Blackfeet) (clergyman)

Education: Loyola University, M.A., 1942; Alma College, M.A., 1949. *Principal occupation:* Clergyman. *Home address:* Box 95, Spokane, Wash. 99107. *Affiliation:* Member, Society of Jesus, Portland, Oreg., 1935-. *Other professional posts:* Teaching grade school, high school, college; administration—mission grade schools, pastoral ministry. *Community activities:* Spokane Urban Indian Health Board; Kona Lodge (chairman of board). *Memberships:* American Indian Historical Association; National Congress of American Indians. *Interests:* "The promotion of studies for and about Indians." *Biographical source: Indians of Today* (Marion E. Gridley). *Published work: Louise Sinxuim, Coeur de Alene Tribe,* 1977.

BROWN, JOSEPH EPES 1920- (professor, writer)

Born September 9, 1920, Ridgefield, Conn. *Education:* Bowdoin College, 1940-1942; Haverford College, B.A. (Anthropology), 1947; University of New Mexico (graduate studies in anthropology), 1954-1956; Stanford University, M.A. (Anthropology), 1966; University of Stockholm (Doctorate, Anthropology and History of Religions, 1970. *Principal occupation:* Professor, writer. *Home address:* Kootenai Creek Ranch, 363 Kootenai Creek, Stevensville, Mont. 59870. *Affiliations:* Teacher, Verde Valley School, Sedona, Ariz., 1952-1953, 1956-1960, 1961-1965; assistant professor, Prescott College, 1966-1969; associate professor, Department of Religious Studies, Indiana University, 1970-1972; University of Montana, Department of Religious Studies (associate professor, 1972-1976; professor, 1977-.) *Editorial work:* Consulting editor, *Parabola: The Magazine of Myth and Tradition;* advisor, "The Zuni Pueblo Film Project," Byron Earhart, Western Michigan

University; editor for Vol. V, *American Indian Traditions,* for Crossroad Press, 25 Vols., World Spirituality Series. *Memberships:* American Anthropological Association; Museum of Northern Arizona; Foundation of North American Indian Culture (advisory board.) *Awards, honors:* Smith-Mundt Grant to teach in Morocco, 1960-1961; The Joseph E. Brown American Indian Scholarship Fund established in Mr. Brown's honor at Verde Valley School, Sedona, Ariz. *Interests:* Research among the Plains Indians; has traveled extensively and has done research in Morocco, North Africa. Major interest within anthropology is the study of diverse cultures. *Published works: The Sacred Pipe* (University of Oklahoma Press, 1953; Penguin Books, with new introduction, 1971; Swedish, Spanish and Japanese translation); *The Spiritual Legacy of the American Indian* (Pendle Hill, 1964, 8th edition, 1976); *The North American Indians: The Photographs of Edward S. Curtis, Aperture,* (Vol. 16, no. 4, Philadelphia Museum of Art, 1972); The Spiritual Legacy of the American Indian, a collection of articles by Mr. Brown (Crossroad Publishing, 1980); *The Gift of the Sacred Pipe* (University of Oklahoma Press, 1982); *chapters in books:* "The Spiritual Legacy of the American Indian, *Sources,* Theodore Roszak, 1972; "The Question of 'Mysticism' with Native American Traditions," *Mystics and Scholars,* Harold Coward and Terence Penelhum, editors (Ross-Erickson Publishers, 1979); "The Roots of Renewal," *Seeing with a Native Eye,* Walter Capps, Editor (Harper & Row, 1977); "Relationship and Unity in American Indian Experience," *The Unanimous Tradition* (Sri Lanka Institute of Traditional Studies, 1982); "Americn Indian Living Religions," *Handbook of Living Religions,* edited by John Hinnells (Penguin Books, 1983); numerous articles, papers and lectures.

BROWN, VINSON 1912- (writer, naturalist, publisher)

Born December 7, 1912, Reno, Nev. *Education:* University of California at Berkeley, A.B., 1939; Stanford University, M.A., 1947. *Principal occupation:* Writer, naturalist, publisher. *Home address:* Happy Camp,

Calif. 96039. *Affiliations:* Lecturer on American Indian religions, University of South Dakota, University of Northern Michigan, Myrin Institute, Haskell Institute; field collector in natural history; lecturer. *Travels:* Visits to many Indian tribes in the U.S., Canada, and Alaska, 1960-1972. *Published works: Exploring Ancient Life* (Science Materials Center, 1958); *Warriors of the Rainbow,* with William Willoya (Naturegraph, 1965); *Pomo Indians of California and Their Neighbors* (Naturegraph, 1969); *Great Upon the Mountain — Crazy Horse of America* (Naturegraph, 1971, cloth ed., Macmillan); *Voices of the Earth and Sky: The Vision-Search of the American Indians* (Stackpole, 1974); *Peoples of the Sea Wind—Native Americans of the Pacific Coast* (Macmillan, 1977); and others which pertain to nature.

BROWN, WILFRED
(B.I.A. superintendent)

Affiliation: Superintendent, Fort Defiance Agency, Bureau of Indian Affairs, P.O. Box 619, Fort Defiance, Ariz. 86504.

BROWNING, ZANE
(B.I.A. superintendent)

Affiliation: Superintendent, Ardmore Agency, Bureau of Indian Affairs, P.O. Box 997, Ardmore, Okla. 73401.

BRUCE, LOUIS R.
(consultant)

Affiliation: President, Native American Consultants, Inc., 725 2nd St., N.E., Washington, D.C. 20002. Branch: 1001 Highland St., Arlington, Va. 22201.

BRUGGE, DAVID M. 1927-
(anthropologist)

Born September 3, 1927, Jamestown, N.Y. *Education:* University of New Mexico, B.A., 1950. *Principal occupation:* Anthropologist.

Affiliations: Various positions, Gallup Community Indian Center, Gallup, N.M., 1953-1957; salvage archaeologist, Four Corners Pipeline Co., Houston, Texas, 1957-1958; anthropologist, The Navajo Tribe, Window Rock, Ariz., 1958-1968. *Other professional posts:* Artchaeologist, Museum of Northern Arizona, Flagstaff, Ariz., 1957; director, Navajo Curriculum Center, Rough Rock, Ariz., 1968; instructor, College of Ganado, Ariz., 1973. *Military service:* U.S. Army, 1945-1947. *Community activities:* Sage Memorial Hospital, Ganado, Ariz. (secretary, advisory board); Title I Committee, Ganado Public Schools. *Memberships:* American Anthropological Association; Society for American Archaeology; Archaeological Society of New Mexico (trustee); American Society for Ethnohistory (secretary-treasurer, 1966-1968); Arizona Archaeological and Historical Society; New Mexico Historical Society; Northern Arizona Society for Science and Art, Inc.; American Association for the Advancement of Science; Plateau Sciences Society. *Interests:* Mr. Brugge writes, "Navajo studies, especially in archaeology, ethnohistory and history, and more generally of the greater Southwest. In addition to my work with the Navajos, I have done field work in northwestern Mexico, principally among the Pima Bajo (Lower Pima) of Sonora. My work with the Navajo Tribe involved research for various land disputes such as the Land Claims Case, the Navajo-Hopi boundary dispute, the McCracken Mesa land exchange and Utah school section case and the Huerfano Mesa land exchange." *Biographical sources: Who's Who in the West; The Official Museum Directory. Published works: Navajo Pottery and Ethnohistory* (The Navajo Tribe, 1963); *Long Ago in Navajoland* (The Navajo Tribe, 1965); *Navajo Bibliography,* with J. Lee Correll and Edith Watson (The Navajo Tribe, 1967); *Navajos in the Catholic Church Records of New Mexico, 1694-1875* (The Navajo Tribe, 1968); *Zarcillos Largos, Courageous Advocate of Peace* (The Navajo Tribe, 1970); *The Story of the Navajo Treaties,* with J. Lee Correll (The Navajo Tribe, 1971); *Navajo and Western Pueblo History* (Tucson Corral of Westerners, 1972); *The Navajo Exodus* (Archaeological Society of New Mexico, 1972.)

BRUNER, EDWARD M. 1924-
(professor of anthropology)

Born September 28, 1924, New York, N.Y. *Education:* Ohio State University, B.A., 1948, M.A., 1950; University of Chicago, Ph.D., 1954. *Principal occuaption:* Professor of anthropology. *Home address:* 2022 Cureton Dr., Urbana, Ill. 61801. *Affiliations:* Assistant professor, Department of Anthropology, Yale University, 1954-1960; associate professor, 1961-1965, professor, 1965-, head of department, 1966-1970, Department of Anthropology, University of Illinois, Urbana, director, Doris Duke American Indian Oral History Project, 1967-1973. *Other professional posts:* Chairman, test committee, Educational Testing Service, Princeton, N.J., 1967-1969. *Memberships:* American Anthropological Association (Fellow); Society for Applied Anthropology; Royal Anthropological Society; American Ethnological Society (past-president, 1981-1982); Association for Asian Studies (member, Indonesian studies committee, 1973-; chairman, 1976-1978.) *Awards, honors:* Fellowship, Center for Advanced Study in the Behavioral Sciences; senior scholarship, East-West Center, University of Hawaii. *Interests:* Anthropological field studies among Navajo Indians, Fort Berthold Indians; among Batak of Sumatra, Indonesia; processes of cultural and social change; urbanization. *Published works: Perspectives in American Indian Culture Change,* with Edward H. Spicer (University of Chicago Press, 1962).

BRUNO, ROBERT LEON
(tribal chairman)

Affiliation: Chairman, Citizen Band Potawatomi Business Committee, Route 5, Box 151, Shawnee, Okla. 74801.

BRYAN, RICHARD P.
(environmental health services)

Affiliation: Chief, Environmental Health Services, U.S. Public Health Service, Indian Health Service, 5600 Fishers Lane, Rockville, Md. 20857.

BUFFALO, GEORGE, Jr.
(B.I.A. superintendent)

Affiliation: Superintendent, Sac and Fox Area Field Office, Bureau of Indian Affairs, Tama, Iowa 52339.

BUFFALOHEAD, W. ROGER
(communications)

Affiliation: Director, Migizi Communications, Inc., 2300 Cedar Ave. South, Minneapolis, Minn. 55404.

BUFORD, BETTIE (LITTLE DOVE)
(Creek and Cherokee) 1935-
(shop owner)

Born February 20, 1935, Ocoee, Fla. *Principal occupation:* Shop owner. *Home address:* P.O. Box 521, Cox Osceola Indian Reservation, Orange Springs, Fla. 32682. *Affiliation:* Owner, Betties Antiques and Osceola Trading Post (furniture store; upholster shop owner, Ocala, Fla. (20 years). *Other professional posts:* Teacher, Indian culture, Osceola Christian Indian School. *Military service:* American Red Cross Military Hospital, Korean conflict. *Memberships:* Southeastern Cherokee Confederation (principal vice-chief); The Concerned Citizens League of America (president); Cox Osceola Cherokee & Creek Indian Reservation (vice chief.) *Awards, honors:* Indian Princess by blood; Marion Education Awards; several awards for teaching Indian culture an crafts. *Interests:* "My major interest is to help improve the lifestyles of my Indian people and to stop some of the prejudice against them. To let all people know what real Indians are, not the stereotypes that they see in the movies and on television. I would like to travel to all tribes." *Work in progress: Indians of the Oklawaka River in Florida.*

BURCH, LEONARD
(tribal council chairman)

Affiliation: Chairman, Southern Ute Tribal Council, P.O. Box 373, Ignacio, Colo. 81137.

BURNS, ROBERT I., S.J. 1921-
(clergyman, historian, educator)

Born August 16, 1921, San Francisco, Calif. *Education:* Gonzaga University, B.A., 1945, M.A., 1947 (D. Litt.), 1968; Fordham University, M.A., 1949; Jesuit Pontifical Faculty (Spokane, Wash., Phil.B., 1946, Phil.Lic., 1947) (Alma, Calif., S.Th.B., 1951, S.Th.Lic., 1953; Postgraduate, Columbia University, 1949, Oxford University, 1956-1957; Johns Hopkins University, Ph.D. (summa cum laude)(History), 1958; University of Fribourg, Switzerland, Doc. es Sc.Hist. (double summa cum laude)(History, Ethnohistory), 1961. *Principal occupation:* Clergyman, historian, educator. *Address:* History Department, Graduate School, University of California, Los Angeles, Calif. 90024. *Affiliations: Assistant archivist, Jesuit and Indian Archives of Pacific Northwest Province, Spokane, 1945-1947; instructor, History Department, University of San Francisco, (instructor, 1947-1948; assistant professor, 1958-1962; associate professor, 1963-1966; professor, 1967-1976); senior professor, History Department, U.C.L.A., 1976-. Other professional posts:* Director, Institute of Medieval Mediterranean, Spain, 1976-; staff, UCLA Center for Medieval-Renaissance Studies, 1977-; staff, UCLA Near Eastern Center, 1979-. *Editorial work:* Board editor, *Trend in History,* 1980; co-editor, Viator (UCLA), 1980; editorial committee, U.C. Press, 1985. *Memberships:* American Historical Association, Pacific Coast Branch (vice president, 1978; president, 1978-1980; presiding-delegate, International Congress of Historical Sciences, 1975, and U.S. Representative, 1980); American Catholic Historical Association (president, 1976); Medieval Association of the Pacific; Society for Spanish and Portuguese Historical Studies; Hill Monastic Library; North American Catalan Society; American Bibliographical Center (board, 1982-1989). *Awards, honors:* Guggenheim Fellow, 1964; ACLS Fellow, 1977; National Endowment for the Humanities grants, 1971-1983; many other grants; Medieval Academy of America (trustee, 1975-1977; executive, 1977-1978); Haskins Gold Medal, 1976 (Life Fellow, 1978); His-

panic Society of America (elected, 1985); five book awards from national historical associations, including American Historical (Pacific Coast Award), American Catholic Historical, and American Association for State and Local History, for *Jesuits and Indian Wars,* 1965; Dr. Burns gave the keynote address at the National Park Service's Sesquicentennial of the sustained Indian-white contact by Americans in the Pacific Northwest states, the (Protestant) Whitman Mission, July 1986 at Whitman College. *Interests:* "I have two fields, allied but distinct, in which I publish regularly. The medieval field is the moving frontier of the 13th-century Catalonia, particularly the absorption by the Catalan peoples of the Valencian kingdom of the Moslems. The American field is the Pacific Northwest, particularly, Indian-white relations and troubles, 1840-1880, as illumined especially by Jesuit documentation here and in Europe. Ethnohistory and the Pacific Northwest frontier is thus seen not in isolation but as illumined by other frontier experiences." *Biographical sources: Who's Who in America; Contemporary Authors;* among others. *Published works:* Co-author, *I lift My Lamp: Jesuits in America,* 1955; *Indians and Whites in the Pacific Northwest: Jesuit Contributions to Peace 1850-1880* (University of San Francisco Press, 1961); *The Jesuits and the Indian Wars* (Yale University Press, 1966); *The Jesuits and the Indian Wars of the Northwest,* reissue of 1966 edition (University of Idaho Press, 1985); articles include, "Northwest Indian Missions," position essay, *Handbook of North American Indians* (U.S. Government Printing Office, 1978; 1986 forthcoming); "Suore Indiane," *Dizionario degli istituti di perfezione,* ed. G. Rocca, 6 vols. (Rome: Edizioni Paoline, 1974); "Jesuit Missions," (North American Indians) *Dictionary of American History* (Charles Scribner's Sons, 1977); "Roman Catholic Missionaries," (to U.S. Indians) *The Reader's Encyclopedia of the Amerian West* (Thomas Y. Crowell Co., 1977); "The Opening of the West," (impact on Pacific Northwest Indians) *The Indian: Assimilation, Integration or Separation* (Prentice-Hall, Canada, 1972); numerous other articles.

**BURTT, J. FREDERIC (Abenaki) 1908-
(professor)**

Born April 4, 1908, Lowell, Mass. *Education:* Lowell Technological Institute, B.S., 1931; Boston University, A.B.A., 1942; Massachusetts Institute of Technology, M.S., 1958. *Principal occupation:* Professor of mechanical and textile engineering. *Home address:* 97 Hoyt Ave., Lowell, mass. 01852. *Affiliations:* Textile engineering, Eaton Rapids, Mich.; supt., assistant general manager, Newmarket Co., Lowell, Mass. (15 years); senior textile technologist, U.S. Research and Engineering Command (QM), Natick, Mass. (two years); professor, Lowell Technological Institute; professor emeritus, visiting lecturer, University of Lowell, 1978-1982. *Community activities:* City of Lowell Conservation Commission (vice chairman); Water Pollution Advisory Board, Northern Middlesex Area. *Memberships:* Society of the Sigma Xi; Massachusetts Archaeological Society (past vice president); New Hampshire Archaeological Society (past president); American Association for the Advancement of Science; AATT; Pennsylvania Institute of Anthropology; Societe Archeologique d'Alexandrie, Egypt; Greater Lowell Indian Cultural Association; Native American Rights Commission; Indian Institute, U.S. Dept. of Education. *Awards, honors:* Medallion of Merit, Alexandria University, Egypt; Chester B. Price Memorial Archaeological Award, New Hampshire Archaeological Society, 1965; Demolay Cross of Honor and Legion of Honor, 1936; honorable member, St. Francis Abenaki Tribe, 1977; Sigma Xi, Omicron Pi, Human Relations Award, 1980. *Interests:* Archaeological work in North and South America; consultant in the textile industry; Fullbright lecturer, Alexandria University, Egypt (two years); worked with Polish archaeologists on Greco-Roman excavations in Egypt; travels to Middle East countries under National Academy of Science's grant. *Biographical sources: Who's Who in American Education; Who's Who in the East; American Men of Science. Published works:* Co-author, *History of the City of Lowell,* 1976; co-editor and publisher, *Colby's Indian History,* 1975; numerous articles to professional journals.

**BUSH, MICHAEL A. (Mohawk Caughnawaga) 1948-
(administrator)**

Born August 10, 1948, Brooklyn, N.Y. *Education:* Brooklyn College, A.A., 1967; Dartmouth College, A.B., 1975. *Principal occupation:* Administrator. *Home address:* 1271 38th St., Brooklyn, N.Y. 11218. *Affiliation:* Executive director, American Indian Community House, Inc., New York, N.Y., 1976-. *Othjer professional post:* Co-director, Community Council of Greater N.Y., Native American Educational Research Program, 1975. *Military service:* U.S. Army, 1967-1970 (Sargeant E-5; five Commendations, 3rd Place Inter Service Annual Leap Fest, 1970). *Community activities:* Governor's Minority Task Force on Mental Health, N.Y. State, 1977; National Low Income Housing Board (executive committee); Minority Task Force, New York State Developmental Disabilities, 1985. *Memberships:* National Congress of American Indians; National Indian Education Association; American Indian Health Care Association (board member, 1984); National Urban Indian Council (former vice-president). *Awards, honors:* Ethnic New York Award, 1984 (Mayor Ed Koch, New York City). *Interests:* American Indian law; reservation economics; carpentry, auto mechanics, iron work; writing; extensive American and Canadian lecture circuit on American Indian Affairs. *Published works:* "Detecting Structural Heat Losses with Mobil Infra Red Thermography," (U.S. Army Corps, 1974); "An Overview of the Socio-Economic Forces Pertaining to Indian Education," (Community Council of Greater N.Y., 1975.)

**BUSH, MITCHELL LESTER, Jr. (Onondaga) 1936-
(chief-tribal enrollment, B.I.A.)**

Born February 1, 1936, Syracuse, N.Y. *Education:* Haskell Institute, 1951-1956. *Principal occupation:* Chief, tribal enrollmen; B.I.A. *Home address:* 519 5th St., S.E., Washington, D.C. 20003. *Affiliation:* Chief, Branch of Tribal Enrollment Services, Bureau of Indian Affairs, Washington,

D.C., 1956-. *Military service:* U.S. Army, 1958-1961 (Specialist 4th Class). *Community activities:* Northern Virginia Folk Festival (board of directors); Haskell Alumni Association of the Nation's Capitol (board of directors); American Indian Inaugural Ball (committee member, 1969, 1973, 1977, 1981, and 1985); American Indian Society, Washington, D.C. (president, 1966-). *Awards, honors:* American Indian Society Distingished Service Award; Maharishi Award conferred by the Maharishi University. *Interests:* Lecturer and Indian dancer for American Indian Society; participant, 1990 Census Planning Conference on Race and Ethnic Items sponsored by the Census Bureau; tour leader to Virginia Indian reservations for Resident Associate Program, Smithsonian Institution; honored at the 1982 Nanticoke (Delaware) Pow wow; judge at the 1978, 1980, 1982, 1984 and 1985 Miss Indian American Pageants held in Sheridan, Wyoming, and Bismarck, North Dakota; photo and bio included in "Shadows Caught: Images of Native Americans," by Stephen Bambaro at Gilcrease Institute, Tulsa, Oklahoma. *Biographical sources: To Live in Two Worlds,* by Brent Ashabranner; *American Indian Wars,* by John Tebbel, 1960; *Successful Indian Career Profiles,* to be published by North American Indian Club, Syracuse, N.Y. *Published works:* Editor, *American Indian Society Cookbook* (American Indian Society, 1975 and 1984 editions); editor, *American Indian Society Newsletter,* 1966-1986; Movies & Television shows: "Lives of the Rich and Famous," segment featuring Connie Stevens; MGM, "George Washington TV Mini-Series"; "Indians," Walt Disney Productions; numerous television programs.

C

CAIN, H. THOMAS 1913-
(museum curator, anthropologist)

Born May 18, 1913, Seattle, Wash. *Education:* University of Washington, B.A., 1938; University of Arizona, M.A. (Anthropology), 1946. *Principal occupation:* Museum curator, anthropologist. *Home Address:* 1824 E. Ocotillo Rd., Phoenix, Ariz. 85016.

Affiliations: Curator of anthropology, San Diego Museum of Man, 1946-1950; director, curator, Heard Museum, Phoenix, Ariz., 1952-. *Other professional posts:* Instructor of museum methods course, Arizona State University. *Military service:* U.S. Marine Corp, 1944. *Memberships:* American Anthropological Association (Fellow); American Association of Museums. *Awards, honors:* Thaw Fellow, Harvard University, 1950; University Fellow, University of Arizona, 1945-1946. *Expeditions:* Field work in Canadian Arctic, Alaska, Georgia, New Mexico, North Dakota. *Published works: Petroglyphs of Central Washington* (University of Washington Press); *Pima Indian Basketry* (Heard Museum Publications in Anthropology.)

CALKIN, LAURIE ARCHER
(Cherokee) 1935-
(designer)

Born February 17, 1935, Corbin, Ky. *Education: Colorado College, B.A., 1959; City College. Principal occupation:* Designer. *Home address:* Route 1, Box 267, Santa Fe, N.M. 87501. *Other professional post:* Former professional dancer, New York City. *Memberships:* Don Juan Little Theatre; Los Alamos Light Opera Association. *Awards, honors:* John Hay Whitney Fellow in theatre; Fulbright Scholar to Peru in dance and the arts.

CALLENDER, CHARLES 1928-
(anthropologist)

Born October 30, 1928, Union Grove, Wisc. *Education:* University of Chicago, Ph.B., 1949, M.A., 1954, Ph.D., 1958. *Principal occupation:* Anthropologist. *Home address:* 2512 Edgehill Rd., Cleveland Heights, Ohio 44106. *Affiliations:* Assistant editor, *Current Anthropology,* 1959-1961; research associate, American University at Cairo, Egypt, 1961-1963; professor, Case Western Reserve University, 1966-. *Memberships:* American Anthropological Association; Midle East Studies Association of North America. *Interests:* "Major professional interests are American Indians and the Middle East. Field work among the Mesquakie

(1954), Sauk (1954), and Prairie Potawato-
mie (1955); in Cairo and Alexandria (1961-
1962), and in Egyptian Nubia (1962-1963).
Published works: Editor, with Sol Tax,
Issues in Evolution (University of Chicago
Prss, 1960); *Central Algonkian Social
Organization* (Milwaukee Public Museum,
1962); *Life-Crisis Rituals Among the Kenuz,*
with Fadwa el Guindi (Case Western
Reserve University Press, 1971).

CANADAY, DAYTON W. 1923-
(historical society director)

Born October 30, 1923, Litchfield, Ill. *Education:* Illinois College, A.B., 1948; Miami
University, 1942, 1946-1947; University of
Illinois, M.S., 1950. *Principal occupation:*
Historical society director. *Home address:*
1906 E. Erskine, Pierre, S.D. 57501. *Affilia-
tions:* Superintendent, South Dakota
Department of History, 1968-1973; director,
South Dakota State Historical Society,
1968-. *Military service:* U.S. Marine Corps
(First Lieutenant; Pacific Medal, Japanese
occupation; American Defense; Good Con-
duct; Korean Service Medal). *Community
activities:* Federal Lewis and Clark Trail
Commission (board member); South
Dakota American Revolution Bicentennial
Commission (board member); South
Dakota Historical Publications Advisory
Committee (member); State Library Advi-
sory Committee (member); South Dakota
Historic Preservation (member); Presbyterian Church (elder); Boy's Club of America
(board); Chamber of Commerce (board).
Memberships: American Association for
State and Local History; State Historical
Administrators Committee; Western His-
torical Association. *Awards, honors:* Key-
man. St. Louis Jr. Chamber of Commerce;
naming of Canaday Room in St. Charles
County Historical Society Museum. *Interests:* Local history; writing; rare books;
travel. *Published works: Collections—
South Dakota History* (South Dakota Historical Society, 1968, 1970, 1971).

CANARD, CURTIS LEE (Muskogee-
Creek) 1932-
(petroleum geologist)

Born February 9, 1932, Wetumka, Okla.

Education: Oklahoma State University,
B.S., 1956. *Principal occupation:* Petroleum
geologist. *Home address:* P.O. Box 35112,
Tulsa, Okla. 74135. *Affiliations:* Senior petroleum geologist (petroleum exploration)
Exxon Corp., Houston, Texas (16 years);
project manager (resource exploration and
evaluations), William Brothers Engineering
Co., Tulsa, Okla. (3 years). *Other professional posts:* Mineral consultant. *Community activities:* Thlopthlocco Tribal Town
(chairman); Oklahomans for Indian Opportunity (board of directors); Oklahoma State
University for Indian Students (geologic
advisor). *Memberships:* American Association for Petroleum Geologists, 1956-; Tulsa
Geologic Scoiety, 1974-. *Awards, honors:*
Scholarship from Congregational Christian
Churches; educational grant, B.I.A. *Interests:* Principal stockholder of minority
owned Deer Stalker Gallery financed
through the Indian Finance Act and deals in
fine Indian art, Tulsa, Okla. *Published
works: Thlophlocco Development Plan*
(Dept. of Housing and Urban Development,
1976), distributed by Oklahoma Indian
Affairs Commission, Oklahoma City, Okla.

CANNON, T.C. *(Pai Doung-U-Day)*
(Kiowa-Caddo) 1946-
(painter, printmaker)

Born September 27, 1946, Lawton, Okla.
Education: Institute of American Indian
Arts, Santa Fe, N.M.; Central State Univer-
sity, Edmond, Okla. *Principal occupation:*
Painter, printmaker. *Home address:* 400 E.
Danforth, #134, Edmond, Okla. 73034. *Mil-
itary service:* U.S. Army (Airbourne
Division-Vietnam, 1968; two Bronze Stars).
Memberships: Council of Regents, Institute
of American Indian Arts: Pacific Northwest
Indian Center. *Exhibitions:* Edinburgh Art
Festival, Scotland; Berlin Festival, Amerika
Haus; National Collection of Fine Arts,
Smithsonian Institution; Bureau of Indian
Affairs, Washington, D.C.; Oklahoma Art
Center, Oklahoma City, Okla.; Museum of
New Mexico, Santa Fe; two-man touring
exhibition, "Two American Painters," with
Fritz Scholder — Madrid, Berlin, Buchar-
est, Warsaw, Ankara, Athens, and London,
1972-1973. *Awards, honors:* Second Prize
and Grand Award, American Indian Expo-

sition; First Prize, Southwestern Scholastic Exhibit, 1962-1964; Governor's Trophy, Scottsdale National Exhibit, 1966. *Biographical sources: Who's Who in American Art; American Indian Painters; Art in America,* summer, 1972.

CARGILE, ELLEN YEAGER 1931-
(educator, artist)

Born January 28, 1931, Dallas, Texas. *Education:* University of Texas, B.S., 1953; University of Arkansas, M.Ed., 1965. *Principal occupation:* Educator, artist. *Home address:* 3059 County Rd. 203, Durango, Colo. 81301. *Affiliation:* Instructor, Division of Cultural Studies, Fort Lewis College, Durango, Colo., 1972-. *Memberships:* Delta Kappa Gamma; AAUW. *Interests:* "(I) teach arts and crafts of the Southwest Indians, and art history of the Southwest; jewelry design; travel; lecture on Indian art forms (International Symposium of Anthropology, Santa Fe, N.M., 1975); consultant/lecturer (Multi-Cultural Education Conference, University of Utah, 1975); has exhibited paintings and sculpture in Texas, New Mexico, Louisiana, Arkansas, Colorado; national travelling exhibitions—one person show in Farmington Civic Center, 1977." *Published works: Understanding and Executing Arts of the Southwest,* 1976; *Walk in Beauty,* Vols. I and II (editor, 1975-1976); *Alecia in Flowerland,* with John R. Tapia, 1976. All published by Basin Reproduction Co.

CARPIO, JOSE
(B.I.A. agency superintendent)

Affiliation: Superintendent, Northern Pueblos Agency, Bureau of Indian Affairs, Box 849, Federal Office Bldg., Santa Fe, N.M. 87501.

CARR, PATRICK J. 1941-
(education specialist)

Born December 16, 1941, New York, N.Y. *Education:* Hunter College, CUNY, B.A., 1966; Northern Arizona University, Flagstaff, M.A., 1974. *Principal occupation:* Education specialist (audio visual services.)

Home address: P.O. Box 2032, Tuba City, Ariz. 86045. *Affiliation:* Tuba City High School, Bureau of Indian Affairs, P.O. Box 160, Tuba City, Ariz. 86045. *Military service:* U.S. Marine Corps, 1966-1968. *Memberships:* Arizona Educational Media Association (past president); National Council of Bureau of Indian Affairs Educators (president); Association for Educational Communication and Technology; Arizona Educational Media Association. *Interests:* "Traveled extensively in Western Europe, Mexico and the U.S. Active in professional educational associations; enjoy writing human interest articles and photography; enjoy balley and visiting art museums."

CARTER, EDWARD RUSSELL, 1910-
(minister)

Born December 8, 1910, Bloomingdale, Ind. *Education:* Earlham College, B.A., 1932; Kansas State University, M.A., 1947. *Principal occupation:* Minister. *Home address:* 66 Linwood St., Bergenfield, N.J. 07621. *Affiliation:* Director, Special Ministries, Division of Christian Life and Mission, National Council of Churches, 1937-. *Memberships:* National Social Welfare Assembly; Council on Indian Affairs; National Fellowship of Indian Workers. *Interests:* "Extensive involvement in Indian life and affairs as well as with seasonal farm workers, Spanish Americans, and natives of Alaska. (I) frequently travel to Alaska and Mexico as well as (to) Indian reservation areas in the U.S." *Published work: The Gift is Rich* (Friendship Prss, 1954).

CASEBOLT, JACK V.
(Indian health service)

Affiliation: Director, Office of Program Planning, Indian Health Service, 5600 Fishers Lane, Rockville, Md. 20857.

CASIUS, EVERLYN
(museum curator)

Affiliation: Curator, Ute Indian Museum, 17253 Chipeta Dr., P.O. Box 1736, Montrose, Colo. 81402.

CASTOR, DELIA FRANKLIN 1913-
(museum curator)

Born July 12, 1913, Cordell, Okla. *Education:* University of Oklahoma, B.F.A., 1936; Oklahoma State University, Library Science, 1965. *Principal occupation:* Museum curator. *Home address:* 408 N. 5th, Ponca City, Okla. 74601. *Affiliation:* Curator, Indian Museum and Cultural Center, Ponca City, Okla. *Community activities:* Teacher and lecturer, Flower Show Schools Organization, National Council of Garden Clubs, 1938-. *Memberships:* Special Libraries Association, 1967-; Oklahoma Historical Society; American Association for State and Local History; American Association of Museums. *Interests:* Fingerweaving or Indian braiding. *Biographical source:* *American Museums Director.*

CHANA, ANTHONY M. (Papago) 1939-
(teacher-elementary education)

Born August 4, 1939, Santa Rosa Village (Ge Aji), Ariz. *Education:* Phoenix College, A.A., 1967; Arizona State Unviersity, B.A., 1970. *Principal occupation:* Teacher-elementary education. *Home address:* 5544 S. Hildreth Ave., Tucson, Ariz. 85706. *Affiliation:* Counselor, Pima Community College, Tucson, Ariz., 1971-. *Memberships:* Arizona State University Alumni Association; Kiwanis Club, 1971-1972; National Indian Education Association, 1973-; American Indian Association (board of directors, 1974-; vice-chairman, 1975-1977; chairman, 1976); Information and Referral Service Board (member, 1975-1976); Committee for Economic Opportunity (board member, 1976-1977); *Interests:* "I am interested in the studies which research the success and failure of students among the urban and reservation Indians. I think the study will demonstrate the phenomenon of success and failure that can be utilized to counsel students effectively. I am also interested in the study of the Papago language and the development of instructional material for the elementary, high school, and college classes. The area that intrigues me most is the Papago that pre-date Spanish influence, which is all but lost."

CHAPMAN, JANE (Mrs. G. Courtney) 1938-
(dealer-Indian arts and crafts)

Born April 11, 1938, Columbus, Ohio. *Education:* University of Chicago, 1953-1955; Ohio Wesleyan University, 1955-1956; University of Illinois, B.A., 1958. *Principal occupation:* Dealer, American Indian arts and crafts—Kiva Indian art. *Home address:* 488 Greenglade Ave., Worthington, Ohio 43085. *Professional post:* Indian Arts and Crafts Association (member, secretary, board of directors). *Community activities:* PTA (president, 1976-1977); Civic Association.

CHAPMAN, ROBERT L.
(tribal official)

Affiliation: President, Pawnee Business Council, P.O. Box 470, Pawnee, Okla. 74058.

CHARLES, ALAN
(tribal chairman)

Affiliation: Chairman, Lower Elwha Community Council, P.O. Box 1370, Port Angeles, Wash. 98362.

CHARLES, RONALD G.
(tribal chairman)

Affiliation: Chairman, Port Gamble Community Council, P.O. Box 280, Kingston, Wash. 98346.

CHASE THE BEAR, LIONEL
(B.I.A. agency superintendent)

Affiliation: Superintendent, Standing Rock Agency, Bureau of Indian Affairs, Fort Yates, N.D. 58538.

CHAVERS, DEAN (Lumbee) 1941-
(president, MANAGE, Inc.)

Born February 4, 1941, Pembroke, N.C. *Education:* University of Richmond, 1960-1962; University of California, Berkeley, B.A. (Journalistic Studies), 1970; Stanford University, M.A. (Anthropology), 1973,

M.A. (Communications), 1975, Ph.D. (Communications Research), 1976. *Principal occupation:* President, MANAGE, Inc. *Home address:* 6709 Esther Ave., N.E., Albuquerque, N.M. 87109. *Affiliations:* President, Native American Scholarship Fund, 1970-1978; president, Bacone College, Muskogee, Okla., 1978-1981; president, Dean Chavers & Associates, 1981-1985; president, MANAGE, Inc., 1985-. *Other professional posts:* Assistant professor, California State University, Hayward, 1972-1974; member, Advisory Panel for Minority Concerns, The College Board, 1980-1985; member, Minority Achievement Program, Association of American Colleges, 1980-1984; board member, National Indian Education Association, 1983-1986. *Military service:* U.S. Air Force, 1963-1968 (Navigator, Captain; Distinguished Flying Cross, Air Medal). *Community activities:* Democratic Party of Wagoner County, Oklahoma (former secretary-treasurer). *Memberships:* National Indian Education Association (board member); National Congress of American Indians; International Communication Association; National Society of Fund Raising Executives; Association for Educational Data Systems. *Awards, honors:* Ford Foundation Graduate Fellow; National Honor Society; Virginia State Spelling Champion, 1959. *Interests:* "Main interest is Indian education, secondary interest is Indian economic development. Have published five books and technical manuals in these areas, as well as some 30 journal articles. Main occupation is providing technical assistance in fund raising, financial management, computer software development, and training for Indian tribes, contract schools, and Indian health clinics." *Published works: How to Write Winning Proposals* (DCA Publications, 1983); *Funding Guide for Native Americans* (DCA Publications, 1983; 2nd ed., 1985); *Grants to Indians* (DCA Publications, 1984); *Tribal Economic Development Directory* (DCA Publications, 1985); *Basic Fund Raising* (Taft Publications, 1986).

CHAVES, ESQUIPULA
(governor-Pueblo)

Affiliation: Governor, Sandia Pueblo, P.O. Box 6008, Bernalillo, N.M. 87004.

CHAVIS, ANGELA YELVERTON (Lumbee) 1950-
(dentist)

Born May 11, 1950, Pembroke, N.C. *Education:* Pembroke State University, B.S., 1971; University of North Carolina, Chapel Hill, School of Dentistry, D.D.S., 1980. *Principal occupation:* Dentist. *Home address:* Route 2, Box 232, Pembroke, N.C. 28372. *Community activities:* Student Health Action Committee; Voter Registration. *Memberships:* North Carolina Association for Preventive Dentistry, 1976-; American Dental Association. *Awards, honors:* Graduated "Cum Laude," Pembroke State University, 1971; scholarship from the American Fund for Dental Health, 1976-1980. *Interests:* "My vocational interest is dentistry. I plan to return to my home town and work to better the dental health of the Indian people in my town and surrounding community." *Biographical source: Who's Who Among Students in American Universities & Colleges, 1971.*

CHIAGO, ROBERT KEAMS (Navajo-Pima) 1942-
(educator and businessman)

Born June 22, 1942, Los Angeles, Calif. *Education:* Arizona State University, B.A., 1965; Northern Illinois University, Dekalb, M.S., 1970; University of Utah, 1974-1976 (61 hours towards Ph.D.). *Principal occupation:* Educator and businessman. *Home address:* 3609 East 3800 South, Salt Lake City, Utah 84109. *Affiliations:* Associate director, American Indian Culture Center, UCLA, 1970; director, Ramah Navajo School Board, Inc., Ramah, N.M., 1970-1971; director, Navajo Division of Education, Navajo Nation, Window Rock, Ariz., 1971-1973; consultant, Mesa Consultants, Albuquerque, N.M., 1973; visiting assistant professor of humanities, University of Utah, Salt Lake City, 1976-1979; director, Native Amerian Studies, University of Utah, 1973-1981; director of Indian Teacher/Counselor Education Programs, University of Utah, 1980-1984; president, Western Indian Technologies, Salt Lake City, Utah, 1984-. *Other professional posts:* Editor and founder, *Utah Indian Journal,* which was a statewide Indian newspaper in 1976 & 1977; founder and coordinator, Western Indian Education

Conference; consulting; proposal writing and evaluation. *Military service:* U.S. Marine Corps, 1965-1968 (Captain, infantry officer; Presidential Unit Citation, Navy Unit Citation, National Defense Service Medal, Vietnam Service Medal and Campaign Medal). *Community activities:* Presidential appointee, National Advisory Council on Indian Education; gubanatorial appointee to the Utah State Board of Indian Affairs; National Congress of American Indians (resolutions committee chairman, 1976-1980); advisory committee for the creation of the Native American Rights Fund, 1971-1972; member, State of Utah ESEA Title IV Advisory Council, 1977-1979; Community Services Council of Utah (board member, 1974-1975; director, Minority Economic Development Council. *Memberships:* National Congress of American Indians; Western Indian Education Conference (coordinator, 1983, 1984, 1986); National Advisory Council on Indian Education, 1983-1986. *Interests:* "Major areas of interest include education, economic development, and employment."

CHIAO, CHIEN 1935-
(professor, researcher)

Born February 6, 1935, China. *Education:* National Taiwan University, B.A., 1958, M.A., 1961; Cornell University, Ph.D., 1969. *Principal occupation:* Professor, researcher. *Home address:* Department of Anthropology, New Asia College, The Chinese University of Hong Kong, Shatin, N.T., Hong Kong. *Affiliations:* Assistant, associate professor, Indiana University, 1966-1976; senior lecturer, chairman, Department of Anthropology, The Chinese University of Hong Kong, 1976-. *Other professional posts:* Adjunct Research Fellow, Institute of Ethnology, Academia Sinica, 1978-; honorary professor, Honan Institute of Museology, 1985-. *Memberships:* Hong Kong Anthropological Society (founder and founding chairman, 1978-1981); American Anthropological Association (Fellow); Royal Asiatic Society - Hong Kong Branch. *Interests:* Cultural anthropology, political anthropology, social structure, religion, culture change; North American with emphasis on the Navajo, with specific focus on Navajo ceremonialism; and East Asia with emphasis on China. *Biographical sources:* "Dr. Chiao Chien Talks About Anthropology," by Bin Xiao *(Readers,* No. 5 1985, Hauiyin, China); "Professor Chiao Chien Returns Home," by Yunho Li *(Unity Weekly,* No. 726, Aug. 24, 1985, Beijing, China). *Published works: Continuation of Tradition in Navajo Society* (Institute of Ethnology, Academia Sinica, 1971).

CHICKS, SHELDON A. (Stockbridge-Munsee) 1928-
(physician)

Born December 20, 1928, Shawano County, Wisc. *Education:* Marquette Univerity, School of Medicine, M.D., 1963. *Principal occupation:* Physician (private practice). *Home address:* 6324 Upper Parkway North, Wauwatosa, Wisc. 53213. *Community activities:* Milwaukee Indian Health Board, Inc. (vice-chairman, board of directors); Milwaukee Indian Community School (board of directors, 1973-1975). *Memberships:* American Psychiatric Association; Association of American Indian Physicians (president, 1974-1975, 1977-1978).

CHIEF, LEROY
(principal)

Affiliation: Principal, Wahpeton Schoo, Bureau of Indian Affairs, Wahpeton, N.D. 58075.

CHILTOSKEY, GOINGBACK (Cherokee) 1907-
(arts and crafts specialist)

Born April 20, 1907, Cherokee, N.C. *Education:* Chicago Art Institute; Purdue University. *Principal occupation:* Arts and crafts specialist. *Home address:* Cherokee, N.C. 28719. *Affiliations:* Instructor, Cherokee Indian School, Cherokee, N.C., 1937-1942, 1947-1953; modelmaker, Engineer Board, Fort Belvior, Va., 1942-1946; partner, Imagineering Associates, Hollywood, Calif., 1946-1947; modelmaker, E.R.D.L., Fort Belvior, Va., 1954-1966; self-employed as craftsmen, Cherokee, N.C., 1966-. *Memberships:* Southern Highlands Handicraft Guild, 1948-; Qualla Arts and Crafts Mutual, 1947-; Washington Society of Artists, 1960-1963; Federal Artists and Designers, 1962-1964. *Awards, honors:* Purchase Award, North Carolina Art Society, 1953; First Prize, Blowing Rock, N.C., Exhibit; Second Prize, Philbrook Art Center, Tulsa, Okla.; prizes at North Carolina State Fair and Cherokee Indian Fair. Work chosen for exhibit at Smithsonian Institution. *Interests:* Mr. Chiltoskey writes, "(My) instructional career included teaching high school students and adults to do wood carving, sculpture, and furniture-making. During spare time and since retirement, (I) design and make wood carvings and sculpture. Lapidary and jewelry making are other interests. Summer camp counseling and personal interests have taken me into most states in the U.S." *Published works: To Make My Bread: Cherokee Cooklore* (Stephens Press, 1951).

CHINO, WENDELL (Mescalero Apache)
(tribal council president)

Affiliation: President, Mescalero Apache Tribal Council, P.O. Box 176, Mescalero, N.M. 88340.

CHOUTEAU, M.M. (Kaw)
(tribal chairman)

Affiliation: Chairman, Kaw Business Committee, Drawer 50, Kaw City, Okla. 74641.

CHRISTIE, JOE C.
(B.I.A. agency superintendent)

Affiliation: Superintendent, Winnebago Agency, Bureau of Indian Affairs, Winnebago, Neb. 68071

CHRISTMAN, RICHARD T, 1937-
(B.I.A. agency superintendent)

Born July 5, 1937, Library, Penna. *Education:* Colorado School of Mines, 1954-1955; California State Teachers College, B.S., 1963; Arizona State University, M.S. (Indian Education), 1967. *Principal occupation:* B.I.A. agency superintendent. *Home address:* 2552 West Capsitrano Rd., Tucson, Ariz. 85706. *Affiliation:* Superintendent,

B.I.A., Papago Agency, Sells, Ariz., 1976-. *Other professional posts:* Education program administrator (supt. of schools, Papago Agency), six years. *Community activities:* American Indian Committee, The Church of Jesus Christ (board member); Quorom of Seventy (vice-chairman). *Awards, honors:* Special Achievement Award for Education Improvement, Bureau of Indian Affairs; Field Management Training Award. *Interests:* "Extensive travel to reservations in the Southwest, Northwest Plains, Canada and Eastern seaboard."

CLAH, HERBERT, Jr. (Navajo) 1949-
(administrator)

Born June 1, 1949, Farmington, N.M. *Education:* Brigham Young University, B.S., 1975, MPA, 1981. *Principal occupation:* Executive director, administrator. *Home address:* 484 West Center St. (46-15), Blanding, Utah 84511. *Affiliation:* Executive director, Utah Navajo Development Council, 1981-. *Community activities:* Rural Commuity Assistance Corporation (board of directors). *Memberships:* Indian Education Advisory Committee; Utah State Board of Education. *Awards, honors:* Exxon Fellowship; Deans Leadership Award, BYU; Janie Thompson Award; Outstanding Young Men of America; Defense Department Recognition, USO Tours, Military Bases in Germany, 1974. *Biographical source: Outstanding Young Men of America,* publication.

CLARK, DONALD E. (Chippewa) 1922-
(teacher)

Born May 16, 1922, Frazee, Minn. *Education:* El Camino College, A.A., 1950; Michigan State University, B.S. (Wildlife Biology), 1954. *Principal occupation:* High school biology teacher. *Home address:* 1220 Furlong Rd., Sebastopol, Calif. 95472. *Military service:* U.S. Navy, 1942-1945. *Community activities:* Native American Club (sponsor). *Memberships:* California Teachers Association; National Educational Association. *Interests:* "Native studies, especially religion and art, and "traditional" photography."

CLARK-PRICE, MARGARET A.
(Wyandotte-Shawnee-Chippewa) 1944-
(publisher, artist)

Born August 2, 1944, Colville Indian Reservation, Nespelem, Wash. *Education:* St. Michael's High School, St. Michael's, Ariz., 1962; Sierra Nevada College, Incline Village, Nev. (2½ years). *Principal occupation:* Publisher and artist. *Home address:* P.O. Box 6338, Incline Village, Nev. 89450. *Affiliation:* Publisher, *Native American* (magazine to develop an information non-political, bridge between the many tribes, extending to the reaches of the general public). *Exhibits:* Her pastels, oils, acrylics, watercolors and pencil works hang in galleries in Arizona, California, and Nevada as well as in many private collections throughout the U.S. *Awards, honors:* Six awards and a Grand prize for a large pastel entitled "Caught in the Middle," at the 1982 annual Navajo Nation Fair, Window Rock, Ariz. *Interests:* "My main interests, obviously, surround the Indian world. I have spect years on my own family genealogy, necessitating journeying across the U.S. and into Canada. I hope to instill such an interest in others through the journey among the pages of the *Native American* annual and its subsequent issues."

CLARKE, FRANK, M.D. (Hualapai)
1921-
(physician/administrator)

Born November 11, 1921, Blythe, Calif. *Education:* Sherman Institute, Riverside, Calif. (seven years); Los Angeles City College (two years); University of California at Los Angeles, B.S., 1946; St. Louis University, School of Medicine, M.D., 1950. *Principal occupation:* Physician/administrator. *Home address:* 7909 Rio Grande Blvd., N.W., Albuquerque, N.M. 87114. *Affiliation:* Clinical director, Albuquerque Service Unit, Public Health Service, Indian Health Service, Albuquerque, N.M., 1975-. *Other profesional post:* Secretary, National Council of Clinical Directors. *Military service:* U.S. Navy, 1942-1946 (Presidential Unit Citation), 1950-1953 (Lt. (MC) USNR). *Memberships:* USPHS Commissioned Officers Association; American Academy of Family Physicians (Charter Fellow); New

Mexico Academy of Family Physicians; Association of American Indian Physicians (president, 1973-1974). *Awards, honors:* Fellow, John Hay Whitney Foundation, 1950; Indian Achievement Award, Indian Council Fire, Chicago, 1961; Man of the Year, City of Woodlake, 1962; Layman of the Year in Education, Tulane County Chapter of California Teacher's Association. *Interests:* Recruitment of Indian students into health professions; lecturer on alcoholism. *Biographical sources: Indians of Today; Who's Who in the West; Community Leaders & Noteworthy Americans.*

CLARY, THOMAS C. (Miami
of Oklahoma) 1927-
(corporate president)

Born March 3, 1927, Joplin, Mo. *Education:* Pace University, New York City, B.B.A. (Marketing); University of Oklahoma, Norman, M.A. (Public Administration); California Western University, Santa Ana, Ph.D. (Psychology). *Principal occupation:* Corporate president. *Home address:* 3410 Garfield St., N.W., Washington, D.C. 20007. *Affiliations:* Director, Light, Inc., Columbus, Ohio (four years); director, Science of Mind Church Counseling and Healing Center, Washington, D.C. (two years); director, Alternative Health Therapies, Washington, D.C. (three years); president, TCI, Inc., Washington, D.C. (ten years). *Other professional posts:* Minister, Science of Mind Church. *Military service:* U.S. Army, 1945-1968 (Lt. Colonel) (Legion of Merit, Army Commendation Medal). *Memberships:* International Transactional Analysis Association (teaching member); American Association of Profesional Hypnotherapists. *Awards, honors:* Silver Anvil Award for International Community Relations by Public Relations Society of America, 1968; Master Hypnotist by Ameriacn Council of Hypnotist Examiners, 1983; Urban Mass Transportation Administration Minority Business Enterprise Award, 1985. *Interests:* Teach courses in "psychic potential," "spiritual healing" and "stress management." *Published works:* "Script Analysis is a New Approach to OD," chapter 12 of *Everybody Wins: Transactional Analysis Applied to Organizations* (Addison-

50

Wesley, 1974); *How to Live with Stress* (NTDS Press, 1977); *At the Organizational Precipice* (NTDS Press, 1977).

CLAUS, TOM (Mohawk) 1929-
(ordained clergyman, administrator)

Born December 26, 1929, Niagara Falls, N.Y. *Education:* High school; private tutoring in theology. *Principal occupation:* Ordained clergyman, administrator. *Home address:* 2302 W. Port au Prince Lane, Phoenix, Ariz. 85023. *Affiliations:* Director, American Indian Crusade, Inc., Glendale, Ariz., 1952-; president, Christian Hope Indian Eskimo Fellowship, Orange, Calif., 1975-. *Other professional posts:* American Indian delegate to World Congress on Evangelism, Berlin, Germany, 1966; delegate to International Congress on World Evangelization, Lausanne, Switzerland, 1974. *Community activities:* Billy Graham Evangelistic Association Crusades (Indian coordinator). *Interests:* "Extensive travels to Indians, Eskimos, Aleuts in Alaska, Canada, U.S., Mexico, Guatamala, Panama, Suriname." *Published works: On Eagles Wings* (Thunderbird Press, 1976); *Christian Leadership in Indian America* (Moody Press, 1977).

CLEGHORN, MILDRED (Fort Sill Apache)
(tribal chairwoman)

Affiliation: Chairwoman, Fort Sill Apache Business Committee, Route 2, Box 121, Apache, Okla. 73006.

CLEMMER, JANICE WHITE
(Wasco-Shawnee-Delaware) 1941-
(professor)

Born February 17, 1941, Warm Springs Reservation, Oregon. *Education:* Brigham Young University, Provo, Utah, B.S. (Archaeology/history), 1964; Dominican College of San Rafael, Calif., M.A. (History), 1975; University of San Francisco, M.A. (Education), 1976; University of Utah, Salt Lake City, (Ph.D., Cultural Foundation of Education, 1979; Ph.D. History, 1980). *Principal occupation:* Professor.

Home address: 1445 E. Princeton Ave., Salt Lake City, Utah 84105. *Affiliations:* Professor, College of Education, Brigham Young University, Provo, Utah, 1980-. *Other professional posts:* Editorial board, *American Indian Culture and Research Journal;* reviewer. *American Indian Quarterly,* University of California at Berkeley. *Community activities:* Boy Scouts-Cub Scouts (merit badge counselor/den mother); leader, Girl Scouts-Brownies; board chairman, Native American Advisory Board, State of Utah Board of Education; committee member, Utah Endowment for the Humanities; board member, American Indian Services; volunteer, Utah State Heart and Lung Association. *Memberships:* SIETAR (Society for Intercultural Education, Training and Research, International Organization); Native American Historians' Association (founding member); American Studies Association; OHOYO - National Native American Women's Program; Association for Supervision and Curriculum Development; State of Utah Bilingual Association; American Historians Western History Association; Utah State Historical Society; Oregon Historical Society; California Historical Society; National Archives (associate); Jefferson Forum; American Association for State and Local History. *Awards, honors:* University of Utah Danforth Foundation Fellowship Candidate; Distinguished Teaching Award Candidate, University of Utah; Tribal Archives Conference Award Recipient; Consortium for Native American Archives; OHOYO One Thousand, Native American Women Award Listing; American Indian Alumni Award, Brigham Young University; Lamanite Award, American Indian Services, BYU; D'Arcy McNickle, Newberry Library Fellowship Research Award, Chicago, Ill.; Spencer W. Kimball Memorial Award, Private Corporation Endowment & AIS, BYU; Phi Alpha Theta; Phi Delta Kappa; Phi Kappa Phi; first Native American woman in U.S. history to earn two Ph.D.s; 1982 Women's Conference "Spotlight", outstanding woman faculty member from the College of Student Life, BYU; Multicultural Week Advisor Awards, BYU; Multicultural Programs Awards, BYU. *Biographical sources:* University of Utah Public Relations Office,

Salt Lake City, Utah rgarding the earning of
two Ph.D.s; stories in *Deseret News,* Church
News Section, 1980; and in Lifestyle section
of the *Salt Lake Tribune,* Salt Lake City,
Spring, 1980; hometown newspapers, *Bend
Bulletin, Bend, Oregon, Spilya Tymoo,*
Warm Springs, Oregon, and *Madras Pio-
neer,* Madras, Oregon. *Published works:*
"The Good Guys and the Bad Guys," *The
Utah Indian,* Journal, Spring, 1979; "Ethnic
Traditions and the Family--The Native
Americans," *Ethnic Traditions and the
Family* series, Salt lake City Board of Edu-
cation, Fall, 1980; editor, *Minority Women
Speak Out* (in progress); various book
reviews pertaining to Native American top-
ics; printed works primarily in-house curric-
ulum development material, Brigham
Young University.

CLIFTON, JAMES A. 1927-
(professor)

Born January 6, 1927, St. Louis, Mo. *Education:* University of Chicago, Ph.B., 1950;
University of Orgon, Ph.D., 1960. *Principal
occupation:* Professor. *Home address:* 332
Bretcoe Dr., Green Bay, Wisc. 54302. *Affili-
ation:* Professor, University of Wisconsin,
Green Bay, 1970-. *Military service:* U.S.
Marine Corps, 1951-1955 (Captain; Purple
Heart). *Memberships:* American Anthropo-
logical Association; American Society for
Ethnohistory; American Historical Associa-
tion. *Awards, honors:* Frankenthal Profes-
sor of Anthropology and History,
University of Wisconsin, Green Bay. *Inter-
ests:* "Research among Klamath of Oregon,
Ute of Colorado, Potawatomi of Kansas,
Wisconsin, Michigan, and Canada. Histori-
cal research on Wyandot and Indians of the
Old Northwest Territory generally; research
in Chile. Expert witness, Indian Claims
Commission and Great Lakes Indians
Treaty Rights." *Published works: Klamath
Personalities* (University of Oregon, 1962);
Cultural Anthropology (Houghton Mifflin,
1967); *A Place of Refuge for All Time*
(Museum of Man, 1974); *The Prairie People*
(Kansas University Press, 1977); *Star
Woman and Other Shawnee Tales* (Univer-
isity Press of America, 1983); *The Pokagons*
(University Press of America, 1985).

CLINCHER, BONNIE MARIE (Sioux)
1952-
(editor-tribal newspaper)

Born July 6, 1952, Poplar, Mont. *Education:* Haskell Indian Junior College, 1973-
1975. *Principal occupation:* Editor of tribal
newspaper. *Home address:* Box 631, Poplar,
Mont. 59255. *Memberships:* Survival of
American Indians Association, 1976-. *Interests:* "I am most interested in the media,
especially when I can assist in informing and
making concerned the Indian people. My
travels only go as far as celebrations across
the northern Plains, on weekends, to just be
among the Indian people and refresh my
spirit in the old ways before returning to the
new ways"; photography.

COCHRAN, GEORGE McKEE
(Cherokee— 1908-
(artist, barber)

Born October 5, 1908, Stilwell, Okla. *Educa-
tion:* Haskell Institute, 1927. *Principal occu-
pation:* Artist, barber. *Home address:* 681
Chase St., Eugene, Oregon 97402. *Com-
munity activities:* Kiwanis Club. *Member-
ships:* Cherokee Foundation, Inc.; Indian
Festival of Arts, Inc. (board member);
Maude I. Kerns Art Center; National Con-
gress of American Indians; Oregon
Archaeological Society (life member), 1964-
Red Dirt or War Paint Clan of the North
American Indian; Mormon Church.
Awards, honors: American Eagle Feather
Award for outstanding work among the
Indian people, American Indian Festival of
Arts, Inc., 1960-1961; Grand Award, All
American Indian Art Exhibit, 1961-1962;
several others. Mr. Cochran's work has been
exhibited in many one-man shows over the
country, including the Seattle Public
Library, Haskell Institute, Philbrook Art
Center, Barnsdall Art Gallery, Truman
Library, University of Oregon, Hotel Utah
Art Gallery, Lloyd's Center Art Gallery,
Wilshire Federal and Loan Art Gallery.
*Published works: Indian Portraits of the
Pacific Northwest* (Binfords and Mort,
1959).

COLLIER, L.W.
(B.I.A. agency superintendent)

Affiliation: Superintendent, Wind River Agency, Bureau of Indian Affairs, Fort Washakie, Wyo. 82514.

COLLIER, LAVERN
(B.I.A. agency superintendent)

Affiliation: Superintendent, Uintah and Ouray Agency, Bureau of Indian Affairs, Fort Duchesne, Utah 84026.

COLLINS, ADELE VICTOR (Chickasaw) 1908-
(painter)

Born January 24, 1908, Blanchard, Okla. *Education:* St. Elizabeth's Academy Indian School, Purcell, Okla.; various art courses at Art League; studied with Emalita Newton Terry. *Principal occupation:* Painter. *Home address:* 1631 Curtis Dr., Las Vegas, Nevada 89104. *Exhibitions:* Oklahoma State Show, Oklahoma City; Oklahoma Indian Show, Philbrook Museum, Tulsa; Arts and Crafts Board, U.S. Dept. of the Interior, Washington, D.C.; Contemporary Indian Art Show, Santa Fe, N.M.; Inter-Tribal Indian Ceremonials, Gallup, N.M.; Scottsdale Contemporary Indian Show, Ariz.; University of South Dakota, Vermillion; La Grande, Oreg. Indian Annual; Smithsonian Institution; Five Civilized Tribes Museum, Muskogee, Okla.; All American Indian Days, Sheridan, Wyoming; Miss Collin's work is in the following permanent collections: U.S. Dept. of the Interior, Washington, D.C.; Vincent Price Collection, Hollywood, Calif.; Heard Museum, Phoenix, Ariz.; Gonzaga University Indian Center, Spokane, Wash.; Southern Nevada University, Las Vegas, Nev. *Awards, honors:* Mis Collins has received many awards and prizes for her art, too numerous to mention.

COLLINS, CARL
(president-Bible Institute)

Affiliation: President, Amerian Indian Bible Institute, 100020 N. 15th Ave., Phoenix, Ariz. 85021.

COLLINS, REBA NEIGHBORS 1925-
(director-Will Rogers Memorial)

Born August 26, 1925. *Education:* Central State University, Edmond, B.A., 1958; Oklahoma State University, M.S. (Journalism), 1959, Ed.D. (Higher Education in Journalism), 1968. *Principal occupation:* Director, Will Rogers Memorial, Claremore, Okla., 1975-. *Address:* c/o Will Rogers Memorial, Box 157, Claremore, Okla. 74018. *Affiliations:* Instructor, professor of journalism, Central State University, 1958-1975; director of public relations, sponsor of alumni publications, school newspaper and college yearbook, Central State University, 1958-1975. *Community activities:* Edmond Guidance Center (board of directors); Claremore Chamber of Commerce (board of directors); member, Claremore Ambassadors; Claremore Pilot Club (charter president); member, Governor's mini-cabinet for tourism and recreation. *Memberships:* Delta Kappa Gamma; Sigma Delta Chi; American Association of Unviersity Women; Oklahoma Public Relations Association for Higher Education (charter president); Oklahoma Education Association (public relations board); CSU Alumni Association; Oklahoma Museum Association (board of directors, treasurer). *Awards, honors:* Outstanding Senior Woman, and Outstanding Future Teacher, Central State University, 1958; (2) First Place Awards, Oklahoma Press Association for Best Feature on Education; Outstanding Communicator Award from Oklahoma Women in Journalism, 1975; Service Award from VFW, 1971; Okie Award from Governor Dewey Bartlet, 1974; Service Award for Helping Organize First Fourth of July Celebration in Edmond, Okla., 1973; Distinguished Former Stduent Award, Central State University, 1979. *Interests:* Genealogy, travel and travel writing. *Published works: In the Shadows of Old North,* 1974; *History of the Janes, Peek Family,* 1975, plus three follow up books; *Will Rogers Memorial Booklet,* 1979; *Roping Will Rogers' Family Tree,* 1982; *Will Rogers and Wiley Post in Alaska,* 1983; editorial staff, *Photolith* magazine (seven years); hundreds of featurer articles for state and national magazines.

COLOMBEL, PIERRE
(Indian health service)

Affiliation: Chief, Human Resource Management, Indian Health Service, 5600 Fishers Lane, Rockville, Md. 20857.

COLOSIMO, THOMAS
(executive secretary-Indian association)

Affiliations: Executive director, Arrow, Inc., 1000 Connecticut Ave., N.W., Washington, D.C. 20036; executive secretary, National American Indian Court Judges Association, 1000 Connecticut Ave., N.W., Suite 401, Washington, D.C. 20036.

COLTON, ALFRED *(Qoyawayma)* (Hopi) 1938-
(professional engineer)

Born 1938, Los Angeles, Calif. *Education:* California State Polytechnic University, B.S., 1961; University of Southern California, M.S. (Mechanical Engineer), 1966, graduate program in water resources and environmental engineering, 1970; Westinghouse International School of Environmental Management, graduate. *Principal occupation:* Professional engineer. *Home address:* 8738 E. Clarendon Ave., Scottsdale, Ariz. 85251. *Affiliations:* Project engineer, Litton Systems, Inc., 1961-1970; supervisor of the Environmental Dept., Salt River Project, Phoenix, Ariz., 1971-. *Other professional posts:* Advisor, University of New Mexico, Native American Program, College of Engineering (NAPCOE); National Representative, Electric Power Research Institute's (EPRI) Environmental Task Force (1974-1977); Bureau of Land Management's (BLM) Arizona Multi-Use Advisory Board (one term). *Community activities:* Western Systems Coordinating Council (WSCC) Environmental Committee (member, past vice-chairman); American Indian Science and Engineering Society (chairman); American Indian Engineering Council (past associate chairman); Heard Museum Men's Council (board of directors); Museum of Northern Arizona (member); Registered Arizona Lobbyist. *Memberships:* Arizona Society of Professional Engineers; Institute of Electrical and Electronic Engineers; American Association for the Advancement of Science; American Public Power Association; Edison Electric Institute Environemntal Committees. *Awards, honors:* First Place Popovi Da Memorial Award for pottery, 1976, Scottsdale National Indian Arts Exhibition,; two blue ribbon awards, 1976, one blue ribbon, 1977, Heard Museum Indian Arts Exhibition, Phoenix, Ariz.; pottery work featured at 1977 Arizona Kidney Foundation Auction, Numkena Studio of Indian Art, Phoenix; individual showing at Santa East, Austin, Texas; first place and special award at the Museum of Northern Arizona's 1977 Hopi Show; second and third place at Gallup Ceremonial, N.M.; holds patents in engineering work in the U.S. and several foreign countries. *Interests:* Pottery and weaving in the Hopi tradition.

CONLEY, ROBERT J. (Cherokee) 1940-
(director of Indian studies)

Born December 29, 1940, Cushing, Okla. *Education:* Midwestern University, Wichita Falls, Texas, B.A., 1966, M.A., 1968. *Principal occupation:* Director of Indian Studies. *Home address:* 3830 Garretson Ave., Sioux City, Iowa 51106. *Affiliations:* Coordinator of Indian culture, Eastern Montana College, 1975-1976; assistant program director, The Cherokee Nation of Oklahoma, 1976-1977; director of Indian studies, Bacone College, 1978-1979; director of Indian studies, Morningside College, Sioux City, Iowa, 1979-. *Military service:* U.S. Marine Corps Reserve, 1957-1962. *Membership:* Western Writers of America. *Interests:* Writing—Mr. Conley writes, "my first novel, *Back to Malachi* (working title) has just been contracted to Doubleday for Fall, 1986 publication;" and acting. *Published works:* Poetry in various magazine and anthologies, including: *Indian Voice* (Feb. and July, 1972), *The Blue Cloud Quarterly* (Vol. 18, #3, 1973), *The Beloit Poetry Journal* (Vol. 30, #2, Winter 1979-1980), *Compages* (Winter and May, 1982); poems such as: *The Rattlesnake Band and Other Poems* (Indian University Press, 1984), "The Hills of Tsa-la-gi," "Morning and Night," and "The Rattlesnake Band," in *The Clouds Threw This Light: Contemporary Native American Poe-*

try, Phillip Foss, editor (Institute of American Indian Arts Press, 1983); "Cherokees 'On the Scout'" in *The Roundup* (Nov.-Dec. 1984); among others. Short Stories in the following periodicals and anthologies: *Indian Voice,* 1972, *Sun Tracks,* Fall 1976; *The Remembered Earth* (Red Earth Press, 1979); and short stories, "Wesley's Story," in *The Greenfield Review* (summer/fall, 1984), and "The Immortals," in *Iowa Archaeological Newsletter* (summer, 1984).

CONN, RICHARD
(curator)

Education: University of Washington, B.A., 1950, M.A., 1955. *Affiliation:* Curator, Denver Art Museum, Denver, Colo. *Military service:* U.S. Army, 1951-1953. *Memberships:* American Association of Museums. *Awards, honors:* McCloy Fellowship in Art, 1979. *Interests:* Native American art in general; fieldwork in eastern Washington, Montana, and Central Canada. *Published works: Robes of White Shell and Sunrise* (Denver Art Museum); *Native American Art in the Denver Art Museum* (Denver Art Museum, 1978); *Circles of the World* (Denver Art Museum, 1982).

CONNER, ROSEMARY
(coordinator-Indian association)

Affiliation: Coordinator, North American Indian Women's Association, National Office, 1411 K St., Suite 200, Washington, D.C. 20005.

COOK, JOHN A. (St. Regis Mohawk) 1922-
(tribal chief)

Born April 22, 1922, Syracuse, N.Y. *Education:* University of Idaho; Loyola University; National Radio Institute; Franklyn Tech. *Principal occupation:* Tribal chief, iron welder. *Home address:* R.F.D., Hogansburg, N.Y. *Affiliation:* Chief, St. Regis Mohawk Tribe. *Military service:* U.S. Air Force, 1942-1945 (Air Medal). *Community activities:* Economic Opportunity Council of Franklyn County (director); Masons; American Legion.

COOK-LYNN, ELIZABETH
(Crow Creek Sioux) 1930-
(associate professor of Indian studies)

Born November 17, 1930, Fort Thompson, S.D. *Education:* South Dakota State College, B.S. (Journalism/English, 1952; University of South Dakota, M.S. (Education/Psychology & Counseling), 1970; University of Nebraska, Lincoln, ABD (all but dissertation) status for Ph.D.; additional graduate work: Stanford University(literary criticism seminar); For teaching credentials - Black Hills State Teachers College and New Mexico State University. *Principal occupation:* Associate professor of Indian studies. *Home address:* Route 12, Box 59, Davenport, Wash. 99122. *Affiliations:* Newspaper work, editing and writing in S.D., 1952-1957; part-time teaching, Carlsbad, N.M., 1958-1964; secondary teaching, Carlsbad, N.M., 1965-1968, Rapid City, S.D., 1968-1969; assistant professor of English, 1970-1980, associate professor of English and Indian Studies, 1980-, Monroe Hall #113, Eastern Washington University, Cheney, Wash. *Other professional posts:* Editor of *The Wicazo SA Review,* a journal of Native Studies, Eastern Washington University. *Professional activities:* Consultant and participant in the curriculum development seminar RMMLA, Flagstaff, Ariz., 1978; project director (planning grant) NEH Media Project: *Indian Scholar's Journal. Published works:* Short stories, poems, and papers: "Problems in Indian Education," *(South Dakota Review),* "A Severe Indictment of Our School Systems," and "Authentic Pictures of the Sioux?" *(Great Plains Observer),* 1970; "Propulsives in Native American Literatures," paper read at National meeting of Conference of College Composition, and Communications, New Orleans, 1973; "The Teaching of Indian Literatures," NCTE, Minneapolis, Minn., 1974; "The Image of the American Indian in Historical Fiction," RMMLA, Laramie, Wyoming; "Delusion: The American Indian in White Man's Fiction," RMMLA, El Paso, Texas; "Three," prose and poetry in *Prairie Schooner,* Fall, 1976; "A Child's Story," short story in *Pembroke Magazine,* 1976; poems published in *Sun Tracks* (University of Arizona, 1977), and *The Ethnic Studies Journal; Then Badger Said This,* collection of poems (Vantage Press, 1978); "The Indian Short Story," and bibliography for *Encyclopedia of Short Fiction,* edited by Walton Beacham (Salem Press, 1980); "The Cure," short story accepted for *Anthology of Native American Literature,* edited by Berud Pryor, UCLA, Davis, 1980; two short stories, "The Power of Horses," and "A Good Chance," accepted by Simon J. Ortiz (Pueblo writer and poet)for inclusion in anthology *The Short Story in Native American Literatures* (Navajo College Press, 1983); 12 poems entitled *Seek the House of Relatives* (Blue Cloud Press, 1983); "Within Walking Distance," Spring issue, 1984, of *Bearing Witness, Sobreviviendo,* an anthology of writing and art by Native American-/Latina women; three poems, *Harper's Book of Twentieth Century Native American Poetry,* 1986, edited by Duane Niatum; among other short stories, articles, and essays.

COOKE, DAVID C. 1917-
(writer)

Born June 7, 1917, Wilmington, Delaware. *Education:* New York University, 1946-1947. *Principal occupation:* Writer. *Home address:* 57 E. Carpenter St., Valley Stream, N.Y. *Awards, honors:* Edgar Award, for *Best Detective Stories of the Year,* 1960: *Interests:* Writing; aviation; the American Indian; travel. *Published works: Famous Indian Tribes* (Random House, 1953); *Fighting Indians of the West* (Dodd, Mead, 1954); *Indians on the Warpath* (Dodd, Meade, 1957); *Tecumseh: Destiny's Warrior* (Julian Messner, 1959); *Indian Wars and Warriors* (Dodd, Mead, 1966).

COOPER, HARRY E. (Nooksack)
(tribal chairman)

Affiliation: Chairman, Nooksack Tribal Council, P.O. Box 157, Deming, Wash. 98244.

COOPER, KAREN COODY (Cherokee) 1946-
(educator, administrator)

Born November 10, 1946, Tulsa, Okla. *Edu-* *cation:* Oklahoma College of Liberal Arts, Chickasha, Okla., 1965-1966; Western Connecticut State University, Danbury, B.A. (Anthropology), 1981. *Princopal occupation:* Educator/administrator. *Home address:* 2192 Litchfield Rd., Watertown, Conn. 06795. *Affiliation:* American Indian Archaeological Institute, Curtis Rd., Washington, Conn. 06793. *Other professional post:* Adjunct instructor, Western State Connecticut State University. *Community activities:* Board member, *Eagle Wing Press,* an American Indian newspaper. *Memberships:* Connecticut Indian Education Council; National Organization for Women; Connecticut Council for Social Studies. *Interests:* Ms. Cooper writes, "I am studying fingerweaving, an ancient craft of American Indians in the Woodlands, and have won prizes and written articles; I am also studying the historic events affecting Connecticut's Indian population; I am a published poet; I enjoy black and white photography."

CORBINE JOSEPH
(tribal chairman)

Affiliation: Chairman, Bad River Tribal Council, Route 39, Ashland, Wis. 54806.

CORNELIUS-FENTON, KAREN
(president-Indian association)

Affiliation: President, National Indian Education Association, 1115 Second Ave. South, Minneapolis, Minn. 55403.

CORNETT, JAMES D. 1923-
(B.I.A. agency superintendent)

Born January 1, 1923, Moorewood, Okla. *Education:* Sayre Jr. College, 1949-1950; Oklahoma State University, B.A., 1952. *Principal occupation:* B.I.A. agency superintendent. *Home address:* Box 425, Warm Springs, Oreg. 97761. *Affiliations:* Soil scientist, Fort Peck Agency, B.I.A., 1952-1956; soil conservationist, Blackfeet Agency, B.I.A., 1956-1962; land operations officer, Zuni Agency, B.I.A.; superintendent, Fort Totten Agency, Zuni Agency; area natural resource officer, Albuquerque Area Office; superintendent, Warm Springs

Agency, Warm Springs, Oreg. *Military service:* U.S. Navy, 1942-1948 (Campaign Medal, Good Conduct Medal). *Community activities:* 4-H; Boy Scouts of America; Lions Club (president, secretary, director).

CORTEZ, RONALD D.
(business committee chairman)

Affiliation: Chairman, Torres-Martinez Business Committee, 1866 E. George, Banning, Calif. 92220.

COSGROVE, STEPHEN FRANCIS (Sioux) 1943-
(ex-professional baseball player)

Born March 8, 1943, Marysville, Kansas. *Education:* Haskell Institute. *Principal occupation:* Ex-professional baseball player, Baltimore Orioles (baseball team).

COTTER, LEONARD N. (Wyandotte) 1906-
(ex-chief, Wyandotte Tribe)

Born July 3, 1906, Wyandotte, Indian Territory, Okla. *Education:* High school. *Principal occupation:* Ex-chief, Wyandotte Tribe; diesel mechanic. *Home address:* Box 15, Wyandotte, Okla. 74370. *Affiliations:* Garage and service station attendant and owner, 1926-1937; staff member, Indian Roads Dept., Okla., 1938-1940; Dunning, James & Patterson Construction Co., Oklahoma City, Okla., 1942-1943; E.A. Martin Machinery Co., Joplin, Mo., 1943-1944; S.E. Evans Construction Co., Ft. Smith, Ark., 1944-1945; diesel mechanic, Oklahoma State Highway Dept., 1946-retirement. *Other professional posts:* Second chief, Wyandotte Tribe, 1932-1936; chief, 1936-1942, 1948-1954, 1963-retirement. *Military service:* U.S. Marines, 1943. *Community activities:* Wyandotte Lions Club (past president); Wyandotte Methodist Church (past lay leader); American Legion. *Published works: Constitutions and By-Laws of the Wyandotte Tribe of Oklahoma* (Dept. of the Interior, 1937); *Corporate Charter of the Wyandotte Tribe of Oklahoma* (Dept. of the Interior, 1937).

COULTER, ROBERT T.
(director-Indian center)

Affiliation: Director, Indian Law Resource Center, 601 E St., S.E., Washington, D.C. 20003.

COURNOYER, FRANK (Yankton Sioux) 1952-
(visual artist)

Born December 26, 1952, Wagner, S.D. *Principal occupation:* Visual artist. *Home address:* Box 551, Wagner, S.D. 57380. *Affiliations:* Member, board of directors, Dakota Plains Institute of Learning, Marty, S.D. 57361, 1984-; chairman, board of directors, Oyate Kin Cultural Society, Marty, S.D., 1984-. *Military service:* U.S. Army, 1971-1974 (Specialist E-4, 82nd Airborne Division) (National Defense Ribbon, Expert Rifleman Badge, Jump Wings). *Community activities:* "Dakota Plains Institute of Learning" is the higher adult education branch of the Yankton Sioux Tribe; "Oyate Kin Cultural Society" is a newly formed organization intent on reviving, preserving and promoting Sioux arts and crafts. *Interests:* Mr. Cournoyer writes, "My major goals include the revival of Sioux arts and crafts to help promote the working artist and teach the future artists/craftspeople the art of marketing, quality, and culture, aiming at a more productive and self-reliant people." *Published works:* "I have an illustration in the book *Remember Your Realtives,* by Renee Sansome-Flood and Shirley A. Bernie, and I'm being considered for some illustrations in an upcoming biography of southeast South Dakota and have been selected to submit an illustration for another upcoming historical biography."

COX, BRUCE 1934-
(professor)

Born June 29, 1934, Santa Rosa, Calif. *Education:* Reed College, B.A., 1956; University of Oregon, M.A., 1959; University of California at Berkeley, Ph.D., 1968. *Principal occupation:* Professor of anthropology. *Home address:* 140 Kenilworth, Ottawa, Ontario, Canada. *Affiliations:* Instructor, Lewis and Clark College, 1964-1965; visiting professor, University of Florida, 1966; assistant professor, University of Alberta, 1967-1969; assistant professor, professor, Carleton University, 1969-. *Memberships:* American Anthropological Association; Law and Society Association. *Interests:* Dr. Cox writes, "I am interested in the cultural ecology of indigenous North American peoples...particularly the disrupted effects of large-scale energy development projects on such peoples' environments. Here, I have in mind the James Bay hydroelectric project in Quebec, the proposed Mackenzie Valley petroleum pipeline corridor in the N.W.T., and coal strip-mining on Black Mesa, and I am collecting information on all these areas." *Published works: Cultural Ecology of Canadian Native Peoples* (Carleton Library, 1973).

COX, CLAUDE (Creek)
(tribal chief)

Affiliation: Chief, Creek Nation, P.O. Box 580, Okmulgee, Okla. 74447.

CRAMPTON, C. GREGORY 1911-
(professor of history)

Born March 22, 1911, Kankakee, Ill. *Education:* Modesto Junior College, 1933; University of California, Berkeley, B.A., 1935, M.A., 1936, Ph.D., 1941. *Principal occupation:* Professor of history. *Home address:* 327 S. 12th E., Salt Lake City, Utah 84102. *Affiliations:* Teaching assistant in history, University of California, Berkeley, 1937-1940; special agent, F.B.I., U.S. Department of Justice, 1943-1945; depot historian, California Quartermaster Depot, U.S. War Department, 1944-1945; professor of history, University of Utah, 1945-; director, Duke Indian Oral History Project, University of Utah, 1967-. *Awards, honors:* Rockefeller Foundation, traveling Fellowship, 1941-1942; postwar Fellowship, Humanities, 1948-1949. *Memberships:* Phi Alpha Theta (vice-president, 1941-1948; president, 1949-1950). *Published works: Outline History of the Glen Canyon Region, 1776-1922* (University of Utah Press, 1959); *Historical Sites in Glen Canyon, Mouth of the San Juan River to Lee's Ferry* (Univerity of Utah Press, 1960); editor with Dwight L. Smight,

The Hoskaninni Papers of Robert B. Stanton, Mining in Glen Canyon, 1897-1902 (Univerity of Utah Press, 1961); *Historical Sites in Glen Canyon, Mouth of Hansen Creek to Mouth of San Juan River* (University of Utah Press, 1962); *The San Juan Canyon Historical Sites* (University of Utah Press, 1964); *Historical Sites in Cataract and Narrow Canyons, and in Glen Canyon to California Bar* (University of Utah Press, 1964); *Standing Up Country, the Canyon Lands of Utah and Arizona* (Alfred A. Knopf; University of Utah Press in association with the Amon Carter Museum of Western Art); *Land of Living Rock, The Grand Canyon and the High Plateaus: Arizona, Utah, Nevada* (Alfred A. Knopf, 1972); *The Zunis of Cibola* (University of Utah Press, 1977); numerous articles in journals.

CRAWFORD, EUGENE
(executive director)

Affiliation: Executive director, National Indian Lutheran Board, 35 E. Hacker Dr., Suite 1847, Chicago, Ill. 60641.

CRAWFORD, MAURICE
(tribal official)

Affiliation: Chairman, Bridgeport General Council, P.O. Box 37, Bridgeport, Calif. 93517.

CRAWFORD, MICHAEL ROBERT
(Penobscot) 1943-
(Indian education administrator)

Born December 5, 1943, Penobscot Indian Reservation, Old Town, Maine. *Education:* Washington State College; University of Maine. *Principal occupation:* Indian education administrator. *Affiliations:* Announcer, WMCS Radio, 1967; teacher of the physically handicapped, Bangor Public Schools, 1967-1968; teacher of Junior high level math and science, Bangor Public Schools, 1968-1969; deputy commissioner, Department of Indian Affairs, State of Maine, 1969-1970;

director, T.R.I.B.E., Inc. (Indian learning center), 1970-. *Interests:* Mr Crawford writes, "I am channeling my career to areas where I can work with other Indians and help find solutions to some of the problems we face. My major interest is in education, and my present position as director of an all-Indian educational center is very challenging. It will give us a chance to show non-Indians what we can do. I expect that T.R.I.B.E., Inc. and its programs will set an example for non-Indian schools."

CROOKS, NORMAN (Mdewakanton Sioux)
(tribal chairman)

Affiliation: Chairman, Shakopee Business Council, Box 150, Sioux Trail, Prior Lake, Minn. 55372.

CROW, JOHN O. (Cherokee) 1912-
(B.I.A. official-retired)

Born September 7, 1912, Salem, Mo. *Education:* Haskell Institute. *Principal occupation:* B.I.A. Official-retired. *Home address:* 9301 Lona Lane, N.E., Albuquerque, N.M. 87111. *Affiliations:* B.I.A. superintendent at Truxton Canyon Agency, Mescalero Agency, Fort Apache Agency, Uintah and Ouray Agency; chief of realty, 1960-1961; acting commissioner, 1961; deputy commissioner, 1961-1965; associate director, Bureau of Land Management, B.I.A., 1965-1971; deputy commissioner of Indian Affairs, B.I.A., 1971-1973. *Awards, honors:* Career Service Award, National Civil Service League, 1964.

CROW, PERCE B. (Lower Brule Sioux) 1925-
(administrative law hearing officer)

Born July 13, 1925, Pierre, S.D. *Education:* Morningside College, Sioux City, Iowa, B.S., 1950, B.S.L., 1972; California College of Law, J.D., 1974. *Principal occupation:* Administrative law hearing officer. *Home address:* 844 Catania Pl., Claremont, Calif. 91711. *Affiliations:* State of California Community Release Board, Sacramento, Calif., 1974-. *Other profesional posts:*

Member, board of directors, American Indian Volunteers; college instructor, Police Science. *Military service:* P.F.C., U.S. Marines, 1943-1946. *Community activities:* Los Angeles County Department of Mental Health Services (member, Citizens Advisory Board).

CROWE, AMANDA (Cherokee) 1928-
(teacher, sculpture)

Born July 16, 1928, Murphy, N.C. *Education:* School of Art, Institute of Chicago, B.F.A., 1950, M.F.A., 1952. *Principal occupation:* Teacher, sculpture. *Home address:* Cherokee, N.C. 28719. *Affiliations:* Teacher of wood-carving and sculptures, Cherokee High School, Cherokee, N.C., 1953-. *Memberships:* Southern Highland Handicraft Guild, 1953- (board of directors, 1958-1961; education committee, 1953-1959; standards committee, 1959-1961); Qualla Arts and Crafts Mutual, 1953- (executive and standards committee, 1954-). *Awards, honors:* Faculty Honorable Mentions in sculpture, anatomy, ceramics, and architectural scupture. *Published work:* Illustrator, *Cherokee Legends* (Tom B. Underwood, 1956).

CROWFEATHER, ISABELLE (Standing RockSioux)
(arts and crafts manager)

Affiliation: Manager, Standing Rock Sioux Arts and Crafts, Fort Yates, N.D. 58538.

CUMMING, KENDALL 1925-
(B.I.A. agency superintendent)

Born August 14, 1925, Nogales, Ariz. *Education:* University of Arizona, B.S., 1949, M.S., 1951. *Principal occupation:* B.I.A. agency superintendent. *Home address:* 549 W. Dublin, Chandler, Ariz. 85224. *Affiliations:* Bureau of Indian Affairs, 1950- (served on Navajo, Hopi, Jicarilla and Pima Reservations; superintendent, Pima Agency, B.I.A., Sacaton, Ariz. *Military service:* 101st Airborne Division in Europe, 1943-1945. *Awards, honors:* Meritorious Service Award, U.S. Department of the Interior. *Interests:* Indian affairs, range management.

CUMMINGS, VICKI
(museum director)

Affiliation: Director, Museum of Indian Heritage, 6040 De Long Rd., Indianapolis, Ind. 46254.

D

DAILEY, CHARLES 1935-
(Native American museum director)

Born May 25, 1935, Golden, Colo. *Education:* University of Colorado, B.F.A.-Fine Arts, 1961. *Principal occupation:* Native American museum director. *Home address:* 412 Sosoya Lane, Santa Fe, N.M. 87501. *Affiliations:* Museum director and museum training coordinator, Institute of American Indian Arts (national junior college, Native American museum), Santa Fe, N.M., 1972-. *Military service:* U.S. Marine Corps, Sergeant, 1953-1956. *Community activities:* National Ski Patrol Member, 1960-1983; Professional Ski Patrolman, 1962-1970. *Memberships:* American Association for State and Local History, 1956-; MPMA, 1960-1980; American Association of Museums, 1964-; New Mexico Association of Museums, 1972-; Native American Museum Association (charter member). *Awards, honors:* Minor painting awards since 1970; numerous awards state and local competitions, 1960-1970; kayacking - invited to participate in World Championships, Italy, 1961; various whitewater championships, 1958-1962. *Interests:* Native American museums survey, 1965-; research, 8,000 slides inventory; museum training interests, 1956-; various sports activities: kayacking, skiing, mountaineering, camping. *Biographical sources: Artists in America,* 1971, 1972; *Santa Fe Artists,* 1968; International Men of Achievement; Who's Who in the West; Contemporary Personage in the Arts. Published works: Creating a Crowd: Mannikens for Small Museums," El Pacio, MNM Press, 1969; "Museum Training Workbooks," IAIA, DOI, BIA, Bureau of Publications, 1973; "Art History; Vol. I/ II," IAIA, DOI, BIA BOP, 1974; "Major Influences, Contemporary Indian Art," IAIA, DOI, BOP, 1982.

DALRYMPLE, KATHRINE C.
(Western Cherokee) 1940-
(fashion designer)

Born January 30, 1940, Pryor, Oklahoma. *Education:* Oklahoma State University, B.A. (Education), 1961. *Principal occupation: Fashion designer (self-employed). Home address:* 917 N. Lexington, Arlington, Va. 22205. *Affiliations:* Associate Home Extension agent for the North Dakota State Extension Service and Standing Rock Sioux Tribe, and taught extension courses at graduate level for University of North Dakota, Grand Forks, 1961-1973; selected representative art objects from Native American artisans from all sections of the U.S., 1961-1973; co-owner, president, Friendship House, Inc. (gift shop specializing in Native American and American-made crafts), 1975-1977; design clothing for specialty shops, catered Native American food, 1977-1978; part-time volunteer coordinator, fashion consultant to executive director, American Indian Heritage Foundation, 1978-1980; owner, American Naturals (design and execute men and women's clothing, jewelry, and accessories based on traditional and contemporary Native American fashions. *Other professional posts:* Ran own catering and fashion design services, Navajo Reservation, 1961-1973; coordianted exhibits featuring her own fashions and jewelry, 1975-1977, Arlington, Va. *Community activities:* Taught crafts classes at various schools and youth clubs in the Washington D.C. area, as well as at the Smithsonian Institution, the Capitol Hill Club, and at a number of Embassies. *Memberships:* American Indian Society of Washington, D.C. *Awards, honors:* Epsilon Sigma Alpha's Outstanding Woman of the Year for Arizona in 1971; her fashions have received three First Prizes at the Gaithersburg, Maryland Exposition, 1973-1978; her fashions have been shown at the Congrssional Club, Capitol Hill Club, and the International Club of Washington, D.C.; her fashions have recently been worn at the Cherry Blossom Parade, Presidntial Inaugural Ball and Parade for Ronald Reagan, several White House teas, and Oklahoma Society Gala; In March, 1982, thirty-one of Mrs. Dalrymple's fashions were worn at the

John F. Kennedy Center for the Performing Arts during the "Night of the First Americans," an event held in celebration of the contributions of the American Indian people; special exhibition, organized by the Indian Arts and Crafts Board's Southern Plains Indian Museum and Crafts Center, the first comprehensive showing of Mrs. Dalrymple's fashions to be presented in the State of Oklahoma; she made the dress worn by the 1983 American Indian Society Princess; in 1976 and 1983, Kathy's work was featured in the *American Indian Society Cookbook*. *Interests:* Mrs. Dalrymple writes, "I feel so fortunate to have grown up among the many Native American cultures in Oklahoma, and especially to have known not only my grandparents, but four of my great grandparents and many of their friends as well. Seeing them create, from necessity, beautiful and useful articles for everyday use from whatever was available was the origin of my interest in the arts of the American Indian. As we have lived and worked in many areas of this great land, I've marveled at the resourcefulness and creativity of the people, and of the women, in particular. No matter how busy and difficult their lives have been, they have always managed to provide many and varied forms of useful, beautiful articles to enrich the lives of the people around them. Trading of ideas, supplies, and patterns as tribes came into contact with each other is greatly apparent. How each group adapted the trade goods brought by the Europeans is a unique and fascinating study of American history. I especially enjoy creating traditional clothing for pow-wow wear." *Works in Progress:* Currently writing a book detailing her family's experiences living on Indian reservations around the country.

DAMAS, DAVID 1926-
(anthropologist)

Born December 27, 1926, Algoma, Wis. *Education:* University of Toledo, B.A., 1950; University of Chicago, M.A., 1960, Ph.D., 1962. *Principal occupation:* Anthropologist. *Home address:* 2160 Lakeshore Rd., Apt. 1202, Burlington, Ontario, Can. *Affiliations:* Arctic ethnologist, National Museum of Canada, Ottawa, Ont., Canada; associate professor of anthropology, McMaster University, Hamilton, Ont., Canada. *Military service:* U.S. Marine Corps, 1945-1946. *Memberships:* American Anthropological Association; American Ethnological Society; Canadian Sociology and Anthropology Association; Northeastern Anthropological Association. *Interests:* Eskimo ethnology; social structure; cultural ecology. *Fieldwork:* Among the Igulik Eskimos, 1960-1961; Copper Eskimos, 1962-1963; Netsilik Eskimos, 1965; Netsilik and Ingulik Eskimos, 1967, 1968. *Published works:* *Iguligmiut Kinship and Local Grouping* (National Museum of Canada, 1963); *Band Societies* (National Museum of Canada, 1969); *Ecological Essays* (National Museum of Canada, 1969).

DANA, RALPH F. (Passamaquoddy)
(reservation governor)

Affiliation: Governor, Pleasant Point Passamaquoddy Reservation, P.O. Box 343, Perry, Maine 04667.

DARDEN, STEVEN
(executive director-Indian center)

Affiliation: Executive director, Flagstaff Indian Center, 15 N. San Francisco, P.O. Box 572, Flagstaff, Ariz. 86001.

DAUGHERTY, JOHN, Jr. (Shawnee-Delaware) 1948-
(health systems administrator)

Born August 9, 1948, Claremore, Okla. *Education:* Northeastern State University, Tahlequah, Okla., B.A. (Social Sciences), B.S. (Business), 1976; University of Minnesota, Minneapolis, 1984- (working toward advanced certificate in health administration). *Principal occupation:* Health systems administrator. *Home address:* 2237 Elmwood Lane, Miami, Okla. 74354. *Affiliation:* Executive director, Native American Coalition of Tulsa, 1978-1979; administrator, USPHS Miami Indian Health Center, Miami, Okla., 1979-. *Military service:* U.S. Air Force, 1969-1972 (in Madrid, Spain) (U.S.A.F. Commendation Medal for Meritorious Service). *Community activities:* Member, Rotary International; chairman, Title IV, Indian Education Parent Committee; officer, Native American Student Association at Northeast Oklahoma A&M Junior College and Northeastern Oklahoma State University, Tahlequah, 1973-1976. *Awards, honors:* Who's Who Among Students in American Universities and Colleges, 1976-1977; golf team; deans honor roll, 1976, NEOSU, Tahlequah; chosen by University of Minnesota Independent Study Program to give presentation on Indian Health in U.S. during International Health Night, July 17, 1985. *Interests:* "My educational and vocational interest is in health care administration. My goals are to better myself in these areas. Indian cultures and the presentation of my tribal ceremonies are of great concern to me. Participating in tribal activities of other tribes, as well as my tribe and encouraging others to participate are very important to me."

DAVIS, GEORGE
(B.I.A. agency superintendent)

Affiliation: Superintendent, Colville Agency, Bureau of Indian Affairs, P.O. Box 111-011, Nespelem, Wash. 99155.

DAVIS, ROBERT C. 1922-
(film producer, lecturer)

Born May 7, 1922, Kansas City, Mo. *Education:* High school. *Principal occupation:* Film producer, lecturer. *Home address:* P.O. Box 12, Cary, Ill. 60013. *Affiliations:* Self-employed. *Military service:* U.S. Signal Corps, 1942-1945. *Memberships:* Film Lecturer's Association, 1970-. *Awards, honors:* Amerian Film Festival Awards for *Arizona Revealed;* Columbus Film Festival Awards for seven other films. *Films produced: Land of the Crimsoned Cliffs,* 1955; *Arizona Utopia,* 1961; *Arizona Revealed,* 1964; *Arizona Adventure,* 1975; many 35mm and 2¼ x 2¼ color transparencies of Navajo, Pima and Hopi Indians.

DAVIS, ROSE-MARIE
(president-Indian community college)

Affiliation: President, Little Hoop Community College, P.O. Box 147, Fort Totten, N.D. 58335.

DAYLEY, JON P. 1944-
(professor of linguistics)

Born October 8, 1944, Salt Lake City, Utah. *Education:* Idaho State University, B.A., 1968, M.A., 1970; University of California, Berkeley, M.A., 1973, Ph.D., 1981. *Principal occupation:* Professor of linguistics. *Home address:* 5953 Eastwood Place, Boise, Idaho 83712. *Affiliations:* Visiting lecturer in linguistics, University of California, Berkeley, 1982; assistant professor of linguistics, Boise State University, 1982-. *Other professional posts:* Linguista - Projecto Linguistico Francisco Marroquin, Guatemala, 1973-1978; writer, resercher, Experiment in International Living, Brattleboro, Vt., 1978-1979. *Memberships:* Linguistic Society of America; Society of Mayanists; Berkeley Linguistics Society; National Association for Foreign Student Affairs; Guatemalan Scholars Network. *Interests:* American Indian languages: Mayan language—Tzutujil Maya, Uto-Aztecon languages—Shoshone; Creole languages; general linguistics. *Published works: Tzutujil Grammar* (University of California Prss, 1985); *Belizean Creaole Handbook,* Vols. I-IV (Experiment in International Living, U.S. Peace Corps, 1979); and many articles on Mayan languages, shoshone and general linguistics.

DeBOER, ROY J. (Lummi) 1936-
(school principal)

Born July 23, 1936, Bellingham, Wash. *Education:* Olympic Junior College, Bremerton, Wash., A.A., 1960; Western Washington State University, Bellingham, B.A., 1962; University of Puget Sound, Tacoma, Wash., M.Ed., 1981. *Principal occupation:* School principal. *Home address:* 3528 S.E. Pine Tree Dr., Port Orchard, Wash. 98366. *Affiliations:* Director of Indian Education, South Kitsap School District, Port Orchard, Wash., 1973-1980; principal, Wolfe Elementary School, Kingston, Wash., 1981-. *Other professional posts:* Seven years on Washington State Advisory Committee, Indian Education to Washington State Supervisor of Schools. *Military service:* U.S. Air Force, 1954-1958 (A 1/C). *Community activities:* Pacific Lutheran Theological Seminary (board of directors); Division of Service and Mission in America, American Lutheran Church (board of dirctors); Chamber of Comerce, Kingston, Wash.; Sons of Norway, Poulsbo, Wash.. *Memberships:* National Education Association; Washington Education Asscoiation; ASCD; ESPA. *Awards, honors:* Outstanding Secondary Teacher of America, 1973; Quill and Scroll Adult Leadership Award, 1969. *Interests:* Reading, travel, photography; singing with Twana Dancers, Skokomish traditional dance group.

DEER, ADA E. (Menominee) 1935-
(social worker)

Born August 7, 1935, Keshena, Wis. *Education:* University of Wisconsin, Madison, B.A., 1957; Columbia University, School of Social Work, M.S.W., 1961. *Principal occupation:* Social worker. *Home address:* 5689 Lincoln Rd., Oregon, Wisc. *Business address:* Native Americn Studies Program, University of Wisconsin, 1188 Educational Sciences Bldg., 1025 W. Johnson St., Madison, Wis. 53706. *Affiliations:* Lecturer, School of Social Work and Native American Studies Program, University of Wisconsin, 1977-. *Other profesional posts:* Chairperson, Menominee Restoration Committee, 1973-1976; vice president and Washington lobbyist, National Committee to Save the Menominee People and Forest, Inc., 1972-1973; chairperson, Menominee Common Stock and Voting Trust, 1971-1973. *Community activities:* American Indian Policy Review Commission (member, 1975-1977). *Memberships:* National Association of Social Workers; National Organization of Women; Common Cause; Girl Scouts of America; Democratic Party of Wisconsin; National Congress of American Indians. *Awards, honors:* Doctor of Humane Letters, University of Wisconsin, 1974; Doctor of Public

Service, Northland College, Ashland, Wisc., 1974; White Buffalo Council Achievement Award, Denver, Colo., 1974; Pollitzer Award, Ethical Cultural Society, N.Y., 1975; Fellow, Harvard Institute of Politics, 1977. *Interests:* Social work; community organization and social action; minority rights. *Biographical sources: I Am the Fire of Time,* Jane B. Katz, editor (E.P. Dutton, 1977); *Ms Magazine,* April, 1973; *Indians of Today,* 4th Edition; *The Circle,* Dec. 1977.

DeGROAT, ELLOUISE (Navajo) 1939-
(social worker)

Born May 12, 1939, Tuba City, Ariz. *Education:* Arizona State University, B.S., 1962, M.S.W., 1966. *Principal occupation:* Social worker. *Home address:* P.O. Box 521, Fort Defiance (Navajo Nation), Ariz. 86504. *Affiliation:* Social worker, Tribal Affairs Officer, Window Rock, Ariz., 1976-. *Other professional posts:* Consultant, American Child Psychiatry (Committee on Indian Affairs) and the Indian Task Force on Mental Health. *Community activities:* St. Michaels Special Education Association (member); instrumental in staging the First Annual Navajo Health Symposium; involvement with education of Indian children and special concern for the handicapped. *Memberships:* American Indian Health Association; National Association of Social Workers; National Conference of Social Workers (national board member, 1972-1974). *Awards, honors:* DFisquisition Service Award, The Navajo Tribe, 2nd Annual Navajo Helth Symposium. *Interests:* Tribal government; national legislation for Indian tribes; advocate for Indian causes, especially health; American Indian woman; served on the Policy Committee on the Indian Policy Statement on national health insurance. *Published work: Navajo Medicine Man* (Psychiatric Annuals, 1974).

DeHOSE, JUDY
(chairperson-Indian school)

Affiliation: Chairperson, Cibecue Community School, Cibecue, Ariz. 85911.

DELACRUZ, JOSEPH (Quinault)
(president-tribal committee)

Afiliation: President, Quinault Business Committee, P.O. Box 189, Taholah, Wash. 98587.

DeLAGUNA, FREDERICA 1906-
(anthropologist, professor emeritus)

Born October 3, 1906, Ann Arbor, Mich. *Education:* Bryn Mawr College, B.A., 1927; Columbia University, Ph.D., 1933. *Principal occupation:* Anthropologist. *Home address:* 221 Roberts Rd., Bryn Mawr, Penna. 19010. *Affiliation:* Professor of anthropology, Brun Mawr College, 1938-1975. *Other professional posts: Visiting professor, University of Pennsylvania; visiting profesor, Univerity of California, Berkeley. Military service:* U.S. Naval Reserve, 1942-1945 (Lt. Commander). *Memberships:* American Anthropological Association (past president); American Ethnological Society; Society for American Archaeology; Society for Pennsylvania Archaeology; Philadelphia Anthropological Society; Arctic Institute of North America; National Academy of Sciences. *Awards, honors:* Postdoctoral fellowships: National Research Council, Viking Fund (Wenner-Gren Foundation), Rockefeller Post-War Fellowship. *Interests:* "Archaeological and ethnological field work among Eskimos (Greenland and Alaska), Indians (Tlingit, Alaskam Athabascans); archaeological work in northern Arizona. Expeditions to Alaska, 1930-1968, Greenland, 1929; to Arizona, 1941. Have tape-recorded and enjoy Indian music." *Biographical sources: American Men of Science; Who's Who in America; International Biography: World Who's Who. Published works: The Archaeology of Cook Inlet, Alaska* (University of Pennsylvania Press, 1934); *The Prehistory of Northern North America* (Society for American Archaeology, 1947); *The Eyak Indians of the Copper River Delta, Alaska,* with Kaj Birket-Smith; *Chugach Prehistory: The Archaeology of Prince William Sound* (University of Washington Press, 1956, 1960); *The Story of a Tlingit Community* (Bureau of American Ethnology, 1960); *Archaelogy of the Yakutat Bay Area, Alaska,* with Riddell, McGeein, Lane,

Freed, Osborne (Bureau of Amerian Ethnology, 1964); *Under Mount St. Elias: The History and Culture of the Yakutat Tlingit* (Smithsonian, 1972); *Voyage to Greenland: A Personal Initiation Into Anthropology* (W.W. Norton, 1977).

DELAWARE, ROBERT
(B.I.A. job placement)

Affiliation: Job Placement, Bureau of Indian Affairs, 1951 Constitution Ave., N.W., Washington, D.C. 20245.

DELORIA, P.S.
(director-Indian law center)

Affiliation: Director, American Indian Law Center, Univerity of New Mexico, School of Law, P.O. Box 4456, Station A, 1117 Stanford, N.E., Albuquerque, N.M. 87196.

DELORIA, VINE, Jr. (Standing Rock Sioux) 1933-
(writer, professor)

Born March 26, 1933, Martin, S.D. *Education:* Iowa State University, B.S., 1958; Lutheran School of Theology, M. Sac. Theo., 1963; University of Colorado, School of Law, J.D., 1970. *Principal occupation: Writer, professor. Address:* Department of Political Science, University of Arizona, Tucson, Arizona 85721. *Affiliation:* Welder, McLaughlin Body Company, Moline, Illinois, 1959-1963; staff associate, United Scholarship Service, Denver, Colorado, 1963-1964; executive director, National Congress of American Indians, Washington, D.C., 1964-1967; consultant on programs, National Congress of American Indians, FUND, Denver, Colorado, 1968; lecturer, College of Ethnic Studies, Western Washington State College, Bellingham, Washington, 1970-1972; lecturer, American Indian Cultural and Research Center, UCLA, Los Angeles, California, 1972-1973; executive director, Southwest Intergroup Council, Denver, Colorado, 1972; special counsel, Native American Rights Fund, Boulder, Colorado, summer-1972; script writer (Indian series), KRMA-TV, Denver, Colorado, 1972-1973; American Indian

64

Resource Associates, Oglala, South Dakota, 1973-1974; American Indian Resource Consultants, Denver, Colorado, 1974-1975. visiting lecturer, Pacific School of Religion, Berkeley, California, summer, 1975; visiting lecturer, New School of Religion, Pontiac, Michigan, summer, 1976; visiting lecturer, Colorado College, Colorado Springs, Colorado, 1977-1978; professor, University of Arizona, Tucson, Arizona, 1978-. *Military Service:* U.S. Marine Corps Reserve, San Diego, Calif. and Quantico, Va., 1954-1956. *Organizational Memberships:* White Buffalo Council, Denver, Colo. (board of directors, 1964-1966); Citizens Crusade Against Poverty, Washington, D.C. (board of directors, 1965-1966); Council on Indian Affairs, Washington, D.C. (vice-chairman, 1965-1968); Board of Inquiry Into Hunger and Malnutrition in the U.S.A., New York, N.Y., 1967-1968; National Office for the Rights of the Indigent, New York, N.Y. (board of directors, 1967-1968); Ad-Hoc Committee on Indian Work, Episcopal Church, New York, N.Y. (chairman, 1968-1969); Executive Council of the Protestant Episcopal Church, New York, N.Y., 1968-1969; Southwest Intergroup Council, Austin, Texas (board of directors, 1969-1971); Institute for the Development of Indian Law, Washington, D.C. (chairman and founder, 1971-1976); Model Urban Indian Centers Project, San Francisco, Calif. (board of directors, 1971-1973); Oglala Sioux Legal Rights Foundation, Pine Ridge, S.D. (board of directors, 1971); National Friends of Public Broadcasting, New York, N.Y., 1971-1976; Colorado Humanities Program, Boulder, Colo., 1975-1977; National Indian Youth Council, Albuquerque, N.M. (advisory council, 1976); American Civil Liberties Union, Denver, Colo. (Indian committee, 1976-1978); The Center for Land Grant Studies, Santa Fe, N.M., 1976; American Lutheran Church, Minneapolis, Minnesota (consultant, 1976-1978); Nebraska Educational Television Network, Lincoln, Neb. (advisory council, American Indian Series, 1976-1978); Denver Public Library Foundation, Denver, Colo. (board of directors, 1977-1978); Museum of the American Indian, New York, N.Y. (board of trustees, 1977-1982); American Indian Development, Inc., Bellingham, Washington, 1978-1981; Day-break Films, Denver, Colo. (board of directors, 1979-1981); Field Foundation, New York, N.Y. (board of directors, 1980); Indian Rights Association, Philadelphia, Pa. (board of directors, 1980); Institute of the American West, Sun Valley, Idaho (national advisory council, 1981-1983); Disability Rights & Education Defense Fund, Berkeley, Calif. (advisory council, 1981); Save the Children Federation, Westport, Conn. (national advisory council, 1983). *Professional Memberships:* American Judicature Society, 1970-; Colorado Authors League, 1970-. *Editorial Boards and Contributing Editorships:* American Indian Historical Society, San Francisco, Calif. (editorial board, 1971-1972); *Handbook of North American Indians, Smithsonian Institution, Washington, D.C. (planning committee, 1971-1972); The World of the American Indian,* (National Geographic Society, 1972-1976); Clearwater Press (consultant, advisory board, 1972-1978); *American Indian Cultural and Research Center Journal,* UCLA (editorial board, 1972); Race Relations Information Center (contributing editor, 1974-1975); *Integrateducation,* University of Massachusetts, Amherst, Mass. (editorial advisory board, 1975); *American Heritage Dictionary of the English Language,* Houghton-Mifflin (usage panel, 1976-1983); *Explorations in Ethnic Studies,* (LaCrosse, Wis., 1977-); *Katallagete,* Berea, Ky. (editorial board, 1977); *The Historical Magazine of the Episcopal Church,* Austin, Texas (editorial board, 1977); *The Colorado Magazine,* Colorado Historical Society, Denver, Colo. (editorial review board, 1979); *National Forum,* Phi Kappa Phi, Johnson City, Tenn. (contributing editor, 1979); *Studies in American Indian Literature,* Columbia University, New York, N.Y. (advisory board, 1981); *Adherent Forum,* New York, N.Y. (contributing editor, 1981). *Special Activities:* White House Conference on Youth (delegate, 1970); Avco-Embassy Pictures on movie *Soldier Blue* (consultant, 1970); Educational Challenges, Inc., Washington, D.C. (consultant, 1971-1972); Senate Committee on Aging, Washington, D.C. (consultant, 1971-1972); Served as expert witness in four trials involving the occupation of Wounded Knee and aftermath as expert on 1868 Fort Laramie treaty and Sioux history (1974); Project 76, National Council of Churches (sponsor, 1974-1976); Served as appointed counsel in "Consolidated Wounded Knee Cases," treaty hearing in federal court (1975); Colorado Centennial-Bicentennial Commission (commissioner, 1975-1977); EVIST, National Science Foundation (advisory board, 1975-1978); Robert F. Kennedy Journalsim Awards (judge, 1975); Sun Valley Center for the Arts and Humanities, Sun Valley, Idaho (advisory council, 1976-1978, 1980-1983); *Handbook of North American Indians,* Volume Two, "Indians in Contemporary Society," Smithsonian Institution (editor, 1978-); American Indian Studies Program, University of Arizona (chairman, 1978-1981). *Special Honors and Awards:* Anisfield Wolf Award, 1970, for *Custer Died for Your Sins;* Special Citation, 1971, National Conference of Christians and Jews, for *We Talk, You Listen;* Honorary Doctor of Humane Letters, 1972, Augustana College; Indian Achievement Award, 1972, Indian Council Fire, Chicago; Named one of eleven "Theological Superstars of the Future," 1974, by Interchurch Features, New York, N.Y.; Honorary Doctor of Letters, 1976, Scholastica College, Duluth, Minn.; Distinguished Alumni Award, 1977, Iowa State University; Honorary Professor, 1977, Athabasca University, Edmonton, Can.; Honorary Doctor of Human Letters, 1979, Hamline University, St. Paul, Minn. *Published works:* Books: *Custer Died For Your Sins* (Macmillan, 1969); *We Talk, You Listen* (Macmillan, 1970); *Of Utmost Good Faith* (Straight Arrow, 1971); *Red Man in the New World Drama,* edited and revised (Macmillan, 1972); *God Is Red* (Grosset and Dunlap, 1973); *Behind the Trail of Broken Treaties* (Delacourte, 1974); *The Indian Affair* (Friendship Press, 1974); *Indians of the Pacific Northwest* (Doubleday, 1977); *The Metaphysics of Modern Existence* (Harper & Row, 1979); *American Indians, American Justice,* with Clifford Lytle (University of Texas Press, 1983); *A Sender of Words,* editor-The Neihardt Centenial Essays (Howe Brothers, 1984); *The Nations Within,* with Clifford Lytle (Pantheon Books, 1984); *The Aggressions of Civilization,* edited with Sandra Cadwalader (Temple University Press, 1984); *American Indian Policy in the Twentieth Century,* edi-

tor (University of Oklahoma Press, 1985). *Special Reports:* "The Lummi Indians," — Center for the Study of Man, Smithsonian Institution, 1972; "Legal Problems and Considerations Involved in the Treaty of 1868," prepared for the John Hay Whitney Foundation, 1974; "Indian Education Confronts the Seventies," editor and contributor, five volumes, Ofice of Indian Education, 1974; "Contemporary Issues of American Indians, A Model Course," prepared for the National Indian Education Association, 1975; "Legislative Analysis of the Federal Role in Indian Education," Office of Indian Education, 1975; "A Better Day for Indians," issued by the Field Foundation, 1977. Also, articles as contributing editor, editorials, and introductions to books—too numerous to mention.

De MAIN, PAUL (White Earth Chippewa) 1955-
(advisor on Indian affairs policy)

Born October 8, 1955, Hayward, Wis. *Education:* University of Wisconsin, Eau Claire, 1975-1977. *Principal occupation:* Advisor on Indian affairs policy. *Home address:* Route 5, Box 5346, Hayward, Wis. 54843. *Affiliations:* Assistant manager and manager, Lac Courte Oreilles Graphic Arts, Inc., 1979-1980; acting director, Great Lakes Indian News Association, 1980-1982; self determination information officer, Lac Courte Oreilles Tribal Government, 1981-1982; managing editor, *Lac Courte Oreilles Journal,* Hayward, Wisc., 1977-1982; owner/manager, Great Lakes Indian News Bureau, Hayward, Wisc., 1981-1982; sectretary, Native Horizons, Inc., 1983-; advisor on Indian affairs policy to Governor Anthony S. Earl, State of Wiscosnin, 1983-. *Community activities:* Governor's representative, State Council on Alcohol and Other Drug Abuse; lay counselor, Lac Courte Oreilles Tribal Court; board member, Lac Courte Oreilles Honor the Earth Education Foundation; faculty, Lac Courte Oreilles Community College; board of directors, Wisconsin Rural Leadership Conference; representative, Governor's Council on Minority Business Development; planning committee, National Indian Media Conference; chairman, Sawyer County Democratic

Party, 1982; advisory board, Center for Mining Alternatives; member, Northwestern Wisconsin Mining Impact Committee; member, Governor's Study Committee on Equal Rights, 1977. *Memberships:* National Congress of American Indians (conference planning committee, 1983). *Interests:* "As advisor on Indian affairs, I currently have the prime responsibility of liaison between the Governor's Office, 11 federally recognized tribes and urban Indian communities. In addition, development of policy, recommendations on state services, legislation, communications outreach and advisory services to Indian and non-Indian organizations is provided. In this capacity, I am consistently in contact with lobbyists, legislators and state agency program directors as well as making presentations to state personnel and public audiences."

DEMPSEY, HUGH A. 1929-
(historian)

Born November 7, 1929, Edgerton, Alberta, Can. *Principal occupation:* Historian. *Home address:* 95 Holmwood Ave., N.W., Calgary, Alberta, Can. *Affiliations:* Reporter, Edmonton *Bulletin;* Publicity Bureau, Province of Alberta, Canada; Glenbow Alberta Institute, Calgary, Alberta (archivist, 1956-1967; technical director, 1967-1970; director of history, 1970-1978; chief curator, 1978-). *Other professional posts:* Editor, *Alberta History,* 1958-; editor, *Canadian Archivist,* 1963-1966; editor, *Glenbow,* 1968-1974; Canadian editor, *Montana Magazine of History;* editorial board, Royal Canadian Geographical Society; contributing editor, *American West. Community activities:* Alberta Indian Treaties Comemeorative Program, 1976-1978; Alberta Heritage Learning Resources Advisory Committee, 1978-. *Memberships:* Historical Society of Alberta (executive committee, 1953; vice president, 1955-1956; president, 1956-1957); Canadian Historical Association (chairman, archives section, 1961-1962); Indian Association of Alberta (secretary, 1959-1964; advisory board, 1959-1968); Canadian Museums Association (executive committee, 1968-1970); Indian - Eskimo Association of Canada (executive committee, 1960-1965); International Coun-

cil of Museums (Canadian committee, 1968-1971). *Awards, honors:* Alberta Historian of the Year, 1962; honorary doctorate, University of Calgary, 1974; Order of Canada, 1975; Alberta Achievement Award, 1974-1975; honorary chief, Blood Tribe, 1967; winner of Alberta Non-Fiction Award, 1975. *Published works: Crowfoot, Chief of the Blackfeet* (University of Oklahoma Press, 1972). Monographs: *A Blackfoot Winter Count,* 1966; *Tailfeathers, Indian Artist,* 1970; *Blackfoot Ghost Dance,* 1968; *Indian Names for Alberta Communities, 1969.*

DENTON, COYE ELIZABETH
(Cherokee) 1914-
(artist)

Born October 14, 1914, Romulus, Okla. *Education:* East Central State College, B.S., M.A., 1969. *Principal occupation:* Artist. *Home address:* Box 444, Ada, Okla. 74820. *Community activities:* Fornightly Tamti (past president); Tanlettes; Wednesday morning music, Salvation Army Auxiliary; Great Books Organization; Salvation Army (advisory board). *Memberships:* Ada Artists Association, 1958- (vice president); Salvation Army (advisory board, 1955-); League of Women Voters; First United Methodist Church. *Interests:* "Human, ecological and environmental resources — esthetic and active;" travel. *Biographical sources: Who's Who of American Women; American Indian Painters.*

DESJARLAIT, PATRICK ROBERT
(Chippewa) 1921-
(commercial artist)

Born March 1, 1921, Red Lake, Minn. *Principal occupation:* Commercial artist. *Home address:* 7641 62nd Ave., N., New Hope, Minn. 55428. *Military service:* U.S. Navy, 1941-1945 — visual education training, slide films, animation, training films. *Memberships:* Minneapolis Art Directors Club. *Awards, honors:* First Prize, Philbrook Art Center, Tulsa, Okla., 1946; First Prize, Elkus Memorial Award, Inter-Tribal Indian Ceremonial, Gallup, N.M., 1964; Second Award, Scottsdale National Indian Arts

Exhibition, 1964. *One-man shows and exhibitions:* Fine Arts Gallery, San Diego, Calif., 1945; St. Paul Art Gallery, 1946; Gallery of American Indian Art, U.S. Dept. of the Interior, Washington, D.C.

DI MAIO, SUE (Pocahantus) 1920-
(owner-trading post)

Born July 6, 1920, Houston, Tex. *Education:* University of Redlands, A.B., Scripps College, Pomona, Calif. (one year-Arts); University of Southern California, M.A., 1977. *Principal occupation:* Owner, Capistrano Trading Post, 31741 Camino Capistrano, San Juan Capistrano, Calif., 1943-. *Home address:* P.O. Box 2142, Capistrano Beach, Calif. 92672. *Memberships:* Indian Arts & Crafts Association (charter member); Southwest Association on Indian Affairs; Hear Museum; Museum of Natural History, Los Angeles. *Awards, honors:* Bronze plaque erected bearing Ms. Di Maio's name for meritorious fund raising for the Navajo Tribal Museum, Window Rock, N.M. *Biographical sources:* Articles in 1973, 1974, *Western Financial Journal* (success story about Indian crafts and follow up story); nine articles published in series by *Indian Trader Paper,* 1974. *Published works:* 1975 Orange County illustrative article about the Hopi; *Blue Gold,* series of nine articles related to Indian crafts (Main St. Press, 1976).

DI PESO, CHARLES C. 1920-
(archaeologist, foundation
and museum director)

Born October 20 1920, St. Louis, Mo. *Education:* Beloit College, B.S. (Anthropology and Geology, 1942); American Institute of Foreign Trade, B.F.T., 1947; University of Arizona, M.A., 1950, Ph.D., 1952. *Principal occupation:* Archaeologist, foundation and museum director. *Address:* The Amerind Foundation, Inc., P.O. Box 248, Dragoon, Ariz. 85609. *Affiliations:* Director, The Amerind Foundation, Inc. *Other professional posts:* Arizona Historical Advisory Commission, 1967-; consultant, Texas Tech University, 1968-; Arizona Landmarks Commission, 1971- (chairman, 1971-1975);

Arizona Commission for State Parks, 1966-; *American Indian Quarterly* (editor, advisory board, 1974-); consultant Educational Expeditions International, television series, 1974-; advisory council, Cochise Chapter, National Society of Arts and Letters, 1972-; board of directors, Sulphur Springs Valley Historical Society, 1974-; editor and advisory board, *American Indian Art Magazine,* 1975-; advisory board, Arizona Historical Records, 1976-1979 (Governor appointed term); board of directors, Arizona Historical Society, 1976-. *Community activities:* Cochise College (board of governors, 1962-; chairman, 1966-1968, 1975-1976; secretary, 1965-1966, 1974-1975); Tucson Art Center (board of directors, 1972-1976); The Explorers Club (Fellow, 1969-). *Memberships:* Society for American Archaeology (Fellow, 1960-; executive committee, 1970-1971; president-elect, 1971-1972; president, 1972-1973); American Anthropological Association (Fellow, 1962-; nominating committee, 1976-1977); American Association for the Advancement of Science (Fellow, 1960-); Society for Historical Archaeology, 1967-; Arizona Academy of Sciences, 1972-; Southwestern Anthropological Association; Amerian Society for Ethnohistory; The American Association pf Museums; Western History Association, 1964-; Association of Borderline Scholars, 1976-; Southwestern Archaeological Research Group; Latin American Studies Association, 1966-; Institue of Andean Research, 1965-; International Congress of Americanists; Pimeria Alta Historical Society; Cochise County Historical and Archaeological Society (Honorary). *Military service:* U.S. Air Force, 1942-1946 (1st Lt., Pilot). *Awards, honors:* Alfred Vincent Kidder Award, for achievement in American archaeology, American Anthropological Association, 1959; Beloit College, Dr.S., 1970. *Interests:* "Anthropology, archaeology, and ethnohistory of the American Southwest and northern Mexico. Excavation of prehistoric ruins and study of prehistoric man in the New World in an attempt to recreate the history of this area as lived by the Chichimecans. The study of frontier urban areas in regard to donor and recipient cultures and the mechanisms of urbanization in arid lands. *Expeditions:* Principal director, Joint Casas Grandes Expedition, northwestern Chihuahua, Mexico. *Biographical sources: Who's Who in the U.S.; Who's Who Honorary Society of America; Who's Who in the West; American Men and Women of Science; Dictionary of International Biography. Published works: The Babaocomari Village Site on the Babocomari River, Southeastern Arizona,* 1951; *The Sobaipuri Indians of the Upper San Pedro Valley, Southeastern Arizona,* 1953; *The Upper Pima of San Cayetano del Tumacacori,* 1956; The Reeve Ruin of Southeastern Arizona, 1958; *Casas Grandes: A Fallen Trading Center of the Gran Chichimeca,* 1974. All published by Amerind Foundation, Inc. Publications.

DIXON, LAWRENCE DWYER (Sioux) 1916-
(director of Indian center)

Born April 14, 1916, Pine Ridge, S.D. *Education:* Pine Ridge Indian School, 1936-1939. *Principal occupation:* Director of Indian center. *Home address:* 6312 Linden Lane, Bremerton, Wash. 98310. *Affiliations:* Director, Kitsap County Indian Center, NW Byron St., Silverdale, Wash., 1975-. *Other professional posts:* Publicity chairman, Off-Reservation Indians Board, 1974-1975; CETA Consortium Board of Small Indian Tribes of Western Washington. *Community activities:* Executive committee, Kitsap County Overall Economic Development Program; Indian child welfare advisory committee, Department of Social/Health Services, State Level, 1977-1979. *Awards, honors:* Washington Central Kitsap School District Recognition Award, 1983; Washington State DSHS Certificate of Appreciation, 1982; CKHS and Bremerton Kiwanis Air Fair Society; Meritorious Performance, 1976; Superior Achievement from Commanding Officer, USS Pueblo, 1967; National Indian Management, 1980; outside Volunteer Award, 1984; Washington State Jefferson Award, 1984. *Interests:* Indian self-determination; Indian program administration, fundraising; Indian program development, publicity; public relations, recruitment, training and supervision; policy making. *Published works: Are You Listening Neighbor? and the People Speak, Will You Listen?* (State of Washington, 1978).

DIXON, PATRICIA A. (Pauma)
(tribal council chairwoman)

Affiliation: Chairwoman, Pauma Tribal Council, P.O. Box 86, Pauma Valley, Calif. 92061.

DOBYNS, HENRY F. 1925-
(consultant, director-Indian project)

Born July 3, 1925, Tucson, Ariz. *Education:* University of Arizona, B.A., 1949, M.A., 1956; Cornell University, Ph.D., 1960. *Principal occupation:* Consultant, director Indian project. *Home address:* 1943 West North Lane No. 9, Phoenix, Ariz. 85021. *Affiliations:* Research associate, Cornell University, 1960-1966; professor, University of Kentucky, 1966-1970; professor, Prescott College, Ariz., 1970-1973; visiting professor, University of Wisconsin, Parkside, 1974-1975; visiting professor, University of Florida, 1977-1979; director, Native American Historical Demography Project, D'Arcy McNickle Center for the History of the American Indian, The Newberry Library, Chicago, Ill., 1979-. *Military service:* U.S. Army, 1943. *Memberships:* American Association for the Advancement of Science (Fellow); American Anthropological Association; American Society for Ethnohistory (former president). *Awards, honors:* Shared Anisfield-Wolff Award, 1968; Malinowski Award, Society for Applied Anthropology, 1952. *Published works: The Apache People (Coyotero)* (Indian Tribal Series, 1971); *The Papago People* (Indian Tribal Series, 1972); *The Mescalero Apache People* (Indian Tribal Series, 1973); *Prehistoric Indian Occupation Within the Eastern Area of the Yuman Complex: A Study in Applied Archaeology* (Garland, 1974); *Spanish Colonial Tucson* (University of Arizona Press, 1976); *Native American Historical Demography* (Indiana University Press, 1976); *From Fire to Flood* (Ballena Press, 1981); *"Their Number Become Thinned"* (University of Tennessee Press, 1983).

DOCKSTADER, FREDERICK J. 1919-
(museum consultant)

Born February 3, 1919, Los Angeles, Calif. *Education:* Arizona State College, B.A.,

M.A.: Western Reserve University, Ph.D., 1951. *Principal occupation:* Museum consultant. *Home address:* 165 West 66 St., New York, N.Y. 10023. *Affiliations:* Teacher, Flagstaff, Arizona schools, 1942-1950; staff ethnologist, Cranbrook Institute of Sciences, 1950-1952; faculty member and curator of anthropology, Dartmouth College, 1952-1955; assistant director, director, Museum of the American Indian, Heye Foundation, 1955-1975. *Other professional posts:* Advisory editor, *Encyclopedia Americana*, 1957-

Indian Arts and Crafts Board (commissioner, 1955-1964; chairman, 1964-1967); visiting professor of art and archaeology, Columbia University, 1961-; member, New York State Museum Advisory Council; trustee, Huntington Free Library, Futures for Children Foundation. *Memberships:* American Association for the Advancement of Science (Fellow); Cranbrook Institute of Sciences (Fellow); American Anthropological Association (Fellow); Society for American Archaeology; New York Academy of Sciences; Cosmos Club; Century Club. *Awards, honors:* First Prize (silversmithing), Cleveland Museum of Art, 1950; Fellow, Rochester Museum of Arts and Sciences. *Biographical sources: Who's Who in America; Who's Who in Art; American Men of Science; Who's Who in the East; American Indian Authors; Who's Who in the World.* Published works: *The Kachina and the White Man* (Cranbrook Institute of Sciences, 1954); *The American Indian in Graduate Studies* (Museum of the American Indian, 1957, revised in two volumes, 1974); *Indian Art in America* (New York Graphic Society, 1960); *Indian Art in Middle America* (New York Graphic Society, 1964); *Indian Art in South America* (Ne York Graphic Society, 1966); *Pre-Columbian and Later Tribal Arts* (Abrams, 1968); *Indian Art of the Americas* (New York, 1973); *Great North American Indians: Profiles of Life & Leadership* (New York, 1977); *Weaving Arts of the North American Indian,* 1978.

DODGE, DONALD (Navajo 1929-
(B.I.A. area director)

Born July 15, 1929, Crystal, N.M. *Education:* Albuquerque Indian School (high school); University of New Mexico. *Principal occupation:* B.I.A. area director. *Home address:* P.O. Box 114, Window Rock, Ariz. 86515. *Affiliation:* Director, Navajo Tribe's Public Service Division, 1969-1970; superintendent, B.I.A., Fort Defiance Agency, Ariz., 1972-1976; director, B.I.A., Navajo Area Office, Window Rock, Ariz., 1977-. *Military service:* U.S. Army - Korean War. *Awards, honors:* Grandson of famous Navajo leader, Chee Dodge, first chairman of Navajo Tribal Council. *Interests:* Mr. Dodge sees the Bureau's relationship to the Tribe as "government-to-government." "We have our government structure and the Tribe has its structure. We need to get together and compare the two and see where the relationship can be improved. Most of our programs are contractable except those involving areas of trust responsibility." Mr. Dodge concludes, "My main objective is to get a good organization going, one that can coordinate and communicate with the Tribe, so that the best interests of the individual will be served."

DODGE, GARY
(public information officer)

Affiliation: Public Information Officer, Lac du Flambeau Tribe, Lac du Flambeau, Wis. 54843.

DODGE, HENRY
(B.I.A. agency superintendent)

Affiliation: Superintendent, Fort Apache Agency, Bureau of Indian Affairs, Whiteriver, Ariz. 85941.

DODGE, MARJORIE T. (Navajo) 1941-
(school administrator)

Born June 5, 1941, Crownpoint, N.M. *Education:* Western New Mexico University, B.A., 1964; Northern Arizona University, M.A., 1970; University of Montana, Certificate for E.S.O.L., summer, 1967; University of Southern California, Certficate for Adult Leadership, summer, 1969; New Mexico State University, Education Specialist - School Administration, 1971-1972. *Principal occupation:* School administrator.

Home address: P.O. Box 717, Shiprock, N.M. 87420. *Affiliations:* Teacher, Crystal Boarding School, Navajo, N.M. (five years); student teacher supervisor, Chuska/Tohatchie Schools, N.A.U. 4th Cycle National Teacher Corps Program, Navajo Reservation (two years); teacher, first grade, Hunter's Point School, St. Michaels, Ariz., (one year); vice principal, Mesa Elementary School, Independent School District #22 (three years); administrative education specialist, B.I.A., Shiprock Agency, Crownpoint, N.M., 1977-. *Other professional post:* Represent San Juan and McKinley County on Governor's Council on Manpower. *Community activity:* Council of Citizens for San Juan County, N.M. (member). *Memberships:* Ding Be Olta Association; Navajo Education Association; National Indian Education Association; American Association for the Advancement of Science; San Juan Business & Professional Women Association. *Awards, honors;* Ten years B.I.A. Service Award & Letter of Commendation for Superior Performance. *Interests:* "My interest is in the education of the Indian children." *Biographical source:* Biography published in 1973 in the "Arizona Historical Society," Western Publishing Co. *Published work:* "Value Teachings in the Classroom," *Journal of American Indian Education,* Jan. 1972.

DOERFORT, HANS M. 1923-
(Indian education)

Born January 9, 1923, Germany. *Education:* University of Rochester, 1947-1949; University of Washington, A.B., 1951; Boston University, Ed.M., 1956. *Principal occupation:* Indian education. *Home address:* 1104 Rio Brazos Rd., Aztec, N.M. 87410. *Affiliation:* Principal, B.I.A., Aztec Dormitory, Aztec, N.M., 1954-. *Military service:* U.S. Air Force, 1943-1946 (Sergeant). *Community activities:* Kiwanis Club of Aztec (president, 1960); Aztec Chamber of Commerce (president, 1971-1973); San Juan Symphony League (president, 1972-1974); Aztec Museum Association (president, 1975-1976).

DOERING, MAVIS (Cherokee) 1929-
(basketweaving artist)

Born August 31, 1929, Hominy, Okla. *Education:* San Jose State University, 1946; Sacramento City College, 1968. *Principal occupation:* Basketweaving artist. *Home address:* 5918 N.W. 58th St., Oklahoma City, Okla. 73122. *Affiliations:* Consultant (Title IV, Indian pupil education), Putnam City School District, Warr Acres, Okla., 1977-1981; cultural consultant, Indian Student Association, University of Oklahoma, Norman, 1981-; consultant, United National Indian Tribal Youth Organization, 1979-. *Other professional posts:* Basketweaving instructor, Lone Grove School District, Western Heights School District, Deer Creek School District, Oklahoma Baptist University for Upward Bound students, Oklahoma Museum of Art, Willard Art Center, St. John's Methodist Church, the Native American Center of Oklahoma City (elderly program), American Indian Institute of the Univerity of Oklahoma, and Cowboy Hall of Fame, 1977-1984. *Community activities:* Advisory board, Oklahoma Indian Artists and Craftsmen Guild; member, Advisory Arts Council, Native American Center of Oklahoma City; member, National Advisory Council, Wheelwright Museum of the American Indian, Santa Fe, N.M.; newsletter editor, Oklahoma Cherokee Organization; member, Arts Advisory Committee, Crosswinds Gallery; precinct chairman for Democratic Party; Arts Advisory Committee, Diamond Jubilee of the State of Oklahoma (selected by the State of Oklahoma to complete a TV public service announcement for the Diamond Jubilee Celebration. *Memberships:* Oklahoma Museum of Art, 1980-; Cherokee Historical Society, 1980-; Oklahoma Cherokee Organization (secretary, newsletter editor, 1978-); Oklahoma Indian Artists and Craftsmens Guild (2nd vice president and board of directors, 1976-); Wheelwright Museum of the American Indian (advisory board, 1981-); Southwestern Associaton on Indian Affairs, Inc.; Goingsnake Historical Society, 1981-; Five Civilized Tribes Museum, 1978-; Oklahoma Anthropological Society, 1985-; Museum of the American Indian, 1985-. *Awards, honors:* Awards for artwork received from:

Oklahoma Indian Artists and Craftsmens Guild, Oklahoma Museum of Art, Five Civilized Tribes Museum, Galleria American Indian Exposition, Rose State College, Oklahoma Indian Women's Federation, Indian Arts and Crafts Association, Southwestern Association on Indian Affairs, "Four Directions Arts Festival"; "Oklahoma Artist of Month," October 1978; featured artist on three "Creative Crafts" television shows, 1978, 1979, 1982; appearances and interviews on "Voices from the Land," "Unity" and "Danny's Day" television shows; selected as a participant in the Smithsonian Folklife Festival in Washington, D.C. in 1982; commissioned to complete baskets for the 50 Governors at the National Governors' Conference in 1982 by the Oklahoma State Arts Council; selected as ambassador of goodwill for the State of Oklahoma by Governor George Nigh in October 1982; made honorary member of Oklahoma State Anthropoogical Society in October 1982; recipient of the Governor's Arts Award, 1984; received "Women in Communications" Arts Award in 1984; selected for one person exhibits at Southern Plains Indian Museum and the Coulter Bay Indian Museum; work selected for permanent collections at Southern Plains Indian Museum, Windstar Foundation, Oklahoma State Arts Collection, Cultural Center for the American Indian in Houston, National Building of Future Homemakers of America in Washington, D.C., and Mabee-Gerrer Museum. *Interests:* "I am interested in all phases of the arts. I am interested in the promotion of young Indian artists, in the promotion of the American Indian culture to the general populace and I am especially interested in the education of American Indian youth in all fields." *Biographical sources: Oklahoma Today,* Fall 1981; *American Craft,* May 1982; *American Indian-Alaskan Native Resource Guide; Daily Oklahoman,* October 1984, August, 1985; *Crafts in America,* 1984.

DONALD, GARY (Chippewa)
  (tribal chairman)

Affiliation: Chairman, Fond du Lac Reservation Business Committee, 105 University Rd., Cloquet, Minn. 55720; Nett Lake Reservation Business (Bois Fort) Committee, Nett Lake, Minn. 55772.

**DOONKEEN, EULA NARCOMEY
(Seminole) 1931-
  (artist)**

Born December 12, 1931, Oklahoma City, Okla. *Education:* Central State College, B.A. (Eduction), 1965. *Principal occupation:* Artist; co-owner, Alco Printing Co., Oklahoma City, Okla. *Home address:* 1608 N.W. 35th, Oklahoma City, Okla. 73118. *Military service:* U.S.A.F. Women's Reserve, 1951-1955. *Community activities:* Shawnee Area Health Advisory Board; Neighborhood Services Organization, Oklahoma City (secretary, 1972); Oklahoma City Community Council; Oklahoma City Area Health Advisory Board; West Central Neighborhood All Sports Association (vice president). *Memberships:* Seminole General Tribal Council (member; assistant chief); Five Civilized Tribes Inter-Tribal Council (seregeant-at-arms); National Congress of American Indians (area vice president, 1967-1968); Kappa Pi; Bacone Alumni Association; Oklahoma Feeration of Indian Women; American Indian Center (secretary, 1968); Feathers and Buckskin Society; American Indian Press Association; Indian Development Center, Inc.; Universal Link, Plains Center, Oklahoma City (vice president). *Awards, honors:* Several awards for painting in acrylics. *Exhibits:* Mrs. Doonkeen writes, "I have exhibited at the Smithsonian Institution (but) I paint mainly on commission and rarely enter competitions because I feel most competitions are based on bias and inherent traditional favoritism, and not on realistic approaches." *Interests:* "I am very interested in athletic events, both as a participant and (an) observer. In 1965, I captured the women's collegiate fencing championship of Oklahoma in the novice division. I have traveled extensively over the U.S. on business for Indian organizations and my own Seminole Nation's business. I also travel extensively for my own business, the Alco Printing Co. I am well known all over the country for my greeting card and stationery designs."

DORRIS, MICHAEL A. (Modoc) 1945-
(chairman-Native American studies)

Born January 30, 1945, Dayton, Wash. *Education:* Georgetown University, B.A. (magna cum laude), 1967; Yale University, M. Phil (Anthropology), 1970. *Principal occupation:* Chairman, Native Studies Department, Dartmouth College, Hanover, N.H., 1972-. *Address:* Hinman Box 6152, Dartmouth College, Hanover, N.H. 03755. *Affiliations:* Assistant professor of anthropology, Johnston College, University of the Redlands, 1970-1971; assistant professor, Franconia College, N.H., 1971-1972; professor, chairman, Department of Native American Studies, Dartmouth College, 1972-. *Community activities:* Explorers Club (Fellow); Society for Values in Higher Education (Fellow). *Memberships:* Society for Applied Anthropology (Fellow); Society for Values in Higher Education; American Anthropological Association; National Congress of American Indians; National Indian Education Association; National Indian Youth Council; Alpha Sigma Nu; *American Indian Culture Center Journal,* UCLA, 1974- (editorial board); *Viewpoint Magazine* (editor); Panel of Native American Scientists, AAAS (member); Minority Commission, MLA (member); Museum of the Ameriacn Indian (trustee). *Awards, honors:* National Endowment for the Humanities, 1976-; Guggenheim Fellow, 1978; Phil Beta Kappa; Danforth Graduate Fellow; Woodrow Wilson Faculty Fellow, 1980; National Institute of Mental Health Fellow. *Interests:* Contemporary Alaska; culture change; politics of energy resource development; sovereignty and international law; curriculum reform. *Biographical sources: Who's Who in America. Published works: Native Americans Today,* 1975; *Grandmother's Watch,* 1975; *Native Americans: 500 Years After,* (T.Y. Crowell, 1975); *Man in the Northeast,* 1976; *A Sourcebook for Native American Studies,* (American Library Association, 1977); chapter: "Native American Curriculum," *Racism in the Textbook* (Council on Interracial Books for Children, 1976); chapter in "Modoc Bibliographies," in *Encyclopedia of Indians of the Americas,* 1975.; *Pre-Contact North America,* textbook (Harper & Row, 1979); *Introduction to Native American Studies,* textbook (Harper & Row, 1980); editor, *Suntracks,* Arizona State University, 1978-.

DOSS, MICHAEL
(company president)

Affiliation: President, Arrow Creek Associates, 2450 Virginia Ave., N.W. #E106, Washington, D.C. 20037

DOWNING, ERNEST V. (Cherokee-Caddo) 1910-
(government official)

Born November 26, 1910, Verden, Okla. *Education:* Oklahoma City University, 1929-1930; University of Kansas, 1931-1932. *Principal occupation:* Government official. *Home address:* 4713 N.W. 29th, Oklahoma City, Okla. 73127. *Affiliations:* Employed in various capacities by the Bureau of Indian Affairs in Arizona, Illinois, New Mexico and Oklahoma, 1933-1935; executive officer, U.S. Public Health Service, Oklahoma City, Okla., 1955-retirement. *Community activities:* Interstate Council on Indian Affairs (governor's representative, 1952-1954). *Interests:* Mr. Downing writes, "I am interested in fine arts. Presently and for the past six years, I have participated in Oklahoma county libraries sponsoring of adult discussion groups in the liberal arts and great books program. I moderated a television series of eight programs on public-interest subjects sponsored by the Oklahoma Better Business Bureau, 1965."

DOYEL, DAVID E.
(museum director)

Affiliation: Director, Pueblo Grande Museum, 4619 E. Washington St., Phoenix, Ariz. 85034.

DRAKE, ELROY (Navajo) 1942-
(financial manager)

Born March 20, 1942, Tuba City, Ariz. *Education:* Northern Arizona University, B.S. (Business Administration), 1972. *Principal occupation:* Financial manager. *Home address:* P.O. Box 805, Window Rock, Ariz. 86045. *Affiliation: Manager, Navajo Sav-*

ings Branch of First Federal Savings, Phoenix, Ariz., 1975-. Other professional post: Industrial developer. *Military service:* U.S. Army, 1964-1966 (Vietnam Service Medal; SP/4 Class-Military Police). *Community activities:* VFW. *Memberships:* Northern Aruzona University Indian Club (social manager). *Awards, honors:* "1977 Young Navajo of Year," The Navajo Tribe. *Interests:* "Established first Savings & Loan Association on Indian Reservation to promote housing."

DRENNAN, ANTHONY, Sr.
(tribal chairman)

Affiliation: Chairman, Colorado River Tribal Council, Tribal Administration Center, Route 1, Box 23-B, Parker, Ariz. 85344/

DREW, ROBERT (Creek) 1922-
(government official)

Born June 12, 1922, Eufala, Okla. *Education:* Bacone Junior College, Certificate, 1947, B.S. (Education), 1949; Southeastern State College, M.S. (Education), 1957; University of Minnesota, graduate work, 1962-1963. *Principal occupation:* Government official. *Affiliations:* Teacher, coach, B.I.A., Parmelee, S.D., 1949-1950; principal, teacher, B.I.A., Mission, S.D., 1950-1952; principal, teacher, B.I.A., Cherry Creek, S.D., 1952-1955; principal, teacher, B.I.A., Eagle Butte, S.D., 1955-1957; community health worker, Public Health Service, Division of Indian Health, Pine Ridge, S.D., 1957-1959; education specialist (health), Public Health Service, Division of Indian Health, Bemidji, Minn., 1959-1962; area tribal affairs officer, Public Health Service, Division of Indian Health, Oklahoma City, Okla., 1963-1965; acting chief, Office of Tribal Affairs, Public Health Service, Division of Indian Health, Silver Spring, Md., 1966-. *Military service:* U.S. Army, 45th Infantry Division, 1940-1941, 1942-1945 (Purple Heart and Silver Star). *Community activities:* American Legion. *Memberships:* National Congress of American Indians, 1965-; Oklahoma Health and Welfare Associaton, 1965-. *Interests:* Mr. Drew writes, "I was an athletic official in high school foot-

ball and basketball, 1951-1958, and organized and managed independent football teams in Indian communities, 1949-1957, in South Dakota."

DU BRAY, ALFRED WILLIAM
(Rosebud Sioux) 1913-
(B.I.A. official)

Born April 1, 1913, Tripp County, S.D. *Education:* Mitchell Business College, 1937. *Principal occupation:* B.I.A. official. *Address:* c/o Bureau of Indian Affairs, Winnebago Agency, Winnebago, Neb. 68071. *Affiliations:* Mr. DuBray has held various positions with the B.I.A. since 1938; ex-superintendent, Winnebago Agency, 1963-retired. *Military service:* U.S. Army, 1945-1946. *Interests:* Mr. DuBray writes, "My entire career in the federal service has been with the B.I.A. I am keenly interested in the affairs of the American Indians and the policies and programs that have been developed for the improvement of conditions on the Indian reservations. My position as superintendent of an Indian agency has provided the opportunity to be associated with various tribal groups and with individual members of the tribes involved. Such experience provides a real opportunity to observe first hand the problems faced by the American Indian people in their struggle to advance socially and economically and to become part of the mainstream of American life."

DUCHENEAUX, FRANKLIN D.
(Cheyenne River Sioux) 1940-
(attorney)

Born January 30, 1940, Cheyenne Agency, S.D. *Education:* University of South Dakota, B.S. (Business), 1963; University of South Dakota Law School, J.D., 1965. *Principal occupation:* Attorney. *Home address:* 11539 Hickory Cluster, Reston, Va. 22090. *Affiliation:* Special Counsel on Indian Affairs, Committee on Interior & Insular Affairs, U.S. House of Representatives, Washington, 1973-.

74

DUFFIELD, LATHEL F. (Cherokee)
1931-
(professor, curator)

Born December 1, 1931, Collinsville, Okla. *Education:* University of Oklahoma, B.A., 1953, M.A., 1963; University of Wisconsin, Ph.D., 1970. *Principal occupation:* Professor, curator. *Home address:* 347 Sheridan Dr., Lexington, Ky. 40503. *Affiliations:* Executive director, Texas Archaeological Research Center, University of Texas, Austin, 1963-1964; assistant professor of anthropology, Eastern Kentucky University, 1964-1966; associate professor and profesor of anthropology, University of Kentucky, 1969-. *Other professional posts:* Curator, Gilcrease Institute of American History and Art; director, Arkansas Museum of Natural History and Antiquities; director, Museum of Anthropology, University of Kentucky. *Memberships:* American Association of University Professors; American Anthropological Associaton (Fellow); Society for American Archaeology; Kentucky Archaeological Association (editor); Texas Archaeological Society; Oklahoma Anthropological Society; Plains Anthropological Association. *Awards, honors:* Will Rogers Fellowship, University of Oklahoma; traineeship, National Science Foundation. *Interests:* "Interested in Southeastern, Southern Plains and Midwestern archaeology, ethnology, and paleontology. Have conducted archaeological investigations in Texas, Kentucky and Arkansas, and have worked on crews in Arizona, North Dakota, Oklahoma, and Guatemala." *Published works: Engraved Shells from the Craig Mound* (Oklahoma Anthropoogical Society, 1964); co-author, *The Pearson Site: A Historic Indian Site at Iron Bridge Reservoir (Dept. of Anthropology, University of Texas, 1964).*

DUNCAN, CLIFFORD
(museum director)

Affiliation: Director, Ute Tribal Museum, P.O. Box 190, Ft. Duchesne, Utah 84026.

DUSHANE, HOWARD S. (Eastern
Shawnee) 1911-
(B.I.A. officer)

Born July 10, 1911, Seneca, Mo. *Education:* Oklahoma Baptist University, 1931-1932. *Principal occupation:* B.I.A. officer. *Affiliations:* Truxton Canyon Agency, B.I.A., 1934-1950; district agent, Hoopa, Calif., 1950-1952; program officer, Hooper, Calif., 1952-1955; area program officer, Portland, Oreg., 1955-1957; superintendent, Fort Belknap Agency, B.I.A., MOnt., 1957-1960; superintendent, Cheyenne Agency, B.I.A., S.D., 1960-1966; area credit officer, Albuquerque Area Office, B.I.A., 1966-retirement). *Military service:* U.S. Army, 1945-1946. *Interests:* "Vocational interests have, of course, been in the development and progress of the Indian people with whom assigned in both cultural and economic fields. Being of Indian extraction, I have been involved and intensely interested in the progress of the American Indian, and my entire adult life has been devoted to this cause." *Biographical source: Indians of Today* (Indian Council Fire).

DYC, GLORIA 1950-
(instructor)

Born April 15, 1950, Detroit, Mich. *Education:* Wayne State University, B.Ph., 1973, M.A. (Speech, Theatre), 1976; Univerity of Michigan, D.A. (ABD-English), 1982. *Principal occupation:* Instructor. *Home address:* Box 66, Mission, S.D. 57555. *Affiliation:* Chair, General Studies Department, Sinte Gleska College, Rosebud, S.D., 1982-. *Other profesional post:* Instructor, Wayne County Community College, Detroit; artist in the schools, Michigan and South Dakota. *Membership:* Phi Beta Kappa. *Awards, honors:* Hopwood Award for Fiction, The University of Michigan, 1982; Wayne State University Playwriting Contest, 1973. *Interests:* "I'm doing community-based sociolinguistic research on Indian English, the ethnography of speaking, bilingual, bicultural education." *Published works:* Fiction and poetry in numerous small press journals.

E

EAGER, GEORGE B.
(assistant director-museum)

Affiliation: Assistant director, Museum of the American Indian, Heye Foundation, Broadway at 155th St., New York, N.Y. 10032.

EBERHART, CHARLES M. 1919-
(shop owner)

Born March 30, 1919, Boulder, Colo. *Education:* High school. *Principal occupation:* President, Western Trading Post, Inc., Denver, Colo., 1953-. *Military service:* Army Air Corps, 1941-1946 (Staff Sergeant). *Community activities:* South Denver, Chamber of Commerce (member); Chief Iron Shell Museum (director, curator, 1968-1975); White Buffalo Council of American Indians (advisor). *Memberships:* Denver Art Museum; Denver Museum of Natural History; Colorado Historical Society; Museum of the American Indian; Indian Arts and Crafts Association. *Awards, honors:* 1969 Friendship Award, White Buffalo Council of American Indians. *Interests:* "While I have made a study of most facets of the material culture of the American Indian, my main interest is in the use of glass beads and other ornamentation. My studies include not only the effect of the use of trade goods on the Indian historically, but also the preference for different items by various groups today. My interest in this material lead to repeated travel to all the Plains Indian reservations and the starting of a business dealing in these items in order to obtain close first hand information. We sell an extensive line of beads of all kinds, especially glass. Also, being in business, we have many Indians of all tribes request materials and in this way can keep up with the current trends of the various groups. We also have a good line of books on Indian topics and current newspapers."

ECHOHAWK, BRUMMETT (Pawnee) 1922-
(artist, writer, actor)

Born March 3, 1922, Pawnee, Okla. *Educa-tion:* Detroit School of Arts and Crafts, 1945; Art Institute of Chicago, 1945-1948; studied creative writing at the University of Tulsa. *Principal occupation:* Artist, writer, actor. *Home address:* P.O. Box 1922, Tulsa, Okla. 74101. *Affiliations:* Staff artist, Chicago *Daily Times* and Chicago *Sun Times;* artist, *Bluebook,* McCall's Magazine Corp., New York. *Military service:* U.S. Army, 1940-1945 (Purple Heart with oak-leaf cluster; did Combat sketches published in the Army's *Yank Magazine,* and 88 newspapers by N.E.A. News Syndicate). *Community activities:* Gilcrease Museum, Tulsa, Okla. (board member). *Exhibitions:* Paintings shown in Pakistan, India through the Art in the Embassies Program, State Department; other works shown at the De Young Museum, San Francisco; Amon Carter Museum, Fort Worth, Texas; Gilcrease Museum; Imperial War Museum. London; Bad Segeberg, Hamburg, West Germany. *Acting:* As stage actor, Mr. Echohawk has appeared in the role of Sitting Bull in Kopit's play *Indians* in Tulsa, Fort Worth, and Lincoln, Neb. Also played at the Virginia Museum Theater, Richmond, Questor's Theater, London, and Karl May Theater, Bad Segeberg, West Germany; he did a TV film in Hamburg, W. Germany. *Awards, honors:* Assisted Thomas Hart Benton with one of the "greatest" mural in America: The Truman Memorial Library mural called "Independence and the Opening of the West," at Independence, Mo.; commissioned by the Aluminum Co. of America for a painting depicting early American history of the Tennessee Valley; commissioned by Leaning Tree Publishing Co., Boulder, Colo. for paintings to be reproduced as Christmas cards; Mr. Echohawk's paintings are of a classic and representational style, which cover the subjects of the Indian and the American West. *Biographical sources: Encyclopedia of the American Indian; Indians of Today; Dictionary of International Biography;* National Geographic's *American Indians. Published works:* Writings, with illustrations, have appeared in the Tulsa *Sunday World, Oklahoma Today* Magazine, *The Western Horseman* Magazine, and others.

**ECHOHAWK, JOHN E. (Pawnee) 1945-
(attorney)**

Born August 11, 1945, Albuquerque, N.M.
Education: University of New Mexico, B.A.,
1967; University of New Mexico, School of
Law, J.D., 1970. *Principal Occupation:*
Attorney. *Home Address:* 2350 Panorama,
Boulder, Colo. 80302. *Affiliations:* Native
American Rights Fund, Boulder, Colo.
(research associate, 1970-1972; deputy direc-
tor, 1972-1973, 1975-1977; executive direc-
tor, 1973-1975, 1977-). *Community
Activities:* Association on American Indian
Affairs (board of directors); American
Indian Lawyer Training Program (board of
directors); National Committee on Respon-
sive Philanthropy (board of directors).
Memberships: American Indian Bar Associ-
ation; American Bar Association. *Awards,
Honors:* Americans for Indian Opportunity,
Distinguished Service Award; White Buf-
falo Council, Friendship Award; National
Congress of American Indians, President's
Indian Service Award. *Interests:* Indian law.

**EDDY, FRANK W. 1930-
(archaeologist-anthropologist)**

Born May 7 1930, Roanoke, Va. *Education:*
University of New Mexico, B.A., 1952; University of Arizona, M.A., 1958; University
of Colorado, Ph.D., 1968. *Principal occupation:* Archaeologist-anthropologist.
Addresses: 2228 Bluff St., Boulder, Colo.
80302 (home); Department of Anthropology, University of Colorado, Boulder, Colo.
(professional). *Affiliations:* Curator,
Museum of New Mexico, researcher and
director of the Navajo Reservoir Salvage
Archaeological Project, 1959-1965; research
assistant at the University of Colorado
Museum—dig foreman at Yellow Jacket
and Jurgens Site excavations, 1965-1968;
executive director, Texas, Archaeological
Salvage Project, University of Texas, Austin, 1968-1970; director, Chimney Rock
Archaeological Project, University of Colorado, 1970-1973; associate professor, profes-
sor of anthropology, University of
Colorado, 1970-. *Other professional posts:*
Director and prinicpal investigator, Two
Forks Archaeological Project, University of
Colorado, 1974-1975; intern, Interagency

Archaeological Services, Denver, National
Park Service, 1975-1976; co-director and
principal investigator of the Bisti-Star Lake
Cultural Resource Inventory, Archaeological Associates, Inc., summer, 1977. *Military
service:* U.S. Army, 1952-1954. *Memberships:* Society for American Archaeology,
1953-; Society for the Sigma Xi, 1965--1973;
American Quaternary Associaton, 1970-;
Colorado Archaeological Society, 1970-;
Society of Professional Archaeologists,
1976- (counselor, standards board); Association of Field Archaeologists, 1977-. *Interests:* Cultural ecology; prehistoric settlement
studies; cultural change as revealed by
archaeology; technology of primitive societies. *Published works: An Archaeological
Survey of the Navajo Reservoir District,
Northwestern New Mexico,* with Alfred E.
Dittert, Jr., and James J. Hester (Mono-
graph, School of American Research,
Museum of New Mexico, 1961); *Excava-
tions at Los Pinos Phase Sites in the Navajo
Reservoir District* (Museum of New Mex-
ico, 1961); "Excavations at the Candelaria
Site, LA 4406," chapter II in *Pueblo Period
Sites in the Piedra River Section, Navajo
Reservoir District,* assembled with A.E. Dit-
tert, Jr. (Museum of New Mexico, 1963);
*Prehistory in the Navajo Reservoir District,
Northwestern New Mexico* (Museum of
New Mexico, 1966); *Archaeological Investi-
gations at Chimney Rock Mesa: 1970-1972*
(Memoirs of the Colorado Archaeological
Society, 1977); *An Archaeoogical Study of
Indian Settlements and Land Use in the
Colorado Foothills,* with Ric Windmiller
(Memoirs of Southwestern Lore, Colorado
Archaeological Society). Several articles in
journals, and papers delivered at regional
meetings and national conferences.

**EDEN, RONALD D.
(B.I.A.-director of administration)**

Affiliation: Director of administration,
Bureau of Indian Affairs, 1951 Constitution
Ave., N.W., Washington, D.C. 20245.

**EDER, EARL A (Sioux) 1944-
(painter)**

Born November 17, 1944, Poplar, Mont.

Education: Institute of American Indian Arts, Santa Fe, N.M.: San Francisco Art Institute, B.F.A.: University of Montana, M.A., 1971. *Principal occupation:* Painter. *Exhibits:* De-Mo-Lay Gallery, Great Falls, Mont., 1965; Alaska Centennial, 1966; American Indian Historical Society, 1968; Philbrook Art Center, 1969; University of San Francisco, 1969; Scottsdale National Indian Arts Exhibit, 1968, 1970. *Awards, honors:* Second Place, Scottsdale National Indian Arts Exhibit, 1970; First Place (sculpture), Heard Museum, 1970; Second Place (sculpture), Heard Museum, 1972. *Interests:* Mr. Eder writes, "I am a painter, and (painting) is what I would eventually like to teach, and keep moving in that direction." *Biographical sources: House Beautiful,* June, 1972; *Art in America,* July, 1972.

EDMO, KESLEY
(tribal chairman)

Affiliation: Chairman, Fort Hall Business Council, Fort Hall Tribal Office, Fort Hall, Idaho 83203

EDMO, LORRAINE P.
(director-Indian organization)

Affiliation: Director, American Indian Scholarships, 5106 Grand Ave., N.E., Albuquerque, N.M. 87108.

EDMONDSON, ED 1919-
(congressman)

Born April 7, 1919, Muskogee, Okla. *Education:* University of Oklahoma, B.A., 1940; Georgetown University, LL.B., 1947. *Principal occupation:* Congressman (member of Congress, 2nd District, Oklahoma). *Home address:* 219 N. 14th St., Muskogee, Okla. *Military service:* U.S. Navy Reserve. *Memberships:* American Bar Association; Oklahoma Bar Association. *Awards, honors:* Honorary memberships in several Oklahoma tribes. *Interests:* Committee on Interior and Insular Affairs (member); Subcommittee on Indian Affairs (second-ranking Democrat); Committee on Public Works, U.S. House of Representatives (member).

EDMUNDS, JUDITH A. 1943-
(dealer-American Indian jewelry)

Born September 8, 1943, Waltham, Mass. *Education:* Massachusetts College of Pharmacy. *Principal occupation:* Dealer of fine American Indian jewelry and related items. *Home address:* Box 788, West Yarmouth, Mass. 02673. *Affiliation:* President-treasurer, Edmonds of Yarmouth, Inc., 1973-. *Other professional posts:* State chairperson, Indian Arts & Crafts Association (served on Education & Public Relations Committee; currently chairperson for Massachusetts). *Interests:* Ms. Edmunds writes, "My business is a retail outlet, but my greatest pleasure is educating the general public on the different Indian tribes and their style of work and their living conditions, and to create collectors of fine Indian art.By educating these people - those dealers that are selling fakes and misrepresenting their wares will soon be out of business, I travel to reservations a couple of times a year and spend time in the Hopi Mesas and San Domingo Pueblos, as well as on the Navajo Reservation, as we have Indian friends spread out through the various reservations, as well as Anglo friends. My interests outside of the Indian field is fine American antiques."

EDWARDS, JOHN
(Indian school principal)

Affiliation: Principal, Concho Indian School, P.O. Box 8, Concho, Okla. 73022.

EID, LEROY V. 1932-
(professor of history)

Born December 22, 1932, Cincinnati, Ohio. *Education:* University of Dayton, B.S. (Education), 1953; St. John's University, M.S. (History), 1958, Ph.D. (History), 1961; University of Toronto, M.A. (Philosophy), 1968. *Principal occupation:* Professor of history. *Home address:* 1181 Kentshire Dr., Centerville, Ohio 45459. *Affiliation:* Professor, Department of History, University of Dayton, Dayton, Ohio, 1961- (chairman of dept. 1969-1983). *Awards, honors:* Ontario Graduate Fellowship, 1967. *Interests:* "Teacher of history of American Indians. Research interest is in American Indian military expertise (Northeast Woodland of the Colonial period. My writing tries to present this military world from the Indian viewpoint, weaknesses as well as strengths. The overall thesis is that Northeast Woodland Indians showed on important occasions (e.g. Braddock's defeat in Pennsylvania and St. Clair's defeat in Ohio) an army with disciplined soldiers who followed skilled leaders who had excellent tactics." *Published works:* Articles: "National War Among Indians of Northeastern North America: Ethnohistorical Insight or Anthropological Nonsense?" *(Canadian Review of American Studies,* Summer, 1985); "The Cardinel Principle of Northeast Woodland Indian War," *(Papers of the Thirteenth Algonquian Conference,* Toronto, 1982); "I Am An Indian," *(Illinois Quarterly,* 1982); "Liberty and the Indian," *(Midwest Quarterly,* 1982); "The Neglected Side of American Indian War in the Northeast," *(Military Review,* Feb. 1981); "The War of the Iroquois Lost," *(Journal of the Order of the Indian Wars,* Spring 1980); "The Ojibwa-Iroquois War," *(Ethnohistory,* 1979). Papers: "Surprise: The Central Indian Military Tactic," Great Lakes Historical Conference, April, 1984; "Two Types of Indian War: Private and National," paper at Joint Conference of CAAS and ASCUS, October, 1982; "The Cardinal Principle of Northeast Indian War," paper at the Algonquian Conference, October, 1981; "I Am An Indian," paper at American Association for Eighteenth Century Studies, October, 1981; "That Unconquered Nation," paper at Great Lakes History Conference, April, 1980; "Teaching American Indian History, Literature, and Values," paper at the Great Lakes Regional Conference of the National Council for the Social Studies, March, 1980; "Liberty and the Indian," paper at Popular Culture Association, April, 1978. Book reviews: Leonard Carlson's *Indians, Bureacrats, and Land,* in *Journal of the West,* Oct., 1982; Francis P. Prucha's *Indian Policy in the United States* in *Journal of the West, Jan. 1983; Vine Deloria Jr. and Clifford M. Lytle's American Indians, American Justice* in *Journal of the West; among others.*

ELAM, EARL H. 1934-
(professor of history, vice president for academic affairs)

Born December 7, 1934, Wichita Falls, Tex. *Education:* Midwestern University, Wichita Falls, Texas, B.A., 1961; Texas Tech University, Lubbock, M.A., 1967, Ph.D., 1971. *Principal occuaption: Professor of history, vice president for academic affairs. Home address:* 407 N. Cockrell, Alpine, Texas 79830. *Affiliations:* Instructor, Texas Tech University, 1967-1971; professor of history, and vice president for academic affairs, Sul Ross State University, Alpine, Texas, 1972-. Military service: U.S. Navy, 1953-1957 (Radioman). *Memberships:* Western History Association; West Texas Historical Association; Texas State Historical Association. *Interests:* American Indian history; Indian land claims; American Indian ethnology and archaeology; Texas history, Southwestern American history, Spanish borderland history. *Published works:* Several articles and reports; thesis, dissertation, and reports on Wichita Indian history and ethnology.

ELGIN, ALFRED G., Jr.
(executive director-Indian council)

Affiliation: Executive director, National Indian Council on Aging, P.O. Box 2088, Albuquerque, N.M. 87103

ELLISON, THOMAS J. (Oklahoma Choctaw) 1924-
(B.I.A. official)

Born June 17, 1924, Choctaw County, Okla. *Education:* Haskell Indian Junior College; Colorado A & M College, B.S. (Agriculture), 1950. *Principal occupation:* B.I.A. official. *Home address:* Route 4, Box 654, Muskogee, Okla. 74401. *Affiliations:* Extension & Soil Conservation, B.I.A., Anadarko, Okla, 1950-1952, Albuquerque, N.M., 1952-1954, Ardmore, Okla., 1954-1957; credit and financing officer, B.I.A., Winnebago, Neb., 1957-1960, Rosebud, S.D., 1960-1962, Muskogee Area Office, 1963-1967; tribal operations and industrial development, B.I.A., Crow Agency, Mont., 1962; superintendents, Stabding Rock

Agency, B.I.A., 1967-1968; B.I.A., Muskogee Area Office (tribal operations officer, 1969-1972; deputy area director, 1972; acting area director, 1973-1974; area director, 1974-). *Military service:* U.S. Army, 1943-1946. *Community activities:* The Native American Legal Defense and Education Fund (advisory committee, Oklahoma Research Project); Muskogee State Fair Board (chairman, Specialty Day Committee); Bacone College (Academic Committee, Board of Trustees, 1975-1978); Fun Country R C & D steering committee, Ardmore, Okla. (technical assistant).

ELROD, SAM
(deputy administrative director, Indian Health Service)

Affiliation: Deputy administrative director, Indain Health Service, 5600 Fishers Lane, Rockville, Md. 20857.

EMELIO, JOHN
(EMS program director)

Affiliation: EMS program director, Indian Health Service, 5600 Fishers Lane, Rockville, Md. 20857.

EMGEE, Sr. JUDITH
(executive director-Indian school)

Affiliation: Executive director, Ojibwa Indian School, Box A-3, Belcourt, N.D. 58316.

ENGELSTAD, KURT (Eskimo) 1937-
(business executive, attorney)

Born October 3, 1937, Corvallis, Ore. *Education:* Oregon State University, Corvallis, B.S. (Education), 1960; Northwest School of Law, Lewis & Clark College, Portland, Ore., J.D., 1972. *Principal occupation:* Business excutive, attorney. *Home address:* 2125 S.E. Sherman St., Portland, Ore., 97214. *Affiliations:* President and chairman of board, The 13th Regional Corporation, Seattle, Wash., 1983-. *Other professional posts:* President and executive producer, Alaska Native Film Productions, Inc.;

member, board of directors, Alaska Federation of Natives; principal, Engelstad & Associates, a private Oregon-based consulting firm. *Military service:* U.S. Air Force (active duty), 1960-1961; active Air Force reserve, 1961-; (Lt. Colonel; Air Force Longevity Service Ribbon with hour glass device; Air Force Reserve Medal with 4 oak leaves; Small Arms Marksmanship Medal). *Community activities:* Former Boy Scout troop leader; former director and board chairman, Multnomah County, Oregon legal services. *Memberships:* Oregon State Bar, 1972-; Multnomah Bar, 1972-; District Court Bar, 1972-; joint committee of Oregon Bar with Press and Broadcasters (1974-1977 member and chairman). *Awards, honors:* Chief Frank White Buffaloman award for Outstanding Service to the Native American community of Portland, Oregon by Portland Urban Indian Council; Outstanding Journalism graduate for 1960 bestowed by Sigma Delta Chi honorary, Oregon State University chapter. *Interests:* Vocational: Indian law, business management and finance; Avocational: Writing, photography, philately. *Biographical source:* "Natives Without a Land Base," by Elizabeth Roderick, October, 1983 edition *Alaska Native News Magazine. Published works:* Editorial staff, *Environmental Law Review of Northwest School of Law of Lewis & Clark College, 1972.*

ENGLES, WILLIAM LYNN (Oneida) 1935-
(commissioner-administration for Native Americans)

Born September 29, 1935, Poplar, Mont. *Education:* The Evergreen State College, Olympia, Wash., B.A., 1974. *Principal occupation:* Commissioner, Administration for Native Americans. *Home address:* 3751 Gunston Rd., Alexandria, Va. 22302. *Affiliations:* Public information officer, Bureau of Indian Affairs, Washington, D.C., 1974-1984; commissioner, Administration for Native Americans, Department of Health & Human Services, Washington, D.C., 1984-. *Other professinal posts:* Reporter and Bureau Chief, Unite Press International. *Military service:* U.S. Army, 1955-1957 (Corporal).

ENGLISH, SAMUEL F. (Turtle
Mountain Band and Redlake Band
Chippewa) 1942-
(artist)

Born June 2, 1942, Phoenix, Ariz. *Education:* Bacone College, Bacone, Okla., 1960-
1962; University of San Francisco,
1967-1968. *Principal occuaption:* Artist.
Home address: 400 San Felipe N.W., Albuquerque, N.M. 87104. *Affiliation: Owner,
Native American Art Gallery, Albuquerque,
N.M., 1982-.*

ERASMUS, GEORGES HENRY (Dene)
1948-
(Dene politician)

Born August 8, 1948, Fort Rae, N.W.T.,
Can. *Education:* High school, Yellowknife,
N.W.T. *Principal occupation:* Dene politician. *Home address:* P.O. Box 222, Yellowknife, N.W.T., Canada. *Affiliations:*
Secretary, Indian Band Council, Yellowknife, N.W.T., Can., 1969-1971; Organizer
and chairman, Community Housing Association, Yellowknife, 1969-1972; advisor to
president, Indian Brotherhood of N.W.T.,
1970-1971; fieldworker and regional staff
director, Company of Young Canadians,
1970-1973; chairman, University Canada
North, 1971-1975; director, Community
Development Program, Indian Brotherhood of Northwest Territories (later the
Dene Nation) (director, Community Development Program, 1973-1976; president,
1976-1983); president, Denedeh Development Corporation, 1976-1983; elected
Northern vice-chief, Assembly of First
Nations, 1983; elected National Chief,
Assembly of First Nations, Ottawa, Canada.
Awards, honors: Representative for Canada
on Indigenous Survival International, 1983;
Canadian delegate to World Council of
Indigenous Peoples International Conferences, 1984-1985; art, school, athletic awards.
Interests: Reading, travel, outdoors, canoeing and art. "Presently working on a book,
due for publication in August, 1987." *Bio-
graphical sources: New Canadian Encyclopedia; Who's Who in Canada.*

ERICKSON, JOHN
(chief-Smoki People)

Affiliation: Chief, Smoki People, P.O. Box
123, Prescott, Ariz. 86302.

ERICKSON, VINCENT O. 1936-
(professor of anthropology)

Born January 17, 1936, Mount Vernon,
Wash. *Education:* University of Washington, B.A., 1958, M.A., 1961, Ph.D., 1968.
Principal occupation: Professor of anthropology. *Home address:* 175 Southampton
Dr., Fredericton, New Brunswick, Can. E3B
4T5. *Affiliation:* University of New Bruns-
wick, Fredericton, Can., 1966-. *Member-
ships:* American Anthropological
Association; American Ethnological
Society; Canadian Ethnology Society;
American Folklore Society; Canadian Folk-
lore Society. *Interests:* Ethnohistory, ethno-
linguistics, ethnography and folklore of the
Eastern Algonkians, especially of the Indi-
ans of New Brunswick. Indian agent to the
Passamaquoddy, 1965-; fieldwork among
Passamaquoddy, 1967-, and among the
Coast Salish Indians of Washington and
British Columbia, 1960-1962.

ESTEVES, PAULINE
(tribal chairwoman)

Affiliation: Chairwoman, Death Valley
Indian Community, P.O. Box 108, Death
Valley, Calif.92325.

EULER, ROBERT C. 1924-
(professor of anthropology)

Born August 8, 1924, New York, N.Y. *Education:* Arizona State College, B.A., 1947,
M.A. (Economics), 1948; University of New
Mexico, Ph.D. (Anthropology), 1958. *Principal occupation:* Professor of anthropology. *Affiliations:* Ranger, National Park
Service, Wupatka National Monument,
1948-1949; anthropological consultant,
Albuquerque Area Office, B.I.A., 1950-
1951; instructor, associate professor, Arizona State College, 1952-1964; curator of
anthropology, Museum of Northern Arizona, 1952-1956; research associate, Museum
of Northern Arizona, 1956-; associate pro-

fessor, professor and chairman, Department of Anthropology, University of Utah, 1964-? *Other professional posts:* Anthropological consultant, Hualapai Tribe, land claim litigation, 1953-1957; member, board of trustees, Museum of Navajo Ceremonial Art, 1954-1964; anthropological consultant, U.S. Department of Justice, Southern Paiute land claim litigation, 1956; consultant in cross-cultural education, Phoenix, Ariz., public school system, 1961, 1964; ethnohistorian, Upper Colorado River Basin Archaeological Salvage Project, University of Utah, 1962; Arizona Governor's Historical Advisory Committee, 1961-1964; ethnohistorical consultant, Arizona Commission on Indian Affairs, 1962-1964; anthropological consultant, Operation Headstart, U.S. Office of Economic Opportunity, involving Navajo, Paiute, Mojave, and Chemehuevi participation, 1965. *Memberships:* Amerian Anthropological Association (Fellow); American Ethnological Society; Society for Applied Anthropology (Fellow); Society for American Archaeology; Current Anthropology (associate); American Association for the Advancement of Science (Fellow); American Indian Ethnohistoric Conference; The Society for Sigma Xi; The Western History Association (member, editorial board, *The American West);* Arizona Academy of Science (charter member; president, 1962-1963); Arizona Archaeological and Historical Society; New Mexico Historical Society; Ne Mexico Archaeological Society; Utah Historical Society. *Interests:* Ethnographic fieldwork involving historical ethnography, ethnohistory and applied anthropology among the Navajo, Hopi, Walapai, Havasupai, Yavapai, Chemehuevi, Southern Paiute, Southern Ute, Isleta Pueblo, and Zia Pueblo; historica archaeological research in Walapai, Havasupai, Yavapai, and Southern Paiute sites. *Published works:* Editor, *Woodchuck Cave, A Basketmaker II Site in Tsegi Canyon, Arizona,* with H.S. Colton (Museum of Northern Arizona, 1953); *Walapai Culture History* (University of New Mexico, doctoral disserttion, University Microfilms, 1958); *Southern Paiute Archaeology in the Glen Canyon Drainage: A Preliminary Report* (Nevada State Museum, 1963); *Havasupai Religion and Mythology* (Anthropolgoical Papers, University of Utah, 1964); numerous articles, reviews and monographs.

EVANS, REX
(executive director-Indian organization)

Affiliation: Executive director, United South and Eastern Tribes, 1101 Kermit Dr., Suite 800, Nashville, Tenn. 37217.

EVANS, WAYNE H. (Rosebud Sioux) 1938-
(Indian academic/student affairs)

Born April 19, 1938, Rosebud, S.D. *Education:* Black Hills State College, B.S., 1962; University of South Dakota, Ed.D., 1976. *Principal occupation:* Indian academic/student affairs. *Home address:* Vermillion, S.D., 57069. *Affiliation:* University of South Dakota, Vermillion, S.D., 1969-. *Memberships:* South Dakota Indian Education Association (president); South Dakota Indian Counselor's Association (board member). *Awards, honors:* Outstanding Young Man of America. *Interests:* Counseling, guidance; family therapy; values - value orientation. *Published work: Indian Student Counseling Handbook* (Black Hills State College, 1977).

EWAN, ROY S. (Athabascan) 1935-
(corporate president)

Born February 2, 1935, Copper Center, Alaska. *Education:* Mt. Edgecumbe High School. *Principal occupation:* Corporate president. *Home address:* P.O. Box 215, Gakona, Alaska 99586. *Affiliations:* President, Ahtna, Inc.; board member, Grandmet/Ahtna; board member, Ahtna Development Corporation. *Other professional posts:* Serves as ex-officio member on all corporate committees, and shareholder committees and subsidiary boards. *Military service:* U.S. Army, 1953-1955 (Corporal). *Community activities:* Gulkana Village Council (Indian education, past president). *Memberships:* Alaska Feeration of Natives (board member); Alaska Native Federation; The Alliance. *Awards, honors:* 1985 AFN Citizen of the Year, Alaska Federation of Natives.

EWERS, JOHN CANFIELD 1909-
(ethnologist emeritus, Smithsonian)

Born July 21, 1909, Cleveland, Ohio. *Education:* Dartmouth College, B.A., 1931, D.Sc., 1968; Yale University, M.A. (Anthropology), 1934; University of Montana, LL.D., 1966. *Principal occupation:* Ethnologist emeritus, Smithsonian. *Home address:* 4432 N. 26th Rd., Arlington, Va. 22207. *Affiliations:* Field curator, Museum Division, National Park Service, 1935-1940; curator, Museum of the Plains Indian, 1941-1944; associate curator of ethnology, planning officer, U.S. National Museum, Smithsonian Institution, 1946-1959; assistant director, director, Museum of History and Technology, Smithsonian, 1959-1965; senior scientist, Office of Anthropology, now ethnologist emeritus, Department of Anthropology, Smithsonian Institution, Washington, D.C. *Other professional posts:* Museum planning consultant, Bureau of Indian Affairs, 1948-1949; Montana Historical Society, 1950-1954; editor, *Journal of the Washington Academy of Sciences,* 1955; member, editorial board, *The American West, Western Historical Quarterly,* and *Great Plains Quarterly,* 1979-; consultant, American Heritage, 1959; research associate, Museum of the American Indian, Heye Foundation, 1979-. *Military service:* U.S. Naval Reserve, 1944-1946. *Memberships:* American Indian Ethnohistoric Conference (president, 1961); American Anthropological Association (Fellow); Washington Academy of Sciences (Fellow); Rochester Museum of Arts and Science (Fellow); Sigma Xi (president, D.C., chapter); Western History Association (honorary life member). *Awards, honors:* Recipient First Exceptional Service Award for contributions to American history and ethnology, Smithsonian Institution, 1965; Oscar O. Winthor Award, Western History Association, 1976; "Distinguished Published Writings in the Field of American Western History," 1985, Western History Association. *Interests:* "Field research in ethnology and ethnohistory conducted among the Blackfeet tribes of Montana and Alberta (Canada), the Assiniboine of Montana, the Flathead of Montana, the Sioux of South Dakota, and the Kiowa of Oklahoma; studies of Indian art since 1932." *Biographical sources: Who's Who in America; The Reader's Encyclopedia of the American West,* 1977, by Howard Lamar, editor; *Plains Indian Studies,* Douglas H. Ubelaker and Herman J. Viola, editors (Smithsonian Contribution to Anthropology) - a collection of essays in honor of John C. Ewers and Waldo R. Wedel (includes a complete list of John C. Ewer's approximately 163 publications through 1981; *Fifth Annual Plains Indian Seminar in Honor of Dr. John C. Ewers,* George Horse Capture and Gene Ball, editors *(Buffalo Bill Historical Center, 1984); Western Historical Quarterly* (April, 1986). *Published works:* Mr. Ewers writes, "I have published more than 20 books and monographs, and over 100 articles on the American Indian, the fur trade of the American West, artists who interpreted Indians, etc. Among the books — *Plains Indian Painting* (Stanford University Press, 1940); *The Horse in Blackfeet Indian Culture* (Smithsonian Institution, 1955); *The Blackfeet: Raiders on the Northwestern Plains* (University of Oklahoma Press, 1958); *Artists of the Old West* (Doubleday, 1965); *Indian Life on the Upper Missouri* (University of Oklahoma Press, 1968); *Murals in the Round: Painted Tipis of the Kiowa and Kiowa-Apache Indians,* 1978; Editor: *Adventures of Zenas Leonard, Fur Trader,* 1959; *Crow Indian Medicine Bundles,* 1960; *Five Indian Tribes of the Upper Missouri,* 1961; *O-Keepa: A Religious Ceremony and Other Customs of the Mandans,* (George Catlin), 1967; *Indians of Texas in 1830* (Smithsonian Institution, 1969); *Indian Art in Pipestone, George Catlin's Portfolio in the British Museum,* 1979; *Plains Indian Sculpture, Traditional Art from America's Heartland* (Smithsonian Institution, 1986).

EXENDINE, LEAH
(director-Indian resource liaison)

Affiliation: Director, Indian Resource Liaison Staff, Indian Health Service, 5600 Fishers Lane, Rockville, Md. 20857.

EXENDINE, Dr. JOSEPH N.
(deputy director-Indian Health Service)

Affiliation: Deputy director, Indian Health Service, 5600 Fishers Lane, Rockville, Md. 20857

F

FADDEN, JOHN KAHIONHES
(Mohawk-Turtle Clan) 1938-
(artist, illustrator)

Born December 26, 1938, Massena, N.Y. (near Akwesasne, St. Regis Indian Reservation). *Education: Rochester Institute of Technology, B.F.A., 1961; St. Lawrence University and SUNY at Plattsburgh, graduate courses. Principal occupation:* Artist, illustrator. *Address:* Six Nations Indian Museum, Onchiota, N.Y. 12968. *Exhibitions:* Six Nationa Indian Museum, 1954-; Pennsylvania State Museum, Harrisburg, 1962; "Art of the Iroquois," Erie County Savings Bank, Buffalo, N.Y., 1974; Ne York State Fair, Syracuse, 1977; The Woodland Indian Cultural - Educational Centre, Brantford, Ontario, 1977, 1980, 1984; American Indian Community Hosue Gallery, New York City, 1977, 1980, 1982, 1984; Akwesasne Museum, Hogansburg, N.Y., 1980; Schoharie Museum of the Iroquois Indian, 1981-1985; Iroquois Indian Festival II, feature artist, Cobleskill, N.Y., 1983; "Akwesasne: Our Strength, Our Spirit," World Trade Center, Ne York City, 1984; among others. *Interests:* As John looks back over the years, he sees the 1961-1968 period as one of experimentation in which he worked with pen and ink and painted in tempera, selling a few of his works at the family museum (Six Nations Indian Museum), and giving away others. As became more aware of the political changes taking place at Akwesasne, and throughout Native America, he began to make more political statements through his art, mainly through drawings and cover illustrations for *Akwesasne Notes,* a nespaper published by the Mohawk Nation at Akwesasne. The details of his work typically show native nationalism and political ascertiveness based on the traditions of the native peoples. He has illustrated many books and periodicals, and has done cover art for many books; also, calendar art for *Akwesasne Notes Calendar,* 1972-. He has taken part in three films: *Who Were the Ones* (National Film Board of Canada, 1970); *Hodenosaunee: People of the Longhouse* (Stiles-Akin Films, 1981); *The Iroquois Creation Myth* (video tape, Image Film, 1982).

FADDEN, RAY
(museum owner)

Affiliation: Owner, Six Nations Indian Museum, Ochiota, N.Y. 12968.

FAIRBANKS, MICHAEL
(B.I.A. agency superintendent)

Affiliation: Superintendent, Blackfeet Agency, Bureau of Indian Affairs, Browning, Mont. 59417.

FALLEY, NANCI
(president-Indian organization)

Affiliation: President, American Indian Horse Registry, Route 1, Box 64, Lockhart, Tex. 78644.

FALLING, LEROY (Cherokee) 1926-
(administrator)

Born June 15, 1926, Estella, Okla. *Education:* Warner Pacific College, Diploma, 1948; Anderson College, B.S., 1950; Oregon College of Education, Diploma, 1951; Arizona State University, M.S., 1966. *Principal occupation:* Administrator. *Address:* c/o Kinlichee Boarding School, Ganado, Ariz. 86505. *Affiliations:* Teacher, Lapwai Public School, York Public School; educational specialist, Window Rock, Ariz. *Military service:* U.S. Navy, 1944-1946 (World War II Victory Medal). *Community activities:* Window Rock, Fort Defiance Lions Club; Kit Carson Council (vice-chairman, Leadership Training); Boy Scouts of America; Indian Workers Conference (president, 1965-1966); National, International Social Concerns Committee, 1964-1966.

FALLS, ALVIN (Sac and Fox)
(tribal chief)

Affiliation: Principal chief, Sac and Fox Business Committee, Route 2, Box 246, Stroud, Okla. 74079.

FAWCETT, JAYNE GRANDCHAMP
(Mohegan of Connecticut) 1936-
(teacher, assistant curator)

Born January 6, 1936, New London, Conn. *Education:* University of Connecticut, B.A., 1957; Eastern Connecticut State College. *Principal occupation:* Teacher, assistant curator. *Affiliations:* Teacher, Ledyard Junior High School, Gales Gerry, Conn., 1972-; assistant curator, Tantaquidgeon Indian Museum. *Other professional posts:* Lecturer, American Field Studies. *Interests:* "Inspired by the travels of my Aunt, Gladys Tantaquidgeon, my family and I have traveled extesnively throughout the western part of America, visiting as many groups of native American as we were able."

FELSEN, DR. JAMES D.
(chief medical officer,
Indian Health Service)

Affiliation: Chief medical officer, Indian Health Service, 5600 Fishers Lane, Rockville, Md. 20857.

FELSMAN, JOSEPH
(tribal chairman)

Affiliation: Chairman, Confederated Salish & Kootenai Tribal Council, P.O. Box 278, Pablo, Mont. 59855.

FELTS, JACK LEON (Choctaw) 1921-
(publisher, writer)

Born January 7, 1921, Blanchard, Okla. *Principal ocupation:* Publisher, writer. *Affiliations:* Founder, Pan Press, Hollywood, Calif.; associate, Beth Kramer Literary Agency, 1953-; scenarist, 1953-1956. *Military service:* U.S. Coast Guard, 1943-1946. *Memberships:* International director, Individualist Society (editor, I.S. *Tablet*); Descendants of the Choctaws. *Interests:* Established Tahlequah Writers' Conference, 1961-1965; exploration and excavation in Mexico and Central America, 1963-1965; directing historical acquisition and study.

FENTON, WILLIAM NELSON 1908
(anthropologist, professor)

Born December 15, 1908, New Rochelle, N.Y. *Education:* Dartmouth College, B.A., 1931; Yale University, Ph.D., 1937; Hartwick College, LL.D., 1968. *Principal occupation:* Anthropologist, professor. *Home address:* 7 N. Helderberg Parkway, Slingerlands, N.Y. 12159. *Affiliations:* Community worker, U.S. Indian Setvice, in charge of Tuscarora and Tonawanda Reservations, 1935-1937; instructor, assistant professor, St. Lawrence University, 1937-1939; ethnologist, Smithsonian Institution, Bureau of American Ethnology, 1939-1951; lecturer, Johns Hopkins University, 1949-1950, Catholic University of America, 1950-1951; executive secretary for anthropology and psychology, National Academy of Sciences, National Research Council, 1952-1954; assistant commissioner, State Museum and Science Service, New York State Education Department, 1954-1968; research professor of anthropology, S.U.N.Y. at Albany, 1968-1974, distinguished professor, 1974-1979. *Military service:* Research associate, Ethnogeographic Board, 1942-1945. *Memberships:* American Anthropological Association (executive board); American Folklore Society (Fellow; past president); American Indian Ethnohistorical Society; American Ethnological Society (past president); American Association for the Advancement of Science (Fellow); Museum of the American Indian (trustee, 1976-1980). *Awards, honors:* Adopted Seneca (Iroquois); Peter Doctor Award, Seneca Nation of Indians, 1958, for outstanding service to Iroquoian peoples; Cornplanter Medal for Iroquois Research, Cayuga County Historical Society, 1965; Hon. LL.D., Hartwick College, 1968; Dartmouth College Class of 1930 Award, 1979; named Dean in Perpetuum of Iroquoian Studies, 30th Conference on Iroquois Research, 1979; Fulbright-Hays research fellow to New Zealand, 1975; National Endowment for the Humanities fellow, Huntington Library, 1977-1979; member, Iroquois Documentary History Project, Newberry Library, 1979-1981. *Published works: The Iroquois Eagle Dance* (Bureau of American Ethnology, 1953); editor, *Symposium on Local Diversity in Iroquois Culture* (Bureau of American

Ethnology, 1955); editor, *Symposium on Cherokee and Iroquois Culture* (Bureau of American Ethnology, 1961); *American Indian and White Relations to 1830* (Institute of Early American History and Culture, University of North Carolina, 1957); *Parker on the Iroquois* (Syracuse University Press, 1968); editor and translated with E.L. Moore, Lafitan's *Customs of the American Indian (1724)* (The Champlain Society, 1974, 1977).

FERGUSON, ROBERT B. 1927-
(writer, producer)

Born December 30, 1927, Willow Springs, Mo. *Education:* Washington State University, B.A., 1954; Vanderbilt University, M.A., 1973. *Principal occupation:* Writer, producer. *Home address:* Box 12392, Nashville, Tenn. 37212. *Affiliations: Conservation film prodcuer, Tennessee Game and Fish Commission, Nashville, Tenn., 1956-1961; senior record producer, RCA Records, Nashville, Tenn., 1963-. Military service:* Field Artillery, 1946-1947; corporal, U.S. Marine Corps, 1950-1951. *Community activities:* Southeastern Institute of Anthropoogy (director of operations, 1966-); Tennessee Council on Archaeology. *Memberships:* Americn Philosophical Society, 1966-; MENSA, 1971-; Choctaw Nation Historical Society, 1971-. *Interests:* Writings on Southeastern Indian ethnohistory and contemporary affairs (editor, *Chahta Anumpa - The Choctaw Times,* 1968-1972); ethnography of the Mississippi Choctaws; related expeditions. *Published works:* Editor, *The Middle Cumberland Culture* (Vanderbilt Unviersity Press, 1972); *Indians of the Southeast, Then and Now,* with Jesse Burt (Abingdon Press, 1973).

FIELD, RAYMOND C.
(executive director-Indian association)

Affiliation: Executive director, National Tribal Chairmen's Association, 818 18th St., N.W., Suite 420, Washington, D.C. 20006.

FIELDS, AUDREY
(museum coordinator)

Affiliation: Coordinator, Dinjii Zhuu Enjit Museum, P.O. Box 42, Fort Yukon, Alaska 99740.

FISHER, DOROTHY D. (½ Coushatta)
1930-
(merchant-Indian arts and crafts)

Born July 7, 1930, Campti, La. *Principal occupation:* Owner, The Indian Maid, 153 Redlands Mall, Redlands, Calif. 92373. *Home address:* 210 E. Sunset Dr., N., Redlands, Calif. 92373. *Membership:* Indian Arts and Crafts Association. *Interests:* Collector and vendor of all types of Indian arts and crafts.

FISHER, JOE (Blackfeet) 1943-
(tribal administrator, photographer)

November 19, 1943, Santa Monica, Calif. *Education:* Haskell Indian Junior College, Lawrence, Kan., A.A., 1964; Northern Montana College, Havre, 1964-1966; University of Montana, Missoula, 1973-1974. *Principal occupation:* Tribal administrator, photographer. *Home address:* P.O. Box 944, Browning, Mont. 59417. *Affiliation:* Blackfeet Tribe, Box 850, Browning, Mont.; historical documentor, photographer. *Community activities:* American Legion; Blackfeet Societies: Rough Rides, Slickfoot, and Crazy Dog. *Military service:* U.S. Army (Sp-5 Engs.) (Vietnam Service Unit Commendation). *Membership:* VFW. *Interests:* Photographic showing, "Indian Pride on the Move," in Browning, Missoula, Helena; Blackfeet art slide presentation. *Published work: Blackfeet Nation,* 1977.

FLEMING, DARRELL (Cherokee) 1911-
(government administrator)

Born June 22, 1911, Bernice, Okla. *Education:* Haskell Institute, 1927-1933. *Principal occupation:* Government administrator. *Home address:* 8906 Knox Ave., S., Minneapolis, Minn. 55431. *Affiliation:* Assistant area director, B.I.A., Minneapolis, Minn. *Military service:* U.S. Navy, 1944-1946. *Awards, honors:* Presidntial Citation in recognition of outstanding contribution to greater economy and improvement in governmental operations, 1964.

FLORES, WILLIAM VANN (Cherokee-Papago) 1927-
(medical illustrator)

Born October 2, 1927, Appleton, Wis. *Education:* Chilocco Indian School, 1947; Kansas City Art Institute, 1949-1951; Art Center School, Los Angeles, 1955-1957; Oklahoma City University, 1958-1959; El Reno Junior College, 1965-1967. *Principal occupation:* Medical illustrator. *Home address:* P.O. Box 84, Concho, Okla. 73022. *Affiliation:* Medical illustrator, Federal Aviation Agency, Will Rogers Field, Oklahoam City, Okla., 1961-. *Military service:* U.S. Army, 1952-1954 (Korean Service Medal with two Bronze Stars; Presidential Unit Citation; Meritorious Unit Commendation; Good Conduct Medal; national Defense Service Medal; United Nations Service Medal). *Memberships:* Association of Medical Illustrators (first American Indian member); Kansas City Art Institute, Alumni; Society of Art Center Alumni, Los Angeles, Calif.

FOGELMAN, GARY L. 1950-
(editor/publisher)

Born January 1, 1950, Muncy, Pa. *Education:* Lock Haven State University, B.S., 1972; West Chester State University (two years; 18 credits for Masters). *Principal occupation:* Editor/publisher. *Home address:* RD# 1, Box 240, Turbotville, Pa. 17772. *Affiliation:* Editor/publisher, *Indian-Artifact Magazine. Memberships:* Local, state and northeastern archaeological societies; SPA (Chapter No. 8, vice president); IACAP (vice president). *Awards, honors:* Catlin Peace Pipe Award. *Interests:* Colecting Indian artifacts; hunting and fishing. *Published works: The Muncy Indians* (Grit Publishing, 1976); *The Pennsylvania Artifact Series (in progress).*

FOGLEMAN, BILLYE Y.S. 1927-
(anthropologist)

Born December 6, 1927, Plainview, Tex. *Education:* Hockaday Junior College, A.A., 1947; University of Texas, Austin, B.A., 1949; Southern Methodist University, M.A., 1971, Ph.D., 1972. *Principal occupation:* Anthropologist. *Home address:* Quail Call, Route 3, Box 44, Moscow, Tenn. 38057. *Affiliations:* Associate professor, Department of Psychiatry, Health Science Center, University of Tennessee, Memphis, 1976-. *Other professional posts:* Instructor, Texas Women's University, Eastfield Community College, Texas Christian University; consultant, Alcohol Abuse Training Project Related to Minority Populations, Memphis State University, 1976-1979; project administrator, Health Careers Opportunity Program, University of Tennessee, Memphis, 1981-1985. *Memberships:* American Anthropological Association (Fellow), 1972-; Society for Applied Anthropology (Sustaining Fellow), 1972-; Southern Anthropological Society, 1972-. *Awards, honors:* Graduated with honors, University of Texas, Austin; National Defense Education Scholarships, 1970-1972; Outstanding Women of Memphis, Chamber of COmmerce, 1975; Sigma Xi Honorary; Delta Kappa Gamma Hnorary; honored for contribution to Family Medicine Student Association, 1985. *Interests:* "Doctoral research on Native Americans in a southern metropolitan area; research on Vietnamese Refugees in a southern metropolitan area; medical student education; cultural considerations in patient care; avocational interests include travel, camping, fishing, theatre, visiting art museums, and family. *Published works:* "The Appropriation Hypothesis: Primary Interaction Among Urban Indians, II," (*International Migration Review,* Fall, 1973); "Abstract, "Will One Intertribal Center Clinic Survive?" (*In* Abstracts, 1974); "The Housewife Syndrome Among Native American Women," (*Tennessee Anthropologist,* 1977).

FOLLIS, WILLIAM (Modoc)
(tribal chief)

Affiliation: Chief, Modoc Tribal Council, P.O. Box 939, Miami, Okla. 74355.

FORBES, JACK D. (Powhatan (Renape) and Lenape) 1934-
(professor-Native American studies)

Born January 7, 1934, Long Beach, Calif. *Education:* University of Southern California, B.A., 1953; M.A., 1955, Ph.D., 1959. *Principal occupation:* Professor, Native American studies. *Home address:* Route 1, Box 23, Yosemite Ave., Davis, Calif. 95616. *Affiliations:* Research program director, Far West Laboratory, Berkeley, Calif., 1967-1969; professor, Native American Studies, University of California, Davis, 1969-. *Other professional post:* Co-editor, *Attan-Akamik. Community activities:* Powhatan Confederation (Chief's Council); California Indian Legal Services, Inc. (board of directors). *Membership:* California Indian Education Association. *Interests:* "Founder, Native American Movement (chairman, 1961-1962); founder of Coalition of Eastern Native Americans; co-founder of the United Native Americans, 1968; co-founder, D-Q University (volunteer instructor); working with Renape, Lenape, and other related languages." *Biographical sources: Who's Who in the West; Contemporary Authors. Published works: Apache, Navajo and Spaniard* (University of Oklahoma Press, 1961); *Warriors of the Colorado* (University of Oklahoma Press, 1965); *The Indian in America's Past* (Prentice-Hall, 1965); *Native Americans of California and Nevada* (Naturegraph, 1969); *Nevada Indians Speak* (University of Nevada Press, 1967); *Handbook of Native American Studies* (Tecumseh Center, 1971); *Aztecas del Norte* (Fawcett, 1973).

FORCE, ROLAND W. 1924-
(anthropologist, museum director)

Born December 30, 1924, Omaha, Neb. *Education:* Stanford University, B.A. (Psychology), 1950, M.A. (Education), 1951, M.A. (Anthropology), 1952, Ph.D. (Anthropology), 1958. *Principal occupation:* Anthropologist, museum director. *Home address:* 21 Rockleigh Rd., Rockleigh, N.J. 07647. *Affiliations:* Assistant curator, Leland Stanford Jr. Museum, Stanford, Calif., 1952-1953; acting instructor in anthropology, Stanford University, 1954; associate in ethnology, B.P. Bishop Museum, Honolulu, 1954-1956; lecturer, Det. of Anthropology, University of Chicago, 1956-1961; curator of Oceanic Archaeology and Ethnology, Chicago Natural History Museum (Field Museum of Natural History), Chicago, 1956-1961; member, Graduate Affiliate Faculty, University of Hawaii, 1962-1977; director, B.P. Bishop Museum, 1962-1976; holder, Charles Reed Bishop Distinguished Chair in Pacific Studies (1976-1977), director emeritus, B.P. Bishop Museum, 1976-; director and secretary, board of trustees, Museum of the American Indian, Heye Foundation, New York City, 1977-. *Other professional posts:* Chairman of the executive committee and member representing Hawaii, Pacific Science Council, Pacific Science Association, 1966-1978; Bishop Trust Company, Honululu, (director, member, board of directors), 1969-1977; honorary consultant, B.P. Bishop Museum, 1977-; trustee, W.T. Yoshimoto Foundation, Hawaii, 1979-. *Military service:* U.S. Army, 1943-1946 (sergeant; Corps of Engineers; combat duty, European Theatre of Operations). *Community services:* Member, advisory board, State-based Humanities Program, Hawaii, 1972-1975; member, Distribution Committees, Sophie Russell Testamentary Trust and Jessie Ann Chalmers Charitable Trust, Honolulu, 1972-1977; member, Barstow Foundation Committee (Samoan Education), Hawaii, 1963-. *Memberships:* Pacific Club, Honolulu, 1962-; Social Science Association, Honolulu, 1962-; American Anthropological Association; American Association for the Advancement of Science; American Association of Museums; International Council of Museums; National Trust for Historic Preservation; Pacific Science Association. *Awards, honors:* Selected by Chicago Junior Chamber of Commerce as one of Chicago's ten outstanding young men, 1958; Honorary Member, Association of Hawaiian Civic Clubs, 1967; Honorary Doctor of Science, Hawaii Loa College, 1973; Honorary Life Member, Bishop Museum Association, 1976; comendation, Senate Concurrent Resolution, Hawaii, 1976; Honoray Life Fellow, Pacific Science Association. *Biographical sources: Who's Who in America; American Men of Science. Published works:* Many articles in the *Museum of the Ameri-*

88

can Indian Newsletter, and other periodicals, including: "Arctic Art: Eskimo Ivory," *American Indian Art Magazine,* 1981); "A Common Misperception," *(MAI Newsletter,* 1984); "That Without Which Nothing," *(MAI Nesletter,* 1984); "Becons in the Night," *(MAI Newsletter,* 1984); "The Owls' Eyes Obsession," *(MAI Newsletter,* 1984); "Solving the Puzzle of the Past," *(MAI Newsletter,* 1985); among others.

FORD, RICHARD IRVING 1941-
(curator of ethnology)

Born June 27, 1941, Harrisburg, Pa. *Education:* Oberlin College, Ohio, M.A., 1963; University of Michigan, M.A., 1965, Ph.D., 1968. *Principal occupation:* Curator of ethnology. *Home address:* 2825 Provincial, Ann Arbor, Mich. 48104. *Affiliation:* Assistant professor of anthropology, University of Cincinnati, 1967-1969; Curator of ethnology and director, Museum of Anthropology, University of Michigan, Ann Arbor, Mich., 1970-. *Other professional post:* Professor of anthropology and botany, University of Michigan. *Memberships:* Conference of Native American Studies (national advisory committee); American Anthropological Association; Society for American Archaeology (executive committee); Society for Economic Botany (editorial board); The Archaeological Conservancy (secretary); American Association for Advancement of Science (section H, chairperson). *Interests:* Expert witness, Zuni Pueblo, N.M.; consultant to San Juan Pueblo, N.M.; North American ethnobotany; origins of American Indian agriculture; excavations, Jemez Cave and Bat Cove, N.M., and Cloudspitter, Ky. *Awards, honors:* Distinguished Service Award, University of Michigan, 1971; National Science Foundation grantee, 1970-1973, 1975-1976, 1978-1979; Weatherhead scholar, School of American Research, 1978-1979; *Biographical source: Who's Who in America. Published works:* co-author, *Paleoethnobotany of the Koster Site* (Illinois State Museum, 1972); editor, *The Nature and Status of Ethnobotany* (University of Michigan, 1978); editor, *Prehistoric Food Production in North America* (University of Michigan, 1985).

FORREST, ERIN (Modoc-Pit River)
1920-
(rancher, health programs administrator)

Born January 12, 1920, Alturas, Calif. *Education:* Riverside Junior College. *Principal occupation:* Rancher, health programs administrator. *Home address:* P.O. Box 763, Alturas, Calif. 96101. *Affiliations:* State Inheritance Tax Appraiser, 1964-1968; administrative assistant, State Assemblywoman Pauline Davis, 1969-1975; president, XL Indian Reservation Board of Directors, 1946-. *Other professional posts:* Chairman, PL 94-437 Policy Council; chairman, NTCA Health Committee; chairman, NCAI Health Committee; national Indian Health Liaison Officer, NTCA. *Community activities:* Modoc County Democratic Central Committee (chairman, 1968-). *Military service:* U.S. Army, ETO, World War II. *Memberships:* National Tribal Chairmens Association; National Congress of American Indians; California Tribal Chairmens Association; National Health Insurance Health Team. *Awards, honors:* Rural Services Award, Sargeant Shriver, 1969; Outstanding Achievements in Indian Community Development, awarded by Division of Indian Community Development, Indian Health Service, 1975; honored by California Senate Resolution, 1970; honored by California Assembly Resolution, 1975. *Interests:* Indian health programs; Appaloosa horses; wild life conservation; Indian artifacts; National Indian health and social concerns.

FOX, DENNIS R. (Mandan-Hidatsa)
1943-
(assistant director-education, B.I.A.)

Born September 8, 1943, Elbowoods, N.D. *Education:* Dickinson State College, Pa., B.S., 1966; Penn State University, M.Ed., 1971, D.Ed., 1977. *Principal occupation:* Assistant director of education, B.I.A. *Home address:* 4133 Conrad Rd., Alexandria, Va. 22312. *Affiliations:* Education program administrator, Johnson O'Malley Program, Bureau of Indian Affairs, Cheyenne River Agency and Aberdeen Area Office, S.D., 1975-1983; assistant director of education, Bureau of Indian Affairs, Washington, D.C. 1983-. *Other professional post:* Teacher, worked in B.I.A. higher education grant program. *Memberships:* National Indian Education Association; Phi Delta Kappa. *Awards, honors:* Gave presentation at National School Administration Conference. *Interests:* Educational administration. *Biographical source: Indians of Today,* 1970 edition.

FOX, SANDRA J. (HARRELL (Oglala Cheyenne River Sioux) 1944-
(education specialist)

Born December 9, 1944, Kadoka, S.D. *Education:* Dickinson State College, N.D., B.S., 1966; Penn State University, M.Ed., 1971, D.Ed., 1976. *Principal occupation:* Education specialist. *Home address:* 4133 Conrad Rd., Alexandria, Va. 22312. *Affiliations:* Education specialist, Bureau of Indian Affairs, Aberdeen Area Ofice, S.D.; education specialist-curriculum, ORBIS, Inc., Washington, D.C., 1985-. *Other professional post:* Education specialist and consultant, B.I.A. *Memberships:* International Reading Association; National Indian Education Association; North American Indian Women's Association. *Awards, honors:* North Dakota Indian Scholarship; invited to join Pi Lambda Theta; given presentations at National Council of Teachers of English Convention, national Reading Conference, and International Reading Association Convention. *Interests:* "Elementary and secondary education reading improvement." *Published work: An Annotated Bibliography of Young People's Books on American Indians* (Bureau of Indian Affairs, 1973).

FRANCISCO, ELDON (Laguna Pueblo)
(elementary school principal)

Education: Brigham Young University, B.S., 1963; New Mexico State University, M.A., 1972. *Principal occupation:* Elementary school principal. *Home address:* Route 2, Box 236, Walnut GHrove, Miss 39189. *Affiliation:* Principal, Standing Pine Day School, B.I.A., Walnut Grove, Miss. *Other profesional posts:* Agriculture Extension Agent, 1963-1968; school counselor. *Awards, honors:* B.I.A. Ten-Year Pin; EPDA Fellowship. *Interests:* "Personal development of Indian poeple nased upon

their own initiative, motivation and resources."

FRANK, EARL
(tribal chairman)

Affiliation: Chairman, Bishop Tribal Council, P.O. Box 548, Bishop, Calif. 93514.

FRANK, ROBERT L. (Washoe)
(tribal chairman)

Affiliation: Chairman, Washoe Tribal Council, Route 2, Box 68, Gardnerville, Nev. 89410.

FRAZIER, GREGORY W. (Crow-Santee Sioux) 1947-
(business executive)

Born September 5, 1947, Richmond, Ind. *Education:* Earlham College, Richmond, Ind., 1965-1967; Temple University, Philadelphia, Pa., B.A. (Business Administration), 1972; University of Puget Sound, Tacoma, Wash., M.B.A. (Finance), 1978. *Principal occupation:* Business executive. *Home address:* P.O. Box 427, Englewood, Colo. 80151. *Affiliations:* Member, National Indian Planning Council, U.S. DOL; instructor/consultant, American Indian Management Institute, Albuquerque, N.M., 1972-1974; executive director, Seattle Indian Center, Inc., 1974-1977; executive director, AL-IND-ESK-A (The 13th Regional Corp.), Seattle, Wash., 1977-1979; chairman, Absarokee Investments, Seattle, Wash., 1977-; chief executive, National Urban Indian Council, Denver, Colo., 1979-; president, national Council for Indian Business, Englewood, Colo., 1980-. *Other professional posts:* Presidential appointee, National Advisory Council on Indian Education; appointee, Secretary's Advisory Group, Department of HUD; appointee, Department of Labor Ad Hoc Advisory Committee. *Community activities:* King County Housing Task Force (member); Billings-Yellowstone Housing Association (member); Indians for United Social Action (member); National Low Income Housing Coalition (member). *Memberships:* National Indian Education Association; Indian Motorcycle Owners Association (vice president); National Indian Business Council (chairman, 1983-); Registered Lobbyist, U.S. House and Senate, Colorado General Assembly; American Management Association, 1980-. *Awards, honors:* Outstanding Contribution Award, CETA Coalition; Individual Personal Achievement Award, IHRC, Inc.; Outstanding Minority Writer, 1985, U.S. Writers Association; Best Business Efforts, Community Chamber of Commerce, 1985. *Interests:* "Business and economic development; developing countries; writing; international travel; collecting motorcycles; motorcycle road racing; fund raising consultant; owns several businesses, including Mountain Area Leasing, Intra City Properties, First Preferred Properties; manages own Montana ranch, commutes between offices in Colorado, Utah and Washington. *Published works: While We're At It, Why Don't We Find You a Job* (NCIB Press, 1984); *American Indian Index* (Arrowstar Publishing, 1985).

FREDERICKS, OSWALD WHITE BEAR (Hopi) 1905-
  (artist)

Born February 6, 1905, Old Oraibi, Ariz. (Hopi Reservation). *Education:* Phoenix Indian School; Haskell Institute, Lawrence, Kan.; Bacone College, Bacone, Okla., B.S. *Principal occupation:* Artist (Hopi traditional arts and crafts). *Home address:* Box 8, Sedona, Ariz. 86336. *Affiliations:* Artist, Art Studio, Oraibi and Sedona, Ariz. *Other professional posts:* Lecturing, publication, teaching, Hopi history and religion. *Community activities:* Art instructor, Boys Club of America, Phoeniz, Ariz.; art instructor, YMCA; judge of Hopi Court, Oraibi, Ariz. *Memberships:* Ancient Astronaut (honorary member); Boy's Club of America; President Club, Univerity of Northern Arizona, Flagstaff. *Awards, honors:* Judge of the Hopi Tribal Court, Oraibi, Ariz.; awards for Hopi arts and crafts, and sports; technical advisor and coordinator, Hopi legend made to movie *Boy and Eagle* (Disney Productions). *Interests:* Ancient Hopi culture and history; relation to ancient ruins and history in Mexico, Yucatan; rock writing; travel;

ancient cultures and their relationship to Hopi culture and religion. *Biographical sources: Community Leaders and Noteworthy Americans* (Bicentennial Edition, 1976-1977). *Published works: Book of Hopi,* with Frank Waters (Viking Press, 1963); *Kasskara,* in German (Dusseldorf, Munich, 1979).

FREEMAN, KING (Pala)
  (tribal chairman)

Affiliation: Chairman, Pala Executive Committee, P.O. Box 43, Pala, Calif. 92059.

FREEMAN, ROBERT LEE (Dakota-Luiseno) 1939-
  (artist, cartoonist, muralist, printmaker)

Born January 14, 1939, Rincon Indian Reservation, Calif. Education: Palomar College, San Marcos, Calif., A.A., 1976, 1974-. *Principal occupation:* Artist, cartoonist, muralist, printmaker. *Home address:* 1697 Curry Comb Dr., San Marcos, Calif. 92069. *Affiliation:* Art instructor, Palomar College. *Military service:* U.S. Army, 1957-1960 (E-2 Korea, 1959). *Exhibitions:* One-man shows: Schiver Gallery, St. Louis, Mo.; Sioux Museum, Rapid City, S.D.; Turtle Mountain Gallery, Phildelphia, Pa.; Gallery of the American Indian, Sedona, Ariz; among others. Group shows: U.S. Department of the Interior, Washington, D.C.; Heard Museum, Phoenix, Ariz.; Scottsdale National Indian Art Exhibit, Ariz.; among others. Murals: Los Angeles Public Library (45 ft.) and five private murals in homes. Numerous selected public and private collections. *Awards, honors:* 150 national Indian art awards from the following: Scottsdale National Indian Art Exhibit, Heard Museum, Red Cloud Art Show, Southern California Exposition, Gallup Ceremonial, and California State Fair. *Interests:* Mr. Freeman works in several media and has won awards in oil, watercolor, woodcarving, etching, pen and ink, bronze, airbrush and drawing, acrylic and lithography. He has instructed the course Native American Art at Grossmont College, San Diego, and Palomar College, San Marcos, Calif. Travel. *Biographical sources: Who's Who in Indian Art; International*

Artists and Writers (Cambridge, England). *Published works:* Mr. Freeman's work has appeared in such periodicals as *Ford Times, Western Horseman, Southwest Art Scene, Indian Voices, Genie, North County Living, Westerner,* and *"Artist of the Rockies."* Paintings included in two books, *I Am These People,* and *Contemporary Sioux Paintings. Mr. Freeman has illustrated two books: The Layman's Typology Handbook,* and *The Luiseno People.* He is author and publisher of two cartoon books, *For Indians Only,* 1971, and *War Whoops and All That Jazz,* 1973; *Robert Freeman Drawings,* 1985.

FRENCH, EDGAR L., Jr. (Delaware)
(tribal chairman)

Affiliation: Chairman, Delaware Executive Committee, P.O. Box 825, Anadarko, Okla. 73005.

FRIEND, DAVID NATHAN
(executive director-Indian organization)

Affiliation: Executive director, National Center for American Indian Alternative Education, P.O. Box 18329, Capitol Hill Station, Denver, Colo. 80218.

FRISCH, JACK A. 1940-
(anthropologist)

Born May 26, 1940, Glen Cove, N.Y. *Education:* Northeastern University, B.A., 1962; Indiana University, M.A., 1964, Ph.D., 1970. *Principal occupation:* Anthropologist. *Affiliations:* Instructor, State University of New York at Plattsburgh, 1965-1967; assistant professor, Wayne State University, 1968-1972; associate professor, Washington State University, 1972-. *Memberships:* American Anthropological Association; American Folklore Society; American Society for Ethnohistory; Society of Sigma Xi; Central States Anthropological Society; American Association of University Professors; Council on Anthropology and Education; Society for Applied Anthropology. *Awards, honors:* Indiana University Graduate School grant-in-aid for summer research among the Maricopa Indians, Salt River

Reservation, Scottsdale, Ariz., 1965; National Museum of Canada Research Contracts for ethnographic research among the St. Regis Mohawks, St. Regis Reserve, N.Y., Quebec, and Ontario, 1967-1971; Wayne State University Faculty grant-in-aid to continue research on St. Regis Mohawk religious ceremonies, 1969. *Interests:* North American Indian ethnology and ethnohistory; cultural anthropology; folklore and culture; linguistic anthropology; cultural dynamics. *Published works:* Numerous papers published in scholarly journals.

FRITZ, LINDA
(native law librarian)

Afiliation: Librarian, Native Law Centre, University of Saskatchewan, 150 Diefenbaker Centre, Saskatoon, Saskatchewan, Can.

FRYE, BILLY J.
(tribal chairman)

Affiliation: Chairman, Las Vegas Colony Council, 1 Paiute Dr., Las Vegas, Nev. 89106.

FULLER, NANCY J.
(coordinator-Native American museums program)

Affiliation: Coordinator, Native American Museums Program, Office of Museum Programs, Smithsonian Institution, Washington, D.C. 20560. *Published works:* Editor, *Native American Museum Program Newsletter,* 1982-1985; *Tribal Archives: An Introduction Slide/Tape Program,* 1983; Native American Museums: Development and Related Issues, A Bibliography, 1984; *Some Sources of Information for Native American Museums and Cultural Organizations,* 1985; *A Brief Reference Guide for Materials Concerning Native American Culture and History,* 1986. All published by the Office of Museums Program, Smithsonian Institution.

FULTON, WILLIAM DINCAN
(president-Amerind Foundation)

Affiliation: President, Amerind Foundation, Inc., Dragoon Rd., Box 248, Dragoon, Ariz. 85609.

FUNMAKER, KENNETH, Sr.
(Wisconsin Winnebago)
(tribal chairman)

Affiliation: Chairman, Wisconsin Winnebago Business Council, P.O. Box 311, Tomah, Wis. 54660.

G

GAHBOW, ARTHUR (Chippewa)
(tribal chairman)

Affiliation: Chairman, Mille Lacs Reservation Business Committee, Star Route, Onamia, Minn. 56359.

GARCIA, ALEX (Pueblo)
(Pueblo governor)

Affiliation: Governor, Santo Domingo Pueblo, P.O. Box 99, Santo Domingo Pueblo, N.M. 87052.

GARCIA, MARCELINO (Tewa Pueblo)
1932-
(instructional aid worker)

Born June 2, 1932, San Juan Pueblo, N.M. *Education:* U.S. Indian School, Santa Fe, N.M. *Principal occupation:* Instructional aid worker, B.I.A. *Home address:* P.O. Box 854, San Juan Pueblo, N.M. *Community Activities:* San Juan Pueblo Church (chairman). *Awards, honors:* Prize for Indian ceremonial sash belt, New Mexico State Fair.

GARCIA, NORMA JEAN
(Indian council chairmwoman)

Affiliation: Chairwoman, Alturas General Council, P.O. Box 1035, Alturas, Calif. 96101.

GARREAUX, HAZEL (Cheyenne River Sioux) 1916-
(tribal official)

Born June 23, 1916, LaPlant, S.D. *Education:* Normal Training School; commercial diploma, Haskell Institute, 1940. *Principal occupation:* Tribal official. *Home address:* Box 44, Eagle Butte, S.D. 57625. *Affiliation:* Secretary, Cheyenne River Sioux Tribal Council, Eagle Butte, S.D., 1946-1949, 1959-.

GARROW, LEONARD (Mohawk)
(tribal chief)

Affiliation: Head chief, St. Regis Mohawk Council, St. Regis Reservation, Hogansburg, N.Y. 13655.

GASHLER, DAN
(public affairs-Indian Health Service)

Affiliation: Public affairs officer, Indain Health Service, 5600 Fishers Lane, Rockville, Md. 20857.

GENTIS, THIERRY 1958-
(assistant curator)

Born March 3, 1958, Bordeaux, France. *Education:* Roger Williams College, Bristol, R.I., B.A., 1981. *Principal occupation:* Assistant curator. *Home address:* Mount Hope Grant, Bristol, R.I. 02809. *Affiliation:* Assistant curator, Haffenreffer Museum of Anthropology, Brown University, Providence, R.I., 1983-. *Awards, honors:* Magna Cum Laude, Roger Williams College, 1981. *Interests:* African ethnographic art; arctic ethnographic arts and culture; familiar with textile and basketry arts; North American Indian ethnography; Oceanic ethnography; Andean culture. *Published work: Traditional Art of Africa* (Haffenreffer Museum of Anthropology), 1984.

GENTRY, BEATRICE (Wampanoag)
1910-
(teacher)

Born August 31, 1910, Gay Head, Mass.

Education: Framingham State College, Mass., B.S. (Education), 1932; Bureau of Indian Affairs Summer Institute, Pine Ridge, S.D., summer, 1935; Tulsa University, Teacher Certificate, 1962; Bridgewater State College, Hyannis, Mass., 1967-1968. *Principal occupation:* Teacher. *Home address:* State Road, R.F.D. #159, Gay Head, Mass. 02535. *Affiliations:* Teacher, Fort Sill Indian School, Lawton, Okla., 1934-1941; teacher, Wagoner Elementary School, Okla., 1960-1964; teacher, Chilmark Elementary School, Mass., 1964-1974. *Other professional posts:* President, Wampanoag Tribal Council of Gay Head, 1972-1976 (helped establish modern organizational structure of tribal government, first governing officer); member, Massachusetts Commission on Indian Affairs, 1974-1976 (helped establish and organize the first Massachusetts Indian Commission in the 20th century, and whose membership was all Native Americans of Massachusetts) *Community activities:* Town of Gay Head (zoning committee; Gay head Public Library (trustee); Gay Head Community Council (charter member); Wagoner School Band (president); Officers' Wives' Club (member, 1943-1958; secretary, 1947-1948; Griffith Air Force Base, Rome, N.Y.). *Memberships:* Oklahoma Education Association, 1934-1942, 1961-1964; Massachusetts Teachers Association, 1964-1975; National Indian Education Association, 1972-1975; National Retired Teachers' Association, 1975-. *Awards, honors:* Alumni Achievement Award, 1982, from Framingham State College Alumni Association at 50th anniversary of graduating class; Ancient Aquinnah (Gay Head) Indian Cemetary on behalf of the Wampanoag Tribal Council of Gay Head; speaker at dedication ceremonies of Gay Head Cliffs as National Landmark, centennial celebration of Town of Gay Head, Oklahoma Education Association Conference, and J.F. Kennedy Bicentennial Memorial Dinner, Natick Democratic Town Committee. *Interests:* "As an Air Force officer's wife, I have had the opportunity to live and travel to all parts of the continental U.S. and Europe. As a Native American educator with experience providing direct services to Native American children from different tribes, and experience working within the public school system in

different parts of the country, I have learned that the only way for Native American people to determine their own destiny economically and politically among the dominant white society is to make the necessary demands upon the educational system of Indians and non-Indians alike: to provide an avenue to attain the goals that each society deems essential and demand respect for those values and cultures. The educational system's complete disregard and disrespect for Native American values and culture along with lack of Native American input in education programs, communication, counselling and advisement, and lack of role models result in not only inadequate preparation for college, but inadequate for life. I feel it is only through those demands on the educational system for all Americans (including Native Americans) that Native American people will be able to realize our basic needs: the preservation of our lands, the preservation of our religion, culture, and history, and the preservation of our families; that is the sacred rights of our people."

GEORGE, EVANS McCLURE, Jr. Catawba) 1932-
(textile worker)

Born January 26, 1932, Rock Hill, S.C. *Education:* Clemson University, 1952-1956. *Principal occupation:* Textile worker. *Home address:* 1119 McDow Dr., Rock Hill, S.C. 29730. *Affiliation:* Celanese Corporation, Celriver Plant, Rock Hill, S.C., 1958-. *Community activities:* Member, Rock Hill Parks & Recreation Commission; member, Catawba Indian Tribe; York County IPTAY Club (past president); Church Youth leader, 1968-. *Awards, honors:* Captain of 1950 South Carolina Shrine Bowl team; Clemson University Footbal team (captain, 1955); drafted by Washington Redskins, 1955; outstanding volunteer, American Cancer Society. *Interests:* Lifelong vocational interest in the American textile industry; coaching football; carpentry; fishing. *Biographical source:* "Red Carolinian - Where Are They Now?" and "People of the River," Evening Herald articles.

**GEORGE, OSWALD C. (Coeur D'Alene)
1917-
    (tribal official)**

Born May 22, 1917, De Smet, Idaho. *Education:* Gonzaga University, 1936-1937. *Principal occupation:* Tribal official. *Home address:* Route 1, Plummer, Idaho 83851. *Affiliation:* Coeur D'Alene Tribal Council. *Military service:* U.S. Army Infantry, 1940-1945. *Community activities:* Boy Scouts of America (institutional representative); Veterans of Foreign Wars. *Memberships:* Affiliated Tribes of Northwest Indians (past president); National Congrss of American Indians (vice president, Portland area); Pacific Northwest Indian Center, Inc., Spokane, Wash. (board of trustees). *Interests:* "My interest lies in the youth of our nation; promoting citizenship, and training the future leaders of our country. I'm also very much interested in the preservation of our Indian culture and heritage; preservation of our treaty rights and the perpetual retention of our land base — these to me are sacred rights and should be respected."

**GERARD, PAT
    (executive director-Indian bank
    and foundation)**

Affiliations: Executive director, American Indian National Bank and American Indian Economic Development Foundation, 1700 K St., N.W., 2nd Floor, Washington, D.C. 20006.

**GIAGO, MILLIE
    (director-Indian center)**

Affiliation: Director, Native American Center, 2900 S. Harvey, Oklahoma City, Okla. 73109.

**GIAGO, ROBERT
    (director-Indian program)**

Affiliation: Director, American Indian Training and Employment Program, 2900 S. Harvey, Oklahoma City, Okla. 73109.

**GIBSON, CLAY (Mississippi Choctaw)
1927-
    (employment assistance program director)**

Born November 1, 1927, Leake County, Miss. *Education:* Clarke M. College, A.A., 1955; Mississippi College, B.A., 1957; Southwestern Baptist Theological Seminary, S.D., 1962; East Central Junior College. *Principal occupation:* Employment assistance program director. *Home address:* Route 7, Box 253, Philadelphia, Miss. 39350. *Affiliation:* Mississippi Band of Choctaw Indians, Philadelphia, Miss., 1967- . *Other professional posts:* Ordained Baptist Minister for thirty years; missionary tribal council member for two terms; tribal chairman, 1965-1967. *Community activities:* Community Development Club; church and religious activities. *Membership:* Baptist Association, 1945- (moderator, six years; clerk, five years). *Interests:* Ministry; business administration; social services; tribal programs, B.I.A.; travel.

**GIDDINGS, RUTH ELIZABETH
WARNER 1919-
    (anthropologist)**

Born June 17, 1919, Yonkers, N.Y. *Education:* University of Arizona, B.A., 1941, M.A., 1945. *Principal occupation:* Anthropologist. *Home address:* Mount Hope Grant, Bristol, R.I. 02809. *Affiliations:* Research assistant, museum assistant, University of Arizona, Arizona State Museum, 1941-1942; excavations on expeditions to Alaska, 1960, 1964-1967; curator, dirctor of public education, Brown Unviersity, Haffenreffer Museum of Anthropology, 1965-. *Memberships:* Amerian Anthropological Association (Fellow); Society for American Archeaology; American Association for the Advancement of Science; Arctic Institute of North America; Archaeological Institute of North America, 1969-1971; Bristol Historical Society. *Awards, honors:* Honorary M.A., Brown University; Sigma Xi. *Interests:* "Anthropological and archaeological study in Alaska; expeditions to Canada, Alaska, Mexico, and Denmark. Special interests — Eskimo and their pottery, origins, earliest men to people of the new world; Indians of the Americas; how to teach school children in a museum setting about non-literate peoples, by using the collections, experiential techniques, and role-playing participation in the lifeways of the cultures being studied." *Published works: Yaqui Folk Literature* (University of Arizona Press, 1942; revised 1967); *Yaqui Myths and Legends* (Univerity of Arizona Press, 1967).

GILL, JOSEPH C. 1926-
(educator)

Born July 15, 1926, Madison, Wis. *Education:* Marquette University, 1944-1946; St. Louis University, B.A., 1950, M.A., 1953, S.T.L., 1961; University of South Dakota, Ed.D., 1971. *Principal occupation:* Station manager of "Kini," a public service FM radio station serving the Rosebud Reservation, St. Francis, S.D. *Home address:* St. Francis Mission, S.D. 57572. *Affiliations:* Kini Radio Station; instructor (part-time), St. Francis Indian School.

GILLILAND, HAP 1918-
(professor of education and Native American culture)

Born August 26, 1918, Willard, Colo. *Education:* Western State College, Gunnison, Colo., B.A., 1949, M.A., 1950; University of Northern Colorado, Greeley, Ed.D., 1958. *Principal occupation:* Professor of eucation and Native Americn culture. *Home address:* 517 Rimrock Rd., Billings, Mont. 59102. *Affiliations:* Director, Northern Cheyenne Campus Experience Project, 1965; director, Crow Indian Reservation Educational Survey, 1966-1967; director, Remedial Reading, Northern Cheyenne Reservation, 1965-1968; director, Indian Upward Bound Project, 1966-1969; director, EPDA and NDEA in Remedial Reading for Indian students, 1967, 1969-1970; reading specialist, Lake Penn Schools, Alaska (14 Indian and Eskimo villages), Fall 1980, 1981, 1983; professor of education and Native American culture, Eastern Montana College, Billings, 1960-. *Community activities:* Chairman, Northern Cheyenne Tribal Scholarship Committee, 1966-1969; Northern Cheyenne Education Planning Committee, 1965-1972;

Indian Education Committee, Eastern Montana College, 1967-1977. *Memberships:* Montana Council for Indian Education (president, 1976-); Committee on Native Americans and Reading, International Reading Association (chairman, 1979-1980); National Indian Edcution Committee; Association on American Indian Affairs, 1965-. *Interests:* "Three extended trips to South America to live with newly contacted Indian tribes; two trips to New Zealand to conduct teacher training for teachers of Maori students." *Published works: Practical Guide to Remedial Reading* (Chas. E. Merrill Publishing, 1974, 1978); *Chant of the Red Man* (Council for Indian Education, 1976); ten children's books books in 1976 for Council for Indian Education.

GIPP, GERALD
(superintendent-Indian college)

Affiliation: Superintendent, Haskell Indian Junior College, Bureau of Indian Affairs, Lawrence, Kan. 66044.

GIPP, WILLIAM C. (Standing Rock Sioux) 1940-
(B.I.A. agency superintendent)

Born November 11, 1940, Fort Yates, N.D. (Standing Rock Reservation). *Education:* Black Hills State College, Spearfish, S.D., B.S., 1968; South Dakota State University, Brookings, M.A., 1973. *Home address:* Box 408, Rosebud, S.D. 57570. *Affiliation:* Superintendent, Rosebud Sioux Agency, Rosebud, S.D., 1984-. *Other professionsal posts:* Board of directors, Boy Scouts of America, Minnesota. *Military service:* U.S. Army, 1963-1967 (Sergeant E-5, Special Forces, Vietnam Vet). *Memberships:* American Legion; Veterans of Foreign Wars; National Congress of American Indians; South Dakota Teachers Association.

GLAZER, SUZY
(editor)

Affiliation: Editor, *Indian Truth,* Indian Rights Association, 1505 Race St., Philadelphia, Pa. 19102.

GLUBOK, SHIRLEY
(writer, lecturer)

Born in St. Louis, Mo. *Education:* Washington University, B.A. (Art and Archaeology); Columbia University, M.A. (Childhood Education). *Principal occupation:* Writer, lecturer. *Affiliation:* Lecturer on art for children, Metropolitan Museum of Art, New York, N.Y., 1958-. *Memberships:* American Archaeological Society; American Association of Museums; Authors League of America. *Published works: The Art of the North American Indian* (Harper and Row, 1964); *The Art of the Eskimo* (Harper and Row, 1964); *The Fall of the Aztecs* (St. Martin's Press, 1965); among others.

GOFF, DAVID J. 1925-
(historical society director)

Born May 3, 1925, Canastoga, N.Y. *Principal occupation:* Historical society director. *Home address:* 6464 Burleson Rd., Oneida, N.Y. 13421. *Affiliation:* Director, Madison County Historical Society, Oneida, N.Y. *Other professional post:* Traditional crafts consultant, New York State Council on the Arts. *Memberships:* New York State Historical Society; American Association for State and Local History. *Awards, honors:* Adopted Blood Brother, Oneida Nation; Certificate of Commendation, American Association for State and Local History. *Interests:* "Traditional crafts of the Oneida Indians; Oneida language, customs, and history; traditional pioneer New York State crafts; conservation; education - taking history from the museum to the school."

GOGOL, JOHN M. 1938-
(university professor, publisher)

Born August 15, 1938, Westfield, Mass. *Education:* Clark University, B.A., 1960; University of Washington, M.A., 1965, ABD Doctoral Candidacy, 1969. *Principal occupation:* University professor, publisher. *Home address:* P.O. Box 66124, Portland, Oreg. 97266. *Affiliations:* Instructor, Colorado State University, 1965-1968; assistant professor of humanities, Pacific University, Forest Grove, Oreg., 1970-1974; publisher,

Mr. Cogito Press, Pacific University, 1973-; publisher, *American Indian Basketry and Other Native Arts,* 1979-; director, Institute for the Study of Traditional American Indian Arts, 1979-. *Memberships:* Oregon Archaeological Society; Oregon Historical Society; Central States Archaeological Society; Coordinating Council of Literary Magazines; COSMEP. *Awards, honors:* Graves Prize Award in the Humanities, 1971. *Interests:* "In a long teaching career (I) taught German, Russian, comparative literature, American Indian studies, American history, European history, mathematics, physics, and humanities; poet and translator of German, Russian and Polish poetry." *Biographical sources:* "Poetic Justice," by Walt Curtis (*Willamette Week,* Oct.-Nov., 1985); "Basketry and Reservation of Culture," by Paul Pintarich (*Northwest Magazine, The Oregonian,* June, 1983); among others. *Published works: Native American Words* (Tahmahnawi's Publishers, 1973); *Columbus Names the Flowers* (Mr. Cogito Press, 1984); articles and other publications in numerous periodicals.

GOLLNICK, WILLIAM
(school administrator)

Affiliation: Administrator, Oneida Tribal School, Box 365, c/o Oneida Tribe, Oneida, Wis. 54155-0365

GOODBEAR, PEARL ROSE GOODSON (Choctaw) 1915-
(teacher, education specialist)

Born November 30, 1915, Tuskahoma, Okla. *Education:* University of New Mexico, 1936-1938; Southeastern State College, B.S., 1939; Southwestern State College, M.T., 1961; Oklahoma State University, graduate assistant in English, 1971-1972; Bureau of Indian Affairs, workshops (education, alcoholism, administration; attended summer courses at the following schools: University of Mexico, Spanish, 1941; U.C.L.A., elementary work, 1954; University of Arizona, management supervision, 1964, 1966, 1970; University of Brockport, N.Y., English, 1968. *Principal occupation:* Teacher, education specialist.

Home address: Route 2, Box 142, Stillwater, Okla. 74074. *Affiliations:* Teacher, Albuquerque Indian School, 1939-1940; teacher, Standing Rock Day School, Crownpoint, N.M., 1941-1942; head teacher, Crownpoint Boarding School, 1942; teacher, supervisor of dorms, Thoreau Boarding School, N.M., 1953, 1957-1958; teacher, Special Navajo Program, Chemawa Indian School, Oreg., 1955-1957; education specialist, Crownpoint, N.M., 1958-1961; department head, Chilocco Indian School, Okla., 1961-1970; graduate assistant, Department of English, Oklahoma State University, 1971-1972; administrator, Indian Recovery (alcoholism program), North Central Oklahoma Intertribal Helth Council, Pawnee, Okla., 1972-1974; director, Native American Alcoholism Program (formerly Indian Recovery), 1974-1977. *Military service:* U.S. Navy (WAVES), 1944-1945. *Awards, honors:* Husband was Paul Flying Eagle Goodbear, Cheyenne artist, deceased, 1954.

GOODMAN, LINDA J.
(professor)

Born in Denver, Colo. *Education:* University of Colorado, Boulder, B.A., 1966; Wesleyan University, Middleton, Conn., M.A., 1968; Washington State University, Pullman, Ph.D., 1978. *Principal occupation:* Professor. *Home address:* 4135 Dover St., Wheat Ridge, Colo. 80033. *Affiliation:* Assistant professor, Department of Music, Colorado College, Colorado Springs, Colo., 1979-. *Other professional posts:* Advisor of Native American students at Colorado College; director of tribes program for pre-college Native American students. *Community activities:* Talks on Native American music and culture to various museum groups, tour groups, and Native American groups; have organizaed various Native American music and dance performances for non-Indian audiences; consultant for Native American music education programs, District II public schools, Colorado Springs, Colo.; member, Colorado Springs Native Americans Women's Association; organized Native American symposia, art shows, and guest speakers at Colorado College. *Memberships:* American Anthropological Association, 1975-; American Folklore Society, 1975-; American Eth-

nological Society, 1975-; Society for Ethnomusicology, 1975-; Native American Women's Association, Colorado College, 1977-. *Awards, honors:* American Philosophical Society grant, 1967, to work on Pueblo Indian music; 1979 Humanities Division Research Grant from Colorado College, to work on life history of Makah Indian singer; 1980 Mellon Grant, to work on Southwest Indian music, to teach as a new course; 1983 American Council of Learned Societies Fellowship for work on life history of a Northwest Coast musician. *Interests:* "Native American music and culture, especially Northwest Coast and American Southwest. (I) have spent much time traveling and living on reservations in both areas, studying music and culture, attending ceremonies, learning from the people in those areas. Have lead many field trips of college students to various reservations in the Southwest so that they could see and talk to the people living there and learn from them first-hand. Have lead a tour group of older people to the Makah Reservation for the same purpose. I am writing books and articles on Native American music and culture. I am very interested in teaching, counseling, and advising Native American young people, helping them find a way to fit into two worlds. Have worked with a number of Native American students over the years, and I'm interested in Indian singing and dancing, and participate on the few occasions when it is appropriate." *Published works: Music and Dance in Northwest Coast Indian Life* (Navajo Community College Press, 1977); "A Makah Biography," in *Dalmoma: Digging for Roots* (Empty Bowl Press, 1985); "Nootka Indian Music," in *New Grove Dictionary of Music in the U.S.* (Macmillan, 1986).

GORANSON, FREDERICK ARNOLD
1926-
(educator)

Born January 11, 1926, Waltham, Mass. *Education:* University of Wyoming, B.S., 1951; University of Oregon, M.S., 1958. *Principal occupation:* Educator. *Home address:* RFD Poudre Canyon Route, Bellevue, Colo. 80512. *Affiliations:* Head the now well known 'Navajo Gourd Rattle Dance' for the Youth Group, Navajo Club of Los Angeles in 1962, adapted to Hopi version of Navajo Yei-bi-chei song of 1917. Hope to put photos, Navajo historical and cultural material I've gathered into book form."

GORMAN, CLARENCE N. (Navajo) 1931-
(monument superintendent)

Born May 28, 1931, Chinle, Ariz. *Education:* Northern Arizona University. *Principal occupation:* Monument superintendent. *Address:* Aztec National Monument, Route 1, Box U, Aztec, N.M. 87410. *Affiliations:* Maintenance foreman, park ranger, Canyon de Chelly National Monument, Chinle, Ariz.; park ranger, Mesa Verde National Park, Colo.; park ranger, White Sands National Monument, Alamagordo, N.M.; superintendent, Wupatki-Sunset Crater National Monument, Flagstaff, Ariz.; superintendent, Pipestone National Monument, Pipestone, Minn.; superintendent, Aztec National Monument, Aztec, N.M. *Other professional posts:* Navajo Tribal Ranger, 1958; teacher, Bureau of Indian Affairs, 1959. *Military service:* U.S. Marine Corps, 1951-1954 (Good Conduct Medal, U.S. Service Medal, National Defense Medal, Presidential Unit Citation, Korean Presidential Unit Citation, Korean Service Medal with three Battle Stars). *Memberships:* National Riflemen's Association; Southwest Parks and Monuments Association, Inc.; Parks & Recreation Association; Pipestone Shrine Association.

GORMAN, FREDERICK JOHN ELIOT 1943-
(professor)

Born August 16, 1943, Maine. *Education:* Northeastern University, B.A., 1966; University of Arizona, M.A., 1972, Ph.D., 1976. *Principal occupation:* Professor of anthropology and archaeology of prehistoric American Indians. *Home address:* 189 Bay State Rd., Boston, Mass. 02215. *Affiliation:* Assistant professor and professor of anthropology, Department of Anthropology, Boston University, Boston, Mass., 1974-. *Other*

professional posts: Director, Boston University Archaeological Field School. *Memberships:* Sigma Xi, 972-; American Anthropological Association, 1974-; Society for American Archaeology, 1974-; Society of Professional Archaeologists, 1976-; Society for Historical Archaeology, 1976-; Society for the Preservation of New England Antiquities, 1975-. *Awards, honors:* National Science Foundation Research Grants awarded to the Southwest Archaeological Expedition, Field Museum of Natural History, 1970-1972; National Park Service, Dept. of the Interior Grants fpr archaeological site development of the New England glass works, 1975-1978. *Interests:* Southwest Archaeological Field Expeditions; early American Indian hunters; rise and fall of ancient American Civilizations; prehistory of Southwestern Indians; Mohave Indian Tribe. *Biographical sources: Who's Who in the West; Dictionary of International Biography; The Archaeologist's Yearbook,* 1975; *Who's Who in the U.S.,* 1975; *American Men of Achievement* (3rd Edition). *Published works:* Numerous articles in journals.

GORMAN, R.C. (Navajo) 1934-
(artist)

Born July 26, 1934, Chinle, Ariz. *Education:* Northern Arizona University; Mexico City College. *Principal occupation:* Artist. *Address:* Navajo Gallery, P.O. Box 1756, Taos, N.M. 87571. Military service: U.S. Navy, 1952-1956. *Memberships:* Pacific Northwest Indian Center, Gonzaga University (board member); Wheelwright Museum, Santa Fe, N.M. (board member); Kellogg Fellowship Screening Committee, Navajo Health Authority, Window Rock, Ariz. (Fellow); Four Corner State Art Conference; New Mexico Arts and Crafts Fair (standards committee, juror). *Exhibitions:* Mr. Gorman's work has appeared in numerous one-man and group shows and is part of public and private collections. *Awards, honors:* Numerous awards and prizes for art from the following exhibitions and shows: All American Indian Days Art Exhibition; American Indian Artists Exhibitions; Center for Arts for Indian America; Heard Museum; National Cowboy Hall of Fame;

teacher, Alaskam Territorial Schools, 1954-1960; adult, elementary, secondary education, and Job Corps, Bureau of Indian Affairs, in Alaska, Navajo, Mescalero Apache, and Cheyenne River Sioux Reservations, 1960-. *Military service:* U.S. Army, 1943-1945 (Europe with 66th Infantry Division). *Interests:* Community schools; continuing education for adults; the role of the federal government in local education.

GORDON, PATRICIA TRUDELL
(Santee Sioux-Mdewakantonwan Band) 1943-
(director, Indian organization)

Born August 24, 1943, Woodbury County, Iowa. *Education:* Morningside College, B.A., 1977. *Principal Occupation:* Executive Director, Indian Youth of America, Inc. *Home Address:* 2600 South Steele, Sioux City, Iowa 51106. *Affiliations:* Camp Director, Indian Youth Camps in Oregon, Arizona, Idaho, and South Dakota, summer of 1976-; Executive Director, Indian Youth of America, Sioux City, Iowa 51106, 1978-. *Other Professional Posts:* Assistant director/counselor, Indian Studies Program, Morningside College, 1977-1984. *Community Activities:* Iowa Supreme Court Commission on Continuing Legal Education (commissioner); Sioux City Human Rights Commission (chairperson); United Way of Siouxland Agency Relations Committee (member); Native American Child Care Center (panel chair, board of directors). *Awards, Honors:* Sertoma Service to Mankind Award, 1983; participant for the Community International Fellows, a program of the International Leadership Development Institute; Robert F. Kennedy Memorial Fellow. *Interests:* "My main concern and interest at this time is working with Indian young people and improving there lives. I am also very interested in the law especially pertaining to American Indians. Women's issues will always be one of my concerns. My work has taken me throughout the U.S. giving lectures and presentations. I have very little time for hobbies, however, I make time for racquetball, bicycling and reading."

GORMAN, CARL NELSON *(Kin-ya-onny beyeh)* **(Navajo) 1907-**
(artist, lecturer)

Born October 5, 1907, Chinle, Ariz. *Education:* Otis Art Institute, Los Angeles, Calif., Graduate, 1951, extension courses, 1952, 1953. *Principal occupation:* Artist, lecturer—Navajo culture. *Address:* P.O. Box 431, Window Rock, Ariz. 86515., or c/o Navajo Gallery, P.O. Box 1756, Taos, N.M. 87571. *Affiliations:* Illustrator and technical illustrator, Douglas Aircraft Co., Santa Monica, Lawndale, Torrance, Calif., 1951-1963; manager, Navajo Arts & Crafts Guild, 1964-1966; director, Navajo Culture Center, ONEO, Fort Defiance, Ariz., 1966-1969; lecturer, Navajo history and culture, and American Indian art in cultural perspective with workshop, and Navajo language, Native American studies, applied behavioral sciences, University of California, Davis, 1970-1973, retired; director, Office of Native Healing Sciences, Navajo Health Authority, Window Rock, Ariz., 1973-1976, retired; coordinator, Navajo Resources/Curriculum Development, Navajo Community College, Tsaile, Ariz., 1977-. *Other professional posts:* Kin-ya-onny beyeh Originals, professional arts and crafts, 1951-; lecturer-consultant, Navajo arts, history, culture, 1964-. *Military service:* U.S. Marine Corps, 1942-1945, "with group that developed Navajo Code." *Community activities:* Inter-Tribal Indian Ceremonial (executive committee, 1964-1965); Navajo Tribal Fair (arts and crafts exhibit chairman, 1964-1965; evening performance chairman, 1968); Navajoland Festival of the Arts (board member, 1976-). *Memberships:* Navajo Club of Los Angeles (board of directors, several offices, 1955-1964); Otis Art Institute Alumni Association, 1952-; 2nd Marine Division Association; Veterans of Foreign Wars (life member); Navajo Code Talkers Association; Kiwanis, 1978. *Exhibitions:* Mr. Gorman's work has appeared in numerous one-man and group shows and is part of public and private collections. *Interests:* "All phases of art, subjects chiefly Navajo, horses, rock art, but including non-Indian subjects, in a variety of styles and media. Interested in improving quality, expanding markets, and promoting new and adaptive Navajo arts and crafts. In dance, I originated

Philbrook Indian Art Exhibitions; Scottsdale National Indian Arts Exhibition. In the Fall of 1973, Mr. Gorman was the only living artist to be included in the show, "Masterworks of the Museum of the American Indian," held at the Metropolitan Museum in New York City. Two of his drawings were selected for the cover of the show's catalog. In 1975, he was honored by being the first artist chosen for a series of one-man exhibitions of contemporary Indian artists held at the Museum of the American Indian. *Interests:* Mexican art and artists; lithography; cave painting and petroglyphs. *Biographical sources: A Taos Mosaic* (University of New Mexico Press); *American Indian Painter; Arrow III* (Pacific Grove Press); *Art and Indian Individuals* (Northland Press); *Dictionary of International Biography; Indian Painter and White Patrons,* J.J. Brody; *Indians of Today; Masterworks from the Museum of the American Indian* (Metropolitan Museum of Art); *Register of U.S. Living Artists; Who's Who in America; Who's Who in the West; Who's Who in American Art. Published works:* Mr. Gorman's works appear in the following books: *American Indian Painters* (Museum of the American Indian); *Great American Deserts* (National Geographic Society, 1972); *Southwest Indian Painting* (University of Arizona Press, 1973); *The Man Who Sent the Rain Clouds* (Viking Pres, 1974); *Gorman Goes Gourmet; The Lithographs of R.C. Gorman* (Northland Press); *Graphics: A Self Portrait of America.*

GOSS, JAMES ARTHUR 1934-
(professor of anthropology)

Born September 14, 1934, Marion County, Ohio. *Education:* University of Oregon, B.A., 1960; University of Chicago, M.A., 1962, Ph.D., 1972. *Principal occupation:* Professor of anthropology. *Address:* Department of Anthropology, Washington State University, Pullman, Wash. 99163. *Affiliations:* Visiting lecturer in anthropology and linguistics, University of California, Los Angeles, 1964-1966; assistant-associate professor of anthropology, Washington State University, 1966-. *Other professional posts:* Co-editor, *Northwest Anthropologi-*

cal Research Notes, 1967-1970. *Military service:* U.S. Air Force, 1954. *Community activities:* Consultant on problems of Nez Perce children learning English, Nez Perce Headstart Program. *Memberships:* American Anthropological Association; Linguistic Society of America; Society for American Archaeology; Society of Sigma Xi; Northwest Anthropological Conference; Great Basin Anthropological Conference; International Salish Conference. *Awards, honors:* NDEA Title IV Fellowship in Anthropology, University of Chicago, 1960-1963; research assistantship and linguistic research grant, Tri-Ethnic Project, University of Colorado, 1961, 1962; Department of the Interior, National Geographic Society Research Grant, Wetherill Mesa Verde National Park, Colo., 1961-1963; UCLA Academic Senate Grant for *A Pilot Demographic Study of the American Indian Community of the Greater Los Angeles Area,* 1965; WSU Grant-in-Aid for *A Survey of Interior Salish Languages,* 1967; consultant grant, Nez Perce Headstart Program, 1971; NEH Postdoctoral Fellowship in American Indian Studies, Indiana University, 1972-1973. *Interests:* Linguistic anthropology; ethnosemantics; culture-historical reconstruction. *Published works:* Various technical articles in professional journals.

GRANT, MORRIS (Sauk-Suiattle)
(tribal business manager)

Affiliation: Business manager, Sauk-Suiattle Tribal Council, 5318 Chief Brown Lane, Darrington, Wash. 98241.

GRAY, GERALD J.
(Indian school principal)

Affiliation: Principal, Chemawa Indian School, 3700 Chemawa Rd., NE, Salem, Ore. 97303.

GRAY, SHORTY "LITTLE SCOUT" (United Lumbee-Cherokee) 1934-
(log scaler)

Born November 2, 1934, Los Angeles, Calif. *Education:* Modesto City Schools, Calif. *Principal occupation:* Log scaler. *Home* address: Star Route, McArthur, Calif. 96056. *Affiliation:* United Lumbee Nation of N.C. and the America's (Deer Clan chief). *Community activities:* Inter Mountain Horseman's Association (vice president, 1984; president, 1985). *Memberships:* United Lumbee Nation (vice-chief, 1984; chief, 1985-); United Lumbee Nation Mantoca Medicine Society; High Eagle Warrior Society (vice-chief, 1985-). *Awards, honors:* California State Horseman's Association (Region 18 High Point Champion Gymkhana Rider, 1983 and 1984; 1983 and 1985 High Point Rider, Inter Mountain Horseman's Association. *Interests:* "Traditional skills: hunting, fishing, scouting; fur training, bow hunting, horse-raising; shelter building, survival living."

GRAYSON, NOLEY (Choctaw) 1943-
(professor, educational administrator)

Born September 4, 1943, Talihina, Okla. *Education:* Southeastern Oklahoma State University, Durant, B.A., 1969; The Pennsylvania State University, M.Ed., 1975, Ph.D., 1979. *Home address:* 1443 N. Allen St., State College, Penn. 16803. *Affiliation:* Assistant professor, educational administration, director of American Indian Leadership Program, The Pennsylvania State University, University Park, Pa. 16802. *Military service:* U.S. Army, 1961-1964. *Memberships:* National Indian Education Association; Amerian Educational Research Association; Phi Delta Kappa. *Awards, honors:* Kellogg Fellowship, 1984-1987, W.W. Kellogg Foundation; Graduate Fellowship, American Indian Leadership Program, 1974.

GREEN, ELWOOD
(museum curator)

Affiliation: Curator, Native American Centre for the Living Arts, Inc., 25 Rainbow Mall, Niagara Falls, N.Y. 14303.

GREEN, RAYNA (Cherokee) 1942-
(program developer)

Born July 18, 1942, Dallas, Tex. *Education:* Southern Methodist University, Dallas, B.A., 1963, M.A., 1966; Indiana University,

Bloomington, Ph.D. (Folklore, American Studies), 1974. *Principal occupation:* Program developer. *Home address:* 1369 F St., N.E., Washington, D.C. 20002. *Affiliations:* Program director, American Association for the Advancement of Science, 1975-1980; program director, Dartmouth College, Hanover, N.H., 1980-1983; planner, Smithsonian Institution, 1983-. *Other professional posts:* Visiting professor, University of Massachusetts, and Yale University; consultant to numerous federal agencies, tribes, tribal/Indian organizations, institutions, museums, and universities. *Community activities:* Ms. Foundation for Women (board member); Indian Law Resource Center, Fund for the Improvement of Post-Secondary Education (board member); Phelps-Stokes Fund (Indian advisory board). *Memberships:* American Folklore Society (president); American Engineering Society; Society for the Advancement of Native Americans and Chicano Scientists; Amerian Anthropological Association. *Awards, honors:* Smithsonian Fellow, 1970; Ford Foundation, National Research Council Fellow, 1983. *Interests:* Ameriacn folklorist; research on Native American women; Southern women; American material culture; Indian traditional science, technology, and medicine; Indian energy/minerals development; poetry/short fiction; film/TV script writing; exhibit production. *Published works: Native American Women: A Contextual Bibliography* (Indiana University Press, 1982); *That's What She Said: Contemporary Poetry and Fiction by Native American Women* (Indiana University Press, 1984); Introduction to Pissing in the Snow: Other Ozark Folktales; Handicrafts in the Southern Highlands; articles and essays in *Ms. Magazine, Southern Exposure, Science, Handbook of American Folklore, Handbook of North American Indians,* and *Signs.*

GREGORY, JACK DWAIN (Cherokee) 1930-
(professor, writer)

Born June 25, 1930, Muskogee, Okla. *Education:* University of Oklahoma, 1951-1952; Northeastern State University, Tahlequah, Okla., B.A., 1951, M.A., 1953; Arizona State University, doctoral work, 1971-1972.

Principal occupation: Professor, writer. *Affiliations:* Teacher, Muskogee Public Schools, Okla., 1953-1963; professor, University of Arkansas, 1964-1968; professor, University of West Florida, 1969-? *Other professional posts:* Director, forensics workshop, University of Arkansas, 1965-1968; director of forensics, University of West Florida. *Awards, honors:* Youth Work Awards, Elks, American Legion, Toastmasters; Chief's Sash Creek Tribal Award, Interfraternity Council Award. *Interests:* Speech communication and debate; forensics; frontier history; Indian history; Five Civilized Tribes; Indian mythology and folklore; archaeology and ethnohistory; oral communication history of tribes; Cherokee-Mexican Sequoyah Expedition; Indian herbs, cures, medicine men and witch doctors. *Published works: Sam Houston With the Cherokees* (University of Texas, 1965); *Cherokee Spirit Tales* (Indian Heritage, 1969); *Creek-Seminole Spirit Tales* (Indian Heritage, 1970); *Hell on the Border* (Indian Heritage, 1971); *Choctaw Spirit Tales* (Indian Heritage, 1972).

GRIFFITH, GLADYS GIBSON 1925-
(artist)

Born March 15, 1925, Piqua, Ohio. *Education:* High School. *Principal occupation:* Artist. *Home address:* 263 E. Main St., Piqua, Ohio 45356. *Other professional post:* Lecturer on Indian affairs. *Memberships:* Museum of Natural History, 1970-; Ohio Archaeological Society, 1970-; Miami County Historical Society, 1970-; Miami County Archaeological Society; Archaeological Society of Ohio (secretary-treasurer, Miami River Valley Chapter). *Awards, honors:* Ms. Griffith's work is displayed at the Indian Museum, Salamanca, N.Y.: Indian Museum, Oberlin, Kan.;; the Satte House, Boston, Mass.; Pacific Northwest Indian Center, Gonzaga University, Spokane, Wash. *Biographical source: Who's Who in the Arts.*

GRINDE, DONALD ANDREW, Jr.
(Yamasee) 1946-
(professor)

Born August 23, 1946, Savannah, Ga. *Edu-*
cation: Georgia Southern College, Statesboro, B.A. (History), 1966; University of Delaware, M.A. (History), 1968, Ph.D. (History), 1974. *Principal occupation:* Professor. *Home address:* 1274 Reba St., San Luis Obispo, Calif. 93401. *Affiliations:* Assistant professor, Mercyhurst College, Erie, Pa., 1971-1973; assistant professor, SUNY, College at Buffalo, 1973-1977; associate professor, California Polytechnic State University, San Luis Obispo, 1977-1978; visiting associate professor, UCLA, 1978-1979; associate professor, California Polytechnic State University, 1979-1981; director, Native American Studies, University of Utah, Salt Lake City, 1981-1984; associate professor of history, California Polytechnic State University, 1984-. *Other professional posts:* Instructor in Native American history, United Southeastern Tribes, Inc., and SUNY, College at Buffalo, Program for Indian Teacher Education at Allegany and Cattaraugus (Seneca) Reservations, 1974-1975; Native American consultant, Buffalo City Schools, 1974-1975; consultant, Smithsonian Institution, 1977; Native American Consultant, Salt Lake City Schools, 1982-1983; editor, *Journal of Erie Studies,* 1971-1973; editorial board, *Indian Historian,* 1976-. *Community activities:* Buffalo North American Indian Culture Center (corresponding secretary and board member, 1974-1977); American Indian Historical Society (board member, 1976-); Central Coast Indian Council, Calif. (vice chairman, 1979-1980); Salt Lake Indian Center (chairman of board, 1983-1984). *Memberships:* National Indian Education Association (member of Resolutions Committee, 1981-1983); American Indian Historian's Association (charter member); American Indian Historical Society; Phi Alpha Theta; Smithsonian Institution. *Awards, honors:* Hagley Fellow, University of Delaware, 1966-1970; Grant-in-Aid Scholar, Eleutherian Mills Historical Library, 1970-1971; project historian and conservation consultant, Southern Railroad Restoration Project, National Park Service; Faculty Seed Grant, UCLA, American Indian Studies Center, 1978-1979; Outstanding Professional Award (Education), 1984, from *Wasatch Regional Minority Business and Professional Directory* (Salt Lake City, Utah). *Interests:* American Indian history including: 20th century Indian policy,

Native American science, American Indian political theory, history of American technology, museum administration. *Biographical sources: Wasatch Regional Minority Business and Professional Directory* (Salt Lake City, Utah, 1984). *Published works:* Contributing editor, *Readings in American History: Bicentennial Edition, II (Guilford, Conn., Dushkin Publishing, 1975); The Iroquois and the Founding of the American Indian* (Indian Historian Press, 1977).

GROBSMITH, ELIZABETH S. 1946-
(professor of anthropology)

Born May 27, 1946, Brooklyn, N.Y. *Education:* Ohio State University, Bachelor of Music, 1967; University of Arizona, M.A. (Anthropology), 1970, Ph.D. (Anthropology), 1976. *Principal occupation:* Associate professor of anthropology. *Home address:* 1901 South 23rd St., Lincoln, Neb. 68502. *Affiliation:* Associate professor of anthropology, University of Nebraska, Lincoln, Neb., 1976-. *Other professional posts:* Consultant, Association on American Indian Affairs, 1984-1985; consultant, Indian Club, Nebraska State Penitentiary, and American Anthropological Association lecture series. *Memberships:* Plains Anthropological Society (board of directors, 1979-1981); Plains Anthropological Society (vice president, 1980-1981); American Anthropological Association; University of Nebraska Graduate Faculty; Sigma Delta Epsilon, Iota Chapter (Graduate Women's Scientific Fraternity). *Interests:* "My major professional interests are in studying and working with American Indian communities, with specific interests in helping them to design strategies and programs which alleviate reservation problems, be they juvenile justice concerns, alcoholism, curriculum development, legal or economic. When possible, I enjoy traveling to observe indigenous peoples to achieve a better understanding of native cultures (e.g. Alaska, Guatemala). *Published work: Lakota of the Rosebud, A Contemporary Ethnography* (Holt, Rinehart and Winston, 1981).

GRISPE, LARRY
(executive director-Indian center)

Affiliation: Executive director, American Indian Center of Dallas, Inc., 1314 Munger Blvd., Dallas, Tex. 75206.

GROSS, MIKE
(school administrator)

Affiliation: Administrator, Lac Courte Oreilles Ojibwa School, Route #2, Hayward, Wis. 54843.

GRUNDE, RICHARD (Chippewa)
(tribal chairman)

Affiliation: Chairman, Red Cliff Tribal Council, P.O. Box 529, Bayfield, Wis. 54814.

H

HABERLAND, WOLFGANG 1922-
(museum vice-director)

Born August 29, 1922, Hamburg, Germany. *Education:* University of Hamburg, Ph.D., 1951. *Principal occupation:* Chief, American Department and vice-director, Hamburgisches Museum fur Volkerkunde, Hamburg, Germany, 1955-. *Memberships:* Society for American Archaeology, 1955-; Royal Anthropological Institute of Great Britain and Ireland, 1952-; other. *Interests:* Archaeology of Central America; Amerindian art, especially of North America; four expeditions to Central America; travel. *Published work: American Indian Art* (Atlantis-Verlag/Zurich, 1971); many others.

HAIL, BARBARA A. 1931-
(museum director/curator)

Born November 2, 1931. *Education:* Brown University, 1948-1951; Cornell University, B.A., 1952, M.A., 1953. *Principal occupation:* Associate director/curator. *Home address:* 220 Rumstick Rd., Barrington, R.I. 02809. *Affiliations:* Associate director/curator, Haffenreffer Museum of Anthropology, Brown University, Providence, R.I., 1973-. *Other professional posts:* American and world history teacher, Ithaca High School, Ithaca, N.Y., and White Plains High School, White Plains, N.Y. *Memberships:* American Association of Museums (curator's committee); New England Museum Association; Association of College and University Museums and Galleries; Amerian Anthropological Association; Native American Art Studies Association. *Awards, honors:* Elisha Benjamin Andrews Scholar, Pembroke College; Phi Beta Kappa, Brown University, 1950; National Endowment of the Arts Fellowship for Museum Professionals, 1976, 1985. *Interests:* History, ethnohistory, ethnology; museology, stylistica and technical aspects of material culture of North America; Peru; Africa; Nepal; current research is in the art and material culture of the Subarctic. *Published work: Hau, Kola! The Plains Indian Collection of the Haffenreffer Museum of Anthropology* (Haffenreffer Museum of Anthropology, 1983).

HAIL, RAVEN (Oklahoma Cherokee) (lecturer, writer)

Born in Dewey, Okla. *Education:* Oklahoma State University; Southern Methodist University. *Principal occupation:* Lecturer, writer. *Home address:* 3061 Cridelle, Dallas, Texas 75220. Membership: North Texas Herb Club (president). *Interests:* Lecture and write on Cherokee Indian culture, particularly wild edible and medicinal plants; wrote 3-act play *The Raven and the Redbird* (Cherokee Life of Sam Houston and his Cherokee wife). *Published works:* Numerous articles in various publications.

HAIR, JOHN (Oklahoma Cherokee) (tribal chief)

Affiliation: Chief, United Keetoowah Cherokee Council, P.O. Box 1329, Tahlequah, Okla. 74465.

HAIRE, WENONAH GEORGE (Catawba) 1953- (dentist)

Born November 27, 1953, York County, Rock Hill, S.C. *Education:* Clemson University, S.C., B.S., 1976; Medical University of S.C., Charleston, D.MD, 1979. *Principal occupation:* Dentist. *Home address:* 191 Country Club Dr., Rock Hill, S.C. 29730. *Community activities:* Education committee, Career Development Center; chairman, Dental Health Month, 1985; Girl Scout Aid. *Memberships:* Tri County Dental Society, Rock Hill, S.C. (secretary, 1985); U.S. Public Health Service (Lieutenant, inactive reserve); Medical University Alumni Association; First Baptist Church. *Interests:* "Enjoys "travel" vacations (Mexico and U.S.); collects Indian jewelry, paintings and pottery; enjoys pottery making (Catawba traditional coil method); enjoys canning. Only female dentist in Rock Hill, S.C.; just had her first child." *Biographical source: Charlotte Observer* article entitled "Rock Hill Dentist Drills by Day, Fills by Night."

HAKKINEN, ELISABETH S. 1914- (museum curator)

Born January 11, 1914, Skagway, Alaska. *Education:* San Bernardino Junior College, 1930-1932; Western College, Oxford, Ohio, B.A., 1935. *Principal occupation:* Museum curator. *Home address:* Box 236, Haines, Alaska 99827. *Affiliation:* Museum curator, The Sheldon Museum and Culture Center, Haines, Alaska, 1960-. *Awards, honors:* Adopted Kag-wan-tan, Eagle Clan, Grizzly Bear House. *Biographical source: Who's Who of American Women.*

HALL, C.R. (CLIFF) 1933- (owner-Indian arts and crafts shop)

Born October 19, 1933, Las Vegas, N.M. *Education:* McMurry College, Abilene, Texas (four years). *Principal occupation:* Owner, Squash Blossom, 304 10th, Alamagordo, N.M., 1973-. *Military service:* U.S. Navy, 1955-1957. *Community activities:* Downtown Merchants Association (president). *Memberships:* Indian Arts and Crafts Association (charter member). *Interests:* "All Indian arts and crafts; extensive travels to all parts of Navaho, Zuni and Hopi Reservations; Hopi kachina dolls."

HAMMACK, LAURENS CARY 1936- (archaeologist)

Born July 11, 1936, Chicago, Ill. *Education:* University of New Mexico, B.A., 1959, M.A., 1964. *Principal occupation:* Archaeologist. *Affiliation:* Curator,

Research Division, Museum of New Mexico, Santa Fe, N.M., 1964-. *Military service:* U.S. Army, 1959-1961. *Membership:* Society for American Archaeology, 1964-. *Interests:* Southwest and northern Mexico archaeology and ethnology; collecting of antique guns and Southwest Indian materials; archaeological excavations throughout New Mexico. *Published work:* Archaeology of the Ute Dam and Reservoir (Museum of New Mexico, 1965).

HAMILTON, RUBY
(resource coordinator)

Affiliation: Resource coordinator, The Seventh Generation Fund, P.O. Box 10, Forestville, Calif. 95436

HAMP, ERIC P. 1920-
(professor of linguistics and behavioral science)

Born November 16, 1920, London, England. *Education:* Amherst College, B.A., 1942; Harvard University, M.A., 1948, Ph.D., 1954. *Principal occupation:* Professor of linguistics and behavioral science, University of Chicago, 1950-. *Military service:* U.S. Army, 1946-1947 (Sergeant). *Community service:* Illinois Place-Name Survey (chairman, 1966-); consultant U.S. Office of Education, NEH, NSF. *Memberships:* Council on International Exchange of Scholars (advisory committee, 1966-); UNESCO (U.S. National Commission, 1972-); American Philosophical Society (Phillips Fund Committee, 1977-); Linguistic Society of America (president, 1971). *Awards, honors:* Collitz Professor, 1960, Linguistic Society of America; hon. LHD, Amherst College, 1972; Guggenheim Fellow, 1973-1974; Fellow, American Academy of Arts and Sciences, 1976-; Robert Maynard Hutchins Distinguished Service Professor, University of Chicago; various guest professorships. *Interests:* Languages and cultures pf the American Indian, the Balkins, and the Celts; travel and fieldwork: Ojibwa, Cheyenne, Quileute, several Salishan, Eskimo, Otomanguean of Oazaca. *Biographical sources:* Who's Who in America; Who's Who in the World; Directory of American Scholars; Dictionary of International Biography;

American Men & Women of Science; Men of Achievement; The Blue Book. Published works: Associate editor, *International Journal of American Linguistics* (University of Chciago Press, 1966-); editor, *Native American Text Series* (University of Chicago Press, 1974-); author of publications on Ojibwa, Narragansett, Algonquian, Wiyot, Yurok, Quileute, Upper Chehalis, Comox, Kwakwala, Karok, Miwok, Zuni, Crow, Eskimo, etc.

HAMPTON, CAROL CUSSEN McDONALD (Caddo) 1935-
(historian)

Born September 18, 1935, Oklahoma City, Okla. *Education:* H. Sophie Newcomb College, New Orleans, La., 1953-1954; University of Oklahoma, B.A., 1957, M.A., 1973, Ph.D., 1984. *Principal occupation:* Historian. *Home address:* 1414 N. Hudson, Oklahoma City, Okla. 73103. *Affiliations:* Teaching assistant, University of Oklahoma, Norman, 1973-1984; associate director and coordinator, Consortium for Graduate Opportunities for American Indians, University of California, Berkeley. *Community activities:* Caddo Indian Tribe of Oklahoma (tribal council, 1976-); Caddo Tribal Constitution Committee, 1975-1976; Oklahoma City Area Indian Health Service (advisory board); Junior League of Oklahoma City, 1965-; National Committee on Indian Work, Episcopal Church (Co-chair, 1986-); World Council of Churches (commissioner, Program to Combat Racism, 1985); Oklahoma State Regents for Higher Education on Social Justice (member, advisory board, 1984-). *Memberships:* National Indian Education Association; National Historical Society; Oklahoma Historical Society; Western Historical Association; Organization of American Historians; American Historical Association. *Awards, honors:* Francis C. Allen Fellowship, D'Arcy McNickle Center for the History of the American Indian, Newberry Library, 1983. *Interests:* "My interests are in history, philosophy and religion of Ameriacn Indians as well as social and racial justice. *Biographical sources:* Who's Who Among American Women; Who's Who in the

World; etc. Published.work: "Indian Colonization in the Cherokee Outlet and Western Indian Territory" *(Chronicles of Oklahoma, 1976).*

HAMPTON, EBER (Chickasaw) 1942-
(director-neighborhood center)

Born August 13, 1942, Talihini, Okla. *Education:* Westmont College, Santa Barbara, Calif., B.A., 1964; University of California at Santa Barbara, A.B.D., 1968; Harvard Graduate School of Education, 1978-. *Principal occupation:* Director, the Neighborhood Center, Minneapolis, Minn., 1975-. *Home address:* Route 3, Box 167-A, Matawan, Minn. 56072. *Other professional post:* Assistant professor of psychology, Mankata State University, Mankato, Minn. *Membership:* National Indian Education Association. *Awards, honors:* Regents Fellow, 1964-1965; Bush Fellow, 1978-1979.

HAMPTON, JAMES MILBURN, M.D.
(Chickasaw-Choctaw) 1931-
(physician, professor)

Born September 15, 1931, Durant, Okla. *Education:* University of Oklahoma, B.A., 1952; University of Oklahoma, School of Medicine, M.D., 1956. *Principal occupation:* Physician, professor. *Home address:* 1414 N. Hudson, Oklahoma City, Okla. 73103. *Affiliations:* Director of Medical Oncology, Baptist Medical Center, Oklahoma City, Okla.; Clincial Professor of Medicine, University of Oklahoma Medical School, 1956-. *Other professional posts:* Professor and head, Hematology-Oncology, University of Oklahoma Medical School, 1971-1977; head hematology research, Oklahoma Medical Research Foundation, 1971-1977. *Community activities:* Oklahoma County Medical Society (community legal service, 1970, 1972; editorial committee, 1976-; planned parenthood committee, 1974-1975); Heritage Hills, Inc. (member, board of dirtors, 1973-); Central Oklahoma American Indian Health Council (member of board, 1974-1975); Faculty House

(member of board, 1974-1975); Frontiers of Science Foundation of Oklahoma, Inc. (member of board, 1974-). *Memberships:* American Association for the Advancement of Science; American Association for Cancer Research, Southwest Section; American Association of Pathologists and Bacteriologist; American Association of University Professors; American Federation for Clinical Research; American Genetic Association; Amerian Meical Association; American Physiological Society; American Psychosomatic Society; American Society for Clinical Pharmacology and Therapeutics; American Society for Clinical Oncology; American Society of Angiology; American Society of Hematology; Central Society for Clinical Research; International Society on Thrombosis and Haemostasis; New York Academy of Sciences; Oklahoma County Medical Society; Oklahoma State Medical Association; Sigma Xi; Southern Society for Clinical Investigation; Southwest Cancer Chemotherapy Study Group; Association of American Indian Physicians; National Hemophilia Foundation; National Institutes of Health; American Heart Association. *Consultations:* Consultant in Medicine, Tinker Air Force Basc Hospital, Oklahoma City, Okla., 1965-; consultant for National Institutes of Health, national Cancer Institute, 1973-1976; National Heart and Lung Institute, 1971-1976; consultant for Navajo Health Authority, 1974-1976; consultant for Regional Breast Cancer Detection and Treatment Center, 1974-. *Awards, honors:* NIH Career Development Award (Heart and Lung), 1965-1975; Angiology Research Foundation Honors Achievement Award, 1967-1968; Preservation and Restortion Award, Heritage Hills Association, 1973; member, Meical School Planning Committee for Native American Medical School, sponsored by the Navajo Health Authority, 1974-1976; associate editor, *Journal of Laboratory and Clinical Medicine,* 1974-1976; member, Blue Cord, 1974. *Biographical sources: Who's Who in the South and Southwest; American Men of Science; The International Registry of Who's Who. Publishe works:* Experimental articles, non-experimental articles, books, pamphlets, editorials in various journals; abstracts presented at national or international meetings; lectures.

**HANSEN, JOAN LOUISE (Cherokee)
1945-
(reporter, photographer)**

Born February 2, 1945, New Orleans, La. *Education:* Bacone College. *Principal occupation:* Reporter, photographer. *Home address:* 2310 E. Broadway, Muskogee, Okla. *Affiliation:* Reporter, photographer, Muskogee *Daily Phoenix* and *Times Democrat. Awards, honors:* Paintings shown at Philbrook Indian Annual, Tulsa, Okla.; paintings shown at Department of the Interior, Washington, D.C.; numerous awards at local fairs. *Interests:* Reading of Plains Indian traditions and legends; art.

**HAOZOUS, BOB (Chiricahua Apache-Navajo) 1943-
(artist)**

Born April 1, 1943, Los Angeles, Calif. *Education:* Utah State University; California College of Arts and Crafts. *Principal occupation:* Artist. *Home address:* Santa Fe, N.M. 87501. *Exhibitions:* Scottsdale National Indian Arts Exhibition; Philbrook Art Center Amerian Indian Artists Exhibitions; Oakland Museum Indian Show; Southwest Fine Arts Biennial-Museum of New Mexico. *Permanent collections:* Heard Museum; Southern Plains Indian Museum; Crafts Center, Anadarko, Okla. *Awards:* First Prize, Sante Fe Indian Market, 1971; Gold Medal, Wood Sculpture I and II, Heard Museum, 1973, 1974; Grand Prize, Heard Museum National Sculpture Competition, 1975; among others.

**HARANAKA, NANCIE
(Indian services)**

Affiliation: Indian/Family Services, Phoenix Indian Center, Inc., 1337 North 1st St., Phoenix, Ariz. 85004.

**HARDY, DEE
(museum curator)**

Affiliation: Curator, Anasazi Indian Village Museum, P.O. Box 393, Boulder, Utah 84716.

**HARDY, JOSEPH (Navajo)
(corporate executive director)**

Affiliation: Executive director, Navajo Small Business Development Corporation, P.O. Drawer L., Fort Defiance, Ariz. 86504.

**HARE, HERBERT
(B.I.A. agency superintendent)**

Affiliation: Superintendent, Yankton Agency, Bureau of Indian Affairs, Wagner, S.D. 57380.

**HARJO, SUSAN SHOWN
(executive director-Indian organization)**

Affiliation: Executive director, National Congress of American Indians, 804 D St., N.E., Washington, D.C. 20002.

**HARLOW, FRANCIS H. 1928-
(physicist)**

Born January 22, 1928, Seattle, Wash. *Education:* University of Washington, B.S., 1949, Ph.D., 1953. *Principal occupation:* Theoretical physicist. *Home address:* 1407 11th St., Los Alamos, N.M. 87544. *Affiliations:* Staff member, Los Alamos Scientific Laboratory, 1953-; research associate, Museum of New Mexico, 1965-. *Military service:* U.S. Army, 1946-1947. *Interests:* Theoretical fluid dynamics and numerical analysis; Pueblo Indian pottery, history, technology, and artistry. *Published works:* Contemporry Pueblo Indian Pottery (Museum of New Mexico, 1965); *Historic Pueblo Indian Pottery* (Museum of New Mexico, 1967; reprinted 1968, 1970); *The Pottery of San Ildefonso,* with Kenneth Chapman (School of American Research, 1970); *Mattepaint Pottery of the Tewa, Keres and Zuni Pueblos* (Museum of New Mexico Press, 1973); *Historic Pottery of the Pueblo Indians, 1600-1880,* with Larry Frank (New York Graphic Society, 1974); *Modern Pueblo Pottery, 1880-1960* (Northland Pres, 1977); *Glazed Pottery of the Southwest Indians (American Indian Art* Magazine, Nov. 1976); *Pueblo Indian Pottery Traditions* (VILTIS, 1978).

HARNEY, ROBERT
(tribal chairman)

Affiliation: Chairman, Winnemucca Colony Council, P.O. Box 1075, Winnemucca, Nev. 89445.

HARRINGTON, VIRGIL N. (Choctaw) 1919-
(former B.I.A. official)

Born 1919, Kiowa, Okla. *Education:* Oklahoma A & M College, B.A. (Agriculture), 1942. *Principal occupation:* B.I.A. Official. *Address:* 221 S. 12th, Muskogee, Okla. 74401. *Affiliations:* Civilian supervisor, U.S. Navy Department, 1943-1948; soil conservationist, Pawnee Indian Agency, 1948-1955; land operations officer, Consolidated Ute Agency, 1955-1958; superintendent, Seminole Indian Agency, 1958-1963; area director, Muskogee Area Office, B.I.A., 1963-? *Military service:* U.S. Army Signal Corps, 1942-1943. *Community activities:* Lions Club (past president); Rotary Club (past president); American Legion; Elk Club; Masons; Oklahoma State Fair (board of directors); Five Civilized Tribes (board of directors, child welfare advisory board). *Interests:* "Improvement and development of human resources from educational, sociological and economic viewpoints."

HARRIS, LaDONNA (Mrs. Fred Harris)(Comanche) 1931-
(president-Indian organization)

Born February 15, 1931, Temple, Okla. *Education:* High school. *Principal occupation:* President, Americans for Indian Opportunity, 1010 Massachusetts Ave., N.W., Suite 200, Washington, D.C. 20001. *Community activities:* Oklahomans for Indian Opportunity, Inc. (past president); Oklahoma Mental Health and Welfare Association (board member). *Awards, honors:* "Outstanding American Citizen of 1965," Anadarko (Okla.) American Indian Exposition and the Tulsa Indian Council, 1965. *Interests:* "Traveled through Argentina, Brazil, Childe, Peru in November, 1965, with (my) husband, Senator Fred Harris, and Senator and Mrs. Birch Bayh of Indiana."

HARRIS, ROBERT N., Sr. (Shoshone)
(tribal chairman)

Affiliation: Chairman, Shoshone Business Council, Fort Washakie, Wyo. 82514.

HARRISON, DAVID C. (Osage-Cherokee) 1945-
(federal Indian service)

Born July 28, 1945, Pawhuska, Okla. *Education:* Grinnell College, B.A., 1967; Harvard Law School, J.D., 1975. *Principal occupation:* Federal Indian service. *Home address:* 5535 Columbia Pike, Arlington, Va. 22204. *Affiliations:* Rights Protection Officer, Bureau of Indian Affairs, Washington, D.C. 1975-. *Military service:* U.S. Marine Corps, 1967-1971 (Captain, Vietnamese Cross of Gallentry, Bronz Star, Purple Heart). *Memberships:* Osage Heloshka Society; Harvard Law School Association. *Awards, honors:* "I served as senior investigator and authored several chapters of report called by *New York Times* editorial, "a magnificent document, sweeping in scope, meticulous in detail, unsparing in assessing blame." *Published work: Attica, Official Report of the New York State Special Commission on Attica* (Bantam, paper, Praeger, hardcover, 1972).

HARRISON, KATHERINE
(tribal chairwoman)

Affiliation: Chairwoman, Confederated Tribes of the Grande Ronde Indian Community, P.O. Box 94, Grande Ronde, Ore. 97347.

HART, ROBERT G. 1921-
(government official)

Born December 28, 1921, San Francisco, Calif. *Education:* American Institute for Banking, 1939-1941. *Principal occupation:* Governmental official. *Home address:* 916 25th St., N.W., Washington, D.C. 20037. *Affiliations:* Manager, Southern Highlanders, Inc., New York, N.Y., 1946-1952; Southwestern representative, Indian Arts and Crafts Board, Santa Fe, N.M., 1954-1957; treasurer, Westbury Music Fair, Inc.,

1957; director, public relations, Constructive Research Foundation, New York, N.Y., 1958-1959; editor, director of publications, Brooklyn Museum, 1959-1961; general manager, Indian Arts and Crafts Board, Department of the Interior, Washington, D.C. 20240, 1961-. *Other professional posts:* Chairman, Federal Inter-Departmental Agency for Arts and Crafts, 1963-; member, national advisory board, Foxfire Fund, Inc., 1981-. *Military service:* U.S. Army, 1943-1945. *Memberships:* Conseil Internationale des Musees; American Association of Museums; American Craftsmen's Council; World Crafts Council; American Political Science Association. *Awards, honors:* N.Y. State Governor's Award for Outstanding Service, 1951. *Interests:* Folk art. *Published works: How to Sell Your Handicrafts* (David McKay, 1953); *Guide to Alaska* (David McKay, 1959); editor, *Masters of Contemporary American Crafts* (Brooklyn Museum Press, 1960); among others.

HARTMAN, RUSSELL P.
(museum director)

Affiliation: Director, Navajo Tribal Museum, P.O. Box 308, Window Rock, Ariz. 86515.

HATATHLI, NED A. (Navajo) 1923-
(administrator)

Born October 11, 1923, Coalmine Canyon, Ariz. *Education:* Northern Arizona University, B.S., 1951. *Principal occupation:* Former president, Navajo Community College; chairman, board of directors, *American Indian Review. Military service:* U.S. Navy, 1943-1945. *Community activities:* Kit Carson Council; Boy Scouts of America. *Memberships:* Task Force on Minority Business Enterprise, Office of Economic Opportunity, Department of HEW; National Indian Education Association (board of directors); N.C.I.O. Special Indian Education Subcommittee; Regional Manpower Development Advisory Committee. *Awards, honors:* Phi Kappa Phi, Northern Arizona University, 1961; L.L.D. (hon.), Eastern Michigan University, 1971. *Biographical source: Indians of Today.*

HAURY, EMIL W. 1904-
(educator, archaeologist)

Born May 2, 1904, Newton, Kan. *Education:* Bethel College, 1923-1925; Univerity of Arizona, B.A., 1927, M.A., 1928; Harvard University, Ph.D., 1934; LL.D., University of New Mexico, 1959. *Principal occupation:* Educator, archaeologist. *Home address:* 2749 E. 4th St., Box 40543, Tucson, Ariz. 85717. *Affiliations:* Assistant director, Gila Pueblo, Globe, Ariz., 1930-1937; Department of Anthropology, University of Arizona (professor, 1937-1970; head of department, 1937-1964; Fred A. Riecker Distinguished professor, 1970-1980; emeritus, 1980-); director, Arizona State Museum, 1938-1964 (advisor, 1964-). *Memberships:* National Historic Parks, Historic Sites, Buildings and Monuments (advisory board); National Academy of Sciences (chairman, Division of Anthropology and Psychology, National Research Council, 1960-1962); National Council for the Humanities; Americn Philosophical Society; American Academy of Arts and Sciences; National Speleological Society (honorary life member); Society for American Archaeology; American Anthropological Association; American Association for the Advancement of Science; Phi Kappa Phi; Sigma Xi. *Awards, honors:* Guggenheim Fellow, 1949-1950; Viking Fund Medalist for Anthropology, 1950; University of Arizona, Alumni Achievement Award, 1957, Faculty Achievement Award, 1962; U.S. Department of the Interior Conservation Service Award, 1976; Alfred Vincent Kidder Award, 1977; Distinguished Citizen Award, University of Arizona Alumni Association, 1980. *Interests:* "Archaeological theory and method; early man in western America; the later Southwestern prehistoric societies." *Travels, expeditions:* National Geographic Society Arcaheological Expedition, Mexico City, Mexico, 1925; archaeological excavations, Bogota, Colombia, 1949-1950; International Congress of Americanists, Vienna, Austria, 1956, 1960; Intrnational Congress of Anthropological and Ethnological Sciences, paris, France. *Published works: The Excavations of Los Muertos and Neighboring Ruins in the Salt River Valley, Southern Arizona* (Peabody Museum Papers, 1945);

The Staratigraphy and Archaeology of Ventana Cave, Arizona (University of Arizona Press, 1950; University of New Mexico Press); *The Hohokam, Desert Farmers and Craftsmen: Excavations at Snaketown, 1964-1965* (University of Arizona Press, 1976); several articles in professional journals.

HAWKINS, RUSSELL (Sisseton-Wahpeton Sioux)
(tribal chairman)

Affiliation: Chairman, Sisseton-Wahpeton Sioux Tribal Council, Route 2, Agency Village, S.D. 57262.

HAYES, CHARLES F., III 1932-
(museum research director)

Born March 6, 1932, Boston, Mass. *Education:* Harvard University, A.B. (Anthropology), 1954; University of Colorado, M.A. (Anthropology), 1958. *Principal occupation:* Museum research director. *Home address:* 246 Commodore Parkway, Rochester, N.Y. 14625. *Affiliations:* Junior anthropologist, 1959-1961, associate curator of anthropology, 1961-1966, curator of anthropology, Rochester Museum; director, curator of anthropology, 1970-1979, research director, 1979- ,Rochester Museum & Science Center, 657 East Ave., Rochester, N.Y. 14603. *Other professional posts:* Associate lecturer in anthropology, University of Rochester, 1970-1973; consultant, New York State Museum in salvage archaeology; trustee, Seneca Iroquois National Museum, 1977-. *Military service:* U.S. Air Force, 1954-1956 (Captain, Military Air Transport Service and Strategic Air Command, Personnel Officer, 1955-1956). *Memberships:* New York Archaeological Association (president, 1967-1969); New York Archaeological Council (president, 1983-); New York Academy of Sciences; Society of Professional Archaeologists; American Association of Museums. *Awards, honors:* One of fifteen U.S. representatives to the American Association of Museums, International Council of Museums, 1974-1977; New York State Representative of the Society for American Archaeology on the Committee

for Public Understanding of Archaeology, 1971. *Interests:* Anthropology, archaeology, ethnology, museology, travel. *Published works:* Books: Editor, *The Iroquois in the American Revolution, 1976 Conference Proceedings,* 1981; *Aspects of Change in Seneca Iroquois Ladles A.D. 1600-1900,* 1982; *Proceedings of the 1982 Glass Trade Bead Conference,* 1983; *The Origin and Development of the Seneca and Cayuga Tribes of N.Y. State,* 1984. All published by Rochester Museum and Science Center. Articles: "The Canoe Builder - Iroquois Artists Conception of an Old Technology," 1959; "New Archaeological Exhibits Illustrate Iroquois Culture Change," 1960; "An Approach to Iroquois - White Acculturation Through Archaeology," 1961; "Prehistoric Iroquois Studies in the Bristol Hills, New York: A Summary," 1963; "Excavating an Early Seneca Longhouse," 1966; "Indian Life During the Archaic - A New Alcove in the Hall of Man," 1967; among other articles published by Museum Service, *Bulletin,* of the Rochester Museum. Numerous archaeological and historical impact studies conducted by Rochester Museum and Science Center.

HAYWARD, RICHARD (Pequot)
(tribal chairman)

Affiliation: Chairman, Mashantucket Pequot Council, P.O. Box 160, Ledyard, Conn. 06339.

HEADLEY, LOUIS R. (Arapahoe) 1948-
(superintendent)

Born February 25, 1948, Fort Washakie, Wyo. *Education:* University of Montana, Missoula, B.A., 1974; University of South Dakota, Vermillion, M.A., 1977; University of Wyoming, Laramie, Ed.S., 1986. *Princi-*

pal occupation: Superintendent. *Home address:* Box 344, St. Stephens, Wyo. 82524. *Affiliations:* Teacher, principal, St. Stephens Indian School, 1977-; minority counselor, special services, University of Wyoming, Laramie, 1984-. *Other professional posts:* Home-school coordinator, Lander Valley High School, Lander, Wyo.; field coordinator, Tri-State Tribes, Inc., Billings, Mont. *Community activities:* Wind River Indian Education Association, Wind River, Wyo. (past chairman); Keepers of the Fire Indian Club, University of Wyoming (advisor); Cub Scout volunteer, St. Stephens, Wyo.; Head Start Policy Council, Ethete, Wyo. (vice chairman). *Memberships:* Phi Delta Kappa; National Association of Elementary School Principals; National Indian Education Association (treasurer); Wyoming Association for Bilingual-Bicultural Education (treasurer). *Awards, honors:* Wyoming Golden Gloves Championship Scholarship Award; Korean Temple Band, Casper, Wyo; Outstanding Young Men of America, U.S. Jaycees, 1978. *Interests:* "I was a member of the Arapahoe and Shoshone Idian Dance Troupe that danced in Switzerland. I was also selected to dance in Washington, D.C. during the 1976 Bicentennial. I have been chosen to be the head dancer in Denver, Steamboat Spring, Colorado and Rocky Boy Reservation."

HEDRICK, HENRY E.
(director-Indian organization)

Affiliation: Director, American Indian Liberation Crusade, Inc., 4009 S. Halldale Ave., Los Angeles, Calif. 90062-1851.

HEELEY, STEVEN J.W.
(vice president-Indian organization)

Affiliation: Vice president, National Indian Education Association, 1115 Second Ave. So., Minneapolis, Minn. 55403.

HEINMILLER, CARL W
(museum director)

Affiliation: Executive director, Alaska Indian Arts, Inc., 23 Fort Seward Dr., P.O. Box 271, Haines, Alaska 99827.

HEINRICH, ALBERT C. 1922-
(professor of anthropology)

Born February 2, 1922, Ill. *Education:* New School for Social Research, B.A.; University of Alaska, M.Ed.; University of Washington, Ph.D., 1960. *Principal occupation:* Professor of anthropology. *Home address:* 56 Capri Ave., N.W., Calgary, Alberta, Canada. *Affilaition:* Professor of anthropology, University of Calgary, Alberta, Canada. *Memberships:* American Anthropological Association; American Association for the Advancement of Science. *Awards, honors:* Seattle Anthropologicl Society Prize, 1962. *Interests:* Linguistics; social structure; arctic; Indians of North America; South Asia; "Have spent extended periods of time in Alaska, Arctic Canada, The Labrador, South America, India, Europe. Have written numerous articles on Athabascans, Eskimos."

HEIZER, ROBERT F. 1915-
(professor of anthropology)

Born July 13, 1915, Denver, Colo. *Education:* Univesity of California, Ph.D., 1940. *Principal occupation:* Professor of anthropology, Department of Anthropology, University of California, Berkeley. *Home address:* 85 Menlo Place, Berkeley, Calif. 94707. *Memberships:* Society for American Archaeology; American Anthropological Association; Societe des Americanistes des Paris; Institute for Andean Research. *Interests:* Archaeology and ethnology of the American Indians. *Published works: Francis Drake and the California Indians, 1579* (University of California Press, 1947); editor, *The California Indians,* with M.A. Whipple (University of California Press, 1951); *The Four Ages of Tsurai,* with John E. Mills (University of California Press, 1952); *Prehistoric Rock Art of Nevada and Eastern California,* with M.A. Baumhoff (University of California Press, 1962); *Man's Discovery of His Past* (Spectrum Books, Prentice-Hall, Inc., 1962); *Anza and the Northwest Frontier of New Spain* (Southwest Museum, 1967); *Hugo Reid's Letters on the Indians of Los Angeles County, 1852* (Southwest Museum, 1968); *Almost Ancestors: The First Californians,* with Theodora Kroeber (Sierra Club, 1968);

HENDRICKSON, JAMES (Chippewa)
(tribal chairman)

Affiliation: Chairman, Grand Portage Reservation Business Committee, P.O. Box 428, Grand Portage, Minn. 55605.

HENDRICKX, LEONARD 1953-
(director of Indian center)

Born July 10, 1953, Kellogg, Idaho. *Education:* State University of New York at Albany, B.A. (Philosophy). *Principal occupation:* Dirctor of Indian center. *Home address:* 2225 First St., Lot 79, Cheney, Wash. 99004. *Affiliations:* Administrative analyst, City of Redondo Beach, Calif., 1979-1982; executive director, Ameican Indian Community Center, Spokane, Wash., 1982-. *Community activities:* Spokane Urban Indian Health Service Board (chairman); Community Housing Resources Board (chairman); The Native American Alliance for Political Action (treasurer); Spokane Planning Affiliates Network (member); Vocational Advisory Council, Community Colleges (member). *Memberships:* Eastern Washington/Northern Idaho MENSA (treasurer). *Awards, honors:* Outstanding Young Man of America, 1985; Mayor's Proclamation/Community Services, City Council and Indian Community; frequent presenter at national and regional Indian employment and training and education conferences. *Interests:* "Extensive travels throughout the U.S. Outdoors enthusiast, particularly interested in the conceptualization and articulation of innovative program development ideas for Indian comunities, with expertise in successful grant and contract preparation, presentation, and negotiation." *Biographical source: Outstanding Young Men of America, 1985.*

HENSLEY, WILLIAM L. (Eskimo)
1941-
(state senator)

Born 1941, Kotzebue, Alaska. *Education:* University of Alaska, 1960-1961; George Washington University, B.A., 1966; Univerity of Alaska, 1966; University of New Mexico Law School, 1967; U.C.L.A. Law School, 1968. *Principal occupation:* State senator. *Home address:* Kotxebue, Alaska.

Affiliations: Alaska House of Representatives, 1966-1970; Alaska State Senate, 1970-. *Community activities:* Rural Affairs Commission, 1968-1972 (chairman, 1972); Land Claims Task Force (chairman, 1968); Northwest Regional Educational Laboratory (board of directors, 1968-1969); Northwest Alaska Native Association Regional Corporation (board of directors). *Memberships:* Alaska Federation of Natives, 1966- (organizer, 1966; president, 1972); Northwest Alaska Native Association (organizer, 1966); National Council on Indian Opportunity, 1968-1970. *Interests:* "Land claims implementation; rural economic development; education facilities in the bush; old-age centers; bilingual programs."

HENSON, C.L.
(B.I.A. agency superintendent)

Affiliation: Superintendent, Truxton Canon Agency, Bureau of Indian Affairs, P.O. Box 37, Valentine, Ariz. 86437.

HENSON, RICHARD ALLEN
(Comanche) 1942-
(B.I.A. employment assistance officer)

Born January 26, 1942, Pawnee, Okla. *Education:* Oklahoma State Tech, 1960-1962; Minot State College, B.A. (Business Administration), 1976. *Principal occupation:* B.I.A. employment assistance director. *Home address:* 13806 Congress Dr., Rockville, Md. 10853. *Affiliations:* Metropolitan Life Insurance Co., Ardmore, Okla., 1967-1971; guidance counselor, United Tribes Employment Training Center, Bismarck, N.D., equal employment opportunity counselor, job developer and employment assistance officer, United Tribes Employment Training Center, Minot, N.D., 1971-1974; employment assistance officer, Fort Berthold Agency, B.I.A., New Town, N.D., 1974-1976; area equal employment opportunity officer, B.I.A., Albuquerque, N.M., 1976-1977; director, equal employment opportunity, Indian Health Service, Rockville, Md. *Military service:* U.S. Air Force, 1963-1967. *Community activities:* Minot Indian Club (president, 1974); Minot Mayor's Human Rights Committee (member);

Minot's Mental Health & Retardation Board (member). *Interests:* "To continue to work with Indian people in Indian affairs and to return to school to earn my master's degree in public health."

HERON, GEORGE DAVID (Seneca) 1919-
(tribal officer)

Born February 22, 1919, Red House, N.Y. *Education:* High school. *Principal occupation:* Tribal officer. *Home address:* R.F.D. J-57, Salamanca, N.Y. 14779. *Affiliations:* Administrator, Seneca Nation; stockholder, Cattaraugus County Builder's, Inc., Fentier Village, Salamanca, N.Y. *Military service:* U.S. Naval Reserve, 1941-1945 (European-African Service Medal with three battle stars; Asiatic-Pacific; Philippine Liberation Medal; Navy Good Conduct Medal; Amerian Caribbean Service Medal). *Community activities:* Veterans of Foreign Wars; American Legion; Governor's Interstate Indian Council (director). *Membership:* National Congress of American Indians. *Awards, honors:* Citizen of the Year Award, Junior Chamber of Commerce. *Interests:* "Lecturing on Indian culture and tradition."

HESSING, VALJEAN McCARTY (Choctaw) 1934-
(artist)

Born August 30, 1934, Tulsa, Okla. *Education:* Mary Hardin-Baylor College, 1952-1954; Tulsa University, 1954-1955. *Principal occupation:* Artist. *Awards, honors:* Numerous awards and prizes at various art exhibitions. *Interests:* Mrs. Hessing writes, "I am interested in illustrating books; I'm also interested in aiding children and adults in art, especially those who have little or no opportunity to have instruction of any kind."

HESTER, JAMES J. 1931-
(anthropologist)

Born September 21, 1931, Anthony, Kan. *Education:* University of New Mexico, B.A., 1953; Univerity of Arizona, Ph.D., 1961. *Principal occupation:* Anthropologist. *Affi-liations:* Assistant curator, Museum of New Mexico, 1959-1964; adjunct professor, Southern Methodist University, 1964-1965; scientist administrator, National Institute of Health, 1965-. *Military service:* U.S. Air Force, 1954-1956. *Memberships:* American Anthropological Association (Fellow); Society for American Archaeology; Sigma Xi; American Society of Naturalists; Current Anthropology. *Interests:* Archaeology of Navajo Indians; prehistory of Sahara desert; directed culture change; relationship of man to his environment. *Published works: An Archaeological Survey of the Navajo Reservoir District, Northwestern New Mexico,* with A.E. Dittert, Jr. and Frank W. Eddy (Museum of New Mexico, 1961); *Early Navajo Migrations and Acculturation in the Southwest* (Museum of New Mexico, 1962); *Studies at Navajo Period Sites in the Navajo Reservoir District,* with Joel Shiner (Museum of New Mexico, 1963); among others.

HETH, CHARLOTTE WILSON (Oklahoma Cherokee) 1937-
(professor, director-Indian center)

Born October 29, 1937, Muskogee, Okla. *Education:* Oklahoma Baptist University, 1955-1956; University of Tulsa, B.A., 1959, M.M., 1960; University of California, Los Angeles, Ph.D., 1975. *Principal occupation:* Professor, director-Indian center. *Home address:* 4040 Grand View #20, Los Angeles, Calif. 90066. *Affiliations:* Associate professor of music, director, American Indian Studies Center, University of California, Los Angeles, Calif., 1974-. *Community activities:* Panel chair, Folk Arts Program, National Endowment for the Arts, 1981-1983; Indian Centers, Inc., Los Angeles (board member). *Memberships:* Society for Ethnomusicology (council chair, 1981-1982); National Indian Education Association; American Indian Historians' Association. *Awards, honors:* Senior Postdoctoral Fellowship, Center for the History of the American Indian, The Newberry Library, 1978-1979; Southern Fellowships Fund, Post-doctoral Fellowship, 1978-1979; National Research Council senior postdoctoral fellowship, 1984-1985 (Ford Foundation Minority Fellowship). *Interests:*

"American Indian music and dance; Cherokee language and culture; previously I was a Peace Corps volunteer in Ethiopia (1962-1964) teaching English as a second language. I also was a high school teacher in Oklahoma, New Mexico, and California from 1960-1972. I have traveled to Europe, the Middle East, East Africa, Mexico, and Canada. *Published works:* General editor, "The Music of the American Indians," (*Selected Reports in Ethnomusicology,* 1982); general editor, "Music and the Expressive Arts," (*American Indian Culture and Research Journal,* 1982); *Issues for the Future of American Indian Studies: A Needs Assessment and Program Guide,* co-authored with Susan Guyette (American Indian Studies Center, UCLA, 1985); general editor, organizer, and contributor, *Sharing a Heritage: American Indian Arts Conference,* No. 3 in the Contemporary American Indian Issues Series (American Indian Studies Center, UCLA, 1984).

HEWITT, ARNOLD (Tuscarora)
(tribal chief)

Affiliation: Chief, Tuscarora Nation, 5616 Walmore Rd., Lewiston, N.Y. 14092.

HIGHWATER, JAMAKE (Blackfeet-Eastern Band Cherokee) 1942-
(author, lecturer)

Born February 14, 1942, Glacier County, Mt. *Education:* Holds degrees in music, comparative literature, and cultural anthropology. *Principal occupation:* Author, lecturer. *Address:* c/o Alfred Hart, agent, 419 East 57th St., New York, N.Y. 10022. *Affiliations:* Lecturer, Indian culture, various Universities in U.S. and Canada; graduate lecturer, New York University, New York, N.Y., Continuing Education, 1979-; founder, host narrator and writer of TV series Songs of the Thunderbird, PBS Network, Miami, Fla., 1977-; consultant, N.Y. State Council on the Arts, 1975-; founding member, Indian Art Foundation, Santa Fe, N.M., 1980-. *Community activities:* Cultural Council of American Indian Community House, New York, N.Y. (past president and founding member); President's Commission on Mental Health (Art Task Panel, 1977);

N.Y. State Council on the Arts (member, task force on individual artist). *Memberships:* National Congress of American Indians; White Buffalo Society of Amerian Indians, Denver, Colo.; Dramatists Guild; Authors Guild; American Federation of Radio and Television Artists (AFTRA); BMI; League of American Authors. *Awards, honors:* Appointed Honorary Citizen by Governor of Oklahoma; appointed Colonel aid-de-camp on the Staff of the Governor of New Mexico; 1978 Newberry Honor Award for novel *Anpao* by the American Library Association; Jane Addams Peace Book Award, 1978, for *Many Smokes, Many Moons;* Anisfield-Wolf Award in race relations, 1980, for *Song From the Earth: American Indian Painting;* featured speaker, along with Ralph Coe, the Lord Mayor of London, the Governor of Missouri and Mrs. Joan Mondale at the opening night diner of "Sacred Circles, 2000 Years of American Indian Art" at the Nelson Gallery in Kansas City; featured speaker, along with Gov. Lamm of Colorado, at the opening night dinner of the Colorado Historical Society Museum in Denver; interviews with Mr. Highwater have appeared in most major American, European, Latin American and Near Eastern newspapers and magazines. *Interests:* Travels extensively and does fieldwork in North and Central Africa, most American Indian communities and resevations in the U.S.; travels to Central America and Mexico, Europe and the Near East; lectures extensively for E. Colston Leigh Bureau; contributing editor, *Stereo Review, 1972-1979;* classical music editor, New York *Soho Weekly News, 1975-1979;* contributing editor, *N.Y. Arts Journals, 1978-;* contributing editor, *Indian Trader,* 1977-1980; Senior editor, Fodor Travel Guides, 1970-1975; columnist, *Lone Star Revue,* 1981-; written and presented talks about American Indian studies for th BBC, Radio Three in London, Radio Pacifica, CBS-Radio, WMCA-Radio, and numerous other radio and television networks and stations. *Biographical sources: Who's Who in America; Directory of American Poetry; Directory of American Fiction Writers; International Who's Who; Dance World; Theatre World; Pop Bibliography; Who's Who in the East. Published works: Rock & Other Four Letter Words* (Bantam

Books, 1968); *Mick Jagger: The Singer Not the Song* (Popular Library, 1970); *Fodor's Europe Under 25,* (David McKay, 1971-1974); *Fodor's Indian American* (David McKay, 1975); *Song From the Earth: American Indian Painting* (New York Graphic Society, Little Brown, 1976); *Ritual of the Wind: American Indian Ceremonies, Music and Dances* (Viking Press, 1977); Anpao: An American Indian Odyssey (J.B. Lippincott, 1977); *Dance: Rituals of Experience* (A & W Visual Library, 1978); *Many Smokes, Many Moons: American Indian History Thru Indian Arts* (J.B. Lippincott, 1978); *Journey to the Sky: In Search of the Lost World of the Maya* (T.Y. Crowell, 1979); *The Sweet Grass Lives On: 50 Contemporary North American Indian Artists* (Viking Press, 1980); *Masterpieces of American Indian Painting,* 8 Vols., 1978-1980; *The Sun, He Dies: The End of the Aztec World,* 1980; *The Primal Mind: Vision and Reality in Indian America,* 1981. Mr. Highwater wrote introductions for: *Indian Boyhood,* by Charles Eastman (Rio Grande Press, 1976); and *Bears Heart: Scenes from the Life of a Cheyenne,* by Burton Supree (J.B. Lippincott, 1977). Also many articles in various journals and magazines.

HILL, ARLEIGH (Seneca) 1909-
(Indian arts and crafts)

Born June 5, 1909, Grand River Reservation, Ontario, Can. *Principal occupation:* Indian arts and crafts. *Home address:* 463 Mt. Read Blvd., Rochester, N.Y. 14606. *Affiliations:* Associate, Education Division, 1933-1944, associate in Indian Arts and Crafts, 1944-, Rochester Museum of Arts and Sciences; consultant on Indian programs for radio and television. *Community activities:* National Youth Administration (Indian camp counselor); Civilian Defense (educational instructor); Neighborhood Indian Society of Rochester (president); Indian Day Programs (chairman). *Memberships:* Imperial Order of Red Men, 1934-1963; Stadium Club of Rochester. *Awards, honors:* Honorary name bestowed by Turtle Clan of the Seneca Indians, 1951; Civil Defense Citation, 1945; Citation of Merit, Rochester Museum, 1959. *Interests:* Local

and national Indian affairs; reserch and writing on the American Indian. *Published works:* Articles for various sports magazines and for the Rochester Museum of Arts and Sciences *Bulletin.*

HILL, JAMES W. (Spokane)
(tribal chairman)

Affiliation: Chairman, Spokane Business Committee, P.O. Box 385, Wellpinit, Wash. 99040.

HILL, JOAN (Cherokee-Creek)
(artist)

Born in Muskogee, Okla. *Education:* Muskogee Junior College, A.A., 1950; Northeastern State College, B.A. (Education), 1952. *Principal occupation:* Artist. *Home address:* Route 6, Box 151, Muskogee, Okla. 74401. *Affiliations:* Art instructor, Tulsa Public Schools, 1952-1956; self-employed artist, 1956-. *Other professional posts:* Consultant, American Association of University Women; teacher, adult education. *Community activities:* Muskogee Art Guild (art director; publicity director; co-chairman). *Memberships:* National League of Amerian Penwomen, Inc., 1968-; Phi Theta Kappa; Northeastern State College Alumni Association (board of directors). *Awards, honors:* Of Ms. Hill's more than 250 awards, more than 100 are from national competitions. She has about 75 works in permanent collections; has had approximately 20 one-woman shows; has had over 450 juried and non-juried exhibitions throughout the U.S. and abroad; has participated in many traveling shows and has received numerous commissions. *Interests:* Ms. Hill works in oil, gouache, collage, acrylics, transparent wtercolor, tempera, ink, pastel, conte, pencil, and mixed media. Her preferred styles are representational realism, subjective expressionism, abstract symbolism, and non-objective. *Biographical sources: Outstanding Young Women of America,* 1965; *Leadership Index, A Who's Who in Oklahoma,* 1964; *A Dictionary of American Indian Painters,* 1968; *American Indian Painting of the Southwest & Plains Areas,* 1968; *Indians of Today,* 1970; *Who's Who in American Art; The World Who's Who of*

Women (London, England); *Who's Who of American Women. Publishe works:* Ms. Hill's work has appeared in more than 30 publications.

HILL, NORBERT S., Jr.
(executive director-Indian society)

Affiliation: Executive director, American Indian Science and Engineering Society, 1310 College Ave., Suite 1220, Boulder, Colo. 80302.

HILLABRANT, WALTER JOHN
(Citizen Band Potawatomi) 1942-
(psychologist)

Born December 17, 1942, Corsicana, Tex. *Education:* University of California, Berkeley, A.B., 1965; University of California, Riverside, Ph.D., 1972. *Principal occupation:* Psychologist. *Home address:* 1927 38th St., N.W., Washington, D.C. 20007. *Affiliations:* Assistant professor, Howard University, Washington, D.C., 1971-1980; psychologist, Support Services, Washington, D.C., 1980-. *Memberships:* American Psychological Association; Washingon Academy of Sciences; National Indian Education Association. *Interests:* "Indian education; cross-cultural psychology; application of computer and telecommunication technology to social problems." *Published work:* *The Future Is Now* (Peacock Press, 1974).

HILLMAN, JAMES
(director-Indian center)

Affiliation: Director, Detroit American Indian Center, 360 John R, Detroit, Mich. 48226.

HINES, MIFAUNWY SHUNTONA
(director-Indian center)

Affiliation: Director, American Indian Information Center, 139-11 87th Ave., Briarwood, N.Y. 11435.

HINKLEY, EDWARD C. 1934-
(educator)

Born December 16, 1934, Bridgewater,

Mass. *Education:* Harvard University, B.A., 1955, M.Ed., 1959. *Principal occupation:* Educator. *Home address:* RFD 1, 2d-1, Mt. Vernon, Maine 04352. *Affiliations:* Elementary school teacher, Bureau of Indian Affairs, Utah and Arizona, 1959-1961; educational specialist, U.S. Public Health Service, Division of Indian Health, Arizona and Nevada, 1961-1965; Commissioner of Indian Affairs, State of Maine, 1965-1969; eduction and management consultant, T.R.I.B.E., Inc. (Teaching and Research in Bicultural Education), Maine and Canada, 1969-. *Interests:* Indian affairs of Canada and the U.S. on a contemporary level; bicultural education; community development; leadership training and counseling.

HINDS, PATRICK SWAZO
(Tewa Pueblo) 1929-
(artist)

Born March 25, 1929, Tesuque Pueblo, N.M. *Education:* Hill and Canyon School of Art (summers, 1947-1948); California College of Arts and Crafts, B.A., 1952; Mexico City College, 1952-1953; Chicago Art Institute, 1953, 1955. *Principal occupation:* Artist. *Home address:* 224 Sena St., Santa Fe, N.M. 87501. *Military service:* U.S. Marine Corps, 1945-1946, 1950-1951 (two Purple Hearts). *Awards, honors:* Many awards for work entered in shows throughout the Southwest, 1964-. About 20 one-man shows in California; work represented in many permanent collection. *Biographical sources: Who's Who of American Indian Artists; The Indian Historian; The Bialac Collection of Southwest Indian Painting; American Indian Painting; American Indian Painters.*

HIRST, STEPHEN MICHAEL 1939-
(writer)

Born December 20, 1939, Dayton, Ohio. *Education:* Miami University, Oxford, Ohio, B.A., 1962; Johns Hopkins School of Advanced International Studies, Washington, D.C., M.A., 1966. *Principal occupation:* Writer. *Home address:* P.O. Box 321, Marquette, Mich. 49855. *Affiliations:* Preschool director, Havasupai Tribe, 1967-1968, 1970-1973; planner, Havasupai Tribe,

1975-1976. *Memberships:* The Authors Guild, 1976-. *Awards, honors:* 1961 Best Columnist Award of Ohio Collegiate Newspaper Association; 1962 Greer-Hepburn Fiction Award; 1966 U.S. Commerce Deartment Service Award; 1976 Havasupai Tribe Service Award; 1979 Cincinnati Arts Consortium Writing Award; 1981 Ohio Arts Council Fiction Award; finalist for 1982 Arizona Commission on the Arts fiction award. *Published works: Life In a Narrow Place: The Havasupai of the Grand Canyon* (David mcKay Co., 1976); *Havsuw'Baaja* (Havasupai Tribe, 1985).

HISER, DONALD H. 1923-
(archaeologist, museum director)

Born November 20, 1923, Columbiana, Ohio. *Education:* University of Arizona, B.A., 1953; Arizona State University, 1957-1958. *Principal occupation:* Archaeologist, museum director, Pueblo Grande Museum, 4619 E. Washington St., Phoenix, Ariz. 85034, 1953-. *Other professional posts:* Lecturer in anthropology, Phoenix Evening College; lecturer, Traveling Science Institute of Arizona Academy of Science (sponsored by the National Science Foundation). *Military service:* U.S. Naval Reserve, 1943-1945, 1946-1950. *Community activities:* Balsz School Parent-Teachers' Association (president, Indian affairs committee, 1960-1961). *Memberships:* Arizona Academy of Science (past secretary, anthropology section); American Anthropological Association (institutional member); Society for American Archaeology; Archaeological Institute of America. *Interests:* Southwestern U.S. archaeology — Hohokam; avophysical anthropology, ceramic rsearch, teaching and lecturing on Southwestern archaeology. *Published works: Pueblo Grande Museum Popular Series* (Pueblo Grande Museum).

HISER, JOHNNY R. (Ysleta Pueblo)
(tribal governor)

Affiliation: Governor, Ysleta Del Sur Pueblo Museum, P.O. Box 17579, El Paso, Tex. 79917.

HOBSON, DOTTIE F. (Navaho) 1945-
(B.I.A. Indian school principal)

Born March 9, 1945, Tohatchi, N.M. *Education:* University of Arizona, B.A., 1972; University of New Mexico, M.A., 1977; Northern Arizona University, M.A., 1977. *Principal occupation:* Principal, Lukachukai School, B.I.A., Lukachukai, Ariz., 1976-. *Home address:* Box 6, Lukachukaim Ariz. 86507. *Affliation:* Chinle Agency, Bureau of Indian Affairs, Chinle, Ariz. *Other professional posts:* Assistant education program administrator, assistant school superintendent, Chinle Agency, 1978-. *Community activities:* Boy Scouts of America (institutional representative); Gir Scouts; Federal Women's Program Coordinator, Chinle Agency. *Memberships:* Navaho School Administratos Association; National Indian Education Association. *Published works: Kee's Grandfather* (Rough Rock Demonstration School, Chinle, Ariz., 1970).

HOEBEL, E. ADAMSON 1906-
(professor emeritus)

Born November 16, 1906, Madison, Wis. *Education:* University of Wisconsin, Madison, B.A., 1928; University of Cologne, Germany, 1928-1929; New York University, M.A., 1931; Columbia University, Ph.D., 1934. *Principal occupation:* Professor emeritus. *Home address:* 48 Groveland Terrace #30, Minneapolis, Minn. 55403. *Affiliations:* Professor of anthropology, New York University, 1929-1948, University of Utah, 1948-1954, University of Minnesota, 1954-1972 (chairman, Department of Anthropology, 1954-1968; Regent's professor, 1966-1972; professor emeritus, 1972-; adjunct professor of law, 1972-1981). *Other professional posts:* Special officer, U.S. Department of State, U.S. Arms Control, Disarmament Agency; Fellow, Center for Advanced Study in the Behavioral Sciences. *Community activities:* Governor's Council on Human Relations, Minnesota, 1955-1960; Association on American Indian Affairs (director, 1936-1955); Science Museum of Minnesota (trustee, 1978-). *Memberships: American Anthropological Association, 1932- (president, 1956-1957); American Ethnological Association, 1932-*

(president, 1947); American Association for the Advancement of Science, 1934-; American Philosophical Society, 1956-. Awards, honors: Fulbright Professor, Oxford University (England), 1956-1957, Catholic University (The Netherlands), 1970; Research Fellow, Laboratory of Anthropology, Santa Fe, N.M.; member, Governor's Commission on Human Relations, 1955-1964. Expeditions: Field research trips: Comanche Indians, Oklahoma, 1933; Northern Shoshone, Idaho, 1934; Northern Cheyenne, 1935-1936; Keresan Pueblos, New Mexico, 1945-1950; West Pakistan, 1961; New Guineau, 1967. Biographical sources: Who's Who in America; Who's Who in the World; International Dictionary of Biography; International Encyclopedia of the Social Sciences; Law and Society Review (Spring, 1972). Published works: Political Organization and Law-Ways of the Comanche Indians (American Anthropological Association, 1941); The Cheyenne Way, with K.N. Llewellyn (Univerity of Oklahoma Press, 1941); Man in the Primitive World (McGraw-Hill, 1948, 1949); The Comanches: Lords of the South Plains, with E. Wallace (University of Oklahoma Press, 1953); The Law of Primitive Man (Harvard University Press, 1954); The Cheyennes: Indians of the Great Plains (Holt, Rinehart & Winston, 1961); editor, A Cheyenne Sketchbook (University of Oklahoma Press); Anthropology: The Study of Man (McGraw-Hill, 1965); The Plains Indians: A Critical Bibliography (Indiana Univrsity Press, 1977); editor, Law and Society Review, 1969-1973; Journal of Natural Law, 1960-1965; American Indian Quarterly, 1972-; also articles and reviews in legal, historical and anthropological journals.

HOFFMAN, MICHAEL P. 1937-
(anthropologist, professor,
museum curator)

Born September 15, 1937, Council Bluffs, Iowa. Education: University of Illinois, Urbana, B.A., 1959; Harvard University, Ph.D., 1971. Principal occupation: Anthropologist, professor, museum curator. Home address: 409 N. Washington, Fayetteville, Ark. 72701. Affiliations: Professor of anthropology, museum curator, University of Arkansas, Fayetteville, 1964-. Community activities: Arkansas Folklore Society (board of directors); ANL Research Laboratory (board of directors); Arkansas Preservation Program (past member, State Review Committee). Memberships: Society for American Archaeology, 1960-; American Anthropological Association (Fellow) 1961- Caddo Conference, 1964-; Southeastern Archaeological Conference, 1975-; Current Anthropology (Associate); American Indian Historical Society; Association for American Indian Affairs; Arkansas Archaeological Society. Awards, honors: Phi Beta Kappa. Interests: Southeastern Indians, past and present; Caddo, Quapaw, and Cherokee ethnology and contemporary life; avocational interests—running, fishing; expeditions: archaeological fieldwork in Arkansas, Missouri, Illinois, Arizona, Massachusetts, and Guatemala. Published works: Three Sites in Millwood Reservoir (Arkansas Archaeological Survey, 1970); "The Kinkaid-Mainard Site," 3PU2 (Arkansas Archaeologist, 1977); Ozark Reservoir Papers (Arkansas Archaeological Survey, 1978); Prehistoric Ecological Crises (Kennikat Press, 1980); "Arkansas Indians," (Arkansas Naturalist, 1984).

HOHNANI, DANIEL
(college president)

Affiliation: President, College of Ganado, Ganado, Ariz. 86505.

HOKANSEN, SHERRY
(librarian)

Affiliation: Librarian, Yakima Nation Museum-Library, P.O. Box 151, Toppenish, Wash. 98948.

HOLLOW, A.E. (TONY) (Assiniboine Sioux) 1918-
(business management, administration)

Born March 8, 1918, Brockton, Mt. Education: Central Washington University, B.A. (Business Administration), 1975, M.A. (Occ. Ed.), 1978. Principal occupation: Business management and administration. Home address: 301 Hilltop Place, Wenatchee, Wash. 98801. Affiliations: President,

Dull Knife Memorial College, Lame Deer, Mt., 1977-. *Other professional posts:* National and State EPDA Research Coordinator, Central Washington State College, Ellensburg, 1973-1975; Higher Education Consultant, Miles Commuity College, Miles City, Mont., 1976-1977. *Military service:* U.S. Army, 1940-1945 (Administrative Assistant, Chief Warrant Officer). *Community activities:* Northwest Indian Economic Development Association (treasurer, 1966-1970); Indian Center, Wenatchee, Wash. (president, 1970-1973); Ethnic Advisory Council, Central Washington State College (chairman, 1973-1975); Washington State Vocational Education Advisory Board (member, 1975-). *Membership:* American Vocational Association. *Interests:* American Indian arts and crafts; business and administration. *Published works: Guidelines for Business Management Training for Native Americans* (Central Washington University, 1976); *Native American Vocational Education: State of the Art (Washington State)* (Central Washington University, 1976).

HOLLOW, MAUDE C. (Assiniboine Sioux) 1921-
(librarian, media specialist)

Born December 11, 1921, Poplar, Mt. *Education:* Central Washington State College, B.A. (Education), 1967, M.A. (Education), 1973. *Principal occupation:* Librarian, media specialist. *Home address:* 301 Hilltop Place, Wenatchee, Wash. 98801. *Affiliation:* Librarian and media specialist, Wenatchee School District #246, Wenatchee, Wash., 1967-. *Memberships:* National Education Association; Washington State Education Association; Wenatchee Education Asociation; Washington Association for Educational Communication and Technology; Washington State Association of School Librarians (secretary, Region 11).

HOLLOW, NORMAN (Assiniboine Sioux)
(tribal chairman)

Affiliation: Chairman, Fort Peck Tribal Executive Board, Poplar, Mont. 59255.

HOLLOWBREAST, DONALD (Northern Cheyenne) 1917-
(artist, newspaper contributor)

Born May 17, 1917, Birney, Mt. *Education:* Chemawa Indian School, Chemawa, Oreg., 1934-1936. *Principal ocupation:* Artist, newspaper contributor. *Home address:* Senior Citizens Center #28, Lame Deer, Mt. 59043. *Affiliations:* Editor, The Birney Arrow (Indian Newspaper), Lame Deer, Mont., 1977-. *Memberships:* National Mustang Association; Montana Institute of the Arts; Northern Cheyenne Landowners Association; *Awards, honors:* First Prize for water-color painting, Rosebud County Fair, Forsyth, Mt. *Interests:* Western art and writing; Indian newspapers; travel. *Biographical source: Montana,* the Magazine of Western History (Fall, 1964); *Great Falls Tribune; The Billings Gazzette; Sheridan Press; Wassaja. Published work:* Editor, The Birney Arrow, 1960-1971.

HOLMES, BEVERLY C. (Cherokee) 1936-
(research program analyst)

Born September 8, 1936, Tulsa, Okla. *Education:* Henager's Business College; Brigham Young University; Utah State University. *Principal occupation:* Research program analyst. *Home address:* 7155 Game Lord Dr., Springfield, Va. 22153. *Affiliations:* Chairperson, Federal Equal Opportunity Council of Utah; instructor, Weber State College's Division of Continuing Education conducting classes in Indian culture and women's programs; research program analyst for the Deputy Chief of the Forest Service. *Memberships:* Intermountain Indian Education Council (board of directors); National Congress of American Indians; Native American Indian Women's Association; Indian Leadership Training Center; American Indian Historical Society; Federal Employed Women. *Awards, honors:* Federal Woman of the Year, Bureau of Indian Affairs, 1973; Sustained Superior Performance Award, 1973; Special Achievement Award, 1975; nominated to receive a special award sponsored by the American Society for Public Administrators, 1976; Mrs. Holmes was a delegate nominee for the State of Utah to the National Women's Year

Conference, 1977, and has received the Outstanding Alumni Award from Henager's Business College. *Biographical sources: Who's Who of American Women; The World Who's Who of Women* (International Bibliographical Centre).

HOMERATHA, PHIL (Otoe-Missouri)
1943-
(education)

Born March 22, 1943, Pawnee, Okla. *Education:* Tarkio College, Mo., B.S., 1968; Northest Missouri State University, M.S., 1972. *Principal occupation:* Education. *Home address:* 901 W. 22nd, Lawrence, Kan. 66044. *Affiliations:* Head football coach, head wrestling coach, instructor of physical education, Haskell Indian Junior College, Lawrence, Kan., 1973-. *Other professional posts:* Teacher/coach. Dexfield Community Schools, Redfield, Iowa; head track, assistant football coach, Huron College, Huron, S.D. *Community activities:* Haskell Alumni Association (board of directors). *Memberships:* National Federal Government Employees; National Football Coaches Association; National WR Coaches Assocaition. *Awards, honors:* Outstanding Young Men of America, 1972; Tarkio College Outstanding Alumni, 1978. *Interests:* Football; "have served as coordinator for division of Indian studies here at Haskell. Have served as consultant to HEW-Westinghouse Learning on Indian Education; major interest at present job is in area of Indian education."

HONANIE, GILBERT, Jr. (Hopi)
1941-
(architect, planning)

Born April 11, 1941, Tuba City, Ariz. *Education:* Pasadena City College, Calif., A.A., 1969; Arizona State University, Bachelor of Architecture, 1972. *Principal occupation:* Architect, planning. *Home address:* 1711 East Missouri, Suite #5, Phoenix, Ariz. 85016. *Affiliation: President, owner, architect, Gilbert Honanie, Jr., Inc., Phoenix, Ariz., 1975-. Other professional posts:* National Council of Architectural Registration Board; American Indian Council of Architects & Engineers; Western & Arizona

Society of Architects. *Community activities:* Member of Hopi Tribe; member, Arizona Indian Chamber of Commerce; member. Central Arizona Chapter of Architects. *Biographical sources:* Articles in the *Arizona Republic & Gazette, Arizona Builder, Progressive Architecture,* and *Architectural Journal.*

HONER, JANELLE A. (Seminole)
1954-
(artist, gardner)

Born February 28, 1954, Hayward, Calif. *Education:* Humboldt State University, Arcata, Calif., B.A. (Art, Native American Studies), 1976; Anderson Ranch, Snowmass Village, Colo. (seminars and workshops), 1978-1982. *Principal occupation:* Artist, gardner. *Home address:* P.O. Box 1302, Basalt, Colo. 81621. *Affiliations:* Owner operator, Doug and Janella's Garden, El Jebel, Colo., 1981-; gallery artist, Janie Beggs Fine Arts Ltd., Aspen, Colo., 1986-. *Community activities:* Advisor, Aspen Dance Connection. *Memberships:* National Gardening Association; American Crafts Council; Aspen Art Museum; Colorado Council on the Arts; Carbondale Council on the Arts & Humanities. *Art exhibitions and shows:* Featured artist, Cohen Gallery, Denver, Colo., 1985; "Roaring Fork Annual," Aspen Art Museum, 1985; Colorado Artists-Craftsmen Exhibit, Boulder, Colo., 1984; one-person show, Sioux National Museum, 1981; Roaring Fork Valley Art Show, Aspen Center for the Visual Arts, 1981; "Objects 81," Western Colorado Center for the Arts, Grand Junction, Colo., 1981; group show, Applequist Gallery, Aspen, Colo., 1980; Colorado Artists-Craftsmen Exhibit, Arvada Center for the Arts, 1980; Heard Museum Annual Art Show, 1979; "Spree 78," Colorado Council on the Arts Invitational, Denver, Colo., 1978; three-person show, Western Colorado Center for the Arts, Grand Junction, Colo., 1978; among others. *Awards, honors:* Magna Cum Laude, Humbodt State University, Arcata, Calif., 1976; 1983 Colorado Biennial (show toured Colorado in 1984), Denver, Colo.; first and second place prizes, Women Art West, Grand Junction, Colo., 1982-1983; *Craft Range* Magazine award for "Buy the Heartland," 1982; first place sculpture, Woman Art West, 1980; third place sculpture, Red Cloud Indian Art Show, 1980; inclusion in Northern Plains, Southern Plains Indian Museum art collections; among others. *Interests:* Vocational: "We are organic farmers with a gourmet produce market garden. We teach people basic skills and give garden tours, sell produce. We educate abou wild edibles, food storage; we both are chefs. I also do mixed media sculpture and ceramic sculpture, that is the art I show. We traveled extensively in 1985. My goal is to help feed the hungry in 1986."

HOOVER, HERBERT T. 1930-
(professor of history)

Born March 9, 1930, Oakwood Township, Wabasha County, Minn. *Education:* New Mexico State University, Las Cruces, B.A., 1960, M.A., 1961; University of Oklahoma, Norman, Ph.D., 1966. *Principal occupation:* Professor of history. *Home address:* Route 2, Box 25, Vermillion, S.D. 57069. *Affiliations:* Assistant professor of history, East Texas State University, Commerce, 1965-1967; professor of history, University of South Dakota, Vermillion, 1967-. *Other professional posts:* Director, Newberry Library Center for the History of the American Indian, Chicago, Ill., 1981-1983; director, South Dakota Oral History Center, 1967-. *Military service:* U.S. Navy, 1951-1955 (Fleet Marine Corpsman with First Marine Division in Korean War). *Community activities:* South Dakota Council of Humanists; South Dakota Committee on the Humanities; National Endowment for the Humanities (review panels); South Dakota Historical Society (board of trustees); South Dakota Fairview Township Bpard of Control; South Dakota Historical Publications and Records Commission. *Memberships:* Western History Association, 1962- (chair, nominating board; local arrangements committee; program committee; membership committee; board of editors); Organization of American Historians, 1970- (nominating board; membership committee); Phi Alpha Theta, 1960- (international councillor; international board of advisors); South Dakota Historical Society; Missouri Historical Society; Minnesota Wabasha County Historical Society.

Awards, honors: Augustana College Center for Western Studies, 1985 Achievement Award, National Board of Advisors; National Endowment for the Humanities, Research Grant Award, 1978-1981; National Teacher of the Year Award, 1985. *Interests:* "Travel and recreation is tied to principal occupational interests: the history of Indian-white relations, and the preservation of natural life." *Published works: To Be An Indian* (Holt, Rinehart & Winston, 1971); *The Practice of Oral History* (Microfilming Corp. of America, 1975); *The Chitimacha People* (Indian Tribal Series, 1975); *The Sioux: A Critical Bibliography* (Indiana University, 1979); *Bibliography of the Sioux* (Scarecrow Press, 1980).

HORSE, BILLY EVANS (Kiowa)
(tribal chairman)

Affiliation: Chairman, Kiowa Business Committee, P.O. Box 369, Carnegie, Okla. 73015.

HORSE CAPTURE, GEORGE P.
(museum curator)

Affiliation: Curator, Plains Indian Museum, Buffalo Bill Historical Center, P.O. Box 1000, Cody, Wyo. 82414.

HORSECHIEF, MARY ADAIR
(Cherokee) 1936-
(executive director-Murrow Indian Children's Home)

Born July 2, 1936, Sequoyah County, Okla. *Education:* Bacone Indian Junior College, A.A., 1955; Northeastern Oklahoma State University, B.A. (Education), 1957; Tulsa University (Art Couses), 1966. *Principal occupation:* Executive director, Murrow Indian Children's Home, Muskogee, Okla. (child care-residence care institution). *Home address:* 224 N. 15, Muskogee, Okla. 74401. *Other professional posts:* Teacher, B.I.A. school, public school, head start program-management at Tinker Air Force Base. *Community activities:* Community Council (board member); Indian Parent Committee; Soroptimist Club; American Baptist Indian Caucus; Oklahoma Association of Children's Institutions and Agencies (secretary-treasurer). *Memberships:* National Indian Education Association (past secretary); American Baptist Homes & Hospitals. *Awards, honors:* Painting awards and entries in the following shows: Philbrook Indian Annual Art Show; Five Tribes Annual Art Show; Cherokee Historical Museum Competition; American Indian Exposition Competition; Red Cloud Indian Art Show; Heard Museum and others. *Interests:* "I have interest in contemporary American Indian affairs, education and art. Have traveled to a number of traditional Indian communities and reservation areas for business and fellowship."

HORSMAN, REGINALD 1931-
(distinguished professor of history)

Born October 24, 1931, Leeds (Yorkshire) England. *Education:* University of Birmingham, England, B.A., 1952, M.A., 1955; Indiana University, Bloomington, Ph.D., 1958. *Principal occupation:* Distinguished professor of history. *Home address:* 3548 North Hackett Ave., Milwaukee, Wisc. 53211. *Affiliations:* Instructor, 1958-1959, assistant professor, 1959-1962, associate professor, 1962-1964, professor, 1964-1973, and distinguished professor of history, 1973-, University of Wisconsin, Milwaukee. *Memberships:* American Historical Association; Organization of American Historians; Society of American Historians; Society for Historians of the Early Republic (advisory council); Phi Beta Kappa (honorary member); Phi Kappa Phi (honorary member); Phi Eta Sigma (honorary member); Phi Alpha Theta. *Awards, honors:* University of Wisconsin Kiehofer Award for Excellence in Teaching, 1961; Guggenheim Fellowship, 1965. *Interests:* Research on race and expansion in American history; shaping of American Indian policy; early American foreign policy; Wisconsin Oneida. *Biographical source: Who's Who in America. Published works: The Causes of the War of 1812* (University of Pennsylvania Press, 1962); *Matthew Elliott: British Indian Agent* (Wayne State University Press, 1964); *Expansion and American Indian Policy, 1783-1812* (Michigan State University Press, 1967); *Napolean's Europe;*

The New America (Paul Hamlyn, London, 1970) *The Frontier in the Formative Years, 1783-1815* (Holt, Rinehart, 1970) *Race and Manifest Destiny: The Origins of American Racial Anglo-Saxonism* (Harvard University Press, 1981); *The Diplomacy of the New Republic, 1776-1815* (Harlan Davidson, 1985); *Dr. Nott of Mobile: Southerner, Physician, and Racial Theorist* (LSU press, forthcoming).

HORTON, DAVID A., Jr.
(B.I.A. agency superintendent)

Affiliation: Superintendent, Southeast Agency, Bureau of Indian Affairs, P.O. Box 3-8000, Juneau, Alaska 99802.

HOULIHAN, PATRICK T. 1942-
(anthropologist, museum director)

Born June 22, 1942, New Haven, Conn. *Education:* Georgetown University, B.S., 1964; University of Minnesota, M.A., 1969; University of Wisconsin, Ph.D., 1972. *Principal occupation:* Anthropologist, museum director. *Home address:* 1220 Wentworth Ave., Pasadena, Calif. 91106. *Affiliations:* Instructor, University of Wisconsin, Oshkosh, 1969-1971; director, Anthropology Museum, University of Wisconsin, Oshkosh, 1969-1971; museum intern, Milwaukee Public Museum, 1971-1972; adjunct professor, Arizona State University, Tempe, Ariz., 1972-1980; director, The Heard Museum, Phoenix, Ariz., 1972-1980; director, New York State Museum, Albany, 1980-1981; instructor, American Indian art, UCLA, Extension Division. 1981-; director, Southwest Museum, Los Angeles, Calif., 1981-. *Memberships:* American Association of Museums (first vice president, Western Regional Conference; American Anthropological Association (council on museum education); California Association of Museums (board of directors, 1985-1986). *Field work:* Urban Indian research for the Indian employment service (BIA sponsored), Minneapolis, Minn., 1967. *Interests:* American Indian art. *Published works:* "Museums and Indian Education," (*Journal of Indian Education*, Oct., 1973) "Southwest Pottery Today," (*Arizona Highways*, May, 1974);

"The Hopi Kachinas," (*Image Roche* Magazine, No. 63, 1974); "Indian Art: Fads and Paradoxes," (*Phoenix* Magazine, Feb., 1975); "Basketry Designs in the Greater Southwest," (Exhibit Catalog, Utah Fine Arts Museum, Salt lake City, April, 1976); "Contemporary Indian Art," (Exhibit Catalog, Mid-America Arts Association, Spring, 1979); "Prints and the American Indian Artist," (*American Indian Arts Magazine,* Spring, 1979); "Indians of the Northwest Coast," (*Reader's Digest,* 1980); various articles in *Masterkey,* a quarterly publication of the Southwest Museum, 1981-. Editorial director for the following Heard Museum publications: *Kachinas: A Hopi Artist's Documentary,* 1973; *Pueblo Shields,* April, 1976; *The Other Southwest: Indian Arts and Crafts of Northeastern Mexico,* April, 1977. Editorial director for the following Southwest Museum publications: *Native Faces: Indian Cultures in American Art,* co-author with Patricia Trenton, Ph.D., 1984; *Kachinas of the Zuni* (Northland Press, 1985); work in progress: *Lummis in the Pueblos* (Northland Press, Fall, 1986); *The American Indian in American Art* (Harry Abrams, Fall, 1987). Television programs: Script author for six one-half hour television programs, "Indian Art at the Heard," produced by KAET, 1975; script researcher/writer for five one-half hour television programs titles, "American Indian Artists," produced by KAET, 1976; script author for a one-half hour television program on "The Craft Arts of Northwestern Mexico," produced by KAET, 1977; guest curator, "Generation in Clay," traveling exhibit of Pueblo Pottery, the American Federation of Art, New York, 1980-1983; principal investigator (1977-1980), Navajo Film Project, KAET, Tempe, Ariz.

HOUSE, ERNEST (Ute Mountain Ute)
  (tribal chairman)

Affiliation: Chairman, Ute Mountain Tribal Council, Tribal Office Bldg., Towaoc, Colo. 81334.

HOUSER, ALLAN (Chiricahua Apache)
1914-
  (artist, art instructor)

Born June 30, 1914, Apache, Okla. *Education:* Santa Fe Indian School; Utah State University; private study. *Principal occupation:* Artist, art instructor. *Home address:* 1020 Camino Carlos Rey, Santa Fe, N.M. 87501. *Affiliation:* Instructor in sculpture and advanced painting, Institute of American Indian Arts, Santa Fe, N.M. (retired). *Membership:* Southwestern Association on Indian Affairs (board of directors). *Exhibitions:* One-man shows: Museum of New Mexico, Santa Fe., 1936; Heard Museum, Phoenix, Ariz., 1970; Southern Plains Museum, Anadarko, Okla., 1971; Philbrook Art Center, Tulsa, Okla., 1972; The Gallery Wall, Phoenix, Ariz., 1976, 1977. *Awards, honors:* Mural commissions: Washington, D.C., San Francisco Exposition and New York World's Fair, 1939; Guggenheim Scholarship for sculpture and painting, 1948; created seven and one-half feet tall marble statue, *Comrade in Mourning,* for Haskell Institute, Lawrence, Kan., 1949; 1954 recipient of *Palmes d3 Academique* from French Government for painting; awarded Waite Phillips Trophy for outstanding contributions to field of Indian art, Philbrook Art Center, 1969; appeared in a documentary film produced by National Educational Television, aired 1976. *Interests:* Sculpture, painting, book illustration, lecturing; writing; recording stories; travels to Navajo Reservtion, New York City, Mexico City. *Biographical sources: Indians of Today,* 1960; *Art and Indian Individualists,* by Guy and Doris Monthan, 1975; *Southwest Indian Painting,* by Clara Lee Tanner (University of Arizona Prss, 1973). *Published works:* Mr. Houser's illustrations have appeared in many books.

HOUSER, SCHUYLER
  (college president)

Affiliation: President, Sisseton-Wahpeton College, P.O. Box 262, Sisseton, S.D. 57262.

HOUSH, RAYMOND E. 1921-
(agricultural education)

Born July 26, 1921, Hay Springs, Neb. *Education:* Colorado State University, CTD, 1942-1943; University of Nebraska, 1946-1948; Chadron State College, Neb., B.A., 1959, B.S., 1965; Northern Arizona State University, M.S., 1968; International University, M.S. (Education Specialist), 1977; California Western University, Ph.D., 1978. *Principal occupation:* Agricultural education. *Home address:* 2200 Hidden Glenn, Farmington, N.M. 87401. *Affiliations:* Extension horticulture, Colorado State University, 1969-1974; director, Navajo Community College, Agriculture Program, 1975-. Military service: U.S. Army, 1942-1946 (pilot, radar, engineering corps). *Memberships:* American Horticultural Society; American Society of Animal Breeders; American Agronomy Society; American Dairy Association (state director, 1970-); National Pilots Association. *Awards, honors:* Spokesman of the Year, American Agriculture, 1975; Top Pilot Award, National Pilots Association. *Interests:* "I organized and developed Navajo Community College, Agriculture Program, to train Navajos to operate the Navajo Indian Irrigation Project." *Biographical sources:* Numerous articles: *Daily Times* (Farmington, N.M.); *Navajo Times* (Window Rock, Ariz.); Navajo Community College, *Annual Report, 1975* (Tsaile, Ariz.); *Published work: Developmental Agriculture* (Ph.D. diisertation, 1978).

HOVI, DOROTHY 1933-
(Indian jewelry sales)

Born April 17, 1933, Trenton, N.J. *Education:* Ursinus College, B.S., 1955. *Principal occupation:* Indian jewelry sales; owner, Way of the Arrow, 72 South St., New Providence, N.J. 07974, 1976-. *Membership:* Indian Arts and Crafts Association.

HOWARD, HELEN ADDISON 1904-
(author, historian)

Born August 4, 1904, Missoula, Mt. *Education:* University of Montana, B.A., 1927; University of Southern California, M.A., 1933. *Principal occupation:* Author, histo-

rian. *Home address:* 410 S. Lamer St., Burbank, Calif. 91506. *Affiliations:* Reporter and feature writer, *Daily Missoulian,* Missoula, Mont., 1923-1929; radio-TV monitor-editor, Radio Reports, Inc., 1943-1956; reviewer of scholarly books on American Indians, 1969-1986, editorial advisory board, 1978-, *Journal of the West,* Kansas State University, Manhattan, Kan. Memberships: Montana Historical Society, 1955-; California Writers Guild, 1973-1978. *Awards, honors: War Chief Joseph* dramatized for radio in commemoration of American Indian Day, over KFI-NBC network, 1949; lecturer on American Indian poetry, 1966-1967; *Saga of Chief Joseph,* transcribed in braille and taped, Library of Congress, 1967, microfilmed for college and library use, 1975; *Northwest Trail Blazers,* also microfilmed, 1975; appointed to editorial advisory board, 1978-, *Journal of the West,* scholarly historical quarterly. *Interests:* American Indians; Western history; ride own Arabian horses. *Biographical sources:* Subject biography, KLAC, Los Angeles, 1970, "Our American Heritage," on Indian radio program; *Contemporary Authors; Who's Who of American Women,* 1983-1984; *The Writers Directory,* 1981-1982; *Two Thousand Women of Achievement,* 1971-1972; *Dictionary of International Biography,* 1985-1986; World Who's Who of Women, 5th Edition; *International Authors & Writers Who's Who; Community Leaders & Noteworthy Americans; Personalities of the West and Midwest. Published works: War Chief Joseph* (Caxton, 1941-1978; *Northwest Trail Blazers* (Caxton, 1963-1968); *American Indian Poetry-Tusas 334* (G.K. Hall & Co., 1979-1985); *American Frontier Tales* (Mountain Press, 1982-); contributed three essays to *Dictionary of Indian Tribes of the Americas,* 4 Vols. (Scholarly Press, 1980); many articles in scholarly and popular history magazines, also in seven horse speciality magazines.

HOWE, OSCAR (Sioux) 1915-
(artist, professor emeritus)

Born May 13, 1915, Joe Creek, S.D. *Education:* Dakota Wesleyan University, B.A., 1952; University of Oklahoma, M.F.A.,

1954. *Principal occupation:* Artist, professor emeritus. *Home address:* 128 Walker St., Vermillion, S.D. 57069. *Affiliations:* Artist in residence, Dakota Wesleyan University, 1948-1952; director of art, Pierre High School, Pierre, S.D., 1953-1957; artist in residence, assistant professor of creative arts, professor emeritus, University of South Dakota, Vermillion, 1957-. *Military service:* U.S. Army, 1942-1945. *Memberships:* Delta Phi Delta; International Institute of Arts and Letters (Fellow). *Awards, honors:* Subject, *This Is Your Life* television program, 1960; Grand Purchase Award, Philbrook Art Center, 1947; named S.D. Artist Laureate, 1960; Certificate of Appreciation, Indian Arts and Crafts Board, 1962; Recognition Award, Foundation of North American Indian Culture, 1964; numerous awards in the following art shows from 1949-: Denver Art Museum, Museum of New Mexico, Philbrook Art Center; numerous one-man shows in the U.S.; paintings on permanent exhibit in several U.S. museums. *Books illustrated: Legends of the Mighty Sioux,* 1941; *The Little Lost Sioux,* 1942; *Bringer of the Mystery Dog,* 1943; *North American Indian Costumes,* 1952; among others.

HOWELL, GEORGE E. (Pawnee-Cheyenne) 1935-
(health systems administrator)

Born December 30, 1935, Pawnee, Okla. *Education:* Westminster College, Salt Lake City, Utah, B.S., 1978; University of Utah, Salt Lake City, M.S.W., 1980. *Principal occupation:* Health systems administrator. *Home address:* P.O. Box 712, Wagner, S.D. 57380. *Affiliations:* Health systems administrator, PHS Indian Health Center, Fort Thompson, S.D., 1983-1985; health systems administrator, PHS Indian Health Hospital, Wagner, S.D., 1985-. *Other professional posts:* Director, Mental Health/Social Services, social worker, clinical instructor, University of Utah. *Military service:* U.S. Air Force, 1954-1959 (A/1c). *Community activities:* Four Corners Gourd Dance Society (president); Alcohol Treatment Program (chairman, board of directors); UNAC (chairman, board of directors). *Memberships:* National Association of Social Workers; Native American-Alaska Native Social Workers Association. *Awards, honors:* CSWE Scholarship Grant.

HOWELL, IRENE (Santee Sioux)
(tribal chairwoman)

Affiliation: Chairwoman, Upper Sioux Board of Trustees, P.O. Box 147, Granite Falls, Minn. 56241.

HOXIE, FREDERICK E. 1947-
(director-Indian center)

Born April 22, 1947, Hoolehua, Molokai. *Education:* Amherst College, Mass., B.A., 1969; Brandeis University, Waltham, Mass., Ph.D., 1977. *Principal occupation:* Director-Indian center. *Home address:* 2717 Lincolnwood Ave., Evanston, Ill. 60201. *Affiliation:* Director, D'Arcy McNickle Center for the History of the Amerian Indian, Newberry Library, 60 W. Walton, Chicago, Ill., 1983-. *Other professional post:* Adjunct professor of history, Univerity of Illinois, Chicago. *Memberships:* American Historical Association; Organization of American Historians; American Society of Ethnohistory. *Awards, honors:* Rockefeller Foundation Humanities Fellowship, 1983-1984. *Published works:* Editor, With the Nez Perces (University of Nebraska Press, 1981); *A Final Promise* (University of Nebraska Press, 1984).

HUDSON, MELVIN, Jr. 1932-
(anthropologist)

Born December 24, 1932, Monterey, Ky. *Education:* University of Kentucky, B.A., 1959; University of North Carolina, Ph.D., 1965. *Principal occupation:* Anthropologist. *Home address:* Route 2, Danielsville, Ga. 30633. *Affiliation:* Professor of anthropology, University of Georgia, Athens, Ga., 1964-. *Memberships:* American Anthropological Association; Southern Anthropological Society (president, 1973-1974). *Awards, honors:* Woodrow Wilson Fellow, 1959-1960; senior fellow, Newberry Library, 1977-1978. *Interests:* "My primary interest is in the historical anthropology of the Indians of the Soutestern U.S." *Published works:*

The Catawba Nation (University of Georgia Press, 1970); editor, *Four Centuries of Southern Indians* (University of Georgia Press, 1975); *The Southeastern Indians* (University of Tennessee Press, 1976; editor, *Black Drink: A Native American Tea* (University of Georgia Press, 1978).

HUERTA, C. LAWRENCE (Yaqui Pasqua Pueblo) 1924-
(chancellor emeritus)

Born August 16, 1924, Nogales, Ariz. *Education:* University of Arizona, LLB & J.D., 1953. *Principal occupation:* Chancellor emeritus. *Home address:* P.O. Box 235, Tsaile (Navajo Reservation), Ariz. 86556. *Affiliations:* President, United Services of America, Inc., Washington, D.C., 1962-1974; holder of the Chair of Economic Development, Navajo Community College, Tsaile, Ariz., 1974-; Chancellor Chancellor Emeritus, Navajo Community College, 1975-. *Other professional posts:* Associate (Navajo) Tribal attorney; special assistant, Attorney General (Arizona); Commissioner, Arizona Industrial Commissione; Judge, Maricopa Superior Court, Phoenix, Ariz.; contract management specialist, U.S. Dept. of Commerce, Washington, D.C. *Community activities:* Founder, Navajo Judicial Systems; founder, American Indian School of Medicine; U.S. Dept. of State, Washington, D.C. (Foreign Service Evaluation/Selection Board). *Memberships:* American Indian Society, Washington, D.C.; Phi Delta Pji; International Legal Fraternity; Arizona State Bar; New Mexico State Bar; Bar of the District of Columbia; United States Supreme Court; Pasqua Yaqui Association; Tsaile Kiwanis Navajo Reservation. *Awards, honors:* Founder, American Coordinating Council on Political Education; Casey Club (businessmen) Vesta Club; 3rd Degree Knights of Columbus. *Interests:* "Copyrights, trademarks; student of Panama and U.S. Canal Zone; lecturer on American Indians (North and South America); Indian law, religion, government; student of Latin American affairs." *Published works: Enriquezca Su Vida* (self, 1968); *Arizona Law & Order* (self, 1968).

HUFF, DELORES (Western Cherokee) 1934-
(principal)

Born May 27, 1934, New York, N.Y. *Education:* Tufts University, B.A., 1972, M.A., 1973; Harvard University, Ed.D., 1978. *Principal occupation:* Principal. *Address:* Pierre Indian Learning Center, Pierre, S.D. 57501. *Affiliation:* Principal, Pierre Indian Learning Center, 1976-. *Other professional posts:* Harvard University, American Indian Program—research in planning for economic development in American Indian communities; planner, Boston Indian Council; director of education, Boston Indian Council; evaluator, Native American Committee Education Program; evaluator, O.E.O. Rural Health Programs. *Community activities:* Advisory council for the State of Massachusetts, Vocational and Technical Education (board member); WINNERS, Inc. (board member, co-founder). *Memberships:* National Indian Education Association; Phi Delta Kappa. *Interests:* "I plan on writing a book on planning education for economic development in American Indian comunities. I enjoy research and planning. I have been co-host of two Indian radio programs: the first, *Red Power,* ran for one year and won the national award for radio; the second, *Pow Wow,* ran for three years. I have visited most all of the reservations in this country. I have also been an evaluator for education and health programs for O.E.O. Health planning is another field that interests me. I was a member of the Institute for the Study of Health and Society. *Published works:* "Planning Indian Education," (*Current* Magazine, Dec., 1976); "Colonialism and Education: The Native American Experience," (*Harvard* Magazine, May, 1976).

HUGHES, J. DONALD 1932-
(professor)

Born June 5, 1932, Santa Monica, Calif. *Education:* Oregon State University, Corvallis, 1950-1952; UCLA, A.B., 1954; Boston University, Ph.D., 1960. *Principal occupation:* Professor. *Home address:* 2568 S. Columbine St., Denver, Colo. 80210. *Affiliation:* Professor of history, University of Denver, Denver, Colo., 1967-. *Other pro-*

fessional post: Visitng professor, University of Colorado, Boulder. *Memberships:* American Historical Society, 1961-; Forest History Society. *Awards, honors:* Burlington Northern Research Prize, 1985; Alumni Fellow, Boston University, 1957-1958; Phi Beta Kappa, 1954-. *Interests:* Teaching, writing; the environment; travel. *Published works: Ecology in Ancient Civilizations* (University of New Mexico Press, 1975); *In the House of Stone and Light* (Grand Canyon N.H.A., 1977); *American Indians in Colorado* (Pruett Press, 1978); *American Indian Ecology* (Texas Western Press, 1983); contributing editor (editor-in-chief, 1983-1985), *Environmental Review; member editorial board, Environmental Ethics.*

HUGHES, JUANITA (Eastern Cherokee) (museum curator)

Affiliation: Curator, Museum of the Cherokee Indian, P.O. Box 770-A, Cherokee, N.C. 28719.

HUNTER, ROBERT L. (B.I.A. agency superintendent)

Affiliation: Superintendent, Western Nevada Agency, Bureau of Indian Affairs, Stewart, Nev. 89437.

HUNTER, TERRY (executive director-Indian association)

Affiliation: Executive director, Association of American Indian Physicians, 6805 S. Western, Suite 504, Oklahoma City, Okla. 73139.

HURT, WESLEY R. 1917- (museum director)

Born September 20, 1917, Albuquerque, N.M. *Education:* University of New Mexico, B.A. (Anthropology), 1938, M.A. (Sociology), 1941; University of Michigan, Ph.D. (Anthropology), 1952. *Principal occupation:* Museum director. *Home address:* 120 Concord Rd., Bloomington, Ind. 47401.

Affiliation: Director, Indiana University Museum, Bloomington, Ind., 1964-. *Other professional post:* Professor of anthropology, Indiana University. *Military service:* U.S. Army, Counter Intelligence Corps, 1942-1945. *Memberships:* American Association of Museums; American Anthropological Association; Society for American Archaeology; Association of Science Museum Directors; Americn Quaternary Association. *Interests:* Arcaeology of the New World; directed archaeological project in Missouri Valley of South Dakota, 1949-1960; archaeological expeditions to South America, 1955, 1958, 1968, 1969. *Published works:* Approximately 100 articles and monographs on American Indian archaeology and ethnology.

HURTADO, ALBERT L. 1946- (assistant professor of history)

Born October 19, 1946, Sacramento, Calif. *Education:* Sacramento City College, Calif., 1964-1966; California State University, Sacramento, B.A., 1969, M.A., 1975; University of California, Santa Barbara, Ph.D., 1981. *Principal occupation:* Assistant professor of history, Arizona State University, Tempe, Ariz., 1986-. *Affiliations:* Assistant professor of history, Indiana University-Purdue University, Indianapolis, 1983-1986, Arizona State University, 1986-. *Other professional posts:* Lecturer, University of Maryland; instructor, Sierra College, Rocklin, Calif. *Military service:* U.S. Army, 1969-1971, Counter Intelligence Agent. *Community activities:* California Committee for the Promotion of History (chair, 1981-1983). *Memberships:* National Council on Public History (treasurer, 1985-1986; board of directors, 1982-1986); American Historical Association; Organization of American Historians; Western History Association; American Society for Ethnohistory; California Historical Society; Indiana Historical Society. *Awards, honors:* Bolton Prize for Spanish Borderlands History for the best article in the field, awarded biennially by the Western Historical Association for, "'Hardly a Farm House--a Kitchen Without Them': Indian and White Households on the California Borderland Frontier in 1860," (*Western Historical Quarterly,* July, 1982). *Interests:* Western history,

Indian history, public history; backpacking, photography. *Published works:* Articles and book reviews in various scholarly journals. "Indian Survival in Frontier California, 1820-1860," in progress.

HUTCHINGS, EVELYN K. (Choctaw-Chickasaw) 1946-
(director of special services)

Born September 19, 1946, Talihina, Okla. *Education:* Southeastern State University, Durant, Okla., B.S. (Business Administration), 1972, M.B.S. (Elementary Education), 1975, M.B.S. (Guidance and Counseling), 1976. *Principal occupation:* Director of special services, Murray State College, Tishomingo, Okla. *Home address:* 101 Faculty Dr., Apt. 10, Tishomingo, Okla. 73460. *Community activities:* Oklahoma Health Systems Agency (Sub-area Council IV - council member). *Memberships:* Southwest Association of Student Assistance Programs; Oklahoma Division of Student Assistance Programs; Oklahoma Personnel & Guidance Association; Indian Adult Advisory Committee, Athletic Committee, Murray State College; Emergency School Aid Assistance, Fillmore Schools (consultant); National Indian Education Association.

HYDE, DOUGLAS (Nez Perce) 1946-
(artist)

Born July 28, 1946, in "Nez Pece country," Idaho. *Education:* Institute of American Indian Arts. *Principal occupation: Artist. Awards, honors:* Numerous awards since 1965.

I

IDE, JOHN H. (Klamath) 1932-
(U.S. Air Force, retired)

Born November 30, 1932, Klamath Agency, Ore. *Education:* University of Tampa, Fla., B.A. (History), 1971; University of Hawaii, Honolulu, M.A. (TESL), 1975. *Principal occupation:* U.S. Air Force, retired. *Home address:* 85-175 Farrington Highway #B424, Waianae, Hawaii 96792. *Affiliation:* Professor of English, Hankuk University of Foreign Studies, Seoul, Korea, 1977-1983; JTPA director, Hawaii Council of American Indian Nations, Honolulu, 1984-. *Military service:* U.S. Army, 1952-1955 (radio operator); U.S. Air Force, 1956-1973 (munitions specialist, retired with rank of technical sergeant E-6). *Community activities:* American Indian Services Corp. (president); American Indian Powwow Association (vice president); Hawaiian Heritage Cultural Center of Waianae, Hawaii (member, board of directors). *Memberships:* Non-Commissioned Officer's Association; Retired Enlistee Association; National Association of Uniformed Services. *Interests:* "Served in Germany, 1949-1955, 1962-1966; Japan, 1957-1960; Taiwan, 1968-1970; Korea, 1972, 1977-1983. Interested in linguistics and history; was judo player and instructor, 1957-1971. Present interest is in educational and vocational counseling. I'm completing studies in counseling and guidance. Pursuing interests in Indian affairs and Klamath restoration." *Published works:* "Multi-Level Reinforcement in Language Teaching (*College English Teacher's Journal,* Korea, 1979); co-author, "North American Culture," (Hankuk University, 1980); "Easy Come, Easy Go," (*The Current English Magazine,* Korea, 1982); "Some Problems Encountered by Korean Students Studying Abroad," with David Cottrell, (*Journal of East-West Education,* Korea, 1981); "Teaching Culturally Appropriate English," (*College English Teacher's Journal,* Korea, 1982).

ISAAC, CALVIN JAMES (Choctaw) 1933-
(education)

Born December 5, 1933, Philadelphia, Miss. *Education:* Delta State University, B.A. (Music Education), 1954. *Principal occupation: Education. Home address:* Route 7, Box 21, Philadelphia, Miss. 39350. *Affiliations:* Education specialist, Title I, B.I.A., Philadelphia, Miss, 1972-1975; former tribal chief, Mississippi Band of Choctaw Indians, Philadelphia, Miss., 1975-1980. *Other professional posts:* Director, Choctaw Head Start Program, Service Unit director; teacher supervisor (elementary), B.I.A.; education specialist (fine arts). *Military ser-*

vice: U.S. Dept. of Defense, Army. *Community activities:* Choctaw Housing Authority (chairman); Choctaw Advisory School Board (chairman); Policy Advisory Council (tribal representative). *Memberships:* Mississippi State Advisory Committee, 1975-; United Southeastern Tribes, Inc., 1975-; National Tribal Chairman's Association, 1975-; Governor's Colonel Staff, 1976-; Goveror's Multicultural Advisory Council, 1976-. *Awards, honors:* John Hay Whitney Fellowship Scholar, 1967-1968; Phi Delta Kappa, Mississippi State University, 1976; Omicron Delta Kappa, Delta State University, 1975.

ISAACS, IDA LUJAN (Taos-San Juan Pueblo)
(owner/manager-Indian House Recordings)

Born Taos Pueblo, N.M. *Principal occupation:* Owner/manager, Indian House Recordings, P.O. Box 472, Taos, N.M. 87571. *Other professional post:* Guest assistant curator, Whitney Museum of American Art, "Two Hundred Years of American Indian Art" show. *Community activities:* Headstart Parents Group; Taos Pueblo School Board; B.I.A. Credit Committee. *Awards, honors:* Minority Business Award, Small Business Administration, 1976; announcer, Indian program, KXRT-FM, Taos.

J

JABBOUR, ALAN ALBERT 1942-
(archivist)

Born June 21, 1942, Jacksonville, Fla. *Education:* Univerity of Miami, B.A. (magna cum laude), 1963; Duke University, M.A., 1966, Ph.D., 1968. *Principal occupation:* Archivist. *Home address:* 3107 Cathedral Ave., N.W., Washington, D.C. 20008. *Affiliations:* Head, Archive of Folk Song, Library of Congress, 1969-1974; head, Folk Arts Program, national Endowment for the Arts, Washington, D.C., 1974-1976; director, The American Folklife Center, Library of Congress, Washington, D.C., 1976- (the Center engages in the preservation, presentation, and dissemination of American folk

cultural traditions, and contributes to the cultural planning and prgramming of the Library, federal government and the nation). *Memberships:* American Folklore Society; Society for Ethnomusicology; Modern Language Association; California Folklore Society; John Edwards Memorial Foundation (advisor); American Folklife Center (member, board of trustees). *Awards, honors:* Phi Beta Kappa; University of Miami Music Scholarship, 1959-1962; Woodrow Wilson Fellowship, 1963; Duke Univerity Scholarship, 1964-1966; Dabforth Teaching Fellowship, 1966-1968; responsible for the initiation of one of the Library's American Revolution Bicentennial projects, an anthology of 15 long-playing records containing examples of major folk music traditions of the U.S. -- Anglo-American, Afro-American, American Indian, and other rural and urban ethnic groups. The series is called, *Folk Music in America. Interests:* Folk music and song; folklore; medieval English literature; musicology; American studies. *Published works:* Numerous papers presented and published.

JACKSON, CHARLES (Cow Creek Band Umpqua)
(tribal chairman)

Affiliation: Chairman, Cow Creek Band of Upqua Indians, 283 S.E. Fowley, Rosebug, Ore. 97470.

JACKSON, DEAN
(college president)

Affiliation: President, Navajo Community College, Tsaile Rural Post Office, Tsaile, Ariz. 86556.

JACKSON, WALTER (Quileute)
(tribal chairman)

Affiliation: Chairman, Quileute Tribal Council, P.O. Box 279, La Push, Wash. 98350.

JACKSON, WILLIAM
"RATTLESNAKE"(Cherokee) 1928-
(civil service; principal chief-Southeastern Cherokee Confederacy)

Born December 23, 1928, Norman Park, Colquitt County, Ga. *Principal occupation:* Civil service; principal chief, Southeastern Cherokee Confederacy. *Home address:* Route 1, Box 111, Leesburg, Ga. 31763. *Affiliations:* Civil service, Albany, Ga., 1964-; principal chief, Southeastern Cherokee Confederacy, Leesburg, Ga., 1978-. *Military service:* U.S. Army (Korean War Medal). *Memberships:* American Legion; VFW. *Awards, honors:* Letter of Appreciation, 20-Year Service Awards with Civil Service; safety awards. "I have received a Proclamation in person from ex-Governor, George Busbee." *Interests:* "I visit different clans and band meetings; attend chiefs of council meetings, annual meetings, and pow wows. I have posed for an artist to paint my portrait for Albany Junior College. I am also the publisher of newsletter for the Southeastern Cherokee Confederacy. We have members all over the United State, and I'm recognized as pricnipal chief of this tribe. We are a nation within a nation."

JACKSON, ZANE, Sr. (Cayuga)
(tribal chairman)

Affiliation: Chairman, Warm Springs Tribal Council, Warm Springs, Ore. 97761.

JACOBS, ALEX A. *(Karoniaktatie)*
(Mohawk) 1953-
(writer, artist, editor)

Born February 28, 1953, Akwesasne Reservation, via Rooseveltown, N.Y. *Education:* Institute of American Indian Arts, Santa Fe, N.M., AFA (sculpture, creative writing), 1977; Kansas City Art Institute, BFA (sculpture, creative writing), 1979. *Home address:* P.O. Box 223, Hogansburg, N.Y. 13655. *Affiliations:* Editor, *Akewesasne Notes,* via Rooseveltown, N.Y., 1979-1985; editor, *Akwekon Literary Journal, Akwesasne Notes,* Hogansburg, N.Y., 1985. *Other professional posts:* Board of directors, CKON-F, Radio Station, Mohawk Nation. *Awards, honors:* 1975 poetry award, Scottsdale

National Indian Art Exhibit; 1979 honorable mention, Society of Western Art, Kansas City, Mo. *Interests:* "Poetry, prose, short stories; graphic arts; sculpture; painting, printmaking; ceramics; video/audio/performance art; editor of Native American literature and journalism; networking national and international native peoples; poetry readings and workshops; travel U.S.A. with White Roots of Peace, 1973-1974 (native touring group/communications). *Published works:* "Native Colours" (*Akwesasne Notes,* 1974); "Landscape: Old & New Poems" (*Blue Cloud Quarterly,* 1984); Anthologies: "Come to Power," "The Remembered Earth," "The Next World, 3rd World Writers, and "Songs From the Earth on Turtle's Back," in various literary magazines, 1972-1985; editor, *Akwekon Literary Journal,* 1985-.

JACOBS, HARVEY
(Indian education)

Affiliation: Indian education, Bureau of Indian Affairs, 1951 Constitution Ave., N.W., Washington, D.C. 20245.

JACOBS, WILBUR R.
(professor of history)

Born in Chicago, Ill. *Education:* University of California, Los Angeles, Ph.D. *Principal occupation:* Professor of history, University of California, Santa Barbara, Calif. *Home address:* 199 Edgemound Dr., Santa Barbara, Calif. 93105. *Military service:* U.S. Air Force (World War II). *Memberships:* American Historical Association (former president, Pacific Coast Branch); American Society for Ethnohistory (former president); American Society for Environmental History (former president); Organization of American Historians. *Awards, honors:* Staford Prize for book, *Wilderness Politics and Indian Gifts,* American Historical Association University Press, Pacific Coast Branch. "Began the first class in American Indian history taught in any branch of the University of California. Class is still offered and graduates from it have gone on to teach Indian history at a number of leading universities and colleges in America." *Interests:* "American Indian environmental studies;

the achievements of American Indian women; the role and place of the Indian in American frontier history and in early American history. (I am) contributor to many historical journals, encyclopedias and to the *Handbook of the American Indians."* *Biographical sources: Encyclopedia of the American West,* edited by Howard Lamar; *Who's Who in America; Who's Who on the Pacific Coast; Who's Who in the World. Published works: The Southern Colonial Indian Frontier* (University of Nebraska Press, 1967); *Wilderness Politics and Indian Gifts* (University of Nebraska Press, 1972); *Dispossessing the American Indians,* Second Edition (University of Oklahoma Press, 1985).

JAEGAR, RONALD
(B.I.A. agency superintendent)

Affiliation: Superintendent, Central California Agency, Bureau of Indian Affairs, 1800 Tribute Rd., P.O. Box 15740, Sacramento, Calif. 95813-0740.

JACOBSEN, WILLIAM H., Jr. 1931-
(professor of English)

Born November 15, 1931, San Diego, Calif. *Education:* Harvard University, A.B., 1953; University of California, Berkeley, Ph.D., 1964. *Principal occupation:* Professor of English, University of Nevada, 1967-. *Home address:* 1411 Samuel Way, Reno, Nev. 89509. *Memberships:* Linguistic Society of America; International Linguistic Association; Society for the Study of the Indigenous Languages of the Americas; American Anthropological Association; Society for Linguistic Anthropology; Great Basin Anthropological Conference. *Awards, honors:* Outstanding Researcher Award, University of Nevada, Reno, 1983. *Interests:* "American Indian languages, primarily Washo and Makah, and the Hokan and Wakashan families; also, fieldwork or publication on Salinan, Yana, Nootka, Nez Perce, Numic, and Chimakuan. *Published work: First Lessons in Makah* (Makah Cultural and Research Center, 1979).

JAEGER, ROBERT
(B.I.A. area director)

Affiliation: Director, Minnesota Sioux Area Field Office, 1330 Sioux Trail, N.W., Prior Lake, Minn. 55372.

JAENEN, CORNELIUS J. 1927-
(professor of history)

Born February 2, 1927, Cannington Manor, Saskatchewan, Canada. *Education:* University of Manitoba, Winnipeg, M.A., 1950; Univerity of Ottawa, Ontario, Ph.D., 1963. *Principal occupation:* Professor of history, University of Ottawa. *Memberships:* American Society for Ethnohistory; Canadian Historical Association; French Colonial Historical Society (vice president); Canadian Ethnic Studies Association (vice president). *Awards, honors:* Ste. Marie Prize, 1973, for *Friend and Foe. Published works: Friend and Foe: Aspects of French-Amerindian Cultural Contact in the Sixteenth and Seventeenth Centuries* (Columbia University, 1976); *The Role of the Church in New France* (McGraw-Hill - Ryerson, Ltd., 1976); *The French Relationship With the Native Peoples of New France* (Indian and Northern Affairs, Canada, 1984); *Identites, Selected Problems and Interpretations in Canadian History* (Prentice-Hall, Canada, 1986); booklets, and numerous chapters of books on the American Indian.

JAFFE, A.J. 1912-
(statistician)

Born in 1912, Mass. *Education:* University of Chicago, Ph.D., 1941. *Principal occupation:* Statistician. *Home address:* 314 Allaire Ave., Leonia, N.J. 07605. *Affiliations:* Special research scholar, Department of Anthropology, Columbia University, New York, N.Y. *Other professional posts:* Research associate, Museum of the American Indian, New York, N.Y. *Memberships:* American Statistical Association; Population Association of America; American Association for the Advancement of Science; International Population Union. *Interests:* "Changing demography of the Native Americans." *Published works: Peo-*

132

ple, *Jobs, and Economic Development* (Free Press, 1959); *Changing Demography of Spanish Americans* (Academic Press, 1980); *Misuse of Statistics* (Marcel Dekker, Inc., 1986).

JAMES, OVERTON (Chickasaw) 1925-
(educator)

Born July 21, 1925, Bromide, Okla. *Education:* Southeastern State College, B.A., 1949, M.A., 1955. *Principal occupation:* Educator. *Home address:* 6033 Glencove Pl., Oklahoma City, Okla. 73132. *Affiliations:* Teacher and athletic coach, public schools of Ravia, Caddo and Shattuck, Okla.; sales manager, *Compton's Pictured Encyclopedia,* 1960-1965; governor, Chickasaw Nation of Oklahoma, 1963-; field representative, assistant director, State Department of Education Division, Oklahoma City, Okla., 1965-. *Military service:* U.S. Navy, 1943-1946. *Community activities:* Choctaw-Chickasaw Confederation (president); Women's Gridiron Club of Oklahoma (board of directors); Oklahoma State Indian Affairs (past chairman); Inter-Tribal Council of Five Civilized Tribes (past president); Five Civilized Tribes Museum (board of directors); Masons; VFW; American Legion. *Memberships:* National Education Association; Oklahoma Education Association; National Congress of American Indians. *Awards, honors;* In October, 1963, Mr. James became the 27th governor of the Chickasaw Nation, and the youngest ever to serve as governor. *Interests:* Sports, hunting and fishing.

JAMES, WABUN 1945-
(writer, lecturer, teacher)

Born April 5, 1945, Newark, N.J. *Education:* George Washington University, B.A., 1967; Columbia University, M.A. (Journalism), 1968. *Principal occupation:* Writer, lecturer, teacher. *Home address:* P.O. Box 9167, Spokane, Wash. 99209. *Affiliation:* Executive director, The Bear Tribe Medicine Society, Spokane, Wash., 1972-. *Published works: The People's Lawyers* (Holt, Rinehart & Winston, 1973); *The Bear Tribe's Self-Reliance Book* (Bear Tribe Publishing, 1977); *The Medicine Wheel Book* (Prentice-Hall, 1980); *Sun Bear: The Path to Power* (Bear Tribe Publishing, 1983).

JAMES, WALTER S., Jr.
(executive director-Indian organization)

Affiliation: Executive director, Council for Native American Indian Progress, 280 Broadway, Suite 316, New York, N.Y. 10007.

JAMES, WILLIE
(B.I.A. agency superintendent)

Affiliation: Superintendent, Chilocco Maintenance and Security Detachment, Bureau of Indian Affairs, P.O. Box 465, Newkirk, Okla. 74647.

JILEK, WOLFGANG GEORGE, M.D. 1930-
(psychiatrist, anthropologist)

Born November 25, 1930, Tetschen, Bohemia. *Education:* Medical schools of the universities of Munich, W. Germany, Innsbruck, Austria, and Vienna, Austria, M.D., 1956; McGill University, Montreal, Quebec, Canada, M.Sc., 1966; University of British Columbia, Vancouver, Canada, M.A. (Anthropology), 1972. *Principal occupation:* Clinical professor of psychiatry. *Home address:* 571 English Bluff Rd., Delta, British Columbia, Canada V4M 2M9. *Affiliations:* Department of Anthropology & Sociology, 1974-; clinical professor of psychiatry, Department of Psychiatry, 1980-, University of British Columbia, Vancouver, Canada. *Other professional posts:* Consultant psychiatrist, Greater Vancouver Mental Health Service; consultant in mental health, World Health Organization, 1984-1985. *Community activities;* American Psychiatric Association (member, Task Force on American Indians, 1971-1977). *Memberships:* Canadian Psychiatric Association (organizer and chairman of the Task Force, later Section, on Native People's Mental Health, 1970-1980); World Psychiatric Association (secretary, Transcultural Psychiatry section, 1983-); Canadian Medical Association; Fellow, Royal College of Physicians and Surgeons of Canada; editorial advisor, *Transcultural Psychiatric Research Review,* Montreal, Canada; editorial advisor, *Curare-Journal of Ethnomedicine and Transcultural Psychiatry,* Heidelberg, W. Germany. *Interests:* "Transcultural psychiatry; traditional medicine and ceremonialism, especially of aboriginal North and South American peoples; ethnomedical and ethnopsychiatric research among aboriginal people of Canada, U.S. (especially Northwest Pacific culture area), and South America; Haiti; East Africa; Southeast Asia; Papua, New Guinea, 1963-)." *Published works: Salish Indian Mental Health and Culture Change* (Holt, Rinehart & Winston, Toronto, 1974); *Indian Healing-Shamanic Ceremonialism in the Pacific Northwest Today* (Hancock House, 1982); *Traditional Medicine and Primary Health Care in Papua, New Guinea* (WHO & Papua, New Guinea University Press, 1985); numerous articles which deal with North American Indians.

JILEK-AALL, LOUISE M., M.D.
1931-
(psychiatrist, anthropologist)

Born April 25, 1931, Oslo, Norway. *Education:* University of Oslo, Norway, 1949-1950; University of Tuebingen, W. Germany, 1951-1955; University of Zurich, Switzerland, M.D., 1958, Dipl. of Trop. Med., 1959; University of Basal, Switzerland, 1959; McGill University, Montreal, Canada, Dipl. of Psychiatry, 1965; University of British Columbia, Vancouver, Canada, M.A. (Social Anthropology), 1972. *Principal occupation:* Psychiatrist, anthropologist. *Home address:* 571 English Bluff Rd., Delta, British Columbia, Can. V4M 2M9. *Affiliations:* Clinical professor of psychiatry, University of British Columbia, Vancouver, B.C., Canada (member, faculty of medicine, 1975-). *Other professional posts:* Consultant psychiatrist, Greater Vancouver Mental Health Service; consultant psychiatrist, Shaughnessy Hospital, Vancouver, B.C. *Military service:* Medical officer, U.N. Congo Mission, 1960-1961 (Citation and Congo Medal of the League of Red Cross Societies, 1961). *Memberships:* Canadian Psychiatric Association (vice chairperson, Section on Native Mental

Health); Canadian Psychiatric Association (member, Task Force/Section on Native Mental Health, 1970-); Royal College of Physicians and Surgeons of Canada, 1966- (Fellow); World Psychiatric Association, 1974- (member, Transcultural Section). *Interests:* "Transcultural psychiatry; ethnomedicine; Canadian, American and Alaskan Native mental health; Native therapeutic resources; alcohol abuse prevention and rehabilitation. Fieldwork and research in transcultural psychiatry and ethnomedicine in North and South America, the Caribbean, Asia, Africa, Oceania; neurological research in epilepsy." *Published works:* Articles in various scientific and professional journals.

JIM, ROGER R., Sr. (Yakima)
(tribal chairman)

Affiliation: Chairman, Yakima Tribal Council, P.O. Box 151, Toppenish, Wash, 98948.

JIMMIE, LUKE, (Mississippi Choctaw)
(chairman-tribal education)

Affiliation: Chairman, Education Committee, Mississippi Band of Choctaw Indians, Route 7, Box 21, Philadelphia, Miss. 39350.

JOHANNSEN, CHRISTINA BARBARA
1950-
(museum director)

Born October 29, 1950, Rahway, N.J. *Education:* Beloit College, Wis., B.A., 1972; Brown University, Ph.D., 1984. *Principal occupation:* Museum director. *Home address:* Star Route 1, Box 144, Warnerville, N.Y. 12187. *Affiliation:* Director, Schoharie Museum of the Iroquois Indian, Box 158, Schoharie, N.Y. 12157, 1980-. *Other professional post:* Trustee, Mohawk Caughnawaga Museum. *Community activities:* Schoharie County Tourism Development Corp. (secretary, board of directors). *Memberships:* American Association of Museums; Mid-Atlantic Association of Museums. *Interests:* "Research and promotion of contemporary Iroquois art. Actively involved in educating the public about the contributions of Iroquois peoples today and to an understanding of their past. Concern in maintaining professional museological standards in small museums and delineating a museum's purposes and goals. Continued field research in Iroquois communities throughout the U.S. and Canada. Special interest in creatively photographing museum objects." *Published works:* "European Trade Goods and Wampanoag Culture in the Seventeenth Century" in *Burr's Hill: A 17th Century Wampanoag Burial Ground in Warren, Rhode Island* (Haffenreffer Museum of Anthropology, Brown University, 1980); *Iroquois Arts: A Directory of a People and Their Work,* co-edited with Dr. John P. Ferguson (Association for the Advancement of Native North American Arts and Crafts, 1984); *Efflorescence and Identity in Iroquois Art,* Ph.D. Dissertation, Brown Univerity, 1984.

JOHN, ANGELO MARVIN (Navajo)
1946-
   (artist)

Born February 5, 1946, Holbrook, Ariz. *Education:* Institute of American Indian Arts, 1962-1965; Arizona State University. *Principal occupation:* Artist. *Home address:* 29 Clark Homes, Flagstaff, Ariz. 86001. *Community activities:* Navajo Youth Conference (president, 1965); Institute of American Indian Arts (student body president, 1965). *Awards, honors:* Awards received from Institute of American Indian Arts, Scottsdale Exhibition, Philbrook Art Center. *Interests:* Mr. John writes, "I am interested in track; Indian art; reading (recent history)."

JOHN, CALVIN (Seneca) 1920-
   (project director)

Born June 15, 1920, Coldspring, N.Y. *Principal occupation:* Project director, Iroquoia, a cultural/recreational/tourism project of the Seneca Nation. *Home address:* P.O. Box 343, Salamanca, N.Y. 14779. *Military service:* U.S. Army, 1942-1945 (Staff Sergeant, 31st Infantry Division). *Community activities:* Kiwanis Club; Congregational Reservation Temperance group; Cattaraugus County Planning Board; Jimersontown Presbyterian Church.

JOHNNY, RONALD EAGLEYE
   (president-Indian organization)

Affiliation: President, American Indian Law Students, American Indian Law Center, University of New Mexico School of Law, 1117 Stanford N.E., Albuquerque, N.M. 87196.

JOHNS, GLENN DAVID (Skokomish)
1947-
   (artist)

Born December 15, 1947, Shelton, Wash. *Education:* Stewart Indian School; Institute of American Indian Arts. *Awards, honors:* Second Place, 1965 Scottsdale National Indian Arts Exhibition. *Exhibits:* Second Annual Exhibition of American Indian Painting (U.S. Dept. of the Interior Art Gallery); Young American Indian Artist (Riverside Museum).

JOHNS, JOSEPH F. *(Cayoni)*
(Creek) 1928-
   (museum manager, artist)

Born January 31, 1928, Okefenokee Swamp, Ga. *Education:* High school (U.S. Armed Forces Institute). *Principal occupation:* Museum manager, artist. *Home address:* 7 Russell St., West Peabody, Mass. 01960. *Affiliation:* Building manager, Peabody Museum, Harvard University, Cambridge, Mass., 1974-. "I am also Indian artist in residence at the Peabody Museum (sculpture and carving in any medium). I maintain a small studio, at my home, for carving the eight traditional masks of the Creek people." *Military service:* U.S. Naval Amphibious Forces (Sniper), 1944-1946 (U.S. Navy P.O. 3; Asiatic Pacific Medal, Silver Star Medal); U.S. Coast Guard (reitired), 1947-1965 (U.S.C.G. P.O. 1; Silver Life Saving Medal presented by President Harry S. Truman in Washington, D.C., 1947). *Community activities:* Masonic Shriner at Aleppo Temple, Wilmington, Mass. *Membership:* Boston Indian Council. *Awards, honors:* "I was a crew member of the Coast Guard Cutter Westwind Expedition to the North Pole (Dew Line), 1953-1954; and a cre member of the Coast Guard's Cutter, Eastwind expedition to the South Pole (Operation Deep Freeze, 1961-1962); (I am) holder of Antarctica Service Medal. A book about my life is now being written by Mitchell Wade."

JOHNSON, PATRICIA LUCILLE PADDLETY (Kiowa) 1938-
(attorney)

Born October 22, 1938, Mountain View, Okla. *Education:* Oklahoma College of Liberal Arts, Chickasaw, B.S. (Economics), 1971; University of Oklahoma, Norman, J.D., 1975. *Principal occupation:* Attorney. *Home address:* Route 3, Anadarko, Okla. 73005. *Affiliation:* Associate Magistrate, Bureau of Indian Affairs, Code of Indian Offenses, Court, Anadarko, Okla. *Community activities:* Indian Capital Baptist Church (member and teacher); Oklahoma Indian Rights Association; Oklahoma Indian Women Association. *Memberships:* Oklahoma Bar Association, 1975- (Minorities Law Committee, 1976); Federal Bar for the Western District of Oklahoma, 1975-. *Interests:* "I am interested in assisting young Indian people to achieve their life's goals, whether in Law or in any other field of training. I work extensively with our church in attempting to inspire and inform Indians in this area of the opportunities available to them. Alcoholism and drug related offenders make up the majority of my clients, and when I have the time, I counsel and encourage them."

JOHNSON, ROBERT
(executive director-Indian association)

Affiliation: Executive director, American Indian Development Association, 1015 Indian School Rd. N.W., Albuquerque, N.M. 87102.

JOHNSON, ROY S. *(Crazy Horse)* (Rappahannock) 1928-
(research writer, lecturer, educator)

Born December 7, 1928, Caroline County, Va. *Education:* Temple University, 1947-1949; University of Pennsylvania, B.A., 1951; College of Metaphysics, Ps.D., 1972. *Principal occupation:* Research writer, lecturer on Indian affairs, educator. *Military service:* U.S. Army, 1943-1946 (1st Lieutenant; six major campaigns—Pacific Theatre

Medal, Silver Star, Bronze Star, Purple Heart, Presidential Unit Citation, Good Conduct Medal). *Community activities:* Coalition of Native Americans. *Memberships:* Rappahannock Tribe, State of Virginia (field chief); Powhatan Indians of Delaware Valley (chairman). *Interests:* Mr. Johnson teaches basic adult education to Native Americans; teaches self-defense and the Powhatan language. *Published work:* East Coast Indian Tribes, with Jack D. Forbes.

JOHNSON, SAM 1938-
(president-Indian village)

Born August 14, 1938, Ashdown, Ark. *Education:* University of Arkansas, Fayetteville, B.A. *Principal occupation:* President, Kado-ha Indian Village, Murfressboro, Ark., 1978-. *Military service:* U.S. Army (four years).

JOHNSON, SAMUEL
(B.I.A. Indian education)

Affiliation: Indian education, Bureau of Indian Affairs, 1951 Constitution Ave., N.W., Washington, D.C. 20245.

JOHNSTON, BASIL H. (Ojibway) 1929-
(teacher)

Born July 13, 1929, Parry Island Reserve, Ontario, Can. *Education:* Loyola College, Montreal (graduate cum laude, 1954); Ontario College of Education, Secondary School Teaching Certificate, 1962. *Principal occupation:* Teacher. *Home address:* 253 Ashlar Rd., Richmond Hill, Ontario, Can. L4C 2W7. *Affiliations:* Assistant manager, 1957-1959, manager, 1959-1961, Toronto Board of Trade; teacher, Earl Haig Secondary School, 1962-1969; lecturer, Royal Ontario Museum, Toronto, 1969-1972; teacher, private English teacher of Ojibway Indians, Toronto, 1974-. *Community activities:* Toronto Indian Club; Canadian Indian Centre of Toronto (executive and vice president, 1963-1969); Indian Eskimo Association (executive, legal committee, speakers committee, 1965-1968); Union of Ontario Indians; Feeral Indian Consultations,

Toronto; Indian Hall of Fame (committee member, 1968-1970); Wigwamen Inc., 1974-1975; Ontario Geographic Names Board, 1977-. *Awards, honors:* 1976 Fels Award for *Many Smokes,* Klamath Falls, Oreg. *Published works:* Numerous stories, essays, articles and poems in various publications.

JOHNSTON, ROBERT (Comanche)
1953-
(lawyer)

Born January 28, 1953, Little Rock, Ark. *Education:* Wichita State University, B.A., 1975; University of Oklahoma, College of Law, J.D., 1978. *Principal occupation:* Lawyer. *Home address:* 1330 Dorchester Dr., Norman, Okla. 73069. *Interests:* Indian law; oil and gas law; natural resources law. *Published work: "Whitehorn v. State:* Peyote and Religious Freedom in Oklahoma" *(American Indian Law Review,* Vol. V, No. 1, winter, 1977).

JOJOLA, TED (Isleta Pueblo)
1951-
(educator, administrator)

Born November 19, 1951, Isleta Pueblo, N.M. *Education:* University of New Mexico, B.A. (Archaeology); Massachusetts Institute of Technology, M.A. (City Planning); University of Hawaii-Manoa, Ph.D. (Political Science), 1982; University of Strasbourg, France, Certificate of International Human Rights Law, 1985. *Principal occupation:* Educator, administrator. *Home address:* Route 6, Box 578, Albuquerque, N.M. 87105. *Affiliations:* Internal planner, National Capital Planning Commission, Washington, D.C., 1973; legal/historical researcher, Institute for the Development of Indian Law, Washington, D.C., 1976; visiting research associate, Institute of Philippine Culture, Manila, 1977-1978; visiting professor of urban planning, UCLA, 1984; assistant professor of planning, University of New Mexico, Albuquerque, 1982-; director, Native American Studies Department, University of New Mexico, 1980-. *Other professional posts:* Consultant, Thurshun Consultants, Albuquerque, N.M., 1980-; coordinator, Ethnic/Minority Directors' Coalition, 1983-. *Community activities:* 9th

Inter-American Indian Congress, Santa Fe, N.M. (U.S. organizing committee, 1985-); Zuni Tribal Museum, Zuni, N.M. (advisory board, 1985-); JOM/Indian Education Parent's Committee, Isleta Pueblo, N.M. (chair). *Memberships:* Native American Studies Association. *Awards, honors:* Postdoctoral Fellow, American Indian Studies, UCLA, 1984; public grantee, Atherton Trust, Honolulu, 1976; recipient of Participant Award, East-West Center, Honolulu. *Interests:* "My main interest lay in the notion of continued tribal "survival," and the various and varying strategies that have ensued in the course of this struggle. Currently, I have been doing research in the notion of tribal (traditional) consensus making and its theoretical modeling toward the idea of using this mechanism for the integration of tribal policy in the regional development process." *Biographical source: Who's Who in the West. Published works: Memoirs of an American Indian House,* 1976; contributing articles to various publications.

JONES, BUDDY CALVIN
(Creek-Cherokee)

Born in Gladewater, Tex. *Education:* University of Oklahoma, M.A., 1968. *Principal occupation:* Archaeologist. *Home address:* Route 3, Box RPGA, Crawfordville, Fla. 32327. *Affiliations:* Curator, Caddo Indian Museum, Longview, Texas (27 years); archaeologist, Bureau of Arcaheological Research, Division of Archives, History and Records Management, Florida Department of State, R.A. Gray Bldg., Tallahasssee, Fla. (18 years). *Military service:* U.S. Army, 1963. *Memberships:* Society of American Archaeology; Southeastern Archaeological Society. *Awards, honors:* Ripley R. Bullon Award, 1983, for lifetime service award, presented by the Florida Anthropological Society. *Biographical sources: Who's Who in the South and Southeast; Men of Achievement,* Cambridge, England, 1976; "Interview with B. Calvin Jones" *(Florida Anthropologist,* 1982-1983 (two part interview). *Published work:* Article: "Southeastern Ceremonial Complex Manifestations at Mound 3, Lake Jackson Site, Leon County, Florida" *(Mid-Continental Journal of Archaeology,* Kent State University); among others.

JONES, DAVID S. (Choctaw) 1928-
(elementary school principal)

Born July 24, 1928, Boswell, Okla. *Education:* Eastern A & M College, Wilburton, Okla., 1950-1951; East Central State College, Ada, Okla., 1951-1952; Central State University, Edmonds, Okla., 1955-1963, B.A., M.A. *Principal occupation:* Elementary school principal. *Home address:* P.O. Box 1223, Navajo, N.M. 87328. *Affiliations:* Principal, Crystal Boarding School, Navajo, N.M., 1983-. *Other professional post:* Council for Exceptional Children, Navajo Area (vice president). *Military service:* U.S. Navy, 1945-1947; U.S. Naval Reserve (18 years); U.S. Army Reserve (Staff Sergeant, 12 years); (Meritorious Service Medal, World War II Victory Medal, Asiatic Pacific Medal, Armed Forces Reserve Medal, Marksman. *Community activities:* El Reno Lions Club, Okla. (past president); Methodist Church (chairman, official board); Methodist Mens Club; Church School (superintendent). *Memberships:* National Indian Education Association (life member); Elementary School Principals Association; Oklahoma Governor's Council for Vocational Education; National Indian Scouting Association. *Awards, honors:* Masonic Teacher of Today Award; American Legions Award for Achievement; Gray-Wolf Award for Outstanding Indian Scouter, Boy Scouts of America. *Interests:* Travels with Naval and Army Reserve trainings. *Published work:* Co-author, *A Guide for Teachers of Indian Students* (Oklahoma Department of Education, 1972).

JONES, JOAN MEGAN 1933-
(socio-cultural anthropologist)

Born September 7, 1933, Laramie, Wyo. *Education:* University of Washington, Seattle, B.A., 1956, M.A., 1968, Ph.D., 1976. *Principal occupation:* Socio-cultural anthropologist. *Home address:* 392 Yokeko Dr., Anacortes, Wash. 98221. *Affiliations:* Educator, Burke Museum, Seattle, 1969-1972; visiting lecturer, Primitive Art, University of British Columbia, 1978; visiting instructor, course: "Indians of the Northwest Coast," Anthropology Department, Western Washington University, Bellingham (Summer), 1981; research asso-

ciate, Department of Anthropolgy, University of Washington, Seattle, 1982-. *Community activities:* Anacortes Arts and Crafts Festival Foundation, (board member, 1981-1983); Anacortes Branch, American Association of University Women (board member, 1982-1984); Skagit Valley Weavers Guild, (board member, 1985-1986). *Memberships:* American Anthropological Association (member, 1968-; Fellow, 1976-); Society for Applied Anthropology (Fellow, 1983-); American Association of Museums, 1969-; National Association for the Practice of Anthropology (charter member); Association for Women in Science, 1983-. *Awards, honors:* Wenner-Gren Foundation for Anthropological Research, Museum Research Fellow, 1967-1968; Ford Foundation, Dissertation Fellowship in Ethnic Studies, 1972-1973. *Interests:* "Professional specialization in Native American art and material culture studies and research with museum collections. Field work: Native basketmakers in southern British Columbia, for National Museum of Man, National Museums of Canada, Urgent Ethnology Research Contract, 1973-1974; anthropologist for basketry research, Quinault Indian Nation, 1976-1977; consultant, fiber arts, Samish Indian Tribe, 1985-. As a handweaver, handspinner, and knitter, I am active in local spinners and weavers groups. Travel." *Published works: Northwest Basketry and Culture Change* (Burke Museum, 1968); *Native Basketry of Western North America* (Illinois State Museum, 1978); *The Art and Style of Western Indian Basketry* (Hancock House, 1982); *Northwest Coast Indian Basketry Styles* (University of Washington Press and Burke Museum) (in press).

JONES, LEO (Pit River)
(tribal chairman)

Affiliation: Chairman, Pit River Tribal Council, P.O. Box 763, Alturas, Calif. 96101.

JONES, STANLEY, Sr. (Tulalip)
(tribal chairman)

Affiliation: Chairman, The Tulalip Board of Directors, 6700 Totem Beach Rd., Marysville, Wash. 98270.

JONES, STEPHEN S. *(Red Dawn)*
(Santee Sioux) 1921-
(lecturer, educator, folklorist,
anthropologist)

Born June 1, 1921, Flandreau, S.D. *Education:* Sioux Falls College, S.D., B.A., 1948; California State University, Fullerton, M.A., 1978. *Principal occupation:* Lecturer, educator, folklorist, anthropologist, American Indian Programs, Anaheim, Calif. *Home address:* P.O. Box 9698, Anaheim, Calif. 92802. *Affiliations:* Curator of anthropology, Science Museum of Natural History, Gastonia, N.C. (six years); American Indian programs, Anaheim, Calif. *Other professional post:* Registered medical technologist. *Military service:* U.S. Army, 1942-1945 (Staff Sergeant). *Memberships:* American Indian Lore Association (director); Continental Confederation of Adopted Indians (director); American Anthropological Association; Southwest Museum; Minnesota Historical Society. *Awards, honors:* 1973 Catlin Peace Pipe Award, American Indian Lore Association. *Interests:* "Field of American Indian dance, ethnology, history and folklore. Lifelong avocation in interpreting Indian lifeways (traveling extensively throughout the nation presenting Indian programs for schools and civil groups). Tour master for college groups into the Southwest; major field of interest—customs and traditions of Southwest Indians. Traveled nationally lecturing and researching, 1976-." *Published work:* Editor, *Great on the Mountain: The Spiritual Life of Crazy Horse* (Naturegraph, 1971); editor, *Master Key* (Southwest Museum, 1972-1982.

JONES, VELMA
(tribal chairwoman)

Affiliation: Chairwoman, Big Pine General Council, P.O. Box 384, Big Pine, Calif. 93513.

JONES, WILLIAM M.
(director-Indian center)

Affiliation: Director, Mid-American All-Indian Center, 650 N. Seneca, Wichita, Kan. 67203.

JORDAN, JANET ETHRIDGE 1947-
(professor of anthropology)

Born February 2, 1947, Denver, Colo. *Education:* Colorado College, 1965-1967; Columbia University, B.A. (magna cum laude), 1969; Yale University, 1969-1971; University of Connecticut, Ph.D., 1974. *Principal occupation:* Professor of anthropology. *Affiliation:* Colorado State University, Fort Collins, Colo., 1974-? *Memberships:* American Anthropological Association; American Society for Ethnohistory; Association for Political and Legal Anthropology (vice president, 1977-1978; chairperson, 1976-1977; editor of newsletter, 1976-. *Awards, honors:* Phi Beta Kappa, Columbia University; Phi Kappa Phi, University of Connecticut. *Interests:* Fieldwork on politics and law of Miccosukees, 1975-1976; "Politics and Religion in a Western Cherokee Community: A Century of Struggle in a White Man's World," unpublished Ph.D. dissertation. *Published works:* "Social Aspects of Illness in a Western Cherokee," paper at Southern Anthropological Society Meetings, April, 1974, Blacksburg, Va.; "Self-Determination Implications of Federal and Local Networks," paper at American Anthropological Association meetings, December, 1977.

JORDAN, SUE ZANN (Mescalero
Apache) 1959-
(teacher)

Born December 17, 1959. *Education:* University of Illinois, Urbana, B.A., 1979; Sangamon State University, M.A., 1983. *Principal occupation:* Teacher, Cibecue Community School, Cibecue, Ariz. 85911, 1984-. *Other professional post:* Part-time teacher, Northern Pioneer College. *Membership:* Arizona Media Association. *Awards, honors:* State of South Dakota Poetry Award and money certificate; Golden Poet Award, World of Poetry. *Interests:* General: Poetry, art, music, education, earth science, and literature. Vocational: Woodworking, graphic arts, ceramics, weaving, and horticulture. Travels: "(I) traveled extensively in North and South America and less extensively overseas." *Published works:* Poetry, too numerous to list.

JORGENSEN, JOSEPH GILBERT 1934-
(professor of anthropology)

Born April 15, 1934, Salt Lake City, Utah. *Education:* University of Utah, Salt Lake City, B.S., 1956; Indiana University, Bloomington, Ph.D., 1964. *Principal occupation:* Professor of anthropology. *Home address:* 1517 Highland Dr., Newport Beach, Calif. 92660. *Affiliations:* Assistant professor, Antioch College, 1964-1965, University of Oregon, 1965-1968; professor of anthropology, Univesity of Michigan, Ann Arbor, 1968-1974, University of California, Irvine, Calif., 1974-. *Other professional post:* Coordinator, Northern Ute Tribe (Unitah and Ouray Ute Indian Reservation, Fort Duchesne, Utah), 1960, 1962; research associate, John Muir Institute, 1970-. *Community activities:* Mariners Community Association (president); Society to Preserve Our Newport (board member); Newport Bech Aquatics Support Group (president). *Memberships:* Human Relations Area Files (board of directors); Native Struggles Support Group (board of directors and co-chair); Anthropology Resource Center (board of directors); American Association for the Advancement of Science (Fellow); Sigma Xi. *Awards, honors:* John Simon Guggenheim Fellow, 1974-1975; C. Wright Mills Book Award for *Sun Dance Religion,* 1972; F.O. Butler Lecturer at South akota State University, 1976; M. Crawford Lectures at the University of Kansas, 1980; Rufus Wood Leigh Lecture at the University of Utah, 1982. *Interests:* "Employed by Northern Ute Tribe in several capacities, 1960-1962. Research among Northern Utes, Southern Utes, Ute Mountain Utes, Fort Hall Shoshone, Wind River Shoshone, Crow, Soboba, and several Eskimo villages, particularly Malakleet. Expert witness for Indian and Eskimo plaintiffs in several federal cases." *Published works: Salish Language and Culture* (Indiana University, 1969); *Sun Dance Religion* (University of Chicago Press, 1972); *Native Americans and Energy Development, I and II* (Anthropology Resource Center, 1978, 1984); *Western Indians* (W.H. Freeman, 1980); *Oil Age Eskimos* (Human Relations Area Files Press, 1987). Editorial board: *Behavioral Science Research,* 1973-; *The Indian Historian,* 1974-; *Southwest Economy and Society,* 1976-; *Social Science Journal,* 1978-; Environmental Ethics, 1978-; *Social Policy Revue,* 1981-; contributing articles to New York Review of Books, and to professional journals

JOSEPHY, ALVIN M., Jr. 1915-
(author, historian)

Born May 18, 1915, Woodmere, N.Y. *Education:* Harvard College, 1932-1934. *Principal occupation:* Author, historian. *Home address:* 4 Kinsman Lane, Greenwich, Conn. 06830. *Affiliations:* Associate editor, *Time* Magazine, 1951-1960; editor-in-chief, American Heritage Publishing Co., Inc., New York, N.Y., 1960-1979. *Other professional posts:* Consultant, Secretary of the Interior, 1963; commissioner and vice chairman, Indian Arts and Crafts Board, Dept. of the Interior, Washington, D.C., 1966-1970; president, National Council, Institute of the American West, Sun Valley, Idaho, 1976-; contributing editor, *American West* Magazine, Tucson, Ariz., 1983-. *Military service:* U.S. Marine Corps, 1943-1945 (Master Technical Sergeant; Bronze Star). *Memberships:* Association on American Indian Affairs (director, 1961-); Museum of the American Indian (trustee, 1976-; president, National Council, 1978-); Western History Association; Society of American Historians; American Antiquarian Society. *Awards, honors:* Western Heritage Award, National Cowboy Hall of Fame, 1962, 1965; Eagle Feather Award, National Congress of American Indians, 1964; Award for Merit, American Association on State and Local History, 1965; Golden Spur, Golden Saddleman and Buffalo Awards, Western Writers of America, 1965; National Book Award nominee, 1968; Guggenheim Fellowship, 1966-1967. *Interests:* History, culture and concerns of the American Indians; western American history; conservation; extensive western travel. *Biographical source: Who's Who in America. Published works: American Heritage Book of the Pioneer Spirit,* co-author (Simon & Schuster, 1959); *The American Heritage Book of Indians* (Simon & Schuster, 1961); *The Patriot Chiefs* (Viking Press, 1961); *The Nez Perce Indians and the Opening of the Northwest* (Yale University Press, 1965); editor, *The American Her-*

itage History of the Great West (Simon & Schuster, 1965); *The Indian Heritage of America* (Knopf, 1968); *Red Power* (McGraw-Hill, 1971); *Now That the Buffalo's Gone* (Knopf, 1982); among others.

JOURDAIN, ROGER (Chippewa)
(tribal chairman)

Affiliation: Chairman, Red Lake Tribal Council, Red Lake, Minn. 56671.

JUANCITO, CHARLES H.
(Rappahannock)
(teacher)

Born in Philadelphia, Pa. *Education:* University of Pennyslvania, 1955-1958; Temple University, 1969-1972. *Principal occupation:* Teacher. *Home address:* 927 N. Sixth St., Philadelphia, Pa. 19123. *Affiliations:* Teacher, Chester-Upland School District, Chester, Pa.; director, Native American Cultural Center. *Other professional posts:* Engineering technician, draftsman. *Memberships:* National Education Association (secretary, First American Task Force); Pennsylvania Education Association; American Vocational Education Association; Pennsylvania Industrial Arts Association; Coalition of Eastern Native Americans. *Awards, honors;* Commendation for work as a teacher of adult basic education and English as a second language, State of Pennsylvania Adult Education Department, Harrisburg, Pa. *Interests:* Education; ethnology and anthropology; geology.

JUANICO, JUAN (Acoma Pueblo)
(museum director)

Affiliation: Director, Acoma Museum, P.O. Box 309, Acoma Pueblo, N.M. 87032.

JUDKINS, RUSSELL ALAN 1944-
(anthropologist)

Born August 8, 1944, Salt Lake City, Utah. *Education:* Brigham Young University, B.S., 1966; Cornell University, Ph.D., 1973. *Principal occupation:* Anthropologist. *Home address:* Homestead Gatehouse,

Geneseo, N.Y. 14454. *Affiliation: Assistant professor, and professor, State University of New York, College at Geneseo, N.Y., 1972-.* Memberships: American Anthropological Association (Fellow); Northeastern Anthropological Association; Society for Medical Anthropology. *Interests:* "Contemporary American Indian society and culture, including medical research; growth and change in community and religious life; nutrition; Iroquoian, especially Seneca; Indians of Intermountain West, including Mormon Indians. *Biographical source: American Men and Women of Science.*

JUMPER, BETTY MAE (Seminole)
1927-
(director-Seminole communications)

Born April 27, 1927, Indiantown, Fla. *Education:* Cherokee Indian School, Cherokee, N.C., 1949 (first Seminole Indian to receive a high school diploma). *Principal occupation:* Director-Seminole communications. *Home address:* Hollywood, Fla. 33024. *Affiliation:* Chairperson, Seminole Tribe, 1967-1971; director of communications and editor-in-chief of the *Seminole Tribune* (the newspaper of the Seminole Tribe), Seminole Tribe of Florida, 6333 Forrest (N.W. 30th) St., Hollywood, Fla. 33024. *Community activities:* Speaker at schools throughout Florida about Seminole Tribe; advisor, Manpower Development and Training Committee for the State of Florida; member, Independent Bible Baptist Church. *Memberships:* Native American Press Association; Florida Press Association. *Awards, honors:* Served on first tribal council as secretary-treasurer, and later resigned to serve as vice chairperson. In 1967, Betty Mae was the first woman elected as chairperson of the Seminole Tribe, serving four years. In 1968, Betty joined three Southeastern Tribes in signing a Declaration of Unity in Cherokee, N.C. The declaration implemented the Inter-Tribal Council, United Southeastern Tribes. While serving as chairperson of the Seminole Tribe, she was appointed by the President of the U.S. to become one of eight Indian members to work with Vice President Agnew. Only two women were chosen to serve on the committee, the National Congress on Indian Opportunity under President Nixon. She was chosen "Woman of the Year" by the Department of Florida Ladies Auxiliary of Jewish War Veterans of the U.S. for her outstanding contributions in the field of humanities. Betty Mae received a medicine peace pipe and a gold pin from the United Southeastern Tribes. *Interests:* "Betty did much to improve the health, education and social conditions of the Seminole people. Through her efforts, the Tribe was one of the first tribes to obtain the CHR (Community Health Representative) Program. She was also effective in her concerns for Indian people on regional, national and state levels." *Published work: ...And With the Wagon - Came God's Word* (Seminole Print Shop, 1984).

JUNALUSKA, ARTHUR SMITH (Cherokee) 1918-
(writer, director, producer, lecturer, choreographer)

Born November 30, 1918, Cherokee Nation, Cherokee, N.C. *Education:* Cherokee Indian School; Haskell Institute; Okmulgee Junior College; Eckels College of Embalming; Lister Institute of Medical Research; London School of Medicine. *Principal occupation:* Executive and artistic director, American Indian Society of Creative Arts, Inc., New York, N.Y. *Other professional posts:* Writer of plays for radio, television and stage; performer; founder, American Indian Drama Company; director of drama, South Dakota Wesleyan University, 1958; creator, writer and producer of "Dance of the Twelve Moons," an American Indian Dance Company production; director and coordinator, Indian Village, Freedomland (New York City Amusement Park), 1960-1961; consultant and technical advisor for motion pictures and plays; director of performing arts, Indian Festival of Arts, LaGrande, Oreg. *Military service:* U.S. Army (World War II0.

JUNEAU, ALFRED LeROY (Blackfeet) 1919-
(public accounting)

Born August 21, 1919, Browning, Mt. *Education:* Southwestern University, Los Angeles, Calif., B.S., 1951. *Principal occu-pation:* Public accounting. *Home address:* 539 Crane Blvd., Los Angeles, Calif. 90065. *Affiliations:* Comptroller, Los Angeles Indian Center, Inc. (four years); Associate consultant, United Indian Development Association (Indian business development), 1976-; United American Indian Council (Indian socio-economic concerns), 1976-; commissioner (appointed by Mayor Bradley), Los Angeles City-County Native American Indian Commission, 1977-. *Other professional posts:* Secretary-treasurer, U.S. Steel Buildings Co., Los Angeles, Calif. *Military service:* U.S. Army Signal Corps, 1941-1945 (Sergeant; two Bronze Stars, Good Conduct Medal, Europe-Africa-Middle Eastern Theatre Servie Medal, Meritorious Unit Award). *Memberships:* California Public Accountants, 1951-; Loyal Order of Moose, 1973-; National Congress of American Indians, 1944-; Parent Teachers Association, Los Angeles, 1955-; Smithsonian Institution, 1975-; Blackfeet Indian Tribe, Browning, Mt. (enrolled member). *Interests:* "General accounting and related financial matters; continuing interest in socio-economic betterment of American Indians in urban areas and on reservations; invited and attended, February 2, 1978, President and Mrs. Carter's prayer breakfast in Washingtn, D.C.; invited on February 3, 1978 to attend an All-Indian prayer breakfast at the U.S. Capitol in Washington, D.C.; have played profesionally a trumpet in the U.S. and Europe." *Biographical source: Vida Reporter* (Los Angeles, April, 1977), a short biographical article with photo.

K

KAHN, FRANKLIN (Navajo) 1934-
(artist)

Born May 25, 1934, Pine Springs, Ariz. *Education:* Stewart Indian School. *Principal occupation:* Artist. *Home address:* 3315 N. Steues Blvd., Flagstaff, Ariz. 86001. *Affiliation:* Sketch artist and sign painter, Federal Sign and Signal Corp., Flagstaff, Ariz.. *Membership:* American Indian Service Committee. *Awards, honors:* Second Prize,

142

Scottsdale National Indian Art Show. *Interests:* Watercolor and oil painting; Indian designs and symbols. *Published work:* Illustrator, *Going Away to School* (Bureau of Indian Affairs, 1951).

KAHRAHRAH, BERNARD (Comanche)
(tribal chairman)

Affiliation: Chairman, Comanche Business Committee, P.O. Box 908, Lawton, Okla. 73502.

KANNON, CLYDE DAVID 1938-
(teacher, special education)

Born November 3, 1938, Maury County, Tenn. *Education:* Emory & Henry College, Emory, Va., B.A. (Psychology and English), 1960; Florida Atlantic University, 1968-1970; University of South Dakota, M.A. (Special Education), 1976. *Principal occupation:* Teacher, special education. *Address:* Community School, Crow Creek Reservation, Fort Thompson, S.D. 57339. *Affiliations:* Teacher, Tulare County School System, Earlimart, Calif., 1962-1963; teacher, Williamson County School System, Tenn., 1963-1968; teacher, South Florida Schools, principal/teacher K-6, Bureau of Indian Affairs (Big Cypress Reservation), Seminole Agency, Hollywood, Fla., 1968-1971; elementary teacher, special education teacher, teacher supervisor, principal, Fort Thompson Community School, B.I.A., Crow Creek Agency, Fort Thompson, S.D., 1971-. *Awards, honors:* Special Education Achievement Award, National Blue Key Honor Society, 1960.

KASCHUBE, DOROTHEA VEDRAL 1927-
(professor of anthropology)

Born November 6, 1927, Chicago, Ill. *Education:* Indiana University, B.A., 1951, M.A., 1953, Ph.D., 1960. *Principal occupation:* Professor of anthropology, Department of Anthropology, University of Colorado, Boulder, Colo., 1955-. *Home address:* 370 S. 36th St., Boulder, Colo. 80303. *Other professional posts:* Research associate, Stanford University (summers). *Memberships:* American Anthropological

Association; Linguistic Society of America; Sigma Xi. *Interests:* "Language of the Crow Indians and of the Siouan language family. Language as both biological and cultural behavior." *Published works: Structural Elements of the Language of the Crow Indians of Montana* (University of Colorado Press, 1967); co-author with Joseph H. Greenberg, *Word Prosodic Systems: A Preliminary Report* (Working Papers on Language Universals, Stanford University, 1976).

KAUFMAN, STEVEN, M.D.
(Indian health service)

Affiliation: Chief, Inpatient Services, Indian Health Service, 5600 Fishers Lane, Rockville, Md. 20857.

KEALIINOHOMOKU, JOANN WHEELE 1930-
(anthropologist)

Born May 20, 1930, Kansas City, Mo. *Education:* Northwestern University, B.S., 1955, M.A., 1958; Indiana University, Ph.D., 1976. *Princpal occupation:* Anthropologist. *Home address:* 518 South Agassiz St., Flagstaff, Ariz. 86001. *Affiliation:* Professor, Department of Anthropology, Northern Arizona State University, Flagstaff, Ariz. *Other professional posts:* Visiting professor for University of Hawaii, Manoa Campus; University of Hawaii, Hilo Campus; New York University; World Campus Afloat. *Community activities:* Native American for Community Action (board of directors, 1977-1982; secretary of board, 1979-1982); Cross-Cultural Dance Resources, Inc. (a non-profit organization - a "living museum" for scholars and performers to talk, study, consult) (president, board of directors). *Memberships:* American Anthropological Association (Fellow); American Ethnological Society; American Folklore Society; Association for the Anthropological Study of Play; Bishop Museum Association, CORD (Congress on Research in Dance) (board of directors, 1974-1977); Cross-Cultural Dance Resources, Inc. (founder and director); Society for Ethnomusicology (council member, 1967-1970, 1980-1983). *Awards, honors:* Weatherhead Resident Scholar, School of American Research,

Santa Fe, N.M. 1974-1975; Research Fellow, East-West Center, Honolulu, Hawaii, 1981; Dedicatee for Tenth Annual Flagstaff Indian Center's Basketball Tournament, 1983. *Interests:* "Cultural anthropology with strong interface to physical anthropology and linguistics; area studies: Southwestern American Indians, Midwestern American Blacks, Pacific peoples, especially Polynesians; focus: performance arts, affective culture, culture dynamics; field work in Southwest U.S., especially with Hopi and other Pueblos. *Biographical sources: Dictionary of International Biography; The World Who's Who of Women; Who's Who in Oceania; Who's Who of American Women. Published works:* "Hopi and Polynesian Dance: A Study in Cross-Cultural Comparison" (*Ethnomusicology,* 1967); with Frank Gillis, "Special Bibliography: Gertrude Prokosch Kurath" (*Ethnomusicology,* 1970); "Dance Culture as a Microcosm of Holistic Culture" (*New Dimensions in Dance Research: Anthropology and Dance—The American Indian,* 1974); *Theory and Methods for an Anthropological Study of Dance,* Ph.D. dissertation, anthropology (University Microfilms, 1976); "The Drama of the Hopi Ogres," chapter in *Southwestern Indian Ritual Drama,* edited by Charlotte Frisbie, (University of New Mexico Press, 1980); "Music and Dance of the Hawaiian and Hopi Peoples," chapter in *Becoming Human Through Music* (Music Educators National Conference, 1985); "The Would-Be Indian," chapter in *Anthropology and Music: Essays in Honor of David P. McAllester,* edited by Charlotte Frisbie (University of Michigan Press, 1985); among other articles, reviews and chapters in various publications.

KEEGAN, MARCIA (Cherokee) 1943-
(free-lance photographer, author)

Born May 23, 1943, Tulsa, Okla. *Education:* University of New Mexico, B.A., 1964. *Memberships:* American Society of Magazine Photographers; American Society of Picture Professionals; Southwestern American Indian Association; Wheelwright Museum; Museum of the American Indian, Heye Foundation; New York Women in Communications, Inc.; North American Indian Women's Association. *Awards,*

honors: Recipient of Creative Artists Program Grant, 1972. *Interests:* Ms. Keegan writes, "I am a writer/photographer specializing in documentation of the Southwest tribes, mainly Pueblo and Navajo. I am interested in presenting to non-Native Americans the traditional life-styles and ceremonies of the Southwest tribes. To this end I have also worked on educational filmstrips, one of which was, *We Are American Indians,* published by Guidance Associates of Harcourt Brace & Jovanovich, 1973. *Published works: The Taos Indians & Their Sacred Blue Lake* (Julian Messner, 1972); *Mother Earth, Father Sky* (Grossman Publishing, 1974); *We Can Still Hear Them Clapping* (Avon Books, 1975); *Pueblo & Navajo Cookery* (Morgan & Morgan, Inc., 1977).

KEELY, KAY
(B.I.A. Indian education)

Affiliation: Indian education, Bureau of Indian Affairs, 1951 Constitution Ave., N.W., Washington, D.C. 20245.

KEEN, RALPH F. (Cherokee) 1934-
(educator)

Born August 31, 1934, Hominy, Okla. *Education:* Northeastern State College, Okla., B.A. (Education), 1951; Kansas State College of Pittsburgh; Kansas State University. *Principal occupation:* Educator. *Affiliation:* Training instructor in painting, Haskell Indian Junior College, Lawrence, Kan. *Military service:* U.S. Air Force, 1958-1961. *Memberships:* Kansas Education Association; National Education Association; American Congress of Parents and Teachers.

KEGG, MATTHEW M. (Chippewa) 1953-
(teacher)

Born October 5, 1953, Brainerd, Minn. *Education:* Bemidji State University, Minn., B.A., 1976. *Principal occupation:* Teacher. *Home address:* Star Route P.O. Box 105, Onamia, Minn. 56359. *Affiliations:* Graduate assistant, Indian Studies Program, Bemidji State University, 1980-1981;

teacher, Mille Lacs Indian Reservation, Onamia, Minn., 1981-. *Awards, honors:* Recipient of Certificate of Appreciation from State Department of Education of Minnesota, 1980, for contributions to Indian education; Most Valuable Player award from hockey team, Bemidji Northland Icers, 1980. *Interests:* "Hockey; published several articles in magazines; poetry; outdoor activities: camping, backpacking, canoeing, biking."

KEHOE, ALICE BECK 1934-
(professor of anthropology)

Born September 18, 1934, New York, N.Y. *Education:* Barnard College, B.A., 1956; Harvard University, Ph.D., 1964. *Principal occupation:* Professor of anthropology. *Home address:* 3014 N. Shepard Ave., Milwaukee, Wis. 53211. *Affiliations:* Assistant professor of anthropology, University of Nebraska, 1965-1968; associate professor, professor of anthropology, Marquette University, Milwaukee, Wis., 1968-. *Memberships:* American Anthropological Association (Fellow); Society for American Archaeology; American Ethnological Society. *Interests:* Cultural anthropology and archaeology; field work among Blackfoot, Cree and Dakota tribes in the U.S. and Canada; archaeological field work in Montana and Saskatchewan. *Published works:* Hunters of the Buried Years (Regina, Sask. School Aids & Text Book Co., 1962); *North American Indians* (Prentice-Hall, 1981).

KEITH, C. HOBART *(Blue Horse)*
(Oglala Sioux) 1922-
(artist, sculptor)

Born March 8, 1922, Pine Ridge, S.D. *Education:* Colorado Springs Fine Arts Center, 1938-1941. *Principal occupation:* Artist, sculptor. *Home address:* P.O. Box 444, Pine Ridge, S.D. 57770. *Affiliations:* Chief judge, Oglala Sioux Tribal Court, 1967-; representative, Oglala Sioux Tribal Council. *Military service:* U.S. Navy, 1942-1946. *Community activities:* Veterans of Foreign Wars; American Legion; Tribal Land Owners Association. *Awards, honors:* Certificate of Appreciation, National Police Officers Association of America, Police Hall of Fame, Inc.

KELLER, GEORGE
(B.I.A. agency superintendent)

Affiliation: Superintendent, San Carlos Agency, Bureau of Indian Affairs, San Carlos, Ariz. 85550.

KELLER, NANCY (Sac and Fox)
(tribal chairwoman)

Affiliation: Chairwoman, Sac and Fox Tribal Council, P.O. Box 38, Reserve, Kan. 66434.

KELLY, ALVIN (Quechan)
(tribal president)

Affiliation: President, Quechan Tribal Council, P.O. Box 1352, Yuma, Ariz. 85364.

KENNEDY, JAMES H.
(school superintendent)

Affiliation: Superintendent, Kickapoo Nation School, P.O. Box 106, Powhattan, Kan. 66527.

KEPLIN, DEBBIE L. (Turtle Mountain Chippewa) 1956-
(general manager-radio station)

Born February 28, 1956, Belcourt, N.D. *Education:* Flandreau Indian School, 1974; University of North Dakota, Grand Forks (two years liberal arts instruction). *Principal occupation:* Public radio station general manager. *Home address:* P.O. Box 236, Belcourt, N.D. 58316. *Affiliation:* General manager, KEYA Radio Station, Belcourt, N.D. *Other professional posts:* Occupied positions at KEYA radio of program director, news director, music director, and executive secretary. *Community activities:* Member, St. Ann's Society, Belcourt, N.D.; assistant-religious education, St. Anthony's Catholic Church, Belcourt; member, Turtle Mountain Musicians; member, Turtle Mountain Historical Society. *Memberships:* National Association of Female Executives, 1985-; Corporation for Public Broadcasting/National Public Radio (authorized representative). *Awards, honors:* Certificate of Native American Leadership Training by the Community Council of the Northern

Plains Teacher Corps, Nov. 1979 & Feb. and April, 1980; Certificate of Training-Explosive Devices Training by the U.S. Department of the Interior, Sept., 1984; dedicated service to the KEYA Radio Station and the Belcourt community by Turtle Mountain Community School, Nov., 1985; for community service by Turtle Mountain Band of Chippewa Indians, Feb., 1985. *Interests:* "To promote and educate the local community and surrounding communities on the history and culture of the Turtle Mountain Band of Chippewa through the use of radio. To develop programs focusing on problems affecting the local community, such as alcoholism, unemployment, housing, recreation, etc...To encourage the training of high school students in the operation of broadcast facilities-radio. *Programs produced:* "All Nations Music," 1980- (features traditional and contemporary Native American music, legends and stories); "Memorial to James Henry," former chairman of Turtle Mountain Band of Chippewa, 5-minute piece aired nationally on radio series "First Person Radio" of Minn. in Sept., 1983; "Music of the Turtle Mountains," 1985- (program features the talents and biographies of local artists, musicians and poets); the music of Floyd Westerman, Sr. Mary Anthony Rogers, many local fiddlers, Adella and Gilbert Kills Pretty Enemy, 1985- (program features biographical sketches of artists through interview and music selections).

KICKINGBIRD, K. KIRKE
(executive director, Indian organization)

Affiliation: Executive director, Institute for the Development of Indian Law, 1104 Glyndon St., S.E., Vienna, Va. 22180.

KILPATRICK, ANNA GRITTS
(Oklahoma Cherokee) 1917-
(teacher, writer)

Born March 7, 1917, Echota, Okla. *Education:* Southern Methodist University, B.S., 1958. *Principal occupation:* Teacher, writer. *Affiliation:* Teacher, Dallas, Tex. public schools. *Published works: Friends of Thunder* (SMU Press); *Walk In Your Soul* (SMU Press); *The Shadow of Sequoyah* (University of Oklahoma Press), all with Jack Frederick Kilpatrick.

KILPATRICK, JACK FREDERICK
(Oklahoma Cherokee) 1915-
(professor of music)

Born September 23, 1915, Stilwell, Okla. *Education:* Bacone College, 1933-1935; Northeastern State College of Okla., 1935; University of Redlands, Mus.B., 1938; Catholic University, Mus.M., 1946; University of Redlands, Mus.D., 1950. *Principal occupation:* Professor of music, School of Arts, Southern Methodist University, Dallas, Texas. *Military service:* U.S. Naval School of Music, 1943-1945 (instructor). *Memberships:* Phi Beta Kappa; American Anthropological Association; Society for Ethnomusicology; American Composers Alliance; Pi Kappa Lambda. *Awards, honors:* National Science Foundation Grant; Danforth Foundation Fellowship; American Philosophical Society Grant; Carnegie Foundation Grant; Tobin Foundation Grant; achievement awards, Cherokee Nation, National Federation of Music Clubs. *Published works: Friends of Thunder* (SMU Press, 1964); *Walk In Your Soul* (SMU Press, 1965); *The Shadow of Sequoyah* (University of Oklahoma Press, 1965); all co-authored with Anna Gritts Kilpatrick; *Sequoyah: Of Earth and Intellect* (Encino Press, 1965).

KING, CLARENCE E., Sr.
(Ottawa) 1909-
(former chief-Ottawa Tribe of Oklahoma)

Born January 1, 1909, Miami, Okla. *Affiliations:* Former Principal Chief, Ottawa Tribe of Oklahoma; self-employed electrician. *Military service:* U.S. Navy, 1944-1946 (Asiatic and Pacific Medals, World War II Medal).

KING, MARY ELIZABETH 1929-
(anthropologist)

Born September 7, 1929, Williamsport, Pa. *Education:* Columbia University, A.B., 1951, M.A., 1958; University of Arizona, Ph.D., 1965. *Principal occupation:* Anthropologist. *Home address:* 515 Askin Rd., St. Davids, Pa. 19087. *Affiliations:* Museum assistant, librarian, and curator of Western Hemisphere textiles, The Textile Museum, Washington, D.C., 1953-1967; lecturer, assistant professor, associate professor of anthropology, Howard University, Washington, D.C., 1963-1971; professor of anthropology and curator of anthropology, The Museum of Texas Tech University, Lubbock, Texas, 1971-1977; keeper of collections, The University Museum, University of Pennsylvania, 1978-. *Memberships:* American Anthropological Association Fellow); Royal Anthropological Institute (Fellow); Society for American Archaeology; Current Anthropology (Associate); American Association for the Advancement of Science (Fellow); Sigma Xi; International Congress of Americanists; American Association of Museums (council member, 1978-). *Interests:* Archaeology and ethnography of North and South America; primitive art; material culture, especially textiles and basketry; human ecology; museology; fieldwork in South Dakota, Peru, Mexico; project director, The Lubbock Lake Site (fieldwork), 1975, 1976. *Published works:* Numerous articles, monographs, and reviews in various publications.

KINGMAN, A. GAY
(superintendent-Indian center)

Affiliation: Superintendent, Pierre Indian Learning Center, Star Route 3, Pierre, S.D. 57501.

KINLEY, LARRY (Lummi)
(tribal chairman)

Affiliation: Chairman, Lummi Business Council, 2616 Kwina Rd., Bellingham, Wash. 98225-9298.

KINNEY, RODNEY P. (Eskimo)
(consultant-engineering)

Education: University of California, San Jose, B.S. (Civil Engineering), 1960; graduate studies at Univerity of California, Berkeley and San Jose, and University of Alaska, Anchorage. *Principal occupation:* Consultant engineering. *Address:* P.O. Box 771102,

Eagle River, Alaska 99577. *Affiliations:* Geotechnical consultant, Woodward Clyde Consultants, Anchorage, Alaska, 1961-1975; engineering coordinator, Alyeska Pipeline Service Co., 1975-1979; manager of Engineering & Planning Division, Anchorage Water & Wastewater Utility, 1979-1980; principal engineer, Rodney P. Kinney Associates, Eagle River, Alaska, 1980-. *Military service:* U.S. Navy, 1951-1959. *Community activities:* Local Chamber of Commerce. *Memberships:* American Society of Civil Engineers; Bering Straits Native Association; American Indian Science and Engineering Society; American Water Works Association; American Public Works Association. *Interests:* "Rodney P. Kinney Associates, a qualified Eskimo firm, was established October 2, 1980. The firm emphasizes consultation and services in general civil engineering, including roads and drainage, water and sewer, as well as soil testing and data collection. We also offer geophysical (seismic refraction and resistivity) and slope inclinometer services, water resource development services, and consultation for private and public systems." *Biographical sources:* Who's Who in the West; Who's Who in Technology Today; International Men of Distinction.

KITTO, RICHARD (Santee Sioux)
(tribal chairman)

Affiliation: Chairman, Santee Sioux Tribal Council, Route 2, Niobrara, Neb. 68760.

KNIGHT, PHILIP (Wintun)
(tribal chairman)

Affiliation: Chairman, Rumsey Community Council, P.O. Box 18, Brooks, Calif. 95606.

KOOMSA, MARLAND
(chief-Indian health education)

Affiliation: Chief, Health Education, Indian Health Services, 5600 Fishers Lane, Rockville, Md. 20857.

KRAFT, HERBERT C. 1927-
(professor of anthropology,
archaeologist)

Born June 1, 1927, Elizabeth, N.J. *Education:* Seton Hall University, 1947-1950, M.A., (History), 1961; Hunter College, C.U.N.Y., M.A. (Anthropology), 1969. *Principal occupation:* Professor of anthropology and director of Archaeological Research Center, Seton Hall University, South Orange, N.J., 1960-. *Home address:* 15 Raymond Terrace, Elizabeth, N.J. 07208. *Other professional posts:* Archaeological consultant for cultural resources surveys. *Military service:* Merchant Marines, 1945-1947. *Community activities:* New Jersey Historic Sites (member, State Review Board). *Memberships:* Society of Professional Archaeologists; Archaeological Society of New Jersey (president, editor of *Bulletin*); Eastern States Archaeological Federation; New York State Archaeological Association (Fellow); New Jersey Academy of Sciences (Fellow); Society for Pennsylvania Archaeology. *Awards, honors:* Archie Award, Society for Pennsylvania Archaeology; recipient of two grants from the New Jersey Historical Commission; ten grants from the National Park Service, for excavations of prehistoric sites in New Jersey. *Interests:* "(My) primary interest is the prehistoric and contact period archaeology of New Jersey, and the Northeast and Middle Atlantic States generally. Since 1964, I have conducted archaeological excavations for the National Park Service, and for Seton Hall University sponsored research in the Upper Delaware Valley, N.J., and on several sites in northeastern New Jersey and Staten Island, N.Y. These excavations have encompassed the entire span from Paleo-Indian to the Historic Contact Period. I have traveled extensively in Meso-America and Europe especially to archaeologically oriented areas." *Biographical sources: Dictionary of International Biography; American Men and Women of Science; Current Biographies of Leading Archaeologists; Outstanding Educators of America, 1971. Published works: The Miller Field Site* (Seton Hall University Press, 1970); *Archaeology in the Upper Delaware Valley* (Pensylvania Historic and Museum Commission, 1972); *A Delaware Indian Symposium* (Pennsylvania

Historic and Museum Commission, 1974); *The Archaeology of the Tocks Island Area* (Archaeological Research Center, Seton Hall University, 1975); numerous articles in *Archaeology of Eastern North Ameica, Annals* of the New York Academy of Sciences, *Researches and Transactions* of the New York State Arcaheological Association, etc.

KREIPE, MARTHA (Prairie Band Potawatomi) 1944-
(museum professional)

Born November 9, 1944, Topeka, Kan. *Education:* Haskell Indian Junior College, Lawrence, Kan., (Certificate, Welding), 1975; University of Kansas, Lawrence, Kan., B.F.A. (Painting), 1978, M.A. (Special Studies-pending). *Principal occupation:* Museum professional. *Home address:* 900 West 190th St. #11-0, New York, N.Y. 10040. *Affiliation:* Manager, Indian Information Center, Museum of the American Indian, New York, N.Y., 1984-. *Community activities:* Indian Center, Lawrence, Kan. (board of directors); Circle of Red Nations, New York, N.Y. (president, board of directors); Native American Education Program, New York, N.Y. (parent's committee); Grupo Aymara Productions (board of directors). *Awards, honors:* HUD Minority Fellowship, University of Kansas. *Interests:* "Vocational interests: Contemporary North American Indian activities—cultural, social, artistic; Andean Indian life and music." *Published works: 49's, A Pan Indian Mechanism for Boundary Maintenance and Social Cohesion* (AAAmeeting, 1980); *Native American Conceptions of Time* (Manhattan Laboratory Museum Symposium, 1983); Teacher's Kit: "The Parfleche," Museum of the American Indian, Heye Foundation, 1985.

KRENZKE, THEODORE
(B.I.A. director-Indian services)

Affiliation: Director, Indian Services, Bureau of Indian Affairs, 1951 Constitution Ave., N.W., Washington, D.C. 20245.

KREPPS, ETHEL CONSTANCE
(Kiowa/Miami) 1941-
(attorney)

Born October 31, 1941, Mt. View, Okla. *Education:* St. John's Medical Center, Tulsa, Okla., R.N., 1971; University of Tulsa, B.S., 1974; Univerity of Tulsa, College of Law, J.D., 1979. *Principal occupation:* Attorney. *Home address:* 3326 South 93rd East Ave., Tulsa, Okla. 74145. *Affiliation:* Lawyer, Native American Coalition of Tulsa, Inc., 1740 West 41st St., Tulsa, Okla. 74107, 1981-. *Other professional posts:* President, National Indian Social Workers Association; president, Oklahoma Indian Child Welfare Association; national vice president, Amerian Indian Nurses Association; secretary, Native American Chamber of Commerce. *Community activities:* Kiowa Tribe of Oklahoma (elected secretary); Native American Chamber of Commerce (secretary); Tulsa Indian Affairs Commission; American Indian Toastmasters. *Memberships:* National Trial Lawyers Association; American Bar Association; Federal Bar Association; Oklahoma Bar Association; Tulsa County Bar Association; Tulsa Women Lawyers Association; Women Lawyers Association of Oklahoma; Phi Alpha Delta Legal Fraternity. *Awards, honors:* Indian Business Person of the Year Award, 1984; Outstanding Leadership Award, 1985, from International Indian Child Conference; Trial Lawyers Association National Award. *Interests:* Writer, painting, collections, travel, photography. *Biographical sources: Who's Who in Finance and Industry; Who's Who in the South and Southwest; Who's Who of American Women; Who's Who in the World; Who's Who in Society; Personalities of the World. Published works: A Strong Medicine Wind* (Western Publications, 1981); *Oklahoma Memories,* chapter (University of Oklahoma Press, 1982); *Oklahoma Images,* chapter (University of Oklahoma Press, 1983).

KUHKLEN, ALBERT
(B.I.A. agency superintendent)

Affiliation: Superintendent, Anchorage Agency, Bureau of Indian Affairs, P.O. Box 100120, Anchorage, Alaska 99510.

KUKA, KING D. (Blackfeet) 1946-
(artist, art instructor)

Born August 13, 1946, Browning, Mt. *Education:* Institute of American Indian Arts, Diploma, 1965; University of Montana, BFA, 1973; Montana State University, M.A. *Principal occupation:* Artist (sculpture and painting), high school art teacher on Blackfeet Reservation; owner-operator, Blackwolf Gallery. *Home address:* Box 182, East Glacier Park, Mt. 59434. *Military service:* U.S. Army, 1965-1967. *Exhibits:* One-man shows: Reeder's Alley, Helena; University of Montana Center, Missoula; Museum of the Plains Indian, Browning; Rainbow Gallery, Great Falls; Flathead Lake Lookout, Lakeside. Painting and sculpture exhibits at Riverside Museum, New York, N.Y.; San Francisco; Philbrook Art Center, Tulsa, Okla.; Gallery of Indian Arts, Washington, D.C. *Awards, honors:* Numerous awards for art and creative writing. *Interests:* Mr. Kuka's main interest is in the arts, Indian culture and outdoor life. *Published works:* Poetry: *The Whispering Wind* (Doubleday); *Voices of the Rainbow* (Viking Press); Anthologies: *The First Skin Around Me* (Terrritorial Press); *The Remembered Earth* (Red Earth Press); among others.

KURATH, GERTRUDE PROKOSCH 1903-
(dance ethnologist, musicologist)

Born August 19, 1903, Chicago, Ill. *Education:* Bryn Mawr College, B.A., 1922, M.A., 1928; Yale School of Drama, 1929-1930. *Principal occupation:* Dance ethnologist, musicologist. *Home address:* 1125 Spring St., Ann Arbor, Mich. 48103. *Affiliations:* Pageant director, Rhode Island School of Design, 1932-1945; teacher of dance, Brown University Extension, 1936-1945; director, Creative Dance Guild, 1937-1946; dance critic, Ann Arbor *News,* 1961-1972. *Other professional posts:* Field employee, New York State Museum, 1952; dance consultant, *Webster's International Dictionary,* third edition; field employee, National Museum of Canada, 1962-1969. *Community activities:* Community Music School, Providence, R.I., (dance director, 1932-1940); Washtenong Youth Groups, Ann

Arbor, Mich., 1954-1959. *Memberships:* Michigan Folklore Society, 1947- (treasurer, editor, president); Dance Research Center, 1963-; Society for Ethnomusicology, 1953- (dance editor, 2nd vice president); Congress on Research in Dance (CORD), 1967-. *Awards, honors:* Adopted Chippewa and Onondaga; research grants: American Philosophical Society, 1949-1968; Indiana University Archives of Traditional Music; Michigan Academy of Science, Arts and Letters; Museum of New Mexico; National Museum of Canada; Wenner-Gren Foundation, 1949-1972; Chicago Folklore Prize for *Music and Dance of the Tewa Pueblos,* Department of Germanic Languages, University of Chicago; Steloff Research Award, CORD, 1983. *Interests:* Field trips: Mexico, 1946; Iroquois (New York and Ontario), 1948-1964; Cherokee (North Carolina), 1949-1952; Algonquians (Iowa, Wisconsin), 1952, 1956, (Michigan), 1953-1967, (Manitoba), 1968; Rio Grande Pueblos (New Mexico), 1957-1969. *Biographical sources: Who's Who of American Women; Who's Who of Music International; Dictionary of American Scholars;* special bibliography of Gertrtude P. Kurath, *Ethnomusicology,* 1970; *Research Method and Background of G.P.K.,* CORD Annual VI, 1972; *Dance Memoirs* (Chimera Press, Cambridge, 1983). *Published works: The Iroquois Eagle Dance,* with William Fenton (Bureau of American Ethnology, 1953); *Songs of the Wigwam* (Cooperative Recreation Service, 1955); *Songs and Dances of the Great Lakes Indians,* recording (Ethnic Folkways Library, 1956); *Algonquian Ceremonialism and Natural Resources of the Great Lakes* (Indian Institute of World Culture, 1957); *Dances of Anahuac: The Choreography and Music of Pre-Cortesian Dances* (Aldine, 1964); *Iroquois Music and Dance: Ceremonial Arts of Two Seneca Longhouses* (Bureau of American Ethnology, 1964); *Michigan Indian Festivals* (Ann Arbor Publishers, 1966); *Dance and Song Rituals of Six Nations Reserve, Ontario* (National Museum of Canada, 1968); *Music and Dance of the Tewa Pueblos, New Mexico* (Museum of New Mexico Press, 1970); "Tutelo Rituals on Six Nations Reserve" (*Ethnomusicology,* 1981); numerous other articles in *Encyclopaedia Britannica* and *Encyclopaedia Americana;* numerous articles and reviews in scholarly journals.

KURTH, REV. E.J.,
(school superintendent)

Affiliation: Superintendent, Red Cloud Indian School, Holy Rosary Mission, Pine Ridge, S.D. 57770.

KUTSCHE, PAUL 1927-
(social anthropologist)

Born January 3, 1927, Grand Rapids, Mich. *Education:* Harvard College, B.A. (cum laude), 1949; University of Michigan, M.A., 1955; University of Pennsylvania, Ph.D., 1961. *Principal occupation:* Social anthropologist. *Address:* Department of Anthropology, Colorado College, Colorado Springs, Colo. 80903. *Affiliations:* Professor, Colorado College, 1959-. *Community activities:* Pikes Peak Gay Community Center (newsletter editor, 1983-1985). *Memberships:* American Anthropological Association (Fellow), 1954-; Western Social Science Association, 1969- (executive council, 1969-1972); Association of Borderland Scholars, 1976- (executive council, 1977-1983); American Ethnological Society, 1975-; Anthropology Research Group on Homosexuality, 1983- (co-chair, 1984-). *Interests:* "Cherokee Indians, especially ethnohistory; New Mexico Hispanic village structure; rural-urban migration; Costa Rica; gender. *Published works: Survival of Spanish American Villages* (Colorado College Studies, 1979); *Canones: Values, Crisis and Survival* (University of New Mexico Press, 1981); *Bibliography of Unpublished Material on the Cherokee* (Scarecrow Press, 1986).

L

LA BARRE, WESTON 1911-
(professor of anthropology)

Born December 13, 1911, Uniontown, Penn. *Education:* Princeton University, A.B. (summa cum laude), 1933; Yale Graduate School, Ph.D. (with honors), 1937. *Principal occupation:* Professor of anthropology. *Home address:* Mt. Sinai Rd., Route 1, Box 171-B, Durham, N.C. 27705. *Affiliations:* Instructor, Rutgers University, 1939-1943; assistant professor, associate professor, James B. Duke Professor of Anthropology, professor emeritus, Duke University, Durham, N.C., 1946-. *Other professional posts:* Instructor, 1955-1959, visiting clinical professor, University of North Carolina Medical School, 1959-. *Military service:* U.S. Naval Reserve (World War II). *Memberships:* American Anthropological Association (Fellow); Current Anthropology (Fellow). *Awards, honors:* Roheim Memorial Award. *Interests:* "Primitive religion and art; culture and personality; psychological anthropology." *Biographical sources: American Men of Science; Who's Who in America; Who's Who in Latin America; International Dirctory of Anthropologists; Directory of American Scholars; Who's Who in the South and Southwest. Published works: The Peyote Cult* (Yale University Publications in Anthropology, 1939; Schocken Books, 1970); *The Aymara Indians of Lake Titicaca Plateau* (Memoir No. 68, American Anthropological Association, 1948); *They Shall Take Up Serpents* (Schocken Books, 1962, 1969); *Normal Adolescence,* with others (Scribners, 1968); *The Ghost Dance: Origins of Religion* (Doubleday, 1970); numerous articles, reviews and notes in scholarly publications, 1939-.

LA CLAIR, LEO JOHN (Muckleshoot) 1941-
(teacher)

Born February 15, 1941, Auburn, Wash. *Education:* Central Washington State College, B.A., 1964; University of Colorado; University of Utah. *Principal occupation:* Teacher. *Affiliation:* Program assistant, Indian Program, American Friends Service Committee, Seattle, Wash. *Community activities:* Committee on Educational Opportunities for American Indians and Alaska Natives (Council on Indian Affairs). *Memberships:* National Association of Intergroup Relations Officials; National Indian Youth Council. *Awards:* United Scholarship Service and American Indian Development, Inc. Scholarships; Eleanor Roosevelt Foundation Grant.

LA COURSE, RICHARD VANCE (Yakima) 1938-
(journalist, editor-in-chief)

Born September 23, 1938, Toppenish, Wash. *Education:* San Luis Rey College, Calif. (philosophical studies), 1957-1961; Old Mission Santa Barbara, Calif. (theological studies), 1961-1963; Portland State University, Wash. (English master's preparation), 1963; University of Washington, Seattle (non-thesis master's study), 1964-1968. Principal occupation: Journalist, editor-in-chief. *Address:* 1228 M St., N.W., Washington, D.C. 20005. *Affiliations:* Copy news editor, photo news editor, correspondent, *Seattle Post-Intelligencer,* Seattle, Wash., 1969-1971; news director, Washington News Bureau, American Indian Press Association, Washington, D.C., and AIPA Southwest News Bureau, Albuquerque, N.M., 1971-1975; managing editor, *Confederated Umatilla Journal,* Pendleton, Oreg., 1975-1976; managing editor, *Yakima Nation Review,* Toppenish, Wash., 1977-1978; founder/managing editor, *Manataba Messenger,* Colorado River Indian Tribes, Parker, Ariz., 1980-1981; managing editor, *CERT Report,* Council of Energy Resource Tribes, Washington, D.C., 1981-1983; president, managing editor, La Course Communications Corp., Washington, D.C., 1983-. *Military service:* U.S. Army Reserve, 1964-1970. *Memberships:* Native American Press Association (co-founder, board of directors); Northwest Indian News Association (co-founder); ASNE-ANPA Foundation (adjunct member, Minorities Committee); National Congress of American Indians; Americans for Indian Opportunity, Norman, Okla. (honorary lifetime member); *Race Relations Reporter,* Nashville, Tenn. (associate editor). *Awards, honors:* Presentor, "The Role of Communications in Indian Life," Native American Teacher Corps. Conference, Denver, Colo., 1973; presenter/panelist, annual conference, Association for Education in Journalism, Fort Collins, Colo./Seattle, Wash., 1974/1978; U.S. representative, work and planning sessions of Canadian Indian journalists of Alberta Native Communications Society, Edmonton, Alberta, Canada, 1972-1975; presenter, History of American Indian Journalism;

Techniques and Strategies of Investigative Journalism, Indian Investigative Journalism Project, National Indian Youth Council, Albuquerque, N.M., 1975; co-author, videoscript on tribal jurisdiction issues, National Congress of American Indians, Washington, D.C., 1975; presenter, Workshop on Investigative Journalism, Freedom of the Press in Indian Country, Minnesota Chippewa Tribes, Bemidji, Minn., 1977; keynote speaker and honoree, Second Annual Indian Media Conference and American Indian Film Festival, San Francisco, Calif., 1978; co-founder, Northwest Indian News Association (author of news network charter for association), 1978; recipient, Indian Media Man of the Year Award, National Indian Media Conference, Anaheim, Calif., 1980; recipient, National Recognition Award for Accomplishment, Americans for Indian Opportunity, Washington, D.C., 1984; co-founder, Native American Press Association, University Park, Pa. (author of news network charter, code of ethics, business plan of operation. *Interests:* "La Course Communications Corp., an Indian-owned media firm organized in October 1983, provides services in publication research and development, graphic design, publication of directories, market analysis and specialized mailing lists related to American Indian concerns. Plans to publish a full-size weekly newspaper, *Native America,* with syndication of its news copy nationally. The corporation will also launch computer programming and software services in the field of American Indian interests." *Published works: American Indian Media Directory* (American Indian Press Association, 1974 edition); editor, "1855 Yakima Treaty Chronicles: May 28, 1855 - June 11, 1855," special collector's edition, *Yakima Nation Review,* June 23, 1978; editor, *The Schooling of Native America,* Native American Teachers Corps, 1978; author-editor, *Northwest Tribal Profiles,* Portland Area Office, B.I.A., 1980); author-editor, *Red Pages: Business Across Indian America* (La Course Communications, 1984); *Native Hemisphere: The Emerging Social Continent* (in progress); *The Sandinista-Meskito War* (working title) (in progress).

**LADD, EDMUND JAMES (Zuni) 1926-
(Pacific archaeologist-retired;
museum curator)**

Born January 4, 1926, Fort Yuma, Calif. *Education:* University of New Mexico, Albuquerque, B.S., 1955, M.A., 1964. *Principal occupation:* Pacific archaeologist-retired; museum curator. *Home address:* 686 Calle Espejo, Santa Fe, N.M. 87505. *Affiliations:* Pacific archaeologist, USDI, National Park Service, Honaunar, Kona, Hawaii, (23 years); curator of ethnology, New Museum of Indian Arts and Culture, Santa Fe, N.M. *Military service:* U.S. Army, 1944-1946. *Memberships:* American Anthropological Association; Society for American Archaeology.

**LAFROMBOISE, RICHARD (Chippewa)
(tribal chairman)**

Affiliation: Chairman, Turtle Mountain Tribal Council, Belcourt, N.D. 58316.

**LAMAR, NEWTON (Wichita)
(tribal president)**

Affiliation: President, Wichita Executive Committee, Wichita Tribal Affairs Office, P.O. Box 729, Anadarko, Okla. 73005.

**LAMB, CHARLES A. 1944-
(museum director)**

Born September 25, 1944, Farragut, Idaho. *Education:* California Western University, B.A. (History), 1966; San Diego State University, Graduate School, 1970-1973. *Principal occupation:* Museum director. *Home address:* 1509 Mohave, Parker, Ariz. 85344. *Affiliations:* National Park Ranger, Crater Lake, Ore., and Yellowstone National Park, Wyo. (eight years); California State Park Ranger and Archaeologic Aid, 1971-1972; Museum director, Colorado River Indian Tribes Museum, Parker, Ariz., 1973-. *Community activities:* Parker Area Historical Society (president); Museums Association of Arizona (Western Regional Representative); Tribal Tourism Committee (chairman); Irataba Society (board member); Tribal Safety Committee (former chairman). *Memberships:* American Association of Museums (education committee); American Association for State and Local History; Society for California Archaeology; National Trust for Historic Preservation. *Awards, honors:* Copely Press Scholarship; graduate of Horace M. Albright Training Center for National Park Service; graduate of Montana State University, Law Enforcement Academy. *Interests:* History, archaeology, anthropology, biology; historic preservation; hunting, fishing, photography, painting. *Biographical sources:* Articles in the following: *Arizona Republic* newspaper; *Parker Pioneer* newspaper; *Yuma Daily Sun* newspaper; among others. *Published works: San Simeon: A Brief History,* illustrations by C. Lamb (Santana Press, 1971).

LAME BULL, LUCINDA (Paiute)
(tribal chairwoman)

Affiliation: Chairwoman, Fort Bidwell Community Council, P.O. Box 127, Fort Bidwell, Calif. 96112.

LAMPMAN, EVELYN SIBLEY 1907-
(writer)

Born April 18, 1907, Dallas, Ore. *Education:* Oregon State University, B.S., 1929. *Principal occupation:* Writer. *Home address:* 3410 W. Rosemont Dr., West Linn, Ore. 97086. *Interests:* Mr. Lampman writes, "History, particularly the Western U.S. I grew up close to a reservation, so I have known and liked Indians all my life. Many visited in our home as guests of my father when I was a child. I have traveled in Mexico." *Published works: Witch Doctor's Son* (Doubleday, 1954); *Navajo Sister* (Doubleday, 1956); *Shy Stegosaurus of Indian Springs* (Doubleday, 1962); *Temple of the Sun* (Doubleday, 1964); *The Tilted Sombrero* (Doubleday, 1966); *Half Breed* (Doubleday, 1967); *Cayuse Courage* (Harcourt Brace, 1970); *Year of Small Shadow* (Harcourt Brace, 1971); *Once Upon a Little Big Horn* (Thomas Y. Crowell, 1971); *Go Up the Road* (Atheneum, 1972).

LANDES, RUTH 1908-
(cultural anthropologist)

Born October 8, 1908, New York, N.Y. *Education:* New York University, B.S., 1928; NYU School of Social Work, MSW, 1929; Columbia University, Ph.D., 1935. *Principal occupation:* Cultural anthropologist. *Affiliations:* Professor of anthropology, McMaster University, Hamilton, Ontario, Can., 1965-? *Other professional posts:* Consultant to national agencies and educational systems, California Social Work Department, and agencies, California Bureau of Mental Hygiene, California Department of Education, California Public Health medicine and nursing, San Francisco Police Department, 1957-? *Membership:* Author's Guild. *Interests:* Cultural anthropology of the Santee Dakota and Prairie Potawatomi Indians; Spanish-speaking peoples of the Southwest; education and minoirty cultures; civil rights; status of women; bi- and multilingualism; culture and personality. *Published works: Ojibwa Sociology* (Columbia University Press, 1937, 1968); *The Ojibwa Woman* (Columbia University Press, 1938, 1968, 1970); *Ojibwa Religion and the Midewiwin* (University of Wisconsin Press, 1968); *Santee Sociology* (University of Wisconsin Press, 1969); *Potawatomi Culture* (University of Wisconsin Press, 1970).

LANG, RICHARD W.
(museum director)

Affiliation: Director, The Wheelwright Museum of the American Indian, P.O. Box 5153, Santa Fe, N.M. 87502.

LaROCHE, HAROLD L. (Lower Brule Sioux) 1931-
(B.I.A. agency superintendent)

Born January 16, 1931, Lower Brule, S.D. *Education:* University of South Dakota, B.S., 1956; University of Minnesota, M.A., 1971. *Principal occupation:* B.I.A. agency superintendent. *Address:* Seminole Agency, Bureau of Indian Affairs, 6075 Stirling Rd.,

Hollywood, Fla. 33024. *Affiliations:* Director of Home Living, Guidance and Counseling, Social and Psychoogical Services, and Student Activities, Flandreau Indian School, Flandreau, S.D., 1972-?; superintendent, Seminole Agency, Bureau of Indian Affairs, Hollywood, Fla. *Military service:* U.S. Marine Corps, 1951-1954 (Sergeant). *Memberships:* American Legion; University of Minnesota Alumni Association. *Biographical source: Who's Who in American Colleges and Universities* (1955-1956).

LASARTE, BERNARD J.
(Coeur D'Alene)
(tribal chairman)

Affiliation: Chairman, Coeur D'Alene Tribal Council, Plummer, Idaho 83851.

LAUBIN, GLADYS W.
(lecturer, entertainer)

Home address: Grand Teton National Park, Moose, Wyo. 83012. *Principal occupation:* Lecturer and entertainer (presentation of Indian dances on the concert stage). *Memberships:* Association on American Indian Affairs; National Congress of American Indians; Chicago Indian Center; Jackson Hole Fine Arts Foundation. *Awards, honors:* Adopted member of Sioux Tribe; dance prizes, Standing Rock and Crow Reservations; Capezio Dance Award, 1972; Catlin Peace Pipe Award, Special Literary Award, American Indian Lore Association, 1976. *Interests:* Research among Sioux, Crow, Blackfeet, Cherokee, Kiowa, and other American Indian tribes related to dance, customs, Indian lore, music; photography; painting; costume making; woodcraft. *Published works:* Co-author, *The Indian Tipi* (University of Oklahoma Press, 1957); documentary art films, produced with Reginald Laubin: *Old Chiefs Dance, Talking Hands, War Dance, Indian Musical Instruments, Ceremonial Pipes and Tipi How* (University of Oklahoma Press, 1951-1958); *Indian Dances of North America and Their Importance to Indian Life* (University of Oklahoma Press, 1977); *The Indian Tipi,* 2nd Edition (University of Oklahoma Press, 1977); *American Indian Archery* (University of Oklahoma Press, 1978).

LAUBIN, REGINALD K.
(lecturer, entertainer)

Home address: Grand Teton National Park, Moose, Wyo. 83012. *Education:* Hartford Art School; Norwich Art School. *Principal occupation:* Lecturer and entertainer (presentation of American Indian dances and lore on the concert stage). *Memberships:* Association on American Indian Affairs; National Congress of American Indians; Chicago Indian Center; Jackson Hole Fine Arts Foundation. *Awards, honors:* Guggenheim Fellowship, 1951; adopted son of Chief One Bull, nephew of Sitting Bull; dance prizes, Standing Rock and Crow Reservations; Capezio Dance Award, 1972; Catlin Peace Pipe Award, Special Literary Award, American Indian Lore Association, 1976. *Interests:* Research among Sioux, Crow, Blackfeet, Cherokee, Kiowa and other tribes on dance, custom, lore, music and general anthropology; archery; photography; duplication of Indian craft techniques; primitive camping and cooking; woodcraft. *Published works: The Indian Tipi* (University of Oklahoma Press, 1957); series in *Boy's Life* on Indian crafts; six documentary films on Indian dance and culture, produced with Gladys Laubin; *Indian Dances of North America, and Their Importance to Indian Life* (University of Oklahoma Press, 1978).

LAVIOLETTE, REV. G., OMI 1911-
(editor and manager-*Indian Journal*)

Born April 7, 1911, Clarence, Ontario, Can. *Education:* University of Ottawa, Ontario, B.A., 1929; Oblate Fathers Seminary, Lebret, Saskatchewan, B.Th, 1934. *Principal occupation:* Editor and manager, *Indian Record,* Winnipeg, 1934-. *Home address:* 480 Aulneau St. #503, Winnipeg, Manitoba, Canada R2H 2V2. *Affiliations:* Founder, editor-manager, *Indian Record,* 1934-; editor of various periodicals, 1938-. *Other professional posts:* Missionary to the Dakota-Sioux Indians in Canada. *Community activities:* Religious Order of the Oblate of M.I. Winnipeg; Latin American Association of Winnipeg (president). *Memberships:* Manitoba Historical Society; St. Boniface Historical Society (advisory board). *Interests:* "Publishing on extensive history of the Dakota-Sioux Indians in Canada, to be published in 1986. Specialized in the Dakota Indian language. Since 1965, worked with Spanish-speaking people in metropolitan Winnipeg. Travels to Europe, Israel, Egypt, Mexico, South American, Japan, Taiwan, Hong Kong, etc." *Biographical source: International Biographical Centre* (Cambridge, England). *Published work: The Sioux Indians in Canada* (Martin Press, Regina, Sask., 1944).

LAWRENCE, ERMA G. (Haida) 1912-
   (native language instructor)

Born August 2, 1912, Hydaburg, Alaska. *Education:* Sheldon Jackson College, A.A. *Principal occupation:* Native language instructor. *Home address:* 320 Baldwin St. #415, Ketchikan, Alaska 99901. *Affiliation:* Ketchikan Gateway Borough School District, Ketchikan, Alaska. *Other professional posts:* Writer and consultant, Haida Society for the Preservation of Language and Literature, 1972-. *Community activities:* Curriculum Review Board (member). *Memberships:* Ketchikan Haida Society (secretary, 1973-); Alaska Native Sisterhood, 1938-. *Interests:* Bilingual education; linguistics; curriculum development; bilingual conferences and workshops. *Biographical sources: Ketchikan Daily News; Tundra Times,* Fairbanks; *Southeastern Log,* Ketchikan. *Published works: Haida Reader,* 1973; *Short Haida Stories,* 1974; compiler, editor, *Haida Noun Dictionary,* 1975, *Haida Verb Dictionary,* 1977; *Haida Teacher's Handbook,* 1976); and others.

LEAP, WILLIAM L. 1946-
   (anthropologist)

Born November 28, 1946, Philadelphia, Pa. *Education:* Florida State University, B.A. (Anthropology and Linguistics), 1967; Southern Merhodist University, Ph.D. (Anthropology), 1970. *Principal occupation:* Anthropologist. *Home address:* 206 G St., N.W., Washington, D.C. 20024. *Affiliations:* Associate professor, professor of anthropology, American University, Washington, D.C., 1970-. *Other professional post:* Director, Indian Education Program, Center for Applied Linguistics,

Arlington, Va., 1974-. *Interests:* "My vocational interests center on Indian self-determination through education. A major component of such a strategy is relevant education, and that means addressing the Indian (e.g. tribal or traditional) as well as the mainstream cultural components of the students interests, lifestyle, and life-options. My work in the field has centered on assisting Tribal governments and Tribal agencies develop programs to provide Tribal members to take charge of and manage such programs without reliance on outside sources of support." *Published works: Language Policies in Indian Education: Recommendations,* 1973, and *Handbook for Staff Development in Indian Education,* 1976 (Center for Applied Linguistics); *Studies in Southwestern Indian English* (Trinity University Press, 1977); *American Indian Language Education* (National Bilingual Research Center, 1980); "American Indian Language Renewal" in *Annual Review of Anthropology,* 1981; and published as book by National Clearinghouse for Bilingual Education, 1982.

LEASK, JANIE (Haida-Tsimshean) 1948-
   (president-Alaskan Native organization)

Born September 17, 1948, Seattle, Wash. *Education:* East Anchorage High School, 1966. *Principal occupation:* Alaska Federation of Natives, 411 W. 4th Ave., Suite 301, Anchorage, 1974- (vice president, 1977-1982; president, 1982-). *Address:* P.O. Box 104836, Anchorage, Alaska 99510. *Community activities:* Enrolled in Cook Inlet Region, Inc. (one of the 12 in-state Alaska Native Regional corporations; The State Board of Education; the Anchorage Organizing Committee for the 1992 Olympics; the Alaska Land Use Council; the ARCO Scholarship Committee. *Awards, honors:* Governor's Award in 1983 for work on behalf of Alaska Native people.

LEE, ROBERT H. 1920-
   (newspaper editor)

Born May 28, 1920, Minneapolis, Minn. *Home address:* Boulder Canyon Route, Sturgis, S.D. 57785. *Affiliations:* Wire, state and Sunday editor, Rapid City *Daily Journal* (nine years); reporter, Minneapolis *Tribune, Rocky Mountain News,* Denver, Colo.; political columnist, *Daily Plainsman,* Huron, S.D., *Public Opinion,* Watertown, S.D., *American News,* Aberdeen, S.D.; vice president, editor, Black Hills Publishers, Sturgis, S.D. *Military service:* U.S. Army, 1940-1945, 1947-1964 (Bronze Star). *Memberships:* South Dakota Historical Society, 1947- (director, 1964-); Crazy Horse Memorial Commission (director); Western Writers of America. *Awards, honors:* Award for coverage of theft of Chief Sitting Bull's body from North Dakota grave and reburial in South Dakota, Associated Press. *Published works: Dakota Panorama* (Mid-West-Bear Printing Co., 1961); *Last Grass Frontier* (Black Hills Publishers, 1964); editor, *Gold, Gals, Guns, Guts, Centennial History of Deadwood, S.D.* (Black Hills Publishers, 1976).

LEE, THOMAS E. 1914-
(archaeologist)

Born April 6, 1914, Port Bruce, Ontario, Can. *Education:* Wayne State University, B.A., 1944; University of Toronto, 1942-1943; University of Chicago, 1947-1948; University of Michigan, M.A., 1949. *Principal occupation:* Archaeologist. *Home address:* 1575 Forlan Dr., Ottawa, Ontario Can. K2C 0R8. *Affiliations:* Biologist, National Museum of Canada, 1950-1959; professor invite, Centre d'Etudes Nordiques, Universite Laval, Quebec, 1966-. *Military service:* Royal Canadian Air Force, 1942-1946 (Corporal; CVSM & CLASP: Defense of Britain; 1939-1945 Star; Burma Star; War Medal). *Other professional posts:* Editor, *Anthropological Journal of Canada,* Ottawa; associate editor, *New World Antiquity,* London; associate editor, *The Chesopian,* Norfolk, Va. *Memberships:* Ontario Archaeological Society, 1953- (Life); Instituto Interamerican, 1958- (Fellow, Life); Anthropological Association of Canada, 1963- (Fellow, Life); Guild of American Prehistorians, 1964- (Co-founder; Life); The Chesopian Archaeological Association. *Awards, honors:* Title of Kitchi Donegachin, conferred by Wykwemikong Band of the Ojibways; Master Archaeologist Award,

Guild of American Prehistorians. *Interests:* Archaeology of the American Indian; historical archaeology; wild life; travel. *Published works: Archaeological Investigation, Lake Abitibi,* 1965; *Arcaheological Discovery Discovery, Payne Bay Region, Ungava 1966,* 1968; *Archaeological Investigation of a Longhouse, Pamiok, Ungava,* 1972; *Archaeological Investigation of a Longhouse Ruin, Pamiok Island,* 1974; *The Fort Abitibi Mystery,* 1974; among others, all published by Laval University. Plus more than 200 papers and book reviews.

LENZ, MONSIGNOR PAUL A. 1925-
(Roman Catholic Priest)

Born December 15, 1925, Gallitzin, Pa. *Education:* St. Vincent College, Latrobe, Pa.; St. Vincent Seminary, Latrobe, Pa.; Penn State University. *Principal occupation:* Executive director, The Bureau of Catholic Indian Missions, Washington, D.C. *Home address:* 2021 H St., N.W., Washington, D.C. 20006. *Other professional posts:* Board of trustees: The Catholic University of America, Washington, D.C.; Xavier University, New Orleans; St. Vincent Seminary, Latrobe; National Catholic Indian Tekakwitha Conference, and The National Catholic Development Conference, Washington, D.C. *Memberships:* Rotary Club of Washington, D.C.; George Washington University Faculty Club.

LERNER, ALBERT L. 1931-
(B.I.A. employment assistance officer)

Born December 6, 1931, New York, N.Y. *Education:* S.U.N.Y., Oswego, B.S., 1956; Oregon State University, M.Ed., 1961. *Principal occupation:* B.I.A. employment assistance officer. *Home address:* 2090 McCormack Lane, Placentia, Calif. 92670. *Affiliations:* Vocational teacher, Stewart Indian School, Nev., 1956-1961; head, Vocational Training Department, Flandreau Indian School, S.D., 1961-1965; adult vocational training officer, Cleveland, Ohio, Chicago, Ill., 1965-1967; employment assistance officer, B.I.A., Chicago, Ill., 1969-1971, Los Angeles, Calif. (director), 1971-. *Military service:* U.S. Navy (Aviation machinist, mate 3).

LESTENKOF, JACOB
(B.I.A. area director)

Affiliation: Director, Juneau Area Office, Bureau of Indian Affairs, P.O. Box 3-8000, Juneau, Alaska 99802.

LESTER, A. DAVID (Creek) 1941-
(executive director-Indian organization)

Born September 25, 1941, Claremore, Okla. *Education:* Brigham Young University, Provo, Utah, B.A. (Political Science and Public Administration), 1967. *Principal occupation:* Executive director, Council of Energy Resource Tribes (CERT), 1580 Logan St., Denver, Colo. 80203. *Home address:* 8688 East Otero Circle, Englewood, Colo. 80112. *Affiliations:* Vice-chairman, American Indian Scholarships, Inc., Taos, N.M. (two years); president, United Indian Development Association, Los Angeles, Calif. (seven years); economic development specialist, National Congress of American Indians, Washington, D.C. *Other professional posts:* Commissioner, Administration for Native Americans, U.S. Department of Health and Human Services, Washington, D.C.; Boards of Directors: American Indian National Bank , Washington, D.C.; Americans for Indian Opportunity, Albuquerque, N.M.; American Indian Scholarships, Inc., Taos, N.M.; National Area Development Institute, and Los Angeles Indian Center, Los Angeles, Calif.. *Community activities:* Served as a Presidential appointee to the National Advisory Council on Minority Enterprise, which advised cabinet-level officials on strategies to stimulate minority business ownership, and to the National Council on Indian Opportunity, devoted to improving social and economic opportunities for American Indians; served as Human Relations Commissioner for the City of Los Angeles and as Chairman of the Los Angeles County American Indian Commission. *Awards, honors:* Received the Indian Council First Indian Achievement Award, the Americans for Indian Opportunity's Distinguished Services "Peace Pipe" Award, a proclamation of "David Lester Day" by the Governor of Oklahoma, recognition by the California State Assembly for contributions to Indian-State relations, the United Indian Development Association's Jay Silverheels

Achievement Award, the White Buffalo Council of American Indians' National-Level Award for Outstanding Service to American Indians; created a self-supporting management institute which trained 2,000 Indian businessmen and women; presented a wide variety of Indian and Native American issues before conferences, coventions, and other meetings and on radio and television. *Interests:* Indian affairs; pow-wows; Indian cultures; "Indian economic progress is my vocational goal."

LESTER, JOAN 1937-
(museum curator)

Born July 4, 1937, New York, N.Y. *Education:* Brown University, B.A. (Art History), 1959; Sorbonne, Paris, France (Certificate of Studies, 1958; University of California, Los Angeles, M.A. (Primitive Art/American Indian Art), 1963. *Principal occupation:* Museum curator. *Home address:* 2 Muster Ct., Lexington, Mass. 02173. *Affiliations:* Museum assistant, 1963-1970, museum coordinator-Native American Advisory Board, 1973-, developer/curator, American Indian Collections and Programs, 1976-, associate curator, 1975-1978, curator of collections, 1978-, Boston Children's Museum, Mass.; coordinator of North American Indian resources and workshop (courses and workshops presenting Indian people in southern New England), co-developer of American Indian people in Greater Boston area, 1971-1974. *Other professional posts:* Chair, National Curator's Committee, 1982- member-at-large, Council for Museum Anthropology, 1983-; principal investigator, American Indian Games, National Endowment for the Humanities Planning Grant, 1983-. *Community activities:* Member, advisory boards: Phoenix School, Cambridge, Mass.; MIT Museum; Native American Studies Department of Plimoth Plantation, Mass.; Tomaquag Indian Memorial Museum, Exeter, R.I. MAP assessor, Museum Assessment Program. *Memberships:* American Association of Museums (curator's committee); International Council of Museums; New England Museum Association; Native American Art Studies Association; Council for Museum Anthropology; Peabody Museum Assocaition (member-at-large). *Awards, honors:* Boston Indian Council Certificate of Merit, 1975; Bay State Historical League Award of Excellence, for "Indians Who Met the Pilgrims," June, 1975. *Interests:* "American Indian art; American Indian arts in New England as they continue today; cooking, bicycling, cross country skiing, theater, classical music, folk dancing, reading." Published works: "The American Indian, A Museum's Eye View," in *Indian Historian,* summer, 1972; "*Indians Who Met the Pilgrims,*" the Match Program, *American Science and Enginnering, Boston, 1974; "A Code of Ethics for Curator's,"* in *Museum News,* Jan./Feb., 1983; chapter I - *The Prodcuction of Fancy Bakets in Maine* (American Indian Archaeological Institute, 1986); *American Indian Art in New England* (Boston Chilren's Museum, 1986); *The Art of Tomah Joseph, Passamaquoddy Artist* (manuscript submitted). Reports: American Indian Art Association, "Tomah Joseph, Passamaquoddy Artist," Sept., 1983; Metropolitan Museum of Art, "The Northeast Native American Program at the Children's Museum," April, 1983; York Institute, Saco, Maine, "Northeast Native American Baskets: A Continuing Tradition," Oct., 1982); Massachusetts Indian Association, "The Significance of the Katherine Hall Newall Collection," Oct., 1982; American Indian Art Association, "They're Still Here, Native American Art in New England," March, 1982; Institute for Contemporary Art, "Native American Ash Splint Basketry in New England," Feb., 1982.

LEVI, JERRY R. (Cheyenne-Arapaho) 1946-
(Indian program administrator)

Born June 27, 1946, Concho, Okla. *Education:* Southeastern Oklahoma State University, B.S., 1971; Oklahoma City University, M.B.A., 1986. *Principal occupation:* Administrator, Potawatomi WIC & Food Distributor Programs. *Home address:* 419 S. Ardalotte, Shawnee, Okla. 74801. *Affiliations:* Chairman, Oklahoma, New Mexico Food Action Committee for Tribes (ONFACT); member, National Association of WIC Directors. *Military service:* U.S. Army, 1968-1970 (SP5-E-5; Soldier of the Month, Feb., 1970; selected for All-Army

Trials). *Community activites:* Tribal chairman, Cheyenne-Arapaho Tribes, 1981; Concho School Board (chairman, 1981); El Reno Title IV Committee vice chairman, 1980-1981; El Reno YMCA wrestling coach; Yukon Jays football coach.

LEVIER, FRANCES ANDREW (Citizen Band Potawatomi) 1950-
(tribal administrator, business committeeman)

Born November 13, 1950, Topeka, Kan. *Education:* Hofstra University, B.A. (Social Science and Secondary Education), 1973; University of Kansas, M.S.Ed. (Edcuational Administration), 1975, Ed.D. (Administration and Higher Education), 1979. *Principal occupation:* Tribal administrator and business committeeman. *Home address:* 13 Lorie Lane, Shawnee, Okla. 74801. *Affiliations:* Acting director, Supportive Educational Services, 1975-1976, instructor, School of Social Welfare, 1977-1979, assistant director of Minority Affairs, 1974-1980, University of Kansas, Lawrence, Kan.; director, Health Programs, Prairie Band Potawatomi Tribe, 1980-1981; acting executive director, Prairie Band Potawatomi Tribe of Kansas, 1980-1981; executive director, Region VI Indian Alcoholism Training Program, 1982-1983; executive director, A proposal, Evaluation, Research, and Training consulting firm (P.E.R.T., Inc.), 1982-; director of economic development, Citizen Band Potawatomi Tribe, 1983-1985; tribal administrator and business committeeman, Citizen Band Potawatomi Tribe, Shawnee, Okla., 1983-. *Other professional post:* Member of the Board of Regents, Haskell Indian Junior College, Lawrence, Kan., 1979-1983; consultant, Rockefeller Foundation, 1979; consultant, instructor, Leavenworth Federal Penitentiary, Kan., 1978-1980; consultant, Kickapoo Tribe of Kansas, 1978; consultant, Powhatten School District, Kan., 1978; assistant director, Topeka Indian Center, Kan., 1977-1978. *Community activities:* Affirmative Action, University of Kansas (board member, 1976-1980); United Indian Recovery Association (board member, 1980-1981); Emergency Services Council, City of Lawrence, Kan. (chairman, 1977-1980). *Awards, honors:* Recipient of Ford Foundation Fellowship for American Indians, 1973-1976; "Elected to five-member Business Committee (governing body) of the Citizen Band Potawatomi Tribe in June, 1985. Was first business committee member ever named to the position of tribal administrator in the history of the 12,000 member tribe." *Published works:* "A Brief History of the Pedigree Papers," 1983; editor, "Using Indian Culture to Develop Alcohol & Drug Materials for Indian Adults and Youth," 1983; "Overview of Inhalent Abuse Among American Indian Youth," 1981; "An Attitude Survey of Urban Indians in N.E. Kansas Toward Higher Education," 1979; all published by the American Indian Institute, University of Oklahoma, 1983. "The Need for Indian Student Organizations in Large Institutions of Higher Edcuation," N.E.C.C.A. Conference Article, K.C., Mo., 1979.

LEWIS, DAVE
(director-Indian association)

Affiliation: Director, Indian Arts and Crafts Association, 4215 Lead SE, Albuquerque, N.M. 87108.

LEWIS, ROBERT E. (Zuni) 1914-
(former tribal official)

Born August 24, 1914, Zuni, N.M. *Education:* High school; U.S. Navy Torpedo School. *Principal occupation:* Former tribal official. *Home address:* Zuni, N.M. 87327. *Affiliation:* Governor, Pueblo of Zuni, N.M (elected Jan., 1965). *Military service:* U.S. Navy, 1942-1945 (Torpedoman; Pacific Theatre Award; Presidential Award. *Community activities:* All-Pueblo Indian Council; New Mexico Governor's Committee of 100 on Economic Development, State Constitutional Convention; Lions Club; American Legion; Committee on Indian Awareness; Dir Rama, Inc. (board of directors). *Awards, honors:* Outstanding Citizen of McKinley County, 1970; Conservation Award, New Mexico Bankers Association; Indian Leadership Award, B.I.A., U.S. Dept. of the Interior. *Interests:* "Traveling; speaking engagements throughout the U.S. on behalf of the genernal Indian movement." *Published work: Zuni Tales* (University of Utah Press, 1972).

LIBHART, MYLES
(director-Indian Arts
and Crafts Board)

Affiliation: Director, Indian Arts and Crafts Board, U.S. Department of the Interior, 18th & C Sts., N.W., Room 4004, Washington, D.C. 20240.

LIEB, BERTHA K.
(executive director-Indian center)

Affiliation: Executive director, The Indian Center of Lawrence, 2326 Louisiana St., P.O. Box 1016, Lawrence, Kan. 66044.

LINCOLN, DARAN
(tribal president)

Affiliation: President, Covelo Community Council, Round Valley Reservation, P.O. Box 448, Covelo, Calif. 95428.

LINFORD, LAURENCE D.
(executive director—Indian association)

Affiliation: Executive director, Inter-Tribal Indian Ceremonial Association, P.O. Box 1, Church Rock, N.M. 87311.

LINK, MARTIN ANDREW 1934-
(former museum director)

Born September 26, 1934, Madison, Wis. *Education:* University of Arizona, B.A., 1957. *Principal occupation:* Former director, Navajo Tribal Museum, Window Rock, Ariz. *Affiliation:* Treasurer, Gallup Museum of Arts and Crafts. *Military service:* U.S. Army Reserve, 1961. *Community activities:* Inter-Tribal Indian Ceremonial Association (board of directors, 1971-); Navajo Centennial Commission (chairman, 1968); Annual Navajo Science Fair (chairman); Knights of Columbus; Lions Club; Gallup Archaeological Society; Plateau Sciences Society (board of directors, 1965-). *Memberships:* Arizona Academy of Sciences; American Association of Museums; New Mexico Association of Museums; Western Museums League; New Mexico Archaeological Society (board of regents, 1971-). *Award:* Annual Award for improvement of the environment from Keep New Mexico Beautiful, Inc., 1970. *Interests:* Photography; western exploration. *Published works: Navajo—A Century of Progress* (KC Publications, 1968); *Navajo Treaty Negotiations of 1868* (KC Publications, 1968); *The Second Long Walk* (St. Michaels Press, 1968); *A Guide to the Navajo Museum* (Navajo Printing Dept., 1971).

LITTLE, HARLEY
(B.I.A. agency superintendent)

Affiliation: Superintendent, Okmulgee Agency, Bureau of Indian Affairs, P.O. Box 370, Okmulgee, Okla. 74447.

LITTLE, STEWART
(B.I.A. executive assistant)

Affiliation: Executive assistant, Bureau of Indian Affairs, 1951 Constitution Ave., N.W., Washington, D.C. 20245.

LITTLE, VINCENT
(B.I.A. area director)

Affiliation: Director, Albuquerque Area Office, Bureau of Indian Affairs, P.O. Box 8327, 5301 Central East, Albuquerque, N.M. 87198.

LITTLE AXE, DANNY (Absentee-Shawnee)
(tribal chairman)

Affiliation: Chairman, Absentee-Shawnee Executive Committee, P.O. Box 1747, Shawnee, Okla. 74801.

LITTLECHIEF, BARTHELL (Kiowa-Comanche) 1941-
(artist-sculptor/painter)

Born October 14, 1941, Kiowa Indian Hospital, Lawton, Okla. *Education:* Cameron University, Lawton, Okla., 1964-1965; University of Oklahoma, Norman, 1966-1967. *Principal occupation:* Artist-sculptor/painter. *Home address:* Route 3, Box 109A, Anadarko, Okla. 73005. *Military service:* U.S. Army National Guard, 1966-1971

(SP/4). *Memberships:* Kiowa TIA-PAIH Society of Oklahoma; Native American Church. *Biographical sources: Who's Who in North American Indian Art; Who's Who in American Art; American Artists; Kiowa Voices;* articles in *Southern Living* magazine, and *Texhoma Monthly* magazine.

LITTLECOOK, OLIVER (Ponca)
(tribal chairman)

Affiliation: Chairman, Ponca Business Committee, P.O. Box 2, White Eagle, Ponca City, Okla. 74601.

LIVERMORE, EARL R. (Blackfeet)
1932-
(artist)

Born November 29, 1932, Browning, Mt. *Education:* Haskell Institute; University of Washington; Burnley Professional School of Art, Seattle, Wash.; Academy of Art, San Francisco, Calif. *Principal occupation:* Artist. *Home address:* 2149 Otis Dr., Apt. 236, Alameda, Calif. 94501. *Affiliations:* Mechanic, Boeing Airplane Co., Seattle, Wash., 1957-1959; operating engineer, Group Health Hospital, Seattle, 1959-1960; treating engineer, J.H. Baxter Co., Kenydale, Wash., 1960-1964; stationary engineer, Children's Hospital, San Francisco, Calif., 1964-1968; director, American Indian Center, San Francisco, 1968-1970; Indian desk director-consultant for American Indian Community Action Programs, Scientific Analysis Corp., San Francisco, 1970; director, Bay Area Alcoholism Program, Oakland, Calif., 1970-1972; consultant, National Institute on Alcohol Abuse and Alcoholism (National Indian Review Panel), Rockville, Md., 1973-1975; director, Native American Alcoholism and Drug Abuse Program/Indian Womens Alcoholism Crisis Center, Oakland, Calif., 1972-? *Military service:* U.S. Coast Guard, 1952-1956. *Community activities:* Lone Mountain College, San Francisco (board member, 1973-1974); Human Rights Commission of the City and County of San Francisco (commissioner, 1968-1975; Native American Advisory Committee to the San Francisco Human Rights Commission (chairman); Youth and Education Committee of the Human Rights

Commission; State Acoholism Advisory Board, 1974-1977); National Indian Alcoholism Board, 1975-1977; San Francisco American Indian Center (president, 1970); California League for American Indians (board member, 1973). *Memberships:* American Indian Historical Society (board member); National Association of Blackfeet Indians, Seattle, Wash. *Exhibitions:* University of California, Berkeley; Philbrook Art Center, Tulsa, Okla.; Heard Museum, Phoenix, Ariz.; Scottsdale National Indian Arts Exhibition; Indian Festival of Arts, LaGrande, Ore.; American Indian Historical Society (one-man show), San Francisco; Oakland Museum; palace of Fine Arts, San Francisco; two paintings in the permanent collection of the Plains Indian Museum, Browning, Mont.; among others. *Interests:* Fine arts; sports.

LOCKLEAR, JUANITA O.
(director-Indian center)

Affiliation: Director, Native American Resource Center, Pembroke State University, Pembroke, N.C. 28372.

LOFTON, GENE TRAVIS (Chickasaw-Choctaw-Creek) 1934-
(museum curator)

Born March 8, 1934, Healdton, Okla. *Education:* Oklahoma A & M (three years). *Principal occuaption:* Curator, Tucker Tower Museum, Lake Murray, Okla., 1971-. *Home address:* P.O. Box 1649, Ardmore, Okla. 73401.

LOLOMA, CHARLES (Hopi) 1921-
(jeweler)

Born 1921, Hotevilla, Ariz. *Education:* School for American Craftsmen, S.U.N.Y. at Albany, Journeyman's Certificate. *Principal occupation:* Jeweler. *Memberships:* Arizona Commission on the Arts and Humanities (member); American Crafts Council (Fellow); Wheelwright Museum (board member); Native American Center for the Living Arts, Inc. (board member). *Interests:* "(I am) extremely active in Hopi ceremonies, ways of life, and farming;"

travel. *Biographical sources:* Numerous articles in *Arizona Highways, New Mexico Magazine,* and *American Indian Art.* PBS special film, *Loloma.*

LOMAHAFTEWA, LINDA (Hopi) 1947-
(teacher, artist)

Born July 3, 1947, Phoenix, Ariz. *Education:* San Francisco Art Institute, BFA, 1970, MFA, 1971. *Principal occupation:* Teacher, artist. *Home address:* Route 11, Box 20 SP 59, Santa Fe, N.M. 87501. *Affiliation:* Assistant professor of Native American Art, California State College, Rohnert Park, Calif., 1971-1973; teacher, painting and drawing, Native American Studies, University of California, Berkeley, 1974-1976; drawing and painting instructor, Institute of American Indian Arts, Santa Fe, N.M.. 1976-. *Exhibitions:* "Festival of Native American Art," Aspen Institute at Baca, 1982; "Contemporary Native American Art," Gardiner Art Gallery, Oklahoma State University, Stillwater, Okla., 1983; "Contemporary Native American Photography," Southern Plains Indian Museum, Anadarko, Okla., 1984; "Shadows Caught Images of Native Americans," Gilcrease Museum, Tulsa, Okla., 1984; "2nd Annual Heard Invitational," Heard Museum, Phoenix, Ariz., 1985; "One Woman Exhibit," American Indian Contemporary Arts, San Francisco, Calif., 1985; "Women of Sweetgrass, Cedar and Sage," Gallery of the American Indian Community House, New York, N.Y., 1985; "The Art of the Native American," Owensboro Museum of Fine Arts, Ky., 1985; "Native to Native," Alchemie Gallery, Boston, Mass., 1986. *Community activities:* City of Santa Fe Arts Board. *Memberships:* San Francisco Art Institute Alumni Association; Institute of American Indian Arts Alumni Association. *Awards, honors:* Indian Festival of Arts - First Place Painting, La Grande, Oreg., 1974; 61st Annual Indian Market - Third Place Painting, Santa Fe, N.M., 1982. *Interests:* Art—displayed at the following permanent collections: Southern Plains Indian Museum, Anadarko, Okla.; Millicent Rogers Museum, Taos, N.M.; University of Lethbridge, Native American Studies Department, Alberta, Canada; Native

American Center for the Living Arts, Inc., Niagara Falls, N.Y.; American Indian Historical Society, San Francisco, Calif.; Center for the Arts of Indian America, Washington, D.C. *Biographical sources: Who's Who in American Art,* 1976; *The Sweet Grass Lives on 50 Contemporary Native American Indian Artists,* by Jamake Highwater (Lippincott, 1980); *American Women Artists,* by Charlotte Streifer Rubinstein (Avon, 1982); *The World Who's Who of Women,* Eighth Edition, 1984; *Bearing Witness Sobreviviendo,* An Anthology of Writing and Art by Native American-/Latina Women (*Calyx:* A Journal of Art and Literature by Women, Corvallis, Ore., 1984); *The American West, The Modern Vision,* by Patricia Janis Broder (Little, Brown, 1984).

LONEFIGHT, EDWARD (Mandan-Hidatsa) 1939-
(B.I.A. Indian education)

Born May 28, 1939, Elbowoods, N.D. *Education:* Dickinson State College, N.D., B.S., 1964; Arizona State University, M.A., 1970. *Principal occupation:* B.I.A. Indian education. *Address:* Bureau of Indian Affairs, Roomm 4871, 1951 Constitution Ave., N.W., Washington, D.C. 20245. *Affiliation:* Superintendent, Riverside Indian School, Anadarko, Okla.; Indian education, B.I.A., Washington, D.C. *Community activities:* Jaycees; Kiwanis Club. *Membership:* National Education Association.

LOOKOUT, CHARLES E. (Osage-Delaware) 1922-
(reference/periodicals librarian)

Born December 29, 1922, Pawhuska, Okla. *Education:* Oklahoma State University, B.A., 1952; University of Oklahoma, Master of Library Science, 1968. *Principal occupation:* Reference/periodical librarian, Tulsa City-County Library System, Tulsa, Okla., 1964-. *Military service:* U.S. Navy, 1942-1946 (Machinist mate 3/C; served aboard aircraft carrier U.S.S. Saratoga; received Asiatic-Pacific American Theatre, Victory Medal, Good Conduct Medal, and six Battle Stars). *Community activities:* V.F.W.: American Legion; Osage War Dance Com-

mittee, Pawhuska, Okla. (member). *Memberships:* American Library Association; Oklahoma Library Association (recruitment committee-two years); Tulsa Library Staff Association (membership chairman-two years); O.U. and O.S.U. Alumni Associations. *Awards, honors:* National Poppy Director Award, 1962, by V.F.W. National Convention, Minneapolis, Minn.; Third Place, Strait War Dancing Contest, 1976, by Kihekah Steh Indian Club. *Interests:* Indian war dancing; theater; travel. "I have initiated a program to list the entire holdings of Tulsa City-County Library System on North American Indians in computer print-out."

LOUDNER, GODFREY, Jr. (Crow Creek Sioux) 1946-
(mathematics instructor)

Born September 30, 1946, Fort Thompson, S.D. *Education:* Black Hills State College, B.S.; South Dakota School of Mines and Technology, M.S.; University of Notre Dame, Ph.D. (Mathematics), 1974. *Principal occupation:* Mathematics instructor, Sinte Gleska College, Rosebud, S.D. *Home address:* Box 432, Mission, S.D. 57555. *Memberships:* American Mathematics Society. *Interests:* Professional: lie groups, differential geometry, harmonic analysis; mountain climbing, cave exploration. "Working on monograph about "Automonophic Forms With Applications."

LOUNSBERRY, GARY RICHARD 1944-
(social worker)

Born May 22, 1944, Wellsville, N.Y. *Education:* University of Rochester, N.Y., A.B., 1966; University of Michigan, M.S.W., 1968; University of Pittsburgh, M.P.H., 1981, Ph.D., 1985. *Principal occupation:* Social worker. *Home address:* R.R. 6, Box 281, Lawrence, Kan. 66046. *Affiliation:* Commissioned officer in the Commissioned Corps of the U.S. Public Health Service, Indian Health Service, 1970-; clinical social worker and service unit director, Sisseton Service Unit, Indian Health Service, Sisseton, S.D., 1970-1974; mental health consultant, Claremore Service Unit, Indian Health Service, Claremore, Okla., 1974-

1979; human service consultant, Haskell Health Center, Lawrence, Kan., 1981-. *Other professional posts:* Guest lecturer at Claremore Junior College (now Rogers State College), 1974-1979; Adjunct faculty, Haskell Indian Junior College, Lawrence, Kan., 1981-; adjunct faculty—field instruction, School of Social Welfare, University of Kansas, Lawrence, 1984-. *Community activities:* Trinity Episcopal Church — various offices and committees in South Dakota, Oklahoma, and Kansas; Douglas County Children's Advisory Committee. *Memberships:* Academy of Certified Social Workers, National Association of Social Workers, 1968-; Public Health Association; American Orthopsychiatric Association; Biofeedback Society of America. *Awards, honors:* U.S. Public Health Service, Career Development Training Award, 1979-1981, Isolated Hardship Service Ribbon, 1984; Employee of the Quarter, Haskell Health Center, 1984; George Abbott Scholarship, New York State Regent's Scholarship; Golden R Award (Rochester); National Merit Scholarship Finalist; Bausch and Lomb Science Award (Scio). *Interests:* "Vocational interests: Cross-cultural mental health and social services; family therapy with alcoholic families; computer applications to human services; human services in rural areas; human sexuality; psychosocial aspects of chronic illness. Avocational: Native American arts and crafts; Indian history during the colonial period; genealogy; regional American food, gardining, traveling, sailing, fishing." "Introduction of Biofeedback Training Into an IHS Mental Health Program," 1977, and "Social Networks and Utilization of Health Services by Urban Indians," 1982 (*Proceedings of the U.S.P.H.S. Professional Association,* April 1977); *Contemporary American Indians and Access to Health Services: Urban and Reservation Differences in Use of Social Networks to Access Health Services* (Dissertation, University Microfilms, 1985).

LOVE, TIMOTHY (Penobscot)
(tribal governor)

Affiliation: Governor, Penobscot Tribe, Six River Rd., Indian Island, Old Town, Maine 04468.

LOVELY, DEBORAH
(executive director, Indian center)

Affiliation: Executive director, United American Indian Education Center, 2100 28th St., Sacramento, Calif. 95818.

LOWRY, IRENE
(executive director-Indian association)

Affiliation: Executive director, North American Indian Association, 360 John R, Detroit, Mich. 48226.

LUCAS, MERLE R. (Sioux) 1944-
(administrator)

Born June 9, 1944, Vanport City, Ore. *Education:* Northern Montana College, Havre, 1963-1964. *Principal occupation:* Administrator. *Home address:* 3305 5th Ave. South, Billings, Mont. 59101. *Affiliations:* Director, Native American Studies, Carroll College, Helena, Mt. (one year); associate professor, Native American Studies, Blackfeet Community College, Browning, Mt. (two years); coordinator of Indian affairs, State of Montana, State Capitol, Helena, Mt. (nine years); associate planner, Department of Planning and Economic Development, State of Montana (three years); executive director, Montana Inter-Tribal Policy Board, 1983-. *Military service:* U.S. Army Airborne, 1965-1968 (E-5; Bronze Star; Army Commendation Medal with one Oak Leaf; Purple Heart; National Defense Service Medal; Vietnam Service Medal with 3 Bronz Service Stars; Republic of Vietnam Campaign Medal). *Community activities:* Helena Indian Center, Mont. (president, three years); Montana United Indian Association, Helena, Mont. (treasurer, two years). *Memberships:* Governors Inter-State Indian Council, 1973-1982; Montana Indian Edcuation Association, 1980-; Montana Indian Education Advisory Board, 1985-. *Awards, honors:* Outstanding Vietnam Era Veteran (1977) of the Nation for outstanding contributions shown to the community, state, and nation since returning to civilian life, No Greater Love Organization, Washington, D.C. *Biographical sources:* *Western Business Magazine* article concerning economic development for Montana reservations; periodic news articles concerning Indian issues relating to Native Americans in Montana. *Published works: Profile of Montana Native American* (State of Montana, 1974); "Annual Report of the Governors' Interstate Indian Council Conference," 1979.

LUCERO, ALVINO (Isleta Pueblo) (tribal governor)

Affiliation: Governor, Isleta Pueblo, P.O. Box 317, Isleta, N.M. 87022.

LUCERO, RICHARD, Jr. (Mescalero Apache-Seminole) 1944- (administrator)

Born September 24, 1944, Billings, Mt. *Education:* University of Wyoming, Laramie, 1964-1966; Eastern Montana College, Billings, 1966-1967; Rocky Mountain College, Billings, Mont., B.A. (Psychology), 1968. *Principal occupation:* Administrator. *Home address:* 3733 Magnolia, Grand Prairie, Tex. 75051. *Affiliations:* Psychology technician, Veterans Administration, Psychiatric Hospital, Sheridan, Wyo., 1971-1972; director, Alcoholism Treatment and Recovery Program, San Acadio, Colo., 1972-1974; director, Alcoholism Family Services Division, Weld Mental Health Center, Inc., Greeley, Colo., 1974-1977; director, Drug Abuse Services Project, Mental Health Center of Boulder County, Inc., Boulder, Colo., 1977-1978; associate professor, University of Northern Colorado, 1977-1978; director, Montana United Indian Association, Health Department, Helena, Mt., 1978-1980; executive director, Dallas Inter-Tribal Center, Tex., 1980-. *Other professional posts:* President, board of directors, American Indian Health Care Association, 1984-; certified management consultant with Performax Systems International, Inc., 1983-. *Community activities:* Colorado Alcohol and Drug Treatment Committee (member, 1976-1978); Indian Health Planners Task Force, (advisory committee, 1978-1979; chairman, 1979-1980; compiled, edited and wrote the National Urban Specific Health Plan submitted to the Secretary of Health and Human Services); Youth Advisory Committee, Fort McKenzie Veterans Administration Psychiatric Hospital (chairman, 1970-1972). *Memberships:* Colorado Association of Professional Alcoholism Counselors, Inc. (member of committee that developed state certification standards); American Indian Health Care Association (chairman, Region VII, Health Directors Board, 1982-1984; treasurer, 1983-1984; president, 1984-); *Awards, honors:* Recipient of Superior Performance Award, 1970, Public Relations Award, 1972, Fort McKenzie V.A. Psychiatric Hospital, Sheridan, Wyo.; guest speaker, National Council on Alcoholism Annual Conference, 1974; appointed by President Gerald Ford to serve on National Drug Abuse and Adolescents Task Force, 1977; developed special proposal to provide therapeutic community treatment center for Eastern Colorado. *Interests:* Music, tennis, coaching baseball, basketball.

LUMSDEN, JOSEPH K. (Chippewa) 1934- (educational administration, tribal chairman)

Born October 10, 1934, Sault Ste. Marie, Mich. *Education:* Michigan Technological University, B.S., 1967; Northern Michigan University, Teaching Certificate, 1969. *Principal occupation:* Educational administration, tribal chairman. *Home address:* 1101 Johnston St., Sault Ste. Marie, Mich. 49783. *Affiliation:* Tribal chairman, Sault Ste Marie Tribe of Chippewa Indians, 1973-. *Military service:* U.S. Marine Corps, 1953-1956 (Corporal). *Community activities:* Michigan Fishery Advisory Committee (chairman); Chippewa-Ottawa Fishery Management Authority. *Memberships:* National Congress of American Indians; National Tribal Chairman's Association. *Awards, honors:* Recognition of Leadership and Achievement, Bureau of Indian Affairs, 1984.

LUPE, RONNIE (White Mountain Apache (tribal chairman)

Affiliation: Chairman, White Mountain Apache Tribal Council, P.O. Box 700, Whiteriver, Ariz. 85941.

LURIE, NANCY OESTREICH 1924-
(museum curator)

Born January 24, 1924, Milwaukee, Wis. *Education:* University of Wisconsin, Madison, B.A., 1945; University of Chicago, M.A., 1947; Northwestern University, Ph.D., 1952. *Principal occupation:* Curator and head, Anthropology Section, Milwaukee Public Museum. *Home address:* 3342 N. Gordon Place, Milwaukee, Wis. 53212. *Affiliations:* Instructor, anthropology and sociology, University of Wisconsin, Milwaukee, 1947-1949, 1951-1953; research associate, North American ethnology, Peabody Museum, Harvard University, 1954-1956; consultant and expert witness for law firms representing tribal clients before the U.S. Indian Claims Commission, 1954-; lecturer in anthropology, Rackham School of Graduate Studies Extension Service, University of Michigan, 1956-1961; lecturer in anthopology, School of Public Health, University of Michigan, 1959-1961; assistant coordinator, American Indian Chicago Conference, University of Chicago, 1960-1961; associate professor of anthropology, University of Wisconsin, Milwaukee, 1963; Fulbright appointment (lectureship, University of Aarhus, Denmark) involved teaching a course on the American Indian and a course on applied anthropology, 1964-1965; professor, 1965-, department chairman, 1967-1970, adjunct professor, 1973-, Department of Anthropology, University of Wisconsin, Milwaukee; curator and head, Anthropology Section, Milwaukee Public Museum, 800 W. Wells St., Milwaukee, Wis. 53233. *Community activities:* Wisconsin Historic Sites Preservation Board, 1972-1979; Wisconsin Humanities Committee, NEH, 1981-1983. *Memberships:* American Anthropological Association (president, 1983-1985); American Ethnological Society; American Society for Ethnohistory; Wisconsin Archaeological Society; Central States Anthropological Society (president, 1967); Council for Museum Anthropology; American Association of Museums; Sigma Xi; Society for Aplied Anthropology; member of editorial board of Northeast Vol. 15 of *Handbook of North American Indians. Awards, honors:* Award of Merit for *Mountain Wolf Woman,* American Society for State and Local History, 1962; Saturday Review Anisfield Wolf Award with co-editor for *The American Indian Today, 1968;* Woman of the Year, Milwaukee Municipal Women's Club, 1975; Honorary Doctorate of Letters, Northland College, Ashland, Wis., 1976; Increase Lapham Medal, Wisconsin Archaeologicl Society, 1977; Merit Award, Northwestern University Alumni Association, 1982; several awards for publications, including *A Special Style,* from Wisconsin State Historical Society, 1985, and from Milwaukee County Historical Society, 1984; with Stuart Levine for *American Indian Today,* from *Saturday Review; Award of Merit, Wisconsin Academy of Sciences, Arts, & Letters, 1984. Interests:* "Major field research, Winnebago Indian communities in Wisconsin and Nebraska; Dogrib Indians, Northwest Territories, Canada; researcher and expert witness in six cases before the U.S. Indin Claims Commission; other Indian-related testimony in U.S. Court of Claims and district courts." *Biographical sources: Who's Who in America; Who's Who of American Women. Published works:* Editor, *Mountain Wolf Woman, Sister of Crashing Thunder* (University of Michigan Press, 1961); *The Substance Economy of the Dogrib Indians of Lac La Marte, Canadian Northwest Territories,* with June Helm (Northern Research and Coordination Centre, Ottawa, 1961); editor, with Stuary Levine, *The American Indian Today* (Everett/Edwards Press, 1968; Penguin, 1970); editor, with Eleanor B. Leacock, *The North American Indian in Historical Perspective* (Random House, 1971); *Wisconsin Indians* (State Historical Society of Wisconsin, 1980); *A Special Style: The Milwaukee Public Museum, 1882-1982* (Milwaukee Public Museum, 1982); *North Amerian Indian Lives* (Milwaukee Public Museum, 1985).

LYNN, SHARON
(B.I.A. Indian education)

Affiliation: Indian Education, Bureau of Indian Affairs, 1951 Constitution Ave., N.W., Washington, D.C. 20245.

Mc

McALLESTER, DAVID P.
(Narragansett) 1916-
(professor-retired)

Born August 6, 1916, Everett, Mass. *Education:* Harvard University, B.A., 1938; Columbia University, Ph.D., 1949. *Principal occupation: Professor-retired. Home address:* Star Route 62, Box 40, Monterey, Mass. 01245. *Affiliations:* Professor of anthropology and music, Wesleyan University, Middletown, Conn., 1947-1986 (retired). *Other professional posts:* Visiting professor, Yale University, University of Hawaii; University of Sydney and University of Queensland, Australia; consultant, American Folklife Festival, Smithsonian Institution, Washington, D.C., 1975-1976; one of the founders and secretary-treasurer, editor, and president of Society for Ethnomusicology. *Community activities:* Valley View Hospital (advisory board); a founder of Middletown Friends Meeting and South Berkshire Friends Meeting. *Memberships:* Society for Ethnomusicology (secretary-treasurer, editor, president, 1953-); American Anthropological Association (Fellow), 1949-1976; American Academy of Arts and Sciences, 1968-; Institute of American Indian Arcaheology, Washington, Conn. (trustee, 1976-). *Awards, honors:* Social Science Research Council Grant, 1950; Guggenheim Foundation Fellowship, 1957-1958 (study Navajo religion); National Science Foundation Grants, 1963-1965 (study Nanavjo religion); J.D.R. III Foundation Grant, 1971; National Endowment for the Humanities Grant, 1976; Fulbright Foundation (senior lecturer in Australia), 1978; Tokyo National Research Institute of Cultural Properties (lecture), 1980. *Interests:* "Studies of American Indian ceremonialism, music, folklore, mythology, religious literature. Field work with Navajos, Apaches, Zunis, Passamaquoddies, Penobscots, Comanches, Hopis. Canoeing, hiking, mountain-climbing, camping. Musical performance of Native American songs. *Biographical source:* Autobiographical sketch in a Festschrift due to be published in 1986, edited by Charlotte Frisbie, Department of Anthropology, Southern Illinois University, Edwardsville, Ill. *Published works: Peyote Music* (Viking Fund, 1949); *Enemy Way Music* (Peabody Museum, 1954); *Myth and Prayers of the Great Star Chant* (Wheelwright Museum, 1956); *Indian Music of the Southwest* (Taylor Museum, 1961); *Reader in Ethnomusicology* (Johnson Reprint, 1971); *Navajo Blessigway Singer,* with Charlotte Frisbie (University of Arizona, 1978); *Hogans: Navajo Houses and House Songs,* with Susan McAllester, (Wesleyan University, 1980); other monographs and pamphlets; about sixty articles and other contributions. *Recordings: Music of the American Indian,* 12" LP with pamphlet (Litton Educational Publishing, 1978; *Music of the Pueblos, Apache, and Navajo,* with Don N. Brown, 12" LP with 7-page pamphlet, texts, photographs (Taylor Museum, 1962); *Navajo Creation Chants,* five 10" 78 rpm records, with pamphlet (Peabody Museum, 1952.

McBRIDE, MARY (San Felipe Pueblo) 1948-
(elementary school principal)

Born June 3, 1948, Albuquerque, N.M. *Education:* Eastern New Mexico University, Portales, B.S., 1971; New Mexico Highlands University, Las Vegas, M.A., 1982. *Principal occupation:* Elementary school principal, B.I.A., Isleta Pueblo, N.M., 1984-. *Home address:* P.O. Box 751, Algodones, N.M. 87001. *Other professional post:* Elementary teacher, Isleta Pueblo. *Community activities:* Bernalillo Public School (parent advisory committee); Five Pueblo Indian Education Section; Save the Children Federation Committee; Parent-Teacher Organization, public and B.I.A. schools. *Awards, honors:* Graduate Professional Opportunity Program. *Interests:* "(My) vocational interest is to return to the university to work on a degree in gifted education and to hopefully have my own school addressing the needs and serving the Indian gifted children."

McCABE, EDWARD, Jr.
(B.I.A. agency superintendent)

Affiliation: Superintendent, Shiprock Agency, Bureau of Indian Affairs, Shiprock, N.M. 87420.

McCARTHY, JOAN DOLORES
(Blackfoot) 1935-
(reservation trader-wholesale/retail)

Born January 14, 1935, Easton, Pa. *Education:* Churchman's Business College, Easton, Pa. (one year). *Principal occupation:* Reservation trader. *Home address:* 1500 Eddy St., Merritt Island, Fla. 32952. *Affiliation:* Owner-two shops: Cocoa Village, Fla.—authentic Native American jewelry and crafts; and Merritt Square Mall—unique gifts and art deco/nouveau access. "I'm known as "Sun Dancer" woman who keeps spirits together and bright, and "Bear Clan" bringer of light (lightening the soul or spiritual healing). (I) started business on my own as a single parent with three children to raise—no outside help or child support." *Community activities:* "Counsel Native Americans on their rights, on or off the reservation, the business or schooling open to them, water rights, etc.; give speeches to youth groups, all sorts of organizations; display in libraries, schools, and banks. *Awards, honors:* Art awards in silversmithing, pen and ink, watercolors, copper and enamel work, and sketching. *Interests:* "My desire is to give back the pride to the Native American encouraging them to protect their culture. It may save the world for all! I travel to all the Southwestern reservations; encourage artists in their work, get publicity for them, set up shows, etc. to show their work or talents. Sell to rock stars and movie stars—promote the beauty of their craftmanship—to people that can help the cause. I worked to keep the water on the Apache Reservation at Fort McDowell several years ago. I'm currently involved in trying to help in the Hopi/Navajo problem and the Taos water supply. Also trying to reinstate the rights of Native Americans to sell in Old Town Albuquerque—they're being displaced by greedy whites." *Biographical source:* The Department of Interior *Source Book.*

McCLELLAND, JOHN
(chairman-Indian organization)

Affiliation: Chairman, Native American Coalition of Tulsa, Inc., 1740 West 41st St., Tulsa, Okla. 74107.

McCLOSKEY, RICHARD J.
(Indian health service)

Affiliation: Director, Office of Legislation and Regulations, Indian Health Service, 5600 Fishers Lane, Rockville, Md. 20857.

McCOMBS, SOLOMON (Creek) 1913-
(artist, former vice chief-
Creek Nation of Oklahoma)

Born May 17, 1913, Eufaula, Okla. *Education:* Bacone College, 1931-1937; Tulsa University (downtown college), 1943. *Principal occupation:* Artist, former vice-chief, Creek Nation of Oklahoma. *Home address:* 3238 East 3rd St., Tulsa, Okla. 74104. *Affiliation:* Foreign service reserve officer, U.S. Department of State, Washington, D.C., 1966-1973. *Other professional posts:* Board of directors, American Indian National Bank, Washington, D.C., 1973-1975; lifetime member of board of directors, designed bank logo. "Served as a member of th Subcommittee on Indian participation during President Johnson's and President Nixon's Inaugural parades--supervised the construction of four American Indian floats." *Memberships:* National Congress of American Indians, 1965-; Five Civilized Tribes (council member, Inter-Tribal Council; chaplain, 1976-); National Council of the Creek Nation (speaker, 1976-); CWYW Club of Tulsa (lifetime member, 1977-). *Awards, honors:* Five Civilized Tribes Museum Seal, 1955; Waite Phillips Special Indian Artists Award for contributions in Indian Art over a period of five years, Philbrook Art Center, Tulsa, Okla., 1965; Grand Award, Philbrook Art Center, 1965; Grand and Gran Masters Award, 1965, 1970, 1973, 1977; Army Award (commissioned to paint depicting one of the American Indian Congressional Medal of Honor recipients of World War II in battle), Washington, D.C., 1976; First Prize Awards, All American Indian Days, Sheridan, Wyo., and Pawnee Bill Museum, Pawnee, Okla., 1970; Bacone College Distinguished Service Award, 1972; Heritage Award, Five Civilized Tribes Museum, Muskogee, Okla., 1977; Grand Prize of $1,000 at Central Washington State College; among others. *Interests:* Graphics, architectural design; lecturing on American

Indian art; Indian painting (traditional); tours of paintings; exhibits and lectures throughout the Middle East, Africa, India, and Burma, sponsored by the U.S. Department of State, Washington, D.C. *Biographical sources: Indians of Today, 1960-1970; Who's Who in the South and Southwest; Register of U.S. Living Artists, 1968; Personalities of the South; Dictionary of International Biography; Notable Americans, 1976-1977. Published works: McCombs Indian Art Calendar, 1978; White Eagle-Green Corn, 1979.*

McCONE, ROBERT CLYDE 1915-
(professor of anthropology)

Born September 30, 1915, Redfield, S.D. *Education:* Wessington Springs College, S.D., B.A., 1946; South Dakota State University, Brookings, M.S., 1956; Michigan State University, Ph.D., 1961. *Principal occupation:* Professor of anthropology. *Home address:* 1901 Snowden Ave., Long Beach, Calif. 90805. *Affiliations:* Professor of anthropology, California State University, Long Beach, Calif., 1961-1986; ordained elder, Dakota District of the Wesleyan Church, Rapid City, S.D., 1952-. *Memberships:* American Anthropological Association (Fellow); Royal Anthropological Institute of Great Britain & Ireland (Fellow); American Scientific Affiliation (Fellow); Phi Kappa Phi. *Interests:* Cultural sources of belief conflict in Christianity; cultural problems of contact of American Indian culture with Christianity. *Biographical sources: International Scholar's Directory; Contemporary Authors. Published works:* "Time and the Dakota's Way of Life," Agricultural Experiment Station, South Dakota State College, 1956; "The Time Concept Perspective and Premise in the Socio-cultural Order of the Dakota Indians," (*Plains Anthropologist,* 1960); "Cultural Factors in Crime Among the Dakota Indian," (*Plains Anthropologist,* 1966); "Death and the Persistance of Basic Personality Structure Among the Lakota," (*Plains Anthropologist,* 1968); *Man and His World* (Creation Science Research Center, 1971); *Culture and Controversy: An Investigation of the Tongues of Pentecost* (Dorrance, 1978).

McCORD, DAVID
(executive director-Indian organization)

Affiliation: Executive director, Confederation of American Indians, P.O. Box 5474, New York, N.Y. 10163.

McDERMOTT, RICHARD S.
(B.I.A. area director)

Affiliation: Director, Palm Springs Area Field Office, Bureau of Indian Affairs, Box 2245, 441 S. Calle Encilia, Palm Springs, Calif. 92262.

McDONALD, ARTHUR LEROY
(Sioux) 1934-
(research consultant)

Born December 26, 1934, Martin, S.D. *Education:* University of South Dakota, A.B., 1962, M.A., 1963, Ph.D., 1966. *Principal occupation:* Research consultant. *Home address:* Box 326, Lame Deer, Mt., 59043. *Affiliation:* Owner, Cheyenne Consulting Service. *Other professional posts:* Acting head, Psychology Department, Central College, 1963-1964; head, Psychology Department, Montana State University, 1968-1971. *Military service:* U.S. Marine Corps, 1953-1956 (Sergeant). *Memberships:* Pine Ridge Sioux Tribe; Sigma Xi; American Association for the Advancement of Science; American Quarter Horse Association. *Interests:* "Indian research in mental health, education, alcohol, and evaluation; raising quality American quarter horses. *Published works: Psychology and Contemporary Problems* (Brooks-Cole, 1974) numerous articles in scientific journals.

McDONALD, JOSEPH
(college president)

Affiliation: President, Salish-Kootenai Community College, P.O. Box 278, Pablo, Mt. 59855.

McDONALD, MIKI 1946-
(museum director)

Born December 10, 1946, Orange, Calif. *Education:* University of Washington, B.A.,

1974, M.A., 1976. *Principal occupation:* Museum director. *Home address:* 343 SW Alfred St., Chehalis, Wash. 98532. *Affiliation:* Director, Lewis County Historical Museum, Chehalis, Wash., 1976-. *Membership:* American Association for State and Local History. *Interests:* "My major fields of interest have been with the cultures of the Native American people of the Northwest region. I have a strong background in genealogical research for Native Americans, physical anthropology of the region, and Native American education."

McDONALD, WALTER (Salish-Nez Perce) 1910-
(rancher)

Born February 16, 1910, St. Ignatius (Flathead Indian Reservation), Mt. *Education:* Haskell Institute. *Principal occupation:* Rancher. *Home address:* St. Ignatius, Mt. *Affiliation:* Liaison officer, State of Montana, working with Indian youth and their parole/probation officers. *Other professional post:* Montana Council on Corrections. *Community activities:* Lake County Rural Development Council; Western Montana Cattle Marketing Association. *Memberships:* Confederated Salish-Kootenai Tribal Council, 1941-1965 (chairman, 14 years). *Awards, honors:* Bronze Buffalo Plaque presented by the Confederated Salish-Kootenai Tribal Council. *Interests:* Congressional lobbying to further tribal interests.

McELVAIN, W. LEE 1939-
(attorney)

Born January 6, 1939, Grand Junction, Colo. *Education:* University of Colorado, B.A., 1961; George Washington University Law School, LL.B., 1964. *Principal occupation:* Attorney. *Home address:* 2123 Natahoa Ct., Falls Church, Va. 22043. *Affiliation:* General Counsel, Committee on Interior & Insular Affairs, U.S. House of Representatives, Washington, D.C., 1967-. *Memberships:* Congressional Staff Club; Federal Bar Association; Virginia Bar Association; National Trust for Historic Preservation; American Forestry Association; U.S. Supreme Court.

McGEE, HAROLD FRANKLIN, Jr. 1945-
(professor of anthropology)

Born June 5, 1945, Miami, Fla. *Education:* Florida State University, B.A., 1966, M.A., 1967; Southern Illinois University, Ph.D., 1974. *Principal occupation:* Professor of anthropology. *Home address:* 3608 Leaman St., Halifax, Nova Scotia, Can. B3K 3Z9. *Affiliations:* Associate professor, Department of Anthropology, Saint Mary's University, Halifax, Nova Scotia, Can. *Other professional post:* Consultant to museums and other institutions. *Memberships:* Canadian Ethnology Society; Royal Anthropological Institute of Great Britain and Ireland (Fellow). *Interests:* Mr. McGee writes, "(My) major area of interest and expertise is with contemporary and historic Micmac and Malecite peoples of Atlantic Canada. In addition to standard ethnological concerns as an academic, I am interested in getting the non-native population to understand the reasons for similarity and difference of the native peoples' life ways to their own so that they will encourage governments to allow for greater local autonomy by the native people. Academically, I am particularly interested in native "world view," politics, aesthetics, and reconstruction of aboriginal society and culture," *Published works:* Native Peoples of Atlantic Canada (McClelland and Stewart, 1974); The Micmac IndiansL The First Migrants in Banked Fires-The Ethnics of Nova Scotia, edited by D. Campbell (Scribbler's Prss, 1978); journal articles and papers.

McGEE, PATRICIA (Yavapai Apache)
(tribal chairwoman)

Affiliation: Chairwoman, Yavapai-Prescott Board of Directors, P.O. Box 348, Prescott, Ariz. 86301.

McGILBARY, RAY (Creek) 1927-
(educational administrator)

Born January 10, 1927, Haskell, Okla. *Education:* University of Oklahoma, B.S., 1953, M.A., 1957. *Principal occupation:* Educational administrator. *Affiliations:* Principal/teacher, Standing Rock Community School, Crownpoint, N.M.; principal, Thoreau Boarding School, Thoreau, N.M.; principal, Many Farms Jr. High School, Many Frams, Ariz. *Military service:* U.S. Army, 1945-1949 (Sergeant). *Community activities:* Booster Club of Chinle; Chinle Navajo Committee. *Memberships:* Association of School Administrators; Common Cause. *Awards, honors:* Distinguished Service Award, Bacone Junior College, Bacone, Okla.

McGRATH, JAMES A. 1928-
(specialist in intercultural education)

Born September 2, 1928, Tacoma, Wash. *Education:* Central Washington State College, 1946-1948; University of Oregon, B.S., 1950; University of Montana, 1951; University of Washington, 1952; University of New Mexico, M.A., 1952. *Principal occupation:* Specialist in intercultural education. *Home address:* 948 Acequia Madre, Santa Fe, N.M. 87501. *Affiliations:* Teacher-director of arts and crafts, U.S. Dependents Education Group Schools, Europe-Germany, France, Italy, Eritrea, 1955-1962; teacher, assistant art director, director of arts, director of special services, Institute of American Indian Arts, Santa Fe, N.M. 1962-. *Other professional posts:* Exhibiting artist and sculptor, 1948-; specialist in American Indian culture, U.S. State Department, 1966-1968; director of first White House Indian Dance Program, 1965. *Community activities:* Community Arts Council (president); New Mexico Arts Commission (consultant). *Memberships:* International Society for Edcuation Through Art. *Awards, honors:* J.K. Gill Arts Media Fellowship, University of Oregon; First Prize in Sculpture, Bellevue, Wash. Fair; First Prize in Painting, Museum of New Mexico; Honorable Mention in Sculpture and Drawing, Museum of New Mexico. *Interests:* Mr. McGrath writes, "Chief interest is art and nature—the use of art as an intercultural education tool; Indian art in the Western Hemisphere; cross-cultural education through the arts; all phases of art education, especially those relating to Native American (Indian) arts and crafts;" travel. *Published works: Quilaut: The Art of Getting in Touch With the Spirits* (Center for the Arts of Indian America, 1967); *Powhoge: The Mar-*

tinez Family of San Ildefonso (Center for the Arts of Indian America, 1968); Art and Indian Children (Bureau of Indian Affairs, 1970); *My Music Reaches to the Sky: Native American Musical Instruments* (Vergara, 1972); *Sound, The Flute Voice: Dance With Indian Children* (Vergara, 1972).

McGREEVY, SUSAN BROWN 1934-
(museum director)

Born January 28, 1934, Chicago, Ill. *Education:* Mt. Holyoke College (two years); Roosevelt University, B.A., 1969; Northwestern University, M.A., 1971. *Principal occupation:* Director, The Wheelwright Museum, Santa Fe, N.M., 1977-. *Home address:* 704 Camino Lejo Box 5153, Santa Fe, N.M. 87502. *Other professional posts:* Curator of North American Ethnology, Kansas City Museum, Mo., 1975-1977. *Memberships:* American Anthropological Association; Society for American Archaeology; American Society for Ethnohistory; Society for Applied Anthropology; American Ethnological Society; Council for Museum Anthropology; American Association of Museums. *Interests:* North American ethnology, specifically southern and central Plains and the Southwest; field work with the Navajos. *Published work:* "The Dyer Collection," (*American Indian Art Magazine*, 1978); *Lullabies From the Earth: Cradles of Native North America,* 1980; contributing articles to professional publications.

McKIBBEN, JESSE (Quapaw)
(tribal chairman)

Affiliation: Chairman, Quapaw Tribal Business Committee, P.O. Box 765, Quapaw, Okla. 74363.

McKINNEY, WHITNEY (Shoshone-Paiute)
(tribal chairman)

Affiliation: Chairman, Shoshone-Paiute Business Council, P.O. Box 219, Owyhee, Nev. 89832.

McLEAN, ROBERT ELDON 1930-
(teacher)

Born August 5, 1930, Salt Lake City, Utah. *Education:* University of Utah, B.S., 1960, M.S., 1961. *Principal occupation:* Teacher. *Home address:* 1105 First Ave., Salt Lake City, Utah 84103. *Affiliation: Teacher, physical education specialist, Salt Lake City Board of Education, 1961-. Military service:* U.S. Navy, 1947-1951. *Memberships:* Utah State Archaeological Society, 1964-1965; Inter-Tribal Indian Ceremonial Group, Utah, 1961. *Awards, honors:* Indian Service Award, Inter-Tribal Pow-Wow, Salt Lake City, Utah; Sweepstake Awards for Indian outfits, Utah State Fair; others. *Interests:* Indian culture—dancing, lore, crafts and history; lectured for sociology/anthropology departments of universities throughout the country. *Published works: American Indian Dances,* with John Squires (Ronald Press); *Recreational Program of the Hopi Indians,* thesis (University of Utah).

M

MacDONALD, GEORGE F. 1938-
(archaeologist)

Born July 4, 1938, Galt, Ontario, Can. *Education:* University of Toronto, B.A., 1961; Yale University, Ph.D., 1966. *Principal occupation:* Archaeologist. *Home address:* RR #1, Cantley, Quebec, Can. J0X 1L0. *Affiliations:* Atlantic Provinces Archaeologist, 1964-1966, head-Western Canada Section, 1966-1969, National Museums of Canada; chief, Archaeology Division, 1969-1971; chief, Archaeological Survey of Canada, 1971-1977, senior archaeologist, Office of the Director, 1977-, National Museum of Man. *Other professional post:* Conjunct professor, Department of Anthropology, Trent University, 1974-. *Memberships:* Canadian Archaeological Association (president, 1969-1970); American Association for the Advancement of Science (Fellow); American Anthrological Association (Fellow); Archaeological Institute of America, Ottawa Chapter (vice president, 1976-1977); Society for American Archaeology (first positions, executive committee, 1977-1978); International Quarternary Association

(head, working group for Eastern North America-Commission for the Paleo-Ecology of Early Man, 1976-1977); Council for Canadian Archaeology; International Union of Prehistoric and Protohistoric Sciences. *Awards, honors:* Numerous awards and research grants. *Interests:* Native peoples of North and South America; prehistory, field research, Atlantic and Pacific Coast of Canada, Ontario and Yukon Territories; traditional Native American arts and crafts; Northwest Coast Indian print-making, scultpure, Ojibwa print-making; "assembled and wrote catalogues for numerous exhibitions of contemporary and traditional Native American art that traveled in Europe, North America, Asia, New Zealand;" study travel. *Published works:* Numerous articles, papers, reports, and reviews, 1965-; directed the prodcution of 45 short study 16mm, color films on West Coast art and technology; production of gallery films and study video tapes and public release films such as *To Know the Hurons,* 1977.

MacDONALD, PETER, Sr. (Navajo) 1928-
(former chairman, Navajo Tribal Council)

Born December 16, 1928, Teec Nos Pos, Ariz. *Education:* Bacone Junior College, A.A., 1951; University of Oklahoma, B.S. (Electrical Engineering), 1957; U.C.L.A., graduate studies, 1958-1962. *Home address:* 9 Chee Dodge Dr., Drawer 685, Window Rock, Ariz. 86515. *Affiliations:* Project engineer, member of technical staff, Hughes Aircrafts Co., El Segundo, Calif., 1957-1963; director, Management, Methods & Procedures, 1963-1965; Office of Navajo Economic Opportunity, 1965-1970, The Navajo Tribe, Window Rock, Ariz.; chairman, Navajo Tribal Council, 1970-? *Military service:* U.S. Marine Corps, 1944-1946 (Corporal; member, "Navajo Code Talkers" in the South Pacific). *Community activities:* New Mexico Governor's Economic Development Advisory Group, 1963-1967; New Mexico State Planning Commission, 1963-1967; Navajo Community College, Tsaile, Ariz. (board of regents, 1971-); Antioch School of Law, Washington, D.C. (board of visitors, 1972-); Patagonia Corporation, Tucson, Ariz. (board of directors, 1972-); Navajo Agricultural Products Industry, Farmington, N.M. (board of directors, 1972-); New Mexico Governor's Energy Task Force, Santa Fe, N.M., 1972-; New Mexico Commission, Regional Housing Authority, Santa Fe, N.M., 1973-; Non-Profit Housing/Community Development Corp., Shiprock, N.M., 1972; Arizona State Justice Planning Agency Governing Board, 1975-; Arizona Advisory Committee of U.S. Commission on Civil Rights, Washington, D.C., 1970-1974. *Memberships:* University of Oklahoa Alumni Association; National Association of Community Development (board of directors, 1968-1970; National Tribal Chairman's Association; American Indian National Bank, Washington, D.C. (board of directors, 1974-). *Awards, honors:* Appointed by President Nixon to the National Center for Voluntary Action, 1970-1974; Presidential Commendation for exceptional services to others, 1970; Citation, Distinguished American, National Institute for Economic Development, 1970; Citation, Distinguished Baconian, Bacone Junior College, Okla., 1971; Arizona Indian of the Year, 1971; Good Citizenship Medal, National Society of Sons of the American Revolution, 1972; Silver Beaver Award, Boy Scouts Of America, Kit Carson Council, 19731 member (appointed by Secretary of Commerce), National Public Advisory Committee on Regional Economic Development, U.S. Department of Comerce, Washington, D.C., 1973-1977; Citation, One of the 200 Rising American Leaders by *Time* Magazine, 1974; inducted into Engineering Hall of Fame, University of Oklahoma, 1975. *Biographical sources: Who's Who in America; Who's Who in the West;* Mr. MacDonald has been written about in magazines and newspapers, such as: *Newsweek; Time; U.S. News & World Report; Signature; People; Washington Post; New York Times; Chicago Times; Los Angeles Times,* etc.

MacLACHLAN, BRUCE B. 1935-
(anthropologist, educator)

Born May 26, 1935, Cambridge, Mass. *Education:* University of Chicago, A.B., 1954, M.A., 1955, Ph.D., 1962. *Principal occupa-*

tion: Anthropologist and educator. *Home address:* 12 Hillcrest, Carbondale, Ill. 62901. *Affiliations:* Associate professor of anthropology, Southern Illinois University, Carbondale, 1964-. *Military service:* U.S. Army Reserve, 1958-? (Major; Army Commendation Medal; Army Reserve Components Achievement Medal). *Memberships:* Royal Anthropological Institute (Fellow); American Anthropological Association (Fellow); American Association for the Advancement of Science (Fellow); American Ethnological Society; Law and Society Association; Reserve Officers Association; Civil Affairs Association. *Interests:* Mr. MacLachlan writes, "Have worked with Indian comunities: Tahltan Indians, British Columbia; Klallam, Washington; Mescalero Apache, New Mexico; Shoshoni and Arapaho, Wind River, Wyo.; with special interest in tribal moral values and tribal law."

MacNABB, ALEXANDER S. (Micmac)
1929-
(government official)

Born August 24, 1929, Bay Shore, N.Y. *Education:* Colgate University, A.B., 1956; Washington and Lee University Law School, J.D., 1959; New York University Law School, postgraduate, 1960-1961. *Principal occupation:* Government official. *Home address:* 10600 Sunlit Rd., P.O. Box 86, Oakton, Va. 22124. *Affiliations:* President, Alexander MacNabb Associates, Bay Shore, N.Y., 1960-1967; president, Town Almanac Publishing Co., Bay Shore, N.Y., 1960-1967; member, President's Comittee on Manpower, U.S. Office of Economic Opportunity, 1966-1967, special assistant to director, Community Action Program, 1967-1969; OEO representative to Presidentially established National Program for Voluntary Action, Washington, D.C., 1969-1970; director, Office of Operating Services, U.S. Department of the Interior, B.I.A., Washington, D.C., 1970-1972, director, Office of Engineering, 1972-1973; director, Office of Indian and Territorial Development, U.S. Dept. of the Interior, 1973-1974; deputy director, Office of Feeral Contract Compliance, Empoyment Standards Administration, Dept. of Labor, 1974-1975; director, Indian and Native American Programs, Employment and Training Adminis-

172

tration, Washington, D.C., 1975-. *Military
service:* U.S. Naval Reserve, 1952-1954.
Memberships: American Political Science
Association; American Academy of Political and Social Sciences; National Congress
of American Indian (Micmac Tribe);
National Indian Youth Council.

MADSEN, BRIGHAM D. 1914-
(professor emeritus of history)

Born October 21, 1914, Magna, Utah. *Education:* Idaho State University, Certificate,
1934; University of Utah, B.A., 1938; University of California, Berkeley, M.A., 1940,
Ph.D., 1948. *Principal occupation:* Professor emeritus of history. *Home address:* 2181
Lincoln Lane, Salt Lake City, Utah 84124.
*Affiliation: University of Utah, Salt Lake
City, 1965-. Other professional posts:* Dean
of Continuing Education, 1965-1966; deputy academic vice president, 1966-1967;
administrative V.P., 1967-1971; director of
libraries, 1971-1973; chairman of History
Department, 1974-1975; professor of history, University of Utah. *Military service:*
U.S. Army Infantry, 1943-1946. *Community activities:* Peace Corps, Washington,
D.C. (assistant director of training, 1964);
Vista Program, Office of Economic Opportunity, Washington, D.C. (first director of
training, 1965. *Memberships:* Western His-
tory Association; Utah State Historical
Society (Fellow); Montana State Historical
Society; Western Writers of America; Idaho
State Historical Society; Utah Westerners
(board member). *Awards, honors:* Distin-
guished Teaching Award, 1977, University
of Utah; Utah Academy, Charles Reed
Award, 1983; Westerners Interantional Best
Non-Fiction Book for 1980, and 2nd Place -
Western Writers of America, Spur Awards,
North to Montana. Interests: Northern
Rocky Mountain region—Utah, Nevada,
Wyoming, Idaho and Montana. Major
interest in Shsohone-Bannock Tribes of
Fort Hall, Idaho, having served as
consultant-historical rsearcher for tribes in
two claims cases against the U.S. Government. Operated building company for ten
years and still hold a Utah contractors
license. *Biographical source:* Who's Who of
America. Published works: The Bannock of
Idaho, 1958; *The Lemhi: Sacajawea's People, 1979; The Northern Shoshoni, 1980; co-

author, *North to Montana,* 1980; *Gold Rush
Sojourners in Salt Lake City, 1849-1850,*
1983; *The Shoshoni Frontier and the Bear
River Massacre,* 1985; *Chief Pocatello: The
White Plume,* 1986.

MAHAN, HAROLD D. (½ Cherokee) 1931-
(biologist, museum administrator)

Born June 11, 1931, Ferndale, Mich. *Education:* Wayne State University, B.A., 1954;
University of Michigan, M.S., 1957; Michigan State University, Ph.D., 1964. *Principal
occupation:* Biologist, museum administra-
tor. *Home address:* 28050 Gates Mill Blvd.,
Pepper Pike, Ohio 44124. *Affiliations:* Pro-
fessor, Central Michigan University, Mt.
Pleasant, Mich., 1957-1972; director, Cen-
tral Michigan University Museum, 1969-
1972; director, Cleveland Museum of
Natural History, 1973-. *Military service:*
U.S. Air Force (Special Services, 1950-
1953). *Community activities:* Michigan
Audubon Society (president); Mid-West
Museums Conference (ex-vice president);
Ohio Museums Association (president).
Memberships: Phi Kappa Phi, 1968-; Sigma
Xi, 1968-; Animal Behavior Society; Associ-
ation of Science Museums Directors (presi-
dent, 1980-); Association of Systematic
Collection (vice president, 1980-). *Awards,
honors:* Recipient, Louis Agassiz Research
Fuertes Award, 1957, Wilson Ornithologi-
cal Society. *Interests:* Ornithology; wildlife
photography; bird distribution research;
travel. *Biographical sources: Who's Who in
America; Who's Who in the Midwest; Who's
Who in Ecology. Published works:* An
Introduction to Ornithology, co-author
(Macmillan, 1975); *The Jack Pine Warbler*
(Michigan Audubon Society, 1967-1972).

MAIN, ELMER
(B.I.A. agency superintendent)

Affiliation: Superintendent, Fort Belknap
Agency, Bureau of Indian Affairs, P.O. Box
80, Harlem, Mt. 59526.

MALLOTT, BYRON (Tlingit) 1943-
(chief executive officer)

Born April 6, 1943, Yakutat, Alaska. *Education:* Western Washington State College, Bellingham, (completed major in political science-no degree), 1961-1964. *Principal occupation:* Chief executive officer, Sealaska Corporation, Juneau, Alaska. *Home address:* P.O. Box 322, Yakutat, Alaska 99689. *Affiliations:* Mayor, City of Yakutat, 1965; elected to City Council, City of Yakutat, 1968; local government specialist, Office of the Governor, Juneau, 1966-1967; special assistant to U.S. Senator Mike Gravel, Washington, D.C., 1969; executive director, Rural Alaska Community Action Program, Inc., Anchorage, 1970; director, Local Affairs Agency, Office of the Governor, 1971-1972; commissioner, Department of Community and Regional Affairs, State of Alaska, 1972-1974; consultant, Alaska Natives Resources, Inc., 1974-1978; president, Alaska Federation of Natives, Inc., 1977-1978; chairman of the board, Sealaska Corporation, Juneau, 1976-1984; chief executive officer, Sealaska Corporation, Juneau, 1982-. *Other professional post:* Owner Yakutat Bay Adventures (commercial fishing), 1974-; director, Alaska Airlines, 1982-; chairman of the board of trustees, Permanent Fund Corp., Seattle, Wash., 1982; board member, Alaska United Drilling, Inc., 1982- director, Federal Reserve Bank, Seattle Branch, 1982-; board member, United Bank of Alaska, 1984-; board member, Colville Tribal Enterprise Corp., 1985-; board member, The Mediation Institute, 1985-. *Community activities:* Rural Affairs Commission, State of Alaska, 1972-1976; Alaska Native Foundation (vice chairman, 1975-1979); Yak-Tat Kwaan, Inc. (Yakutat Village Corp.) (board of directors, 1974-1978; chairman, 1976-1977); B.M. Behrends Bank (director, 1975-1984); Capital Site Planning Commission, State of Alaska, 1977-1979; Governor's Rapportionment Board, State of Alaska (chairman, 1979-1980); White House Fellowship Selection Commission-Western Region, 1978-1983; Commercial Fisheries & Agricultural Bank, State of Alaska (director, 1979); University of Alaska Foundation (director, 1980-1985). *Awards, honors:* Governor's Award for Service to Alaska, 1982; recipient of the "Alaska Native Citizen of the Year Award" from the Alaska Federation of Natives, 1982; Honorary Doctorate Degree in the Humanities by the University of Alaska, 1984. *Published works:* Several recent articles are "One Day in the Life of a Native Chief Executive," in two parts, *Alaska Native Magazine,* Sept. and Oct., 1985; "Byron's Brew," *Alaska Business Monthly,* Oct., 1985; "Sealaska: Soon to Rival Oil Companies in Power?" an interview with Byron Mallott, *Alaska Industry,* Sept., 1981.

MANKILLER, WILMA P. (Oklahoma Cherokee)
(tribal chief)

Affiliation: Principal Chief, Cherokee Nation of Oklahoma, P.O. Box 948, Tahlequah, Okla. 74465.

MANN, ROBERT C.
(B.I.A. agency superintendent)

Affiliation: Superintendent, Choctaw Agency, Bureau of Indian Affairs, 421 Powell, Philadelphia, Miss. 39350.

MANNERS, ROBERT A. 1913-
(professor emeritus)

Born August 21, 1913, Ne York, N.Y. *Education:* Columbia University, B.S., 1935, M.A., 1939, Ph.D., 1950. *Principal occupation:* Ralph Levits professor emeritus. *Home address:* 134 Sumner St., Newton Centre, Mass. 02159. *Affiliation:* Professor of anthropology, Brandeis University, Waltham, Mass., 1952-1979; Ralph Levitz Professor Emeritus, Brandeis University, 1980-. *Other professional post:* Editor-in-chief, *American Anthropologist,* 1974-1976; president, Northeastern Anthropological Association, 1978. *Military service:* AUS, 1942-1946 (Captain). *Memberships:* American Anthropological Association (Fellow), 1946-; American Ethnological Society; Northeast Anthropological Association. *Awards, honors:* Fellowships and grants. *Interests:* Field work in Caribbean area; ethnohistorical research, North American Indians, 1952-1953; anthropological field work in Kenya, 1957-1959, 1961-1962. *Biographi-*

cal source: Who's Who in America. Published works: Culture Theory (Prentice-Hall, 1972); *Ethnohistory of Southern Paiute* (Garland, 1974); *Ethnohistory of Walapai* (Garland, 1974); *Ethnohistory of Havasupai* (Garland, 1974); *Southern Paiute and Chemehuevi, An Ethnohistorical Report* (Garland, 1974); *An Ethnological Report on the Hualapai Indians of Arizona* (Garland, 1975); numerous articles in professional journals.

MANSON, SPERO M. (Pembina Chippewa) 1950-
(mental health researcher)

Born May 2, 1950, Everett, Wash. *Education:* University of Washington, B.A., 1972; University of Minnesota, M.A., 1975, Ph.D. (Anthropology), 1978. *Principal occupation:* Mental health researcher. *Affiliations:* Director, National Center for American Indian and Alaska Native Mental Health Research, Denver, Colo., 1986-; professor, Department of Psychiatry, Univerity of Colorado Health Sciences Center, Denver, Colo., 1986-. *Other professional posts:* Professor and director, Institute on Aging, School of Urban and Public Affairs, Portland State University, Ore., 1982-1986; associate professor and director, Social Psychiatric Research, Department of Psychiatry, School of Medicine, Oregon Health Sciences University, Portland, 1982-1986; adjunct associate professor of anthropology, Portland State University, 1982-1986. *Consultantships:* Billings Area Office, Indian Health Service, Mt., 1984-; Northwest Portland Area Indian Health Board, 1985-; Alaska Native Health Board, 1985-. *Community activities:* National Institute of Mental Health Epidemiology and Services Research Review Committee, 1983-1987; NIDA Advisory Committee on Prevention, 1983-1985; Oregon State Governor's Task Force on Alcohol and Drug Abuse, 1984-1986. *Memberships:* American Anthropological Association; Gerontological Society of America; Society for Applied Anthropology. *Awards, honors:* 1984 Oregon State System of Higher Education, Faculty Excellence Award; Fulbright-Hays Scholar; CIC Traveling Scholar; National Science Foundation Scholarship. *Interests:* Professional: psychiatric epidemiology; diagnostic instru-

ment construction; preventive intervention research. Avocational: Photography, writing, upland game bird hunting; travel. *Published works:* Co-editor, books in preparation: *American Indian Youth: Seventy-five Years of Psychosocial Research* (Greenwood Press); *Health and Behavior: A Research Agenda for American Indians* (Oregon Health Sciences University); editor, *Medical Anthropology: Implications for Stress Prevention Across Cultures* (National Institute of Mental Health, Government Printing Office). Numerous articles in professional journals.

MARACLE, BRIAN (Cayuga-Mohawk) 1947-
(editor, reporter, writer)

Born March 18, 1947, Six Nations, Ontario, Can. *Education:* Dartmouth College, B.A., 1969. *Principal occupation:* Editor, reporter, writer. *Home address:* 86-1947 Pendrell, Vancouver, British Columbia, Can. *Affiliation:* Editor, *Nesika* newspaper, Vancouver, B.C., 1975-. *Community activities:* British Columbia Native People's Credit Union (charter member, 1972; president, 1974-).

MARCHAND, THELMA (Colville) 1932-
(tribal officer)

Born April 17, 1932, Okanogan County, Wash. *Education:* Wenatchee Junior College. *Principal occupation:* Secretary, Colville Business (Tribal) Council. *Home address:* 320 Columbia St., Omak, Wash. 98841.

MARKEN, JACK W. 1922-
(professor, writer)

Born February 11, 1922, Akron, Ohio. *Education:* University of Akron, B.A., 1947; Indian University, M.A., 1950, Ph.D., 1953. *Principal occupation:* Professor of English, South Dakota State University, Brookings, S.D., 1967-. *Military service:* U.S. Army Air Force, 1946. *Community activities:* South Dakota Committee on the Humanities (chairman). *Memberships:* Midwest Modern Language Association (chairman, seminar on the American Indian); National

Indian Education Association; American Association of University Professors. *Awards, honors:* Fulbright lecturer, University of Jordan, 1965-1966; lecturer on the American Indian, U.S.I.S. and Finnish-American Society, Sept., 1970. *Interests:* "Literature of the American Indian (paper on it a CCCC in Ne Orleans, April, 1973; lectured on it at Miami University, Ohio, May, 1973). Interested in Indian stories and photographs; also in English literature, especially William Godwin. Director of two major programs on the American Indian in the summers of 1969 and 1970 funded by the National Endowment for the Humanities." *Biographical sources: Who's Who in American Education; Directory of American Scholars; Personalities of the West and Midwest; Dictionary of International Biography. Published work: Bibliography of Books By and About the American Indian in Print, 1972* (Dakota Press, 19730.

MARKS, PATRICIA ANN 1954-
(lobbyist, consultant)

Born March 2, 1954, Brockport, N.Y. *Education:* S.U.N.Y. at Brockport, B.S. (Political Science), 1976; Georgetown University Law Center (J.D. expected May, 1987). *Principal occupation:* Lobbyist, consultant. *Home address:* 4226 34th St., Mt. Ranier, Md. 20712. *Affiliations:* Personal staff member, U.S. Senator James Abourezk, Washington, D.C., 1975-1976 (during this period, Sen. Abourezk was chairman of the Senate Indian Affairs Subcommittee of the Senate Interior and Insular Affairs Committee); professional staff member, Amerian Indian Policy Review Commission, Washington, D.C., 1976-1977; legislative assistant, U.S. Senate Select Committee on Indian Affairs, Washington, D.C., 1977-1979; vice president and co-founder, Karl A. Funke & Associates, Inc., Washington, D.C., 1979- (a lobbying and consulting firm which represents Indian tribes, national Indian organizations, business and local governments). *Other professional post:* Co-founder and officer, AAA Roofing Co., Inc. *Memberships:* National Congress of American Indians; ABA Student Bar Association. *Awards, honors:* National Indian Health Board Award for Service, 1983. *Interests:*

Indian health; Indian legislative specialist; Indian Child Welfare Act; national Indian budget issues; Indian economic development. *Published work:* American Indian Policy Review Commission "Final Report," U.S. Congress.

MARTIN, JAMES
(B.I.A. Indian education)

Affiliation: Indian Education, Bureau of Indian Affairs, 1951 Constitution Ave., N.W., Washington, D.C. 20245.

MARTIN, JOY
(B.I.A. Indian education)

Affiliation: Indian Education, Bureau of Indian Affairs, 1951 Constitution Ave., N.W., Washington, D.C. 20245.

MARTIN, PETER J. (White Earth Chippewa) 1937-
(federal government administrator-Indian affairs)

Born July 21, 1937, White Earth Indian Reservation, White Earth, Minn. *Education:* North Dakota State School of Science, 2-year drafting/trade course), 1958; University of New Mexico, B.A. (Public Administration), 1967. *Principal occupation:* Federal government administrator-Indian affairs. *Home address:* P.O. Box 363, White Earth, Minn. 56591. *Affiliations:* Administrative manager, Albuquerque Indian School, 1966-1969; administrative director, Institute of American Indian Arts, Santa Fe, N.M., 1969-1970; executive assistant, 1970, chief, 1970-1972, Plant Management Engineering Center, B.I.A., Denver, Colo.; chief, Indian Technical Assistance Center, Denver, Colo., 1972-1977; program specialist, Muskogee Area Office, B.I.A., 1977-1980; owner, Indian consultant business, American Indian Programs, White Earth, Minn., 1980-. *Memberships:* Anishnabe Akeeng (The People's Land); National Congress of American Indians; Minnesota Indian Contactor's Association; Minnesota Democratic Farm Labor Party - National Roster of Buy Indian Contractor's. *Awards, honors: Certificate of Superior Perfor-*

mance, Department of the Interior, Bureau of Indian Affairs (For service in connection with the placement of 220 Job Corps employees, July 1969); Department of the Interior, Bureau of Indian Affairs, 20-year Service Pin, April, 1978. *Interests:* "Interested in and work for betterment of all American Indians; presently engaged as nationwide consultant in American Indian Programs (sole proprietorship enterprise); have visited over 200 Indian reservations and worked with respective tribal councils and program heads; research, writing articles and books, and study of American Indian tribes and involvement with Indian-Federal-State-Municipal programs and relationships."

MARTIN, PHILLIP (Mississippi Choctaw) 1926-
(chief, Mississippi Band of Choctaw Indians)

Born March 13, 1926, Philadelphia, Miss. *Education:* Cherokee High School, Cherokee, N.C., 1945; Meridian Junior College, Meridian, Miss., 1955-1957. *Principal Occupation:* Chief, Mississippi Band of Choctaw Indians. *Address:* Route 7, Box 256, Philadelphia, Miss. 39350. *Affiliations:* Tribal Chairman, Mississippi Band of Choctaw Indians, 1959-1965, 1971-1975; President, National Indian Management Service, Philadelphia, Miss., 1975-; Chief, Mississippi Band of Choctaw Indians, 1979-. *Other Professional Posts:* President, United South and Eastern Tribes, 1968-1969, 1971-1972; President, National Tribal Chairmen's Association, 1981-1983. *Military Service:* U.S. Air Force, 1945-1955. *Community Activities:* Mississippi Band of Choctaw Indians (councilman, 1957-1966, 1971-1975, 1977-1979); Choctaw Housing Authority (chairman of board, 1964-1971); Choctaw Community Action Agency (executive director, 1966-1971); Chata Development Company (president-board of directors, 1969-1975); Haskell Indian Junior College (president-board of regents, and board member, 1970-; Chahta Enterprise, Choctaw Greetings Enterprise, and Choctaw Electronics Enterprise (chairman). *Memberships:* National Tribal Chairmen's Association; National Congress of American Indians; United South and Eastern Tribes; Americans for Indian Opportunity; American Indian Policy Review Commission (member, Task Force #7); Master's in Public Health for Native Americans Program, University of California at Berkeley (advisory committee); Neshoba County Chamber of Commerce. *Awards, Honors:* Indian Council Fire, Indian Achievement Award; United South and Eastern Tribes Leadership Award, 1984. *Interests:* Indian tribal government development and economic development.

MARTIN, ROBERT (Serrano)
(tribal spokesman)

Affiliation: Spokesman, Morongo General Council, 11581 Potrero Rd., Banning, Calif. 92220.

MASON, K. GOYLE
(executive director-Indian organization)

Affiliation: Executive director, Union of Ontario Indians, 27 Queen St. East, Toronto, Ontario, Can. M5C 2M6.

MASSEY, EDNA H. (Mrs. Fred H.) (Oklahoma Cherokee) 1913-
(artist, designer, teacher)

Born July 11, 1913, Stilwell, Okla. *Education:* Haskell Institute; George Washington University. *Affiliation:* Artist, art teacher, textile designer; interior designer, arts and crafts specialist, Bureau of Indian Affairs, U.S. Dept. of the Interior, Washington, D.C. *Memberships:* Creative Crafts Council, Smithsonian Institution; American Craftsmans Council. *Awards, honors:* First Prize, Textile Design, 1960, Second Prize, 1962, Creative Crafts Biennial.

MATSON, DANIEL SHAW 1908-
(teacher)

Born May 17, 1908, Mediapolis, Iowa. *Education:* University of Arizona, A.B., 1930; San Luis Rey Seminary, San Luis Rey and Santa Barbara, Calif., M.A., 1944. *Principal occupation:* Teacher of Papago language, culture, and linguistics; and German, Univerity of Arizona, 1950-1954, 1969-. *Awards, honors:* Honorary Spanish Fraternity. *Interests:* "Study and analysis of Papago and Pima language—structure, vocabulary, tradition; transcription, translation and analysis of historical documents relating to the history of Mexico and Southwest U.S." *Published works: A Colony on the Move* (School of American Research, 1965); *Friar Brings Reports to the King* (University of Arizona Press, 1977).

MATTE, SARA J. (Gros Ventre-Flathead) 1952-
(personnel officer)

Born March 14, 1952, St. Ignatius, Mt. *Education:* Montana State University, Bozeman, B.S., 1974. *Principal occupation:* Personnel officer, Bureau of Indian Affairs, Washington, D.C., 1984-. *Home address:* 3372 Gunston Rd., Alexandria, Va. 22302. *Other professional post:* Personnel management specialist, Bureau of Reclamation, Sacramento, Calif., 1980-1984.

MATTHEWS, ANN M. 1942-
(museum curator)

Born July 25, 1942, Carmel, Calif. *Education:* Tallahassee State University, B.A., 1971. *Principal occupation:* Curator, Tallahassee Junior Museum, 1970-. *Home address:* Box 474, Havana, Fla. 32333. *Memberships:* American Association of Museums; American Association for State and Local History. *Interests:* 19th century history, architecture, and decorative arts, historic farms and farming; Florida Indians (pre-Columbian); native wildlife. *Published work: Apalachee Indian Farm Guide Book* (Tallahassee Junior Museum, 1976).

MAUDLIN, STANISLAUS IRVIN 1916-
(founder/executive director-American Indian Cultural Research Center)

Born December 16, 1916, Greensburg, Ind.

Education: St. Meinrad College, Ind., B.A., 1936; Collegio di St. Anselmo, Rome, 1939; Institute of Alcoholism, N.D., 1966. *Principal occupation:* Founder and director of American Indian Culture Research Center, Marvin, S.D. 57251. *Professional posts:* Associate pastor, work in adolescent and adult eduction, Liaison with Turtle Mountain Chippewa Tribe, Belcourt, N.D., 1941-1950; superintendent of schools, St. Michael, N.D., 1950-1956; member of Industrial Development Committee, Devils Lake, N.D., 1954-1956; president of five state Tekakwitha Indian Missionar Conference, 1955-1956; fundraising on Fort Totten Indian Reservation; founder and pastor of St. John Indian Mission, Pierre, S.D., 1955-1966; counselor, Pierre Indian School, Belcourt, N.D., 1966-1968; founder and executive director, American Indian Culture Research Center, 1968-. *Community activities:* South Dakota Committee for the Humanities (executive committee, 1972-), *Awards, honors:* Adopted into the Yankton Band of Dakota Tribe, 1941 (*Wambdi Wicasa*); adopted into Fort Totten Band, Dakota Tribe, 1954 (*Tikdisni*); adopted into Crow Creek Band, Dakota Tribe, 1961 (*Nasdad Mani*); adopted into Turtle Mountain Chippewa Tribe, 1966 (*Mahcheekwaneeyash*); Citation from South Dakota Association of Counselors and Student Personnel Service Directors for Outstanding Service to Youth, 1971; Citation from South Dakota Social Welfare Conference for services to the social, cultural and humanitarian development of individuals in our State, 1972. *Service activities:* Invited to Washington, D.C., as advisor to Senator McGovern and the late Senator Humphrey, in first anti-poverty legislation, 1964; wrote first Teacher and Student *Handbook,* Stephen High School, Stephan, S.D., 1964; requested by Governor's Commission on Youth (North Dakota) to write position paper on "Juvenile Delinquincy Among Indian Youth: Causes, Forms, Possible Means of Solution," 1967; lecturer to numerous groups, especially to college and university audiences, as well as state and national Church conferences; director of workshops on Indian culture, religion and education; member of evaluation board for Methodist Fund for Reconciliation (South Dakota region).

178

MAY, CHERYL (Oklahoma Cherokee)
1949-
(journalist)

Born February 22, 1949, Kansas City, Mo. *Education:* University of Missouri, K.C., B.A. (English), 1974; Kansas State Univerity, Manhattan, M.S. (Journalism), 1985. *Principal occupation:* Journalism. *Home address:* 1301 Overlook Dr., Manhattan, Kan. 66502. *Affiliations:* Communications director, American Maine-Anjou Association, Kansas City, Mo., 1975-1979; deputy managing editor/research editor, University Relations, Kansas State University, Manhattan, Kan., 1979-. *Community activities:* United Way, KSU publicity chair, 1985; Riley County Historical Society volunteer (organized "Celebrate American Indian Heritage"); 4-H project leader. *Memberships:* National Association of Science Writers; Council for Advancement and Support of Education (CASE). *Awards, honors:* Special Merit Award for "Cattle Research in Kansas," Council for Advancement and Support of Education CASE, writer, 1984; scholarship winner, "Communicating University Research," CASE, 1983; selected for listing in *Ohoyo 1000,* 1982, and for the *Resource Directory of Alaskan and Native American Indian Women,* 1980; Award for Merit for "Artificial Insemination of Beef and Dairy Cattle, " slide script, Society for Technical Communication, 1980; Award for Achievement for "Safety in Handling Livestock," slide script, Society for Technical Communication, 1980; Award for Outstanding News Reporting, Carlsbad, Calif. Chamber of Commerce, 1969. *Interests:* "I'm a journalist specializing in science writing. I developed and edit a research magazine, *Perspectives,* which provides a view of all types of research at Kansas State University. I'm also interested in photography and have won several awards for both writing and photography. In my current position I supervise several units in the KSU University Relations office including photo services, public affairs, news, publications, and support staff." *Published works: Cattle Management* (Reston-Prentice-Hall, 1981); *Legacy, Engineering at Kansas State University* (KSU Press, 1983).

MAYOTTA, RAYMOND
(B.I.A. agency superintendent)

Affiliation: Superintendent, Minnesota Agency, Bureau of Indian Affairs, RR #2, FC 200, Cass lake, Minn. 56633.

MEANS, RUSSELL (Oglala Sioux)
(co-founder-American Indian Movement)

Affiliation: Co-founder, American Indian Movement (AIM), 1209 Fourth St., S.E., Minneapolis, Minn. 55414.

MEANS, WARREN W. (Oglala Sioux)
1937-
(organization executive)

Born November 17, 1937, Pine Ridge, S.D. *Education:* University of Montana, B.A., 1971; University of Montana School of Law, 1971-1972. *Principal occupation:* President-owner, Means Development Corporation. *Other profesional post:* Executive director, United Tribes Educational Technical Center, 1972-1976; "liaison between North American Indian Alliance of Butte, Mt. with federal and state agencies involved in the delivery of services to Indian people." *Memberships:* Montana Adult Education Association; National Advisory Council on Vocational Education (Presidential appointee, 1977-1978); South Dakota Indian Contractors Association.

MEANS, WILLIAM A.
(executive director-Indian organization)

Affiliation: Executive director, International Indian Treaty Council, 777 U.N. Plaza, Room 10F, New York, N.Y. 10017.

MECKLENBURG, ROBERT,
(Indian health service)

Affiliation: Chief, Dental Services Branch, Indian Health Service, 5600 Fishers Lane, Rockville, Md. 20857.

MEDFORD, CLAUDE, Jr. (Choctaw) 1941-
(artist)

Born April 14, 1941, Lufkin, Tex. *Education:* University of New Mexico, B.A., 1964; Oklahoma State University, 1969. *Principal occupation: Artist. Home address:* Natchitoches, La. 71457. *Affiliations:* Museum director, Alabama-Coushatta Indian Reservation; manager of the Coushatta Cultural Center, La.; taught classes and workshops at the American Indian Archaeological Institute in Washington, Conn. in 1979, and the Clifton Choctaw Indian Community west of Alexandria, La. in 1981; received a folk arts apprenticeship fellowship from the Louisiana State Arts Council, Division of the Arts, and now teachers basketry to any interested Indian among the five surviving tribes of Louisiana. Mr. Medford is a gifted craftsman and practitioner of Southeast Indian arts, including basketry, pottery, wood working, shell working, metalworking, fingerweaving, beadwork, featherwork, horn and hoofwork, brain tanning of deer hides, leatherworking and gourd work. His baskets are in numerous private collections as well as several public collections, that of the Southern Plains Indian Museum, the Museum of the Red River in Idabel, Okla., Tantaquidgeon Mohegan Museum in Uncasville, Conn. and a traveling exhibit to be circulated by the Smithsonian Institution Traveling Exhibition Service. Since 1972, he has show his work each year at the New Orleans Jazz and Heritage Festival. *Interests:* To perpetuate the arts and culture of the Southeastern Indian tribes. *Published works: numerous articles for various publications.*

MEDICINE BULL, BERTHA (Northern Cheyenne) 1950-
(newspaper editor)

Born June 1, 1950, Crow Agency, Mt. *Education:* University of Montana, 1974-1976. *Principal occupation:* Newspaper editor, 1976-. *Other professional posts:* Artist and photographer, *Award:* Best Write-Up Award, *Wassaja,* San Francisco, Calif. *Interests:* Art; radio/TV.

MEINHOLTZ, ROLLAND R. (Cherokee) 1937-
(drama instructor)

Born August 20, 1937, Oklahoma City, Okla. *Education:* Northwestern University, B.S., 1959; University of Washington, M.A. (Drama), 1964. *Principal occupation:* Drama instructor. *Affiliations:* Teacher, public schools of Washington and California; instructor in drama, Institute of American Indian Arts, Santa Fe, N.M. *Interests:* Acting; direction and adaptation of plays; travels throughout the U.S. in connection with the Festival of Indian Performing Arts, Washington, D.C.

MENARD, NELLIE (STAR BOY) (Rosebud Sioux) 1910-
(arts and crafts specialist)

Born June 3, 1910, Rosebud, S.D. *Affiliations:* Manager, Rosebud Arts and Crafts, 1937-1942; manager, Northern Plains Arts and Crafts, 1943-1946; arts and crafts specialist, Sioux City Museum and Crafts Center, Rapid City, S.D., 1953-. *Community activities:* Rosebud Reservation delegate to Museum of Modern Art and Museum of the American Indian; attended Indian Arts and Crafts Conference, Central Office, B.I.A., Washington, D.C. *Awards, honors:* Pendleton Robe, for submitted blanket design, Pendleton Mills, 1929; Superior Performance Award, Indian Arts and Crafts Board, U.S. Dept. of the Interior; numerous awards bestowed by the Sioux people. *Interests:* Sioux culture.

MEREDITH, HOWARD L. (Cherokee) 1938-
(historian)

Born May 25, 1938, Galveston, Tex. *Education:* University of Texas, B.S., 1961; S.F. Austin State University, M.A., 1963; University of Oklahoma, Ph.D., 1970. *Principal occupation:* Historian. *Home address:* 623 Lulbertson Dr., Oklahoma City, Okla. 73105. *Affiliations:* Chairman, Cookson Institute, Oklahoma City, Okla., 1974-. *Memberships:* Oklahoma Historical Society (director, 1975-?); Cherokee National Historical Society; Oklahoma Heritage Association; Western Historical Association. *Interests:* "History of American Indian thought; cross cultural education—late maturing youth." *Biographical source: Oklahoma Monthly* (June, 1977). *Published works: The Native American Factor* (Seabury Press, 1973); *Native Response...Rural Oklahoma* (Oklahoma Historical Society, 1977).

MERRELL, JAMES H. 1953-
(professor of history)

Born October 19, 1953, Minneapolis, Minn. *Education:* Lawrence University, Appleton, Wis., B.A., 1975; Oxford University, England, B.A., 1977; Johns Hopkins University, M.A., 1979, Ph.D., 1982. *Home address:* Vassar College, Box 527, Poughkeepsie, N.Y. 12601. *Affiliation:* Assistant professor of history, Vassar College, Poughkeepsie, N.Y., 1984-. *Memberships:* American Historical Association, 1977-; Organization of American Historians, 1977-; American Society for Ethnohistory, 1983-. *Awards, honors:* Rhodes Scholarship; Danforth Fellowship; Predoctoral Fellowship, Newberry Library; Postdoctoral Fellowship, Institute of Early American History and Culture; American History and Life Award, and Robert F. Heizer Award for article, "The Indians New World: The Catawba Experience."

MESSINGER, CARLA J.S. (Lenni Lenape Delaware) 1949-
(founder and president, Lenni Lenape Historical Society)

Born May 20, 1949, Allentown, Pa. *Education:* Kutstown University, Pa., B.S., 1971; Lehigh University, Bethlehem, Pa., M.Ed., 1973. *Principal occupation:* Founder and president, Lenni Lenape Historical Society, Fish Hathcery Rd., Allentown, Pa. 18103. *Home address:* 1819½ Linden St., Allentown, Pa. 18104. *Other professional post:* Former substitute teacher of elementary education and special education (12 years); special consultant on Lenape culture to other organizations, such as Philadelphia school district. *Awards, honors:* 1985 President's Volunteer Action Award, Citation by the House of Representatives, Pa.; Keystone

Award of Merit, Governor's Private Sector Initiatives Task Force for Lenni Lenape Historical Society. *Interests:* Multi-media, cultural programs for all ages given at the Lenni Lenape Historical Society. *Biographical sources: Allentown Neighbors,* "Call/Chronicle, July 8, 1982; *Daily Record,* N.J. You Magazine feature, July 21, 1985; *Easton Express,* Discover-Travel/Leisure, Sept. 15, 1985.

MIKE, LORNA J. (Lower Elwha Klallam) 1955-
(fisheries manager)

Born May 16, 1955, Tacoma, Wash. *Education:* Peninsula College, Port Angeles, Wash. (one year-working on degree). *Principal occupation:* Fisheries manager. *Home address:* 1123 East Columbia St., Port Angeles, Wash. 98362. *Affiliations:* Fisheries manager, Lower Elwha Fisheries, Point No Point Treaty Council, Kingston, Wash., 1985- (fisheries secretary, 1979-1985). *Other professional posts:* Chairman of Tribal Fisheries Committee; vice chairman of the Lower Elwha Tribal Business Committee; board member of the Lower Elwha Indian Child Welfare Consortium.

MILAM, JAMES (Oklahoma Seminole)
(tribal chief)

Affiliation: Chief, Seminole General Council, P.O. Box 745, Wewoka, Okla. 74884.

MILITAIRE, DELBERT
(executive director-Indian organization)

Affiliation: Executive director, National Indian Business Council, 3575 S. Fox, Box 1263, Englewood, Colo. 80150-1263.

MILLER, FRED (Cocopah)
(tribal chairman)

Affiliation: Chairman, Cocopah Tribal Council, P.O. Box Bin G, Somerton, Ariz. 85350.

MILLER, HURON
(president-Indian centre)

Affiliation: President, Native American Centre for the Living Arts, Inc., 25 Rainbow Mall, Niagara Falls, N.Y. 14303.

MILLER, JAY (Delaware) 1947-
(professor of anthropology)

Born April 7, 1947. *Education:* University of New Mexico, B.A., 1969; Rutgers University, Ph.D., 1972. *Principal occupation:* Professor of anthropology, University of Washington, Seattle, Wash. 98195. *Affiliations:* Teaching assistant, lecturer, instructor of anthropology, Rutgers University at Livingston and Newark, 1969-1972; assistant professor of anthropology, Montclair State College. *Other professional posts:* Adjunct curator, North American Ethnology, Washington State Memorial Thomas Burke Museum; executive committee, Indian Studies Program, University of Washington, 1975-; consultant, San Juan County Archaeological Research Project, 1973-; reviewer, National Science Foundation, 1977; contributor, *Smithsonian Handbook of North American Indians.* *Memberships:* American Anthropological Association (Fellow); Society fpr American Archaeology. *Awards, honors:* National Science Foundation Predoctoral Fellowship, 1969; grant-in-aid for research in New Jersey history from the New Jersey Historical Commission, 1973; Summer Salary Award, University of Washington Graduate Research Fund, 1974; research grant from the Alcoholism and Drug Abuse Institute, University of Washington, 1974; "Delaware Indian Music," University of Washington Graduate Research Fund, Interdisciplinary Grant, 1975-1976; "Social Context of Southern Tsimshian," Jacobs Research Fund, Whatcom County Museum, 1977; among others. *Field research:* Archaeology, Anasazi Origins Project (summers, 1966-1967); ethnography, Southwestern Pueblos, 1966-1969; ethnography, Unami Delaware, 1972-; Southern Tsimshian: new language and ethnography at Hartley Bay, 1976 and Kelmtu, 1977, British Columbia; Colville Reservation: conceptual landscape, 1977-. *Dissertation: The Anthropology of Keres Identity* (A Structural Study of the Ethnographic and Archaeological Record of the Keres Pueblos). *Published works:* Numerous papers and articles; books in review and preparation.

MILLER, LEON, Jr. (Mohican)
(tribal chairman)

Affiliation: Chairman, Stockbridge-Munsee Tribal Council, RR 1, Bowler, Wis. 54416.

MILLER, MICHAEL R. (Chippewa-Stockbridge Munsee) 1946-
(director-Native American programs)

Born April 26, 1946, Minneapolis, Minn. *Education:* Appalachian State University, Boone, N.C., B.S. (Business), 1968; University of Minnesota, Duluth, M.S.W., 1984. *Principal occupation:* Director of Native American programs. *Home address:* 113 Emory Dr., River Falls, Wis. 54022. *Affiliations:* Indian education coordinator-supervisor, Title IV-A, Superior Public Schools, Wis., 1974-1981; Native American Outreach Coordinator, Northland College, 1981-1984; director of Native American programs, international student advisor, University of Wisconsin, River Falls, Wis., 1984-. *Memberships:* Wisconsin Indian Education Association, 1985-; National Association for Foreign Student Affairs, 1985-. *Interests:* "My main areas of interest include Indian education, the social aspects of education, improving the image of Native Americans as this image relates to alcoholism, and learning more about international problems and how they relate to the U.S. and Native American experience."

MILLER, ROLAND E. (Stockbridge-Munsee) 1918-
(B.I.A. officer)

Born April 21, 1918, Gresham, Wis. *Education:* Haskell Institute, 1932-1937. *Principal occupation:* B.I.A. officer. *Affiliations:* Various administrative positions with the Bureau of Indian Affairs, 1937-. *Military service:* U.S. Army, 1940-1945, 1950-1952. *Community activities:* Lutheran Church.

MILLER, STEPHEN
(monument superintendent)

Affiliation: Superintendent, Navajo National Monument, Tonalea, Ariz. 86044.

MILLER, THOMAS G.
(school administrator)

Affiliation: Administrator, Hannahville Indian School, Route #1, Wilson, Mich. 49896.

MILLER, VIRGINIA P. 1940-
(professor of anthropology)

Born October 28, 1940, Patterson, N.J. *Education:* Smith College, 1958-1960; University of California, Berkeley, B.A., 1962; University of California, Davis, M.A., 1970, Ph.D., 1973. *Principal occupation:* Assistant professor of anthropology, Dalhousie University, Halifax, Nova Scotia, Can., 1974-. *Memberships:* American Anthropological Association; American Society for Ethnohistory; Canadian Ethnological Society. *Interests:* "Ethnohistory of North America, especially California and Eastern Canada; historical demography." *Published work: Ukomno'm: The Yuki Indians of Northern California* (Ballena Press, 1978).

MILLER, WALLACE W. (Omaha)
(tribal chairman)

Affiliation: Chairman, Omaha Tribal Council, Macy, Neb. 68039.

MILLETT, JERRY (Shoshone)
(tribal chairman)

Affiliation: Chairman, Duckwater Shoshone Tribal Council, P.O. Box 68, Duckwater, Nev. 89314.

MILLIGAN, HARRIET
(museum curator)

Affiliation: Curator, Kaw Indian Mission, 500 N. Kission, Council Grove, Kan. 66846.

MILLS, EARL H. (Mashpee Wampanoag) 1929-
(teacher, tribal officer)

Born March 30, 1929, Mashpee, Mass. *Education:* Arnold College, B.S., 1952; Bridgewater State College, M.A., 1959. *Principal occupation:* Teacher, tribal officer. *Address:* Box 22, Falmouth, Mass. 02541. *Affiliation:* Director of physical education and athletics, Falmouth High School. *Military service:* U.S. Army, 1946-1948. *Community activities:* Old Indian Meeting House Authority, Inc. (president); Mashpee Wampanoag Tribe (tribal executive). *Memberships:* Massachusetts Coaches Association; Athletic Directors Association; Massachusetts Teachers Organization.

MILLS, WALTER R.
(B.I.A. agency superintendent)

Affiliation: Superintendent, Colorado River Agency, Bureau of Indian Affairs, Route 1, Box 9-C, Parker, Ariz. 85344.

**MINER, MARCELLA HIGH BEAR
(Cheyenne River Sioux) 1935-**
(tribal official)

Born July 31, 1935, Cheyenne Agency, S.D. *Education:* Cheyenne River Boarding School; Aberdeen School of Commerce. *Principal occupation:* Tribal official. *Home address:* Eagle Butte, S.D. 57625. *Affiliations:* Tribal treasurer, 1962-1966, assistant finance officer, 1968-1969, bookkeeper, 1969-, Cheyenne River Sioux Tribal Council. *Community activities:* Cheyenne River Mission, Episcopal Church (treasurer, 1963-1966).

MITCHELL, JIMMY
(contract health services)

Affiliation: Chief, Contract Health Services, Indian Health Services, 5600 Fishers Lane, Rockville, Md. 20857.

MITCHELL, LOUIS (Sac and Fox)
(tribal chairman)

Affiliation: Chairman, Sac and Fox Tribal Council, Route 2, Box 52C, Tama, Iowa 52339.

MITCHELL, WAYNE LEE
(Santee Sioux-Mandan) 1937-
(educator, social worker)

Born March 25, 1937, Rapid City, S.D. *Education:* Bacone College, A.A., 1957; University of Redlands, Calif., B.A., 1959; Arizona State University, M.S.W., 1970, Ed.D., 1979. *Principal occupation:* Educator, social worker. *Home address:* P.O. Box 61, Phoenix, Ariz. 85001. *Affiliations:* Professional social worker, various county, state and federal agencies, 1962-1970; social worker, B.I.A., Phoenix, Ariz., 1970-1977; social worker, 1977-1984, supervisor, 1984-, U.S. Public Health Service, Phoenix, Ariz. *Other professional post:* Assistant professor, Arizona State University. *Military service:* U.S. Coast Guard, 1960-1966. *Community activities:* Phoenix Indian Community School (board of directors); Phoenix Indian Center (board of directors); Phoenix Area Health Advisory Board, 1975; Community Behavioral Mental Health Board, 1976. *Memberships:* National Congress of American Indians; National Association of Social Workers; Association of American Indian Social Workers; American Orthopsychiatric Association; Phi Delta Kappa; Kappa Delta Pi; Chi Sigma Chi. *Awards, honors: Delegate to White House Conference on Poverty, 1964; nominated, Outstanding Young Men of America, 1977; Phoenix Indian Center Community Service Award, 1977; Temple of Islam Community Service Award, 1980. Interests: World traveler—China (twice), Russia, India, Nepal, Thailand, Egypt, Israel, Mexico, Central American countries, Colombia, Peru, Equador, European countries, etc. Biographical sources: Who's Who in the West; Who's Who in the World; Men of Achievement. Published works: A Study of Cultural Identification on the Educational Objectives of Hopi Indian High School Seniors* (master's thesis), (Arizona State University, 1970); *Native American Substance Abuse* (Arizona State University Press, 1983); *American Indian Families: Developmental Strategies and Community Health* (Arizona State University Press, 1983).

MITHUN, MARIANNE 1946-
(linguist, professor of linguistics)

Born April 8, 1946, Bremerton, Wash. *Education:* Pomona College (Calif.), B.A., 1969; Yale University, M.A., M.Phil., Ph.D., 1969-1974. *Principal occupation:* Linguist, professor of linguistics. *Address: Department of Linguistics, University of California, Santa Barbara, Calif. 93106. Affiliations:* Assistant professor of linguistics, S.U.N.Y. at Albany, 1973-1981; professor of linguistics, University of California, Berkeley, 1981-1986; professor of linguistics, University of California, Santa Barbara, Calif., 1986-. *Community activities:* Organizer, Iroquois Conference, 1973-1985. *Memberships:* Society for Linguistic Anthropology (president); American Anthropological Association (executive committee, board of directors, administrative advisory committee); Society for the Study of the Indigenous Languages of the Americas (executive board); *Interests:* "American Indian languages and linguistics, especially Iroquoian (Mohawk, Oneida, Onondaga, Cayuga, Seneca, Tuscarora, Huron), Pomo (Central Pomo), Siouan (Dakota, Lakota, Tutelo), Algonquian (Cree)." *Published works: A Grammar of Tusarora* (Garland Press, 1976); *Kanien'keha'Okara'shon:'a (Mohawk Stories)* and *Iontenwennaweienstahkhwa' (Mohawk Spelling Dictionary)* (New York State Museum *Bulletin, 1976,1977); The Languages of Native America* (University of Texas Press, 1979); *Watewayestanih: A Grammar of Cayuga* (Woodland Indian Culture & Education Centre, 1982); *Extending the Rafters: An Interdisciplinary Approach to the Iroquois* (SUNY Press, 1984).

MODUGNO, REV. THOMAS A.
(director-Indian organization)

Affiliation: Director, Marquette League for Catholic Indian Missions, 1011 First Ave., New York, N.Y. 10022.

MOFFETT, WALTER L. (Nez Perce)
1927-
(pastor)

Born June 23, 1927, Kamiah, Idaho. *Education:* College of Idaho, B.A., 1955. *Principal occupation:* Pastor. *Home address:* P.O. Box 668, Kamiah, Idaho 83536. *Affiliations:* Clerk-stenographer, U.S. Department of the Interior, Standing Rock Reservation, N.D., 1949-1950; intern pastor, Brigham City, Utah, 1955-1958; clerk and sanitarian, U.S. Public Health service, Indian Health Service, Idaho and Washington, 1958-1962; pastor, Kamiah-Kooshia United Presbyterian Churches, Kamiah, Idaho, 1964-; council member, Nez Perce Tribal Executive Committee, 1970-. *Other professional posts:* Guidance counselor, Kamiah Public Schools (two years). *Military service:* 945-1947 (Corporal). *Community activities:* Northwest Regional Eductional Laboratory (past member, board of directors); Small Business Administration (advisory council); State Advisory Council, Title III ESEA, Idaho; Idaho Historic Sites Review Board; Community Relations Council, Cedar Flats Job Corps Center, Kooshia, Idaho (past chairman). *Memberships:* Affiliated Tribes of Northwest Indians (president); National Congress of American Indians (area vice president); National Indian Council on Aging. *Interests:* Politics—1974 Republican candidate for State Senator; held pastorate fourteen years. *Biographical source: Personalities of the West and Midwest,* 1971.

MOFSIE, LOUIS (Hopi-Winnebago)
1936-
(art instructor)

Born May 3, 1936, Brooklyn, N.Y. *Education:* S.U.N.Y. at Buffalo, B.S., 1958; Pratt Institute; Hofstra University, M.S. *Principal occupation:* Art instructor, East Meadow, N.Y. *Community activities:* Thunderbird American Indian Dancers of New York (director); Indian League of the Americas of New York (president, 1961-1963); *Memberships:* New York State Art Teachers Association; Classroom Teachers Association. *Awards, honors:* Association of Southwestern Indians Award for painting submitted to the Annual Indian Artists Exhibition, Santa Fe Art Museum. *Interests:* Art instruction; Indian dance; travel. *Published work: The Hopi Way* (M. Evans & Co., 1970).

MOHAWK, JOHN (Seneca) 1945-
(journalist)

Born August 30, 1945, Buffalo, N.Y. *Education:* Hartwick College, B.A., 1968; State University of New York at Buffalo, Ph.D., 1975. *Principal Occupation:* Journalist. *Home Address:* Route 438, Gowanda, N.Y. 14070. *Affiliations:* Editor, *Akwesasne Notes,* 1976-1983; President, Associated Indigenous Communications, 1985. *Other Professional Post:* Lecturer, State University of New York at Buffalo, American Studies Program. *Community Activities:* Seventh Generation Fund (chairman of board); Indian Law Resource Center (board member). *Published Work: A Basic Call to Consciousness* (Akwesasne Notes, 1978).

MOLLENHOFF, LORI
(president-Indian organization)

Affiliation: President, Migizi Communications, Inc., 2300 Cedar Ave. South, Minneapolis, Minn. 55404.

MOMADAY, AL (Kiowa) 1913-
(artist, educator)

Born July 2, 1913, Mountain View, Okla. *Education:* University of New Mexico; U.C.L.A.: Famous Artists Schools. *Principal occupation:* Artist, educator. *Home address:* Jemez Pueblo, N.M. 87024. *Affiliation:* Principal, Jemez Day School, N.M. *Memberships:* National Congress of American Indians; Artists' Equity Association; National Education Association; New Mexico Indian Arts Committee. *Awards, honors:* Grand Award, Indian Painting, All American Indian Days, Sheridan, Wyo., 1955; Grand Award, Indian Painting, American Indian Exposition; Outstanding Southwestern Indian Artists Award, Dallas Exchange Club, 1956; First Prize, Indian Painting, Philbrook Art Center, Tulsa, Okla., 1956; First Prize, Indian Painting, Scottsdale National Indian Arts Exhibition, 1964; among others.

MOMADAY, NATACHEE SCOTT
(Eastern Cherokee) 1913-
(artist, writer, teacher)

Born February 13, 1913, Fairview, Ky. *Education:* Haskell Institute; Crescent College, B.A., 1933. *Principal occupation:* Artist, teacher, writer. *Home address:* Jemez Pueblo, N.M. 87024. *Affiliations:* Civil service teacher, Albuquerque, Shiprock, Chinle, Navajo Service, Ariz. *Other professional posts:* Personnel director, H.A.A.F., Hobbs, N.M.; former newspaper reporter. *Memberships:* Delta Kappa Gamma; National League of American Pen Women; United Daughters of the Confederacy; Daughters of the American Revolution. *Awards, honors:* Arts and Crafts Fair, Albuquerque, N.M.; Inter-Tribal Indian Ceremonial Association. *Published works:* *Woodland Princess,* a book of 24 poems (McHughes Co., 1931); co-author, *Velvet Ribbons,* 1942; *Owl in the Cedar Tree* (Ginn & Co., 1965).

MOMADAY, NAVARRE SCOTT
(Kiowa-Cherokee) 1934-
(author, educator)

Born February 27, 1934, Lawton, Okla. *Education:* University of New Mexico, B.A., 1958; Stanford University, M.A., 1960, Ph.D., 1963. *Principal occupation:* Author, educator. *Address:* Department of English, Stanford University, Stanford, Calif. 94305. *Affiliations:* Assistant professor, associate professor of English, University of California, Santa Barbara, 1962-1969; professor of English and Comparative Literature, University of California, Berkeley, 1969-1972; professor of English, Stanford University, 1972-. *Other professional posts:* Consultant, National Endowment for the Humanities, 1970-; trustee, Museum of the American Indian, 1978-. *Memberships:* American Studies Association; MLA. *Awards, honors:* Guggenheim Fellowship, 1966; Recipient Pulitzer Prize for fiction, 1969; Premio Letterario Internazionale Mondello, Italy, 1979. *Biographical source: Who's Who in America. Published works: The Complete Poems of Frederick Goddard Tuckerman,* 1965; *House Made of Dawn,* 1968; *The Way to Rainy Mountain,* 1969; *Angle of Geese*

and Other Poems, 1973; *The Gourd Dancer,* 1976; *The Names,*1976.

MONETTE, GERALD
(college president)

Affiliation: President, Turtle Mountain Community College, P.O. Box 340, Belcourt, N.D. 58316.

MONSEN, MARIE A. 1939-
(federal government program analyst)

Born October 18, 1939, New York, N.Y. *Education:* Bucknell University, Lewisburg, Pa., B.A. (Sociology), 1961; East-West Center, Honolulu, Hi., M.A. (Sociology), 1963. *Principal occupation:* Federal government program analyst. *Home address:* 6807 Hopewell Ave., Springfield, Va. 22151. *Affiliations:* Training officer, Peace Corps, Thailand Program, 1964-1970; evaluation specialist, Department of the Interior, Washington, D.C., 1971-1979; chief, Local and Indian Affairs, Department of Energy, Washington, D.C., 1979-. *Community activities:* Annandale Christian Community for Action (vice president); Shelter House, Fairfax County (board of directors); elder in Presbyterian Church. *Membership:* Women's Council on Energy and the Environment, 1983-. *Awards, honors:* Certificate of Special Achievement, Bureau of Indian Affairs, 1979; Outstanding Achievement Award, 1984, Americans for Indian Opportunity; Superior Job Performance Awards, 1984-1985, Department of Energy. *Interests:* Indian energy; tribal government.

MONTAGUE, FELIX J.
(B.I.A. agency superintendent)

Affiliation: Superintendent, Fort Yuma Agency, Bureau of Indian Affairs, P.O. Box 1591, Yuma, Ariz. 85364.

MONTGOMERY, JOHN
(B.I.A. agency superintendent)

Affiliation: Superintendent, Zuni Agency, Bureau of Indian Affairs, P.O. Box 338, Zuni, N.M. 87327.

MONTOYA, GERONIMA CRUZ
(Pueblo) 1915-
(artist, teacher)

Born September 22, 1915, San Juan Pueblo, N.M. *Education:* St. Joseph's College, B.S., 1958; University of New Mexico; Claremont College. *Principal occupation:* Art teacher, Santa Fe, N.M. *Home address:* 1008 Calle de Suenos, Santa Fe, N.M. *Community activities:* Community Concert Association (captain); San Juan Pueblo Choir (secretary-treasurer). *Awards, honors:* School of American Research Purchase Award; Museum of New Mexico Special Category Prize, Inter-Tribal Indian Ceremonial, Gallup, N.M.; Special Prize, Philbrook Art Center, Tulsa, Okla.; DeYoung Museum Purchase Prize; among others.

MONTOYA, SAMUEL
(B.I.A. agency superintendent)

Affiliation: Superintendent, Southern Pueblos Agency, Bureau of Indian Affairs, P.O. Box 1667, Albuquerque, N.M. 87103.

MOORE, DAISY POCAHONTAS
(Wampanoag) 1931-
(director-Wampanoag Indian program)

Born July 6, 1931, Mashpee, Mass. *Education:* Boston University, B.A., 1958. *Principal occupation:* Director, Wampanoag Indian Program, Living History Museum, Plimoth Plantation, Plymouth, Mass., 1983-. *Home address:* 400 Plymouth St., Middleboro, Mass. 02346. *Other professional post:* Member, Mashpee Tribal Council (Wampanoag). *Membership:* American Museum Association. *Interest:* "Primary area of interest—museum; have traveled throughout Africa; taught school in Africa for three years under the auspices of the Methodist Church; limited travel to Europe; attended the University of Grenoble, France for one year." *Biographical sources:* Articles in local newspapers: "In Harmony With Nature," *Cape Cod Times,* June 13, 1985; "Collection at Mashpee Wampanoag Museum Enhanced by Plimoth Plantation Loan," *The Enterprise* (Falmouth, Mass., May 24, 1985).

MOORE, JOHN H. 1939-
(anthropologist)

Born February 27, 1939, Williston, N.D. *Education:* New York University, Ph.D., 1974. *Principal occupation:* Associate professor of anthropology, University of Oklahoma, Norman, Okla. *Home address:* 1311 Spruce Dr., Norman, Okla. 73072. *Other professional posts:* Consultant, Sand Creek Descendents Association, Muskogee Creek Tribal Towns, Inc. *Military service:* U.S. Army, 1962-1964 (lieutenant). *Memberships:* American Anthropological Association; American Ethnological Society; American Association for the Advancement of Science. *Interests:* Treaty rights; health; demography. *Biographical source:* "Search for the Sand Creek Descendents," *Sooner Magazine,* Spring, 1983. *Published works: Ethnology in Oklahoma* (Papers in Anthropology, 1980); *The Cheyennes in Moxtavhohona* (Northern Cheyenne Tribe, Inc., 1981); *The Cheyenne Nation* (University of Nebraska Press, 1986).

MOORE, JOSIAH N. (Papago)
(tribal chairman)

Affiliation: Chairman, Papago Tribal Council, P.O. Box 837, Sells, Ariz. 85634.

MOORE, LOUIS (Miami)
(tribal chief)

Affiliation: Chief, Miami Business Committee, P.O. Box 636, Miami, Okla. 74355.

MOORE, PAUL V.
(college president)

Affiliation: President, Bacone College, East Shawnee, Muskogee, Okla. 74402.

MOORE, RAMONA
(president-Indian association)

Affiliation: President, North American Indian Women's Association, 1411 K St., N.W., Suite 200, Washington, D.C. 20005.

MOORE, TRACEY ANN *(E-ne-opp-e)*
(Pawnee-Otoe-Osage-Sac and Fox)
1964-
  (student)

Born August 14, 1964, Fairfax, Okla. *Education:* Northern Oklahoma College, Tonkawa, 1982-1984; University of Oklahoma, 1984-. *Principal occupation:* Student, University of Oklahoma, Norman. *Home address:* 401 Tallchief Dr., Fairfax, Okla. 74637. *Affiliations:* Vice president, American Indian Student Association, University of Oklahoma, 1985-1986; Intramurals Committee for Minority Students, University of Oklahoma Student Association, 1985-1986; American Indian Student Service, University of Oklahoma, Norman, 1986-. *Other professional posts:* CETA Summer Youth Progam, The Osage Nation, 1981-. *Awards, honors:* Nominated twice for Outstanding Young Women of America, 1985; Osage Nation representative for Miss National Congress of American Indians Pageant, 1985; University of Oklahoma, American Indian Student Association Princess, 1985-1986; Tulsa Powwow Princess, 1984; Miss Indian Oklahoma, 1st runner-up-most talented; National Viet Nam Veterans Powwow Princess & Association Princess, 1982-1984; Osage Tribal Princess, 1980 and 1983; recommended to submit autobiography for International Youth in Achievement, Cambridge, England. *Interests:* "My major is physical education. I hope to teach or be a women's basketball coach, I feel education is the key to life and I stress it to the Native American youth that it is important, and that they can also compete in sports as well. I enjoy traveling across the U.S. to Native American celebrations of every kind. I have represented my tribe at powwows, state and national organizations which involved me traveling to all 4 directions. My parents are Ted Moore, Sr., a former world champion fancy dancer for a number of consecutive years at the American Indian Exposition in Anadarko, Okla., and Thomasine Moore, a former Osage princess and current Osage Tribal Director at the American Indian Exposition. My great-grandfather was See-Haw, a great leader of the Osage Nation."

MORAN, ERNEST T. (BUD)
(Confederated Salish & Kootenai
-Chippewa Cree) 1939-
  (B.I.A. agency superintendent)

Born August 27, 1939, Harlem, Mt. *Education:* Oceanside Junior College, 1960; Santa Ana Junior College, 1962-1963; received numerous training courses in administration and management while in the U.S. Marines. *Principal occupation:* B.I.A. agency superintendent. *Home address:* #14 Phinney Dr., Lapwai, Idaho 83540. *Affiliations:* Credit and business development officer, director of economic development program, Confederated Salish & Kootenai Tribes; Indian Community Action Program, University of Montana, Missoula; Bureau of Indian Affairs: housing officer, Rocky Boy, Mt.; reservation programs officer, Lame Deer, Mt.; credit and business development, Jicarilla Agency, Dulce, N.M.; tribal operations officer, Western Nevada Agency, Stewart, Nev.; field representative in Klamath, Calif.; superintendent, Northern Cheyenne Agency, Lame Deer, Mont., 1980-1985; superintendent, Northern Idaho Agency, Lapwai, Idaho, 1985-. *Other professional posts:* President, Indian American Foundation; past president, NFFE Union, Jicarilla Apache Agency Post, N.M. *Military service:* U.S. Marine Corps, 1958-1967 (Navy Unit Citation; Vietnam Unit Citation with Star; Vietnam Service Medal with Star; National Defense Service Medal with Star; Armed Forces Expeditionary Medal with 2 Stars). *Community activities:* Active Corps of Executives (member); Aide de Camp to Governor of New Mexico; Toastmasters Club, Lame Deer, Mt. (past president); coached four years of Little League, Lame Deer. Mt. *Memberships:* Confederated Salish & Kootenai Tribe; tribal affiliations with Chippewa Cree Tribe and Rocky Boy Tribe. *Awards, honors:* Special Achievement Award from Bureau of Indian Affairs; Letter of Appreciation from Jicarilla Apache Tribe and Northern Cheyenne Tribe; guest speaker (at Dull Knife Memorial College on numerous occasions) on government and their relations with tribes.

MORGAN, DONALD I. (Blackfeet) 1934-
(B.I.A. official)

Born June 12, 1934, Browning, Mt. *Education:* College of Great Falls, Mt.; University of New Mexico; Central Washington University. *Principal occupation:* B.I.A. official. *Home address:* P.O. Box 654, Fort Thompson, S.D. 57339. *Affiliations:* Administrator, Wind River Agency, B.I.A., Fort Washakie, Wyo.; administrator, vocational training and job placement worker, Los Angeles Field Employment Office, Los Angeles, Calif.; vocational counselor, Blackfeet Agency, Browning, Mt., Northern Cheyenne Agency, Lame Deer, Mt., Yakima Agency, Toppenish, Wash.; administrator, Crow Creek Agency, B.I.A., Fort Thompson, S.D. *Military service:* U.S. Army, 1957-1959.

MORGAN, GUY (Navajo) 1921-
(tribal official)

Born September 15, 1921, Woodspring (Kinlichee), Ariz. *Education:* Various B.I.A.-operated schools, 1930-1940. *Principal occupation:* Tribal official. *Home address:* Woodspring Trading Post, Ganado, Ariz. 86505. *Affiliations:* Owner, Woodspring Trading Posts #1 & 2, Ariz. *Other professional posts:* Delegate, Navajo Tribal Council, Window Rock, Ariz.; Navajo Tribal Welfare Committee, 1963-1966; Navajo Tribe Commission on Alcoholism, 1967-1971; Navajo Tribe Transportation and Roads Committee, 1971-. *Awards, honors:* Ten-year pin, B.I.A. *Interests:* As chairman of the Navajo Tribe Transportation and Roads Committee, Mr. Morgan is concerned that taxes paid by his tribe to four different states result in better facilities for his people.

MORGAN, MARILYN ELIZABETH 1944-
(technical editor)

Born June 30, 1944, Bremerton, Wash. *Education:* California State University, San Francisco, B.A., 1972. *Principal occupation:* Technical editor. *Home address:* 2858 North Highview Ave., Altadena, Calif. 91001. *Affiliations:* Technical editor, Jet Propulsion Laboratory, California Institute of Technology, Pasadena, Calif. *Other professional post:* Editor, *Native American Annual.* *Memberships:* Society for Technical Communication (audio-visual committee); Astronomical Society of the Pacific. *Interests:* Technical communiction; astronomy and science in general; Native American progress and cultural integrity. *Published work:* Editor, *Native American Annual* (Native American Publishing Co., Margaret Clark-Price, Publisher, 1985).

MORGAN, RONALD JOSEPH WHITEWOLF (¼ Blackfeet) 1940-
(writer, photographer, jeweler)

Born October 4, 1940, Seattle, Wash. *Education:* Bachelor degree in history from Universal Life Church, Modesto, Calif., 1974. *Principal occupation:* Writer, photographer, jeweler. *Home address:* P.O. Box 297, Redwater, Tex. 75573. *Occupational activities:* "I'm a public speaker, lecturer and dancer. I give talks on the Old West and Indians, also have slide shows and relic displays using artifacts from my collections. As a dancer, I've demonstrated Indian dances for tourists, school and youth groups. I have appeared in three video movies, filmed on the Alabama-Coushatta Reservation, Livingston, Texas. I speak the Dakota Sioux language, sign language and Spanish." *Memberships:* Smithsonian Institution; National Archives. *Awards, honors:* Awarded honorary title, "Special Consultant-American Indian Affairs," 1969; "I have been consulted by writers, U.S. Senators and many Indian organizations over the years." *Interests:* "Research is one of my main interests. I'm an Indian historian and always try to learn the old ways. My interests are many: archaeology, linguistics, publishing and law. I'm especially interested in state and federal law books relating Indian court cases. Collecting Indian artifacts; documents, photographs and original historical newspapers are just some of my interests, As a professional photographer, I'm busy recording western and Indian historical sites, graves of famous Indians and Indian powwows. I'm a part-time jeweler, casting in both gold and silver. My future plans are to produce video movie documentaries pertaining to Indian ceremonies and wild life. I'm currently working on fictional book about intertribal wars. The University of South Dakota, Institute of Indian Studies, has expressed an interest in using my photographs in a future publication, *Who's Who Among the Sioux." Biographical sources: Source Directory* (U.S. Dept. of the Interior, B.I.A., 1985-1987); *The American Indian Index: A Directory of Indian Country* (Arrowstar Publishing, 1986-1987). *Published works:* Articles: "I Fought With Geronimo" by Jason Betzinez as told to Ronald Morgan (*The Westerner,* Stagecoach Publishing, 1971); series, "The Indian Side," in *The Frontier, Real West, True West,* and *American West* Magazines; among others.

MORRIS, ELIZABETH (Athabascan) 1933-
(director-Indian organization)

Born February 16, 1933, Holikachuk, Alaska. *Education:* Seattle Community College, 1969-1970. *Principal occupation:* Former executive director, Seattle Indian Center, 1971-? *Home address:* 946 16th Ave., E., Seattle, Wash. 98112. *Community activities:* Candidate for Washington State Legislature, 1970; Seattle Community Council (advertising screening committee). *Interests:* Ms. Morris writes, "(I am) interested in the welfare of my people, and devote most of my time toward improving the quality of (their) lives. Because of my own experiences and difficulties, I am interested in helping (my people) maintain their identity and unique culture, (while) at the same time adapt(ing) to the urban scene."

MORRIS, C. PATRICK 1938-
(professor of Native American studies)

Born December 5, 1938, Watsonville, Calif. *Education:* Arizona State University, B.A. (History), 1964, M.A., 1970, Ph.D. (Anthropology), 1974. *Principal occupation:* Professor of Native American Studies, Center for Native American Studies, Montana State University, Bozeman, Mt. *Home address:* 8210 Balsam Dr., Bozeman, Mt. 59715. *Community activities:* Assist tribal colleges organize International Exchange Program

for 23 Indian tribes with Norway and France. *Memberships:* National Indian Education Association; Montana Indian Education Association. *Awards, honors:* Marshall Fellowship, Norway; Fulbright Award, Norway, University of Oslo; Goodwill Award for International Understanding, Norway. *Interests:* "Indian law and policy; international human rights and indigenous people; Indian reservation economies; tribally controlled colleges; American Indian religious thought; Indian literature—oral and written. *Published works:* "As Long As the Water Flows: Indian Water Rights, A Growing National Conflict in the U.S.," in *Native Power,* edited by J. Brosted, et al. (University of Oslo, 1985); *The Hill of Sorrow: Ethnohistory of the Little Shell Chippewa (in press).*

MORRISON, GEORGE (Chippewa) 1919-
(artist, art teacher)

Born September 30, 1919, Grand Marais, Minn. *Education:* Minneapolis School of Art, Certificate, 1943; Art Students League, New York, N.Y., 1943-1946; University of Aix-Marseilles, France, 1952-1953; M.F.A. (hon.), Minneapolis College of Art and Design, 1969. *Principal occupation:* Artist, art teacher. *Home address:* 2050 Stanford Ave., St. Paul, Minn. 55105. *Affiliations:* Assistant professor, associate professor, Rhode Island School of Design, 1963-1970; visiting professor of art and American Indian Studies, University of Minnesota, 1970-1973, professor, 1973-. *Memberships:* Audubon Artists, New York, 1955-; Federation of Modern Painters and Sculptors, New York, 1955-. *Exhibitions:* Numerous one-, two-, and three-man shows, invitational exhibitions and group shows in the U.S., France, The Netherlands, South America and Japan. Mr. Morrison's work is in the permanent collections of the Whitney Museum, New York City, New York University, Rochester Memorial Museum, St. Lawrence University, Canton, N.Y., Penn State University, Altoona, Pa., The Philadelphia Museum, University of Massachusetts, Virginia Museum of Fine Arts, Minneapolis Institute of Art, University of Minesota, Duluth, Amon Carter Museum of Western Art, Pacific Northwest Indian Center, Spokane, Wash. and many others. *Awards, honors:* Scholarship grants, Consolidated Chippewa Agency, 1941-1943; Fulbright Scholarship (FRance), 1952-1953; John Hay Whitney Fellowship, 1953-1954; numerous prizes and awards for paintings. *Biographical source: George Morrison: The Story of an American Indian,* by Dragos Kostich (Dillon Press, 1976).

MOSE, E.
(executive director-Nevada
Indian Commission)

Affiliation: Executive director, Nevada Indian Commission, 472 Galleti Way, Reno, Nev. 89431.

MOSES, DAVID (Sauk-Suiattle)
(tribal chairman)

Affiliation: Chairman, Sauk-Suiattle Tribal Council, 5318 Chief Brown Lane, Darrington, Wash. 98241.

MOSES, LILLY L. (Nez Perce)
1949-
(economic development planner)

Born November 8, 1949, Seattle, Wash. *Education:* Oregon State University, B.S. (Education), 1976; University of Idaho, College of Law, 1979-1980. *Principal occupation:* Economic development planner. *Home address:* Route 1, Box 24, Kamiah, Idaho 83536. *Affiliations:* Cooperative education coordinator, American Indian Higher Education Consortium, Denver, Colo., 1973-1974; teacher intern, Madras Public Schools, Madras, Oreg., 1975-1976; grants/contracts specialist, Planning Department, Warm Springs Confederated Tribes, Warm Springs, Oreg., 1976-1977; community service manager, Nez Perce Tribe, Lapwai, Idaho, 1977-1979; researcher, Cobe Consultants, Portland, Ore., 1980-1981; economic development planner/manager, Limestone Enterprise, Nez Perce Tribe, P.O. Box 365, Lapwai, Idaho 83540. *Community activities:* Kamiah Revitalization Committee, Kamiah, Idaho (member, 1983-); elected to Housing Board of Commissioners, Nez Perce Tribal Hous-

ing Authority, 1985-1989). *Memberships:* Association for the Humanities in Idaho , 1978-1981. *Awards, honors:* 1971 After Dinner Speech Award; All-Indian Debate Tournament, Dartmouth College. *Interests:* "To gain a professionally gratifying position in the federal government that assists American Indian tribes in achieving self-sufficiency;" camping, hunting, fishing, beadwork, dancing.

MOYLE, ALVIN (Paiute-Shoshoni)
(tribal chairman)

Affiliation: Chairman, Fallon Paiute-Shoshini Business Council, 8955 Mission Rd., Box 232A, Fallon, Nev. 89406.

MUNGER, LYNN 1918-
(museum curator)

Born May 24, 1918, Steuben County, Ind. *Education:* Manchester College, Ind. *Principal occupation:* Museum curator. *Home address:* Box 486, Fremont, Ind. 46737. *Affiliations:* Teacher, Steuben County School System (15 years); Curator, Potawatomi Museum, Fremont, Ind. *Military service:* U.S. Navy, 1939-1945 (Presidential Unit Citation; Pearl Harbor Survivor; European Theatre Decoration). *Memberships:* Central States Archaeological Society (consultant); Ohio Primitive Art Society (consultant); Smithsonian Institution. *Interests:* "Although my interests are many and diversified, I retain the major focus of interest on the American Indian, working with school groups, service clubs and archaeological societies to dispel some of the common misconceptions concerning the heritage of the American Indian. Other fields of interest are ecology and entomology."

MURPHY, CHARLES W. (Standing Rock Sioux) 1948-
(tribal chairman)

Born December 27, 1948, Fort Yates, N.D. *Education:* Saint Benedict College, Atchison, Kan., 1968-1969. *Principal occupation:* Tribal chairman. *Home address:* P.O. Box D, Fort Yates, N.D. 58538. *Affiliations:* Police officer, B.I.A., Fort Yates, N.D., 1970-1972; range technician, B.I.A., Standing Rock Sioux Tribe, 1972-1976; agricultural director, 1976-1979, economic development planner, 1979-1981, vice chairman and councilman, 1981-1983, chairman, 1983-, Standing Rock Sioux Tribe, Fort Yates, N.D. *Military service:* U.S. Army, 1969-1970 (Vietnam Veteran; Army Commendation Medal; Bronze Star). *Community activities:* Standing Rock Irrigation Board, Standing Rock Sioux Tribe (chairman, 1981-); United Tribes Educational Technical Center, Bismarck, N.D. (board of directors, 1983-); Aberdeen Area Roads Commission (chairman, 1985-); Aberdeen Tribal Chairman's Association (chairman, 1986-); Theodore Jamerson Elementary School, Bismarck, N.D. (school board, 1984-); Saint Alexius Medical Center, Bismarck, N.D. (board of directors, 1985-). *Memberships:* National Tribal Chairman's Association, 1983-; United Sioux Tribes, Pierre, S.D. (chairman, 1985-. *Awards, honors:* Certificate of Special Achievement, Department of the Interior, 1980. *Interests:* "Elected by the enrolled members of the Tribe (Standing Rock Sioux), (I) serve as the chair of the Tribal Council and the chief executive officer of the tribal government. Specialized experience or other related background in personnel management, administration, planning and budgeting, and land and resource management. Responsible for implementation of tribal law; and represent the Tribe before Congress and government agencies."

MURRAY, DONALD CLYDE
(Micmac-Algonquian) 1932-
(engineering manager)

Born April 11, 1932, Bayside, N.Y. *Education:* University of Louisville, B.A. (Physics), 1952; University of Southern California, M.A. (Psychology), 1965; U.C.L.A., Ph.D. (Psychology), 1973. *Principal occupation:* Engineering manager, Hughes Aircrafts Co., Los Angeles, Calif., 1953-. *Home address:* 2106 West Willow Ave., Anaheim, Calif. 92804. *Other professional posts:* Licensed psychologist, State of California; senior associate, Al. J. Murray & Associates (mechanical consultants). *Military service:* U.S. Marine Corps, 1952-1954 (Captain; Reserves-retired). *Memberships:* American Association for the Advancement

of Science; Amerin Physical Society. *Awards, honors:* Howard Hughes Doctoral Fellowships, 1968-1973; Order of the Chevalier, Cross of Honor, and Legion of Honor recipient, International Order of DeMolay. *Interests:* Consultant and lecturer; management psychology; executive counseling. *Biographcial source:* Registry of Native American Professionals.

MURRAY, WALLACE C. (Ioway)
(tribal chairman)

Affiliation: Chairman, Iowa Business Committee, Iowa Veterans Hall, P.O. Box 190, Perkins, Okla. 74059.

MUSKRAT, JEFF W. (Oklahoma Cherokee) 1922-
(former B.I.A. official)

Born June 17, 1922, Grove, Okla. *Education:* Northeast Oklahoma Junior College, 1941-1942; Tulsa University, 1946-1947. *Principal occupation:* Former superintendent, Cherokee Agency, B.I.A., Cherokee, N.C., 1974-? *Home address:* P.O. Box 245, Cherokee, N.C. 28719. *Military service:* U.S. Army, 1942-1967 (Lt. Col.-retired; Silver Star; Bronze Star with Oak Leaf Cluster; Army Commendation Medal with two Oak Leaf Clusters; Presidential Citation). *Community activities:* Cherokee Boys Club (board of directors); Museum of the Cherokee Indian (board of directors). *Memberships:* Retired Officer's Association; Veterans of Foreign Wars; American Legion; Quarter Horse Association; American Indian Cattleman's Association.

N

NARANJO, TITO E. (Santa Clara Pueblo) 1937-
(professor of social work)

Born August 8, 1937, Santa Clara Pueblo, N.M. *Education:* Baylor University, Waco, Tex., 1956-1958; Hardin-Simmons University, Abilene, Texas, 1958-1959; New Mexico Highlands University, Las Vegas, B.A., 1962, M.A., 1963; University of Utah, M.S.W., 1967. *Principal occupation:* Associate professor of social work. *Home address:* P.O. Box 516, Mora, N.M. 87732. *Affiliations:* Director of social services, Mora County, N.M., 1970-1971; assistant professor, College of Santa Fe, N.M, 1972-1975; associate professor of social work, New Mexico Highlands, University, Las Vegas, N.M., 1976-. *Other professional post:* Mora Valley Health Services, Inc. (board of directors). *Community activities:* Intermountain Centers for Human Development (board member); tribal secretary for Santa Clara Pue, 1976. *Memberships:* American Indian Higher Education (board of directors). *Interests:* "I am a part time rancher, part-time artist and writer. I enjoy hunting, fishing and photography. I am a distance runner in the mastes category and I also love to canoe, hike and adventure in Alaska and Mexico. *Biographical source:* "A Conversation With Tito Naranjo," in (*Confluencia, summer, 1980*).

NARCIA, LEROY (Papago)
(tribal chairman)

Affiliation: Chairman, Ak Chin Community Council, Route 2, Box 27, Maricopa, Ariz. 85239.

NASH, GARY B. 1933-
(historian)

Born July 27, 1933, Philadelphia, Pa. *Education:* Princeton University, B.A., 1955, Ph.D., 1964. *Principal occupation:* Historian. *Home address:* 16174 Alcima Ave., Pacific Palisades, Calif. 90272. *Affiliations:* Assistant to the Dean of the Graduate School, 1959-1961, assistant professor, Department of History, 1964-1966, Princeton University; assistant professor, 1966-1968, associate professor, 1969-1972, professor, 1972-, Department of History, University of California at Los Angeles. *Other professional posts:* Dean, Council on Educational Development, U.C.L.A., 1980-1984; dean of Undergraduate and Intercollege Curricula Development, U.C.L.A., 1984-; faculty advisory committee, American Indian Studies Center, U.C.L.A., 1973-1982; editorial board, *American Indian Culture and Research Journal,* 1980-. *Memberships:* American Historical Association; Institute of Early American History and Culture; Organization of American Historians (nominating committee, 1980-1983; American Antiquarian Society. *Awards, honors:* Research grants from University of California Institute of Humanitics and Research Committee, UCLA, 1966-1983; Guggenheim Fellowship, 1970-1971; Prize from the American Historical Association, Pacific Coast Branch, 1970, for best book, *Quakers and Politics: Pennsylvania, 1681-1726;* American Council for Learned Society Fellow, 1973-1974; American Philosophical Society grants, 1977, 1981, 1984; runner-up Pulitzer Prize in History for *The Urban Crucible,* 1979; 1980 Commonwealth Club of California, Silver Prize in Literature for *The Urban Crucible. Published works:* Co-edited, *Struggle and Survival in Colonial America* (University of California Press, 1981); *Red, White and Black: The Peoples of Early America* (Prentice-Hall, 1974; 2nd Ed., 1982); The American People: Creating a Nation and a Society (Harper and Row, 1986); *Retracing the Past: Readings in the History of the American People* 2 volumes (Harper and Row, 19860; among others. Numerous articles in various professional journals.

NASON, JAMES D. (Comanche) 1942-
(museum curator, social anthropologist)

Born July, 1942, Los Angeles, Calif. *Education:* University of California, Riverside, B.A., 1964; University of Washington, M.A., 1967, Ph.D., 1970. *Principal occupation:* Museum curator, social anthropologist, Thomas Burke Memorial Washington State Museum, University of Washington, Seattle, Wash. *Affiliations:* Chairman, Anthropology Division and Curator of Ethnology, Thomas Burke Memorial Museum; professor, Department of Anthropology, University of Washington. *Other professional posts:* Commissioner, Kings County Arts Commission, Wash. *Memberships:* American Anthropological Association, 1970 (Fellow); American Association for the Advancement of Science, 1970- (Fellow); American Ethnological Society, 1970- (Fellow); American Association of Museums; International Council of Museums; Association for Social Anthropology in Oceana, 1971- (Fellow). *Interests:* Social anthropology and museology; culture change and modernization; Oceana (Micronesia) and North America; ethnohistory research. Field research. *Published works:* Edited with Mac Marshall, *Micronesia, 1944-1974* (Human Relations Area Files Press, 1976).

NAUMAN, CHARLES W. 1925-
(motion picture production)

Born December 14, 1925, Gettysburg, S.D. *Education:* University of Iowa, M.A., 1950. *Principal occupation:* Motion picture production. *Home address:* Box 232, Custer, S.D. 47730. *Affiliation: Nauman Films, Inc., Custer, S.D., 1955-. Military service:* U.S. Air Force, 1944-1946 (Sergeant; Presidential Unit Citation; Battle Star, Central Europe). *Awards, honors:* Cine "Golden EagleE Award (twice); New York Film Festival; American Film Festival; among others. *Interests:* Native American Indian Culture; travel; "interested in any world travel involving filmmaking or other positive involvement with cultures; expedition into canyons of Sierra Madre Occidental of Mexico to film Tarahumara Indian culture and Easter festival. *Films produced: The Grass That Never Breaks; Tahtonka,* 16mm documentary of Plains Indians from prehorse era to Wounded Knee Massacre—1967, voted best film of the week on B.B.C.—voted among 100 best educational films in the U.S.—awarded top honors at most major international film festivals in U.S. and abroad; *The Child Is A Piper,* best cable film of the year for television, 1970; *Johnny Vik,* 35mm full length feature film, 1971; *Sioux Legends,* 16mm documentary of Plains Indians culture, 1972 (Cine "Golden Eagle Award; Martin Luther King, Jr. Award).

NAUMAN, H. JANE 1929-
(motion picture production)

Born May 4, 1929, Grinnell, Iowa. *Education:* University of Iowa, B.A., 1950. *Principal occupation:* Motion picture production. *Home address:* Box 232, Custer, S.D. 57730. *Affiliaitons:* Nauman Films, Custer, S.D., 1955-; president, Sun Dog Distributing

(motion pictures), 1976-. *Awards, honors:* Fulbright Scholarship Award. See previous listing of husband, Charles W. Nauman for more information.

NAYLOR, JACK
(B.I.A. agency superintendent)

Affiliation: Superintendent, Miami Agency, Bureau of Indian Affairs, P.O. Box 391, Miami, Okla. 74354.

NEAMAN, KENNETH L. (Shoshoni)
(tribal chairman)

Affiliation: Chairman, Northwestern Band of Shoshoni Nation, Star Route 2 W, Rock Springs, Wyo. 82901.

NEELY, SHARLOTTE 1948-
(anthropologist)

Born August 13, 1948, Savannah, Ga. *Education:* Georgia State University, B.A., 1970; University of North Carolina, M.A., 1971, Ph.D., 1976. *Principal occupation:* Anthropologist. *Home address:* 3010 Marshall Ave., Cincinnati, Ohio 45220. *Affiliation:* Assistant professor, associate professor of anthropology, Northern Kentucky University, Highland Heights, Ky., 1974-. *Memberships:* American Anthropological Association, 1970- (Fellow); Southern Anthropological Association, 1974-; Central States Anthropological Society, 1975-; American Society for Ethnohistory, 1976-. *Awards, honors:* Predoctoral Research Fellowship, National Institutes of Mental Health, 1974; Alternate for Postdoctoral Fellowship, (D'Arcy McNickle) Center for the History of the American Indian, Newberry Library, Chicago, Ill., 1974. *Interests:* "Major research with Southeastern Indians, especially the Eastern Band of Cherokee Indians of North Carolina -- on-going research, including fieldwork, since 1971; also travel experience in the Indian areas of the Southwest, Plains, and Mexico. Major topical interests relating to Indians: ethnohistory, politics, ethnic relations, education, and the role women." Unpublished Ph.D. dissertation *Ethnicity in a Native American Community, and unpub-*

lished M.A. thesis, The Role of Formal Education Among the Eastern Cherokee Indians, 1880-1971, University of North Carolina, Chapel Hill. *Published works:* Numerous articles and papers.

NELSON, MICHAEL (Navajo) 1941-
(corporate president)

Born February 2, 1941, Whitecone (Navajo Nation), Ariz. *Education:* Fort Lewis College, Durango, Colo., B.A. (Business Administration), 1966. *Principal occupation:* President, Michael Nelson & Associates, Inc., Window Rock, Ariz.. *Home address:* P.O. Box 614, Window Rock, Ariz. 86515. *Affiliation:* Michael Nelson & Associates, Inc. maintains retail outlets in Teesto, Tuba City and Kayenta, Ariz. *Memberships:* Navajo Business Association (president, 1974-1978). *Awards, honors:* National Indian Businessperson of the Year, 1983; Minority Retail Firm of the Year, 1985; other local awards. *Interests:* "Travels to other parts of the world; recent travels to Hawaii, Hong Kong, Bahamas, and all the small islands in the Caribbean, Mexico." *Biographical source: The Maazo Magazine,* Vol. 1, No. 3, entitled "Business on the Navajo Reservation, The Maazo Interview with Michael Nelson a Successful Navajo Businessman." *Published work:* Publisher and editor of 1979 and 1980, *Airca Rodeo Championship Edition* (All Indian Rodeo Cowboy Association).

NENEMA, GLEN (Kalispel)
(tribal chairman)

Affiliation: Chairman, Kalispel Business Committee, P.O. Box 38, Usk, Wash. 99180.

NESETH, EUNICE (Aleut) 1907-
(elementary teacher-retired)

Born January 6, 1907, Afognak, Alaska, *Eduction:* Western Washington College of Educatin, B.A., 1942. *Principal occupation:* Elementary teacher-retired, Grades 1-6, Kodiak, Alaska, 1943-1967. *Home address:* Box 456, Kodiak, Alaska 99615. *Other professional posts:* Acquisitions Committee, Alaska Museum; instructor of basket weaving. *Community activities:* Senior Citizens,

Afognak Native Association (board member); Koniag and Kodiak Islands Native Association (member); *Memberships:* Alaska Education Association; Kodiak Education Association; Alaska Historical Society; Kodiak Historical Society (curator, 1957-1975; life member, 1975-). *Interests:* Education; travel; languages: "grass basket weaving, having learned from Anfesia Shapsnikoff of Unalaska during ten sessions while she lived in with us."

NESPOR, ELSIE PASCHAL 1927-
(principal)

Born October 3, 1927, Marvell, Ark. *Education:* University of Tulsa, B.S., 1971, Graduate School, 1971-1973; Black Hills State College, M.S. (Education), 1976. *Pirncipal occupation:* Principal, Loneman School (Oglala Sioux Tribe), Oglala, S.D. *Home address:* Oglala, S.D. 57764. *Affiliations:* Owner-manager, Nespor Ranch, Okemah, Okla., 1952-1959; curriculum specialist, Tulsa Public Schools, 1971-1973. *Memberships:* Kappa Delta Pi (membership chairman); South Dakota Educatin Association; South Dakota Indian Education Association. *Awards, honors:* Outstanding Educator, Elementary and Secondary Education, 1976. *Interests:* Early childhood; Indian educational research and curriculum development; "employed by Creek Nation of Oklahoma, Okmulgee, Okla., to do field research study preparatory to writing Early Childhood Family Development Program for Creek Nation, 1977, summer;" consulting; poetry (published in *Nimrod,* University of Tulsa, and *Obsidian*). *Biographical sources: Who' Who in American Education; Notable Americans,* 1977. *Published works: Environment for Early Learning* (Tulsa Public Schools, 1972); *Student Handbook (Loneman School)* (Bureau of Indian Affairs, 1974); *Young Creek Americans and Their Families: Possibilities for Change* (Creek Nation, 1977).

NEW, LLOYD H. (professional name- Lloyd Kiva) (Cherokee) 1916-
(artist, craftsman)

Born February 18, 1916, Fairland, Okla. *Education:* Oklahoma State University,

1933-1934; Art Institute of Chicago, 1934-1935; University of New Mexico, 1937; University of Chicago, B.A.E., 1938; Laboratory of Anthropology, Santa Fe, N.M. , 1939. *Principal occupation:* Artist, craftsman. *Address:* Institute of American Indian Arts, Cerrillos Rd., Santa Fe, N.M. 87501. *Affiliations:* Director, Indian Exhibit, Arizona State Fair, 1939-1950; instructor in arts and crafts, U.S. Indian School, Phoenix, Ariz., 1939-1941; established Lloyd Kiva Studios, Scottsdale, Ariz., 1945; instructor in art education, U.S. Indian summer schools for teachers, 1949-1951; co-director, Southwest Indian Arts Project (sponsored by the Rockefeller Foundation), University of Ariozna, 1959-1961; art director, Institute of American Indian Arts, 1962-? *Awards, honors:* Mr. New writes, referring to the period during which he established the Lloyd Kiva Studios in Scottsdale, Ariz., "During this period (I) was devoted to the problem: Can Indian craftsmen produce contemporary craft items for general use, enabling the craftsmen to earn a living, pursuing their crafts in a general society? This implies some understanding of design inspiration from Indian tradition, careful craftsmanship, fashion, and marketing. (My) 'Kiva Bags' (a craft item Mr. New created) have been marketed by outstanding fashion stores throughout the country. Top fashion publications have featured these and other Kiva fashions from time to time." Mr. New has attended various conferences relating to indigenous arts and crafts forms in the U.S. and Mexico. *Published work: Using Cultural Differences as a Basis for Creative Expression* (Institute of American Indian Arts, 1964).

NEWCOMB, WILLIAM W., Jr. 1921- (professor of anthropology)

Born October 30, 1921, Detroit, Mich. *Education:* University of Michigan, B.A., 1943, M.A., 1946, Ph.D., 1953. *Principal occupation:* Professor of anthropology, University of Texas, Austin, Texas, 1962-. *Home address:* 6206 Shoal Creek Blvd., Austin, Texas 78757. *Other professional post:* Director, Texas Memorial Museum, 1957-1978. *Military service:* U.S. Army Infantry, 1943-1946. *Memberships:* American Anthropological Association (Fellow);

Texas Archaeological Society. *Awards, honors:* Awards for *Indians of Texas,* Texas Institute of Letters, Dallas Public Library. *Interests:* American Indian ethnology, particularly Plains and Texas; culture change; primitive art; ethnographic field work with Delaware Indians; archaeological field work in Arkansas and Texas; rock art of the Texas Indians; ethnohistory of Wichita. *Published works: The Culture and Acculturation of the Delaware Indians* (University of Michigan Press, 1956); *The Indians of Texas* (University of Texas Press, 1961); *The Rock Art of Texas* (Univerity of Texas Press, 1967); *A Lipan Apache Mission, San Lorenzo de la Santa Cruz, 1762-1771,* with Curtis Tunnell (Texas Memorial Museum, 1969); *North American Indians: An Anthropological* (Texas Memorial Museum, 1974); *The People Called Wichita* (Texas Memorial Museum, 1976); *German Artist of the Texas Frontier, Richard Friedrich Petro* (University of Texas Press, 1978).

NEWMAN, HARRISON 1912- (writer)

Born April 17, 1912, Newark, Ohio. *Education:* Centre College, B.A., 1933. *Principal occupation:* Writer. *Home address:* 296 Pine St., Lockport, N.Y. 14094. *Awards, honors:* Honorary adoption into Turtle Clan, Tonawanda Band of Seneca Indians, 1933. *Interests:* American Indians; archaeology. *Published works: Primitive Peoples of Western New York,* and *The Iroquois,* both with Richard L. McCarthy (Buffalo and Erie County Historical Society).

NICKLASON, FRED 1931- (historian)

Born May 5, 1931, Swatara, Minn. *Education:* Gustavus Adolphus College, St. Peter, Minn., B.S., 1953; University of Pennsylvania, M.A., 1955; Yale University, Ph.D., 1967. *Principal occupation:* Historian. *Home address:* 6323 Utah Ave., N.W., Washington, D.C. 20015. *Affiliations:* Assistant professor, University of Maryland, College Park, Md., 1967-; director, Nicklason Research Associates, Washington, D.C., 1971-. *Military service:* U.S. Army, 1955-1957 (Research Analyst). *Mem-*

berships: American Historical Association; Western Historical Association; Southern Historical Association; American Studies Association; American Ethnohistorical Association. *Awards, honors:* American Philosophical Society Grant. *Interests:* American Indian policy; American Southwest travel.

NICHOLSON, MARY EILEEN
(Colville) 1924-
(tribal official)

Born March 1, 1924, Okanogan County, Wash. *Education:* St. Mary's Mission. *Principal occupation:* Member, Colville Business (Tribal) Council, Nespelem, Wash. *Home adress:* Route 1, Box 90, Tonasket, Wash. 98855. *Community activities:* Western Farmers Association; Agricultural Stabilization Conservation Service (committee member).

NICHOLSON, NARCISSE, Jr.
(Colville) 1925-
(tribal official)

Born February 5, 1925, Tonasket, Wash. *Education:* High school. *Principal occupation:* Tribal official. *Home address:* 618 S. Index, Omak, Wash. 98841. *Affiliation:* Former chairman, Colville Business (Tribal) Council, Nespelem, Wash. *Other professional post:* Recreation Development Committee, Grand Coulee and Coulee Dam Chambers of Commerce (executive committee). *Military service:* U.S. Army, 1943-1946 (European-African-Middle Eastern Service Medal; American Theatre Service Medal; Victory Medal; Good Conduct Medal).

NIELSEN, ANITA G. (Wampanoag) 1922-
(educational program supervisor)

Born June 21, 1922, Mashpee, Mass. *Education:* Massasoit Community College (two years). *Principal occupation:* Wampanoag educational program supervisor (teacher), Plimoth Plantation, Living Museum, Plymouth, Mass., 1983-. *Membership:* Wampanoag Tribal Council (life membership). *Awards, Honors:* Honorable Mention, Heard Museum; National Competition,

Contemporary Craft - Finger-Twined Bag. *Interests:* "Native tribal peoples' uses of natural resources—for food, shelter, clothing, crafts (i.e. basketry, mats, twining bags); would like to pursue research in natural native plants for dye."

NIMOHOYAH, SEKON (JIM) (Kiowa)
(Indian health service)

Education: University of Oklahoma, B.A., 1966, M.A. (Anthropology), 1972; University of Houston, B.S. (Optometry), 1976; University of Texas, School of Public Health, M.P.H., 1977. *Principal occupation:* Indian health service. *Home address:* P.O. Box 13, White Earth Ojibwa Nation, Ogema, Minn. 56569. *Affiliations:* Chief, Area Director of all Vision Care Programs in Minnesota, Michigan and Wisconsin for the Indian Health Service, White Earth, Minn. 56591. *Other professional post:* Consultant to Minnesota Chippewa Tribe on PL 94-437. *Military service:* U.S. Army, 1966-1968 (Sergeant E-5, Special Forces Group, Medic, Airborne Pathfinder, Jungle Expert; Bronze Star for Valor; two Purple Hearts, Vietnamese Service Ribbon, Presidential Unit Citation). *Memberships:* Association of American Indian Physicians, 1973-; American Optometric Association, 1972-; Beta Sigma Kappa Optemtric Honor Fraternity International, 1975-; Texas Optometric Society, 1973-; American Public Health Association, 1975-; U.S. Public Health Service Commissioned Officer Society, 1976-. *Awards, honors:* Better Vision Institute Scholarship, 1973-1975; Most Outstanding 2nd Year Vision Analysis Clincian, 1974;Public Health Teaching Fellowship, 1975-1976; Community Health Optometry Award, 1976; invited to lecture to Academy of Optometry and Physiological Optics, Public Health Section, December, 1975, on my grant and project, "Native American Vision Care Project to Navajo Nation." *Biographical source:* Who's Who in American Health Care (Hanover Publications). *Published articles:* "Vision Anomalies of Clinical Patients, Navajo Nation," 1975; "Vision Anomalies, A Demographic and Epidemiological Study of Cheyenne River Sioux Nation," 1977; "Anaphylactic Shock and Other Ocular Emergencies," with William R. Jones, 1975; among others.

NITSCH, TWYLAH HURD (Seneca) 1912-
(teacher, lecturer)

Born December 5, 1912, Irving, N.Y. *Education:* Empire State College, S.U.N.Y. at Buffalo. *Principal occupation:* Teacher, lecturer. *Home address:* 12199 Brant-Reservation Rd., Irving, N.Y. 14081. *Affiliation:* Founder and president, Seneca Indian Historical Society. *Interests:* "Lecturer devoted to the dissemination of the wisdom, prophecy and philosophy of the Seneca Nation; programs presented at home and away to this end. Showing through these programs and lectures how the ancient wisdom of the Senecas can enrich the lives and increase the awareness of other cultures in the present. Programs in Scotland, Ireland, England, Italy, Hawaii, Canada, Mexico, most of the U.S." *Biographical sources: Medicine Power,* and *Medicine Talk* by Brad Steiger; *Flight of the Seventh Moon* by Lynn Andrews (dedicated to Twylah Nitsch) (Human Dimension Institute, Columbus, N.C.). *Published works: Wisdom of the Senecas* (S.U.N.Y.-Dept. of Bilingual Education, 1979); *Entering Into the Silence—The Seneca Way,* 1976, *Language of the Stones,* 1980/1983, *Language of the Trees,* 1982, *Nature Chants and Dances,* 1984 (all published by The Seneca Indian Historical Society).

NOLEY, GRAYSON (Choctaw) 1943-
(director-Indian program)

Born September 4, 1943, Talihina, Okla. *Education:* Southeastern Oklahoma State University, Durant, B.A., 1969; The Pennsylvania State University, University Park, M.Ed., 1975, Ph.D., 1979. *Principal occupation:* Director, American Indian Leadership Program, Penn State University. *Home address:* 1443 North Allen St., State College, Pa. 16802. *Affiliations:* Director, American Indian Leadership Program, The Pennsylvania State University, Education Policy Studies, University Park, Pa., 1979-. *Other professional posts:* Assistant professor of education; assistant director, American Indian Special Education Teacher Training Program; director, American Indian Education Policy Center, Pennsylvania State University. *Military service:* U.S. Army,

1961-1964. *Community activities:* Partnership Coordinating Committee; Committee for Understanding Others (local school district); Minorities Committee (graduate record examination board), *Memberships:* American Educational Research Association; Comparative and International Education Society; National Indian Education Association. *Awards, honors:* Kellogg Foundation, National Fellowship Program, 1984-1987; participant, Phoenix Seminar, Penn State University, 1975; American Indian Ledership Program Fellowship, Penn State University, 1974-1979; Music Scholarship, Southeastern State University, Durant, Okla. *Interests:* "Federal policies on Native American education; drug and alcohol abuse in adolescent Native Americans; travel." *Published work:* Two chapters in *The Choctaw Before Removal* (Mississippi University Press, 1985); articles in various education journals and American Indian journals.

NORDWALL, CURTIS
(B.I.A. agency superintendent)

Affiliation: Superintendent, Papago Agency, Bureau of Indian Affairs, Sells, Ariz. 85634.

NORMAN, MARGARET JANE
(museum curator)

Affiliation: Curator, Seminole Nation Museum, P.O. Box 1532, Wewoka, Okla. 74884.

NORRIS, LEONARD
(director-Indian organization)

Affiliation: Director, Organization of the Forgotten American, 1020 Pine St., Klamath Falls, Ore. 97601.

NUVAYESTEWA, EVANGELINE (Tewa-Hopi) 1940-
(elementary teacher)

Born February 17, 1940, Keams Canyon, Ariz. *Education:* Phoenix College, A.A., 1961; Northern Arizona University. *Principal occupation:* First grade teacher,

Polacca, Ariz., 1971-. *Home address:* P.O. Box 637, Polacca, Ariz. 86042. *Community activities:* Save the Children Federation (advisor-secretary). *Award:* Outstanding Elementary Teachers of America, awarded by Gilbert Beers, Ph.D., director.

O

OANDASAN, WILLIAM (Yuki of the Covelo Indian Community) 1947-
(senior editor, poet)

Born January 17, 1947, Santa Rosa, Calif. *Education:* University of California, Santa Cruz, B.A., 1974; University of Illinois, Chicago, M.A., 1981; Vermont College, Montpelier, M.F.A., 1984. *Principal occupation:* Senior editor, poet. *Home address:* 2852 Sawtelle Blvd., #42, Los Angeles, Calif. 90064. *Affiliations:* Senior editor, *American Indian Culture and Research Journal,* American Indian Studies Center, U.C.L.A., Calif., 1980-; executive director, A Publications, Los Angeles, Calif., 1976-1984. *Other professional post:* Poet in residence at the Dorland Mountain Colony for writers, artists and composers. *Community activities:* California Arts Council (member of multicultural arts panel); A Writers Circle (member of board of directors); tutor for elementary and high school students for Indian centers of Los Angeles. *Memberships:* A Writers Circle; Native American Education Service; MLA; RMMLA; MELUS. *Awards, honors:* 1985 American Book Award from Before Columbus Foundation. *Interests:* "Traveled to Canada, Mexico and the Philippine Islands. Poet, writer, editor and publisher. (I) Compiled a bibliography of the tribes of the Round Valley Reservation in northern California for the D'Arcy McNickle Center for the History of the American Indian at the Newberry Library, and compiling a bibliography of the northern California Indian tribes for the American Indian Bibliography Series of Scarecrow Press. Consultant on American Indian affairs; poetry reading. *Published works: A branch of California Redwood* (UCLA-American Indian Studies Center, 1981); *Moving Island* (A Publications, 1984); *Round Valley Songs* (West End Press, 1984); editor, *American Indian Cul-*

ture and Research Journal (UCLA-American Indian Studies Center, 1980-); editor, *A,* a journal of contemporary literature, 1976-1984.

O'BRIEN, PATRICIA J. 1935-
(North American archaeologist)

Born April 1, 1935, Chicago, Ill. *Education:* University of Illinois, Urbana, B.A., 1962, Ph.D., 1969. *Principal occupation:* North American archaeologist. *Home address:* 1902 Blue Hills Rd., Manhattan, Kan. 66502. *Affiliation:* Professor of anthropology, Kansas State University, Manhattan, Kan., 1969-. *Community activities:* Kansas Antiquity Commission (member). *Memberships:* Society for American Archaeology; American Anthropological Association; Sigma Xi; American Association for the Advancement of Science. *Interests:* "Archaeological research in north-central Kansas, the Kansas City, Mo. area, the Quad City area in Illinois, and in the Yucatan, Mexico." *Published works: Formal Analysis of Cahokia Ceramics: Powell Tract* (Illinois Archaeological Survey Monograph No. 3, 1972); *Archaeology of Kansas* (Museum of Natural History, University of Kansas, 1984).

O'CONNOR, LEO
(B.I.A. agency superintendent)

Affiliation: Superintendent, Lower Brule Agency, Bureau of Indian Affairs, Lower Brule, S.D. 57548.

OESTREICHER, DAVID M. 1959-
(writer, salvage ethnographer, student, teacher)

Born December 5, 1959, New York, N.Y. *Education:* S.U.N.Y. at Purchase, B.A. (with honors), 1981; New York University, M.A., 1985; currently in graduate program at N.Y.U. *Principal occupation:* Writer, salvage ethnographer, student, teacher. *Home address:* 19 Forbes Blvd., Eastchester, N.Y. 10709. *Interests:* "Participated in government funded expedition lead by Nicholas A. Shoumatoff to visit the last remnants of the

Delaware (Lenape) Indians in Oklahoma, November, 1977. Thereafter, worked individually to record the culture and language of the Delaware. Much of the work is recorded on tapes, notes and video, and has been a major contribution to the Delaware Indian Resource Center at the Ward Pound Reservation in New York. His research comprises one of the main bodies of information on this vanishing tribe. Mr. Oestreicher has lectured widely on the subject of the Delaware Indians. He has taken part and helped arrange various symposiums and programs at Yale University, Tulsa University, Seton Hall, CUNY at Purchase, New York City Hall and elsewhere. He has appeared as a guest on WOR radio in New York with Ed and Pegeen Fitzgerald. David Oetreicher was a teacher for the Title IV American Indian Education Program in Mahwah, New Jersey for a period of two years. His students, members of the Ramapo Mountain Indian Tribe, studied Delaware language and culture with him. For seven years until her death in November of 1984, he worked intensely with Nora Thompson Dean, "Touching Leaves Woman," the last full-blooded traditionalist of the Unami Delaware. The results of the work are chronicled in a book that tells not only the tragic story of a tribe on the verge of extinction but also the human element involved in being the last of a people. The book is entitled *Conversations With Touching Leaves: Voices of the Lenape,* and will soon be published. Before her death in 1984, Touching Leaves blessed the manuscript and expressed the hope that "through this book my people will be remembered." Oestreicher has also been a consultant for films and book in connection with the Delaware Indians. Other interests include: ancient Near Eastern and Jewish history, poetry, classical and folk music, art, conservation, canoeing and the outdoors."

OFFICER, JAMES E. 1924-
(professor of anthropology)

Born July 28, 1924, Boulder, Colo. *Education:* University of Kansas, 1942-1943; University of Arizona, B.A., 1950, Ph.D., 1964. *Principal occupation:* Professor of anthropology, University of Arizona. *Home address:* 621 North Sawtelle Ave., Tucson,

Ariz. 85716. *Affiliations:* Information officer, Department of State, 1950-1953; instructor, University of Arizona, 1957-1960; associate commissioner, Bureau of Indian Affairs, 1961-1967; assistant to the Secretary of the Interior, 1967-1969; coordinator of international programs, University of Arizona, 1969-1976; professor of anthropoogy, University of Arizona, Tucson, Ariz., 1969-. *Community activities:* U.S. Representative, Interamerican Indian Institute (Mexico City), 1968-1978; Democratic Precinct Committeeman, 1970-1976. *Memberships:* Arizona Historical Society (board of directors); American Anthropological Association (Fellow), 1958-; Society for Applied Anthropology (Fellow), 1958-; Tucson Corral of the Westerners, 1969-(board of directors); Tucson Rotary Club, 1973-; Phi Beta Kappa, 1950-; Pacific Council on Latin American Studies, 1973-. *Awards, honors:* Distinguished Service Award, Department of the Interior, 1968; Quill and Scroll National Journalism Scholarship, 1942; Tucson-Mexico Goodwill Award, Tucson Trade Bureau, 1982; Creative Teaching Award, University of Arizona Foundation, 1983. *Interests:* "Social history of the Indians of the Americas; land tenure among pre-Columbian and contemporary Indian groups in Mexico, Chile, and the U.S.; Indian servitude in Spanish colonial America. Have lived among and worked with Indian and mextizo groups in Mexico and Chile; and have been closely associated with various Indian groups in the U.S. *Published works: Indians in School* (University of Arizona Press, 1956); *Anthropology and the American Indian* (Indian Historian Press, 1974); *Arizona's Hispanic Perspective* (Arizona Academy, Phoenix, 1982); *Hispanic Arizona, 1536-1956* (forthcoming-University of Arizona Press, 1987).

OKLEASIK, M. LaVONNE 1936-
(clerk, teacher)

Born July 4, 1936, Iowa. *Education:* Luther College, Decorah, Iowa, B.A., 1960. *Principal occupation:* Clerk, teacher. *Home address:* Box 356, Nome, Alaska 99762. *Affiliations:* Clerk, City of Nome, Alaska; financial secretary, education chairman, bible study teacher, Our Savior's Lutheran Church, Nome. *Other professional post:*

200

Private piano teacher. *Community activities:* Community alcohol program in Nome since 1980. "These activities have been with the Eskimo people. My husband is an Eskimo from Teller, Alaska. My desire for the people in this area is for them to be confident, to be happy about themselves and able to look at problems realistically and try to solve them in a satisfying manner. This I have tried to do in a volunterr basis through the church and the community alcohol program, working with all ages—children and elderly."

OLD COYOTE, BARNEY (Crow) 1923-
(government official, professor)

Born April 10, 1923, St. Xavier, Mt. *Education:* Morningside College, 1945-1947, *Principal occupation:* Government official, professor. *Address:* Montana State University, Bozeman, Mt. *Affiliations:* National Park Service, Crow Agency, Mt.; Bureau of Indian Affairs: Fort Yates, N.D., Crow Agency, Mt., Aberdee, S.D., Rocky Boys, Mt., Rosebud, S.D.; spccial assistant to the secretary, U.S. Department of the Interior, 1964-1969; assistant area director, B.I.A., Sacramento, Calif., 1969-1970; professor and director, American Indian Studies, Montana State University, Bozeman, Mt., 1970-. *Military service:* U.S. Army Air Corps, 1941-1945. *Community activities:* American Legion (post commander); Knights of Columbus (grand knight). *Memberships:* National Federation of Federal Employees (president, credit union; chairman, board of directors). *Awards, honors:* Special Achievement Award and Management Training Intern, Bureau of Indian Affairs; Doctor of Humane Letters (honor), Montana State University, 1968; Distinguished Service Award, U.S. Department of the Interior, 1968. *Interests:* Mr. Coyote writes, "Genberal interest is in the welfare of Indians and youth of all races, particularly in the education and general participation in the American way of life of all citizens during formative years; conservation of natural and human resources and the general appreciation of the aesthetic values of the American way of life."

OLD PERSON, EARL (Blackfeet)
(tribal chairman)

Affiliation: Chairman, Blackfeet Tribal Business Council, Browning, Mt. 59417.

OLDS, FOREST D. (Miami) 1911-
(farmer, stockman)

Born March 5, 1911, Miami, Okla. *Principal occupation:* Farmer, stockman. *Home address:* Route 2, Miami, Okla. *Affiliations:* Former chief, Miami Tribe of OKlahoma; clerk, North Fairview School Board. *Community activities:* Ottawa County Farm Bureau; Ottawa County Soil and Water Conservation District. *Memberships:* Oklahomans for Indian Opportunity (board of directors); Miami Co-Op Association, Inc. (former vice president). *Awards, honors:* Goodyear Tire and Rubber Co. Award for soil conservation, 1964. *Interests:* "Conservation; research into history of Miami Tribe; travel to former homesites of the Miami Tribe in Indiana, Kansas and Ohio; trip to Washington, D.C. to testify before Congressional committees as a representative of the Miami Tribe.

OLIVIERO, MELANIE BETH
(executive director-Indian Rights Association)

Affiliation: Executive director, Indian Rights Association, 1505 Race St., Philadelphia, Pa. 19102.

OLNEY, HIRAM
(B.I.A. agency superintendent)

Affiliation: Superintendent, Yakima Agency, Bureau of Indian Affairs, P.O. Box 632, Toppenish, Wash. 98948.

OLSON, MARTIN L. (Eskimo) 1927-
(commercial pilot, merchant)
Born June 24, 1927, White Mountain, Alaska. *Education:* Spartan School of Aeronautics, Tulsa, Okla.(aircraft and engine mechanic license, commercial pilot license). *Principal occupation:* Commercial pilot, merchant. *Home address:* 5 Front St., Golovin, Alaska 99762. *Affiliations:* Presi-

dent, Olson Air Service, Golovin, Alaska. *Military service:* U.S. Navy. *Community activities:* Bering Straits Native Association, Nome, Alaska (first vice president); Golovin Village Council (past president).

OPLER, MORRIS EDWARD 1907-
(professor emeritus)

Born May 16, 1907, Buffalo, N.Y. *Education:* University of Buffalo, B.A. (Sociology), 1929, M.A. (Anthropology), 1930; University of Chicago, Ph.D. (Anthropology), 1933. *Principal occupation:* Professor emeritus. *Home address:* 4006 Brookhollow Rd., Norman, Okla. 73069. *Affiliations:* Research assistant and associate, Department of Anthropology, University of Chicago, 1933-1935; assistant anthropologist, Bureau of Indian Affairs, 1936-1937; assistant professor of anthropology, Claremont College, 1938-1942; visiting and assistant professor, Howard University, 1945-1948; professor of anthropology and Asian studies, Cornell University, Ithaca, N.Y., 1948-?; director, Cornell University Indian Program, 1948-?; professor emeritus, Department of Anthropology, Cornell University. *Other professional post:* Associate editor, *Journal of American Folklore,* 1959-? *Memberships:* Sigma Xi; Phi Delta Kappa; Phi Beta Kappa; Alpha Kappa Delta; American Association of University Professors; American Sociological Association; American Anthropological Association (Fellow; executive board, 1949-1952; president-elect, 1961-1962; president, 1962-1963); Society for Applied Anthropology; Association for Asian Studies; American Ethnological Society; American Folklore Society (Fellow; first vice president, 1946-1947; executive committee, 1950; council member, 1957-1960). *Published works:* The Ethnobiology of the Chiricahua and Mescalero Apache, with E.F. Castetter (*Bulletin,* University of New Mexico Press, 1936); *Dirty Boy: A Jicarilla Tale of Raid and War* (American Anthropological Association, Memoirs No. 52, 1938); *Myths and Tales of the Jicarilla Apache Indians* (Stechert, 1938); *Myths and Legends of the Lipan Apache Indians* (J.J. Augustin, 1940); *An Apache Life-Way: The Economic, Social,* *and Religious Institutions of the Chiricahua Indians* (University of Chicago Press, 1941; University Microfilms; Cooper Square Publishers, 1966); *Myths and Tales of the Chiricahua Apache Indians* (Banta, 1942); *The Character and Derivation of the Jicarilla Holiness Rite* (University of Ne Mexico, 1943); *Childhood and Youth in Jicarilla Apache Society* (The Southwest Museum, 1946); among others.

ORR, CAROL (Colville) 1943-
(artist)

Born August 21, 1943, Republic, Wash. *Education:* University of Washington, B.A., 1965. *Principal occupation:* Freelance artist (portraits, murals, Indian theme paintings). *Awards:* Four-year scholarship, Colville Tribe; Federal Scholarship for four years (art studies, University of Washington); award, Philbrook Art Exhibit; second prize, Indian Show, La Grande, Oreg., 1965. *Interests:* Portraits on commission, book jackets and illustrations, feature illustrations, mural commissions on any theme, etc. Ms. Orr's work appears in various museums and private collections.

ORR, HOWELL McCURDY (Chickasaw) 1929-
(artist)

Born May 20, 1929, Washington, Okla. *Education:* Bacone College; Northeastern Oklahoma State College, B.F.A.; University of Tulsa, graduate work; University of Gto San Miguel Allende, Mexico, M.F.A.; University of the Americas, Mexico City; Univerity of Nevada, Las Vegas. *Principal occupation:* Artist. *Address:* New Mexico Highlands University, Las Vegas, N.M. 87701. *Affiliations:* Indian studies coordinator and assistant professor of art, New Mexico Highlands University. Las Vegas, N.M. *Military service:* U.S. Army, 1952-1954. *Awards, honors:* Numerous awards and exhibitions in the U.S. and Mexico. *Biographical sources: Indians of Today,* 4th Edition; *American Indian Painters* (Museum of the American Indian, 1968).

ORTIZ, ALFONSO ALEX
(San Juan Pueblo) 1939-
(professor of anthropology)

Born April 30, 1939, San Juan Pueblo, N.M. *Education:* University of New Mexico, B.A., 1961; Arizona State University, postgraduate studies, 1961-1962; University of Chicago, M.A., 1963, Ph.D., 1967. *Principal occupation:* Professor of anthropology. *Home address:* 830 E. Zia Rd., Santa Fe, N.M. 87501. *Affiliations:* Assistant professor, Pitzer College, Claremont, Calif., 1966-1967; assistant professor, associate professor, Princeton University, 1967-1974; professor of anthropology, University of New Mexico, Albuquerque, N.M., 1974-. *Other professional posts:* Charles Charropin visiting scholar, lecturer, Rockhurst College, 1977; chairman, Native American advisory group, Division of Performing Arts, Smithsonian Institution, 1975-1976; chairman, selection committee, Doctoral Fellowships for American Indians, Ford Foundation, 1975-1978; member, advisory council, National Indian Youth Council; board of directors, Social Science Research Council, 1972-1974; board of directors, Institute for the Development of Indian Law; member, advisory council, D'Arcy McNickle Center for the History of the American Indian, Newberry Library, 1972-, chairman, 1978-; member, National Humanities Faculty, 1972-; member, national advisory council, Institute of the American West, Sun Valley Center for the Humanities, 1976-; member, minority advisory panel, Danforth Graduate Fellowship Program, 1976-1979. *Memberships:* Committee for the Education of Women and the Minorities in the Sciences, NRC, 1975-; National Commission for the Minorities in Higher Education, 1979-1981; American Anthropological Association (Fellow); Royal Anthropological Institute (Fellow); Association on American Indian Affairs (director, 1967-; president, 1973-). *Awards, honors:* Roy D. Albert Prize for outstanding master's thesis in anthropology, University of Chicago, 1962-1963; keynote speaker, Second National Indian Education Conference, August, 1970; distinguished lecturer, Department of Religion, University of Oregon, Jan., 1973; distinguished Bicentennial professor, University of Utah, 1976;

Guggenheim Fellow, !975-1976; Fellow, Center for Advanced Study in the Behavioral Sciences, 1977-1978; Weatherhead scholar in residence, Navajo Community College, 1976; numerous other educational and civic panels. *Interests:* "Contemporary American Indian affairs; religion and society; space, time, color and number in world view; the oral tradition." *Biographical source: Who's Who in America.* Published works: *The Tewa World: Space, Time, Being, and Becoming in a Pueblo Society* (University of Chicago Press, 1969); editor, *New Perspectives on the Pueblos* (University of New Mexico Press, 1972); *To Carry Forth the Vine: An Anthology of Traditional Native American Poetry;* editor, southwest volumes, *Handbook of North American Indians,* Vol. 9 (Smithsonian Institution, 1980).

ORTIZ, ROXANNE DUNBAR
(Southern Cheyenne) 1938-
(professor-Native American studies)

Born September 10, 1938, Oklahoma. *Education:* San Francisco State University, B.A., 1963; U.C.L.A., M.A., 1965, Ph.D. (History), 1974. *Principal occupation:* Professor, Native American Studies, California State University, Hayward, Calif., 1974-. *Home address:* 275 Grand View Ave., San Francisco, Calif. 94114. *Community activities:* Staff member, International Indian Treaty Council (non-governmental organization in consultative status with U.N.). *Published work: The Great Sioux Nation* (Random House, 1977).

ORTIZ, SIMON J. (Acoma Pueblo) 1941-
(writer, poet, teacher)

Born May 27, 1941, Albuquerque, N.M. *Education:* Fort Lewis College, Durango, Colo., 1961-1962; University of New Mexico, Albuquerque, 1966-1968; University of Iowa, Iowa City, 1968-1969. *Principal occupation:* Writer, poet, teacher. *Home address:* P.O. Box 263, Mission, S.D. 57555. *Affiliation:* Instructor and co-director, Creative Writing Program, Sinte Gleska College, Mission, S.D. *Other professional posts:* Consulting editor to Pueblo of

Acoma, Institute of American Indian Arts Press, and Navajo Community College Press. *Military service:* U.S. Army, 1963-1966. *Community activities:* National Indian Youth Council (community organizer, 1970-1973); Adult Community Education, Acoma Pueblo, N.M. (director, 1975); AIM House, Oakland, Calif. (member of board, 1977-1979). *Memberships:* Americans Before Columbus Foundation (board of directors, 1978-); American PEN, 1980-. *Awards, honors:* Discovery Award (Creative Writing, 1970), Fellowship (Creative Writing, 1981), National Endowment for the Arts. *Interests:* "Avocational interests include listening to music, long distance running, travel. Places I've traveled include all of the areas of the U.S., including Alaska in 1979, 1981, and 1984; I traveled to Europe, including Holland, Belgium, and Germany. *Biographical sources:* "This Song Remembers" (article-interview)(Macmillan, 1980); "Coyote Said This" (biographical article)(University of Aarhus, Denmark, 1984); "I Tell You Now" (autobiographical article)(University of Nebraska Press, 1986). *Published works: Naked In The Wind* (Quetzal-Vihio Press, 1971); *Going For The Rain* (Harper & Row, 1976); *A Good Journey* (Turtle Island Press, 1977); *Howbah Indians* (Blue Moon Press, 1978); *The People Shall Continue* (Children's Press Books, 1978); *Fight Back* (INAD-University of New Mexico, 1980); *From Sand Creek* (Thunder's Mouth Press, 1981); *A Poem Is A Journey* (Pternandon Press, 1982); *Fightin'* (Thunder's Mouth Press, 1983); *Blue and Red* (Acoma Pueblo Press, 1983); *The Importance of Childhood* (Acoma Pueblo Press, 1983).

OTT, WILLIAM
(B.I.A. area director)

Affiliation: Eastern Area Director, Bureau of Indian Affairs, 1951 Constitution Ave., N.W., Washington, D.C. 20245.

OVERFIELD, THERESA 1935-
(professor of nursing; research professor of anthropology)

Born July 22, 1935, Buffalo, N.Y. *Education:* D'Youville College, Buffalo, N.Y., B.S.

(Nursing), 1958; Columbia University, M.P.H. (Public Health), 1962; University of Colorado, M.A. (Anthropology), 1972, Ph.D. (Physical Anthropology), 1975. *Principal occupation:* Professor of nursing, research professor of anthropology. *Home address:* 172 Braewick Rd., Salt Lake City, Utah 84103. *Affiliations:* Intinerant public health nurse, Alaska Department of Health, Bethel, Alaska, 1959-1961; nurse epidemiologist, Arctic Health Research Center, USPHS, Anchorage, Alaska, 1962-1965; nursing consultant, Colorado Department of Public Health, Denver, 1966-1969; research assistant professor, 1975-1976, assistant professor of nursing, 1976-1978, College of Nursing, University of Utah, Salt Lake City; associate professor, College of Nursing, Brigham Young University, Salt Lake City, 1978-1984; adjunct assistant and associate professor, 1976-1985, research professor, 1985-, Department of Anthropology, University of Utah, Salt Lake City; director of research, 1979-, professor, 1984-, College of Nursing, Brigham Young University, Salt Lake City. *Other professional posts:* Advisory board, 1978-1982, reviewer, 1979-, *Western Journal of Nursing;* reviewer, *Research in Nursing and Health. Community activities:* Western Commission on Higher Education in Nursing, Boulder, Colo. (research steering committee member, 1978-1982); Transcultural Nursing Conference Group, Utah Nurses Association, Salt Lake City (chairperson, 1978-1980); Salt Lake Indian Health Center, Inc. (advisory committee member and board of directors, 1981-1982); Veterans Administration Medical Center, Salt Lake City (nursing research committee member, 1982-; member, Health Services Research and Development Review Board, 1983-); Utah Nurses Association *Newsletter,* Salt Lake City, (committee on research, 1985-); various college and university committees. *Memberships:* American Nurses Association (Utah); Utah Public Health Association (board member, 1983-); American Association of Physical Anthropologists; Society for Medical Anthropologists; Human Biology Council; American Association for the Advancement of Science; Western Society for Research in Nursing; Council for Nursing and Anthropology; Society for the Study of Human Biology; American Public Health Association. *Awards, honors:* USPHS, Special Nurse Predoctoral Fellowships, 1969-1974; American Nurses Foundation, Inc. Grant for Pseudocholinesterase Silent Allele in Alaskan Eskimos, 1974; University of Utah, Demography Study Group, Grant for computer use on Eskimo data for fertility study, 1976-1977; *American Journal of Nursing,* Excellence in Writing Award, 1981; Brigham Young University, Womens Research Institute Grant and College of Nursing Research Grant, 1985. *Interests:* Racial variation; biomedical research; Eskimos—western Alaska; papers, lectures, workshops and conferences presented on the Alaskan Eskimo and the American Indian, too numerous to mention. *Published works:* Numerous articles in various professional journals.

OWENS, ROGER C. 1928-
(anthropologist, professor)

Born September 14, 1928, Port Arthur, Tex. *Education:* Michigan State University, B.A., 1953; University of Arizona, M.A., 1957; U.C.L.A., Ph.D. (Anthropology), 1962. *Principal occupation:* Anthropologist, professor. *Home address:* 54 Fort Hill Rd., Huntington, N.Y. 11743. *Affiliations:* Instructor, assistant and associate professor of anthropology, University of California, Santa Barbara, 1959-1967; professor of anthropology, Queens College, C.U.N.Y., Flushing, N.Y., 1967-. *Other professional post:* Curriculum development consultant, Holt, Rinehart and Winston, Inc., 1968-1977. *Military service:* U.S. Army, 1946-1947. *Memberships:* American Anthropological Association (Life Fellow); Current Anthropology (Associate); Sigma Xi (Fellow); numerous nonprofessional organizations devoted to topics in anthropology and Native American affairs. *Awards, honors:* National Science Foudnation Undergraduate Research Participation Award, 1961-1963; Research Grants, University of California, Santa Barbara, 1961-1966; Grant-in-aid, Holt, Rinehart and Winston, Inc., 1969-1971; Distinguished Teacher of the Year, Queens College, 1983-1984; Mellon Foundation Fellowship, Queens College, 1983-1984. *Interests:* American Indians; Latin America. *Biographical*

source: Who's Who in the East. Published works: Senior editor, *North American Indians: A Sourcebook* (Macmillan, 1967); "The Contemporary Ethnography of Baja, California, Mexico," chapter in *Handbook of Middle American Indians* (Tulane University Press, 1969); "American Indian Society and Culture: A Conspectus," in *Encyclopedia of Indians of the Americas,* Vol. 1 (Scholarly Press, 1974); *Native North Americans: The Anthropology of Americans Original Inhabitant* (Queens College Reprographics, 1977); "Indians, American," in *Academic American Encyclopedia* (Arete Publishing Co., 1980); *The Mountain Pai; An Ethnography of the Indians of Baja, California, Mexico* (typescript, 1984); among others; numerous papers on the American Indian read at meetings.

OWHI, HARRY (Colville) 1928-
(tribal officer)

Born November 14, 1928, Nespelem, Wash. *Education:* North Idaho Colege of Education; Kinman Business University; University of Ne Mexico. *Principal occupation:* Executive secretary, Colville Business (Tribal) Council, Nespelem, Wash. *Home address:* P.O. Box 324, Nespelem, Wash. *Military service:* U.S. Army, 1946-1947.

OXENDINE, THOMAS (Lumbee) 1921
(naval officer, government
information officer)

Born December 23, 1921, Pembroke, N.C. *Education:* Pembroke State College, B.A., 1948; Armed Forces Information School, 1966. *Principal Occupation:* Naval Officer and Government Information Officer. *Home Address:* 1141 North Harrison St., Arlington, Va. 22205. *Affiliations:* U.S. Navy, Naval Aviator, 1942-1947, Commander, 1951-1970; Public Information Officer, Bureau of Indian Affairs, Washington, D.C., 1970-. *Military Service:* Naval Aviator-World War II, United States Navy, 1942-1947 (Distinguished Flying Cross-Air Medal); Navy Jet Fighter Pilot, 1951-1960; Commanding Officer, Training Squadron Two, Naval Air Basic Training Command,

Pensacola, Florida, 1960-1962; Deputy Fleet Information Officer, Staff of the Commander-in-Chief, U.S. Pacific Fleet, 1962-1965; Public Affairs Officer, Commander Task Force 77, Gulf of Tonkin, 1965; Aviation Plans Officer/Director, Plans Division, Office of Information, Department of Navy, The Pentagon, Washington, D.C., 1965-1968; Public Affairs Officer, Naval Air Systems Command, Department of Navy, Washington, D.C., 1968-1970. *Memberships:* National Congress of American Indians; National Aviation Club; National Press Club. *Awards, Honors:* First Distinguished Alumnus Award, 1967, Pembroke State College; Athletic Hall of Fame, 1980, Pembroke State University; extensive press coverage as "First American Indian to complete Naval Aviation Cadet Flight Program." *Biographical Sources: Who's Who in Government; Who's Who in the East.*

P

PABLO, MATT
(museum director/curator)

Affiliation: Director/curator, Malki Museum, Inc., 11-795 Fields Rd., Morongo Indian Reservation, Banning, Calif. 92220.

PADILLA, JOE A. (Tesuque Pueblo)
(Pueblo governor)

Affiliation: Governor, Tesuque Pueblo, Route 11, Box 1, Santa Fe, N.M. 87501.

PADILLA, NICOLAS J.
(Rancheria chairman)

Affiliation: Chairman, Susanville Indian Rancheria Business Council, Drawer 'U', Susanville, Calif. 96130.

PALE MOON, PRINCESS
(president-Indian foundation)

Affiliation: President and executive director, American Indian Heritage Foundation, 6051 Arlington Blvd., Falls Church, Va. 22044.

PARASHONTS, TRAVIS N.
(Southern Paiute) 1953-
(director-Utah Indian affairs)

Born October 10, 1953, Cedar City, Utah. *Education:* Southern Utah State College, Ceadr City, B.A., 1979; University of Utah, Salt Lake City (Masters of Social Work candidate). *Principal occupation:* Director, Utah Division of Indian Affairs, 6220 State Office Bldg., Salt Lake City, Utah. *Home address:* 689 S. Pitford Dr., Centerville, Utah 84014. *Other professional posts:* Former tribal chairman, Paiute Tribe; American Indian Service, Brigham Young University, Provo, Utah (board member); American Indian Cultural Foundation, Page, Ariz. (board member); Indian Affiliates, Orem, Utah (board member). *Awards, honors:* Spencer W. Kimball Award for working with Indian people; Paiute Tribal Award for service as tribal chairman; Cedar City Chamber of Commerce Award. *Interests:* "I assisted the Paiute Tribe in getting federal recognition in 1980 and helped them get back 5,000 acres of land and established a 2.5 million dollar irrevocable trust fund for economic development." *Published work: Paiute Language—For Beginner* (Southern Utah State College, 1980).

PARENT, ELIZABETH ANNE
(Athabascan) 1941-
(associate professor)

Born January 12, 1941, Bethel, Alaska. *Education:* Harvard Graduate School of Education, M.Ed and CAS, 1972-1974; Stanford University, M.A. and Ph.D., 1974-1984. *Principal occupation:* Associate professor, American Indian Studies, San Francisco State University, 1600 Holloway Ave., San Francisco, Calif., 1980-. *Memberships:* Society for Values in Higher Education; American Association for Higher Education; National Indian Education Association. *Awards, honors:* Postdoctoral Fellow, American Indian Studies Center, U.C.L.A., 1985-1986; Ford Fellow; Danforth Fellow. *Interests:* American Indian education, history and politics; educational psychology; women's issues; child development and pedagogy. *Published work: The Educational Experiences of the Residents of Bethel, Alaska,* Ph.D. dissertation (Stanford University).

206

PARKER, ALAN
(president-American Indian
National Bank)

Affiliation: President, American Indian
National Bank, 1700 K St., N.W., Suite
2000, Washington, D.C. 20006.

PARKER, E.M., Sr. 1902-
(museum curator)

Born April 19, 1902, Hopkins, Pa. *Educa-
tion:* Detroit School of Lecturing; DuBois
Business College. *Principal occupation:*
Museum curator. *Home address:* 247 East
Main St., Brookville, Pa. 15825. *Affilia-
tions:* Sign writer, 1924-1967; curator, E.M.
Parker Indian Museum, Brookville, Pa.
Memberships: Genuine Indian Relics
Society; American Association of Museums; Pennsylvania Archaeological Society;
Ohio Archaeological Society. *Awards,
honors:* Adopted into the Seneca Indian
Wolf Clan, 1954; Cold Spring Longhouse;
received 25 trophies for displaying Early
Flint Locks from 1730-1847, plus displaying
fine Indian artifacts from western Pennsyl-
vania, Ohio, and western New York. *Inter-
ests:* "History of the American Indian,
particularly the Iroquois; American military
arms before 1900; interested in cultures of
the Ohio Basin, Ohio and Pennsylvania,
Adena and Hopewell, late B.C. and early
A.D. *Biographical sources: Who's Who in
Indian Relics,* Third Edition (Cameron
Park, 1972); *Dictionary of International
Biography; Men of Achievement; Commun-
ity Leaders and Noteworthy Americans;
Notable Americans of the Bi-Centennial
Era,* 1976.

PARKER, JOE
(B.I.A. agency superintendent)

Affiliation: Superintendent, Tahlequah
Agency, P.O. Box 828, Tahlequah, Okla.
74465.

PARKER, SHARON
(program coordinator)

Affiliations: Coordinator, American Indian
Lawyer Training Program, and chairwoman, National Institute for Women of

Color, 1712 N. St., N.W., Washington, D.C.
20036.

PARKER, WAYNE (Comanche) 1938-
(farmer and rancher)

Born September 23, 1938, Spur, Tex. *Edu-
cation:* West Texas State University, B.S.,
1961. *Principal occupation:* Farmer and
rancher. *Home address:* HCR 2, Box 127,
Ralls, Tex. 79357. *Affiliations:* Archaeologi-
cal curator, Pioneer Memorial Museum,
Crosbyton, Texas, and Ralls Historical
Museum, Ralls, Texas; editorial staff for
Artifacts Society of Ohio, and *La Tierra*
archaeological journal. *Community activi-
ties:* Cotton Gin Board (member); Museum
Board (member); Boy Scout Commission;
Crosby County Historical Commission.
Memberships: Texas Archaeological
Society; Central States Archaeological
Society; South Plains Archaeological
Society; Artifacts Society; Southern Texas
Archaeological Society (editorial board,
Journal). *Awards, honors:* Life Saving
Award signed by President Eisenhower;
"Best Committee Member," Texas Histori-
cal Commission, 1971; guest speaker at
"History Day at the Ranch," Matador
Ranch, 1984 and 1985; 4th cousin to Chief
Quanah Parker (Kwahadi Comanches).
Interests: "I have written over 95 articles
concerning Indian artifacts which have been
published throughout the U.S. (I) hunted
bull elk in Colorado for 20 years. *Biographi-
cal sources: Arrowheads and Projectile
Points; North American Indian Artifacts;
Selected Preforms, Points and Knives of the
North American Indians. Published works:
The Bridwell Site* and *The Roberson Site*
(Crosby County Museum Association, 1982
and 1986.

PARKS, DOUGLAS R. 1942-
(linguist)

Born August 28, 1942, Long Beach, Calif.
Education: University of California, Berke-
ley, B.A., 1964, Ph.D., 1972. *Principal occu-
pation:* Linguist. *Home address:* 8275 East
State Road 46, Bloomington, Ind. 47401.
Affiliations: Director, Title VII Program,
White Shield School District, Roseglen,
N.D. (three years); research associate,

Department of Anthropology, Indiana University, Bloomington, 1983-. *Other professional post:* Associate director, American Indian Studies Research Institute, Indiana University. *Memberships:* Plains Anthropological Society (board of directors, 1980-1982; president, 1982); American Anthropological Association; American Society for Ethnohistory. *Awards, honors:* American Council of Learned Societies Fellow, 1982-1983; Smithsonian Fellow (Smithsonian Institution, 1973-1974). *Published works: A Grammar of Pawnee* (Garland Publishing, 1976); *An Introduction to the Arikara Language* (Title VII Materials Development Center, Anchorage, Alaska, 1979); *Ceremonies of the Pawnee,* 2 Vols. (Smithsonian Institution Press, 1981); *Arikara Coyote Tales: A Bilingual Reader* (White Shield School, 1984); *An English-Arikara Student Dictionary* (White Shield School, 1986).

PARMAN, DONALD L. 1932-
(historian)

Born October 10, 1932, New Point, Mo. *Education:* Central Missouri State College, B.S., 1958; Ohio University, M.A., 1963; University of Oklahoma, Ph.D., 1967. *Principal occupation: Historian. Home address:* 614 Rose St., West Lafayette, Ind. 47906. *Affiliation:* Department of History, Purdue University, West Lafayette, Ind., 1966-. *Military service:* U.S. Army, 1953-1955 (Corporal). *Memberships:* Organization of American Historians; Western History Association; Agricultural History Society; American Society for Ethnohistory; Indian Association of Historians. *Interests:* "Main research interests are Navajo Indian history and twentieth century Indian affairs; main travels are in the Southwest and elsewhere in 'Indian Country'." *Biographical sources:* Directory of American Scholars, Vol. 1; *Dictionary of International Biography; Contemporary Authors. Published works:* Co-editor, *American Search,* 2 Vols. (Forum Press, 1973); *Navajos and the New Deal* (Yale University Press, 1976).

PARRA, DONNA C. (Navajo) 1941-
(counseling services)

Born September 7, 1941, Rehoboth, N.M. *Education:* University of New Mexico, B.A., 1970, M.A., 1974. *Principal occupation:* Counseling services. *Home address:* 819 Gonzales Rd., Santa Fe, N.M. 87501. *Affiliations:* Medical secretary, USPHS Indian Hospital, Gallup, N.M., 1961-1963, 1965; research assistant, National Institutes of Mental Health (Alcoholism Project: "A Community Treatment Plan for Navajo Problem Drinkers"), Family Service Agency, 1966-1968; director of counseling services, Institute of American Indian Arts, Sante Fe, N.M., 1976-. *Other professional posts:* Instructor of English, counselor, Gallup High School, 1970-1975; consultant to teach workshops on ethnic literature, 1973-1975, consultant, Curriculum Development, Native American Literature, 1974-1975, Gallup-McKinley County Schools; consultant, University of New Mexico Cultural Awareness Center, Albuquerque, N.M., 1975. *Community activities:* Santa Fe Public Schools Title IV Indian Education Parent Committee (officer); New Mexico Human Rights Commission Film Project (scholar and advisor); Ford Canyon Youth Center, Gallup, N.M. (advisory board); Gallup Inter-Agency Alcoholism Coordinating Committee (member); New Mexico International Women's Year Convention, June, 1977 (workshop leader on "Indian Women"). *Memberships:* League of Women Voters; New Mexico Association of Women Deans and Counselors; National Indian Education Association. *Awards, honors:* Four-year Navajo Tribal Scholarship recipient; Charles S. Owens Future Teachers of America Scholarship (Gallup High School, 1959); Sequoyah Indian Fellowship, University of New Mexico, 1970. *Interests:* "Ms. Parra writes, "I have great interest in the field of human rights, specifically issues of Indian sovereignty, because I feel that this whole issue relates directly to the survival of the American Indian as a group. I also have great interest in Native American literature and have developed a curriculum on this which has been adopted by the Gallup-McKinley County School district. I have been involved in alcohol research among the American Indian in a National Institutes of

Mental Health Project in Gallup, "A Community Treatment Plan for Indian Problem Drinkers" (1966-1968), and am presently directing a program I designed with students and staff of our educational facility.

PARRISH, RAIN (Navajo) 1944-
(museum curator)

Born February 8, 1944, Tuba City, Ariz. *Education:* University of Arizona, B.A. (Anthropology), 1967. *Principal occupation:* Museum curator. *Home address:* 704 Kathryn Ave., Santa Fe, N.M. 87501. *Affiliation:* Curator of American Indian Collections, Wheelwright Museum of the American Indian, Santa Fe, N.M., 1979-. *Membership:* New Mexico Museum Association. *Awards, honors:* Navajo Woman of the Year in the Arts, 1985; "10 Who Made a Difference," 1985 *The New Mexican Newspaper). Interests:* "Travel, art history, anthropology, sports, skiing, hiking, reading, writing." *Published works: The Stylistic Development of Navajo Jewelry* (Minneapolis Institute of the Arts, 1982); *Woven Holy People* (Wheelwright Museum, 1983); *The Pottery of Margaret Tafoya* (Wheelwright Museum, 1984).

PARSONS, NEIL (Blackfoot) 1938-
(art instructor)

Born March 2, 1938, Browning, Mt. *Education:* Montana State University. B.A. (Art), 1961, M.S. (Applied Art), 1964. *Principal occupation:* Art instructor. *Home address:* 513 Salazar, Santa Fe, N.M. 87502. *Affiliations:* Graphic illustrator, Boeing Aircraft Co.; art instructor, Institute of American Indian Arts, Santa Fe, N.M. *Military service:* U.S. Air Force Reserve, 1961-1964. *Memberships:* Pi Kappa Alpha; Delta Phi Delta; Montana Insitute of Arts. *Award:* Joseph Kinsey Howard Memorial Fellowship, 1963. *Exhibitions:* Museum of New Mexico—Contemporary American Indian Artists, and New Mexico Biannual; Bureau of Indian Affairs—Indian Invitations; Montana Institute of Arts State Festival; Seattle Art Museum; Atkins Museum, Kansas City, Mo.; and others. Work featured in collections of Dr. Verne Dusenberry, Lloyd Kiva New, Museum of the Plains Indian.

PARTON, PETRY D.
(B.I.A. agency superintendent)

Affiliation: Superintendent, Jicarilla Agency, Bureau of Indian Affairs, Dulce, N.M. 87528.

PATAWA, ELWOOD (Umatilla)
(tribal chairman)

Affiliation: Chairman, Umatilla Board of Trustees, P.O. Box 638, Pendleton, Ore. 97801.

PATTERSON, ELMA (JONES)
(Tuscarora) 1926-
(social worker)

Born August 13, 1926, Lockport, N.Y. *Education:* Cornell University, B.S., 1949; S.U.N.Y. at Buffalo, School of Social Work, M.S.W., 1963. *Principal occupation:* Social worker. *Home address:* 1162 Ridge Rd., Lewiston, N.Y. 14092. *Affiliations:* Supervisor of Field Services for Indians...A State Agency. *Community activities:* New York Iroquois Conference, Inc. (founder; past chairman; board of directors); Seneca Nation Educational Foundation, Inc. (trustee); Americans for Indian Opportunity (AIO)(past vice chairman and secretary-treasurer); Governor's Interstate Indian Council (chairman); New York State Library Services for Indians (advisory committee); Leisuretimers of the Tonawanda Indian Reservation (advisory committee); Niagara County Department of Social Services (advisory committee). *Memberships:* American Indian Social Workers Association (charter member).

PATTERSON, PATRICK *(Kemoha)*
(Apache-Seneca) 1914-
(artist)

Born December 29, 1914, Centralia, Ill. *Education:* University of Oklahoma, B.F.A. *Principal occupation:* Artist. *Home address:* 201 Main St., Woodward, Okla. 73801. *Affiliation:* Director, Woolaroc Museum (32 years). *Art:* Glass design; marble design; church murals. *Community activities:* Girl Scout Board. *Interests:* Autropological trips to Panama, Guatemala, Mexico and Peru.

Helped excvate Spiro Mound in Oklahoma. *Published work: Woolaroc Museum* (Frank Phillips Foundation, Inc.).

PAUL, BLAIR F. (Tlingit) 1943-
(lawyer)

Born July 5, 1943, Juneau, Alaska. *Education:* Western Washington State College, B.A., 1966; University of Washington Law School, J.D., 1970. *Principal occupation:* Lawyer. *Home address:* 6810 31 N.E., Seattle, Wash. 98115. *Community activities:* Pioneer Square Historic Preservation Board, 1974-; Washington Trust for Historic Preservation (president, 1976-1977); United Indians of All Tribes (board member, 1969-1971): Seattle Indian Health Board, 1970-1973; Seattle Indian Services Commission, 1972-1973. *Memberships:* American Trial Lawyers; Washington Trial Lawyers; Seattle-Kings County Bar.

PAYNE, SUSAN F.
(president-Indian Institute)

Affiliation: President, American Indian Archaeological Institute, Route 199, Box 260, Washington, Conn. 06793.

PAYTON, KENNETH L. (Cherokee)
1926-
(former B.I.A. agency superintendent)

Born August 3, 1926, Picher, Okla. *Education:* Oklahoma State University, B.S., 1949. *Affiliation:* Former superintendent, Mescalero Agency, B.I.A., Mescalero, N.M. *Military service:* U.S. Navy, 1944-1946. *Membership:* Soil Conservation Society of America.

PEACOCK, KENNETH 1922-
(musicologist)

Born April 7, 1922, Toronto, Can. *Education:* University of Toronto, Mus.B., 1943. *Principal occupation:* Musicologist. *Home address:* 540 Brierwood Ave., Ottawa, Can. *Affiliation:* Musicologist, National Museums of Canada, Ottawa, Ontario, Can. *Memberships:* Canadian Folk Music Society; Canadian Authors Association.

Interests: Musicological research among Indian tribes of Ontario, Manitoba, Saskatchewan, Alberta and British Columbia. *Published works: The Native Songs of Newfoundland,* 1960; *Survey of Ethnic Folkmusic Across Western Canada,* 1963; *Twenty Ethnic Songs from Western Canada,* 1965; *Music of the Doukhobors,* 1966 (all published by Queen's Printer); among others.

PEARSON, BILLY
(environmental health)

Affiliation: Director, Environmental Health, Indian Health Service, 5600 Fishers Lane, Rockville, Md. 20857.

PEASE-WINDY BOY, JANINE
(college president)

Affiliation: President, Little Big Horn Community College, P.O. Box 370, Crow Center, Education Commission, Crow Agency, Mt. 59022.

PEASLEY, BOB D. (½ Oglala-Omaha)
1932-
(artist)

Born August 23, 1932, Sioux City, Iowa. *Education:* Portland Community College; Clark College, Vancouver, Wash., 1964-1968; University of Washington, 1968-1971; University of British Columbia (art and anthropology studies). *Principal occupation:* Artist. *Affiliation:* Artist-master carver, director, Indian Arts Studies Centre, Estacada, Ore. *Other professional post:* Retired police chief. *Military service:* U.S. Army, 1950-1951. *Membership:* Indian Arts & Crafts Association, Albuquerque, N.M., 1975- (board of directors; appointed, National Security Chief, Oct., 1977). *Awards, honors:* Numerous awards for art from the following: New Mexico State Fair; Heard Museum; among others. *Interests:* "Contemporary production, instruction, research of all seven major tribal areas of Northwest Coast Indian art; theatrical arts of Indian productions, music ethnographical studies; participant in "The American West Program," Colorado State University,

1977 (first artist in residence, Fort Collins City Museum, Colo.); selected by Department of State and The African-American Institute for a cultural exchange trip to several countries in West Africa in 1979; family documents and antique photographs; family heir-looms. *Biographical sources:* Featured in "Community Focus, *Coloradoan* Newspaper (July 10, 1977); *The Indian Trader,* news Magazine (Sept. 1977). *Published work:* "Masks & Meanings of the Northwest Coast Indians" *(The Indian Trader,* December, 1977).

PENA, GILBERT M. (Pueblo)
(chairman-All Indian Pueblo Council)

Affiliation: Chairman, All Indian Pueblo Council, 2401 12th St., N.W., Albuquerque, N.M. 87197.

PENCILLE, HERBERT W. (Chemehuevi) 1927-
(businessman)

Born January 29, 1927, Los Angeles, Calif. *Education:* Los Angeles Valley College (Business Law). *Principal occupation:* Businessman. *Home address:* 12243 Hartland St., N. Holywood, Calif. 91605. *Affiliations:* General manager, Hydrex Termite Control Co. of Southern California, 1969-?; chairman, Chemehuevi Indian Tribal Council, 1972-?; Owner, Hydrex Pest Control Co., East San Fernando Valley, 1975-. *Military service:* U.S. Army Air Corps, 1946-1947. *Memberships:* National Pest Control Association, 1949- (director, 1962); Pest Control Operators of California, Inc. (president, 1959; director, 1959, 1960). *Awards, honors:* Man of the Year Award, Pest Control Operators of California, Inc., 1968. *Interests:* Private pilot license.

PENISKA, JOSEPH N. (Northern Ponca-Santee Sioux) 1932-
(junior college administrator)

Born April 27, 1932, Niobrar, Neb. *Education:* Deane College, Crete, Neb., B.A., 1956; University of South Dakota, M.Ed., 1961; College of Idaho; Arizona State University; Northeastern Oklahoma State University. *Principal occupation:* Director of

student affairs, The College of Ganada, Ganado, Ariz., 1974-. *Other professional posts:* College track coach, assistant professor and director of physical education; guidance director; director of Indian studies. *Military service:* U.S. Army, 1953-1955 (Corporal; Good Conduct Medal). *Memberships:* Arizona Native American Education Association; National Indian Education Association. *Awards, honors:* First American Indian Leadership Program Award, Arizona State University, 1970. *Published work:* Co-author, *American Indians in Higher Edcuation* (Region IV West, national Association of Student Personnel Administrators, 1977).

PENSONEAU, RALPH
(B.I.A. agency superintendent)

Affiliation: Superintendent, Southern Ute Agency, Bureau of Indian Affairs, P.O. Box 315, Ignacio, Colo. 81137.

PENTEWA, RICHARD SITKO (Hopi) 1927-
(artist)

Born April 12, 1927, Oraibi, Ariz. *Education:* Oklahoma A & M College, School of Technical Training, 1957. *Principal occupation:* Artist (painting and sculpture). *Home address:* P.O. Box 145, Oraibi, Ariz. *Military service:* U.S. Army (Koran Service Medal; Combat Infantry Badge; U.N. Service Medal; National defense Service Medal). *Membership:* Hopi Tribal Council. *Awards, honors:* Numerous awards for art. *Interests:* Art; travel.

PEPION, DONALD D. (Blackfeet)
(college president)

Born in Browning, Mt. *Education:* New Mexico State University, Las Cruces, B.S., 1974; Montana State University, Bozeman, M.Ed., 1979. *Principal occupation:* President, Blackfeet Community College. *Home address:* P.O. Box 812, Browning, Mt. 59417. *Affiliations:* Executive director, Blackfeet Housing Programs, Browning, Mt. (seven years); instructor, Native American studies, Blackfeet Community College, Browning, Mt. (four years). *Other professional posts:* Accountant; vocational education and training. *Community activities:* Blackfeet Developmental Disabilities (chairman); Blackfeet Indian Preference Committee (member). *Memberships:* American Indian Higher Education Consortium; National Indian Education Association.

PERATROVICH, ROY (Tlingit) 1910-
(former B.I.A. agency superintendent)

Born May 1, 1910, Klawock, Alaska. *Principal occupation:* Former superintendent, Anchorage Agency, Bureau of Indian Affairs, Anchorage, Alaska, 1968-? *Home address:* 1002 W. 30th #15, Anchorage, Alaska 99503. *Other professional posts:* Chief territorial tax collector, and director of land registration, Territory of Alaska. *Community activities:* Alaska Native Brotherhood (grand president, five terms; executive committee). *Memberships:* Federal Executive Committee, 1968-. *Awards, honors:* United Nations Fellowship; John Hay Whitney Fellowship; Boss of the Year, Anchorage Agency, 1976.

PEREAU, JOHN
(B.I.A. agency superintendent)

Affiliation: Superintendent, Rocky Boy's Agency, Bureau of Indian Affairs, Box Elder, Mt. 59521.

PEREZ, DAVID (Nambe Pueblo)
(Pueblo governor)

Affiliation: Governor, Nambe Pueblo, Route 1, Box 117-BB, Santa Fe, N.M. 87501.

PEREZ, FRANKLIN (RANDY)
(Assiniboine Sioux)
(tribal president)

Affiliation: President, Fort Belknap Community Council, Harlem, Mt. 59526.

PESHEWA, MACAKI (Shawnee) 1941-
(priest-Native American Church)

Born May 23, 1941, Spartanburg, S.C. *Education:* Spartanburg Junior College, S.C., A.A., 1966; Wofford College, Spartanburg, B.A., 1968; Furman University (postgraduate work, 1969); University of South Carolina (post-graduate work, 1971-1973); Univerity of Tennessee, Knoxville, M.S., 1974 (post graduate work, 1976-1977); Auburn University (post-graduate work, 1974-1975); Native Americas University (Doctorate-Human Development, 1975; Doctorate-System Theory of Life Science, 1976). *Principal occupation:* Priest-Native American Church, Knoxville, Tenn. *Home address:* P.O. Box 53, Strawberry Plains, Tenn. 37871. *Affiliations:* Chairman, Tennessee Indian Council, Knoxville, Tenn.; chairman and founder, Native American Indians in Media Corporation, Knoxville, Tenn.; chairman, Indian Historical Society of the Americas, Knoxville, Tenn. *Other professional post:* Chairman, Systems Theories and Human Development Corporation, P.O. Box 16115 U.T. Station, Knoxville, Tenn., 1977-. *Military service:* U.S. Air Force. *Commuity activities:* Work with off-reservation Indians; Tennesse Band of Cherokees (medicine man, business advisor); The American Indian Movement (urban Indian, Shawnee Nation); Native American Church of the Southeast (incorporator and head); National Lenape Band of Indians (medicine man); Consciousness Expansion Movement of Native Americans (president, chairman of the board); Tuskegee Alumni Foundation, Knoxville, Tenn. (advisory board); Knoxville Communications Cooperative (advisory board); Native Americas University (Southeast regional coordinator; board of regents; Indian Voters League. *Memberships:* Association of Humanistic Psychology; XAT-Amerian Indian Medicine Society; International Minority Business Council/Association; Phi Delta Kappa; Alpha Delta Omega. *Awards, honors:* Notary-at-Large, Tennessee; Key-to-City Certificate of Appreciation, Knoxville, Tenn.; Governor Recognitions: Appreciation Certificate, and Colonel-past and present administration. *Interests:* "Archives of living elders in America today; art collector for Native American Church collection. Parapsychology; existential philosophy; existential phenomenology; altered states of consciousness and metaphysics; herbal medicine; yoga; handball; travel. *Published work:* Film produced: *Amonita Sequoyah* (Native American Media, 1982); *Archives: Longest Walk for Survival,* 1981; *Archives: Black Elk, Sun Bear, AmyLee, Simon Brasquepe.*

PETERSON, FRANK R. (Aleut) 1940-
(former chief executive-
Alaska Native association)

Born July 9, 1940, Lazy Bay, Alaska. *Education:* Yale University; Sheldon Jackson Junior College, Sitka, Alaska, 1965-1966. *Home address:* Waldo Apartments, Kodaik, Alaska 99615. *Affiliation:* Former chief executive, Kodiak Area Native Association, Kodiak, Alaska, 1973-? *Other professional posts:* Ayakulik, Inc. (president, Regional Village Corporation); president, Association of Small Koniag Tribes; assemblyman, Kodiak Island Borough; advisory board member, Kodiak Baptist Mission; board of directors, Kodiak Public Broadcasting Corp. (KMXT); KANA Housing Authority; ex-officio, Kodiak Community College Advisory Board; ex-officio member, Board of Commissioners. *Military service:* U.S. Marine Corps, 1960-1965 (Corporal E-4).

PETERSON, GARY (Skokomish)
(tribal chairman)

Affiliation: Chairman, Skokomish Tribal Council, Route 5, Box 432, Shelton, Wash. 98584.

PETTIGREW, JACKSON D. (Chickasaw)
1942-
(artist, business manager)

Born July 2, 1942, Ada, Okla. *Education:* East Central University, Ada, Okla., B.A., 1973. *Principal occupation:* Artist, business manager. *Home address:* 3727 Governor Harris Dr., Ada, Okla. 74820. *Affiliations:* Owner, Native American Arts (retail-/wholesale), Ada, Okla., 1984-. *Other professional post:* Chairman of the board, First American Foundry Arts, Inc. (art bronze), Ada, Okla. *Community activities:* Teach art classes for young people, J.O.M. Indian pro-

gram. *Membership:* Southern Oklahoma Artist Association. *Interests:* "Artistic growth and sharing concepts with young people who are interested in art as a career. Also interested in civil rights. I was an equal opportunity specialist at the Dallas Regional Office of Civil Rights, Dallas, Tex., 1973-1979. I was also vice chairperson for the Regional Indian Affairs Council from 1974-1978. We served as an advocate for Native Americans in Region VI and the nation. Other interests include: silversmithing, painting and sculpturing. I have competed in various national juried art shows."

PHILEMON, HENRY, Sr. (Potawatomi)
(tribal chairman)

Affiliation: Chairman, Hannahville Indian Community Council, Route 1, Community Center, Wilson, Mich. 49896.

PHILLIPS, GEORGE HARWOOD 1934-
(professor of history)

Born January 27, 1934, San Diego, Calif. *Education:* San Diego State University, B.A. (English), 1959; University of California, Los Angeles, M.A. (African History), 1967, Ph.D. (American History), 1973. Ph.D. dissertation: *Indian Resistance and Cooperation in Southern California: The Garra Uprising and Its Aftermath.* *Principal occupation:* Professor of history. *Home address:* 1065 8th St., Boulder, Colo. 80302. *Affiliations:* Lecturer in history, University of West Indies, Jamaica, 1969-1971; lecturer in Afro-Ethnic Studies, Fullerton State University, Calif., 1972-1973; acting assistant professor of history, U.C.L.A., 1973-1975; visiting lecturer in history, 1977-1978, assistant professor of history, 1978-1981, associate professor of history, University of Colorado, Boulder, 1981-. *Other professional posts:* Contributing editor, *The Journal of California and Great Basin Anthropology;* board of editors, *Pacific Historical Review. Military service:* U.S. Marine Corps, 1954-1956. *Memberships:* American Historical Association (Pacific Coast Branch). *Published works: Chiefs and Challengers: Indian Resistance and Cooperation in Southern California* (University of California-Berkeley Press, 1975); *The*

Enduring Struggle: Indians in California History (Boyd & Fraser, 1981). Articles: "The Indian Paintings from Mission San Fernando: An Historicl Interpretation" *(The Journal of California Anthropoogy,* Summer, 1976); "Indians and the Breakdown of Spanish Mission System in California" *(Ethnohistory,* Fall, 1974); "Indians in Los Angeles, 1781-1875: Economic Integration, Social Disintegration" *(Pacific Historical Review,* August, 1980).

PHILP, KENNETH 1941-
(professor of history)

Born December 6, 1941, Pontiac, Mich. *Education:* Michigan State University, B.A., 1963, Ph.D., 1968; University of Michigan, M.A., 1964. *Principal occupation:* Professor of history, University of Texas, Arlington, 1968-. *Memberships:* American Historical Association; Western History Association; Organization of American Historians. *Interests:* American Indian history; federal Indian policy. *Published works:* Co-editor, *Essays on Walter Prescott Webb* (University of Texas Press, 1976); *John Collier's Crusade for Indian Reform* (University of Arizona Press, 1977); editor, *Indian Self-Rule: From Roosevelt to Reagan* (Howe Brothers, 1986).

PHOENIX, ANDREW (Paiute)
(tribal chairman)

Affiliation: Chairman, Cedarville Community Council, P.O. Box 142, Cedarville, Calif. 96104.

PICOTTA, ALVIN
(B.I.A. agency superintendent)

Affiliation: Superintendent, Michigan Agency, Bureau of Indian Affairs, Federal Square Office Plaza, P.O. Box 884, Sault Ste. Marie, Mich. 49783.

PICO, ANTHONY (Diegueno)
(tribal spokesman)

Affiliation: Spokesman, Viejas Tribal Committee, P.O. Box 908, Alpine, Calif. 92001.

PIERCE, LYMON
(director-Indian center)

Affiliation: Director, Los Angeles Indian Center, Inc., 1610 West Seventh St., 3rd Floor, Los Angeles, Calif. 90017.

PIETROFORTE, ALFRED 1925-
(speech instructor)

Born March 25, 1925, Philadelphia, Pa. Education: College of the Sequoias, A.A., 1952; Fresno State College, B.A., 1954, M.A., 1961. *Principal occupation:* Instructor in speech and general semantics, College of the Sequoias. *Home address:* 2113 S. Church St., Visalia, Calif. *Interests:* English; public speaking; general semanitcs; American folk music—especially the music of the California Indians. Mr. Pietroforte writes, "My publication, *Songs of the Yokuts and Paiutes,* took two years to complete. This meant extensive travel to a number of Indian reservations and rancherias as well as visiting informants who have left the reservations and have made their homes in the cities and towns of California."

PIGSLEY, DELORES (Siletz)
(tribal chairwoman)

Affiliation: Chairwoman, Confederated Tribes of Siletz Indians Tribal Council, P.O. Box 549, Siletz, Ore. 97380.

PINKHAM, ALLEN V. (Nez Perce)
(tribal chairman)

Affiliation: Nez Perce Tribal Executive Committee, P.O. Box 305, Lapwai, Idaho 83540.

PINO, AUGUSTIN (Zia Pueblo)
(Pueblo governor)

Affiliation: Governor, Zia Pueblo, General Delivery, San Ysidro, N.M. 87053.

PINTO, TONY J. (Diegueno)
(tribal chairman)

Affiliation: Cuyapaipe General Council, P.O. Box 187, Campo, Calif. 92006.

PLUMMER, EDWARD O.
(B.I.A. agency superintendent)

Affiliation: Superintendent, Eastern Navajo Agency, Bureau of Indian Affairs, P.O. Box 328, Crownpoint, N.M. 87313.

POLESE, RICHARD 1941-
(editor)

Born November 16, 1941, Berkeley, Calif. *Education:* San Jose State College, 1959-1961; Hanover College, Hanover, Ind., B.A., 1962. *Principal occupation:* Editor. *Home address:* P.O. Box 1295, Santa Fe, N.M. 87501. *Affiliations:* Editor, *El Palacio,* Southwestern Quarterly; book editor, Museum of New Mexico Press, 1969-. *Other professional posts:* Columnist for the Santa Fe *Reporter. Awards, honors:* Edited and designed the award-winning book, *Music and Dance of the Tewa Pueblos,* by Dr. Gertrude Kurath. *Interests:* Mr. Polese has written and edited publications on the Southwest and its people since 1962. These include several articles in *El Palacio* magazine, and editing and designing of several books and is recognized as an authority on the New Mexico Zia sun symbols, its origins and variations. *Published works: Original New Mexico Cookery,* 1965; editor, *Pueblo Pottery of New Mexico Indians,* 1977; editor, *Music and Dance of the Tewa Pueblos,* 1969; editor, *In Search of Maya Glyphs,* 1970; editor, *Navajo Weaving Handbook,* 1977. All published by Museum of New Mexico Press.

POOCHA, FRITZ T. (Hopi) 1933-
(school administrator)

Born February 26, 1933, Polacca, Ariz. *Education:* Arizona State University, B.A., 1961; Penn State University, M.A., 1971. *Principal occupation:* School administrator. *Home address:* P.O. Box 1247, Tuba City, Ariz. 86045. *Affiliations:* Teacher, Tuba City Boarding School, 1961-1971; principal, Polacca Day School, Polacca, Ariz., 1971-1975; principal, Moenkopi Day School, Tuba City, Ariz., 1975-. *Military service:* U.S. Army, 1953-1955 (Corporal-79th Army Engineer, Korean Conflict). *Community activities:* American Legion (special services officer, 1971-); V.F.W., 1974-. *Inter-ests:* Mr. Poocha writes, "Bilingual and bicultural education; minorities have languages that are structured differently and consist of sounds not found in the English language. In teaching the English language, thought process must be changed. Cultural values are perceived differently."

POOLAW, LINDA S. (Delaware-Kiowa) 1942-
(tribal cultural consultant, writer-playwrite)

Born April 8, 1942, Lawton, Okla. *Education:* University of Sciences and Arts of Oklahoma, Chickasha, B.A. (Sociology), 1974; University of Oklahoma (two years Masters work in Communications). *Principal occupation:* Tribal cultural consultant, Delaware Tribe of Western Oklahoma, Anadarko, Okla. *Home address:* P.O. Box 986, Anadarko, Okla. 73005. *Other professional post:* Playwrite. *Community activities:* Salvation Army, Caddo County (chairperson); Delaware Tribe of Western Oklahoma (treasurer); Riverside Indian School Board (vice president); American Indian Exposition (vice president). *Memberships:* Indian and Western Arts Association (vice president). *Interests:* "Writing fiction and history about American Indians. (I) have traveled coast to coast to develop relationships with tribes. In 1986, I plan to research and write a book on my deceased father's work in photography, "50 Years of Life on the Southern Plains," (Horace Poolaw)." *Plays:* "Skins," 1974; "Happiness Is Being Married to a White Woman," and "Written, Spoken and Unspoken Word" (University of Oklahoma Press, 1982); "The Day the Tree Fell," children's play (American Indian Institute, Norman, Okla., 1983).

POPOVI DA (Tewa Pueblo) 1922-
(potter)

Born April 10, 1922, Santa Fe, N.M. *Education:* Canyon School of Art. *Principal occupation:* Potter. *Home address:* San Ildefonso Pueblo, Santa Fe, N.M. 87501. *Military service:* U.S. Army, 1943-1946 (Good Conduct Medal; special recognition for service under the Manhattan Engineers). *Community activities:* San Ildefonso Pueblo (governor); All-Pueblo Indian Council (chairman); New Mexico State Art Commission (board of directors). *Memberships:* New Mexico Assocaition on Indian Affairs (board of directors); Gallup Inter-Tribal Ceremonial Association (board of directors). *Awards, honors:* National Indian Arts Council, Scottsdale, Ariz.; Inter-Tribal Ceremonial; New Mexico Craft Fair; Philbrook Museum, Tulsa, Okla.; Museum Fur Volkerkunde, Germany; among others. *Interests:* "Preservation of traditional art and culture of the Pueblos."

POPE, JERRY L. (Shawnee) 1941-
(artist)

Born April 26, 1941, Greenfield, Ind. *Education:* John Heron School of Art; Indiana University, B.F.A., 1964. *Principal occupation:* Artist. *Affiliations:* Curator, American Indian People's Museum, Indianapolis, Ind.; editor, *Tosan,* American Indian People's News, Indianapolis, Ind.; principal chief, United Remnant Band, Shawnee nation of Indiana, Ohio, Kentucky and Pennsylvania; director, Three Feather Society (Native-professional-social organization). *Other professional post:* Assisted in the compilation of Smithsonian Institution's list of native publications. *Memberships:* League of Nations, Pan-American Indians; National Association of Metis Indians; Three Feather Society (director); Mide Widjig, Grand Medicine Lodge Brotherhood, Albuquerque, N.M. *Awards, honors:* First Prize, national Exhibition of Small Paintings; selected to preside over and organize dedication of world's largest collection of Cuna Indian art, Dennison University, Granville, Ohio, 1972; among others. *Interests:* Mr. Pope writes, "1. Professional Native artist, by voction; 2. editing and publishing of the Inter-Tribal Native publiction, *Tosan;* 3. rebuilding the United Remnant Band of the Shawnee Nation, beginning in 1970 with seven persons; we now have reestablished all twelve clans; 4. re-education of my people in traditional ways, instilling due pride in knowledge of their birthright; 5. work with in-prison Native groups." *Published work: Native Publications in the United States and Canada* (Smithsonian Institution, 1972).

PORTER, FRANK WILLIAM, III 1947-
(ethnohistorian)

Born July 9, 1947, Charleston, W.V. *Education:* University of Maryland, M.A., 1973, Ph.D., 1978. *Principal occupation:* Ethnohistorian. *Home address:* 409 Ridge Rd., Gettysburg, Pa. 17325. *Affiliation:* Director, American Indian Research and Resource Institute, Gettysburg College, Gettysburg, Pa. 17325. *Military service:* U.S. Air Force, 1967-1971. *Memberships:* American Society of Ethnohistory; Maryland Historical Society. *Awards, honors:* Phi Alpha Theta Award, 1973. *Interests:* Photography, woodworking, oil painting, organic gardening, book collecting. *Published works: Indians in Maryland and Delaware* (Indiana University Press, 1979); *Maryland Indians* (Maryland Historical Society, 1983); *Strategies for Survival* (Greenwood Press, 1986); *In Pursuit of the Past* (Scarecrow Press, 1986).

POWELL, DICK & DONNA 1934-, 1939-
(Indian store owner/operators)

Born (Dick) February 13, 1934, Oakland, Calif.; (Donna) October 6, 1939, Sacramento, Calif. *Principal occupation:* Owner/operator, Bear Track Trader, Ludington, Mich., 1976-. *Military service:* (Dick) U.S. Army, 1956-1958 (1st Sergeant). *Membership:* Indian Arts and Crafts Association, 1976-. *Interests:* "We have traveled throughout the Southwest extensively in the 1960-1970 period. Now that we have our own retail store we hand select all merchandise we sell, and usually are not able to go more than once a years to the reservation area."

POWERS, MARIA N. 1938-
(anthropologist)

Born January 8, 1938, Cranston, R.I. *Education:* Brooklyn College, C.U.N.Y., B.A. (Psychology; magna cum laude), 1973; Rutgers University, M.A. (Anthropology), 1979, Ph.D. (Anthropology; dissertation: *Oglala Women in Myth, Ritual, and Reality), 1982. *Principal occupation:* Anthropologist. *Home address:* 74 Stillwell Rd.,

Kendall Park, N.J. 08824. *Affiliation:* Visiting research associate, Institute for Research on Women, Rutgers University, New Brunswick, N.J., 1983-. *Other professional posts:* Associate editor, *Powwow Trails: American Indians, Past and Present,* Somerset, N.J., 1964-1966; consultant, Title IV Bilingual Health Program, Pine Ridge Indian Reservation, Pine Ridge, S.D., Summer, 1976; consultant, Psychiatric Nursing Program, University of South Dakota and U.S. Public Health Service satellite program, Oglala Sioux Community, Pine Ridge Reservation, Summer, 1976; consultant, Lakota Culture Camp (program evaluation for Dept. of Special Education, State of S.D.), Pine Ridge Indian Reservation, Summer, 1980; member of thesis committee in Psychiatric Nursing, Rutgers University—thesis title: *An Exploratory Study of Mentoring Relationships Among Indian Women in the Profession of Nursing,* 1982; also thesis committee in anthropology—Ph.D. thesis entitled: *Comanche Belief and Ritual,* 1985. *Memberships:* American Anthropological Association; Society for Medical Anthropology; Society for Visual Anthropology; American Folklore Society; American Ethnological Society; Philadelphia Anthropological Society; Society for Ethnomusicology; Nebraska State Historical Society; American Dance Therapist Association; American Craftsman's Council; Actor's Equity; American Federation of Television and Radio Artists. *Fieldwork:* Pine Ridge, South Dakota, Oglala ("Sioux"), also various tribes of New Mexico, Arizona, Oklahoma and Wyoming; urban U.S. "I have done extensive anthropological research among the Oglala Lakota on the Pine Ridge Indian Reservation in South Dakota. A major part of the research focused on native subsistence, food procurement, preparation, storage, distribution, and nutrition. I also studied native therapeutic techniques, particularly treatment of psychosomatic disorders." *Awards, honors:* Wenner-Gren Foundation Grant-in-aid, Summer, 1980 (field research on the relationship of Oglala traditional women's roles to social structure); National Endowment for the Humanities, Research Assistant on "Oglala Music and Dance," September, 1980 - August, 1982, January, 1983 - December, 1983; Douglass Fellows Grant for Research on photo-

graphs of American Indian women, Spring, 1983, 1984; National Endowment for the Humanities, Planning Grant: principal investigator, "Lakota Women: A Photographic Retrospective," January, 1985 - December, 1985; Minnesota Historical Society, grant for field research on Lakota medicine, Summer, 1985. *Interests:* "American Indians, particularly Northern Plains, urban U.S.; intercultural health care systems; anthropology of gender, medicine, art, and dance." Dance: "have appeared in numerous Broadway and off-Broadway shows; on major network television shows; taught dance." American Indian art: "have studied traditional crafts among the Sioux and Comanches and am proficient in various techniques of American Indian beadwork, quillwork, and ribbonwork." *Papers presented:* "Images of American Indian Women: Myth and Reality," Rome, Italy, 1984, tour in West Germany-1985; "Symbols in Contemporary Oglala Art," Vienna, Austria; "Workshop on American Indian Music and Dance" (with William K. Powers), Budapest, Hungary, 1985; "Stereotyping American Indians," Cologne, West Germany, 1985; "Native American Motherhood: A View From the Plains," Rutgers University, 1985; among others. *Published works:* Co-editor, *Lakota Wicozanni-Ehank'ehan na Lehanl (Lakota Health Traditional and Modern),* three volumes plus teacher's guide (Oglala Sioux Community College, 1977); "Metaphysical Aspects of an Oglala Food System," in *Food and the Social Order* (Russell Sage Foundation, 1984); *Oglala Women: Myth, Ritual, and Reality* (University of Chicago Press, 1986); "Puting on the Dog: Ceremoniousness in an Oglala Stew," with William K. Powers, in *Natural History* (American Museum of Natural History-in press); *Lakota Foods,* with William K. Powers (in preparation); *Lakota Medicine* (Minnesota Historical Society Press-in preparation).

POWERS, WILLIAM K. 1934-
(professor of anthropology, journalist)

Born July 31, 1934, St. Louis, Mo. *Education:* Brooklyn College, B.A. (summa cum laude, honors in anthropology), 1971; Wesleyan University, M.A. (Anthropology; thesis: *Yuwipi Music in Cultural Context*), 1972; University of Pennsylvania, Ph.D. (Anthropology; dissertation: *Continuity and Change in Oglala Religion*). *Principal occupation:* Professor of anthropology, journalist. *Home address:* 74 Stillwell Rd., Kendall Park, N.J. 08824. *Affiliations:* Associate editor, *American Indian Tradition, 1960-1962; editor and publisher, Powwow Trails,* 1964-1966; consulting editor, *American Indians Then and Now Series* (G.P. Putnam's Sons), 1968-; instructor, North American Indian music and dance, Wesleyan University, 1971-1972; teaching fellow, 1972-1973, lecturer, 1973-1977, (North American Indians),University of Pennsylvania; visiting lecturer, assistant professor and acting chairman, Department of Anthropology, Rutgers University, New Brunswick, N.J., 1974-. *Fieldwork:* Primarily among the Oglala Sioux, Pine Ridge, South Dakota, 1966-; also various tribes in New Mexico, Arizona, Oklahoma and Wyoming. *Grants and fellowships:* Research in American Indian religion, linguistics, and music, American Philosophical Society, 1966, 1967, 1977; among others. *Awards, honors:* Award of Excellence in Juvenile Literature, New Jersey State Teachers of Enblish, 1972, 1973; Faculty Merit Award, Rutgers University, 1977; among others. *Memberships:* American Anthropological Association; Society for Applied Anthropology; Washington Anthropological Society; Philadelphia Anthropological Society; Society for Ethnomusicology; Indian Rights Association (director, 1977-?). *Interests:* North American Indian studies—historical and contemporary Indian affairs; urban U.S.; social organization; comparative religion; history of anthropology; sociolinguistics; ethnomusicology; culture change. *Published works: Indian Dancing and Costumes* (G.P. Putnam's Sons, 1966); *Young Brave* (For Children, Inc., 1967); *Crazy Horse and Custer* (For Children, Inc., 1968); *Indians of the Northern Plains* (G.P. Putnam's Sons, 1969); *The Modern Sioux: Reservation Systems and Social Change* (University of Nebraska Press, 1970); *Indians of the Southern Plains* (G.P. Putnam's Sons, 1971); *Continuity and Change in the American Family,* with Marla N. Powers (Dept. of HEW); *Indians of the Great Lakes* (G.P. Putnam's

Sons, 1976); co-author, *Lakota Wicozani - Ehank'ehan na Lehanl* (Indian Health- Traditional and Modern), 1976; *Oglala Religion* (University of Nebraska Press, 1977); *Lakota Foods,* with Marla N. Powers (in preparation); numerous papers, articles in scholarly journals, notes, book reviews, abstracts, etc.

POWLESS, PURCELL (Oneida)
(tribal chairman)

Affiliation: Chairman, Oneida Executive Committee, P.O. Box 365, Oneida, Wis. 54155.

PRESCOTT, MICHAEL (Sioux)
(tribal president)

Affiliation: President, Lower Sioux Indian Community Council, RR 1, Box 308, Morton, Minn. 56270.

PRESS, DANIEL S.
(tribal employment)

Affiliation: General counsel, Council on Tribal Employment, 918 16th St., N.W., Suite 503, Washington, D.C. 20006.

PRICE, B. LEIGH 1939-
(attorney)

Born June 15, 1939, Waco, Tex. *Education:* University of California, Berkeley, B.A., 1961; Yale University Law School, J.D., 1972. *Principal occupation:* Attorney. *Home address:* 6705 Tomlinson Terrace, Cabin John, Md. 20818. *Affiliation:* American Indian coordinator, Environmental Protection Agency, Washington, D.C. *Other professional post:* Visiting professor, Arizona State College of Law, 1985-1986. *Military service:* U.S. Marine Corps, 1966-1969 (Captain; Vietnam Service Medal). *Memberships:* New Mexico State Bar Association. *Awards, honors:* A&O Distinguished Service Award, 1981. *Interests:* "Indian law and environmental law; design and development of pollution control programs for tribes and state governments; land use; land rcordation and registration."

PRICE, FRANK
(president-Alaskan Native
organization

Affiliation: President, Thirteenth Regional Corporation, 4241 21st Ave. West, Suite 100, Seattle, Wash. 98199.

PRICE, JOHN A. 1933-
(professor of anthropology)

Born February 16, 1933, Merced, Calif. *Education:* University of Utah, B.A., 1959, M.A., 1962; University of Michigan, Ph.D., 1967. *Principal occupation:* Professor of anthropology, York University, Downsview, Ontario, Can. *Other professional posts:* Editor, *Canadian Journal of Native Studies;* editor, Canadian Society for Applied Anthropology. *Military service:* U.S. Army, 1952-1955 (Sergeant; Korean Battle Ribbon). *Interests:* Computer programming. *Published works: Native Studies: American & Canadian Indians* (McGraw-Hill-Ryerson, 1978); *Indians of Canada* (Prentice-Hall-Canada, 1979); *The Washo Indians* (Nevada State Museum, 1980).

PRINTUP, MARIBEL
(B.I.A. Indian education)

Affiliation: Indian Education, Bureau of Indian Affairs, 1951 Constitution Ave., N.W., Washington, D.C. 20245.

PRUCHA, FRANCIS PAUL 1921
(professor of history)

Born January 4, 1921, River Falls, Wis. *Education:* River Falls State College, B.S., 1941; University of Minnesota, M.A., 1947; Harvard University, Ph.D., 1950; St. Louis University, 1952-1954; St. Mary's College, s.t.l, 1958. *Principal occupation:* Professor of history. *Address:* Department of History, Marquette University, Milwaukee, Wis. 53233. *Affiliations:* Society of Jesus, 1950; ordained priest, 1957; professor of history, Marquette University, Milwaukee, Wis., 1960-. *Military service:* U.S. Army Air Force, 1942-1946. *Memberships:* American Historical Association, 1949-; Organization of American Historians, 1954-; State Historical Society of Wisconsin, 1960- (board of

curators, 1972-1978, 1981, president, 1976-1978); Western History Association, 1962- (president, 1983); Milwaukee County Historical Society (board of directors, 1964-. *Published works: Broadax and Bayonet* (State Historical Society of Wisconsin, 1953); *Army Life on the Western Frontier* (University of Oklahoma Press, 1958); *American Indian Policy in the Formative Years* (Harvard University Press, 1962); *Guide to Military Posts of the U.S., 1789-1895* (State Historical Society fo Wisconsin, 1964); *The Sword of the Republic* (Macmillan, 1969); *Indian Peace Medals in American History* (State Historical Society of Wisconsin, 1971); *The Indians in American History* (Holt, Rinehart & Winston, 1971); Americanizing the American Indians: Writings by the "Friends of the Indians" 1880-1900 (Harvard University Press, 1973); *Documents of the United States Indian Policy* (University of Nebraska Press, 1975); *American Indian Policy in Crisis: Christian Reformers and the Indian, 1865-1900* (University of Oklahoma Press, 1976); *A Bibliographical Guide to the History of Indian-White Relations in the U.S.* (University of Chicago Press, 1977); *United States Indian Policy: A Critical Bibliography* (Indiana University Pres, 1977); *The Churches and the Indian Schools, 1888-1912* (University of Nebraska Press, 1979); editor, *Cherokee Removal: The "William Penn" Essays and Other Writings,* by Jeremiah Evarts (Univrsity of Tennessee Press, 1981); *Indian Policy in the United States: Historical Essays* (University of Nebraska Press, 1981); *Indian-White Relations in the United States: A Bibliography of Works Published, 1975-1980* (University of Nebraska Pres, 1982); *The Great Father: The United States Government and the American Indians,* 2 vols. (University of Nebraska Press, 1984); *The Indians in American Society: From the Revolutionary War to the Present* (University of California Press, 1985).

PULLAR, GORDON L. (Koniag)
1944-
(president-Kodiak Area Native
Association)

Born January 22, 1944, Bellingham, Wash. *Education:* Western Washington Univerity, Bellingham, B.A., 1973; University of

Washington, Seattle, M.P.A. (Tribal Administration Program - course of study designed to meet the contemporary management needs of Native American corporations, organizations, and tribal governments as well as federal and state agencies dealing with Native American issues and programs), 1983. *Principal occupation:* President/executive director, Kodiak Area Native Association, Kodiak, Alaska 99615. *Home address:* P.O. Box 4331, Kodiak, Alaska 99615. *Affiliations:* Rewind operator/supervisor, Georgia Pacific Corp., Bellingham, Wash., 1963-1979; business analyst/marketing specialist, Small Tribes Organization of Western Washington, Sumner, Wash., 1979-1981; associate editor, *Nations* magazine (National Communications, Inc., Seattle, Wash.), 1981; owner/publisher, *Kodiak Times,* Kodaik, Alaska, 1983-1985; president/executive director, Kodiak Area Native Association, Kodiak, Alaska, 1983-. *Other professional post:* Assistant editor, business editor, *The Indian Voice* (Small Tribes Organization of Western Wash.), 1979-1981. *Community activities:* Volunteer work in social programs involving Native Americans: Washington State Dept. of Social and Health Services, Whatcom County Detoxification Center, and Whatcom County Juvenile Probation Dept.; Northwest Indian News Association (board of directors, 1979-1981); Governor's Minority and Women's Business Development Advisory Council (appointed by Governor of State of Washington, 1980-1981); Native American Business Alliance (board of directors, vice president-publicity chairman, 1981-1983); Alaska Regional Energy Association (board of directors, 1984-1985); Kodiak Area State Parks Advisory Board, 1983; Alaska Federation of Natives, Inc. (board of directors, 1983-). *Memberships:* Koniag, Inc. (regional Native corporation); Leisnoi, Inc, Woody Island ANCSA Corp.; National Congress of American Indians; American Society for Public Administration (South Central Alaska Chapter).

PUNLEY, RANDOLPH J.
(director-Indian center)

Affiliation: Director, National Indian Employment Resource Center, 2258 South Broadway, Denver, Colo. 80210.

PURICH, DON
(director-Indian law center)

Affiliation: Director, Native Law Centre, Univerity of Saskatchewan, 150 Diefenbaker Centre, Saskatoon, Saskatchewan, Can.

Q

QUIMBY, GEORGE IRVING 1913-
(museum director; professor of anthropology)

Born May 4, 1913, Grand Rapids, Mich. *Education:* University of Michigan, B.A., 1936, M.A., 1937, Graduate Fellow, 1937-1938; University of Chicago (Postgraduate work),1938-1939. *Principal occupation:* Museum director. *Home address:* 6001 52nd Ave., NE, Seattle, Wash. 98115. *Affiliations:* Director, Muskegon (Mich.) Museum, 1941-1942; Assistant curator, 1942-1943, curator, 1954-1965, research associate, 1965-, North American Archaeology and Ethnology (Field Museum), curator of exhibits, anthropology, 1943-1954, Field Museum of Natural History, Chicago, Ill.; curator of anthropology, 1965-1968, director, 1968-, Thomas Burke Memorial Museum, professor of anthropology, University of Washington, Seattle, Wash., 1965- *Other professional posts:* Lecturer, University of Chicago, 1947-1965, Northwestern University, 1949-1953. *Archaeological expeditions and field work:* Michigan, 1935, 1937, 1942, 1956-1963; Wisconsin, 1936; Hudson's Bay, 1939; Louisiana, 1940-1941; New Mexico, 1947; Lake Superior, 1956-1961. *Memberships:* American Association for the Advancement of Science (Fellow); American Anthropological Association; Society for American Archaeology (president, 1958); American Society for Ethnohistory; Wisconsin Archaeological Society; Society for Historical Archaeology (council, 1971-1974, 1975-1978); Association of Science Museum Directors (president 1973-); Norwegian Totemic Society; Arctic Institute of North America; American Association of Museums (council, 1971-1974); Sigma Xi. *Published works: Aleutian Islanders, Eskimos of the North Pacific* (Chicago Natural History Museum, Anthropology Leaflet No. 35,

1944); *The Tehefuncte Culture, An Early Occupation of the Lower Mississippi Valley* (Memoirs-Society for American Archaeology, No. , 1945); *Indians Before Columbus*, with Paul Martin and Donald Collier (Chicago, 1947); *Indians of the Western Frontier, paintings of George Catlin* (Chicago Natural History Museum, 1954); *Indian Life in the Upper Great Lakes, 11,000 B.C. to A.D. 1800* (University of Chicago Press, 1960); *Indian Culture and European Grade Goods*, 1966; co-editor, documentary film, *In the Land of the War Canoes*, 1973; (with Bill Holm-two documentary films) *The Image Maker and the Indians*, 1979, and *Edward S. Curtis in the Land of the War Canoes: A Pioneer Cinematographer in the Pacific Northwest*, 1980; contributing articles to professional journals.

R

RAGAN, CONNIE SEABOURN
(Oklahoma Cherokee) 1951-
(artist-painter/printmaker)

Born September, 20, 1951, Purcell, Okla. *Education:* University of Oklahoma, B.F.A., 1980. *Principal occupation:* Artist-painter/printmaker (self-employed). *Home address:* 2605 SW 99 St., Oklahoma City, Okla. 73159. *Interests:* "My entire life is devoted to doing art and being a good wife and mother." *Biographical sources: Who's Who in American Art*, 1984; *Community Leaders of the World*, 1984; *Directory of Distinguished Americans*, Third Edition; *The International Who's Who of Contemporary Achievement*, 1984; *Personalities of the South*, 1985; *The World Who's Who of Women*, 1985; "The Emergence of an Artist," *Art Gallery International*, 1980; "The Rising Star of Connie Seabourn Ragan," *Indian Trader*, 1982.

RAGSDALE, WILLIAM P.
(B.I.A. area director)

Affiliation: Director, Anadrko Area Office, Bureau of Indian Affairs, WCD - Office Complex, P.O. Box 368, Anadarko, Okla. 73005.

RAMIREZ, DAVID (Yaqui)
(tribal chairman)

Affiliation: Chairman, Pascua Yaqui Tribal Council, 4821 West Calle Vicam, Tucson, Ariz. 85706.

RAMIRIZ, RAYMOND
(museum superintendent)

Affiliation: Superintendent, Ysleta Del Sur Pueblo Museum, P.O. Box 17579, El Paso, Tex. 79917.

RAPHAEL, JOSEPH (Chippewa)
(tribal chairman)

Affiliation: Chairman, Grand Traverse Band Tribal Council, Route 1, Box 118, Suttons Bay, Mich. 49682.

RATON, ELI SEO, Sr. (Santa Ana Pueblo)
(Pueblo governor)

Affiliation: Governor, Santa Ana Pueblo, P.O. Box 37, Bernalillo, N.M. 87004.

RAVE, AUSTIN JERALD
(Minneconjou Sioux) 1946-
(artist)

Born August 5, 1946, Cheyenne River Sioux Reservation, S.D. *Education:* Institute of American Indian Arts, Santa Fe, N.M., 1964-1966; San Francisco Art Institute, 1966-1967; Engineering Drafting School, Denver, Colo., 1970-1972. *Principal occupation:* Artist. *Home address:* Eagle Butte, S.D. 57625. *Other professional posts:* Draftsman, technical illustrator. *Awards, honor:* Numerous awards for art. *Biographical source: Dictionary of International Biography.*

REASON, JAMIE TAWODI
(Southeastern Cherokee) 1947-
(carver/painter)

Born March 11, 1947, Muncie, Ind. *Principal occupation:* Owner/manager, Sacred Earth Studio, Mastic Beach, N.Y., 1980- (Native American art studio). *Home address:* 197 Longfellow Dr., Mastic Beach, N.Y. 11951. *Military service:* U.S. Air Force, 1966 (A/3/C; Vietnam Veteran; National Defense Expert Marksman; Air Police). *Community activities:* Committee for Annual Paumanoke Inter-Tribal Pow-Wow (publicity director/head judge); member of "The Painted Fan Singers." *Memberships:* Indian Arts & Crafts Association; Vietnam Er Veterans Inter-Tribal Association; East End Arts & Humanities Council; Ani-Yvwiya Association of New York. *Interests:* "My art has been exhibited at the Museum of the American Indian, The Gallery of the American Indian Community House (New York City), Red Cloud Indian Art Show, Dartmouth College, Native American Symposium at Old Westbury College (N.Y.), Rhode Island Indian Council, and many galleries. My work is in over 100 private collections." Mr. Reason is probably best known for his solid carved cedar feather boxes, mirror boards, horse memorial sticks, and his traditional bone roach spreaders. *Biographical sources:* The Museum of the American Indian *News,* Sept. 24, 1983; *Suffolk Life,* 1983-1984; Southeastern Cherokee *News; American Indian Community House Newsletter,* 1984; *The Knoxville Journal,* April 7, 1984; *Daily News,* April 4, 1984; *New York Times,* August 18, 1985.

RED SHE BEAR (DEANNA BARNES) (Ute) 1938-
(teacher, craftswoman)

Born June 25, 1938, Boise, Idaho. *Education:* College of the Redwoods, Eureka, Calif.; Humboldt State University, Arcata, Calif.; Lela Center for Holistic Therapy, Arcata, Calif.; Indian Survival Society, Bandon, Ore. *Principal occupation:* Founder-/manager, Red Bear Creations, Bandon, Ore. *Home address:* 358 N. Lexington Ave., Bandon, Ore. 97411. *Affiliations:* Founder, Indian Survival Society; founder and president, Women's Center. *Community activities:* American Red Cross (provider and secretary); Coos and Curry Area Agency on Aging (provider); Intertribal Sweat Lodge Board (officer); District 7 Sub-Area Health Advisory Council (provider); Women's Crisis Service (advisory board). *Membership:* National Indian Health Care Association

(spokeswoman). *Interests:* "Making traditional quilts and blankets. Preserving our old culture and traditions is very important to me. I am an elder, pipecarrier, sweatleader, storyteller in the winter, tech survival skills in the woods, lecture on traditional uses of indigenous plants as food and medicine, and on Indian women's roles in society. I'm currently writing book, *Crystal Wind Warrior,* about a crystal who became a human to help the people (manuscript, 1986)."

REDCLOUD, MERLIN (Winnebago) (tribal chairman)

Affiliation: Chairman, Winnebago Business Committee, P.O. Box 311, Tomah, Wis. 54660.

REED, SILVER STAR (United Lumbee-Cherokee-Choctaw) 1929- (homemaker, national chieftain)

Born November 29, 1929, Vanita, Okla. *Home address:* P.O. Box 512, Fall River Mills, Calif. 96028. *Affiliation:* National chieftain, United Lumbee Nation of N.C. and America, 1983-. *Other professional posts:* Parent committee of Title IV and Johnson O'Malley Indian Education Program, Tulare-Kings Counties, Calif; National Secretary (four years), and Grand Council (member-board of directors)(six years), United Lumbee Nation of N.C. and America. *Memberships:* Native American Wolf Clan (secretary, 1977-); Chapel of Our Lord Jesus, 1974-. *Published works:* Compiler, *Over the Cooking Fires,* featuring traditional Lumbee recipes (United Lumbee Nation, 1982); *Lumbee Indian Ceremonies* (United Lumbee Nation, 1982).

REESER, RALPH R. 1932- (B.I.A. attorney)

Born November 26, 1932, Fairbanks, Alaska. *Education:* Seattle University, 1952-1955; Univerity of Washington, B.A., 1956; George Washington University Law School, J.D., 1960. *Principal occupation:* Attorney. *Home address:* 3702 Spruell Dr., Wheaton, Md. 20902. *Affiliations:* Attorney-advisor, Public Housing Administration, Washing-

222

ton, D.C., 1961-1966; director, Housing Development, Bureau of Indian Affairs, Washington, D.C., 1966-1970; deputy director, Publicly Financed Housing, Department of HUD, Washington, D.C., 1970-1972; director, Congressional & Legislative Affairs, Bureau of Indian Affairs, Washington, D.C., 1972-. *Military service:* U.S. Air Force, 1951-1952 (S/Sgt.).

REUTLINGER, BARBARA N. 1933-
(journalist-editor)

Born March 14, 1933, Scholls, Ore. *Education:* Central Oregon Community College (one year). *Principal occupation:* Editor, *Rawhide Press,* Times Publishing Co., Wellpinit, Wash., 1971-. *Home address:* P.O. Box 393, Wellpinit, Wash. 99040. *Other professional post:* Free-lance article writer. *Memberships:* Washington Press Women; National Federation of Press Women; Northwest Indian Press Association (board member, 1977-). *Awards, honors: Rawhide Press,* nominated as on of top ten Indian papers in the nation; numerous editorial awards. *Interests:* "Writing is my vocation and avocation, with spare time spent in painting and fine arts and crafts."

REYES, JOYCE (Yakima) 1937-
(organization executive)

Born May 21, 1937, Redmond Ore. *Education:* University of Washington. *Affiliation:* President, American Indian Women's Service League, Seattle, Wash. *Community activities:* Seattle Human Rights Commission (social and health services advisory committee); United Indians of All Tribes Foundation (secretary). *Interests:* Ms. Reyes writes, "I am active now in the development of an Indian cultural/educational facility to be located on 17 acres in the City of Seattle."

REYES, LUANA L.
(Indian health service)

Affiliation: Director, Division of Program

Formulation, Indian Health Service, 5600 Fishers Lane, Rockville, Md. 20857.

REYHNER, JON ALLAN 1944-
(school administrator)

Born April 29, 1944, Fountain Hill, Pa. *Education:* University of California, Davis, B.A., 1966, M.A., 1967; Northern Arizona University, Flagstaff, M.A., 1973, Ed.S., 1977; Montana State University, Bozeman, Ed.D., 1984. *Principal occupation:* School administrator. *Home address:* General Delivery, Cibecue, Ariz. 86435. *Affiliations:* Math/science teacher, Chinle Junior High School, Chinle, Ariz., 1971-1973; social studies teacher, Fort Defiance Junior High School, Fort Defiance, Ariz., 1973-1975; assistant principal, Navajo Public School, Navajo, N.M., 1975-1977; principal, Wallace Public School, Parker, Ariz., 1977-1978; principal, Rocky Boy Public School, Box Elder, Mt., 1978-1980; university supervisor of professional and student teachers, Department of Elementary Education, Montana State University, Bozeman, 1980-1981; principal/federal projects director, Heart Butte Public Schoos, Mt., 1982-1984; administrator/principal, Havasupai School, Supai, Ariz., 1984-1985; academic coordinator, Cibecue Community School, Ariz., 1985-. *Memberships:* International Reading Association, 1982-; American Association of School Administrators, 1984-; National Indian Education Association, 1984-; Council for Indian Education, 1984-; Phi Delta Kappa, 1973-; Phi Alpha Theta. *Interests:* Bilingual education; photography; historical research on Western America. *Published works: Heart Butte: A Blackfeet Indian Community,* 1984; editor, *Stories of Our Blackfeet Grandmothers,* 1984; editor, *The Story of Running Eagle,* by James Willard Schultz, 1984; editor, *Famine Winter,* by James Willard Schultz, 1984; editor, *The Loud Mouthed Gun,* by James Willard Schultz, 1984; all published by Council for Indian Education. Articles: "The Self Determined Curriculum: Indian Teachers as Cultural Translators" (*Journal of American Indian Education,* Nov., 1981).

RHOADES, EVERETT RONALD, M.D.
(Oklahoma Kiowa) 1931-
(physician, director-Indian
Health Service)

Born October 24, 1931, Lawton, Okla. *Education:* Lafayette College, 1949-1952; University of Oklahoma College of Medicine, M.D., 1956. *Principal occupation:* Physician, director-Indian Health Service, Rockville, Md. *Affiliations:* Chief, Infectious Diseases, Wilford Hall, U.S. Air Force Hospital, 1961-1966; professor of medicine, Chief, Infectious Diseases, University of Oklahoma College of Medicine, Oklahoma City, 1966-?; director, Indian Health Service, Room 5A-55, Parklawn Bldg., 5600 Fishers Lane, Rockville, Md. 20857. *Military service:* U.S. Air Force, 1957-1966 (Major; Certificate of Merit, 1967). *Community activities:* Association of American Indian Physicians (president, 1972, 1976); Oklahoma Lung Association (board of directors); Association on American Indian Affairs (vice president, 1977-); Task Force on Health of American Indian Policy Review Commission (chairman, 1975); National Advisory Allergy and Infectious Disease Council (NIH), 1971-1975; Central Oklahoma Indian Health Project (board of directors; chairman, 1976); Kiowa Tribal Business Committee (vice chairman, 1973-1975); founder and donor, Dorothy Rowell Rhoades Prize to outstanding graduating Indian student, Elgin High School, Okla. *Memberships:* American Thoracic Society, 1960-; American Federation for Clinical Research, 1960-; American College of Physicians, 1963- (Fellow); American Society for Microbiology, 1967-; National Congress of American Indians; Sigma Xi. *Awards, honors:* Markle Scholar, Academic Medicine, 1967-1972; John Hay Whitney Opportunity Fellow, 1952-1956; Student Research Achievement Award, 1956; Outstanding Achievement, Veterans Administration Hospital, 1960, 1961; Recognition Award, Association of American Indian Physicians, 1973, 1976; Breath of Life Award, Oklahoma Lung Association, 1977; Public Health Service Recognition Award, 1977; among others. *Interests:* Internal medicine; infectious diseases; Kiowa Gourd Clan; Kiowa Blacklegging Society; dancing and powwows; amateau archaeology; history of medicine and Indians; travel. *Biographical sources: Directory of Medical Specialists; Dictionary of International Biography; Who's Who in the South and Southwest; American Men & Women of Science; Indians of Today; Contemporary American Indian Leaders. Published works:* Numerous articles in scientific journals relating to infectious diseases, microbiology, and Indian life; author of "Kiowa Tribe" for *World Book Encyclopedia*; edited "Task Force Report" to American Indian Policy Review Commission (Health), U.S. Government Printing Office, 1975.

RICHARDSON, BARRY
(director-Indian center)

Affiliation: Baltimore American Indian Center, 113 South Broadway, Baltimore, Md. 21231.

RICHARDSON, KENNETH (Paiute)
(tribal chairman)

Affiliation: Chairman, Yerington Tribal Council, 171 Campbell Lane, Yerington, Nev. 89447.

RICHARDSON, PATRICIA ROSE
(BREWINGTON)(Coharie-Cherokee)
1933-
(crafts consultant)

Born July 21, 1933, Clinton, N.C. *Education:* East Carolina Indian School, 1952; Nash Technical College, Rocky Mt., N.C., A.A. (Education), 1986. *Principal occupation:* American Indian crafts consultant-/pottery and beadwork. *Home address:* P.O. Box 130, Hollister, N.C. 27844. *Affiliations:* Instructor, Title IV Indian Education, Halifax Board of Education, N.C. (six years); crafts instructor, Haliwa-Supai Indian Tribe, Hollister, N.C. (five years). *Memberships:* North Carolina Crafts Association (board member); American Indian Heritage Foundation. *Awards, honors:* First Place Awards—Excellence in Beadwork, Schiele Museum Indian Festival, 1978/1986; Good Medicine Crafts Award, 1980/1986. *Interests:* Exhibitions at major Indian festivals: Grand Prairie, Tex., Hunter Mountain, N.Y., Palm Beach, Fla., North Carolina Indian festivals, National Indian Festival, Washington, D.C.

RIDDLES, LEONARD *(Black Moon)* **(Comanche) 1919-**
   (artist, farmer/rancher)

Born June 28, 1919, Walters, Okla. *Education:* High school. *Principal occupation:* Artist, farmer/rancher. *Hoe address:* Route 1, Walter, Okla. *Military service:* U.S. Army, 1941-1945 (Service Ribbon, American Defense Ribbon). *Community activities:* Comanche Tribal Council (former officer); Masons. *Membership:* American Indian Artists Association. *Awards, honors:* Numerous awards from 1963-. *Exhibitions:* Philbrook Art Center, Inter-Tribal Indian Ceremonial; Museum of New Mexico; U.S. Department of the Interior Gallery; among others. *Interests:* Mr. Riddles writes, "I am interested in the history of the American Indian and in any phase of archaeological study. We do research on the Comanche Tribe, so (I) find all expeditions of real interest. Museums are also of great interest to me." Mr. Riddles illustrated the jacket for *Buried Colts,* by Harley Smith.

RIDENHOWER, MARILYN
   (college president)

Affiliation: President, Fort Peck Community College, P.O. Box 575, Poplar, Mt. 59255.

RIDINGTON, ROBIN 1939-
   (professor of anthropology)

Born November 1, 1939, Camden, N.J. *Education:* Swarthmore, B.A., 1962; Harvard University, Ph.D., 1968. *Principal occupation:* Professor of anthropology. *Home address:* 3464 W. 27th Ave., Vancouver, British Columbia, Can. V6S 1P6. *Affiliation: Assistant and associate professor of anthropology, Univerity of British Columbia, Vancouver, B.C., 1967-. Memberships:* Society for Humanistic Anthropology (Canadian representative); Canadian Ethnology Society; American Anthropological Association. *Interests:* Field research among Beaver Indians, 1964-; writing about Omaha ceremony, 1985-1986. *Published works:* Articles: "From Artifice to Artifact: Stages in the Industrialization of a Northern Native Community" (*Journal of Canadian Studies,* 1983); "Laurie Anderson: Shaman of the Post-Modern Era" (*The Vancouver Literary News,* May, 1983); "Stories of the Vision Quest Among Dunne-za Women" (*Atlantis,* 1983); "Beaver Indians" (*The Canadian Encyclopedia,* Hurtig, 1985); "Native People, Subarctic" (*The Canadian Encyclopedia,* Hurtig, 1985); "Fix and Chicadee: The Writing of Indian White History" in volume edited by Calvin Martin (in press); "Mottles As By Shadows: A Sacred Symbol of the Omaha Tribe" in *First Voices of the First America* (New Scholar, in press); among others.

RINER, REED D. 1941-
   (anthropologist/futurist)

Born December 22, 1941, Mentone, Ind. *Education:* University of Colorado, Ph.D., 1977 (dissertation: *A Study of Attitudes Toward Formal Education Among Indian Parents and Students in Six Communities. Principal occupation:* Associate professor of anthropology, Northern Arizona State University, Flagstaff, 1975-. *Home address:* 506 Charles Rd., Flagstaff, Ariz. 86001. *Other professional post:* Advisor, Native American Indian Studies Program, Northern Arizona University; editor/publisher, *Cultural Futures Research. Military service:* U.S. Naval Reserve, 1963-1968. *Memberships:* American Anthropological Association; Society for Appplied Anthropology; High Plains Society for Applied Anthropology (past president); World Future Studies Federation; World Future Society; Contact Cultures of the Imagination (board of directors); Cross-Cultural Dance Resources (board of directors). *Interests:* "My primary professional interests are applied futures research; Native American Indian studies, especially Indian education; and the application of anthropology in the solution of—especially institutional—organizational problems such as the future of Native American Indians." *Published works:* Numerous articles in professional journals.

ROACH, MILBURN H.
(administrative director-
Indian Health Service)

Affiliation: Administrative director, Indian Health Service, 5600 Fishers Lane, Rockville, Md. 20857.

ROBERTS, HOLLIS (Choctaw)
(tribal chief)

Affiliation: Chief, Choctaw Tribal Council, Drawer 1210, 16th & Locust St., Durant, Okla. 74701.

ROBERTSON, ELLEN (Oklahoma Cherokee) 1945-
(librarian)

Born March 7, 1945, Washington, D.C. *Education:* University of California, Berkeley, B.A., 1973, M.L.S., 1974. *Principal occupation:* Librarian, American Indian Law Center, University of New Mexico School of Law, Albuquerque, N.M., 1975-. *Home address:* 1125 Lafayette, N.E., Albuquerque, N.M. 87110. *Other professional post:* Editor, *American Indian Law Newsletter,* Univerity of New Mexico School of Law. *Interests:* Photography and literature; Pece Corps, 1966-1968 (Tunesia); travel.

ROBINSON, GARY (Cherokee-Mississippi Choctaw) 1950-
(film/video producer)

Born January 12, 1950, Dallas, Tex. *Education:* University of Texas, Austin, B.S., 1973; M.A. (Radio, TV, Film), 1978. *Principal occupation:* Film/video producer. *Home address:* P.O. Box 781, Okmulgee, Okla. 74447. *Affiliations:* Production assistant, Instructional Media Department, Tulsa Public Schools, Tulsa, Okla., 1973-1974; media specialist, Texas Department of Mental Health/Mental Retardation, Austin, Tex., 1975-1978; branch sales manager, Magnetic Media Corp., Austin, Tex., 1978-1979; independent media producer/writier, 1980; communication specialist, Creek Nation, Okmulgee, Okla., 1981-; owner-producer, Pathfinder Communications (production and consultant company),

Okmulgee, Okla. *Membership:* Oklahoma Film & Tape Professionals Association. *Interests:* "Develop, produce and direct educational and promotional programs about Creek Indian Tribe. Regularly produce informational videotapes on Creek culture, history, art and current tribal activities. Currently developing a feature film for the tribe on Alexander Posey and the Creek Nation of Oklahoma. Avocational interests include: music, religion, movies, travel." *Video productions: The Green Corn Festival* (documentary of ancient Creek ceremony), 1982, 20 minutes; *1,000 Years of Muscogee (Creek) Art,* 1982, 26 minutes; Folklore of the Muscogee People (Creek Indian legends), 1983, 28 minutes; *Continuing Progress for the Muscogee People* (public relations on Creek Tribe), 1983, 13 minutes; *Nova-Make My People Live* (nationally broadcast documentary on the Indian health crisis), 1983, 58 minutes; *Strength of Life: Knokovitee Scott* (Creek/Cherokee artist), 1984, 28 minutes; *Stickball: The Little Brother of War* (documentary on ancient Creek game), 1984, 12 minutes; *Consider Your Future* (medicine employment recruitment), 1984, 10 minutes; *Bacone College: Headed for the Future* (promotional fundraiser program for Muskogee based private college), 1984, 11 mintues; *Estee Muskogee (The Muskogee People),* 1985, 24 minutes; *Indian Law/Theology Symposium Highlights* (project of the National Indian ministries task force), 1985, 90 minutes; *Bingo Is Our Business* (information about Creek Nation's business enterprise), 1985, 20 minutes; *Native American Producers Showcase* (film/video work of six Indian produers, for the Native American Public Broadcasting Consortium), 1985, 28 minutes.

ROBINSON, NATHAN WINFIELD
(Eastern Band Cherokee) 1938-
(motel/restaurant owner)

Born October 29, 1938, Ashland, Wis. *Education:* Southern Tech, Atlanta, Ga., 1957-1958. *Principal occupation:* Owner/operator, El Camino Motel, and El Camino Craft Gallery, 1960-. *Home address:* P.O. Box 482, Cherokee, N.C. 28719. *Military service:* U.S. Army, 1961-1962. *Community activities:* Cherokee (Tribal) Health Board (vice chairman and chairman, 1974-1976); Cherokee Sheltered Workshop (board of directors); Cherokee Baptist Church (youth committee). *Interests:* "Own and operate El Camino Motel; own restaurant, but have leased to another party; own and operate El Camino Craft Gallery, dealing in hand made crafts from all over the U.S. Hobbies: gardening, vintage cars, phhotography, racing karts."

**ROBINSON, ROSE W. (Hopi) 1932-
(director-American Indian programs,
writer-editor)**

Born March 27, 1932, Winslow, Ariz. *Education:* Haskell Institute, 1951; American University (Journalism Studies), 1970-1971. *Principal occupation:* Director-American Indian programs, writer-editor. *Home address:* 3805 Windom Pl, N.W., Washington, D.C. 20016. *Affiliations:* Writer-editor, Indian Arts and Crafts Board, U.S. Department of the Interior, Washington, D.C., 1963-1968; information officer, Office of Public Instruction, Bureau of Indian Affairs, Washington, D.C., 1968-1972; executive director, American Indian Press Association, Washington, D.C. 1972-1975; assistant director, Bicentennial Program, Bureau of Indian Affairs, 1975-1976; vice president and director, American Indian Program, Phelps-Stokes Fund, Washington, D.C., 1976-; editor, Native American Philanthropic News Service publications, Phelps-Stokes Fund, 1976-. *Other professional posts:* Chairman, Eastern Region, National Indian Lutheran Board, Lutheran Church in the U.S.A., 1976-; president, D.C. Chapter, North American Indian Women's Association, 1976-; board of directors, College of Ganado, Ganado, Ariz.; board of directors, American Indian Scholarships, Inc., Albuquerque, N.M. *Community activities:* American Indian Society of Washington, D.C., 1964- (vice president, 1967-1969; publicity chairman, 1969-1971); National Endowment for the Arts, 1977- (expansion arts advisory panel). *Memberships:* National Indian Education Association (board of directors, 1985-); Native American Science Education Association (board of directors, 1982-); National Congress of American Indians, 1969-1985; Women in Foundations, 1977-; North American Indian Women's Association, 1970-. *Biogra-*

phical source: Directory of Significant 20th Century American Minority Women, Vol. I, (Gaylord Professional Publications, Fisk University, Nashville, Tenn., 1978). Published works: Editor, *IDRA News* (Interior Dept. Recreation Association newsletter), 1957-1961; editor, *Smoke Signals* (Indian Arts and Crafts Board monthly publication), 1965-1968; editor, *Indian Record* (B.I.A. monthly publication), 1968-1972, 1975); *Indian Funding Programs* (Joint Strategy and Action Committee pamphlet on church funding sources for Indian programs, 1974); compiler and editor, *American Indian Directory* (National Congress of American Indians, 1972, 1974); co-editor, with Richard LaCourse, *American Indian Media Directory* (American Indian Press Association, 1974); editor, conference report, *Conference on Indian Higher Education for Private Philanthropists and Indian Educators* (Phelps-Stokes Fund, 1975); editor, *The Exchange, The Roundup,* and *Bulletins* (Native Philanthropic News Service, the Phelps-Stokes Fund, 1976-).

**RODRIGUEZ-SELLAS, JOSE E. 1954-
(outreach intake coordinator)**

Born May 4, 1954, Ponce, Puerto Rico. *Education:* University of New Haven (Conn.), B.A. (History), 1978; University of Puerto Rico/Rio Piedras, Labor Relations Institute, 1979-1981; Labor Education Institute, Santurce, P.R., 1981. *Principal occupation:* Outreach Intake Coordinator for American Indians for Development. *Home address:* 1450 Ella T. Grasso Blvd., New Haven, Conn. 06511. *Other professional posts:* Editor of American Indians for Development *Newsletter;* Connecticut journalist for *Que Pasa* (the only Latin American newspaper in Connecticut). *Community activities:* President of Latin Student Organization (1978), University of New Haven, West Haven, Conn. *Memberships:* Brother-/Sisterhood of People of the Caribbean and Latin America (spokesperson and coordinator of "Hermandad Caribena y Latinoamericana). *Awards, honors:* Certificate of Appreciation for services rendered to the members of Hermandad de Trabajadores de Servicios Sociales de Puerto Rico by the National Leadership of the Brotherhood of Social Services Workers of Puerto Rico,

1979-1981. *Interests:* "My main interests at present are : journalism, graphic arts, printing, photography and writing. I write in Spanish and English. I write about history, culture, politics and I also write poems. My main concerns are the daily struggles of the so-called "minorities" for civil rights and economic justice, and the struggle for self-determination of all the people of Latin America."

ROEHL, ROY F.
(Chairman-Alaskan Native corporation)

Affiliation: Chairman, Chugach Alaska Corporation, Chugach Alaska Bldg., 3000 A St., Suite 400, Anchorage, Alaska 99503.

ROESSEL, ROBERT A., Jr. 1926-
(teacher, administrator)

Born August 26, 1926, St. Louis, Mo. *Education:* Washington University, St. Louis, Mo., B.A., 1949, M.A., 1951; University of Chicago; Arizona State University, Ph.D., 1960. *Principal occupation:* Teacher, administrator. *Affiliation:* Teacher and administrator, Navajo Reservation, B.I.A.; director of Indian education, Arizona State University, Tempe, Ariz.; director, Rough Rock Demonstration School, Chinle, Ariz.; chancellor, Navajo Community College, Tsaile, Ariz.. *Military service:* U.S. Army, 1944-1946. *Awards, honors:* Distinguished Service Award in Navajo Education, 1967. *Interests:* "Indian control over Indian education is a major concern and interest. (I am) also interested in developing materials reflecting positive aspects of Navajo life and culture for various classrooms." *Published works: Arizona Cultures* (Arizona State University, 1960) *Success and Failure of Southwestern Indians in Higher Education,* (Arizona State University, 1961); *Indian Communities in Action* (Amerindian, 1961; Arizona State University, 1967); *Education of the Indian Adult,* (Arizona State University, 1962); *Cases and Concepts in Community Development (Arizona State University, 1963).*

ROESSEL, RUTH (Navajo) 1934-
(teacher)

Born April 14, 1934, Round Rock, Ariz. *Education:* Univerity of Northern Arizona, 1955; Arizona State University, B.A., 1969. *Principal occupation:* Teacher. *Affiliations:* Teacher, Low Mountain School, B.I.A., 1955-1958; director of dormitory services, Rough Rock Demonstration School, Rough Rock, Ariz., 1966-1968; director of Navajo and Indian studies, Navajo Community College, Tsaile, Ariz., 1968-? *Community activities:* Dine Bi Olta Association (board of directors). *Memberships:* American Association for Higher Education; National Indian Education Association; American Anthropological Association. *Awards, honors:* Navajo Woman of the Year, State Fair Commission, State of Arizona, 1960. *Interests:* "Interested in Indian and Navajo history and culture; arts and crafts, especially weaving. Involved in producing materials (publication) by Navajo, about Navajo, and for Navajo. Visiting on a continuing basis, major Indian groups in the U.S. and Canada." *Published works: Papers on Navajo Life and Culture,* 1971; *Navajo Studies at Navajo Community College,* 1972; *Stock Reduction: A National Disgrace,* 1973; all published by Navajo Community College Press.

ROESSLER, PAUL ALBERT (Navajo) 1920-
(economic consultant)

Born October 8, 1920, Buckman, N.M. *Education:* Georgetown University, B.S. (Foreign Service), 1949, postgraduate, 1949-1951; University of Maryland, postgraduate, 1965-. *Principal occupation:* Economic consultant. *Addresses:* P.O. Box 3045, Tucson, Ariz. 85701; P.O. Box 34137, Bethesda, Md. 20817. *Affiliations:* Field representative, War Claims Commission, Washington, D.C., 1949-1951; lesgislative analyst, Foreign Claims Settlement Commission, 1951-1952; Philippine Liaison officer, 1952-1953; foreign liaison officer, 1952-1956; staff assistant, Atomic Energy Commission (AEC), 1956-1957; assistant atomic energy attache, Japan, 1957-1961; senior foreign affairs officer, 1961-1963; associate program director, National

Science Foundation, Washington, D.C. 1963-1965; international economist, U.S. Department of the Army, 1965-1975; director, Office of Policy Planning, 1975-1975, chief, Division of Economic Development, 1976-1980, Bureau of Indian Affairs, Department of the Interior; president, American Economic Consultants, Inc., Tucson, Ariz., 1980-, Bethesda, Md., 1982- *Military service:* U.S. Army, 1941-1946, PTO; col., U.S. Army Reserve, 1956- (Purple Heart with cluster; Philippine Defense Medal; Philippine Liberation Medal; Philippine Presidential Unit Citation with two clusters; others). *Memberships:* National Economists Club; Society of Government Economists; American Political Science Association; DAV; VFW; American Legion; Delta Phi Epsilon. *Biographical sources: Who's Who in the East; Who's Who in the South and Southwest; Who's Who in the U.S.; American Men of Science; International Biographic Dictionary* (London); *Men of Distinction* (London); and others.

ROGERS, EDWARD S. 1923-
(ethnologist)

Born May 2, 1923, Lee, Mass. *Education:* Massachusetts Institute of Technology, 1942-1944; 1946-1947; Middlebury College, B.A., 1951; University of New Mexico, M.A., 1953, Ph.D., 1958. *Principal occupation:* Curator, Department of Ethnoogy, Royal Ontario Museum, 100 Queen's Park, Toronto, Ontario, Can. M5S 2C6. *Other professional post:* Part-time professor of anthropology, McMaster University, Hamilton, Ontario, Can. *Military service:* U.S. Army, 1943-1946 (Army Specialized Training Program, 1943-1944; Infantry, 1944-1945). *Community activities:* Archaeological and Historic Sites Board of Ontario, 1966-1972; Ministry of Natural Resources, 1962-1975; Northern Studies Committee, University of Toronto, 1971-1973. *Memberships:* Arctic Institute of North America; American Anthropological Association. *Interests:* Consultation on contemporary matters concerning North American Indians. *Publshed works: The Round Lake Ojibwa* (Royal Ontario Museum, 1962); *The Hunting Group-Hunting Territory Complex Among the Mistassini Indians* (National Museums of Canada, 1963); *Bibli-*

ography of Ontario Anthropology (Royal Ontario Museum, 1964); *An Athapaskan Type of Knife* (National Museums of Canada, 1965); *Sibsistence Areas of the Cree-Ojibwa of the Eastern Subarctic: A Preliminary Study,* two parts (National Museums of Canada, 1963-1966); *North Pacific Coast Indians* (Canadian Antiques Collector, 1967); *The Material Culture of the Mistassini* (National Museums of Canada, 1967); *Indian Farmers of Parry Island* (Royal Ontario Museum, 1967); *Canadian Indians* (Swan Publishing, 1967); *Indians of Canada* (Clarke, Irwin, 1969); *Forgotten Peoples* (Royal Ontario Museum, 1969); *Band Organization Among the Indians of Eastern Subarctic Canada* (National Museums of Canada, 1969); *Natural Environment-Social Organization-Witchcraft: Cree Versus Ojibwa-A Test Case* (National Museums of Canada, 1969); *Indians of the North Pacific Coast* (Royal Ontario Museum, 1970); *Iroquoians of the Eastern Woodlands* (Royal Ontario Museums, 1970); *Indians of th Subarctic* (Royal Ontario Museum, 1970); *Indians of the Plains* (Royal Ontario Museum, 1970); *Algonkians of the Eastern Woodlands* (Royal Ontario Museum, 1970); *The Indians of Canada/A Survey* (Royal Ontario Museum, 1970); *The Quest Food and Furs-The Mistassini Cree, 1953-1954* (National Museums of Canada, 1973); *Parry Island Farmers: A Period of Change in the Way of Life of the Algonkians of Southern Ontario,* with Flora Tobobondung (National Museum of Man, 1975); and others; also numerous papers, reviews, and articles in scholarly journals.

ROGERS, JAMES BLAKE (Oklahoma Cherokee) 1915-
(cattle rancher and feeder)

Born July 25, 1915, New York, N.Y. *Education:* Pomona Colege, 1935-1937. *Principal occupation:* Cattle rancher and feeder. *Home address:* 1 Greenfair Court, Bakersfield, Calif. 93309. *Affiliations:* Actor, Hal Roach and Harry Sherman Studios, 1942-1943; associate publisher, *Beverly Hills Citizen,* newspaper., 1943-1953. *Military service:* U.S. Marine Corps, 1944-1945 (Staff Sergeant). *Community activites:* Cherokee Historical Society (director); Will

Rogers Memorial Commission, State of Oklahoma (member). *Memberships:* The Pacific Coast Hunter, Jumper and Stock Horse Association (past director); California Professional Horsemen's Association (past director).

ROGERS, WILL, Jr. (Cherokee) 1911-
(publisher, journalist)

Born October 20, 1911, New York, N.Y. *Eduction:* Stanford University, B.A., 1935. *Principal occupation:* Publisher, journalist. *Home address:* Santos Ranch, Tubac, Ariz. 85646. *Affiliations:* Publisher/journalist, *Beverly Hills Citizen,* newspaper, 1935-1953; U.S. Congressman, 16th District, California, 1942-1944; special assistant to the Commissioner of Indian Affairs, 1967-1969; creative coonsultant, George Spota Theatre Production of "Will Rogers, U.S.A." starring James Whitmore, 1968-. *Other professional posts:* Motion picture actor, television commentator, lecturer. *Military service:* U.S. Army, 1944-1945 (Bronze Star). *Community activities:* Beverly Hills Chamber of Commerce; chairman, Southern California Truman campaign committee, 1948; Will Rogers Memorial Commission, State of Oklahoma (member); California State Parks Commission (chairman). *Memberships:* Arrow, Inc. (founder and honorary president); National Congress of American Indians, 1946-; Oklahoma Cherokee Tribe. *Interests:* "In recent years he has divided his energies between his real estate business in Beverly Hills and his ranch in Tubac, Arizona. He continues to be active in Indian affairs, making occasional trips for the Bureau of Indian Affairs. A well known lecturer, he continues active in this field. He has worked with the Alaskan Federation of Natives. *Theatrical activities:* Movies: Star in *The Will Rogers Story,* (Warner Brothers, 1951); *The Boy From Oklahoma,* and *Wild Heritage.* Plays: *Ah, Wilderness,* and *Street Scene* (Pasadena Playhouse). Radio: *Rogers of the Gazette.* Television: *Good Morning Show,* CBS.

ROHN, ARTHUR HENRY 1929-
(professor of anthropology, archaeologist)

Born May 15, 1929, Elmhurst Ill. *Education:* Harvard College, B.A., 1951; University of Arizona, 1955-1956; Harvard University, Ph.D., 1966. *Principal occupation:* Professor of anthropology, Wichita State University, Wichita, Kan., 1970-. *Home address:* 320 North Parkwood, Wichta, Kan. 67208. *Military service:* U.S. Navy, 1951-1954 (Lieutenant; Korean Service Medal with one star K7; United Nations Service Medal; National Defense Service Medal). *Memberships:* Society for American Archaeology, 1953- (review editor, *American Antiquity, 1967-1970*); *Current Anthropology,* 1960-; *American Anthropological Association (Fellow),* 1966-; *American Association for the Advancement of Science, 1966-1976; American Society for Conservation Archaeology, 1973-; Archaeological Institute of America; Tree Ring Society. Awards, honors:* Outstanding Educators of America, 1973; City of Wichita, Distinguished Service Citation, 1976; Leadership Award, Wichita State University, 1978. *Interests:* "Pueblo Indian culture history, especially social organization and economics; archaeology of the Central Plains; especially Kansas; New England archaeology; Delaware culture history; research focused most heavily on archaeology of the Southwest and Plains—expeditions at Mesa Verde and Yellowjacket, Colo.; Wolf Creek, Marion, and Hillsdale, Kan.; and Marshfield, Mass. *Biographical sources: American Men and Women of Science; Who's Who in the Midwest; Contemporary Authors; Who's Who Among Authors and Journalists. Published works: Mug House, Mesa Verde National Park, Colorado* (National Park Service, 1971); *Prehistoric Ceramics of the Mesa Verde Region* (Museum of Northern Arizona, 1974); *Cultural Change and Continuity on Chapin Mesa* (Regents Press, of Kansas, 1977) among others; also numerous articles, chapters, and book reviews.

ROKWAHO (DAN THOMPSON)
(Mohawk) 1953-
(publications/graphic design consultant)

Born November 7, 1953, Akwesasne Territory. *Education:* High school. *Principal occupation:* Publications and graphic design consultant. *Home address:* P.O. Box 166, Rooseveltown, N.Y. 13683. *Affiliations:* Media specialist, St. Regis Mohawk Language Program, 1980-1982; co-founder (with John Fadden) and production manager, Pictographics, P.O. Box 166, Rooseveltown, N.Y., 1977-. *Other professional posts:* Literary editor, artist and photographer, *Akwesasne Notes,* 1982-1983; founding editor, *Indian Time,* an Akwesasne biweekly newspaper, 1983; art director for Indian Studies, Cornell University, Ithaca, N.Y., 1984; editor, *Akwesasne Notes* and *Indian Time,* 1984-1985; co-founder of *Akwekon,* a literary and arts quarterly published by Akwekon/Akwesasne Notes; co-founder of "Suntracks," a tracking and nature observation school in the Adirondack Mountains near Ochiota, N.Y. *Membership:* Association for the Advancement of Native North American Arts and Crafts (administrative executive; project, *Iroquois Arts: A Directory of a People and Their Work,* published, 1984). *Interests:* "Music, literature, theatre, computer science, electronic and mechanical gaggetry, the sciences, and archaic Mohawk words and semantics (compiling a dictionary of terms)." *Published works:* Editor and designer, *Trail of Broken Treaties.* B.I.A. *I'm Not Your Indian Anymore* (Akwesasne Notes, 1974); translator and illustrator, *Teiohakwente,* a Mohawk language textbook (Dept. of Indian Affairs, Ottawa, Can., 1977); author and artist, *Covers* (poetry, illustrations) (Strawberry Press, 1982); contributor of poetry to numerous anthologies; cover art and illustrations for many publications, as well as design production for *Akwesasne Notes Calendars.*

ROLATOR, FRED S. 1938-
(professor of history)

Born July 22, 1938, McKinney, Tex. *Education:* Wake Forest University, B.A., 1960; University of Southern California, M.A., Ph.D., 1960-1963. *Principal occupation:* Professor of history, Middle Tennessee State University, Murfreesboro, Tenn., 1967-. *Home address:* Route 8, Box 467, Murfressboro, Tenn. 37130. *Other professional post:* Associate professor of history and chairman of the History and Social Sciences Department, Grand Canyon College, Phoenix, Ariz., 1964-1967. *Community activities:* Frequent speaker on Indian matters for civic organizations and school in area; co-director, The American Indian and the Jacksonian Era: The Impact of Removal: A Sequi-centennial Symposium (The national symposium on the adoption of the Indian Removal Bill of 1830) held Feb., 1980; Rutherford County Heritage Commission (member, 1978-1980). *Memberships:* Tennessee Baptist Historical Society (vice president; former president); Southern Baptist Historical Commission (commissioner); *Baptist History and Heritage* (board of directors); Organization of American Historians; The Western Historical Association; The Southern Historical Society; The Society for Historians of the Early American Republic. Awards, honors: National Merit Scholar, Wake Forest, 1956-1960; national Defense and Haynes Fellow, USC, 1960-1963; Tennessee Baptist Convention, Heritage Award, 1984. *Interests:* "History of the American Indian, especially previous to 1492; American church history; director of Historic Preservation effort, Camp Palma, located near Tupa, Sao Paulo state, Brazil (1976). extensive travel to several states and Mexico." *Biographcial sources: Directory of American Scholars; Dictionary of International Biography; Who's Who in the South and Southwest. Published works: The Continental Congress: A Study in the Origins of American Public Administration* (Xerox, 1971); *Charles Thompson* (Harrington Associates, 1977); *The Triumphant Indians: The History of North America to 1492* (in preparation).

ROSELEIGH, PATRICIA F.
(chief-nutrition & dietetics- Indian Health Service)

Affiliation: Chief, Nutrition & Dietetics Branch, Indian Health Service, 5600 Fishers Lane, Rockville, Md. 20857.

ROSEN, LAWRENCE 1941-
(professor of anthropology)

Born December 9, 1941, Cincinnati, Ohio. *Eduction:* Brandeis University, B.A., 1963; University of Chicago, M.A., 1965, Ph.D., 1968, J.D., 1974. *Principal occupation:* Professor of anthropology, Princeton University, Princeton, N.J., 1977-. *Home address:* 180 Prospect Ave., Princeton, N.J. 08540. *Other professional posts:* Former summer clerk, Native American Rights Fund, Boulder, Colo., 1972; visiting professor of law, Columbia University, Spring, 1979. *Memberships:* American Anthropological Association; North Carolina and Federal bars. *Interests:* American Indian legal problems. *Biographical source: American Men and Women of Science. Published work:* Editor, *The American Indian and the Law* (Transaction Books, 1978).

ROSS, AGNES ALLEN (Santee Sioux) 1910-
(educator)

Born October 27, 1910, Flandreau, S.D. *Education:* Haskell Institute, A.A., 1931; Northern Arizona University, Flagstaff, B.S., 1938; Nebraska State, Chadron, M.S., 1960. *Principal occupation:* Educator. *Home address:* Flandreau, S.D. 57028. *Affiliations:* Teacher, Day School, Rosebud, S.D., 1938-1941; teacher, teacher supervisor, education specialist, Pine Ridge, S.D., 1951-1970. *Other professional posts:* Instructor, Pine Ridge Community College, affiliated with Black Hills State College and University of Colordo, Boulder; Title I coordinator, Flandreau Indian School, 1970-1973. *Community activities:* State Cultural Preservation (board member); Tribal Health Board; National Advisory Board for Teacher Corp.; Santee Sioux Tribal Council (chairperson, 1972-1976). *Memberships:* Delta Kappa Gamma; North American Indian Women's Association; South Dakota Indian Education Association; Veteran's of Foreign Wars Aux (past president); American Legion Aux. (past president). *Awards, honors:* South Dakota's Teacher of the Year, 1958; B.I.A. Outstanding Performance, 1959, 1970; recognized as first woman chairperson in the United Sioux Tribes. *Interests:* Ms. Ross writes, "Now

retired—however—still involved in consultant services in Indian education and bilingual education; assists colleges and universities as an advisor in Indian education, and (I) enjoy speaking to school groups.

ROSS, DONALD
(school superintendent)

Affiliation: Superintendent, Crow Creek Reservation High School, Stephen, S.D. 57346.

ROSSE, WILLIAM, Sr. (Shoshone)
(tribal chairman)

Affiliation: Chairman, Yomba Tribal Council, Route 1, Box 24A, Austin, Nev. 89310.

ROUBIDEAUX, NANETTE S. (Ioway of Kansas/Nebraska) 1940-
(museum professional)

Born July 20, 1940, Porcupine, S.D. *Education:* Haskell Indian Junior College, A.A.S., 1975; Univerity of Kansas, B.A. (Honors), 1977, Ph.D. candidate, 1977-. *Principal occupation:* Museum professional. *Home address:* 900 West 190 St., Apt. 11-O, New York, N.Y. 10040. *Affiliations:* Teaching assistant, research assistant, assistant instructor, graduate assistant, University of Kansas, Lawrence, Kan., 1977-1983; co-director, Kansas Committee for the Humanities Project "Change, Continuities, and Challenges, Haskell Indian Junior College, 1884-1984," 1984-1985; intern fellowship, Museum of the American Indian, Ne York, N.Y., 1985-. *Other professional posts:* Consultant: KANU Radio, University of Kansas, 1981-; Women's Transitional Care, Lawrence, Kan., 1982-; Haskell Indian Junior College, 1984-; Museum of the American Indian, 1985-; chairperson, Grand Review Committee for Department of Health and Human Services, Office of Human Development Services, 1985-. *Memberships:* American Historical Association; American Anthropological Association; Phi Alpha Theta; Society for Values in Higher Education. *Awards, honors:* Danforth Foundation Fellowship, 1979-1982; Outstanding

Americans Program, listed in *Outstanding Young Women in America,* 1977; American Indian Scholarship Program, 1977-1980; Lawrence Professional and Business Women's Outstanding Haskel Indian Junior College Student, 1975; Merwlyn Foundation Research Grant, 1976; Commission of the Status for Women, Outstanding Student in Contributions to a Minority Culture, 1976; Minority Affairs Teaching Assistant Award, 1977; Graduate School, Dissertation Fellowship, 1984-1985. *Interests:* Contemporary Native American activities. *Biographical source: Outstanding Young Women in America,* 1977. *Published works: The Native American Woman: A Cross-Disciplinary Bibliography* (in preparation); "Up Before Dawn: A Study of the Family Farm," paper given at regional meeting of American Anthropological Association, Memphis, Tenn., 1979.

ROUFS, TIMOTHY G. 1943-
(professor)

Born August 30, 1943, Cokato, Minn. *Education:* University of Notre Dame, A.B., 1965; University of Minnesota, Ph.D., 1971. *Principal occupation:* Professor, Department of Sociology, Anthropology, Geography, University of Minnesota, Duluth, 1970-. *Community activities:* A.M. Chisholm Museum, Duluth, Minn. (board of directors). *Memberships:* American Ethnological Society; Society for Applied Anthropology (Fellow); American Anthropological Association (Fellow); The Royal Anthropological Association of Great Britain and Ireland (Fellow); Current Anthropology (Associate); Sigma Xi, 1980-. *Awards, honors:* 1973 Service Award from *Anishnabe,* University of Minnesota-Duluth, American Indian Student Association; 1976 City of Duluth Bicentennial Award; 1980 Outstanding Young Men of America. *Interests:* Anishnabe, Chippewa, and Ojibwa ethnohistory; culture and personality studies. *Biographical source: Who's Who in the Midwest. Published works: The Anishnabe of the Minnesota Chippewa Tribe* (Indian Tribal Series, Phoenix, 1975); *Working Bibliography of the Anishnabe and Selected Related Works* (Lake Superior Basin Studies Center, Duluth, 1981, 1984); editor, with Larry P. Atkins, *Information Relating*

to *Chippewa Peoples* (from the *Handbook of American Indians North of Mexico, 1907-1910*) (Lake Superior Basin Studies Center, Duluth, 1984).

ROUILLARD, JOHN C. (Santee Sioux)
1928-
(professor-American Indian studies)

Born December 31, 1928, Rapid City, S.D. *Education:* Northwestern Univerity, B.M.Ed., 1952, M.M., 1958. *Principal occupation:* Professor-American Indian studies. *Home address:* 6040 Manon St., La Mesa, Calif. 92041. *Affiliation:* Chairman, American Indian Studies, San Diego State University, San Diego, Calif., 1971-. *Military service:* U.S. Army, 1946-1948. *Memberships:* California Indian Education Association; National Indian Education Association, 1972-; National Congress of American Indians, 1972-; Santee Sioux Tribe (enrolled member); Pi Kappa Lambda. *Interests:* Educational program development--main interest in post secondary education, alternative school development; music—amateau and professional performance and research in American Indian music. *Published works:* "The Tale of Iktomi and the Sheeo," in *Spectrum of Music* (Macmillan, 1974); "Contemporary Indian Education," in *The People Cabrillo Met* (Third Annual Cabrilla Festival Historical Seminar, 1975).

ROUSE, IRVING 1913-
(professor and curator emeritus
of anthropology)

Born August 29, 1913, Rochester, N.Y. *Education:* Yale University, B.S., 1934, Ph.D., 1938. *Principal occupation:* Professor and curator emeritus of anthropology, Peabody Museum and Department of Anthropology, Yale University, New Haven, Conn., 1938-. *Other professional post:* Research associate, Museum of the American Indian, New York, N.Y. *Memberships:* American Anthropological Association, 1935-; Society for American Archaeology, 1935-; Association for Field Archaeology, 1974-. *Awards, honors:* A. Cressy Morrison Prize in Natural Science, New York Academy of Sciences, 1948; Viking Fund Medal and

Award in Anthropology, 1960; Distinguished Service Award, American Anthropological Association, 1984; Fiftieth Anniversary Award, Society for American Archaeology, 1985. *Interests:* Archaeological fieldwork. *Published works: A Survey of Indian River Archaeology, Florida* (Yale University Publications in Anthropology, 1951); *Introduction to Prehistory: A Systematic Approach* (McGraw-Hill, 1972); among others.

ROWLAND, ALLEN (Northern Cheyenne)
(tribal president)

Affiliation: President, Northern Cheyenne Tribal Council, Lame Deer, Mt. 59043.

ROWLAND, DARIUS
(college president)

Affiliation: President, Dull Knife Memorial College, P.O. Box 206, Lame Deer, Mt. 59043.

RUBY, ROBERT H., M.D., 1921-
(physician and surgeon)

Born April 23, 1921, Mabton, Wash. *Education:* Whitworth College, B.S., 1943; Washington University School of Medicine, M.D., 1945. *Principal occupation:* Physician and surgeon. *Home address:* 1022 Ivy, Moses Lake, Wash. 98837. *Affiliations:* Director, USPHS Hospital, Pine Ridge Indian Reservation, 1953-1955; private practice of medicine, Moses Lake, Wash., 1955-. *Other professional post:* Instructor (course on Native Americans), Department of Anthropology, Big Bend Community College, Moses Lake, Wash. *Military service:* U.S. Army Air Corps, 1946-1948. Schiffner Military Museum (board member); Washington State Library Association; Grant County Historical Society; Moses Lake Migrant Committee; Moses Lake Public Library. *Memberships:* Amerian Medical Association, 1945-; Washington State Medical Society, 1955-; American College of Surgeons, 1954-. *Awards, honors:* The Robert Gray Medal Award by the Washington State Historical Society;

The Distinguished Author of History Award of the Esatern Washington State Historical Society; Certificate of Recognition at the Governor's Writers Day in 1967, 1971, 1983; the Pacific Norhwest Booksellers Award, 1966; The Northwest Author's Award for nonfiction, 1966; a resolution of commendation by the Moses Lake City council, Dec., 1971. *Interests:* "Writing and traveling. My writing consists of many articles on the Native Americans for newspapers, and magazines, besides the numerous books (listed below). I have also written a portion of a text book for Native Americans used in some Spokane (Wash.) schools." *Biographical sources: Who's Who in the West. Published works: The Oglala Sioux* (Vantage Press, 1955); *Myron Eels and the Puget Sound Indians* (Superior Publishing, 1975); *Half-Sun on the Columbia,* 1963, *The Spokane Indians,* 1970, *The Cayuse Indians,* 1972, *The Chinook Indians,* 1975, *Indians of the Pacific Northwest: A History,* 1981, and *A Guide to the Indian Tribes of the Pacific Northwest,* 1986, all published by the University of Oklahoma Press.

RUDDELL, J. PRESTON, Jr. 1949-
(attorney)

Born December 20, 1949, Schenectady, N.Y. *Education:* University of North Carolina, B.A., 1971; UNC Law School, J.D., 1975. *Principal occupation:* Attorney. *Home address:* Box 985, Eagle Butte, S.D. 57625. *Affiliations:* Attorney, South Dakota Legal Services, Fort Thompson and Eagle Butte, S.D., 1976-1977; attorney general, Cheyenne River Sioux Tribe, Eagle Butte, S.D., 1977-. *Military service:* U.S. National Guard, SP-4, 1970-1976. *Community activities:* Crow Creek Commission on Alcoholism, Fort Thompson, S.D. *Membership:* South Dakota Bar Association. *Awards, honors:* Reginald Heber Smith Community Lawyer Fellowship Program, 1975-1977. *Interests:* Indian law; "have played professional baseball and am interested in all sports. I'm an eastern transplant who loves South Dakota and working with Native American people."

RUSSELL, JERRY
(chairman-Indian organization)

Affiliation: National chairman, Order of the Indian Wars, P.O. Box 7401, Little Rock, Ark. 72217.

RUSSELL, NED (Yavapai-Apache)
(tribal chairman)

Affiliation: Chairman, Yavapai-Apache Community Council, P.O. Box 1188, Camp Verde, Ariz. 86322.

S

SABATTIS, CLAIR (Maliseet)
(tribal chairwoman)

Affiliation: Chairwoman, Houlton Maliseet Band Council, P.O. Box 576, Houlton, Maine 04730.

SAINTE-MARIE, BUFFY (Cree) 1942-
(folksinger, poet)

Born February 20, 1942, Craven, Saskatchewan, Can. *Education:* University of Massachusetts, B.A. (Philosophy), 1963. *Principal occupation:* Folksinger, poet. *Affiliations:* Recording artist, Vanguard Recording Society. *Other occupation:* Free-lance writer on Indian culture and affairs; associate editor, *The Native Voice* (Vancouver, B.C., Can.). *Interests:* Lecturing on Indian affairs; composing, singing. Miss Sainte-Marie writes, "I am best known for songs and poems directly related to past and present American Indian affairs. (I have contributed) to *The Native Voice, Thunderbird, American Indian Horizons,* and *Boston Broadside* in the fields of North American Indian music and Indian affairs. Have lived on and visited reserves (reservations) in fifteen states and four provinces; have traveled, lectured and sung in England, France, Canada, Italy, and Mexico, and have given performances in concert and on television internationally and in all major American cities."

ST. CLAIR, ROBERT N.
(professor of linguistics;
consultant-Indian affairs)

Education: Univerity of Hawaii, B.A., 1963; University of Kansas, Ph.D., 1974. *Principal occupation:* Professor of linguistics, University of Louisville, Louisville, Ky., 1973-; consultant in Indian affairs. *Military service:* U.S. Army, 1957-1960. *Professional activities:* Xth International Conference on Salish Languages (chairman); editor, *Lektos;* editor, *Language Today;* editorial board: language problems and language planning, invisible speech, Annuario (Santo Domingo); co-editor, *Philosophical Linguistics. Memberships:* National Council of Teachers of English; Modern Language Association; International Conference on Salishan Languages; Linguistics Society of America; American Association for the Advancement of Science. *Awards, honors:* Outstanding Educator Award, 1975; Distinguished Visiting Professor (New Mexico State University), 1977. *Field work:* Salishan languages: Skagit, Lummi; Sahaptian languages: Yakima, Wanapam; Eskimo: Yupik Eskimo. *Interests:* Bilingual education; sociolinguistics; political linguistics; travel. *Dissertation;* "Theoretical Aspects of Eskimo Phonology," University of Kansas, Department of Linguistics. *Biographical sources: Who's Who in the South and Southwest; Dictionary of International Biography. Published works:* Numerous articles, papers, monographs, and book reviews in scholarly journals.

SALABIYE, VELMA
(librarian)

Affiliation: Librarian, American Indian Studies Center Library, 3220 Campbell Hall, U.C.L.A., Los Angeles, Calif. 90024.

SALISBURY, NEAL 1940-
(historian, teacher)

Born May 7, 1940, Los Angeles, Calif. *Education:* University of California, Los Angeles, B.A., 1963, M.A., 1966, Ph.D., 1972. *Principal occupation:* Historian, teacher. *Address, Affiliation:* Associate professor, Department of History, Smith College, Northamtpon, Mass. 01063 (1973-). *Memberships:* American Historical Association; American Society for Ethnohistory; Organization of American Historians. *Awards, honors:* Fellow, Smithsonian Institution, 1972-1973; Fellow, Newberry Library Center for History of the American Indian, 1977-1978; Fellow, National Endowment for the Humanities, 1984-1985. *Published works: Manitou and Providence: Indians, Europeans, and the Beginnings of New England, 1500-1643* (Oxford University Press, 1982); *The Indians of New England: A Critical Bibliography* (Indiana University Press, 1982).

SALVADOR, LILLY (Acoma Pueblo) 1944-
(potter)

Born April 6, 1944, McCartys Village, Acoma Pueblo, N.M. *Education:* New Mexico State, Grants, N.M. (one year). *Principal occupation:* Self-employed potter. *Home address:* P.O. Box 342, Acoma Pueblo, N.M. 87034. *Affiliations: Pottery is displayed at the following museums and galleries: Boston Museum of Fine Arts, Boston, Mass.; The Heard Museum, Phoenix, Ariz.; The Museum of Man, San Diego, Calif.; The Natural History Museum, Los Angeles, Calif.; The Whitehorse Gallery, Boulder, Colo. Other institutional affiliation:* National Indian Council on Aging Catalogue. *Community activities:* Native needle embroidery instructor, Acoma Adult Education Programs; secretary, Sky City Community School; member, parent-student association of Saint Joseph School, San Fidel, N.M. *Memberships:* Southwest American Indian Arts Association, 1964-; National Indian Arts & Crafts Association (Albuquerque, N.M.), 1985-1986; Smithsonian Institution, 1985. *Awards, honors:* 1st and 2nd Prize Awards for handcrafted pottery from Whitehorse Gallery, Boulder, Colo; 1st and 3rd Prize Award Ribbons from New Mexico State Fair; 1st, 2nd and 3rd Prize Awards for handcrafted/handpainted pottery from the Southwest American Indian Arts Association, 1st, Honorable Mention Awards from the Gallup Intertribal Indian Ceremonial; 1st, Special Award Ribbon from the Heard Museum, Phoenix, Ariz. *Interests:* "To develop and expand my present pottery gallery (the first at the Pueblo Acoma) into a major showcase for collectors, tourists (who visit annually the oldest inhabited village in the U.S.) and discriminating curators of various museums throughout the U.S. With the private invitations extended by the above mentioned museums and galleries, I have traversed the southwest and northwest region of the U.S. exhibiting my traditional handcrafted-handpainted Acoma Pueblo pottery and figurines." *Biographical sources: American Indian Pottery,* 2nd Edition; *Amerika* newsletter, Chicago, Ill.; National Indian Council on Aging *Catalogue.*

SALZMANN, ZDENEK 1925-
(professor of anthropology)

Born October 18, 1925, Prague, Czechoslovakia. *Education:* Caroline University, Prague, 1945-1947 (Absolutorium, 1948); Indiana University, M.A., 1949, Ph.D., 1963. *Principal occupation:* Professor of anthropology, University of Massachusetts, Amherst, 1968-. *Home address:* 25 Chapel Rd., Amherst, Mass. 01002. *Other professional posts:* Visiting professor, Yale University; consultant to Wind River Reservation schools on Arapaho language and culture curriculum, 1979-. *Memberships:* Linguistic Society of America, 1949-; American Anthropological Association, 1954-; Current Anthropology, 1961-; Ameriacn Folklore Society, 1966-. *Awards, honors:* Research grants from the following: American Philosophical Society; National Endowment for the Humanities; Senior Fulbright-Hays Scholar, International Research and Exchange Board; American Council of Learned Societies. Given in a public ceremony and with the approval of Arapaho elders, the name *hinono'ei neecee* ("Arapaho Chief"). *Interests:* Fieldwork among Northern Arapaho Indians, 1949-; numerous trips to the Wind River Reservation under various auspices. *Biographical sources: American Men and Women of Science; Contemporary Authors; Directory of American Scholars. Published works: Dictionary of Contemporary Arapaho Usage* (Arapaho Language and Culture Commission, 1983); *Analytical Bibliography of Sources Concerning the Arapaho Indians* (Arapaho Language and Culture

Commission, 2nd revised edition); among others; numerous articles in various scholarly journals.

SAM, JIMMY L.
(executive director-Indian center)

Affiliation: Executive director, Boston Indian Council, Inc., 105 S. Huntington, Jamaica Plain, Mass. 02130.

SAMUELSON, LILLIEN THOMPSON 1926-
(owner/manager-Indian shop)

Born July 13, 1926, Mecklenburg County, Va. *Education:* Virginia Polytechnic Institute, 1945-1947; Illinois Institute of Technology, B.S., 1949. *Principal occupation:* Owner/manager, American Indian Treasures, Inc., 2558 Western Ave., Guilderland, N.Y. 12084., 1968-. *Home address:* P.O. Box 595, Guilderland,N.Y. 12084. *Community activities:* Sponsors Native American art show at Sienna College, Loudonville, N.Y. each Spring; co-sponsors celebration of American Indian Day each Fall at the Albany, N.Y. Library. *Memberships:* American Home Economic Association, 1949-; National Congress of American Indians; Association on American Indian Affairs, Inc.; Indian Arts and Crafts Association (board of directors, 1976; vice president, 1978). *Interests:* Ms. Samuelson writes, "My interest in the American Indian goes back to early childhood, with serious studies of the arts and crafts of living Indians having been pursued the last 20 years, Travel has been extensive during this time, and I've come to know the products of most reservations in the U.S. (I) worked as a consultant on Indian education for the New York State Education Department. I started American Indian Treasures in 1967, selling only jand-made Indian crafts from a broadrange of tribes and cultures. Items sold are personally collected to assure authenticity, with buying trips made regularly throughout the year." *Published works:* Articles published in monthlies, distributed nationally, about American Indian artists.

SANBORN, JAMES H. (Penobscot) 1931-
(Indian school principal)

Born January 2, 1931, Milford, Maine. *Education:* University of Alaska, Anchorage, B.S., 1971; University of Southern Maine, Gorham, M.S. (Education), 1973; University of Maine, Orono, C.A.S. (Administration), 1983. *Principal occupation:* Principal, Indian Township School, Princeton, Maine. *Home address:* Box 96, Princeton, Maine 04668. *Military service:* U.S. Air Force, 1948-1971 (retired-Msgt; Air Medal/6OLC; Combat Readiness Badge; Vietnam Service; Korean Service). *Memberships:* American Association of School Administrators; Council for Exceptional Children; Maine Reading Association; International Reading Association. *Interests:* Outdoor sports; travel.

SANCHEZ, GILBERT (San Ildefonso Pueblo)
(Pueblo governor)

Affiliation: Governor, San Ildefonso Pueblo, Route 5, Box 315A. Santa Fe, N.M. 87501.

SANDERS, E. FRED (Catawba) 1926-
(machinist, assistant chief)

Born April 9, 1926, Catawba Indian Reservation, York County, S.C. *Education:* Catawba Indian School; vocational and technical school—machinist courses. *Principal occupation:* Maintenance machinist, General Tire Corp, Charlotte, N.C., 1967-. *Home address:* Reservation Rd., Rural Box 327, Rock Hill, S.C. 29730. *Other professional post:* Master barber. *Military service:* U.S. Army, 1944-1950 (1st Sergeant; Infantry, World War II: Combat Infantry Badge; Bronze Star; 2 Campaign Battle Stars; V.E. Ribbon; Army Occupation Award-Austria). *Community activities:* Assistant chief, Catawba Nation, S.C., 1975-; Charlotte-Mecklenburg Public School System—Indian Education (chairperson-Title IV Program). *Memberships:* National Congress of American Indians; Veterans of Foreign Wars, Rock Hill, S.C.; American Legion, Rock Hill, S.C. *Interests:* "Travel as

official tribal delegate to many National
Congress of American Indians' conferences
and conventions in various states. Support
tribal leaders with positive attitude and assu-
rance that Native Americans will continue to
have a voice and input concerning the future
destiny of tribal government and its people."

SANDO, JOE SIMON *(Paa Peh)*
(Jemez Pueblo) 1923-
   (teacher, writer)

Born August 1, 1923, Jemez Pueblo, N.M.
Education: Eastern New Mexico State University, Portales, B.A., 1949; University of
New Mexico, 1950-1951, 1973; Vanderbilt
University, 1959-1960. *Principal occupation:*
Instructor (ethnohistory), Institute of Amer-
ican Indian Arts, Sante Fe, N.M., 1982-.
Other professional posts: Lecturer on his-
tory, Pueblo Indian Cultural Center; education specialist and teacher of Pueblo Indian
history, University of New Mexico. *Military
service:* U.S. Navy, 1943-1946 (Yeoman 2nd;
World War II; Pacific Campaign Ribbon
with four stars). *Community activities:* All
Indian Pueblo Council (chairman of education, 1970); New Mexico State Judicial
Council (chairman, 1970); American Indian
Scholarships (secretary/treasurer - 14
years); Ancient City Toastmasters Club,
Santa Fe, N.M. (president, 1968). *Awards,
honors:* Alumnus of the Year, 1970, Eastern
New Mexico University. *Interests:* "Gardening with numerous blue ribbons for garden
crops from New Mexico State Fair; woodworking; writing for publication on Indian
history and education; lecture tour of New
Zealand Maori area in 1979; lecture tour of
Switzerland and West Germany in 1981; lecturing to civic groups in State and other
states on Indian history. *Biographical sources: Personalities of the West and Midwest,*
1971; *Indians of Today,* Fourth Edition,
1971. *Published works: The Pueblo Indians*
(Indian Historian Press, 1976, 1982); *Pueblo
Indian Biographies* (S.I.P.I. Press, Albuquerque, 1976); *Nee Hemish, The History of
Jemez Pueblo* (University of New Mexico
Press, 1982); *Pope* (World Book Encyclopedia, 1970); many articles in *New Mexico
Magazine, The Indian Historian, HUD
Magazine.*

SANDOVAL ANNA (Diegueno)
   (tribal spokeswoman)

Affiliation: Spokeswoman, Sycuan General
Council, P.O. Box 2929, El Cajon, Calif.
92021.

SANDOVAL, JOSEPH C. (Taos Pueblo)
   (Pueblo governor)

Affiliation: Governor, Taos Pueblo, P.O.
Box 1846, Taos, N.M. 87571.

SANDOVAL, WILLIAM
   (B.I.A. agency superintendent)

Affiliation: Superintendent, Umatilla
Agency, Bureau of Indian Affairs, P.O. Box
520, Pendleton, Ore. 97801.

SATZ, RONALD N. 1944-
   (professor of history)

Born February 8, 1944, Chicago, Ill. *Education:* Illinois Institute of Technology, B.S.,
1965; Illinois State University, M.A., 1967;
University of Maryland, Ph.D., 1971 (Dissertation: *Federal Indian Policy, 1829-
1849). Principal occupation:* Professor of
history. *Home address:* 4015 White Pine
Dr., East, Eau Claire, Wis. 54701-7465. *Affiliations:* Assistant professor, 1971-1975,
associate professor with tenure, 1977-1980,
dean of graduate studies, 1976-1983, dean of
research, 1977-1893, professor with tenure,
1980-1983, University of Tennessee at Martin; dean, School of Graduate Studies, director, Office of University Research, and
professor of history, The University of Wisconsin, Eau Claire, Wis., 1983-. *Other professional posts:* Proposal reviewer, National
Endowment for the Humanities, 1978-; editorial committee, The Council of Graduate
Schools in the U.S., 1983-; advisory committee on minority student affairs, and undergraduate teaching improvement council,
University of Wisconsin, Madison, 1984-;
camous liaison, University of Wisconsin
System Committee on University/Industry
Cooperation, 1985-; Publications Commit-
tee, Midwestern Association of Graduate
Schools, 1985-1988. *Community activities:*
Ad Hoc Commission on Racism of the Lac
Courte Oreilles Lae Superior Ojibwa Tribal

Governing Board (member); Parent-Teacher Organization, Manz Elementary School and South Junior High School, Eau Claire, Wis. (member); The Heritage Club of the Chippewa Valley Museum, Eau Claire (member). *Memberships:* American Association for Higher Education; American Association of University Professors; American Historical Association; Organization of American Historians; Society for American Indian Studies and Research; Society for Historians of the Early American Republic; Western History Association; Sigma Xi; Pi Gamma Mu; Phi Alpha Theta; Phi Kappa Phi; Delta Tau Kappa; among others. *Award, honors:* University of Tennessee at Martin Liberal Arts Merit Award, 1974, and Phi Kappa Phi Scholar Award, 1983; National Defense Education Act Fellow, University of Maryland, 1970; Fellow in Ethnic Studies, Ford Foundation, 1971; Younger Humanist Research Fellow, National Endowment for the Humanities, 1974; Title III Grant, U.S. Office of Education, University of Tennessee at Martin, 1978, 1981, 1982; University of Wisconsin System Undergraduate Teaching Improvement Council Grant for Critical Thinking Across Disciplines Project, 1985. *Interests:* "Indian-white relations, especially the 19th century; American Indian policy; tribal history; Indian-black relations; Indian religious beliefs and the impact of Christian missionary efforts on Indian religions." *Biographical sources: Outstanding American Educators,* 1974-1975; *Directory of American Scholars,* 6th-8th Eds.; *Contemporary Authors,* 1982; *Dictionary of International Biography,* 1976-1977; *Who's Who in the South and Southwest,* 16th-18th Eds.; *Personalities of the South,* 1978-1979, 1979-1980 Eds.; *International Who's Who in Education,* 1980 Ed.; *Who's Who in the Midwest,* 20th Ed. *Published works: American Indian Policy in the Jacksonian Era* University of Nebraska Press, 1975); *Tennessee's Indian Peoples: From White Contact to Removal, 1540-1840* (University of Tennessee Press, 1979); co-author: *America: Changing Times,* textbook, 1979- (John Wiley & Sons, 1979-1984; Alfred A. Knopf, 1984-); contibutor: *Heroes of Tennessee* (Memphis State University Press, 1979); *The Commissioners of Indian Affairs, 1824-1977* (University of Nebraska Press, 1979);

American Vistas, 1607-1877, 3rd-4th Eds. (Oxford University Press, 1979, 1984); *After Removal: The Choctaw in Mississippi* (University Press of Mississippi, 1986); *Handbook of North American Indians,* 4th Ed. (Smithsonian Institution Press-in press).

SAUBEL, KATHERINE SIVA
(Cahuilla) 1920-
(museum trustee)

Born March 7, 1920, Los Coyotes Reservation, Calif. *Principal occupation:* Trustee and president, Malki Museum, Inc., Banning, Calif. *Home address:* Box 373, Banning, Calif. 92220. *Other professional posts:* Advisory representative, County of Riverside, Calif., Historical Commission; consultant-lecturer, California State College at Hayward, Calif., University of Colorado, and University of California. *Community activities:* Los Coyotes Tribal Council; Mothers Club, Morongo Indian Reservation. *Interests:* Ms. Saubel participated in the Indian Leadership Training Program at the University of California; other interests are Indian history and ethnography, and linguistics. She writes, "I have traveled extensively in the Southwest and California, visiting reservations and museums which display Indian history and culture." *Published works: Cahuilla Ethnobotanical Notes: Oak,* and *Mesquite and Screwbean,* both with Lowell J. Bean (University of California, Archaeological Survey Annual Report, 1962, 1968); *Temalpah: Economic Botany of the Cahuilla Indians,* with Lowell J. Bean (Malki Museum, 1969); *Kunvachmal, A Cahuilla Tale* (The Indian Historian, 1969).

SAUL, C. TERRY *(Tobaksi)*
(Choctaw-Chickasaw) 1921-
(artist)

Born April 2, 1921, Sardis, Okla. *Education:* Bacone Junior College, 1940; University of Oklahoma, B.F.A., 1949. *Principal occupation:* Commercial artist, Phillips Petroleum Co., Bartlesville, Okla., 1955-; "I have a studio in my home and paint for various Indian shows and exhibits and commissioned murals and paintings." *Military service:* U.S.

Army, 1940-1945 (Infantry; Purple Heart, Bronze Star, American Defense Service Ribbon). *Memberships:* Art Students' League (life member). *Awards, honors:* Numerous awards received at various national Indian art shows and exhibitions, such as: American Indian Exposition, Anadarko, Okla.; National Indian Art Show, Bismarck, N.D.; Denver Art Museum; Museum of New Mexico; and National Indian Art Exhibition, Scottsdale, Ariz. Numerous one-man and group shows, traveling exhibitions, etc. Represented in many private and public collections throughout the U.S. and elsewhere.

SAULQUE, JOSEPH C. (Paiute) 1942-
(tribal administrator)

Born October 20, 1942, Bishop, Calif. *Education:* West Valley Community College, Campbell, Calif., A.A., 1970; Brigham Young University, B.A., 1973. *Principal occupation:* Administrative officer, Indian reservation. *Home address:* P.O. Box 1212, Bishop, Calif. 93514. *Affiliation:* Chairman, Utu Utu Gwaitu Paiute Tribe, Benton Paiute Reservation, Benton, Calif. (six years). *Military service:* U.S. Army, 1961-1964 (E-4/Sp-4 Airborne Division). *Memberships:* National Congress of American Indians, 1974-; California Tribal Chairman's Association, Sacramento, Calif. (secretary-three years). *Interests:* Indian affairs.

SAUNOOKE, OSLEY BIRD, Jr. (Eastern Cherokee) 1943-
(attorney, business consultant)

Born April 6, 1943, Jacksonville, Fla. *Education:* East Tennessee State University, 1962-1963; Brigham Young University, B.S., 1965; Univerity of New Mexico Law School, J.D., 1972. *Principal occupation:* Attorney, business consultant. *Home address:* 2435 Gulf Gate Dr., Sarasota, Fla. 33581. *Affiliations:* Teacher-guidance counselor, Cleveland, Ohio, Chicago, Ill., 1965-1969; executive director, United Southeastern Tribes, Inc., 1972-1973; executive director, Florida Governor's Council on Indian Affairs, 1973-1974. *Memberships:* National Congress of American Indians

(Southeast area vice president, 1972-1973; first vice president, 1973-1974; board member, American Indian Scholarships, 1974-).

SAVALA, DELORES (Paiute)
(tribal chairwoman)

Affiliation: Chairwoman, Kaibab Tribal Council, Tribal Affairs Bldg., Pipe Springs, Ariz. 86022.

SAVARD, REMI 1934-
(professeur)

Born March 27, 1934, Quebec, Can. *Education:* Universite Laval, Quebec, Maitrise (Sociologie); Sorbonne, Paris France, Doctorate (Ethnologie). *Principal occupation:* Associate professeur, Dept. D'Anthropologie, Universite de Montreal, Montreal, Quebec, Can. *Memberships:* Canadian Association in Support of the Native People; Canadian Sociology and Anthropology Association. *Interests:* Northeastern Indian mythology; Indian land claims; Indian-non-Indian relationships. *Published works: Carcajou et le Sens Du Monde Recits Montagnais-Naskapi* (Editeau Officiel du Quebec, 1971, 1972, 1974 - 3rd ed.); *Signes et Langages des Ameriques* (Recherches Amerindiennes au Quebec, 1973); *Lerire Precolumbien Dans le Quebec D'Aujourd Hui* (L'Hexagone/Parti Pris, 1977).

SAVILLA, ELMER
(executive director-Indian association)

Affiliation: Executive director, National Tribal Chairman's Association, 818 18th St., N.W., Suite 420, Washington, D.C. 20006.

SCHAAFSMA, POLLY DIX 1935-
(artist, archaeologist)

Born October 24, 1935, Springfield, Vt. *Education:* Mt. Holyoke Colege, B.A., 1957; University of Colorado, M.A., 1962. *Principal occupation:* Artist, archaeologist. *Home address:* Box 289, Arroyo Hondo, N.M. 87513. *Affiliation: Non-staff research archaeologist, Museum of New Mexico, 1963-1967; research assistant, Peabody*

Museum, Harvard University, 1968-1969; author, *School of American Research.* *Memberships:* American Rock Art Research Association; Society for American Archaeology; Taos Art Association (exhibiting artist, 1969-). *Interests:* Prehistoric Indian rock art, particularly of the Southwest; evolution and stylistic development of art forms; Indian religion; primitive art; travels to Mexico. *Published works: Rock Art of the Navajo Reservoir District,* (Museum of New Mexico, 1963); *Southwest Indian Pictographs and Petroglyphs,* (Museum of New Mexico, 1965); *Early Navaho Rock Paintings & Carvings* (Museum of Navaho Ceremonial Art, 1966); *Rio Grande Petroglyphs of the Cochiti Reservoir* (Museum of New Mexico, 1975); *The Rock Art of Utah* (Peabody Museum, 1971); *Indian Rock Art of the Southwest* (University of New Mexico, School of American Research).

SCHEIRBECK, HELEN MAYNOR (Lumbee) 1935-
(human resources administrator)

Born August 21, 1935, Lamberton, N.C. *Education:* Berea College, Berea, Ky., B.A., 1957; VPI - SU, Blacksburg, Va., Ed.D., 1980. *Principal occupation:* Human resources administrator. *Address, Affiliation:* Director, American Indian Programs, Save the Children Federation, 54 Wilton Rd., Westport, Conn. 06880 (1983-). *Other professional posts:* Chairwoman, Indian Education Task Force, American Indian Policy Review Commission, U.S. Congress; director, Office of Indian Affairs, U.S. Office of Education, Dept. of HEW; professional staff, U.S. Senate Subcommittee on Constitutional Rights. *Memberships:* United Indians of America (project advisor); National Indian Education Association (vice president). *Awards, honors:* John Hay Whitney Foundation, Opportunity Award; Outstanding Lumbee Award; Outstanding American Indian Award; Pepsi People Pour It On Award. *Interests:* "Dr. Scheirbeck has traveled and worked throughout the U.S. She has worked with the majority of Indian tribes in the U.S. She has served on Legislature and Executive Task Forces investigating various issues affecting Indian people. Her hobbies include photography, writing,

collecting legends, and swimming." *Biographical sources: Outstanding Indians in USA; Indians of the Southwest; Outstanding Minority Women; Biographies of Outstanding American Indian Women.* *Published works:* "Indian Education: Tool for Cultural Politics" (Harvard Center for Law & Education, Dec., 1970); "The First Americans" (American Red Cross Youth News, Nov., 1972); *The History of Federal Indian Education Policy* (American Indian Policy Review Commission, 1976); *A Study of Three Selected Laws & Their Impact on American Indian Education* (House of Interior & Insular Affairs, Oct., 1976); *Public Policy and Contemporary Education of the American Indian* (Ph.D. Dissertation, 1980).

SCHINDLER, DUANE E. (Turtle Mountain Chippewa) 1944-
(Indian high school principal)

Born April 22, 1944, Turtle Mountain Indian Reservation, Belcourt, N.D. *Education:* University of North Dakota; Valley City State College, N.D.; University of Wisconsin, Eau Claire; Arizona State University; University of South Dakota. *Principal ocupation:* Principal, Turtle Mountain Chippewa High School, Belcourt, N.D. *Home address:* Belcourt, N.D. 57318. *Affiliations:* Program development specialist, Eastern Montana State College, Billings, Mt. (two years); program specialist, University of New Mexico, Albuquerque, N.M. (one year); instructor, Adult Programs, Wenatchee Valley College, Omak, Wash. (two years); director, Adult Education, Colville Confederated Tribes, Nespelem, Wash. (one year); director, American Indian Student Division, University of Washington, Seattle, Wash. (one year). *Other professional posts:* Field reader, consultant: Logo language; computer applications, computer literacy, computer office systems; curriculum development; school board training; program evaluation management. *Community activities:* American Indian Center, Spokane, Wash. (chairman). *Memberships:* National Association of Secondary School Principals; National Indian Education Association; ASCD, NABE. *Awards, honors:* Outstanding Teacher, Oglala Community Schools, Pine Ridge, S.D. *Interests:*

Computers in the classroom; research in mathematics. *Biographical source: Outstanding Young Men of America, 1973. Published works: Concepts of American Indian Learners* (Education, Tempe, Ariz.); *Language, Culture and the Mathematics (Journal of the American Indian, 1986).*

SCHLENDER, JAMES
(Attorney)

Affiliation: Attorney, Lac Courte Oreilles, Route 2, Box 421, Hayward, Wis. 54843.

SCHOLDER, FRITZ (Mission) 1937-
(artist)

Born October 6, 1937, Breckenridge, Minn. *Education:* Sacramento State College, B.A., 1960; University of Arizona, M.F.A., 1964. *Principal occupation:* Artist. *Home address:* 1008 Canton Rd., Santa Fe, N.M. 87501. *Other professional posts:* Participant, Southwest Indian Art Project, Rockefeller Foundation, 1961-1963; chairman, Fine Arts Committee, First Convocation of Amerian Indian Scholars, Princeton University, 1970. *Awards, honors:* Numerous awards for painting at the following exhibitions: Southwestern Drawing and Print Exhibition, Dallas Museum of Fine Arts; Mid-America Exhibition, Nelson Gallery of Art, Kansas City, Mo.; National Indian Exhibition, Scottsdale, Ariz.; among others. *Biographical sources: Who's Who in the West; Who's Who in American Art; Dictionary of International Biography.*

SCHUSKY, ERNEST L. 1931-
(professor of anthropology)

Born October 13, 1931, Portsmouth, Ohio. *Education:* Miami University, Ohio, A.B., 1952; University of Chicago, M.A., 1957, Ph.D. (Anthropology), 1960. *Principal occupation:* Professor of anthropology, Southern Illinois University, Edwardsville, Ill., 1960-. *Home address:* 412 Willowbrook, Collinsville, Ill. 62234. *Other professional post:* Author. *Military service:* U.S. Army, 1953-1954 (Corporal; served in Korea).

Memberships: American Anthropological Association; Royal Anthropological Society of Great Britain. *Awards, honors:* Fulbright Professor, 1982 (taught a course on the American Indian at Seoul National University). *Interests:* Mr. Schusky writes, "My interest in American Indians started in 1953 with the Papagos. Later field trips were made among New England Indians. Fieldwork occured among the Lower Brule and Pine Ridge Sioux between 1958-1960. The political and economic problems of Native Americans has been a professional interest throughout." *Published works: Introducing Culture* (Prentice-Hall, Inc., (four editions) 1967, 1972, 1978, 1986); *The Right to Be Indian* (Institute of Indian Studies, Vermillion, S.D., 1965; Indian Historian Press, 1970); *The Forgotten Sioux* (Nelson Hall, 1975); editor, *Political Organization of Native North Americans* (University Press of America, 1980).

SCHWIND, MARIE N.
(president-Alaskan Native association)

Affiliation: President, Maniilaq Association, P.O. Box 256, Kotzebue, Alaska 99752.

SCOTT, JAMES ROBERT 1947-
(tribal education-measurement and evaluation specialist)

Born July 7, 1947, Norman, Okla. *Education:* Oklahoma State University, B.A., 1970; University of Texas, Ph.D., 1975. *Principal occupation:* Measurement and evaluation specialist. *Home address:* Route 3, Box 556, Philadelphia, Miss. 39350. *Affiliations:* Choctaw Department of Education, Philadelphia, Miss., 1975-; Choctaw Bilingual Education Project, Route 7, Box 21, Philadelphia, Miss., 1975-. *Memberships:* National Indian Education Association; National Amerian Bilingual Education Committee; Phi Delta Kappa. *Interests:* Program development and evaluation; improving Indian education programs; legislative interaction with tribes; educational management; curriculum development.

PRINCESS ROSE SCRIBNER
(Penobscot) 1940-
(president/founder, White Cloud Cultural Center, Inc.)

Born April 3, 1940, Gardiner, Maine. *Education:* Mohegan Community College, Norwich, Conn., A.A., 1978. *Principal occupation:* President/founder, White Cloud Cultural Center, Inc., Norwich, Conn., 1975-. *Home address:* 89 Broad St., Norwich, Conn. 06361. *Memberships:* National Historic Preservation Society; National Indian Education Association; Indian Rights Association. *Awards, honors:* Outstanding Minority Award, Mohegan Community College; American Education Award, University of Connecticut. *Interests:* "My main goal in life (vocational) is to become a good Indian leader in serving our Native American people. I've traveled throughout the U.S. in observing model education programs much needed for Indian people. I hope to be appointed by the President of the U.S. in serving on the National Indian Education Advisory Board, Washington, D.C. I feel by this appointment, I can have the opportunity of getting more school books portraying Indian children properly, so that other children can read and learn what Indian people are all about. To wipe out the present stereotype Indian. Any expeditions I plan for the future will be one of taking a canoe trip down the "Allegash," this area is one in which my famous grandfather guided many famous authors, Lord's of England, Countess's of Canada, on many a trip or expedition." *Published work: Ethnic People of Connecticut* (University of Connecticut, 1979).

SEAMAN, P. DAVID 1932-
(professor of linguistics)

Born January 31, 1932, Connellsville, Pa. *Education:* Asbury College, A.B., 1957; University of Kentucky, M.A., 1958; Indiana University, Ph.D. (Linguistics), 1965. *Principal occupation:* Professor of Linguistics, Department of Anthropology, Northern Arizona University, Flagstaff, Ariz., 1967-. *Home address:* 3600 Moore Circle, Flagstaff, Ariz. 86001. *Other professional posts:* Bilingual/bicultural consulting for Zuni Tribal Council, 1970-1972; linguistic consulting for Bureau of Indian Affairs, 1968-1969, 1970-1976; cross-cultural management consulting for Hopi Tribal Council, 1974-1979; accounting and management consulting for Fort Mojave Tribal Council, 1977-1980. *Military service:* U.S. Army, 1951-1954 (Sergeant; U.S. Army Commendation Medal for efficient administration of U.S. Army field hospital in Korea, 1953). *Community activities:* University Heights Corporation, Flagstaff (director and corporate secretary, 1972-); Flagstaff Medical Center (finance committee, 1980-). *Memberships:* Linguistic Society of America; Society for Study of Indigenous Languages in America; Society for Linguistic Anthropology; Friends of Uto-Aztecan. *Awards, honors:* Distinguished Faculty Award, Northern Arizona University, 1980; among others. *Research:* Hopi dictionary project; traditional Havasupai culture; American Indian language/cultures; Alfred F. Whiting Indian archives. *Interests:* American Indian languages and culture; Greek language and culture. *Paper delivered:* "Hopi Dictionary and Computers," joint meeting, Arizona Humanities Association and Arizona Alliance for Arts Education, Scottsdale Community College, 1983 (article—Arizona Humanities Association *Journal,* Feb., 1984). *Published works: Modern Greek and American English in Contact* (Mouton & Co., The Hague, 1972); co-editor, *Havasupai Habitat: A.F. Whiting's Ethnography of a Traditional Indian Culture* (University of Arizona Press, 1985); *Hopi Dictionary: Hopi-English, English-Hopi* (Northern Arizona University Anthropoogical Paper No. 2, 1985); article: "Hopi Linguistics: An Annotated Bibliography (*Anthropological Linguistics,* 1977).

SECAKUKU, ALPH
(B.I.A. agency superintendent)

Affiliation: Superintendent, Hopi Agency, Bureau of Indian Affairs, Keams Canyon, Ariz. 86034.

SENECA, WILLIAM
(B.I.A. agency superintendent)

Affiliation: Superintendent, New York Liaison Office, Bureau of Indian Affairs, Federal Bldg., 100 S. Clinton St., Syracuse, N.Y. 13202.

SEVELLA, GWENDOLYN (Luiseno)
(tribal chairwoman)

Affiliation: Chairwoman, La Posta General Council, P.O. Box 894, Boulevard, Calif. 92005.

SHAKE SPEAR, VERNON (Paiute)
(tribal chairman)

Affiliation: Chairman, Burns-Paiute General Council, P.O. Box 71, Burns, Ore. 97720.

SHARLOW, JAMES
(chief-personnel operations,
Indian Health Service)

Affiliation: Chief, Personnel Operation Branch, Indian Health Service, 5600 Fishers Lane, Rockville, Md. 20857.

SHAW, CARL F.
(director of public affairs-B.I.A.)

Affiliation: Director of Public Affairs, Bureau of Indian Affairs, 1951 Constitution Ave., N.W., Washington, D.C. 20245.

SHAW, FRANCES (Diegueno)
(tribal chairman)

Affiliation: Chairman, Manzanita General Council, P.O. Box 1302, Boulevard, Calif. 92005; chairman, Southern Indian Health Council, P.O. Box 20889, El Cajon, Calif. 92021.

SHAW, WILFRED (Paiute)
(tribal chairman)

Affiliation: Chairman, Pyramid Lake Paiute Tribal Council, P.O. Box 256, Nixon, Nev. 89424.

SHEA, ESTHER S. (Mrs.)
(Tlingit-Haida) 1917-
(Tlingit language instructor)

Born April 21, 1917, Ketchikan, Alaska. *Principal occupation:* Tlingit language instructor, Ketchikan Indian Education, Ketchikan, Alaska, 1974-. *Community activities:* Alaska Native Sisterhood (Tlingit Naa president, 1976-1977; board); Ketchikan Indian Corporation (board of directors, 1978). *Interests:* Native language preservation; curriculum development; bilingual conferences; bicultural exchange. *Published works:* Three children's books in Tlingit, 1975; *Tlingit Conversation Book,* 1977; numerous Tlingit daily lesson plans and worksheets; Tlingit number and animal coloring books; song translations into Tlingit, like "Jingle Bells."

SHEA, JAMES
(chief-health services planning,
Indian Health Service)

Affiliation: Chief, Health Services Planning Branch, Indian Health Service, 5600 Fishers Lane, Rockville, Md. 20857.

SHEA, W. TIMOTHY 1936-
(public health analyst)

Born December 22, 1936, Columbus, Ohio. *Education:* Xavier University, B.S., 1961; University of Michigan, M.P.H., 1971. *Principal occupation:* Director, Division of Program Evaluation and Policy Analaysis, Indian Health Service, 5600 Fishers Lane, Washington, D.C., 20245, 1971-. *Home address:* 16205 Oak Meadow Dr., Rockville, Md. 20855. *Memberships:* Toastmasters International; American Management Association; Public Health Advisors Association; American Public Health Association. *Awards, honors:* Four recent awards from the Health Resources and Service Administration. *Interests:* Program evaluation; policy analysis; management sciences; contemporary political analysis; decision theory resource allocation; sports; military science; philosophy.

SHEMAYME, HENRY (Caddo)
(tribal chairman)

Affiliation: Chairman, Caddo Tribal Council, P.O. Box 487, Binger, Okla. 73009.

SHENANDOAH, LEON (Onondaga)
(tribal chief)

Affiliation: Chief, Onondaga Nation, P.O. Box 270A, Nedrow, N.Y. 13120.

SHEPPARD, LAVERNE (Shoshone-Bannock) 1960-
(editor)

Born April 17, 1960, Blackfoot, Idaho. *Education:* University of Arizona (one year); Washington State University (three years); Idaho State University, B.A. (Journalism), 1984. *Principal occupation:* Editor, *Sho-Ban News,* 1984-. *Home address:* S033 Hawthorne Rd. #23, Chubbuck, Idaho 83202. *Affiliations:* News editor, Idaho State University student newspaper (one year); reporter, American Microsystems, Inc. magazine (six months); reporter, *Indian Youth Magazine* (one year); reporter, *The Exchange,* Phelps-Stokes Fund, Washington, D.C. (one year—. *Community activities:* Fort Hall Voter Education Committee (chairperson); Tribal Safety Committee (training coordinator); Washington State University Indian Club (president). *Memberships:* Native American Indian Women's Association; Native American Press Association. *Awards, honors:* 1985 Native American Press Association Award: Best Advertisement; honorable mention, best news series and best editorial; commendation by Idaho Governor for contribution to state's grasshopper spraying effort; Ben Davis Scholarship. *Interests:* "Since entering college back in 1978, I have interned at the Idaho Human Rights Commission, Boise, the Phelps-Stokes Fund in Washington, D.C., and American Microsystems, Inc. in Pocatello, Idaho. I participated in the Indian Business Development Program at University of Arizona, Tucson (one year) and have attended many major Indian conferences." *Biographical source: Sho-Ban News,* Fall, 1984.

SHING, LE ROY NED (Hopi) 1942-
(Indian education)

Born August 4, 1942, Keams Canyon, Ariz. *Education:* Northern Arizona University, B.S. (Sociology), 1969; Pennsylvania State University, M.Ed. (Administration), 1972. *Principal occupation:* Indian education. *Home address:* 4532 N. 18th St., Apt. 17, Phoenix, Ariz. 85016. *Affiliations:* Education Committee, education coordinator, 1969-1971, Hopi Tribe; teacher, staff trainer, principal, Hopi Reservation, Ariz. (six years); Title IV Cooridnator, Philipsburg, Pa. (one year); teacher supervisor, secondary education, Phoenix, Ariz., 1976-. *Community activities:* Urban Advisory Indian Board, Phoenix, Ariz.; chairperson, Title IV-JOM, Madison School District, Phoenix, Ariz. *Memberships:* National Indian Education Association; American Indian Research Association; Phi Delta Kappa. *Interests:* Mr. Shing writes, "(My) major interest is to better the educational opportunities for Indian students and tribes. Develop materials and curriculum that will help to upgrade the education of Indian people in the world. Do research that will improve and help others improve education." *Biographical source: International Who's Who in Community Service.* Published work: *Teacher Training Handbook* (State of Pennsylvania, 1976).

SHIPEK, FLORENCE C. 1918-
(professor of anthropology)

Born December 11, 1918, North Adams, Mass. *Education:* University of Arizona, B.A., 1940, M.A., 1940; University of Washington (Geology), 1940-1941, 1944-1946; University of Hawaii, Ph.D. (Anthropology), 1977. *Principal occupation:* Professor of anthropology. *Address:* Department of Anthropology, University of Wisconsin-Parkside, Box N-2000, Kenosha, Wis. 53141. *Affiliation:* Director, Program for Community Development Education for Southern California Indian Reservation, Sociology Department, University of San Diego, Calif., 1970-1972; assistant professor, associate professor, University of Wisconsin-Parkside, 1977-. *Other professional posts:* Anthropologist for the enrollment committee of the San Pascual Band of

Mission Indians, 1956-1968; ethnohistorical researcher, Mission Indian Land Claims Case (land use and identity of Diegueno-Kamia-Kumeyaay), 1959-1964; ethnohistorical researcher, Water Claims Case of San Luis Rey Indian reservations, 1965-1985; consultant to Environmental Impact Firms such as Wirth Associates, Cultural Systems Research, Inc., 1976-; consultant to Indian Freedom Ranch, San Diego County (a rural alcoholic rehabilitation center for Indians), 1978-1982; consultant for Southern California Indian Law Seminar, 1979; consultant for San Pascual Band Education Project, 1981; consultant to Kumeyaay Elders Association, 1981-1983; consultant for Kumeyaay Elders and Cayapaipe Reservation, 1982-; consultant and seminar lecturer for Rincon Band of San Luiseno Indians, 1984; with Dr. Lowell Bean of Cultural Systems Research, Inc., expert witness for water claims case for six southern California Indian Bands (San Luis Rey, Cuyapaipe, Pechanga, Santa Rosa, Morongo, and La Posta), 1984-; with Dr. Lowell J. Bean, consultant to San Luis Rey Band of Mission Indians in its quest for Federal recognition, 1985; consultant to Santa Ynez Reservation on membership genealogies for enrollment, 1986. *Memberships:* American Anthropological Association (Fellow); Society for Applied Anthropology (Fellow); Royal Anthropological Institute (Fellow); American Ethnological Association; American Society for Ethnohistory; Council on Anthropology and Education; Malki Museum Association; Phi Kappa Phi. *Awards, honors:* Grant from Wenner-Gren Foundation for Anthropological Research (autobiography of the last traditional leader of the Kumeyaay), 1982; appointed by the Society for American Archaeology and Society of Professional Archaeology to the Subcommittee to consider revisions to the ethics code and procedures for handling excavation and reburial of American Indian human remains and suggest modifications for state laws concerning unmarked graves, 1985. *Interests:* North American Indians; California and Southwest Indians; Research and consulting: "From 1954 to the present, I have been working directly for and with the various Southern California Indian bands and individuals, doing research for them aimed at solving specific problems.

Research included the history of changing land use and tenure rights, economic and agriculture, socio-political changes, genealogies. I have been meeting with their various political bodies and providing information directly to them. I have appeared as a witness or submitted prepared testimonies to various governmental agencies, such as the Commissioner of Indian Affairs, Indian Claims Commission, Department of Public Welfare, etc. *Published works: Lower California Frontier 1870: Articles from the San Diego Union, 1870* (Dawson's Book Shop, 1965); *The Autobiography of a Diegueno Woman, Delfina Cuero* (as told to Florence C. Shipek) (Dawson's Book Shop, 1969; paperback edition, Malki Museum Press, 1970; available in Talking Books from Library of Congress, 1975); *Pushed Into the Rocks: Changes in Southern California Indian Land Tenure, 1769-1985* (in preparation); *A Strategy for Change: The Luiseno of Southern California* (in preparation); numerous chapters in books, journal articles, book reviews, limited circulation reports, social impact assessments, written legal testimonies, papers presented; Audio Visual Material: *The Indian Heritage—The Life of Delfina Cuero* (videotape prepared for "Heritage San Diego" Educational TV series, San Diego County Education Department.

SHOPTEESE, JOHN T. (Prairie Band Potawatomi) 1938-
(Indian health service)

Born February 28, 1938, Mayetta, Kan. *Education:* Haskell Indian Junior College, 1956-1958. *Principal occupation:* Indian health service. *Home address:* 724 Parkside Dr. N.E., Albuquerque, N.M. 87123. *Affiliation:* Real Property Officer, Office of Administrative Management, Indian Health Service, Albuquerque, N.M., 1958-. *Military service:* U.S. Army, 1962-1964. *Memberships:* Albuquerque Artist Association; Indian Arts and Crafts Association (board of directors; chairman, Native Arts Committee, 1982-1983); Eight Northern Pueblos Arts Guild, 1982-1984. *Awards, honors:* Several awards for achievement in the arts (I am a jeweler—gold/silver smith); sculpture in bronze, pewter, clay; received several juried art show awards throughout the Southwest. *Interests:* "Pursuing excellence in Native arts; to enhance cultural awareness and enact the trends of art through significant application of contemporary overtones. (I) have displayed my arts/crafts at major art shows of Native American artists."

SHIPP, CECIL
(B.I.A. agency superintendent) *Affiliation:*

Superintendent, Wewoka Agency, Bureau of Indian Affairs, P.O. Box 1060, Wewoka, Okla. 74884.

SHOEMATA, JACK
(B.I.A. agency superintendent)

Affiliation: Superintendent, Osage Agency, Bureau of Indian Affairs, Pawhuska, Okla. 74056.

SHOUMATOFF, NICHOLAS A. 1942-
(museum curator)

Born August 20, 1942, Glen Cove, N.Y. *Education:* Pembroke College, Oxford, England; Stanford University; Western Connecticut State College; Empire State College (N.Y.), B.A., 1972. *Principal occupation:* Museum curator. *Home address:* R.D. #2, Route 100, Katonah, N.Y. 10518. *Affiliations:* Instructor, Fairfield University, Fairfield, Conn.; curator, Trailside Nature Museum, Cross River, N.Y. *Memberships:* New York Archaeological Association; New Jersey Archaeological Society; Society for Pensylvania Archaeology; Connecticut Archaeological Society; American Indian Archaeological Institute. *Awards, honors:* Historic Tomahawk Award, Westchester County Historical Society, 1972. *Interests:* Delaware expeditions, 1976 and 1977; directed linguistic and ethnobotanical fieldwork among the Delaware Indians and related tribes of Oklahoma, Wisconsin, and Ontario, Can. *Published works:* Numerous articles in various journals.

SHUNATONA, GWEN
(president-Indian education organization)

Affiliation: President, ORBIS, Inc., 1411 K St., N.W., Suite 200, Washington, D.C. 20005.

SHUNK, HAROLD W. (Yankton Sioux) 1907-
(lecturer)

Born July 25, 1907, Philip, S.D. *Education:* Southern State College, B.S., 1931; South Dakota State University (graduate work). *Principal occupation:* Lecturer. *Home address:* Rimrock Hiway, R.R. 1, Box 115, Rapid City, S.D. 57701. *Affiliations:* Teacher, school administrator, superintendent of Indian agencies, Bureau of Indian Affairs, 1933-1968. *Military service:* U.S. Army, 1943-1946. *Memberships:* American Forestry Association; American Association for State and Local History; South Dakota State Historical Society (lifetime member; president, 1963-1969); The Cowboy and Western Heritage Hall of Fame, State of South Dakota, Fort Pierce, S.D. (vice chairman; chairman-Selection Comittee; chairman, 1977-). *Awards, honors:* Citation for Service Rendered, Rosebud Sioux Tribal Council; Meritorious Service Award, U.S. Department of the Interior, 1968; appointed by President Nixon to the National Council on Indian Opportunity, 1970. *Published works:* Written historical stories for *The Dakotan,* South Dakota State University, and Kansas State historical publications.

SIDNEY, IVAN (Hopi)
(tribal chairman)

Affiliation: Chairman, Hopi Tribal Council, P.O. Box 123, Oraibi, Ariz. 86039.

SIMLA, MARLENE R (Yakima) 1939-
(director-Indian center)

Born January 1, 1939, Toppenish, Wash. *Education:* Institute for American Indian Arts (four Certificates), 1963; Fort Lewis College, Durango, Colo., B.A., 1967; Fort Wright College of Holy Names, Spokane,

Wash., 1976-1979 (lack thesis for Masters degree in Education); Bank St. College (Child Development Associate), 1982. *Principal occupation:* Director, Toppenish Center, Yakima Tribal Preschool Program. *Community activities:* Toppenish Chamber of Commerce; Eagles Auxiliary #2229; Speelyi-me Arts & Crafts Club, 1975-. *Memberships:* Yakima Valley Museum; National Indian Education Association; Allied Arts Council of Yakima; Fort Lewis College Alumni Association. *Awards, honors:* Won Blue & Red ribbons at various art shows for painting (oil, water color, and acrylic); honorable mention at Southwest Indian Art Show, Santa Fe, N.M. *Interests:* "Coordinate and co-direct small traditional dance groups for local community events and celebrations; travel throughout Oregon, Washington and Canada and promote White Swan Rodeo, All-Indian Rodeo Association for 26 years." *Published work: Multi-Cultural Early Childhood Curriculum for the Yakima Indian Nation* (Yakima Indian Nation/Fort Wright College, 1978).

SIMMS, RUSSELL
(executive director-Indian center)

Affiliation: Executive director, Council of Three Rivers American Indian Center, Inc., 200 Charles St., Pittsburgh, Pa. 15238.

SIMON, BRO. C.M.
(director-Indian center)

Affiliation: Director, The Heritage Center, Box 100, Pine Ridge, S.D. 57770.

SIMPLICO, CHAUNCEY (Zuni Pueblo)
(Pueblo governor)

Affiliation: Governor, Zuni Pueblo Tribal Council, P.O. Box 737, Zuni, N.M. 87327.

SIMPSON, DANA
(editor)

Affiliation: Editor, *American Indian Law Review,* Univerity of Oklahoma, College of Law, 300 Timberdell Rd., Norman, Okla. 73019.

SINGER, LAWRENCE (Santa Clara Pueblo)
(Pueblo governor)

Affiliation: Governor, Santa Clara Pueblo, P.O. Box 580, Espanola, N.M. 87532.

SINYELL, EDGAR (Hualapai)
(tribal chairman)

Affiliation: Chairman, Hualapai Tribal Council, P.O. Box 168, Peach Springs, Ariz. 86434.

SINYELLA, WAYNE (Havasupai)
(tribal chairman)

Affiliation: Chairman, Havasupai Tribal Council, P.O. Box 10, Supai, Ariz. 86435.

SIRIA, LARRY
(editor)

Affiliation: Editor, *American Indian Law Review,* University of Oklahoma, College of Law, 300 Timberdell Rd., Norman, Okla. 73019.

SISK, KENNETH (Pit River)
(tribal president)

Affiliation: President, Big Bend General Council, P.O. Box 255, Big Bend, Calif. 96001.

SKENANDORE, PAUL A. (Shenandoah)
(Scan doa) **(Oneida) 1939-**
(lecturer, editor/publisher, owner/operator of bookstore)

Born January 21, 1939, Kaukauna, Wis. *Education:* High school. *Principal occupation:* Lecturer, editor/publisher, owner/operator of bookstore. *Home address:* 736 W. Oklahoma, Appleton, Wis. 54911. *Affiliations:* Editor/publisher of *Shenandoah* monthly Oneida newsletter begun in 1973; owner/operator, Shenandoah Books, 133 E. Wisconsin Ave., Appleton, Wis. *Other professional post:* Lecturer. *Military service:* U.S. Army, 1962-1964 (E-4 Sergeant). *Interests:* History; to see Native nations reestablished with sovereign powers to include treaty-rights; taking the U.S. (Government) to World Court and charging them with trespass and genocide."

SKENADORE, FRANCIS
(attorney)

Affiliation: Attorney, Oneida Tribe, P.O. Box 129, Oneida, Wis. 54155.

SKENEDORE, LYNN (Menominee)
(tribal chairman)

Affiliation: Chairman, Menominee Tribal Legislature, P.O. Box 397, Keshena, Wis. 54135.

SKYE, CLARENCE
(executive director-Indian organization)

Affiliation: Executive director, United Sioux Tribes of South Dakota, P.O. Box 1193, Pierre, S.D. 57501.

SLICKPOO, ALLEN P., Sr.
(Nez Perce-Walla Walla-Cayuse) 1929-
(tribal historian, tribal
councilman-administrator)

Born May 5, 1929, Slickpoo Mission, Culdesac, Idaho. *Education:* Chemawa Indian School, 1945-1948; University of Idaho, 1953-1955. *Principal occupation:* Tribal historian, councilman, administrator, Nez Perce Tribal Executive Committee, Lapwai, Idaho. *Home address:* P.O. Box 311, Kamiah, Idaho 83536. *Affiliation:* Nez Perce Tribal Executive Committee, Box 305, Lapwai, Idaho, 1955-. *Other professional post:* Consultant to the Northwest Regional Educational Laboratory on Indian education and curriculum; served on the Governor's Indian Advisory Council, Idaho. *Military service:* U.S. Army, 1948-1952 (Japanese Occupation/Korea/UN Service). *Community activities:* Veterans of Foreign Wars (Kamiah, Idaho); 2nd Presbyterian Church of Kamiah; Mat'alym'a (Upriver Nez Perce) Culture Club. *Awards, honors:* Outstanding Achievement Award, Indian Child Welfare, 1983; Governor of Idaho Award for "Promotor of the Week,"

1961. *Interests:* "Have traveled to Mexico City and Canada to participate and/or speak at conference relating to the Indian of North America; bilingual/bicultural activities; consultant on historical and cultural concerns (recognized as authority on the history and culture of the Nez Perce people; has lectured in public schools, colleges and universities, to students and organizations relative to American Indian history, culture, government, education, and economic status; has been a reader and/or panelist for the National Endowment for the Humanities." *Published works: NuMeePoom Tit-Wah-tit* (Pruitt Press, Colo., 1973); *Noon Nee MePoo* (Pruitt Press, 1974); wrote a paper for the *Northwest Quarterly on Anthropology,* relating to Indian fishing rights controversy; articles for *World Book Encyclopedia,* 1983-.

SLOBODIN, RICHARD 1915-
(professor emeritus)

Born March 6, 1915, New York, N.Y. *Education:* City College of New York, B.A., 1936, M.S., 1938; Columbia University, Ph.D., 1959. *Principal occupation:* Professor emeritus, Department of Anthropology, McMaster University, Hamilton, Ontario, Can., 1964-. *Military service:* U.S. Army Air Force; U.S. Navy, 1942-1946 (Lieutenant, U.S. Naval Reserve) (Soldier's Medal; Silver Star). *Memberships:* American Anthropological Association; Canadian Sociology & Anthropology Association; Northeastern Anthropological Association. *Interests:* Subarctic American people—Indian and Metis (fieldwork, 1938-). Areas of special interest are, social organization, ethnohistory, folklore, mythology, and religion. *Published work: Band Organization of the Peel River Kutchin* (National Museum of Canada, 1962); *Metis of the Mackenzie District* (Canadian Research Centre for Anthropology, 1966).

SMITH, DON LELOOSKA (Cherokee) 1933-
(woodcarver)

Born August 31, 1933, Sonora, Calif. *Principal occupation:* Woodcarver. *Home address:* Ariel, Wash. *Affiliation:* Lecturer, dance programmer, Oregon Museum of Science and Industry. *Award:* Inter-Tribal Indian Ceremonial, Gallup, N.M., 1966. *Interests:* Woodcarving, Northwest Coast styles; Indian dance and drama; Indian music; various forms of Indian arts and crafts.

SMITH, GERALD L. (Confederated Tribes of Warm Springs-Jemez Pueblo) 1949-
(justice services manager)

Born August 24, 1949, Albuquerque, N.M. *Education:* Univerity of Oregon, B.S. (Personnel and Industrial Management), 1972. *Principal occupation:* Justice Services Manager, The Confederated Tribes of Warm Springs, Warm Springs, Ore., 1984-. *Home address:* P.O. Box 937, Warm Springs, Ore. 97761. *Community activities:* Warm Springs Boxing Club (coach/president). *Memberships:* National Indian Traders Association (director); National Indian Business Council (director); International Association of Chiefs of Police (member-Tribal/State & Local Police Cooperation Committee); Oregon Association-USA Amateur Boxing Federation (vice president). *Awards, honors:* Selected as referee and judge to represent Region XII at the National Junior Olympic Boxing Championships. *Interests:* "Interesting in assisting Indian tribes and organizations In their business endeavors. *Published works: Economic Analysis of National Indian Cultural/Education Centers* (UIATF, 1974); *National Indian Planning Assessment* (UIPA, 1977); *The American Indian Index* (Arrowstar Publishing, 1985).

SMITH JAMES G.E.
(museum curator)

Affiliation: Curator of North American Ethnology, Museum of the American Indian, Heye Foundation, Broadway at 155th St., New York, N.Y. 10032.

SMITH, JAMES R.
(associate director-intergovernmental affairs-Indian Health Service)

Affiliation: Associate director for Intergo-

vernmental Affairs, Indian Health Service, 5600 Fishers Lane, Rockville, Md. 20857.

SMITH, LaMARR
(museum director)

Affiliation: Director, Memorial Indian Museum, P.O. Box 483, Broken Bow, Okla. 74728.

SMITH, LOUISE (Mescalero Apache) 1920-
(teacher)

Born September 9, 1920, Los Lunas, N.M. *Education:* University of New Mexico, B.A. (Music), 1940; Temple University, Harcum College, Fairfield University (graduate courses). *Principal occupation:* Teacher. *Home address:* 53-2 Revere Rd., Drexel Hill, Pa. 19026. *Affiliations:* Co-owner, Springfield Children's House—A Montessori School, 741 Beatty Rd., Springfield, Pa. *Other professional post:* Teacher, Ivy Leaf School, St. Barnabas School, Wyndmoor Montessori School, and Walden Montessori School, Drexel, Pa.; director of education, United American Indians of Delaware Valley, 225 Chestnut St., Philadelphia, Pa. 19106. *Interests:* Music; travel.

SMITH, MICHAEL H.
(B.I.A. agency superintendent)

Affiliation: Superintendent, Ute Mountain Ute Agency, Bureau of Indian Affairs, Towaoc, Colo. 81334.

SMITH, NOREEN
(director-Indian health board)

Affiliation: Director, Indian Health Board of Minnesota, 1315 E. 24th St., Minneapolis, Minn. 55404.

SMITH, ROBERT
(museum director)

Affiliation: Director, Oneida Nation Museum, P.O. Box 365, Oneida, Wis. 54155.

**SMITH, SHEILA S. (Oneida
of Wisconsin) 1962-**
(artist)

Born September 19, 1962, Green Bay, Wis.
Education: University of Wisconsin, La
Crosse, Wis. *Principal occupation:* Artist.
Home address: 1795 Poplar Lane, Seymour,
Wis. 54165. *Affiliation:* Volunteer, Oneida
Nation Museum, Oneida, Wis., 1980-.
Awards, honors: 1st Place, University of
Wisconsin, Stevens Point, 1985 Woodlands
Indian Arts Festival; "proclaimed a master
of my art by the U.S. Department of the
Interior and the Wisconsin Arts Board."
Interests: "I have brought back the last art of
the Iroquois costume designs. I have sold
four costumes to the U.S. Department of the
Interior for their permanent colection of
Indian artifacts. I had two costumes worn
during President Reagan's Inaugural Festiv-
ities. I was also a selected artist from Wis-
consin to be videotaped and exhibited by the
National Endowment of the Arts and Wisconsin Arts Council as a national traveling
exhibit. I have also had a cover of the Stevens Point *Magazine* published in Stevens
Point, Wisconsin." *Biographical sources:*
Wisconsin Arts Board Source Directory,
1986-1987; U.S. Department of the
Interior—Indian Owned and Operated
Businesses, 1985-1987.

SNAKE, REUBEN A., Jr. (Winnebago)
(tribal chairman)

Affiliation: Chairman, Winnebago Tribal
Council, Winnebago, Neb. 68071.

SNEVE, VIRGINIA DRIVING HAWK
(Rosebud Sioux) 1933-
(author, lecturer)

Born February 21, 1933, Rosebud, S.D.
Education: South Dakota State University,
B.S., 1954, M.Ed., 1969. *Principal occupation:* Author, lecturer. *Home address:* 723
Wright Court, Rapid City, S.D. 57701. *Affiliations:* Teacher-counselor, Flandreau
Indian School, Flandreau, S.D., 1966-1970;
editor, Brevet Press, Sioux Falls, S.D.,
1970-1972; consultant, producer-writer,
South Dakota Public TV, Brooking, S.D.,
1973-1980; educational counselor, Flandreau Indian School, 1981-1985. *Commun-

ity activities: South Dakota State Library
Association (Precentennial Project Advi-
sory Advisory Board); St. Mary's School
Board; Emanual Episcopal Church. *Mem-
berships:* South Dakota Press Women
(secretary, 1976-1978); National Federation
Press Women; South Dakota Diocese of the
Episcopal Church (historiographer, 1977-
1985); Diocese Commission of the Dakota-
/Lakota Culture; Enrolled member of
Rosebud Sioux Tribe. *Awards, honors:*
South Dakota Press Woman of the Year,
1974; National Federation Press Alumnus
Women, Achievement, 1974; Distinguished
Alumnus Award, South Dakota State Uni-
versity, 1974; Special Contribution to Edu-
cation, South Dakota Indian Education
Association, 1975; Honorary Doctorate of
Letters, Dakota Wesleyan University, 1979;
Distinguished Contribution to South
Dakota History, Dakota History Confer-
ence, 1982; Council on Interracial Book
Award for *Jimmy Yellow Hawk,* 1972;
Western Writers of America Award for
Betrayed, 1974. *Interests:* "Education;
teacher and counselor at the Flandreau
Indian School for ten years." *Biographical
source: Who's Who of American Women.*
Published works: Jimmy Yellow Hawk
(Holiday House, 1972); *High Elk's Treasure*
(Holiday House, 1972); editor, *South
Dakota Geographic Names* (Brevet Press,
1973); *Betrayed* (Holiday House, 1974);
When Thunders Spoke (Holiday House,
1974); *The Dakota's Heritage* (Brevet Press,
1974); *The Chichi Hoohoo Bogeyman,* Ms.
Sneve wrote the script for the screen play of
the same title for the "Vegetable Soup Child-
ren's TV series" (Holiday House, 1975);
They Led a Nation (Brevet Press, 1975);
That They May Have Life: The Episcopal
Church in South Dakota, 1859-1976 (Seabury Press, 1981); short stories and non-
fiction articles.

SNYDER, FRED (Chippewa-Colville)
1951-
(director-consultant, editor/publisher)

Born March 8, 1951, Pennsylvania. *Education:* Rutgers University, Camden, N.J. (two
years). *Principal occupation:* Director-
consultant, National Native American Co-
Operative, San Carlos, Ariz. *Home address:*
P.O. Box 301, San Carlos, Ariz. 85550.

Other professional posts: Editor/publisher, *Native American Directory—Alaska, Canada, U.S.;* educator. *Community activities: American Indian Market,* monthly, Phoenix, Ariz. (sponsor); Pow Wow Attender for North America. *Awards, honors:* Blue Ribbon (three years), Beadwork Competition, Heard Museum of Anthropology, Phoenix, Ariz.; numerous awards from Indian cultural programs, Title IV, Indian education, ethnic fairs. *Interests:* "Most of all my time is shared between directing the Co-Op (2,700 members), distribution of *Native American Directory* (40,000 copies), traveling extensively throughout North America to Indian powwows, rodeos, craft shows and conventions, and establishing the first Watts Line American Indian Information Center and Chamber of Commerce." *Biographical sources: Arizona Republic,* "Close Up" feature article (May, 1984); *Intertribal Enterprise,* "Close Up" feature article (April, 1985); *Navajo Times Today* (May, 1985). *Published work: Native American Directory—Alaska, Canada, U.S.* (National Native American Co-Op, 1982).

SOBOLEFF, SASHA (Puyallup)
(superintendent-tribal education system)

Affiliation: Superintendent, Puyallup Nation Education System, 2002 East 28th St., Tacoma, Wash. 98404.

SOBOLEFF, WALTER A. (Tlinget
of Southeast Alaska) 1908-
(clergy)

Born November 14, 1908, Killisnoo, Alaska. *Education:* University of Dubuque, Iowa, B.A., 1937, B.D., 1940. *Principal occupation:* Clergy, Presbyterian Church, 1940-1970. *Home address:* P.O. Box 535, Tenakee Springs, Alaska 99841. *Affiliations:* Clergy, 1940-1970, minister-at-large, 1962-1970, Presbyterian Church, Juneau, Alaska. *Other professional post:* Head, Department of Native Studies, University of Alaska, Juneau, 1970-1974. *Military service:* Army National Guard (Alaska Distinguished Service Medal). *Community service:* Lions Club (board of directors, secretary); Mason, Eastern Star, Scottish Rite 33rd; Knight Templar; American Legion; Alaska Native

Brotherhood (president); State Board of Education (chairman); Alaska Presbytery (state clerk; moderator; Synod-Washington-Alaska (moderator). *Memberships:* Southeast Alaska Adult Education Advisory Board, 1982-; Sealaska Heritage Foundation (trustee, 1986-); National Congress of American Indians (life member); Alaska Historical Society (life member); Commerce-Commission on Strategic Planning for the 1990's, 1985-1986; National Indian Education Association; American Indian, Athletic Hall of Fame (board of directors); Alaska Heritage Writers Association. *Awards, honors:* Christian Citizenship Award, Sheldon Jackson College Junior College, 1965; Alaska 49'er, 1973; Public Service Award by U.S. Department of the Interior, 1980; U.S. Forest Service 75th Anniversary Award, 1980; United Presbyterian Church, USA Board of National Missions, 25 Year Servie Award. *Biographicl sources: Who's Who in the West,* 1971; *Indians of Today,* 4th Edition; *Who's Who in Education,* 1970; *International Who's Who in Community, Service,* 1976-1977. *Publications:* "Historic Origin of the Cross," Bachelor of Divinity Thesis; *Grand Camp Alaska Native Brotherhood and Alaska Native Sisterhood, Manual of Ceremonies; Philosophy of Education for Alaska Natives;* numerous bulletins, brochures and articles.

SOCKYMA, MICHAEL C., Jr. (Hopi)
1942
(silver/gold smith, artist)

Born June 4, 1942, Hotevilla, Ariz. *Education:* Phoenix Indian High School. *Principal occupation:* Silver/gold smith, artist. *Home address:* P.O. Box 96, Kykotsmovi, Ariz. 86039. *Awards, honors:* "(I) have won ribbons for jewelry at Jemez Indian art shows, and Gallup Indian art shows." *Interests:* "21 years in making overlay jewelry in silver and gold; custom jewelry in precious stones; artist in oil and acrylic; council member for the Hopi Tribe; active in traditional cultural activities." *Biographical source: Government Directory of Indian Arts; Hopi Silver I & II,* by Margaret Wright.

**SOPIEL, SYLVIA (Passamaquoddy)
1929-**
   (editor)

Born November 3, 1929, Peter Dana Point, Me. *Education:* Hasson College, Bangor, Me. *Principal occupation:* Editor, *Mawiw Kilun,* Princeton, Me., 1977-. *Home address:* Box 186, Princeton, Me. 04668. *Other professional post:* Ex-Justice of the Peace. *Community activities:* Vista volunteer. *Interests:* "(I) have flown all over the country— met a lot of "new" Indian tribes. Life sports, outdoors, serving and making clothes, basket weaving, braiding sweet grass, making necklaces of beads."

SORENSEN, CAROLYN (Santee-Sioux)
   (tribal president)

Affiliation: President, Flandreau Santee-Sioux Executive Committee, P.O. Box 292, Flandreau, S.D. 57028.

SORRELL, CHERYL
   (executive director-Indian center)

Affiliation: Executive director, Winslow Indian Center, 110 E. Second St., Winslow, Ariz. 86047.

SOWMICK, ARNOLD (Saginaw-Chippewa)
   (tribal chief)

Affiliation: Chief, Saginaw-Chippewa Tribal Council, 7070 E. Broadway Rd., Mt. Pleasant, Mich. 48858.

SPEAKS, STANLEY M. (Oklahoma Chickasaw) 1933-
   (B.I.A. area director)

Born November 2, 1933, Tishomingo, Okla. *Education:* Northeastern State College, Tahlequah, Okla., B.S., 1959, M.Ed., 1962. *Principal occupation:* B.I.A. area director. *Address:* Portland Area Office, B.I.A., 1425 N.E. Irving St., P.O. Box 3785, Portland, Ore. 97208. *Affiliations:* Acting supervisor, Intermountain School, Brigham City, Utah, 1974-1975; superintendent, Anadarko Agency, B.I.A., 1975-1977; area director,

Anadarko Area Office, B.I.A., Anadarko, Okla., 1976-1980; director, Portland Area Office, B.I.A., Portland, Ore. *Community activities:* Boy Scouts of America (member-American Indian Relations Committee); 16th American Indian Tribal Leader's Seminar on Scouting (chairman, 1972-1973); Rotary International (member); Oklahoma Governor's Committee on Small Business (member). *Interests:* Boating, fishing, hunting, golf; Boy Scouts of America.

SPEARS, PATRICK (Lower Brule Sioux)
   (tribal chairman)

Affiliation: Chairman, Lower Brule Sioux Tribal Council, Lower Brule, S.D. 57548.

SPENCER, HARGLE
   (B.I.A. agency superintendent)

Affiliation: Superintendent, Sisseton Agency, Bureau of Indian Affairs, Sisseton, S.D. 57262.

SPENCER, ROBERT F. 1917-
   (professor of anthropology)

Born March 30, 1917, San Francisco, Calif. *Education:* University of California, Berkeley, B.A., 1937, Ph.D., 1946; University of New Mexico, M.A., 1940. *Principal occupation:* Professor of anthropology, University of Minnesota, Minneapolis, Minn. *Home address:* 1577 Vincent St., St. Paul, Minn. 55108. *Other professional post:* Editor, American Ethnological Society, 1968-. *Memberships:* American Ethnological Society; Arctic Institute of North America; Royal Anthropological Institute; American Folklore Society. *Interests:* "Anthropology and ethnology of North America—field research among American Indian groups: Keresan, 1938-1940; Klamath, 1947-1948; Eskimo, Point Barrow, Anaktuvuk Pass, etc., 1952-1953, 1968." *Published works:* *The North Alaskan Eskimo* (Smithsonian Institution, 1959, 1969); *The Native Americans,* with J.D. Jennings, et al (Harper & Row, 1965; revised, 1977).

SPICER, EDWARD HOLLAND 1906-
(professor emeritus)

Born November 29, 1906, Cheltenham, Pa. *Education:* University of Arizona, B.A., 1932, M.A., 1933; University of Chicago, Ph.D., 1939. *Principal occupation:* Professor emeritus, University of Arizona. *Home address:* 5344 E. Fort Lowell Rd., Tucson, Ariz. 85712. *Affiliation:* Instructor, 1939-1941, associate professor, 1946-1950, professor, 1950-1978, professor emeritus, 1978-, Department of Anthropology, University of Arizona, Tucson, Ariz. *Military service:* War Relocation Authority, Washington, D.C., 1943-1946. *Other professional posts:* Editor, *Journal* of the American Anthropological Association, 1960-1963; director, Pascua Yaqui Development Project, OEO, Tucson, Ariz., 1966-1969; consultant, U.S. Bureau of Indian Affairs, 1967-1969; member, Arizona Commission on Indian Affairs, 1964-1966. *Memberships:* American Anthropological Association (Fellow-'(president, 1974; editor, executive board); Society for Applied Anthropology (vice president); American Association for the Advancement of Science; American Philosophical Society; National Academy of Sciences. *Awards, honors:* Southwestern Library Association for best book on the Southwest, 1964; Malinowski Award, 1976, Society for Applied Anthropology; Guggenheim Fellow, 1941-1942, 1955-1956; National Science Foundation, Senior Postdoctoral Fellowship, 1963-1964; Senior Fellow, National Endowment for the Humanities, 1970-1971. *Interests:* Acculturation; Southwestern U.S.; Northwestern Mexico; research in Mexico and Peru. *Published works: A Yaqui Village in Arizona* (University of Chicago Press, 1940); *Potam, A Yaqui Village of Sonora* (American Anthropological Association, 1954); editor, *Human Problems in Technological Change* (Russell Sage, 1952; John Wiley, 1965); editor, *Perspectives in American Indian Culture Change* (University of Chicago Press, 1962); *Cycles of Conquest: The Impact of Spain, Mexico, and the U.S. on the Indians of the Southwest, 1533-1960* (University of Arizona Press, 1963); *A Short History of the Indians of the U.S.* (Van Nostrand, 1969); *The Yaquis; A Cultural History,* 1980.

SPIVEY, TOWANA (Chickasaw) 1943-
(curator, archaeologist)

Born November 8, 1943, Madill, Okla. *Education:* Southeastern State University, Durant, Okla., B.A., 1968; University of Oklahoma, 1970-1971. *Principal occupation:* Curator, archaeologist. *Home address:* 2101 Oak St., Duncan, Okla. 73533. *Affiliation:* Curator of anthropology, Museum of the Great Plains, Lawton, Okla., 1974-. *Other professional posts:* Curator-archaeologist, Oklahoma Historical Society, 1974-; archaeologist, Oklahoma Archaeological Survey (two years). *Military service:* Army National Guard, 1960-1968. *Memberships:* Oklahoma Anthropological Society, 1963- (board member); Oklahoma Museums Association, 1973- (council member); Society for Historic Archaeology, 1973-; Council on Abandoned Military Posts (vice president of Oklahoma Department, 1975-). *Interests:* Historic sites-restoration, archaeology, etc.; 19th century military forts and camps; fur trade and exploration of the Trans-Mississippi West; conservation of cultural material or artifacts; wagon restoration. *Published works:* Co-author, *An Archaeological Reconnaissance of the Salt Plains Areas of Northwest Oklahoma* (Museum of the Great Plains, 1976); co-author, *Archaeological Investigations Along the Waurika Pipeline* (Museum of the Great Plains, 1977).

SPOTTED EAGLE, CHRIS
(president-Indian society)

Affiliation: President, American Indian Talent Society, 2225 Cavell Ave., North, Golden Valley, Minn. 55427.

SPOTTED BEAR, ALYCE (Mandan-Hidatsa)
(tribal chairman)

Affiliation: Chairman, Fort Berthold Tribal Business Council, P.O. Box 220, New Town, N.D. 58763.

STALLING, STEVEN L.A.
(San Luiseno Band of Mission Indians
at Rincon Reservation)
(president-Indian association)

Education: California State University, Long Beach, B.S.; University of Southern California, M.B.A. *Principal occupation:* President, United Indian Development Association, 1541 Wilshire Blvd., Suite 418, Los Angeles, Calif. 90017, 1976-. *Home address:* 28776 Charreadas, Laguna Niguel, Calif. 92677. *Affiliations:* Prior to joining the UIDA, Mr. Stalling was executive director of a consulting firm in San Francisco, Calif. and supervised a job creation program which trained 300 American Indians. *Other professional posts:* Session chairman, Fifth International Symposium on Small Business, 1978; delegate to the White House Conference on Small Business, 1978. *Community activities:* Coordinator for the National Congress of American Indians, a lobbying group; former member of the steering committee for the National Indian Education Association; member of Board of Directors for a beginning Development Band directed at solving the domestic financing needs of American Indians; member of Advisory Committee for 1984 Olympics; served on Los Angeles Bicentennial Commission and the Los Angeles Private Industry Council; appointed to the Los Angeles City/County Indian Commission by Republican Supervisor Dean Dana. *Awards, honors:* Cited and recognized by the State Assembly of California for his contributions and efforts in small business and economic development. *Interests:* UIDA assists over 600 businesses annually and has secured over $52 million in financing and contracts for its clients. Long interested in developing American Indian talent, an interest that has accelerated since the formation of UIDA's Management Institute which trains Indian managers, Mr. Stallings has conducted dozens of workshops and seminars. Two of his training books are used throughout America by Indians learning planning and management. *Biographical sources: Who's Who in Finance and Industry,* 1982-1983; *Who's Who in the West,* 1982-1983.

STANDING, NETTIE L. (Kiowa) 1916-
(manager-OKlahoma Indian
Arts & Crafts Cooperative)

Born August 15, 1916, Caddo County, OKla. *Education:* Riverside Indian School; Santa Fe Indian Boarding School, 1934-1935. *Principal occupation:* Founding member and manager, Oklahoma Indian Arts & Crafts Cooperative, Anadarko, Okla., 1962-. *Home address:* P.O. Box 114, Gracemont, Okla. 73042. *Membership:* Oklahoma Federation of Indian Women. *Awards, honors:* 1975 National Endowment Award, recipient of grant for $5,000, for outstanding crafts person and teacher, and to research Kiowa beadwork; Grand Award Winner, 1977, Great Western Shows, Los Angeles, Calif.; 1976 Award from the Department of the Interior, Indian Arts and Crafts Board, for outstanding service to promote, prserve and develop all Indian crafts; 1985 O.I.O—one of the finalists for Indian Business Person of the Year for Oklahoma. *Interests:* "Kiowa beadwork; travel to Smithsonian Institution, and to the Museum of the American Indian in New York City in 1975-1976, to view collection, and to visit the Indian Arts and Crafts Board in Washington, D.C.."

STANDING ELK, DONALD
(B.I.A. Indian Education)

Affiliation: Indian Education, Bureau of Indian Affairs, 1951 Constitution Ave., N.W., Washington, D.C. 20245.

STARBLANKET, NOEL V.
(Saskatchewan) 1946-
(president-National Indian Brotherhood)

Born September 27, 1946, Starblanket Indian Reserve, Balcarres, Saskatchewan, Can. *Principal occupation:* President, National Indian Brotherhood, Ottawa, Ontario, Can., 1976-. *Affiliations:* President-elect, Canadian Indian Youth Council, Ottawa, 1967-1968; employed as an Indian filmmaker by the National Film Board of Canada, Montreal, 1968-1969; liaison officer, National Indian Brotherhood of

Canada, Winnipeg, Manitoba, 1970; chief, Starblanket Indian Reserve, Baclarres, Saskatchewan, 1971-1973; vice president, 1973, 1975-1976, director, Indian Rights and Treaties Research Program, Provincial Indian Organization, Federation of Saskatchewan Indians. *Community activities:* Economic Development for Indian People, Department of Indian and Northern Affairs (numerous committees). *Honors:* Great-great grandson of Chief White Calf, who signed treaty No. 4, 1875; great grandfather Starblanket, inherited chieftainship, Reserve and band named after him; father Victor was chief for 16 years on Starblanket Resrve. *Films:* Developed documentary film, *Starblanket,* produced and telecasted on National TV by the National Film Board of Canada and the Canadian Broadcasting Corporation; consultant, and acted bit part in *Cold Journey, commercial documentary feature developed by Indian film crew for National Film Board.*

STARCHILD, ADAM ARISTOTLE 1946-
(business consultant, author)

Born September 20, 1946, Minneapolis, Minn. *Education:* Sussex College of Technology (England), M.B.A., 1978; Blackstone School of Law (England), J.D., 1982. *Principal occupation:* President, Minerva Consulting Group, New York, N.Y., 1978-. *Address:* P.O. Box 5474, New York, N.Y. 10163. *Community activities:* Council of American Indian Artists (chairman, 1981-); Confederation of American Indians (trustee, 1981). *Memberships:* World Future Society; International Tax Planning Association; Mensa; Associated Business Writers of America. *Awards, honors:* Presidential Sports Award, 1975, 1982; Financial Writers Award, 1981. *Interests:* Canoeing and horsemanship; travels to Europe, Hong Kong, Soviet Union, Caribean. *Published works:* Author of hundreds of articles and over a dozen books.

STEELE, CHESTER (Goshute)
(tribal chairman)

Affiliation: Chairman, Goshute Tribal Council, Ibapah, Utah 87034.

STEELE, WILLIAM OWEN 1917-
(author)

Born December 22, 1917, Franklin, Tenn. *Education:* Cumberland University, B.A., 1940; University of Chattanooga, 1951-1952, *Principal occupation:* Author. *Home address:* 808 Fairmount Ave., Signal Mt., Tenn. *Awards, honors:* Numerous awards for books written. *Published works: The Buffalo Knife* (1952); *Wilderness Journey* (1953); *Tomahawks and Trouble* (1955); *Flaming Arrows* (1957); *Perilous Road* (1958); *Westward Adventure: The True Stories of Six Pioneers* (1962); all published by Harcourt, Brace & World; *Wayah of the Real People* (1964) and *Tomahawk Border* (1966) published by Colonial Williamburg; *The Wilderness Tattoo: A Narrative of Juan Ortiz* (Harcourt, Brace, Jovanovich, 1972); *Surgeon, Trader, Indian Chief: Henry Woodward of Carolina* (Sandpiper Press, 1972); *The Cherokee Crown of Tannassy* (John F. Blair, Publisher, 1977); *Talking Bones: Secrets of Indian Burial Mounds* (Harper & Row, 1978); and others.

STEIN, WAYNE
(college president)

Affiliation: President, Standing Rock Community College, P.O. Box 450, Fort Yates, N.D. 48438.

STEPHENSON, BONNIE (Delaware)
(tribal administrator)

Affiliation: Administrator, Delaware Executive Committee, P.O. Box 825, Anadarko, Okla. 73005.

STEVENS, CONNIE (Iroquois-Cherokee) 1938-
(actress)

Born August 8, 1938, Brooklyn, N.Y. *Principal occupation:* Actress (25 years). *Address:* 243 Delfern Dr., Los Angeles, Calif. 90077. *Affiliation:* Founder, president, executive director, Windfeather Foundation. *Memberships:* Screen Actors Guild, AFTRA, Actors Equity.

256

STEVENS, JOHN W. (Passamaquoddy) 1933-
(tribal governor)

Born August 11, 1933, Washington County, Me. *Education:* High school. *Principal occupation:* Tribal governor, Indian Township—Passamaquoddy Tribal Council, P.O. Box 301, Indian Township, Me. 04668. *Home address:* Peter Dana Point, Indian Township Reservation, Washington County, Me. *Military service:* U.S. Marines, 1951-1954 (Presidential Unit Citation; Korean Presidential Unit Citation; United Nations Medal). *Interests:* Mr. Stevens writes, "Being the chief of an Indian tribe of about a thousand members who are struggling in court and on all fronts to overcome local discrimination and poverty and to have our reservation treaty rights respected by the State of Maine is enough of a task, and doesn't leave much time for anything else."

STEWART, DONALD, Sr. (Crow)
(tribal chairman)

Affiliation: Chairman, Crow Tribal Council, Crow Agency, Mt. 59022.

STEWART, OMER C. 1908-
(anthropologist, ethnogeographer, educator, professor emeritus)

Born August 17, 1908, Provo, Utah. *Education:* University of Utah, B.A., 1933; University of California, Berkeley, Ph.D., 1939. *Principal occupation:* Anthropologist, ethnogeographer, educator, professor emeritus. *Home address:* 921 5th St., Boulder, Colo. 80302. *Affiliations:* Professor of anthropology, 1945-1974, professor emeritus, 1974-, University of Colorado, Boulder, Colo. *Military service:* Liaison officer to Ethnographic Board, Office of Chief of Staff, War Department, Washington, D.C., 1942-1943. *Memberships:* American Anthropological Association (Fellow); Society for American Archaeology; Society for Applied Anthropology (Fellow); Colorado Archaeological Society; American Association for the Advancement of Science; American Ecological Association; Sigma Xi. *Interests:* Expeditions and field work—archaeology of Ute and northern

Arizona, 1931-1933; ethnography of Pomo Indians, northern California; culture element distribution of Northern Paiute and Washo Indians of Nevada, Oregon and California, and Ute and Southern Paiute of Utah, Arizona, and Colorado; study of peyote cult of Washo and Northern Paiute of Nevada and eastern California, University of California, 1935-1938; study of primitive child development, Zuni, N.M., and community study of Morman vilage of Alpine, Ariz., Social Science Research Council, 1940-1941; community analysis, Ignacio, Colo., University of Colorado, 1948-1950; ethnohistory of Pit River, Washo, Northern Paiute, Ute, Chippewa, and Ottawa, 1953-1958; values and behavior on the Ute Reservation, U.S. Department of H.E.W., 1959-1963. *Published works: Ute Peyotism* (Series in Anthropology, University of Colorado, 1948); *Navaho and Ute Peyotism: A Chronological and Distributional Study,* with David F. Aberle (University of Colorado, 1957); editor, *Southwestern Lore,* 1949-1953; contributor to Encyclopedia Americana and Britannica; numerous articles, papers, and chapters in books.

STONE, WILLARD (Cherokee) 1916-
(artist, wood sculptor)

Born February 26, 1916, Oktaha, Okla. *Education:* High school. *Principal occupation:* Artist, wood sculptor. *Home address:* Star Route East, Locust Grove, Okla. *Other professional occupations:* Die finisher, designer, patternmaker, inventor. *Memberships:* Five Civilized Tribes Museum, Muskogee, Okla.; National Cowboy Hall of Fame, Oklahoma City, Okla.; Philbrook Art Center, Tulsa, Okla.. *Awards, honors:* Numerous awards for art and sculptor; special award, Indian Arts and Crafts Board, Department of the Interior, 1966; Outstanding Indian Award, Council of American Indians, 1969; inducted into the Oklahoma Hall of Fame, 1970, Oklahoma Heritage Association; Special Service Award, Cherokee Nation, 1971; Distinguished Service Award, Bacone College, Muskogee, Okla., 1972; Distinguished American Citizen Award, Oklahoma Christian College, Oklahoma City, Okla., 1974; Doctor of Humanities Degree, Oklahoma Christian College, 1976; Citizen of the Year Award, Locust Grove, Okla., 1976. *Interests:* Sculpture, painting, sketching. Mr. Stone is an official representative of the Cherokee Tribe.

STOTT, MARGARET 1945-
(museum curator; honorary
assistant professor)

Born September 25, 1945, Vancouver, Can. *Education:* University of British Columbia, B.A. (Honours), 1966; McGill University, M.A., 1969; University of London (England), Ph.D., 1982. *Principal occupation:* Museum curator of ethnology, honorary assistant professor, Department of Anthropology and Sociology, University of British Columbia, Vancouver, 1979-. *Memberships:* British Columbia Museums Association; Canadian Museums Association; American Association of Museums; Canadian Ethnology Society; Canadian Anthropology and Sociology Association; Mediterranean Institute; Modern Greek Studies Association; Council for Museum Anthropology. *Interests:* "Northwest Coast Indian material culture and art with particular emphasis on the Bella Coola Indians; material culture studies; museum studies; Mediterranean ethnography with particular emphasis on modern Greece; tourism studies, particularly in the Mediterranean." *Published works: Bella Coola Ceremony and Art* (National Museums of Canada, 1975); *Material Anthropology: Contemporary Approaches to Material Culture* (University Press of America, in press). *Exhibitions:* "Northwest Coast Indian Art," exhibition of contemporary Indian art (20 pieces), displayed in four cases at Air Canada Maple Leaf Lounge, Vancouveer International Airport, 1980-; numerous other exhibitions in the past. *Audio-visual productions: The Raven and the First Man,* visuals of the sculpture carved by Haida artist Bill Reid, with the artist narrating the Haida origin myth depicted in the carvings; *Salish Art and Culture,* an interview with an anthropologist in the Museum exhibition "Visions of Power, Symbols and Wealth; among others.

STOUT, RICHARD ALAN
(executive director-Native American
studies program)

Affiliation: Executive director, Southeastern Native American Studies Program, P.O. Box 953, Gastonia, N.C. 28053-0953.

STOUT, SADIE
(chief of nursing—Indian Health Service)

Affiliation: Chief of Nursing, Indian Health Service, 5600 Fishers Lane, Rockville, Md. 20857.

STRICKLAND, RENNARD JAMES
(Cherokee-Osage) 1940-
(professor of law)

Born September 26, 1940, St. Louis, Mo. *Education:* Northeastern State College, Tahlequah, Okla., B.A., 1962; University of Virginia, J.D., 1965, S.J.D., 1970; University of Arkansas, M.A., 1966. *Principal occupation:* Professor of law. *Affiliations:* Professor, University of Arkansas, 1965-1969; professor of law, University of Tulsa, 1972-. *Other professional posts:* Director, Indin Heritage Association, Muskogee, Okla., 1966-; director, Oral History Project, University of Florida, 1969-1971. *Memberships:* American Society of Legal History; Selden Society; Communications Association of America; Oklahoma Historical Society; American Ethnohistory Society. *Awards, honors:* Sacred Sash of the Creeks for Preservation Tribal History; Fellow in Legal History, American Bar Association, 1970-1971. *Interests:* Mr. Strickland writes, "Primary interest (is in) law and the American Indian, including programs to attract Indian students to the law as a profession, and programs to make the law responsive to the needs of Indian citizens; culture of the American Indian, with primary emphasis upon myths and legends and upon the arts and crafts of native tribes; contemporary American Indian paintings, and the evolution of Indian culture as reflected in evolving styles; ethnohistory of specific tribes—the Cherokee, Creek. Seminole, Choctaw and Chickasaw; development of traditional legal systems among the tribes." *Published works: Sam Houston With the Cherokees,* with Jack Gregory (University of Texas Press, 1967); *Starr's History of the Cherokees* (1968); *Cherokee Spirit Tales* (1969); *Cherokee Cook Book* (1969); *Creek-Seminole Spirit Tales* (1971); *Choctaw Spirit Tales* (1972); *Hell on the Border* (1971); *Adventures of an Indian Boy* (1973); *American Indian Spirit Tales* (1973); all with Jack Gregory, published by Indian Heritage Association; *Cherokee Law Ways* (University of Oklahoma Press, 1972).

STRUCHER, JIM
(general manager-Alaskan Native corporation)

Affiliation: General manager, Ahtna Development Corporation, 406 W. Fireweed Lane, Suite 101, Anchorage, Alaska 99503.

STUMP, ROCKY, Sr. (Chippewa Cree)
(tribal chairman)

Affiliation: Chairman, Chippewa Cree Business Comittee, P.O. Box 137, Box Elder, Mt. 59521.

SULCER, PATRICIA KAY 1951-
(editor, assistant administrator)

Born July 30, 1951, Charlotte, Mich. *Education:* Lansing Community College, Lansing, Mich. (two years); Thomas Jefferson College, Allendale, Mich., B.A. (Philosophy). *Principal occupation:* Editor, *HowNiKan,* Potawatomi newspaper, 1983-; assistant administrator, Citizen Band Potawatomi Tribe, Shawnee, Okla., 1983-. *Home address:* 22 E. Severn St., Shawnee, Okla. 74801. *Other professional post:* Board of directors, Native American Publishing Co. *Memberships:* Smithsonian Institution; National Press Photographers Association; Oklahoma Press Association; Native American Press Association (charter member-board of directors); American Association of University Women. *Awards, honors:* 1985 Native American Press Association, Honorable Mention for General Excellence, First Place News or Photo Series. *Interests:* "Cultural reclamation work, organizing council meetings for tribal members across the country, currently writing a Potawatomi dictionary." *Published work:* Editor, *Grandfather, Tell Me a Story* (Citizen Band Potawatomi Tribe, 1984).

SUMMERS-FITZGERALD, DIOSA
(Mississippi Choctaw) 1945-
(director of education, artist)

Born December 23, 1945, New York, N.Y. *Education:* State University College at Buffalo, B.A., 1977; Northwestern University Arcaeological Center, Kampsville, Ill. (Certificate), 1981; Harvard University Graduate School of Education, Ed.M., 1983. *Principal occupation:* Director of education, artist. *Home address:* 226 Ward Ave., Staten Island, N.Y. 10304. *Affiliations:* Instructor, History Department and Continuing Education Department, State University College at Buffalo, N.Y., 1975-1977; instructor, Haffenreffer Museum of Anthropology, Bristol, R.I., 1979-1980; acting tribal coordinator, Narragansett Tribal Education Project, Inc., 1980; administration, instructor, proposal writer, program coordinator, 1980-1981, education director, instructor, 1982-1985, Tomaquag Indian Memorial Museum, Exeter, R.I.; Native American historical and educational consultant, Plimoth Plantation, Plymouth, Mass., 1981-1982; artist in residence, Folk Arts Program, Rhode Island State Council on the Arts, Providence, 1982-1985; artist, Native American Art Forms Nishnabeykwa Productions, Charlestown, R.I., 1982-1985; education director, Jamaica Arts Center, Jamaica, N.Y., 1985-. *Other professional post:* Owner, artist, consultant, Nishnabeykwa Productions, Staten Island, N.Y., 1982-. *Memberships:* Harvard Club of Rhode Island. *Awards, honors:* 1st Prize, Photography, Thomas Indian School Exhibit; Kappa Delta Pi, national Undergraduate Honor Society; Phi Alpha Theta, International History Honor Society. *Interests:* "Over the years, I have devoted most of life to Native American art, and a clear understanding of the roots of Native American tradition through art. I have also sought to develop a better understanding of the Native American through art as well as in the classroom initially as a teacher, and more recently a curriculum developer, and program developer." *Other expertise:* Cultural consultant and educational consultant; craft demonstrations; curator of exhibitions. *Published works: Native American Foods; Fingerweaving,* narrative and instruction; *Ash Splint Basketry;* Tomaquag Indian Museum brochures.

SUMNER, DELORES T. (Comanche) 1931-
(special collections librarian)

Born May 11, 1931, Lawton, Okla. *Education:* Northeastern State University, Okla., B.S., 1964, Masters in Teaching, 1967; University of Oklahoma, Masters in Library Science, 1981. *Special collections librarian. Home address:* Route 3, Box 264C, Tahlequah, Okla. 74464. *Affiliations:* Coordinator/director, Comanche Cultural Center, Comanche Complex, Lawton, Okla. (2½ years); SPC librarian, John Vaughn Library, Northeastern State University, Tahlequak, Okla., 1982-. *Other professional post:* Public school teacher (five years). *Community activites:* Northeastern State University Symposium on the American Indian (appointed member-four years). *Memberships:* American Indian Library Association, 1980-; Tahlequah Arts and Humanities Council, 1980-; Oklahoma Library Association, 1981-; American Library Association, 1981-; Western History Collection Association (Oklahoma University), 1981-; Philbrook Friends of American Art, 1983-; Delta Kappa Gamma Society International (Alpha Eta Chapter), 1984-; Gilcrease Museum Association, 1985-. *Awards, honors:* Certificate of Appreciation, Oklahoma Library Association . *Intersts:* "Supporting the traditional artists in Native American art by traveling to exhibits, showings, and galleries is one of my main interests. I am very much interested in the preservation of Native American culture and tradition through oral history, art work, and the retention of the native language, of which I have accomplished only a small portion while working for my tribe as their cultural director. Today, I am still working toward this goal by personally contacting elders to record their songs, stories, and memories. I also record Comanche hymns whenever possible." *Published work: Numa-Nu: The Fort Sill Indian School Experience* (Oklahoma Humanities Committee, 1980).

SUN BEAR (Chippewa) 1929-
(author, lecturer, teacher, founder of the Bear Tribe)

Born August 31, 1929, White Earth Reservation, Minn. *Principal occupation:* President, The Bear Tribe Medicine Society, Spokane, Wash., 1970-. *Home address:* P.O. Box 9167, Spokane, Wash. 99209. *Other professional posts:* Editor/publisher, *Many Smokes* magazine; motion picture actor and extra, 1955-1965; technical director, "Wagon Train," "Bonanza," and "Wild, Wild West," television series. *Membership:* National Congress of American Indians. *Interests:* "I have been involved in Indian affairs most of my life, and I've spent some time teaching survival living to Indian and non-Indian people. I'm concerned with our Indian people, and other people, becoming more self-sufficient on the land, and learning a better balance with each other, and the Earth Mother." Sun Bear is a world traveler and lecturer, his travels having taken him to Europe, Australia, and India. *Published works: At Home in the Wilderness* (Naturegraph, 1968); *Buffalo Hearts* (Bear Tribe Publishing, 1970); *The Bear Tribe's Self-Reliance Book* (Bear Tribe Publishing, 1977); *The Medicine Wheel Book* (Prentice-Hall, 1980); *Sun Bear: The Path of Power* (Bear Tribe Publishing, 1983).

SUNDOWN, CHIEF CORBETT (Tonawanda Seneca) 1909-
(retired chief)

Born February 21, 1909, Tonawanda Indian Reservation, Basom, N.Y. *Education:* Reservation school, Basom, N.Y. *Professional post:* Chairman, Tonawanda Band of Senecas Chief's Council. *Home address:* 299 Lone Rd., Basom, N.Y. 14013. *Military service:* U.S. Air Force, 1941-1942. *Honor:* Cited by the Iroquois Conference for his role as a leader and educator among Indian people. *Interests:* "Traveled to Geneva, Switzeralnd to attend an International Non-Governmental Organizations Conference on Discrimination Against Indigenous Populations."

260

SURRETT, CLIFTON R. (Moapa)
(tribal chairman)

Affiliation: Chairman, Moapa Business Council, P.O. Box 56, Las Vegas, Nev. 89025.

SURVEYOR, VIRGIL R. (Cheyenne) 1937-
(school superintendent)

Born November 28, 1937, Canton, Okla. *Education:* Oklahoma City University, B.A., 1969, M.A.T., 1978. *Principal occupation:* Superintendent, Kickapoo Nation School, Powhattan, Kan. *Home address:* P.O. Box 53, Powhattan, Kan. 66527. *Affiliations:* Physical education teacher and coach, Concho School (eleven years); social studies teacher, Crescent Public School, Crescent, Okla. (two years); principal, Canton Public School, Canton, Okla. (one year); principal, Winnebago Public School, 1984-1985. *Other professional post:* Athletic director, Kickapoo Nation School. *Military service:* U.S. Army, 1959-1960. *Community activities:* Lions Club, Canton, Okla.; Cub Scouts Den Father, Canton, Okla.; Canton Indian High School Club, 1982-1984. *Memberships:* Kansas Athletic High School Coaches Association, 1985-; Oklahoma Indian Education Association; Oklahoma Middle School Association, 1984-; Kansas Education Association, 1986-.

SWAMP, CHIEF JAKE (Mohawk)
(tribal chief)

Affiliation: Chief, Mohawk Nation, via 188C Cook Rd., Hogansburg, N.Y. 13655.

SWETTER, DONALD A.
(resource coordinator-Indian Health Service)

Affiliation: Director, Division of Resource Coordination, Indian Health Service, 5600 Fishers Lane, Rockville, Md. 20857.

SWIMMER, ROSS O. (Oklahoma Cherokee) 1943-
(Assistant Secretary-Indian Affairs-U.S. Department of the Interior)

Born October 26, 1943, Oklahoma. *Education:* University of Oklahoma, B.S. (Political Science), 1965; University of Oklahoma School of Law, J.D., 1967. *Principal occupation:* Assistant Secretary-Indian Affairs, U.S. Department of the Interior. *Address: Bureau of Indian Affairs, Room 4160 N, 1951 Constitution Ave., N.W., Washington, D.C. 20245. Affiliations:* Law partner, Hansen, Peterson and Thompkins, Oklahoma City, Okla., 1967-1972; general counsel, 1972-1975, principal chief, 1975-1985, Cherokee Nation of Oklahoma, Tahlequah, Okla.; executive vice president, 1974-1975, president, 1975-1985, First National Bank in Tahlequah, Okla.; assistant secretary-Indian Affairs, 1985-. *Other professional post:* Co-chairman, Presidential Commission on Indian Reservation Economies (a panel of tribal leaders appointed to seek ways to help tribes improve economic conditions), 1983-1984. *Community activities:* Boy Scouts of America in Eastern Oklahoma (executive committee); Cherokee National Historical Society (past president); Tahlequah Planning and Zoning Commission (former chairman); Eastern Oklahoma Indian Health Advisory Board (secretary-treasurer); Inter-Tribal Council of the Five Civilized Tribes (advisory board, director). *Memberships:* Oklahoma and American Bar Association; Oklahoma Historical Society; Oklahoma Industrial Development Commission. *Interests:* Interior Secretary Donald Hodel said of Swimmer, "He combines a solid knowledge of tribal and Indian affairs with understanding and skill in modern business management." Swimmer has frequently expressed his views that Indian tribes should be less dependent on the federal government. When nominated for the position of Assistant Secretary, Swimmer said of President Reagan: "I know he is committed to an Indian policy that supports tribal self-determination, which is something I have worked for during my ten years at the Cherokee Nation."

T

TALL CHIEF, GEORGE EVES
(Osage) 1916-
(tribal chief, coach, teacher)

Born November 16, 1916, Arkansas City, Kan. *Education:* Central State College, Edmond, Okla., B.A., 1952; Pacific University, Forest Grove, Ore., M.A., 1957. *Principal occupation:* Principal Chief, Osage Tribe of Oklahoma. *Home address:* P.O. Box 14, Fairfax, Okla. 74637. *Other professional posts:* Coach and teacher. *Community activities:* Rotary Club; Chamber of Commerce; Quarterback Club. *Membership:* National Tribal Chairman's Association (vice president). *Awards, honors:* Iron Eyes Cody Peace Medal; Golden Glove Champion of Oklahoma (in college); Little All-American Coach of the Year in Pacific Coast Wrestling Conference. *Interests:* "My interests at the present time is to better the lot of the American Indian; sports; raise Appaloosa Show horses."

TANNER, CLARA LEE 1905-
(professor emerita)

Born May 28, 1905, Biscoe, N.C. *Education:* University of Arizona, B.A., 1927, M.A. (Archaeology), 1928. *Principal occupation:* Professor emerita. *Home address:* P.O. Box 40904, Tucson, Ariz. 85717. *Affiliation:* Instructor, 1928-1935, assistant professor, 1935-1957, associate professor, 1957-1968, professor, 1968-1978, professor emerita, 1978-, Department of Anthropology, University of Arizona, Tucson, Ariz. *Other professional posts:* Editor, *The Kiva,* 1938, 1948; editorial advisory board, *American Indian Art,* and *Indian America;* numerous University of Arizona committees. *Community activities:* Cummings Publication Council; Southwest Indian Arts and Crafts Committee; Tucson Fine Arts Association; judging of grant applications for the National Endowment for the Humanities, National Science Foundation, and Wenner-Gren Foundation for Anthropological Research. *Memberships:* Southwest Association of Indian Affairs, Sante Fe, N.M. (life member); Arizona Archaeological and Historical Society, Tucson, Ariz. (life member); American Anthropological Association; American Ethnological Society; Society of American Archaeology; National Federation of Press Women; Phi Beta Kappa; Society of Sigma Xi; Delta Kappa Gamma (educational honorary); Arizona Academy of Science; Arizona Historical Society; Arizona Press Women; Society of Southwest Authors; Archaeological Society of New Mexico. *Awards, honors:* Sharlot Hall Award, 1985; LLD Honorary Doctor of Letters, University of Arizona, 1983; Tucson Panhellenic Athena Award for Professional Achievement, 1983; Mortar Board Hall of Fame, University of Arizona, 1977; University of Arizona Alumni Association Faculty Achievement Award, 1974; Faculty Recognition Award, Tucson Trade Bureau, 1972-1973; Woman of the Year, Arizona Press Women, 1971-1972; 50th Anniversary Award of the Gallup Inter-Tribal Indian Ceremonial Association, 1971; Univerity of Arizona, 75th Anniversary Award, 1960; One of Outstanding Tucson Women of 1957; Arizona Press Women First Awards for books written, 1960- (the latest for *Apache Indian Baskets,* 1984); National Federation of Press Women awards, 1969- (the latest for *Apache Indian Baskets,* 1984); Society of Southwestern Authors awards; Border Regional Library Award, 1984 for *Apache Indian Baskets. Interests:* "Public lectures, 1928 to present, predominantly on the subject of Indians of the Southwest and their arts and crafts, to organizations throughout Arizona and in New Mexico, Colorado, California, Texas and Florida; lectures to school classes throughout southern Arizona; craft judging; travel." *Biographical sources: Who's Who in America, Who's Who of American Women; Who's Who in the West; American Men and Women of Science; Contemporary Authors. Published works: Southwest Indian Painting* (1957); *Southwest Indian Craft Arts* (1968); *Southwest Indian Painting, A Changing Art* (1973); *Prehistoric Southwest Craft Arts* (1978); *Apache Indian Baskets* (1982); *Indian Baskets of the Southwest* (1983).

TANNER HELEN HORNBECK 1916-
(consultant historian, expert witness)

Born July 5, 1916, Northfield, Minn. *Education:* Swarthmore College, B.A., 1937; University of Florida, M.A., 1949; University of Michigan, Ph.D., 1961. *Principal occupation:* Consultant historian, expert witness. *Home address:* 1319 Brooklyn Ave., Ann Arbor, Mich. 48104. *Affiliation:* Project director, 1976-1981, research associate, 1982-, The Newberry Library, Chicago, Ill. *Other professional post:* Expert witness in cases before the Indian Claims Commission, and Court of Claims, as well as state and circuit courts, 1962-1982. *Community activities:* Commission on Indian Affairs, State of Michigan, (member, 1965-1969). *Memberships:* American Historical Association; Conference on Latin American History; American Society for Ethnohistory (president, 1983-1984); Historical Society of Michigan. *Awards, honors:* Grantee, 1976, National Endowment for the Humanities (for Atlas of Great Lakes Indian History project). *Interests:* "Special interest in mapping and geographic background of Indian history-location of towns, hunting camps, fishing stations, and trails over land as well as canoe routes." *Biographical sources: Directory of American Scholars; Who's Who of American Women; Who's Who of the Midwest; Historians of Latin America in the U.S. Published works: Zespedes in East Florida, 1784-1790* (University of Miami Press, 1963); *Territory of the Caddo* (Garland, 1974); *Bibliography of the Ojibwa* (Indiana University Press, 1975); editor, *Atlas of Great Lakes Indian History* (University of Oklahoma Press, 1986).

TANTAQUIDGEON, GLADYS
(Mohegan1899-
(museum curator)

Born June 15, 1899, New London, Conn. *Education:* University of Pennsylvania. *Principal occupation:* Co-owner, curator, Tantaquidgeon Indian Museum, Uncasville, Conn. (40 years). *Home address: 1819 Norwich-New London Tpke., Uncasville, Conn. 06382. Other professional posts:* Surveyor of New England tribes for the Bureau of Indian Affairs; field specialist in Indian arts and crafts (area served-Northern

Plains), U.S. Department of the Interior, Washington, D.C. *Memberships:* Archaeological Society of Connecticut; American Indian Archaeological Institute. *Awards, honors:* Honorary member, Alpha Kappa Gamma; Deconess Emeritus, Mohegan Congregational Church, Uncasville, Conn. *Published works: Mohegan Medicine Practices and Folk Beliefs,* 1928; *Notes on the Gay Head Indians of Massachusetts,* 1930; *Newly Discovered Basketry of the Wampanoag Indians of Masachusetts,* 1930; *Lake St. John Medicine Lore,* 1932; *Delaware Indian Designs,* 1933; *Uses of Plants Among the Indians of Southern New England,* 1940; *Delaware Indian Art Designs,* 1950); *Mohegan,* 1947); *Folk Medicine in the Delaware and Realted Algonkian Indians,* 1972).

TAPAHE, LOREN (Navajo) 1953-
(publishing)

Born September 17, 1953, Fort Defiance, Ariz. *Education:* Brigham Young University, A.A., 1974. *Principal occupation:* General manager, Navajo Time Publishing, Window Rock, Ariz., 1977- *Home address:* P.O. Box 481, Window Rock, Ariz. 86515. *Other professional post:* Assistant director, Office of Business Management, The Navajo Tribe, Window Rock, Ariz. *Interests:* Journalism; advertising; photography; river expeditions; personal journal composition; travel—Northwestern tribes of North America, Southwestern tribes, Europe.

TAULBEE, DANIEL J. (Comanche) 1924-
(artist)

Born April 7, 1924, Montana. *Education:* Famous Artists School, Westport, Conn. *Principal occupation:* Artist. *Home address:* 2712 Nettie, Butte, Mt. *Affiliations:* Illustrator, Anaconda Co.; proprietor, Heritage American Award Gallery. *Military service:* U.S. Army. *Awards, honors:* Gold Medal, Burr Gallery, New York, N.Y. *Interests:* One-man exhibits of oil paintings, watercolors, pen and ink drawings throughout the U.S.; depicts "authentic Indian and Western life as I saw and lived them." *Permanent collections:* Farnsworth Museum, Maine; Peabody Museum, Harvard University,

Cambridge, Mass.; Philbrook Art Center, Tulsa, Okla.; Russell Museum, Mt.; Statesville Museum, N.C.; Whitney Museum, Cody, Wyo.

TAX, SOL 1907-
(professor emeritus)

Born October 30, 1907, Chicago, Ill. *Education:* University of Wisconsin, Ph.B., 1931; University of Chicago, Ph.D., 1935. *Principal occupation:* Professor emeritus. *Home address:* 1700 E. 56th St., Chicago, Ill 60637. *Affiliation:* Professor, professor emeritus of anthropology, University of Chicago, 1948- (dean, University Extension, 1963-1968). *Other professional posts:* Director, Fox Indian Project, 1948-1962; research associate, Wenner-Gren Foundation for Anthropological Research, 1958-; editor, *Current Anthropology,* 1959-1974; consultant, U.S. Office of Education, 1955-; founding director, Center for the Study of Man, Smithsonian Institution, 1968-1976. *Community activities:* American Indian Development (board of directors, 1965-1972); Center for the History of the American Indian, Newberry Library, Chicago, Ill. (board of directors, 1975-); Native American Education Services (board of directors, 1976-). *Memberships:* American Anthropological Association (Fellow); president, 1958-1959); National Research Council; American Association for the Advancement of Science; Society for Applied Anthropology; American Folklore Society. *Awards, honors:* Distinguished Service Award, American Anthropological Association, 1977. *Interests:* Social anthropology of North and Middle American Indians; originator of concept of "action" anthropology. *Published works: Heritage of Conquest* (Free Press, 1952); editor, *Indian Tribes of Aboriginal America* (University of Chicago Press, 1952); editor, *Acculturation in the Americas,* (University of Chicago Press, 1952; *Penny Capitalism: A Guatemalan Indian Economy,* (Smithsonian Institution Press, 1953); editor, *Appraisal of Anthropology Today* University of Chicago Press, 1953); among others; general editor, *World Anthropology,* 92 volumes; associate editor, 1948-1953, editor, 1953-1956, *American Anthropologist.*

TAYLOR, GENE (St. Croix Chippewa)
(tribal chairman)

Affiliation: Chairman, St. Croix Council, Star Route, Webster, Wis. 54893.

TAYLOR, GERALD W.
(B.I.A. agency superintendent)

Affiliation: Superintendent, Seattle Support Center, Bureau of Indian Affairs, P.O. Box 80947, Seattle, Wash. 98108.

TAYLOR, PETER S. 1937-
(lawyer)

Born June 9, 1937, St. Paul, Minn. *Education:* Washburn University, Topeka, Kan., B.A., 1959; George Washington University, School of Law, LLB, 1963. *Principal occupation:* Lawyer. *Home address:* 1819 North Lincoln St., Arlington, Va. 22207. *Affiliations:* Co-director, Indian Civil Rights Task Force, Office of the Solicitor, Department of the Interior, 1971-1975 (projects were the compilation of the Opinions of the Solicitor on Indian affairs; updating Kappler's, *Indian Affairs, Laws and Treaties;* development of a Model Procedural Code for use in courts of Indian offenses; and revision of Felix Cohen's, *Handbook of Federal Indian Law);* chairman, Task Force on Revision and Codification of Federal Indian Law, with the American Indian Policy Review Commission, 1975-1977 (upon completion of the Task Force report, served on the editorial board of the Commission in preparation of the AIPRC report; special counsel, 1977-1980, general counsel, 1981-1985, staff director, 1985-, Senate Select Committee on Indian Affairs. *Memberships:* District of Columbia Bar Association; Virginia State Bar Association. *Published works: Opinions of the Solicitor, Department of the Interior, Indian Affairs* (U.S. Government, 1976); editor, *Kappler's, Indian Affairs, Laws and Treaties* (revision, U.S. Government, 1976); *Development of Tripartite Jurisdiction in Indian Country* (Kansas Law Review, 1974).

TAYLOR, RHONDA HARRIS
(president-Indian association)

Affiliation: President, American Indian Library Association, American Library Association, Office of Outreach Services, 50 East Huron St., Chicago, Ill. 60611.

TAYLOR, VIRGINIA (Cherokee) 1922-
(graphic and commercial artist)

Born September 15, 1922, Los Angeles, Calif. *Education:* Art Center School, Los Angeles, Calif. *Principal occupation:* Graphic and commercial artist. *Home address:* 4754 Hwy. 20 NW, Albany, Ore. 97321. *Affiliation:* Staff artist, Office of Publications, Oregon State University, art coordinator and designer, Oregon State University Press, 1963-1967; assistant professor of art, Oregon State University, 1966, 1976; graphic designer and assistant to museum coordinator, Marine Science Laboratory, Department of Oceanography, Oregon State University, Corvallis, Ore., 1969-. *Other professional posts:* Taught Indian history and crafts, Linn Benton Community College; taught basic design, Oregon State University, 1975. *Interests:* Jury Indian art exhibitions; "(I) frequently speak to civic, school and other organizations on Indian art. Numerous awards, joint and one-man exhibitions; work in private and public collections."

TAYLOR-GOINS, ELISE
(director-Indian organization)

Affiliation: Director, Bird Clan Associates, 102 Longfellow St., N.W., Washington, D.C. 20011.

TEBBEL, JOHN (Ojibwa) 1912-
(teacher, writer)

Born November 16, 1912, Boyne City, Mich. *Education:* Central Michigan University, B.A., 1935, Litt.D., 1948; Columbia University, School of Journalism, M.S., 1937. *Principal occupation:* Teacher, writer. *Affiliations:* Writer, *Newsweek* Magazine, 1937; reporter, *Detroit Free Press,* 1937-1939; feature writer, roto news editor, *Providence Journal,* 1939-1941; managing editor,

American Mercury, 1041-1943; Sunday staff writer, *New York Times,* 1943; associate editor, E.P. Dutton, 1943-1947; assistant in journalism, School of Journalism, Columbia University, 1943-1945; chairman, Department of Journalism, N.Y.U., 1954-1965, professor of journalism, N.Y.U., 1965- *Other professional post:* Consultant, Ford Foundation, 1966-. *Biographical source: Who's Who in America. Published works: George Washington's America* (1954); *The Magic of Balanced Living* (1956); *The American Indian Wars* (Harper & Row, 1960); *The Inheritors* (Putnam, 1962); *Compact History of the Indian Wars* (1966); among other books; contibutor to *Saturday Review* and other magazines.

TEEPLE, WADE (Chippewa)
(tribal president)

Affiliation: President, Bay Mills Executive Council, Route 1, Box 313, Brimley, Mich. 49715.

TENORIO, FRANK (San Felipe Pueblo)
(Pueblo governor)

Affiliation: Governor, San Felipe Pueblo, P.O. Box A, San Felipe Pueblo, N.M. 87001.

THEISZ, R.D. 1941-
(professor)

Born May 4, 1941. *Education:* Middlebury College, Vt., M.A., 1965; New York University, Ph.D., 1972. *Principal occupation:* Professor. *Home address:* 14 W. Pine, Spearfish, S.D. 57783. *Affiliations:* Professor, Sinte Gleska College, Rose Bud, S.D., 1972-1977; professor, Center on Indian Studies, Black Hills State College, Spearfish, S.D., 1977-. *Memberships:* Modern Language Association; South Dakota Indian Education Association; National Council of Teachers of English; Porcupine Singers (traditional Lakota singing group). *Awards, honors:* 1972 Excellence in Scholarship Award, N.Y.U.; 1981 Special Contribution to Education, South Dakota Indian Education Association. *Interests:* "Native American cultural history, especially literature, music, dance, and art; cross cultural education." Published works: Buckskin Tokens (Sinte Gleska College, 1974); *Songs and Dances of the Lakota* (Sinte Gleska College, 1976); *Perspectives on Teaching Indian Literature* (Black Hills State College, 1977); *Lakota Art Is An American Art* (Black Hills State College, 1981); Readings in Traditional and Contemporary Sioux Art (Black Hills State College, 1985).

THOMAS, ARTHUR
(director-tribal affairs-Indian Health Service)

Affiliation: Director, Office of Tribal Affairs, Indian Health Service, 5600 Fishers Lane, Rockville, Md. 20857.

THOMAS, DAVID HURST 1945-
(archaeologist, museum curator)

Born May 27, 1945, Oakland, Calif. *Education:* University of California, Davis, B.A., 1967, M.A., 1968, Ph.D., 1971. *Principal occupation:* Museum curator. *Home address:* 210 Myrtle Ave., New Milford, N.J. 07646. *Affiliations:* Assistant curator, 1972-1977, associate curator, 1977-, chairman, Department of Anthropology, 1976-, American Museum of Natural History, New York, N.Y. *Memberships:* Society for American Archaeology; American Anthropological Association; American Association for the Advancement of Science; Sigma Xi. *Interests:* Mr. Thomas writes, "I am primarily involved in archaeological investigations in North America. These include ten years of directing excavations in the Great Basin, primarily in central Nevada. I also have directed a project on the prehistory of St. Catherine's Island, Georgia. I am interested in genernal archaeological theory, and have written two textbooks on this topic." *Biographical source: Who's Who in America;* 30 minute educational film on Mr. Thomas' Nevada excavations: *Gatecliff, An American Indian Rock Shelter. Published works:* "A Test of Shoshonean Settlement Patterns" (*American Antiquity,* 1973); *Predicting the Past* (Holt, Rinehart & Winston, 1974); *Figuring Anthropology* (Holt, Rinehart, 1976); "Shoshonean Bands" (*American*

Anthropologist, 1976); "Western Shoshoni" (*Handbook of the American Indians,* Smithsonian Institution Press); *Archaeology,* (1979).

THOMAS, FREDERICK R. (Kickapoo) 1946-
(tribal chairman)

Born February 21, 1946, Horton, Kan. *Education:* Haskell Indian Junior College, A.A., 1966. *Principal occupation:* Tribal chairman, manager, Kickapoo Tribal Council, Horton, Kan. *Home address:* Route 1, Horton, Kan. 66439. *Other professional posts:* Chairman, Kansas Service Unit, Health Advisory Board. *Military service:* U.S. Army, 1966-1968. *Community activities:* Powhattan Precinct (past board member); Kickapoo Housing Authority (past president); community fundraising projects; community food and clothing bank (founding member); Horton Chamber of Commerce; Horton City Commissioner for Economic Development. *Memberships:* National Tribal Chairman's Association; American Legion; Kickapoo Chapter, Lions International; National Indian Gaming Association (treasurer). *Awards, honors:* Goodyear—Tire Builder of the Year. *Interests:* Member of Delaware Singers; enjoys hunting and fishing, farming, traveling.

THOMPSON, DUANE F.
(B.I.A. agency superintendent)

Affiliation: Superintendent, Fort Hall Agency, Bureau of Indian Affairs, Fort Hall, Idaho 83203.

THOMPSON, EDMOND
(B.I.A. agency superintendent)

Affiliation: Superintendent, Pima Agency, Bureau of Indian Affairs, Sacaton, Ariz. 85247.

THOMPSON, RUPERT
(B.I.A. agency superintendent)

Affiliation: Superintendent, Anadarko Agency, Bureau of Indian Affairs, P.O. Box 309, Anadarko, Okla. 73005.

THUNDER, FAYE ESTHER
(Winnebago) (social worker)

Education: University of Wisconsin, Eau Claire (Sociology), 1976-1980; University of Wisconsin, La Crosse, 1986-. *Principal occupation:* Social worker. *Home address:* Route 1, Fairchild, Wis. 54741. *Affiliations:* Indian child welfare consultant and case-finder, case management for women, Department of Health and Social Services, Wisconsin Winnebago Business Committee, Tomah, Wis. (three years); secretary, Department of Natural Resources. *Military service:* Wisconsin Army National Guard, 1985-1993 (food service specialist). *Community activities:* American Indian Student Council (treasurer, 1976-1980); American Indian Studies Committee, 1976-1980, 1982); Black River Falls Health Commission (chairperson, 1981); Native American Church (secretary, 1979-1980); West Central Native American Community (health committee, 1975). *Memberships:* Mental Health Association, Jackson County (board of directors, 1982-1986); Wisconsin Women's Network, 1983; National Congress of American Indians. *Awards, honors:* State Advisory Council for Legal Services, 1984-1986 (appointed by the Governor); Certificate of Appreciation, Board of Directors, Advisory Council, Eau Claire County Human Services, 1984. *Interests:* "Complete my degree in Sociology; hopefully attend law school or graduate school. I do plan on running for public office (tribal/local).

THUNDER HAWK, MADONNA
(Cheyenne River Sioux) 1940-
(community organizer)

Born June 18, 1940, South Dakota. *Education:* University of San Francisco, 1967-1969; Black Hills State College, Spearfish, S.D., 1980-1982. *Principal occupation:* Community organizer. *Home address:* Eagle Butte, S.D. 57625. *Affiliations:* Dakota Women of All Red Nations; Dakota American Indian Movement. *Community activities:* Musicians for Safe Energy (board member); Nationwide Womens Program—American Friends Service Committee (board member); Black Hills Alliance (board member). *Memberships:* South

Dakota Women's Advocacy Network; Native American Task Force (Rural Coalition). *Interests:* "International advocate for Native American treaty rights; travels: Europe, Japan, Mexico, Honduras, Nicaragua, Costa Rica; attended U.N. Sub-Committee on Racism, Apartheid and Decolonialization, Geneva, Switzerland.

THURMAN, ROBERT
(health care administrator)

Affiliation: Chief, Health Care Administration Branch, Indian Health Service, 5600 Fishers Lane, Rockville, Md. 20857.

TIGER, BUFFALO (Miccosukee-Creek)
(tribal chairman)

Affiliation: Chairman, Miccosukee Business Committee, Box 44021, Tamiami Station, Miami, Fla. 33144.

TIGER, GEORGIANA
(Indian education)

Affiliation: Staff Associate, Indian Education Information Service, Com Tec, Inc., 1228 M St., N.W., Washington, D.C. 20005.

TIPPECONNIC, THOMAS
(B.I.A. area director)

Affiliation: Director, Navajo Area Office, Bureau of Indian Affairs, P.O. Box M, Window Rock, Ariz. 86515.

TITLA, PHILLIP, Sr. (San Carlos Apache) 1943-
(artist)

Born September 17, 1943, Miami, Ariz. *Education:* Eastern Arizona College, Thatcher, Ariz., A.A., 1979. *Principal occupation:* Artist. *Home address:* P.O. Box 497, San Carlos, Ariz. 85550. *Affiliations:* Director of development, San Carlos Apache Tribe, San Carlos, Ariz., 1967-1981; director, Phillip Titla Apache Galleria, San Carlos, Ariz., 1981-. *Other professional post:* Board member, San Carlos Arts and Crafts Association, 1981-. *Community activities:*

Bylas Recreation Program (chairman); San Carlos Powwow Association, 1980-; San Carlos Pageant Committee, 1978-; Cobke Valley Fine Arts Guild, Inc., 1985-1986. *Awards, honors:* Sculpture Award, Best of Show, Pasadena, Calif. Art Show. *Interests:* "My interest is to continue to grow in the art field; prsently doing some gallery shows and lecture at various clubs on Apache culture; also sing Apache songs; shows at colleges, high schools and elementary schools of my work—for education." *Biographical source: Art West,* Sept./ Oct., 1984.

TODD, JOHN G., M.D.
(Chief of staff-Indian Health Service)

Affiliation: Chief of Staff, Indian Health Service, 5600 Fishers Lane, Rockville, Md. 20857.

TOLONEN, MYRTLE (Chippewa)
(tribal president)

Affiliation: President, Keweenaw Bay Tribal Council, Tribal Center Bldg., Route 1, Baroga, Mich. 49908.

TOMHAVE, JEROME
(B.I.A. agency superintedent)

Affiliation: Superintendent, Southern California Agency, Bureau of Indian Affairs, 5750 Division St., Suite 201, Riverside, Calif. 92506.

TOPASH, BERNARD
(B.I.A. agency superintendent)

Affiliation: Superintendent, Siletz Agency, Bureau of Indian Affairs, P.O. Box 539, Siletz, Ore. 97380.

TOWNSEND, JOAN B. 1933-
(anthropologist, professor)

Born July 9, 1933, Dallas, Tex. *Education:* University of California, Los Angeles, B.A., 1959, Ph.D., 1965 (Dissertation: *Ethnohistory and Culture Change of the Iliamna Tanaina). Principal occupation:* Anthropologist, professor. *Home address:* 85 Tunis Bay, Winnipeg, Manitoba, Can. R3T 2X2.

Affiliation: Lecturer, assistant professor, associate professor, professor of anthropology, University of Manitoba, Winnipeg, Manitoba, Can., 1964-. *Other professional posts:* Consultation and assistance in gathering data on Tanaina society and archaeological sites; for Cook Inlet Region, Inc. (Alaskan Native organization). *Field research:* Archival and ethnohistoric research of the 18th-20th centuries of southern Alaska with special emphasis on social, political, and economic conditions of Indians, Eskimos and Aleuts. *Memberships:* American Anthropological Association (Fellow); Arctic Institute of North America (Fellow); Society for Applied Anthropology (Fellow); Current Anthropology; Canadian Ethnology Society (editorial board, *Culture,* 1980). *Interests:* Ethnohistory and sociocultural change: North American Indians— Athapaskan Indians; primary focus on Tanaina; Alaskan Pacific Rim ranked societies (Aleuts, Koniag and Chugach Eskimo; Tanaina, Ahtna, Eyak, and Tlingit Indians; traditional trading systems and alliances; mercantile and the fur trade in Alaska; political evolution; new religions and revitalization movements. *Published works:* Monographs: *Kijik: An Historic Tanaina Settlement* (Field Museum of Natural History, 1970); *Russian Mercantilism and Alaskan Native Social Change* (in preparation); *Tanaina Ethnohistory, Social and Economic Change* (in preparation); *The Archaeology of Pedro Bay, Alaska* (in preparation); numerous papers and book reviews.

TOYA, RONALD GEORGE
(Jemez Pueblo) 1948-
(B.I.A. assistant area director)

Born March 8, 1948, Albuquerque, N.M. *Education:* Westmont College, Santa Barbara, Calif., B.A. (Economics and Business Administration), 1970, B.A. (Psychology), 1971; A.A. (Political Science), 1971. *Principal occupation:* B.I.A. assistant area director. *Home address:* 5017 La Fiesta, Albuquerque, N.M. 87109. *Affiliations:* Chief, Branch of Reservation Programs, Southern Pueblos Agency, B.I.A., Albuquerque, N.M.; chief, Branch of Self-Determination Services, assistant area director, B.I.A., Albuquerque Area Office;

268

superintendent, Mescalero Agency, B.I.A., Mescalero, N.M.; superintendent, Southern Ute Agency, B.I.A., Ignacio, Colo.; special assistant to the Assistant Secretary of the Interior for Indian Affairs, Washington, D.C.; special assistant to the Commissioner of Indian Affairs; chief, Branch of Tribal Government Services, U.S. Department of Interior, B.I.A., Albuquerque Area Office. *Other professional post:* Executive director and chairman of the board, Tribal Government Institute. *Community activites:* Conduct radio show on Indian affairs entitled "Native American Perspective"; involved in youth activities, including baseball and special olympics. *Memberships:* New Mexico Industrial Development (board of directors, 1975-1981; CEDAM - international scuba and archaeological association; Society for American Baseball Research. *Awards, honors: Special and Superior Achievement Awards, B.I.A., 1972, 1979, 1981, 1982; various letters and citations. Interests:* Interested in the management of tribal governments; economic development and preservation of Indian culture; travel; baseball; scuba diving; car racing; hang gliding; dancing. *Published work: Pueblo Management Development* (Southwest Indian Polytechnic Institute, 1976).

TRAHANT, MARK N. (Shoshone-Bannock) 1957-
(editor-in-chief)

Born August 13, 1957, Fort Hall, Idaho. *Education:* Pasadena City College; Idaho State University. *Principal occupation:* Editor-in-chief, *The Sho-Ban News,* Fort Hall, Idaho, 1976-. *Home address:* P.O. Box 488, Fort Hall, Idaho 83203. *Membership:* Northwest Indian Press Association. *Interests:* "Also make films on available topics (16mm).

TREADWELL, ERWIN *(Red Fox)* (Unkechaug) 1918-
(tribal chief)

Born January 17, 1918, Roslyn Heights, N.Y. *Principal occupation:* Tribal chief, Unkechaug Indian Tribe. *Community activities:* AFL-CIO (committeeman); Boy

Scouts of America. *Awards, Honors:* Award for aircraft work, Grumman Aircraft Co. *Interests:* Lecturing on Long Island Indian tribes; Indian dance group. Mr. Treadwell is working on a history of the Long Island tribes.

TRIBBETT, NORMAN HENRY (Wisconsin Potawatomi) 1948-
(tribal librarian)

Born November 5, 1948, Hayward, Wis. *Education:* University of Wisconsin, Oshkosh, B.S., 1981; University of Wisconsin, Madison, M.A., 1983. *Principal occupation:* Librarian, Seminole Tribe, Hollywood, Fla. *Address:* 6073 Stirling Rd., Hollywood, Fla. 33204.

TRUJILLO, JOSE EMELIO (San Juan Pueblo) (Pueblo governor)

Affiliation: Governor, San Juan Pueblo, P.O. Box 1099, San Juan Pueblo, N.M. 87566.

TRUSSELL, LARRY (Tigua Pueblo) (tribal chairman)

Affiliation: Chairman, Tigua Indian Tribal Enterprise, P.O. Box 17579, Ysleta Station, El Paso, Tex. 79917.

TSABETSAYE, ROGER JOHN (Zuni) 1941-
(artist, craftsman)

Born October 29, 1941, Zuni, N.M. *Education:* Institute of American Indian Arts; School for American Craftsmen, Rochester Institute of Technology. *Principal occupation:* Artist, craftsman. *Home address:* Box 254, Zuni, N.M. 87327. *Affiliation:* Owner-founder, Tsabetsaye Enterprises, Box 254, Zuni, N.M. (Zuni jewelry—wholesale/retail). *Membership:* Zuni Craftsmen's Coop Association. *Awards, honors:* Numerous awards from various exhibitions and shows, 1968-.

TSINAJINNIE, ANDY (Navajo) 1919-
(artist)

Born November 16, 1919, Chinle, Ariz. *Education:* College of Arts and Crafts, Oakland, Calif. *Principal occupation:* Artist. *Home address:* Box 542, Scottsdale, Ariz. *Military service:* U.S. Army Air Force, 1940-1945. *Awards, honors:* Numerous awards from various exhibitions and shows. *Published works:* As illustrator, *Spirit Rocks and Silver Magic,* and *Peetie the Pack Rat and Other Desert Stories* (Caxton Printers, Ltd.); Who Wants to Be a Prairie Dog? (Haskell Institute); and others.

TSOSIE, LORETTA A.W. (Navajo) 1943-
(teacher)

Born March 13, 1943, Morenci, Ariz. *Education:* University of New Mexico, B.S., 1971, M.A., 1976. *Principal occupation:* Home economics instructor, Navajo Community College, Tsaile, Ariz., 1972-. *Home address:* P.O. Box 112, Window Rock, Ariz. 86515. *Other professional post:* Chairperson, Career Education Division, Navajo Community College.

TWO HAWK, WEBSTER (Rosebud Sioux)
(tribal president)

Affiliation: President, Rosebud Sioux Tribal Council, Rosebud, S.D. 57570.

TYNDELL, WAYNE
(executive director-Indian center)

Affiliation: Executive director, American Indian Center of Omaha, Inc., 613 South 16th St., Omaha, Neb. 68102.

TYNER, JAMES W. (Cherokee) 1911-
(historian)

Born September 13, 1911, Tahlequah, Okla. *Education:* Haskell Institute. *Principal occupation:* Historian. *Home address:* 112 Cowley Ave., Chouteau, Okla. 74337. *Affiliation:* Historian for Indian history project, American Indian Institute, University of

Oklahoma, Norman, Okla. *Military service:* U.S. Navy, 1942-1945 (Chief Petty Officer, World War II). *Awards, honors:* National Certificate of Commendation for published work, *Our People and Where They Rest* (Hooper Publishing, 1969-1972), American Association for State and Local History. *Interests:* Indian history, including research and recording old cemetaries; woodcarving; cartridge collecting.

U

UNGER, STEVEN
(executive director-Indian association)

Affiliation: Executive director, Association of American Indian Affairs, 95 Madison Ave., New York, N.Y. 10016

V

VANATTA, SHIRLEY PRINTUP (Seneca) 1922-
(writer, artist)

Born October 29, 1922, Red House, N.Y. *Education:* Bacone College. *Principal occupation:* Writer, artist. *Home address:* 116 Jimersontown, Salamanca, N.Y. 14779. *Affiliation:* Editor, *O He Yoh Noh, newsletter of the Seneca Nation. Community activities:* Iroquois Indian Conference of New York (artist; publicist); Everson Museum (board of directors). *Memberships:* Society for Pennsylvania Archaeology. *Awards, honors:* New York State Indian of the Year, Iroquois Temperance League, given by Governor Nelson Rockefeller, 1972; numerous others. *Interests:* Ms. Vanatta writes, "(I was) instrumental in bringing about archaeological research on the Allegany Reservation through the Carnegie Museum—work on 'Vanatta Archaeological Site,' 900-1,000 A.D. Iroquois village, where ceremonial masks (were) uncovered. I instituted the annual Inter-Community Christmas Party, where all children of Indian descent receive gifts; also the elderly, the infirm and the imprisoned. I am an oil and wastercolor artist."

VASKA, ANTHONY (Yup'ik Eskimo) 1948-
(B.I.A. agency superintendent)

Born August 25, 1948, Kalskag, Alaska. *Education:* University of Alaska, Fairbanks, B.A.; Stanford University, M.A. *Principal occupation:* Superintendent, Bethel Agency, Bureau of Indian Affairs, Bethel, Alaska. *Home address:* P.O. Box 1495, Salmon Berry St., Bethel, Alaska 99559. *Other professional post:* Alaska State Legislature, 1980-1984. *Awards, honors:* Ford Foundation Fellow. *Interests:* Arctic anthropology; U.S. American Indian policy.

VASQUEZ, JOSEPH C. *(Lone Eagle)*
(Sioux-Apache) 1917-
(Indian programs administrator)

Born February 21, 1917, Primero, Colo. *Education:* U.S. Armed Forces Institute; Los Angeles City College Extension; U.C.L.A. Extension. *Principal occupation:* Indian programs administrator. *Home address:* 5208 11th St., South, Arlington, Va. 22204. *Affiliations:* Small business coordinator/minority representative, Hughes Aircraft Co., El Segundo, Calif., 1947-1968; appointed Los Angeles City Commissioner, Los Angeles, Calif., 1968-1970; National Council on Indian Opportunity, Washington, D.C., 1970-1972; director, Indian Office, U.S. Department of Commerce, Office of Minority Business Enterprise, Washington, D.C., 1972-. *Other professional posts:* President and council chairman, Los Angeles Indian Center, 1958-1970; founded and promoted the National Business Development Organization (Indian), Los Angeles, 1968-1970. *Military service:* U.S. Army Air Corps, 1943-1945 (Pilot-Flight Engineer). *Community activities:* UCLA Cultural Center (chairman); Los Angeles Mayor's Advisory Committee (board member); California Attorney General's Advisory Committee (board member). *Memberships:* National Indian Education Association (board member); United Indian Development Association (founder). *Awards, honors:* Family of the Year, Hughes Aircraft Co., 1956; Resolution by Governor Pat Brown, California, 1956; plaque for being first Indian to drive car in parade for a President of the U.S., 1964;

Resolution, Indians of Los Angeles, 1967; Resolution, Indian Leader of the Year, National Congress of American Indians, 1968; appointment by President Nixon, 1970. *Biographical sources: Who's Who in Government,* 1972, 1973; *Contemporary Indian Leaders of America,* 1973; *Community Leaders and Noteworthy Americans,* 1975-1976; *Who's Who Honorary Society,* 1976.

VIARRIAL, JACOB (Pojoaque Pueblo)
(Pueblo governor)

Affiliation: Governor, Pojoaque Pueblo Tribal Council, Route 11, Box 71, Santa Fe, N.M. 87501.

VIOLA, HERMAN J. 1938-
(historian)

Born February 24, 1938, Chicago, Ill. *Education:* Marquette University, B.A., 1962, M.A., 1964; Indiana University, Ph.D., 1970. *Principal occupation:* Historian. *Home address:* 7307 Pinewood St., Falls Church, Va. 22046. *Affiliation:* Director, National Anthropological Archives, Smithsonian Institution, Washington, D.C., 1972-. *Other professional post:* Founder and first editor of *Prologue,* The Journal of the National Archives, 1968-1972. *Military service:* U.S. Navy, 1960-1962. *Memberships:* Society of American Archivists; Western History Association; Organization of American Historians. *Biographical source: Who's Who in America. Published works: Thomas L. McKinney, Architect of America's Early Indian Policy, 1816-1830* (Swallow Press, 1974); *The Indian Legacy of Charles Bird King* (Smithsonian Institution Press, 1976); *Diplomats in Buckskin* (Smithsonian Institution Press, 1981); *The National Archives* (Harry N. Abrams, 1984).

VOZNIAK, DEBBIE
(administrative officer-Indian education)

Affiliation: Administrative Officer, National Advisory Council on Indian Education, 2000 L St., N.W., Suite 574, Washington, D.C. 20002.

VIZENOR, GERALD ROBERT
(Chippewa) 1934-
(teacher, poet)

Born October 22, 1934, Mineapolis, Minn. *Education:* New York University; University of Minnesota, B.A., 1960. *Principal occupation:* Teacher, poet. *Affiliations:* Executive director, American Indian Employment Center, Minneapolis, Minn.; staff writer, Minneapolis *Tribune,* 1968-1969; lecturer, Department of Anthropology, Lake Forest College, Lake Forest, Ill., 1970-? *Military service:* U.S. Army, 1952-1955. *Published works: Raising the Moon Vines* (The Nodin Press, 1964); *Seventeen Chirps* (The Nodin Press, 1964); *Summer in the Spring: Ojibway Lyric Poems* (The Nodin Press, 1965); *Empty Swings* (The Nodin Press, 1967); *Escorts to White Earth* (The Four Winds, 1968); *Anishnabe Adisokan,* tales (The Nodin Press, 1970); *Anishnabe Nagamon,* song poems (The Nodin Press, 1970); *New Voices fromthe People Named the Chippewa* (Crowell-Collier, 1971).

VOGET, FRED W. 1913-
(professor emeritus)

Born February 12, 1913, Salem, Ore. *Education:* University of Oregon, B.A., 1936; Yale University, Ph.D., 1948. *Principal occupation:* Professor emeritus. *Home address:* 4020 SW 75th, Portland, Ore. 97225. *Affiliation:* Professor of anthropology, 1965-1981 (chairman, 1969-1971), professor emeritus, 1981-, Southern Illinois University at Edwardsville. *Military service:* U.S. Army, 1942-1946 (Sergeant Major; European Theatre). *Memberships:* American Anthropological Association (Fellow); Society for Applied Anthropology (Fellow; executive committee, 1974-1976; Malinowski Award Committee, 1976-1977); American Ethnological Society; Central States Anthropological Society; American Association of University Professors; Sigma Xi; Lambda Alpha; Alpha Kappa Delta; Current Anthropology (Associate). *Awards, honors:* Canada Council Grant, 1964-1965; Senior Fulbright-Hay Award, Germany, 1971. *Interests:* Ethnological theory; culture change and acculturation; ethnoogy of North America and Africa; ethnology of the Plains, North America; religious movements and culture change; institutional and value analysis of culture as systems; social organization. *Published works: Osage Indians I. Osage Research Report* (Garland, 1974); *A History of Ethnology* (Holt, Rinehart & Winston, 1975); *The Shoshoni-Crow Sun Dance* (University of Oklahoma Press, 1984); *Storia dell'etnologia contemporanea* (Laterza & Figli, 1984).

VOIGHT, VIRGINIA FRANCES 1909-
(writer)

Born March 30, 1909, New Britain, Conn. *Education:* Yale School of Fine Arts; Austin School of Commercial Art. *Principal occupation:* Writer. *Home addres:* 1732 Dixwell Ave., Apt. 1 H, Hamden, Conn. 06514. *Awards, honors: New York Times,* 100 best books of the year, *Uncas, Sachem of the Wolf People. Interests:* Historical research; book and field research on wildlife and natural history in general. *Biographical sources: More Junior Authors* (H.W. Wilson Co.); *Contemporary Authors; The Directory of British and American Authors (St. James Press). Published works: Uncas, Sachem of the Wolf People* (Funk & Wagnalls, 1963); *Mohegan Chief: The Story of Harold Tantaquidgeon* (Funk & Wagnalls, 1965); *Sacajawea, Guide to Lewis and Clark* (Putnam, 1966); *The Adventures of Hiawatha* (Garrard, 1969); *Massasoit, Friend of the Pilgrims* (Garrard, 1971); *Close to the Rising Sun, Algonquian Indian Legends* (Garrard, 1972); *Red Blade and the Black Bear* (fiction (Dodd, Mead, 1973); *Red Cloud, Sioux War Chief* (Garrard, 1975); *Indian Patriots East of the Mississippi* (Anthology) (Garrard, 1976); *Pontiac, Mighty Ottawa Chief* (Garrard, 1977); *Bobcat* (Dodd, Mead, 1978).

W

WADE, JON C.
(college president)

Affiliation: President, Institute of American Indian Arts, College of Santa Fe Campus, Alexis Hall, St. Michaels Dr., Santa Fe, N.M. 87501.

WADENA, DARRELL (Minnesota Chippewa)
(tribal chairman)

Affiliations: Chairman, White Earth Reservation Business Committee, P.O. Box 418, White Earth, Minn. 56591; presdident, Minnesota Chippewa Tribal Executive Committee, P.O. Box 217, Cass Lake, Minn. 56633.

WAHPEHAH, JAMES (Kickapoo)
(tribal chairman)

Affiliation: Chairman, Kickapoo Business Committee, P.O. Box 58, McCloud, Okla. 74851.

WAKEMAN, RICHARD K. (Flandreau Santee Sioux) 1923-
(tribal officer)

Born February 9, 1923, Flandreau, S.D. *Education:* Haskell Institute. *Principal occupation:* Tribal officer. *Home address:* R.R. 1, Flandreau, S.D. 57028. *Affiliation:* Former president, Flandreau Santee Sioux Business Council. *Military service:* U.S. Marine Corps, 1942-1945; U.S. Army, 1951-1953 (Presidential Unit Citation; Commendation; Asiatic Pacific Award). *Community activities:* South Dakota Indian Commission; South Dakota Letter Carriers (president); Dakota Prebytery (moderator); Masonic Lodge. *Interests:* Tribal history.

WALDRAM, JAMES B. 1955-
(professor)

Born August 20, 1955, Oshawa, Ontario, Can. *Education:* University of Waterloo, Ontario, B.A. (Honors), 1978; University of Manitoba, Winnipeg, M.A., 1980; University of Connecticut, Ph.D. (Anthropology), 1983. *Principal occupation:* Professor. *Home address:* 247 Sylvian Way, Saskatoon, Saskatchewan, Can. *Affiliation:* Assistant professor, Department of Native American Studies, University of Saskatchewan, Saskatoon, Saskatchewan, Can., 1983- *Other professional post:* Associate editor, *Native Studies Review. Memberships:* Canadian Ethnology Society; Canadian Indian-Native Studies Association; Canadian Association for Medical Anthropology;

American Anthropological Association; Society for Applied Anthropology. *Awards, honors:* Social Sciences and Humanities Research Council of Canada Doctoral Fellowship. *Interests:* "The impact of hydroelectric development of northern Canadian Native communities. Dietary change in the Canadian north; education needs assessment of urban Native people; health and health care delivery of urban Native people." *Published work: 1885 and After: Native Society in Transition* (Canadian Plains Research Center, Regina, Can., 1986).

WALKER, JERRY CLAYTON 1937-
(school principal, educator)

Born February 2, 1937, Fort Sumner, N.M. *Education:* Eastern New Mexico University, Portales, B.S., 1964, EDSp., 1981; Northern Arizona University, Flagstaff, M.A. (Education), 1971. *Principal occupation:* School principal, educator. *Home address:* P.O. Box 906, Teecnospos, Ariz. 86514. *Affiliations:* Teacher-Special Education,Tuba City Boarding School, Tuba City, Ariz. (nine years); education specialist, Western Navajo Agency, B.I.A., Tuba City, Ariz. (eight years); principal, Teecnospos Boarding School, Teecnospos, Ariz., 1982-. *Memberships:* National Council of Bureau of Indian Affairs Educators (charter member); Council for Exceptional Children, 1967-1982.

WALKER, JOE B.
(B.I.A. agency superintendent)

Affiliation: Superintendent, Shawnee Agency, Bureau of Indian Affairs, Federal Bldg., Shawnee, Okla. 74801.

WALKER, WILLARD 1926-
(professor of anthropology)

Born July 29, 1926, Boston, Mass. *Education:* Harvard College, B.A., 1950; University of Arizona, M.A., 1953; Cornell University, Ph.D., 1964. *Principal occupation:* Professor of anthropology, Wesleyan University, Middletown, Conn., 1967-. *Home address:* Culver Lane, Portland, Conn. 06480. *Memberships:* American Anthropological Association (Fellow);

Society for Applied Anthropology (Fellow); Linguistics Society of America; American Ethnological Society; American Society for Ethnohistory; Southern Anthropological Association; Northeast Anthropological Association ; Museum of the Cherokee Indian Association. *Interests:* "Indian American languages, cultures, ethnohistory. Particular interest in Creeks and Cherokees in the Southeast, the Zuni, Hopi and Yaqui pueblos in the Southwest, and the Algonquian peoples of the Maine-Maritime area. *Published works: Cherokee Primer* (Carnegie Corp. Cross-Cultural Project of the University of Chicago, 1965); co-author, *Cherokee Stories* (Laboratory of Anthropology, Wesleyan University, 1966); co-editor, *Hopis, Tewas, and the American Road* (Wesleyan University, 1983).

WALKING BULL, CHARLES GILBERT, Jr. (Oglala Sioux) 1930-
(artist, singer, writer)

Born June 18, 1930, Hot Springs, S.D. *Education:* Oregon College of Education (two years). *Principal occupation:* Self-employed artist, singer, writer. *Home address:* 11750 Mistletoe Rd., Monmouth, Ore. 97361. *Community activities:* Oregon College of Education, Native American Student Association (president, 1976-1977); singer at Cross-Cultural Dialogue, Sun Valley. *Memberships:* Inter-Tribal Council, Portland, Ore.; National Indian Education Association (Project Media evaluation team); Independent Indian Arts and Crafts Persons Association (helped to organize). *Awards, honors:* Award for Distinction for Art, La Grande Indian Arts Festival, 1974; First Prize Award for Traditional Sioux Fancy Dance, Siletz, Ore., 1973; First Prize Award for Traditional Sioux painting, 1976, 1977, La Grande Indian Arts Festival. *Interests:* "Do traditional Sioux geometrical designs on canvas in oil and acrylics; do Sioux crafts in beadwork and leather. (I am a) soloist, singing in the Lakota language with guitar and drum in public performance. Fancy dancer and participator in Indian gatherings since youth, winning many awards. At present, I am concentrating on traditional Sioux art, translating the legends of my people. I am traditional and bilingual. In my books, I am recording tales from the reservation,

writing original poetry, transalting songs and scoring songs." *Published works: O-hu-kah-kan (Poetry, Songs, Legends, Stories),* 1975; *Wo ya-ka-pi (Telling Stories of the Past and Present),* 1976; *Mi ta-ku-ye (About Our People),* 1977; all books co-authored with Montana Walking Bull, printed by the *Itemizer Observer,* Dallas, Ore., and may be purchased from the Walking Bulls at their home address.

WALKING BULL, MONTANA HOPKINS RICKARDS (Oklahoma Cherokee) 1913-
(professor)

Born January 22, 1913, Butte, Mt. *Education:* University of Oklahoma, B.F.A., 1935, M.A. (Education), 1942; University of Oregon, Ed.D., 1967. *Principal occupation:* Professor of humanities/education, Oregon College of Education, Monmouth, Ore., 1963-. *Home address:* 11750 Mistletoe Rd., Monmouth, Ore. 97361. *Community activities:* Independent Indian Arts and Crafts Persons Association of the Northwest (coordinator); Sun Valley Cross-Cultural Dialogue (participant); book reviewer, *Daily Oklahoman;* speaker for "A Look at Native American Treaty Rights," Glenedon Beach, Ore. *Memberships:* National Indian Education Association (Project Media); National Council of Teachers of English; National School Public Relations Association (NEA); Oregon Education Association (chairman). *Interests:* Reading, writing, music and art; travel; speaker at meetings; attended the first and second Convocations of American Indian Scholars at Princeton University and at Aspen, Colo. *Biographical sources: Directory of American Scholars; Who's Who of American Women, 1972-1973; Who's Who in the West; Dictionary of International Biography; Two Thousand Women of Achievement,* 1970. *Published works:* Co-author, *Two by Two,* in Eugene, Ore. (late 1950's); co-author, *Duo,* with sister, Rosemary Bogart, Euegen, Ore. (late 1950's); co-editor, *Calapooya Collage of Poetry* for Oregon College of Education, Humanities poets, 1970-1976; co-author, with Gilbert Walking Bull, *O-hu-kah-kan,* 1975; *Wo ya-ka-pi,* 1976; and *Mi ta-ku-ye,* 1977; writer for "Search for America," 1970, for NCTE Task Force on Racism and Bias in the Teaching of English.

WALKING ELK, MITCH *(Mo-o-da-me-yotz)* **(Cheyenne-Arapaho-Hopi) 1950-**
(Native American drug/alcohol/cultural counselor)

Born December 28, 1950, Claremore, Okla. *Education:* Augustana College (Social Work major), 1984-. *Principal occupation:* Native American drug/alcohol/cultural counselor. *Home address:* P.O. Box 264, Hatfield, Minn. 56135. *Community activities:* Indian youth worker, Marty and Sioux Falls, S.D., 1979-1982. *Awards, honors:* 2nd Place music competition, Pipestone Vocational "Snow Week" competition, Community Event, Pipestone, Minn. *Interests:* "I auditioned for "You Can Be A Star" competition, Opryland USA, Nashville, Tenn.— results not yet in; currently working on first album of original composition. One song published by George B. German, Music Archives, Sioux Falls, S.D.—title, *Washita River,* a contemporary Indian tune."

WALLACE, ANTHONY F.C. 1923-
(professor of anthropology)

Born April 15, 1923, Toronto, Can. *Education:* University of Pennsylvania, B.A., 1947, M.A., 1949, Ph.D., 1950. *Principal occupation:* Professor of anthropology. *Home address:* 614 Convent Rd., Chester, Pa. *Affiliations:* Professor of anthropology, University of Pennsylvania, 1961-; medical research scientist, Eastern Pennsylvania Psychiatric Institute, 1961-. *Other professional posts:* Member, National Research Council, Division of Behavioral Sciences; U.S. Office of Education, Research Advisory Committee; member, Behavioral Science Study Section, National Institute of Mental Health. *Military service:* U.S. Army, 1942-1945. *Memberships:* American Anthropological Association (Fellow); American Association for the Advancement of Science (Fellow; chairman, Section H); American Sociological Association (Fellow); Sigma Xi; Philadelphia Anthropological Society. *Published works: The Modal Personality Structure of the Tuscarora Indians, as Revealed by the Rorschach* 952); editor and author of introduction, *The Ghost-Dance Religion and the Sioux Outbreak of 1890* (Univerity of Chicago Press, 1965); *The Death and Rebirth of the Seneca*

(Knopf, 1970); other books and numerous articles in professional journals.

WALTERS, GEORGE A.
(B.I.A. agency superintendent)

Affiliation: Superintendent, Nome Agency, Bureau of Indian Affairs, P.O. Box 1108, Nome, Alaska 99762.

WARE, KENT C., II (Kiowa) 1941-
(Indian affairs director)

Born October 5, 1941, Lawton, Okla. *Education:* Arizona State University, B.S., 1966, Law School, J.D., 1970. *Principal occupation:* Director of Indian Affairs, Gulf Oil Corp., Denver, Colo., 1975-. *Home address:* 3724 S. Fairplay Way, Aurora, Colo. 80014.

WARREN, DAVE (Chippewa-Tewa Pueblo) 1932-
(educator)

Born April 12, 1932, Santa Fe, N.M. *Education:* University of New Mexico, B.A., 1955, M.A., 1961, Ph.D. *Principal occupation:* Educator. *Affiliations:* Instructor, Department to History, Oklahoma State University, 1964-1966; assistant professor, Department of History, University of Nebraska, 1966-1968; director of curriculum and instruction, 1968-1970, director, research and cultural studies materials development, 1970-, Institute of American Indian Arts, Santa Fe, N.M. *Other professional posts:* Member, advisory board, Center for Studies of the American West, University of Utah; member, advisory committee, University of New Mexico Indian Studies Program; chairman, selection committee, National Graduate Indian Scholarship Program (Donner Foundation); member, editorial board, *Indian Historian,* American Indian Historical Society, *Military service:* U.S. Air Force, 1955-1957 (Captain). *Memberships:* Latin American Studies Association; National Congress of American Indians. *Interests:* Mr. Warren writes, "Basic area of professional training has been with studies of the advanced Indian cultures of Mexico, prconquest and at the time of Spanish contact. Investigation of the Indian pictorial documents (codices) has been part of this professional study and interest. Currently, my work concerns the organization of cultural studies material into the instructional programs of the Bureau of Indian Affairs and other systems requiring information and resources about the American Indian—materials which reflect the history and current development of American Indians in the U.S., Canada, and Latin America. Of particular concern is finding programs and materials initiated by the Indian people, therefore reflecting their ideas and interpretations of issues, events or other concerns affecting Indian life and history, and utilizing such information in educational programs. Other areas of interest and activity: curriculum development, historical/ethnological writing and research." *Published works:* Articles in scholarly publications.

WARREN, WANDA EVANS GEORGE (Catawba) 1960-
(consultant, student) Born November 16, 1960, Rock Hill, S.C. *Education:* Georgetown University, B.S., 1983; Clemson University, M.A. (Economics), 1986; Georgia State University, 1986- (J.D. expected in 1989). *Principal occupation:* Consultant. Home address: 2986 Whispering Hills Dr., Chamblee, Ga. 30341. *Affiliations:* W.E., Desk Officer (NMFS), U.S. Department of Commerce, Washington, D.C. (three years); International Internship Planning Committee, Clemson University (two years); private consultant, Atlanta, Ga., 1986-. *Community activities:* Governor's Youth Advisory Council, 1979-1980; Governor's Council on Education, 1980-1981. *Memberships:* International Law Society, 1985; Student Bar Association, 1985; Lawyer's Guild Society, 1985; Georgetown Alumni Association; Atlanta Club. *Awards, honors:* Delegate to National Junior Achievements Convention, 1976; Junior Achievement President of the Year; American Indian Scholar, 1984-1985. *Interests:* "Interested in international trade and development as well as international law. (I) speak German and French. Recreational interests include international travel, and downhill skiing."

WASHBURN, WILCOMB E. 1925- (historian)
Born Januaery 13, 1925, Ottawa, Kan. *Education:* Dartmouth College, A.B. (summa cum laude), 1948; Harvard University, M.A., 1951, Ph.D., 1955. *Principal occupation:* Historian. *Home address:* 2122 California St., N.W., #157, Washington, D.C. 20560. *Affiliations:* Curator, Division of Political History, U.S. National Museum, Smithsonian Institution, 1958-1965; chairman, Department of American Studies, National Museum of History and Technology, Smithsonian Institution, 1965-1968; director, American Studies Program, Smithsonian Institution, Washington, D.C., 1968-. *Other professional posts:* Adjunct professor, American University, Washington, D.C., 1976-; consultant in research, Graduate School of Arts and Sciences, The George Washington University, Washington, D.C., 1966-. *Military service:* U.S. Marine Corps, 1943-1946, 1951-1952; presently Colonel, U.S. Marine Corps Reserves (retired). *Memberships:* American Anthropological Association (Fellow); American Antiquarian Society; American Association for the Advancement of Science; American Association of Museums; American Historical Association; American Society for Ethnohistory (president, 1957-1958); American Studies Association (president, 1978-1979); Anthropological Society of Washington; Indian Rights Association; Institute for Early Amerian History and Culture; Organization of American Historians; Society for the History of Discoveries (president, 1963-1965); Society for American Historians; among others. *Awards, honors:* Honorary Doctor of Letters, St. Mary's College of Maryland, 1970; Honorary Doctor of Humanities, Assumption College, Worcester, Mass., 1983; Phi Beta Kappa Lecturer, Spring, 1980. *Published works: Editor, The Indian and the White Man* (Doubleday, 1964); *Red Man's Land/White Man's Law: A Study of the Past and Present Status of the American Indian* (Scribner's, 1971); editor, *The American Indian and the U.S.: A Documentary History,* 4 volumes (Random House, 1973); *The Indian in America* (Harper & Row, 1975); *The Assault on Indian Tribalism: The General Allotment Law (Dawes Act) of 1887* (Lippincott, 1975;

reprint, Robert E. Krieger Publishing, 1986); *The American Heritage History of the Indian Wars,* with Robert M. Utley (American Heritage Publishing, 1977); numerous chapters in books, and articles in professional and scholarly journals.

WASILE, JEANNE
(executive director-Indian corporation)

Affiliation: Executive Director, International Vice President, American Indian International Development Corporation, Woodward Bldg., Suite 438, 733 15th St., N.W., Washington, D.C. 20005.

WATERS, DEANA J. HARRAGARRA
(library director)

Affiliation: Dirctor, National Indian Law Library, Native American Rights Fund, 1506 Broadway, Boulder, Colo. 80302-6296.

WATKINS, MARY BETH OZMUN
(Creek)
(library director)

Education: University of Oklahoma, B.S., 1959, M.L.S., 1968, post-graduate, 1968-1971. *Principal occupation:* Library director. *Home address:* 2503 Margaret Lynn Lane, Muskogee, Okla. 74401. *Affiliations:* Elementary field librarian, 1968-1970, media consultant, 1970-1971, Oklahoma City Public Schools; associate director, Eastern Oklahoma District Library, Muskogee, Okla., 1971-1977; director of libraries, Bacone College, Muskogee, Okla. 1977-. *Memberships:* Oklahoma Library Association, 1968- (secretary, 1972-1973; chairperson, membership committee, 1972-1976; chairperson, publicity committee, 1972-1973; chairperson, Sequoyah Children's Book Award, 1971-1972; chairperson, intellectual freedom committee, 1976-1977; co-chairperson, ad hoc committee serving as Humanities Council Project liaison, 1976-1977, chairperson, 1977-1978); Southwest Library Association, 1968- (SWLA membership chairperson for OLA, 1975-1976, 1977-1978); Oklahoma Education Association; National Education Association; Oklahoma Association of School Librarians

(district chairperson, 1969-1971); American Library Association, 1971- (member, Membership Task Force; chairperson, Southwest Region, 1976-1978); Oklahoma Association for Educational Communication and Technology, 1975-; Bacone Professional Association, 1977- (program committee; by-laws committee; vice president); Oklahoma Humanities Committee, 1977-1980; American Association of University Women (treasurer, 1976-1978; first vice president, program chairperson, 1978-1980). *Awards, honors:* Outstanding Young Women of America, 1970. *Published works:* Articles in *Oklahoma Librarian.*

WATSON, GEORGE (Narragansett)
(tribal chief)

Affiliation: Chief, Narragansett Indian Tribe, RFD #1, Kenyon, R.I. 02836.

WATTS, STEVEN M. 1947-
(Native American studies)

Born July 25, 1947, Lincoln County, N.C. *Education:* Appalachian State University, Boone, N.C., B.A., 1969; Duke University, M.Div., 1972. *Principal occupation:* Native American studies program specialist, Schiele Museum, Gastonia, N.C., 1984-. *Home address:* 622 Caroline Ave., Gastonia, N.C. 28052. *Other professional posts:* Workshop leader and consultant to museums and Native American organizations and groups in the field of aboriginal technologies. *Past work experience:* Minister, school counselor, classroom teacher, camp director, and substance abuse educator. *Community activities:* Commission on the Status of Women; Southeastern Indian Culture Study Group (director); American Indian Cultural Association (past director); Mental Health Association; volunteer work with schools, churches, scout groups, etc. *Memberships:* Center for the Study of Early Man; The Archaeological Society of N.C.; Continental Confederacy of Adopted Indians; Southeastern Cherokee Confederacy, 1980-1981. *Awards, honors:* Statewide speaker for N.C. Mental Health Association (1984); Master of ceremonies, N.C. Comission of Indian Affairs—"Unity Conference"

Intertribal Dance (1981); Outstanding Service Award, Mental Health Association, 1985. *Interests:* "Major interests is replication and experimental use of Native American tools, weapons, utensils, etc.—with the goal of (through educational programs) increasing the appreciation of native skills and lifestyles among participants—helping to rediscover and preserve native technologies for generations to come. Most "spare" time is spent visiting native communities in the Southeast and historic and prehistoric native sites to increase the understanding and collection of knowledge." *Biographical sources:* Approximately a dozen newspaper articles in local and statewide newspapers (copies available upon request). *Published works:* "The Old Bearskin Report," journal (Schiele Museum, 1985); "Southeastern Craft Articles," series (*The Backwoodsman*, Tex., 1984 & 1985).

WAUNEKA, ANNIE DODGE (Navajo) 1910-
(tribal council member)

Born April 10, 1910, Sawmill, Ariz. *Principal occupation:* Tribal council member, Navajo Tribal Government, Window Rock, Ariz., 1951-. *Other professional post:* Lecturer. *Home address:* Box 629, Ganado, Ariz. *Community activities:* President, "School For Me," Navajo Project Concern, Project Hope; Navajo Nation School Board Association (board member); Navajo Tribal Utility Authority (board member); Navajo Health Authority (board member). *Memberships:* National Public Health Education; American Public Health Association; National TB Association; Society for Public Health (honorary lifetime member). *Awards, honors:* President's Freedom Medal Award, 1963; Woman of the Year in Arizona; Honorary Doctor of Humanities Degree, University of Albuquerque, N.M., 1972; Woman of the Year, 1976, *Ladies Home Journal. Interests:* "Main interest is in health of American Indians; education and tribal government." *Biographical sources: Indian Women of Today; Navajo Biography.*

WAX, MURRAY L. 1922-
(professor)

Born November 23, 1922, St. Louis, Mo. *Education:* University of Chicago, B.S., 1942, Ph.D., 1959; University of Pennsylvania, 1947. *Principal occupation:* Professor. *Home address:* 7030 Dartmouth Ave., #2, University City, Mo. 63130. *Affiliations:* Professor of Sociology & Anthropology, University of Kansas, Lawrence, Kan., 1964-1973, Washington University, St. Louis, Mo., 1973-. *Other professional posts:* Executive associate, Workshop on American Indian Affairs, University of Colorado, Boulder, 1959-1960; director, Oglala Sioux Education Research Project (Emory University), 1962-1963; director, Indian Education Research Project (University of Kansas), 1965-1968. *Memberships:* American Anthropological Association (Fellow); American Association for the Advancement of Science (Fellow); American Sociological Association (Fellow); Current Anthropology (Associate); Royal Anthropological Institute of Great Britain and Ireland (Fellow); Society for Applied Anthropology (Fellow); Society for the Study of Religion; Society for the Study of Social Problems; American Educational Research Association; Midwest Sociological Society; Council on Anthropology and Education. *Awards, honors:* Adopted by Oglala Sioux Tribe; Phi Beta Kappa; Sigma Xi; National Institute of Education Grants, 1973-1974, 1978-1979; National Science Foundation Grant, 1978-1981; grants from: U.S. Office of Economic Opportunity, U.S. Office of Education, Wenner-Gren Foundation. *Editorial boards, advisory editor: Human Organization* (editorial board, 1966-); *Journal of Cultural & Educational Futures* (1979-); *Phylon* (1973-); *Qualitative Sociology* (1982-); *Symbolic Interaction* (1983-). *Published works: Formal Education in an American Indian Community* (Monograph #1, Society for the Study of Social Problems, 1964); co-editor, *Indian Education in Eastern Oklahoma: A Report of Fieldwork Among the Cherokee* (U.S. Office of Education, 1969); *Indian Americans: Unity and Diversity* (Prentice-Hall, 1971); *Solving "The Indian Problem"* (New Viewpoints/Franklin Watts, 1975); numerous articles and essays in professional journals.

WEATHERFORD, ELIZABETH 1945-
(museum curator-film and video)

Born July 30, 1945, Anson County, N.C. *Education:* Duke University, B.A., 1966; The New School for Social Research, New York, N.Y., M.A., 1970. *Principal occupation:* Museum curator-film and video. *Address:* Museum of the American Indian, Heye Foundation, Broadway at 155th St., New York, N.Y. 10032. *Affiliations:* Assistant professor, School of Visual Arts, New York, N.Y., 1970-1981; adjunct curator, Museum of the American Indian, New York, N.Y., 1981-. *Memberships:* Educational Film Library Association; American Anthropological Association; Association for Independent Video and Film Makers; Media Alliance; National Alliance of Media Arts Centers, New York Women's Anthropological Caucus; Society on Visual Anthropology; Cultural Survival. *Interests:* "Recent and archival documentary films and videotapes about Native Americans." *Published works: Native Americans on Film and Video (Museum of the American Indian, 1981); Native Americans on Film and Video II* (Museum of the American Indians, 1986); "Anthropology" and "Native Americans" in *Good Reading* (R.R. Bowker, 1985).

WEATHERLY, JOHN
(college president)

Affiliation: President, Nebraska Indian Community College, P.O. Box 752, Winnebago, Neb. 68071.

WEBSTER, EMERSON C. (Seneca)
(tribal chief)

Affiliation: Chief, Tonawanda Band of Senecas, Council of Chiefs, 7027 Meadville Rd., Basom, N.Y. 14013.

WELCH, KAY
(B.I.A. agency superintendent)

Affiliation: Superintendent, Warm Springs Agency, Bureau of Indian Affairs, Warm Springs, Ore. 97761.

WELLS, RICHARD (Nisqually)
(tribal chairman)

Affiliation: Chairman, Nisqually Indian Community Council, 4820 She-Na-Num Dr., S.E., Olympia, Wash. 98503.

WELLS, VINE (Mdewakanton Sioux)
(tribal president)

Affiliation: President, Prairie Island Community Council, Route 2, Welch, Minn. 55089.

WELLS, WALLACE (Crow Creek Sioux)
(tribal chairman)

Affiliation: Chairman, Crow Creek Sioux Tribal Council, P.O. Box 658, Fort Thompson, S.D. 57339.

WERITO, CECILIA
(coordinator-Indian women's program)

Affiliation: Coordinator, Federal Women's Program, Indian Health Service, 5600 Fishers Lane, Rockville, Md. 20857.

WESLAGER, CLINTON ALFRED 1909-
(professor emeritus)

Born April 30, 1909, Pittsburgh, Pa. *Education:* University of Pittsburgh, B.A., 1933. *Principal occupation:* Professor emeritus, Widener University. *Home address:* RD 2, Box 104, Old Public Rd., Hockessin, Dela. 19707. *Memberships:* Archaeological Society of Delaware (past president); Eastern States Archaeological Federation (past president). *Awards, honors:* Christian Lineback Award for excellence in teaching; Archibold Crozier Award; two awards for outstanding books, Association for State and Local History; Fellow, Archaeological Society of New Jersey; Fellow, Holland Society of New York. *Interests:* "Ethnohistorical research among survivors of Eastern Woodland tribes, especially Nanticoke, Delaware, Conoy, Minquas, Mahican, and Munsee." *Published works: Delawares Forgotten Folk,* (1943); *Delaware's Buried Past* (1944); *The Nanticoke Indians* (1948);

Indian Place-Names in Delaware (1950); Red Men on the Brandywine (1953); *Magic Medicines of the Indians* (1973); *The Delaware Indians, A History* (Rutgers University, 1973); *The Delawares: A Critical Bibliography* (1978); *The Delaware Indian Westward Migration;* (Middle Atlantic Press, 1979); *Magic Medicine of the Iroquois* (Middle Atlantic Press, 1980); *The Nanticoke Indians, Past and Present* (University of Delaware, 1983); among others.

WEST, W. RICHARD (DICK)
(Wah-pah-nah-yah) (Southern Cheyenne) 1912-
(teacher, artist, consultant, lecturer, sculptor)

Born September 8, 1912, Darlington, Okla. *Education:* Concho Indian School; Haskell Institute; Bacone Junior Colege, A.A., 1938; University of Oklahoma, B.F.A., 1941, M.F.A., 1950. *Principal occupation:* Teacher, artist, consultant, lecturer, sculptor. *Home address:* RR #1, Box 447, Fort Gibson, Okla. 74434. *Affiliations:* Director, Art Department, Bacone College, Muskogee, Okla., 1947-1970; chairman, Division of Humanities, Haskell Indian Junior College, Lawrence, Kan., 1970-. *Military service:* U.S. Navy, 1942-1946. *Community activities:* Muskogee Art Guild; Bacone College Education Association (president); Indin Club sponsor. *Memberships:* Delti Phi Delta; Southwestern Art Association; Oklahoma Education Association (chairman of art section, district). *Awards, honors:* Outstanding Cheyenne of the Year, 1968, by Cheyennes of Oklahoma; Teacher of the Year, 1969, Bacone College; Outstanding Alumnus, 1973, Haskell Alumni Association; contract artist, Franklin Mint, Franklin Center, Pa., 1974, 1975, to create subject drawings for a series of fifty medallions to be struck or cast on the history of the American Indians; Outstanding Professor, 1976-1977, Haskell Indian Junior College. *Exhibitions:* Numerous one-man shows and art awards throughout the U.S., 1949-. *Interests:* "Mr. West speaks and lectures on his art in general, often on Indian art, and very often on his series of oils portraying Christ as a Plains Indian. He has juried numerous Indian art shows, non-Indian art competitions, and more recently has served as a aconsultant to colleges and universities on Indian studies programs and education of Indian youths. Dick West has been the inspiration of many artists all over America. Dick's prime aim in his art is to show that the Indian, with his priceless heritage of history, legend and color could make himself an important place in contemporary American art. Possibly the best known of his paintings is the "Indian Christ in Gethsemane" at the alter of Bacone's beautiful chapel. Included in his religious series are "The Madonna and Child," The Annunciations," "The Last Supper," "The Crucifixion," and "The Ascension." *Biographical sources: Who's Who in American Art; Who's Who in the South and Southwest; Who's Who in Oklahoma; Personalities of the South; Community Leaders and Noteworthy Americans; International Who's Who in Art and Antiques.* A filmstrip of the life and works of Dick West was made and produced by the American Baptist Films, Valley Forge, Pa., in 1969. Also in 1969 a biography of the artist was written by Charles Waugamen and published by Friendship Press, New York.

WESTERMEYER, JOSEPH, M.D. 1937-
(psychiatrist)

Born April 8, 1937, U.S.A. *Education:* University of Minnesota, M.D., 1961, M.A., M.P.H., Ph.D., 1969-1970, *Principal occupation:* Psychiatrist. *Home addres:* 1935 Summit Ave., St. Paul, Minn. 55105. *Affiliation:* Professor of psychiatry, Department of Psychiatry, University of Minnesota Hospitals and Clincis (UMHC), Minneapolis, Minn., 1970-. *Other professional posts:* Director, Alcohol-Drug Dependence Program, (UMHC), 1982-; director, International Clinic (UMHC), 1984-. *Community activities:* Indian Guest House (halfway house for Indian alcoholics), Minneapolis, Minn. (board member, 1969-1972); Juel Fairbanks House (halfway house for Indian alcoholics, St. Paul, Minn. (board member, 1970-1973); South Side Receiving Center (a detoxification unit for American Indian alcoholics), Minneapolis, Minn. (consultant, 1974-1975); Association of American Indian Affairs, including Senate subcomittee hearing on American Indian child welfare, 1973-1976. *Memberships:* American

Anthropological Association (Fellow); American Association for the Advancement of Science; American Medical Society on Alcoholism; American Psychiatric Association (Fellow); American Public Health Association; American Association of Family Practice (Fellow); Association of Academic Psychiatrists; Minnesota Psychiatric Association; Society on Medical Anthropology; World Psychiatric Association, Transcultural Section ; among others. *Awards, honors:* Meritorious Service Award, U.S. Agency for International Development, 1967; Ginzburg Fellow, Group for the Advancement of Psychiatry, 1969-1970; numerous research grants. *Published works:* Chapters in books and monographs: "The Ravage of Indian Families in Crisis," in *The Destruction of Indian Fanily Life,* ed., S. Unger (Association of American Indian Affairs, 1976); "Alcoholism and American Indian Alcoholism," in *Alcoholism Development, Intervention and Consequences,* with J. Baker, ed., E. Heinman (1986).

WETMORE, RUTH L. (Mrs.) 1934-
(Indian museum curator)

Born 1934 in Nebraska. *Education:* Park College, B.A., 1956; University of Kansas, M.A., 1959. *Principal occupation:* Curator, Indian Museum of the Carolinas, Laurinburg, N.C., 1974-. *Home address:* 811 S. Main St., Laurinburg, N.C. 28352. *Memberships:* Archaeological Society of North Carolina; Oklahoma Anthropological Society; North Carolina Museums Council; Phi Beta Kappa; Pi Sigma Alpha. *Interests:* Philatelic writing and exhibiting. *Published work: First on the Land: The North Carolina Indians* (John F. Blair, Publisher, 1975).

WHITE, ELMER, Sr. (Devil's Lake Sioux)
(tribal chief)

Affiliation: Chief, Devil's Lake Sioux Tribal Council, Sioux Community Center, Fort Totten, N.D. 58335.

WHITE, HARTLEY (Chippewa)
(tribal chairman)

Affiliation: Leech Lake Reservation Business Committee, Box 308, Cass Lake, Minn. 56633.

WHITE,LINCOLN C.
(executive director-Indian education)

Affiliation: Executive director, National Advisory Council on Indian Education, 2000 L St., N.W., Suite 574, Washington, D.C. 20036

WHITE, LONNIE J. 1931-
(professor of history)

Born February 12, 1931, Haskell County, Tex. *Education:* West Texas State College, B.A., 1950; Texas Tech University, M.A., 1955, University of Texas, Ph.D., 1961. *Principal occupation:* Professor of history, Memphis State University, Memphis, Tenn., 1961-. *Home address:* 4272 Rhodes Ave., Memphis, Tenn. 38111. *Military service:* U.S. Army, 1951-1953 (Sergeant). *Memberships:* Western History Association; Southern Historical Association; American Military Institute; American Historical Association; *Journal of the West* (editorial advisory board). *Interests:* Teacher of course on history of American Indians at Memphis State University from 1968 to the present. *Biographical source: Who's Who in the South and Southwest. Published works:* Editor, co-author, *Hostiles and Horse Soldiers: Indian Battles and Campaigns in the West* (Pruett Press, 1972); editor, *The Miles Expedition of 1874-1875: An Eyewitness Account of the Red River War, by Scout J.T. Marshall (Encino Press, 1971); editor, Chronicle of a Congressional Journey: The Doolittle Committee in the Southwest, 1865* (Pruett Press, 1975); *Panthers to Arrowheads: The 36th (Texas-Oklahoma) Division in World War I* (Presidial Press, 1984); *Politics on the Southwestern Frontier: Arkansas Territory, 1819-1836* (Memphis State University Press, 1964); numerous articles in professional journals.

WHITE HAT, ALBERT H. (Rosebud Sioux) 1938-
(bilingual teacher)

Born November 18, 1938, St. Francis, S.D. *Education:* Sinte Gleska College, A.A. (Lakota Studies), 1986. *Principal occupation:* Bilingual teacher. *Home address:* Box 168, St. Francis, S.D. 57572. *Affiliations:* Indian studies program teacher, St. Francis Indian School, 1974-1980; part-time teacher, Lakota Medicine, 1979-1985, director of Title VII, Bilingual Teacher Training Program, Sinte Gleska College, Rosebud, S.D., 1983-. *Other professional posts:* Tribal council (Rosebud Sioux) representative and committee work, 1979-1981; president, board of directors, Sinte Gleska College, 1981-1983. *Community activities:* Rosebud Community Action Program, 1967-1970; Rosebud Ambulance Service, 1970-1972; St. Francis Indian School (chairman of the board). *Memberships:* National Association for Bilingual Education; South Dakota Association for Bilingual Education; South Dakota Indian Education Association. *Awards, honors:* Fellowship award in 1978 to research Native American History for high school history course at Newberry Library, Chicago, Ill. *Interests:* Carpentry, woodwork and construction; horse training; cultural and traditional activities. "Presently, I am coordinating three instructional pamphlets in the areas of Lakota kinship—early childhood development, bilingual science, and bilingual language arts." *Published work:* Co-editor, *Lakota Ceremonial Songs* (song book with cassette tape) (Sinte Gleska College).

WHITEBEAR, BERNIE
(executive director-Indian center)

Affiliation: Executive director, Daybreak Star Arts Center, P.O. Box 99253, Seattle, Wash. 98199.

WHITECROW, JAKE L. (Quapaw-Seneca-Cayuga of Oklahoma) 1928-
(health administrator)

Born July 2, 1928, Miami, Okla. Education: Oklahoma State University, Stillwater, B.S. (Agriculture), 1951. *Principal occupation:*

Health administrator, National Indian Health Board, Denver, Colo. *Home address:* 5100 Leetsdale Dr., #241, Denver, Colo. 80222. *Affiliations:* Americans for Indian Opportunity, Washington, D.C. (board member, seven years); American Indian Heritage Foundation, Washington, D.C. (board member, advisory council, two years). *Other professional posts:* Health committee chairman, National Congress of American Indians; founder, Native American Free Loan Society, Denver, Colo. *Military service:* U.S. Army, 1951-1978 (Major-U.S. Army Reserve-retired; U.N. Medal; Korean War Medal with two Battle Stars; National Defense Medal; Army Reserve Medal). *Community activities:* Quapaw Tribe (chairman); American Legion (precinct co-chairman, post commander); Native American Cattle Co. of Oklahoma (president). *Memberships:* Oklahoma State Historical Society (listed speaker); Thomas Jefferson Forum of Washington, D.C. (listed speaker). *Awards, honors:* Honorary member of 4-H Clubs of Oklahoma; "I was the only Oklahoma Indian to serve as a commissioner with the American Policy Review Commission (U.S. Congress, 1975-1977)." *Interests:* "My avocational interests are: sport of rodeo, Indian customs and history, football, basketball, Indian dice, horse training, dog training. *Biographical source: Indians of Oklahoma* (University of Oklahoma Press). *Published work: American Indian Policy Review Commission Final Report* (U.S. Government Printing Office, 1977).

WHITEHEAD, RUTH HOLMES EVERETT (Sioux) 1947-
(ethnologist, assistant curator)

Born October 10, 1947, Charleston, S.C. *Education:* College of Charleston, B.A., 1971. *Principal occupation:* Ethnologist, assistant curator, Nova Scotia Museum, Halifax, Nova Scotia, Can., 1972-. *Home address:* Box 2, Site 24, R.R. One, Tantallon, Nova Scotia, Can. B0J 3J0. *Interests:* Porcupine quillwork as practiced by the Micmac Indians from 1500-9150; Micmac art in general. *Published works: The Micmac Ethnology Collection of the Nova Scotia Museum* (The Nova Scotia Museum, 1974); *Christina Morris: Micmac Artist and Artist's Model* (National Museums of Canada, 1977); "Decorating Bark With Porcupine Quills (*Ahoy,* children's magazine, 1977); *Micmac Quillwork* (Nova Scotia Museum, 1978); *Inventory of Micmac Material Culture Outside Canada,* with Dr. Harold McGee (Nova Scotia Museum, 1978); "Micmac Quillwork in the Nineteenth Century" (National Museums of Canada, 1978).

WHITELY, PETER M. 1953-
(anthropologist)

Born March 13, 1953, Leicester, England. *Education:* Cambridge University (England), B.A., 1975, M.A., 1980; University of New Mexico, Ph.D., 1982. *Principal occupation:* Assistant professor of anthropology, Sarah Lawrence College, Bronxville, N.Y., 1985-. *Memberships:* American Anthropological Association; American Ethnological Society; Royal Anthropological Institute; Sigma Xi. *Interests:* Hopi ethnology. *Published works: Deliberate Arts: Changing Culture in a Hopi Community* (University of Arizona Press, 1987); *Journey to Reed Springs: A History of the Hopi Village of Bacari* (Northland Press, 1987).

WHITEMAN, DENNIS
(B.I.A. agency superintendent)

Affiliation: Superintendent, Red Lake Agency, Bureau of Indian Affairs, Red Lake, Minn. 56671.

WHITENER, DONALD E.
(B.I.A. agency superintendent)

Affiliation: Superintendent, Crow Creek Agency, Bureau of Indian Affairs, P.O. Box 616, Fort Thompson, S.D. 57339.

WHITESIDE, DON *(Sin-a-paw)*
(Creek) 1931-
(research analyst)

Born May 9, 1931, Brooklyn, N.Y. *Education:* Wisconsin State University, B.S., 1958; University of Wisconsin, M.S., 1960; Stanford University, Ph.D., 1967. *Principal occupation:* Research analyst. *Home address:* 4 Newgale St., Nepean, Ontario, Can K2H 5R2. *Affiliations:* Assistant professor, University of Alberta, Edmonton, Can., 1967-1970; consultant, Government of Canada, Ottawa, 1970-1972; research director, National Indian Brotherhood, Ottawa, 1972-1973; professor, Manitou College, LaMacaza, Quebec, 1973-1975; INA, 1976-1979; owner, Whiteside and Associates, 1979-1982; research analyst, Government of Canada (NHW), 1982-. *Military service:* Merchant Marine, 1947-1948; U.S. Army, 1948-1954. *Community activities:* Alberta Human Rights Association (president, 1969-1970); Civil Liberties Association, National Capital Region (president, 1970-1971, 1973, 1974, 1977-); Canadian Rights and Liberties Federation (secretary/treasurer, 1972-1974; president, 1974-1977, 1983- Aboriginal Institute of Canada (president, 1973-). *Memberships:* United Native Americans. *Awards:* National Science Foundation Fellowship, 1963; Stanford University Fellow, 1963-1964. *Interests:* Genealogy. *Published works: Aboriginal People: A Selected Bibliography* (National Indian Brotherhood, 1973); *Aboriginal People: A Selected Bibliography,* Vol. II (Canadian Association in Support of Native peoples, 1977); *A Look Into Indian History* (Aboriginal Institute of Canada, 1983); *Indians, Indians, Indians* (National Library of Canada, forthcoming).

WHITFORD, THOMAS
(B.I.A. agency superintendent)

Affiliation: Superintendent, Eastern Nevada Agency, Bureau of Indian Affairs, P.O. Box 28, Elko, Nev. 89832.

WHITISH, RACHEL (Shoalwater)
(tribal chairwoman)

Affiliations: Chairwoman, Shoalwater Bay Tribal Council, P.O. Box 579, Tokeland, Wash. 98590.

WHITMAN, KATHY (ELK WOMAN) (Manadan-Hidatsa-Arikara) 1952- (designer, sculptor, painter)

Born August 12, 1952, Bismarck, N.D. *Education:* University of South Dakota; Sinte Gleska College, Rosebud, S.D.; Standing Rock Community College, Ft. Yates, N.D. *Principal occupation:* Professional artist— designer, sculptor, painter. *Home address:* 111 San Salvador, Santa Fe, N.M. 87501. *Affiliations:* Owner, Nux-Baga Lodge, New Town, N.D., 1981-1985; owner, Recreation Center, New Town, N.D., 1985. *Other professional post:* Art instructor, Standing Rock Community College and Sinte Gleska College. *Community activities:* Parent representative-Headstart, Ft. Yates, N.D.; Ft. Berthold Community College, New Town, N.D. (board of directors); Pow-Wow, Canonball, N.D. (president, committee member). *Memberships:* Indian Arts and Crafts Association; North Dakota Council on the Arts (artist-in-residence; board member). *Awards, honors:* Governors Award, Directors and Choice Merit Award, United Tribes Educational Training Center, Bismarck, N.D. *Interests:* "Demonstrated and exhibited paintings in New York City at Museum of the American Indian; danced and exhibited artwork in Charleroi, Belgium and Dijon, France; started a recreation center on Ft. Berthold Reservation for the youth and sponsored an alternative camp for youth. Presently, moved south to Santa Fe, N.M. and promoting own work in stone sculptor with the help of art agents at the Flute Player Gallery, Colorado Springs, Colo." *Biographical sources: Wanbli Ho* (Sinet Gleska College, 1976); *Minot Daily News* (Minot, N.D., 1982); *Denver Post* (Denver, Colo., 1982); *Beulah Beacon* (Beulah, N.D., 1983); *Draw* Magazine (Brookville, Ohio, 1984).

WHITTENER, DAVID (Squaxin Island) (tribal chairman)

Affiliation: Chairman, Squaxin Island Tribal Council, W. 81 Hwy. 108, Shelton, Wash. 98584.

WICKCLIFFE, DENNIS L. (Oklahoma Cherokee) 1944- (B.I.A. public information officer)

Born April 18, 1944, Claremore, Okla. *Education:* Northeastern State University, Tahlequah, Okla., B.A, 1966; University of Oklahoma, M.Ed., 1973. *Principal occupation:* Area public information officer, Bureau of Indian Affairs, Anadarko, Okla., 1976-. *Home address:* P.O. Box 1195, Anadarko, Okla. 73005. *Military service:* U.S. Air Force, 1968-1972 (E-5 highest rank; Air Force Commendation Medal for service in Southeast Asia). *Other professional posts:* English teacher/journalism teacher/Title I coordinator, Riverside Indian School, Anadarko, Okla., 1972-1976; acting principal, Riverside Indian School, 1976. *Memberships:* University of Oklahoma Alumni Asociation, 1973-; Cherokee Tribe of Oklahoma. *Interests:* Travel; sports; working with and for Indian people through the Bureau of Indian Affairs.

WILCOX, U. VINCENT, III, 1945- (museum anthropologist and curator)

Born September 26, 1945, Washington, D.C. *Education:* Yale University, B.A., 1967; Harvard University, M.A., 1968; Columbia University, M.Phil., 1974. *Principal occupation:* Museum anthropologist and curator. *Home address:* 7434 Colshire Dr. #3, McLean, Va. 22101. *Affiliations:* Curator of North American Archaeology and Ethnology, and head of the Research Branch, Museum of the American Indian, Heye Foundation, New York, N.Y. , 1968-1977; collections manager, Department of Anthropology, National Museum of Natural History, Smithsonian Institution, Washington, D.C., 1977-? *Memberships:* American Anthropological Association; Society for American Archaeology; American Association of Museums; International Council for Museums; Council for Museum Anthropology; The Explorers Club. *Interests:* Material culture of the North American Indian—the curation and conservation of anthropological collections, general museology; archaeological fieldwork. *Published works:* Numerous articles in scientific and popular journals.

WILDCAT, WILLIAM (Chippewa)
(tribal president)

Affiliation: President, Lac du Flambeau Tribal Council, P.O. Box 67, Lac du Flambeau, Wis. 54538.

WILKINSON, GERALD
(executive director-Indian organization)

Affiliation: Executive director, national Indian Youth Council, 201 Hermosa, N.E., Albuquerque, N.M., 87108.

WILLIAMS, DAVID EMMETT *(Tosque)* (Kiowa-Apache-Tonkawa) 1933- (artist)

Born August 20, 1933, Redstone, Okla. *Education:* Bacone College. *Principal occupation:* Artist. *Membership:* American Tribal Dancers and Singers Club, 1963- (head drummer and singer). *Awards, honors, exhibits:* Numerous art awards and one-man shows; work represented in permanent collections of several museums.

WILLIAMS, DEAN V (Seneca) 1925- (tribal official)

Born April 30, 1925, Cattaraugus Reservation, N.Y. *Home address:* Route 438, Gowanda—Irving Rd., Irving, N.Y. 14081. *Affiliation:* Former president, Seneca Nation of Indians, Cattaraugus Reservation, N.Y. *Military service: U.S. Navy Submarine Service, 1943-1946.*

WILLIAMS, DELLA R. (SAM) (Papago) 1936- (school principal)

Born February 13, 1936, Ventana Village, Papago Reservation, Ariz. *Education:* Phoenix Junior College, A.A., 1958; Arizona State University, B.A., 1962. *Principal occupation:* School principal. *Home address:* Star Route, Box 92, San Simeon School, Sells, Ariz. 85634. *Affiliations:* Teacher, Santa Rosa Boarding School, B.I.A., 1962-1975; principal, San Simeon School, B.I.A., Papago Indian Agency, 1977-. *Community activities:* Papago Tribal Education Com-

mittee (chairperson, 1965-1970); OEO's Community Action Program; tribal representative at various state and national conferences and workshops, as well as at congressional hearings. *Honor:* Inducted into the Phoenix Indian High School Hall of Fame as a charter member, 1977. *Interests:* Consulting with students, teachers and administrators concerning grades and adjustment; higher education students, consultant and advisor; directed Tribal Education Grants and assisted with other financial needs of higher education; monthly reports to the General Council; participated and assisted in the introduction, planning and development of the first poverty program on the Papago Reservation; participated in supervising and hiring the first Head-Start school teachers, evaluated and made recommendations; participated as guest speaker in Indian education conferences in Tempe, Indian Clubs, The Papago Council, Phoenix Indian High School, Tucson Indian Center, and Papago District Councils.

WILLIAMS, FLOYD (Skagit) (tribal chairman)

Affiliation: Chairman, Upper Skagit Tribal Council, 2284 Community Plaza, Sedro Woolley, Wash. 98284.

WILLIAMS, ROBERT A., Jr. (Lumbee) 1955- (law professor)

Born March 11, 1955, Baltimore, Md. *Education:* Loyola College, Baltimore, Md., B.A., 1977; Harvard Law School, J.D., 1980. *Principal occupation:* Assistant professor of law, University of Wisconsin, Madison, 1980-. *Home address:* 1621 Adams St., Madison, Wis. 53711. *Other professional post:* Legal consultant. *Community activities:* Indian Rights Association, Philadelphia, Pa. (vice president, 1984; board of directors, 1980-1985). *Awards, honors:* American Council of Learned Societies-/Ford Foundation Fellowship recipient, 1985-1986; National Endowment for the Humanities Fellowship recipient, Summer, 1982. *Interests:* American Indian legal history, and economic development.

WILLIAMS, WALTER L. 1948-
(professor)

Born November 3, 1948, Durham, N.C. *Education:* Georgia State University, B.A., 1970; University of North Carolina, Chapel Hill, M.A., 1972, Ph.D., 1974. *Principal occupation:* Associate professor, Anthropology Department, University of Southern California, Los Angeles, Calif. *Home address:* 3400 Ben Lomond Place #130, Los Angeles, Calif. 90027. *Other professional post:* Consultant, American Indian Studies Center, UCLA. *Community activities:* Gay American Indians, Inc. (consultant); Museum of the Cherokee Indians (consultant); International Gay and Lesbian Archives (president, board of directors). *Memberships:* American Anthropological Association; Organization of American Historians, *Awards, honors:* Woodrow Wilson Fellow, 1970; American Council of Learned Societies grant awards, 1977, 1983; UCLA American Indian Studies Center Fellow, 1980, 1982; Newbery Library Fellow, 1978. *Interests:* Fieldwork: Eastern Cherokees, Lakotas, Mayas. *Published works:* Editor, *Southeastern Indians Since the Removal Era* (University of Georgia Press, 1979); editor, *Indian Leadership* (Sunflower University Press, Manhattan, Kan., 1984); *The Spirit and the Flesh: American Indian Androgyny and Male Sexuality* (Beacon Press, 1986. Articles: "Detour Down the Trail of Tears: Southern Indians and the Land" (*Southern Exposure,* Fall, 1974); "The Proposed Merger of Apaches with Eastern Cherokees in 1893" (*Journal of Cherokee Studies,* Spring, 1977); book reviews on Southeastern Indians in: *Ethnohistory, North Carolina Historical Review, American Indian Journal,* and *Journal of Southern History.*

WILLIE, ELVIN, Jr. (Paiute)
(tribal chairman)

Affiliation: Chairman, Walker River Paiute Tribal Council, P.O. Box 220, Schurz, Nev. 89427.

WILNOTY, JOHN JULIUS (Cherokee) 1940-
(stone carver)

Born April 10, 1940, Cherokee, N.C. *Principal occupation:* Stone carver. *Home address:* Cherokee, N.C. 28719. *Membership:* The Qualla Indian Arts and Crafts Cooperative. *Interests:* Building toys for children; rebuilding and designing machinery. Mr. Wilnoty's work is displayed at the Smithsonian Institution and the Museum of the American Indian.

WILSON, DUFFY
(museum director)

Affiliation: Executive director, Native American Centre for the Living Arts, Inc., 25 Rainbow Mall, Niagara Falls, N.Y. 14303.

WILSON, RAYMOND 1945-
(professor of history)

Born April 11, 1945, New Kensington, Pa. *Education:* Fort Lewis College, Durango, Colo., B.A., 1967; University of Nebraska, Omaha, M.A., 1972; University of New Mexico, Ph.D., 1977. *Principal occupation:* Assistant-associate professor of history, Fort Hays State University, Hays, Kan., 1979-. *Home address:* 1721 Haney, Hays, Kan. 67601. *Other professional post:* History instructor, Sam Houston State University, 1977-1979. *Memberships:* Western History Association; Indian Rights Association; Kansas Council for the Social Studies; Kansas Corral of the Westerners; Phi Alpha Theta; Pi Gamma Mu; Phi Delta Kappa; Phi Kappa Phi. *Interests:* "My major area of study is the American West with an emphasis on 19th and 20th century American Indian history. I enjoy traveling throughout western America." *Published works:* Administrative History, Canyon de Chelly National Monument, Arizona (U.S. Dept. of the Interior/National Park Service, 1976); co-author, David M. Brugge, Ohiyesa: Charles A. Eastman, Santee Sioux (University of Illinois Press, 1983); Native Americans in the Twentieth Century (Brigham Young University Pres, 1984); co-author, James S. Olson, Indian Lives:

Essays on 19th and 20th Century Native American Leaders (University of New Mexico Press, 1985).

WILSON, WILLIAM
(assistant director-Indian Health Service)

Affiliation: Assistant director, Indian Health Service, 5600 Fishers Lane, Rockville, Md. 20857.

WINDER, NATHAN W. (STRONG ELK)
(Ute-Navajo-Paiute) 1960-
(counselor-grants/contracts administrator)

Born October 2, 1960, Albuquerque, N.M. *Education:* Stanford University, B.A., 1983; University of Oregon, School of Law, 1984-1985. *Principal occupation:* Counselor, grants/contracts administrator, Pyramid Lake Paiute Tribal Council, Nixon, Nev., 1985-. *Home address:* P.O. Box 242, Nixon, Nev. 89424. *Other professional post:* Director, Wambli Gleska Indian Program. *Community activities:* Native American Church (vice president, Pyramid Lake chapter); Save the Children Committee (chairman). *Interests:* "I am interested in returning back to law school or applying to medical school. I am interested in some day becoming a spiritual leader or a medicine man. I am also interested in sponsoring a sun dance for the four colors of humanity."

CHARITY WING (Sioux) 1902-
(nursing, homemaking)

Born March 9, 1902, Montana Territory. *Education:* Haskell Institute, Lawrence, Kan., A.A., 1926. *Principal occupation:* Nursing, homemaking. *Home address:* P.O. Box 64, Poplar, Mt. 59255. *Affiliation:* Member, Indian Tribal Affairs, Citizens Committee, Fort Peck Sioux Tribe, Poplar, Mt. (20 years); advocate, Fort Peck Sioux Claims Committee for Black Hills (ten years). *Other professional post:* Presbyterian Church Elder; Ladies Aid Healer (70 years; president, three terms). *Awards, honors:* Woman of the Day, Presbyterian Church, Special Recognition, 1981. *Interests:* "Sewing—starquilt construction;

travel; guest lecturer for Indian history, lore, crafts, life styles, method of rearing Indian children; Grandfather Basil Reddoor was first ordained minister of Presbyterian Church on the Fort Peck Reservation in Montana."

CHIEF WISE OWL (Tuscarora) 1939-
(chief and medicine man)

Born February 16, 1939, Robeson County, N.C. *Principal occupation:* Chief and medicine man, Tuscarora Indian Tribe, Drowning Creek Reservation. *Home address:* Route 2, Box 108, Maxton, N.C. 28364. *Other professional posts:* Businessman; teacher of herbs to next medicine man. *Community activities:* Built tribal community center. *Membership:* National Congress of American Indians.

WITTSTOCK, LAURA WATERMAN
(Seneca) 1937-
(administrator)

Born September 11, 1937, Cattaraugus Indian Reservation, N.Y. *Education:* University of Minnesota, B.S. candidate. *Principal occupation:* Non-profit administrator. *Home address:* 3031 Dakota Avenue South, St. Louis Park, Minn. 55416. *Affiliations:* Editor, *Legislative Review,* 1971-1973; executive director, American Indian Press Association, Washington, D.C., 1975; associate director, Red School House, St. Paul, Minn., 1975-1977; director, Project Media, National Indian Education, Minneapolis, Minn., 1973-1975; office manager, Native American Research Institute, Minneapolis, Minn., 1981; administrator, Heart of the Earth Survival School, Minneapolis, Minn., 1982-1985; independent education consultant, 1976-; director, curriculum project, Migizi Comunications, Inc., Minneapolis, Minn., 1985-. *Community activities:* Minnesota Governor's Job Training Council (vice chair, 1983-); Minneapolis Community Business Employment Alliance (vice chair, 1983-); Migizi Communications, Inc. (president-on leave); United Way Planning and Priorities Committee (member); Christian Sharing Fund, Minneapolis-St. Paul Archdiocese (chair, 1981-1986); Minnesota Women's Fund (executive comittee, 1983-);

Children's Theatre and School, Minneapolis (board member, 1984-). *Interests:* Journalism, writing; American Indian education— program designer, evaluator, administrator; American Indian alcoholism and related problems; employment-program designer, board member, policy-maker; American Indian urban studies. *Biographical sources: Let My People Know: American Indian Journalism,* James E. and Sharon M. Murphy (University of Oklahoma Press, 1981); *I Am the Fire of Time: The Voices of Native American Women,* Jane Katz, editor (E.P. Dutton, 1977); *Minnesota Women's Yearbook,* 1978, 1984; *Who's Who in the Midwest; Who's Who of American Women; Contemporary Native American Address* (Brigham Young University, 1977; *Women of Color poster series* (St. Paul Public Schools, 1980). *Published works: Indian Alcoholism in St. Paul,* study with Michael Miller (University of Minnesota, 1981); "Native American Women: Twilight of a Long Maidenhood," *Comparative Perspectives of Third World Women,* Beverly Lindsay, editor (Praeger, 1980); "On Women's Rights for Native Peoples" (Akwesasne Notes, 1975); editor, *Indian Education,* National Indian Education Association, 1973-1974; "The Federal Indian Relationship," *Civil Rights Digest,* Oct., 1973; editor, *Legislative Review,* 1971-1973.

WOODARD, DON 1935-
(Indian arts dealer)

Born May 12, 1935, Gallup, N.M. *Education:* University of New Mexico, B.A., 1957; North Arizona University, M.A., 1972. *Principal occupation:* Indian arts dealer. *Home address:* Box BBB, Cortez, Colo. 81321. *Affiliation:* Owner, Woodard's Indian Arts, Gallup, N.M., 1952-1972; owner, Don Woodard's Indian Trading Post, Cortez, Colo., 1972-. *Other professional posts:* Land claims archaeologist for the Pueblos of Zia, Santa Anna, Jemez, Acoma and Laguna; group leader for Navajo Long Walk Re-enactment. *Memberships:* Inter-Tribal Indian Ceremonial, Gallup, N.M. (board member; program director; exhibition hall chairman); American Society of Appraisers; Indians Arts and Crafts Association (board member; ethics committee chairman). *Interests:* Indian arts and crafts; anthropology .

WOODARD, TOM 1936-
(Indian arts and crafts dealer)

Born August 15, 1936, Gallup, N.M. *Education:* University of Arizona, 1958-1964. *Principal occupation:* Indian arts and crafts dealer, Gallup, N.M., 1960-. *Home address:* 1100 S. Grandview, Gallup, N.M. 87301. *Other professional post:* Collector f Indian art. Memberships: Indian Arts and Crafts Association (president); New Mexico Retail Association (president-elect). *Interests:* Judge at Indian arts and crafts shows.

WOOSLEY, ANNE I.
(director-Amerind Foundation)

Affiliation: Director, The Amerind Foundation, Inc., Dragoon, Ariz. 85609.

WOPSOCK, FRANK (Ute)
(tribal chairman)

Affiliation: Chairman, Uintah and Ouray Tribal Business Council, Fort Duchesne, Utah 84026.

WRIGHT, BARTON A. 1920-
(B.I.A. chief administrator)

Born December 21, 1920, Bisbee, Ariz. *Education:* University of Arizona, B.A., 1952, M.A., 1954. *Principal occupation:* B.I.A. chief administrator. *Address:* Bureau of Indian Affairs, Room 3519N, 1951 Constitution Ave., N.W., Washington, D.C. 20245. *Affiliations:* Archaeologist, Amerind Foundation, Dragoon, Ariz., 1952-1955; curator, Museum of Nothern Arizona, Flagstaff, Ariz., 1955-1957; scientific director, Museum of Man, San Diego, Calif., 1977-1982; chief, Administration, Bureau of Indian Affairs, Washington, D.C., 1982-. *Military service:* U.S. Army, 1943-1946. *Memberships:* American Association of Museums, 1971-; Western Museums League (vice president, 1964-); Society for American Archaeology, 1950-; Arizona-Nevada Academy of Science, 1958-; Indian Arts and Crafts Association (board member); Societe des Amerinistes de Paris, 1978-. *Interests:* Mr. Wright writes, "Museology, especially in the fields of anthropology and geology; ethnology of Hopi Indians; arts and crafts of

Southwestern Indians; painting and drawing the U.S. Southwest; history of the U.S. Southwest; judging arts and crafts shows; advising on the establishment and care of cultural centers." *Biographical sources: Who's Who in the West; Who's Who in American Art. Published works: Kachinas: A Hopi Artist's Documentary* (Northland Press-Heard Museum, 1973); *Kachinas: The Goldwater Collection* (Heard Museum, 1975); *The Unchanging Hopi* (Northland Press, 1975); *Pueblo Shields* (Northland Press, 1976); *Hopi Kachinas, Guide to Collecting Dolls* (Northland Press, 1977).

WRIGHT, FRANK, Jr. (Puyallup)
(tribal chairman)

Affiliation: Chairman, Puyallup Tribal Council, 2002 E. 28th St., Tacoma, Wash. 98404.

WYNECOOP, JOSEPH A. (Spokane)
1919-
(manager, aerospace-information support)

Born March 22, 1919, Reardan, Wash. *Education:* Eastern Washington University, B.A., 1946; Glendale University College of Law, B.S.L., 1971. *Principal occupation:* Manager, aerospace-information support. *Home address:* 3832 Hillway Dr., Glendale, Calif. 91208. *Affiliations:* Training director, 1968-1971, administrative specialist, 1971-1974, advisory committee for minority affairs, 1970-1976, Affirmative Action Program representative, 1970-, Jet Propulsion Laboratory, California Institute of Technology, Pasadena, Calif. *Military service:* U.S. Air Force, 1942-1968 (Lt. Colonel, retired; Air Force Outstanding Unit Award; Medal for Humane Action; Joint Chiefs of Staff Commendation Medal; Air Force Commendation Medal; Alexander the Great Medal (Greece); Greek Joint Chiefs Letter of Commendation). *Community activities:* All American Indian Celebration Corporation (vice president and director, 1969-1970); Governor's "California Indian Assistance Project" (representative, 1969-1974); American Indian Enterprise (vice president, 1969-1975); Pacific Northwest Indian Center (financial commissioner, 1971-1973). *Memberships:* Indian Scholarship Fund Associa-

tion (director and vice president, 1969-1975); Urban Indian Development Association (vice president, 1969-1975); Retired Officers Association, 1968-; Air Force Association, 1976-; National Congress of American Indians (member of board, Indian Scholarship Committee, 1977-).

Y

YELLOWHAMMER, JOYCE
(office manager-Indian association)

Affiliation: Office manager, National Indian Education Association, 1115 Second Ave. South, Minneapolis, Minn. 55403.

YORK, KENNETH HAROLD
(Mississippi Choctaw) 1948-
(educational consultant)

Born May 15, 1948, Neshoba County, Miss. *Education:* Northeastern Oklahoma State University, Tahlequah, B.A., 1971; University of Minnesota, M.A. (Educational Administration), 1975. *Principal occupation:* Educational consultant. *Home address:* 807 Black Jack Rd., Philadelphia, Miss. 39350. *Affiliations:* President, Tisho and Associates, Philadelphia, Miss. (ten years); president, Choctaw Associated Members for Progress, Philadelphia, Miss. (three years). *Other professional post:* Adjunct professor, Mississippi State University. *Community activities:* Choctaw Federal Credit Union (president, 1976-1983); Pearl River Choctaw Commuity Development Club (president, 1985-1986); St. Theresa Catholic Church Council, 1985-. *Memberships:* National Indian Education Association; National Association of Bilingual Education; International Reading Association. *Awards, honors:* American Legion's Boys State, 1966; Pearl Service Award, 1982; Outstanding Young Men of America, 1976. *Interests:* Bilingual bicultural education; literacy among Native Americans; farming and agribusiness; business and management development among Native Americans; sovereignty and human rights.

Biographical sources: Meridian Star, 1983; "Faces," video program on Mississippi ETV; "Mississippi Roads," video documentary on Mississippi ETV. *Published works: Recommended Teacher Training Curriculum for Native American Bilingual Education Programs* (Mississippi State University, 1977); *Working with the Bilingual Commuity* (National Clearinghouse for Bilingual Education, 1979) *Made By Hand: Mississippi Folk Art* (Mississippi History and Archives, 1980); *LaSalle and His Legacy: Frenchmen and Indians in the Lower Mississippi Valley* (University of Mississippi Press, 1982).

YOUCKTON, PERCY (Chehalis)
(tribal chairman)

Affiliation: Chehalis Community Council, P.O. Box 536, Oakville, Wash. 98568.

YOUNGDEER, ROBERT (Eastern Band Cherokee)
(tribal chief)

Affiliation: Chief, Eastern Band of Cherokee Indians, P.O. Box 455, Cherokee, N.C. 28719.

Z

ZAH, PETERSON (Navajo) 1937-
(tribal chairman)

Born December 2, 1937, Low Mountain, Ariz. *Education:* Phoenix College, A.A., 1960; Arizona State University, B.A. (Education), 1963. *Principal occupation:* Chairman, Navajo Nation, Window Rock, Ariz., 1983-. *Home address:* P.O. Box 308, Window Rock, Ariz. 86515. *Other professional posts:* Education-secondary education techer; executive director of DNA—People's Legal Services. *Community activities:* Wide Public School Association; Window Rock School Board (past president); National Association of the Indian Legal Services (founder); Arizona State Advisory Committee to the U.S. Civil Rights Commission (member). *Memberships:* Navajo Education & Scholarship

Foundation; National Tribal Chairmen's Association; Council of Energy Resource Tribes. *Awards, honors:* Humanitarian Award, City of Albuquerque, N.M.—Mayor Harry Kinney; Honorary Doctorate (Humanitarium), Santa Fe College.

ZAHARLICK, ANN MARIE, 1947-
(professor of anthropology)

Born March 24, 1947, Scranton, Pa. *Education:* Cedar Crest College, B.A., 1969; Lehigh University, M.A., 1973; The American University, Ph.D., 1977 (Dissertation: *Picuris Syntax). Principal occupation:* Professor of anthropology. *Home address:* 4071 Garrett Dr. West, Columbus, Ohio 43214. *Affiliations:* Instructor and curriculum development specialist, Bilingual/Multicultural Teacher Training Program for Native Americans, The University of Albuquerque, N.M., 1975-1977; assistant professor and language development specialist, Native American Bilingual Teacher Education Program, The University of Albuquerque, 1977-1979; assistant professor, Department of Anthropology, The Ohio State University, Columbus, Ohio, 1979-. *Other professional posts:* Instructor, Acoma Pueblo Bilingual Education Program, 1978; instructor, Sandia Pueblo Language Program. *Research/fieldwork:* Research on the Picuris language, Picuris Pueblo, N.M., 1973; research on Picuris syntax, Picuris and Taos, N.M., 1974-1976; development of Keresan language spoken by the pueblos of Acoma, Cochiti, Santo Domingo, Laguna, Zia, Santa Ana, and San Felipe, and development of curriculum guides and bilingual education materials in Keres and Picuris; analysis of Picuris syntax and semology—updating of John P. Harrington's *Picuris Children's Stories* and preparation of a dictionary and grammar for use in the Picuris bilingual education program, 1976-; linguistic research on passive construction and tone in Picuris, Picuris, N.M., 1980-1981. *Community activities:* Assisted in the establishment of bilingual education programs at Acoma, Laguna, Cochiti, Santa Ana, and Picuris Pueblos, 1975-1979; produced teaching guides and materials for the Picuris Bilingual Education Programs (10 stories and booklets in Picuris, 1975-); presentations on

American Indians to 4th and 5th grade students in the Albuquerque and Columbus Public Schools, 1978-1982. *Memberships:* American Anthropological Association (Fellow); American Association for the Advancement of Science; American Ethnological Society; Linguistic Association of the Southwest; Linguistic Society of America; New Mexico Association for Bilingual Education; New York Academy of Sciences; Society for Applied Anthropology (Fellow), Society for the Study of the Indigenous Languages of the Americas; Southwestern Anthropological Association; The Southwest Circle; *Southwest Journal of Linguistics* (editorial board, 1985-1987); among others. *Awards, honors:* Distinction awarded for Ph.D. comprehensive examination: Language Acculturation, 1974; The American University Dissertation Fellowship, 1974-1975; The Honor Society pf Phi Kappa Phi; Edward Sapir Award in Linguistics (for *Picuris Syntax*), The New York Academy of Sciences, 1978; nominated for Outstanding Teaching Award, College of Arts and Sciences, The Ohio State University; Certificate of Award, Ohio Coalition of Refugee Mutual Assistance Association, for volunteer service with the Laotian refugee community. *Interests:* Cultural and linguistic anthropology. *Biographical sources: Outstanding Young Women of America; Who's Who in the Midwest; The International Directory of Distinguished Leadership; Personalities of America; The World Who's Who of Women. Published works: Picuris Syntax* (University Microfilms, 1977); A Picuris/English Dictionary (in progress); *Picuris Grammar* (in progress); editor, *Native Languages of the Americas* (special issue of the *Journal of the Linguistic Association of the Southwest,* 1981); numerous book chapters, articles, book reviews, papers and presentation.

ZEPHIER, ALVIN (Yankton Sioux)
(tribal chairman)

Affiliation: Chairman, Yankton Sioux Tribal Business and Claims Committee, Route 3, Box 248, Marty, S.D. 57361.

ZILKA, CAROL L. (Cheyenne River Sioux) 1949-
(B.I.A. special educator)

Born December 24, 1949, Sioux Falls, S.D. *Education:* Mankato State University, Mankato, Minn., B.S., 1972; Pennsylvania State University, M.Ed., 1984. *Principal occupation:* Special educator. *Home address:* 9063 Giltinan Ct., Springfield, Va. 22153. *Affiliations:* Special education teacher, Hennepin Technical Centers, Hennepin, Minn. (two years); educational case manager (seven years), special education coordinator, 1984-, Office of Indian Education Programs, Eastern Area Office, Bureau of Indian Affairs, 1951 Constitution Ave., N.W., Washington, D.C. 20245. *Memberships:* Council for Exceptional Children, 1977- (Minnesota board of directors, 1979-1981; 1980 local arrangements chairperson for National Topical Conferences on seriously emotionally disturbed; 1978-1981 Minnesota convention director; 1978 Minnesota chapter #32, president; 1977 Minnesota chapter #32 publicity and membership chairperson. *Awards, honors:* 1985 Certificate of Special Achievement, Department of the Interior, Bureau of Indian Affairs; 1983 Graduate Fellowship, Pennsylvania State University, American Indian Special Education Teacher Training Program (member of first graduating class); 1980 National Council for Exceptional Children, Certificate of Appreciation (served as local arrangements chairperson for national conference on seriously emotionally disturbed; 1980 Minnesota Council for Exceptional Children, President's Award for Personal Contribution, dedicated effort and planning of Minnesota's first CEC Topical Conference; 1980 Hennepin Technical Center, Superintendent's Award for advancing professional development.

ZIOLKOWSKI, RUTH
(foundation chairperson)

Affiliation: Chairperson, Crazy Horse Memorial Foundation, Ave. of the Chiefs, Black Hills, Crazy Horse, S.D. 57730.

GEOGRAPHICAL INDEX

ARKANSAS

Fayetteville
Hoffman, Michael P.
Little Rock
Brown, Dee Alexander
Russell, Jerry

ALASKA

Anchorage
Kuhklen, Albert
Leask, Janie
Peratrovich, Roy
Roehl, Roy F.
Strucher, Jim
Bethel
Vaska, Anthony
Delta Junction
Alfonsi, John
Eagle River
Kinney, Rodney P.
Fort Yukon
Fields, Audrey
Gakona
Ewan, Roy S.
Golovin
Olson, Martin L.
Haines
Hakkinen, Elisabeth S.
Heinmiller, Carl W.
Juneau
Antiqua, Clarence
Horton, David A., Jr.
Lestenkof, Jacob
Ketchikan
Lawrence, Erma G.
Kodiak
Peterson, Frank R.
Neseth, Eunice
Pullar, Gordon L.
Kotzebue
Hensley, William L.
Schwind, Marie N.
Murfreesboro
Johnson, Sam
Ninilichik
Bouwens, William
Nome
Okleasik, M. LaVonne
Walters, George A.

Tenakee Springs
Soboleff, Walter A.
Yakutat
Mallott, Byron

ARIZONA

Camp Verde
Russell, Ned
Chandler
Cummings, Kendall
Cibecue
DeHose, Judy
Reyhner, Jon Allen
Dragoon
Di Peso, Charles C.
Fulton, William Dincan
Woosley, Anne I.
Flagstaff
Ambler, J. Richard
Darden, Steven
John, Angelo Marvin
Kahn, Franklin
Kealiinohomoku, Joann
Riner, Reed D.
Seaman, P. David
Fort Defiance
Brown, Wilfred
DeGroat, Ellouise
Hardy, Joseph
Ganado
Falling, LeRoy
Hohnani, Daniel
Morgan, Guy
Wauneka, Annie Dodge
Glendale
Artichoker, John Hobart
Keams Canyon
Secakuku, Alph
Kykotsmovi
Sockyma, Michael C., Jr.
Lukachukaim
Hobson, Dottie F.
Maricopa
Narcia, Leroy
Oraibi
Pentewa, Richard Sitko
Sidney, Ivan
Parker
Drennan, Anthony, Sr.
Lamb, Chalres A.
Mills, Walter R.

Peach Springs
Sinyell, Edgar
Phoenix
Blue Spruce, George, Jr.
Cain, H. Thomas
Claus, Tom
Collins, Carl
Dobyns, Henry F.
Doyel, David E.
Haranaka, Nancie
Honanie, Gilbert, Jr.
Mitchell, Wayne Lee
Shing, Le Roy Ned
Pipe Springs
Savala, Delores
Polacca
Nuvayestewa, Evangeline
Prescott
Erickson, John
McGee, Patricia
Rough Rock
Begay, Jimmie C.
Sacaton
Thompson, Edmond
San Carlos
Keller, George
Snyder, Fred
Titla, Phillip, Sr.
Scottsdale
Colton, Alfred
Tsinajinnie, Andy
Sedona
Fredericks, Oswald
Sells
Christman, Richard T.
Moore, Josiah N.
Nordwall, Curtis
Wiliams, Della R.
Somerton
Miller, Fred
Supai
Sinyella, Wayne
Teecnospos
Walker, Jerry Clayton
Tonalea
Miller, Stephen
Tsaile
Begay, Ruth Tracy
Huerta, C. Lawrence
Jackson, Dean
Tuba City
Carr, Patrick J.

Poocha, Fritz T.
Tubac
Rogers, Will, Jr.
Tucson
Bahti, Mark
Chana, Anthony M.
Deloria, Vine, Jr.
Haury, Emil W.
Officer, James E.
Ramiriz, David
Roessler, Paul Albert
Spicer, Edward Holland
Tanner, Clara Lee
Valentine
Henson, C.L.
Whiteriver
Bradley, Russell
Dodge, Henry
Lupe, Ronnie
Window Rock
Atkinson, La Verne D.
Dodge, Donald
Drake, Elroy
Gorman, Carl Nelson
Hartman, Russell P.
MacDonald, Peter, Sr.
Nelson, Michael
Tapahe, Loren
Tippeconnic, Thomas
Tsosie, Loretta A.W.
Zah, Peterson
Winslow
Sorrell, Cheryl
Yuma
Kelly, Alvin
Montague, Felix J.

CALIFORNIA

Alameda
Livermore, Earl R.
Alpine
Pico, Anthony
Altadena
Morgan, Marilyn Elizabeth
Alturas
Forrest, Erin
Garcia, Norma Jean
Jones, Leo
Anaheim
Jones, Stephen S.
Murray, Donald Cylde

Bakersfield
Rogers, James Blake
Banning
Cortez, Ronald D.
Martin, Robert
Pablo, Matt
Saubel, Katherine Siva
Berkeley
Heizer, Robert F.
Big Bend
Sisk, Kenneth
Big Pine
Jones, Velma
Bishop
Frank, Earl
Saulque, Joseph C.

Bridgeport
Crawford, Maurice
Brooks
Knight, Philip
Buena Park
Aguilar, Jose V.
Burbank
Howard, Helen Addison
Campo
Pinto, Tony J.
Capistrano Beach
Di Maio, Sue
Cedarville
Phoenix, Andrew
Claremont
Batalille, Gretchan M.
Crow, Perce B.
Covelo
Lincoln, Daran
Davis
Forbes, Jack D.
Death Valley
Esteves, Pauline
El Cajon
Sandoval, Anna
Fall River Mills
Boyer, Momma Quail
Reed, Silver Star
Forestville
Hamilton, Ruby
Bidwell
Lame Bull, Lucinda
Glendale
Wynecoop, Joseph A.

Happy Camp
Brown, Vinson
Hollywood
Pencille, Herbert W.
Hoopa
Bennett, Ruth
Laguna Niguel
Stalling, Steven L.A.
Long Beach
McCone, Robert Clyde
Los Angeles
Burns, Robert I.
Hedrick, Henry E.
Heth, Charlotte Wilson
Juneau, Alfred LeRoy
Oandasan, William
Pierce, Lymon
Salabiye, Velma
Stevens, Connie
Williams, Walter L.

McArthur
Gray, Shorty
Newport Beach
Jorgennsen, Joseph G.
Oakland
Bean, Lowell John
Pacific Grove
Adams, Margaret B.
Pacific Palisades
Nash, Gary B.
Pala
Freeman, King
Palm Springs
McDermott, Richard S.
Pasadena
Houlihan, Patrick T.
Pauma Valley
Dixon, Patricia A.
Placentia
Lerner, Albert L.
Redlands
Fisher, Dorothy D.
Riverside
Beatty, Patricia
Tomhave, Jerome
Sacramento
Jaegar, Ronad
Lovely, Deborah
San Francisco
Ortiz, Roxanne D.

San Luis Obispo
Grinde, Donald A., Jr.
San Marcos
Freeman, Robert Lee
Santa Barbara
Jacobs, Wilbur R.
Sebastopol
Clark, Donald E.
Stanford
Momaday, Navarre S.
Susanville
Padilla, Nicolas J.
Visalia
Pietroforte, Alfred

COLORADO

Aurora
Ware, Kent C., II
Basalt
Honer, Janelle A.
Bellevue
Goranson, Frederick A.
Boulder
Echohawk, John E.
Eddy, Frank W.
Hill, Norbert S., Jr.
Kaschube, Dorothea V.
Phillips, George H.
Stewart, Omer C.
Waters, Deana J. H.
Cortez
Austin, Frank
Woodard, Don
Denver
Friend, David N.
Hughes, J. Donald
Punley, Randolph J.
Whitecrow, Jake L.
Durango
Cargile, Ellen Y.
Englewood
Frazier, Gregory W.
Lester, A. David
Militaire, Delbert
Fort Collins
Becenti, Francis D.
Ignacio
Burch, Leonard
Pensoneau, Ralph

Montrose
Casius, Everlyn
Towaoc
House, Ernest
Smith, Michael H.
Wheat Ridge
Goodman, Linda J.

CONNECTICUT

Greenwich
Josephy, Alvin M., Jr.
Hamden
Voight, Virginia F.
Ledyard
Hayward, Richard
New Haven
Rodriguez-Sellas, Jose E.
Norwich
Princess Rose Scribner
Portland
Walker, Willard
Uncasville
Tantaquidgeon, Gladys
Washington
Payne, Susan F.
Waterbury
Benedict, Patricia
Watertown
Cooper, Karen Coody
Westport
Scheirbeck, Helen M.

DELAWARE

Hockessin
Weslager, Clinton A.

DISTRICT OF COLUMBIA

Blumer, Thomas J.
Bush, Mitchell L., Jr.
Clary, Thomas C.
Colosimo, Thomas
Conner, Rosemary
Coulter, Robert T.
Delaware, Robert
Doss, Michael
Eden, Ronad D.

Field, Raymond
Gerard, Pat
Green, Rayna
Harjo, Susan Shown
Hart, Robert G.
Hillabrant, Walter J.
Jabbour, Alan A.
Jacobs, Harvey
Johnson, Samuel
Keely, Kay
Krenzke, Theodore
La Course, Richard V.
Leap, William L.
Lenz, Msr. Paul A.
Libhart, Myles
Little, Stewart
Lonefight, Edward
Lynn, Sharon
Martin, James
Martin, Joy
Moore, Ramona
Nicklason, Fred
Ott, William
Parker, Alan
Parker, Sharon
Press, Daniel S.
Printup, Maribel
Robinson, Rose W.
Savilla, Elmer
Shaw, Carl F.
Shunatona, Gwen
Standing Elk, Donald
Swimmer, Ross O.
Taylor-Goins, Elise
Tiger, Georgiana
Vozniak, Debbie
Washburb, Wilcomb E.
Wasile, Jeanne
White, Lincoln C.
Wright, Barton A.

FLORIDA

Crawfordville
Jones Buddy C.
Havana
Matthews, Ann M.
Hollywood
Jumper, Betty Mae
LaRoche, Harold L.
Tribbett, Norman H.
Merritt Island
McCarthy, Joan D.

Miami
Tiger, Buffalo
Orange Springs
Buford, Bettie
Sarasota
Saunooke, Osley B., Jr.

GEORGIA

Atlanta
Bealer, Alex W., III
Chamblee
Warren, Wanda E.G.
Danielsville
Hudson, Melvin, Jr.
Leesburg
Jackon, William

HAWAII

Waianae
Ide, John H.

IDAHO

Boise
Dayley, Jon P.
Chubbuck
Sheppard, Laverne
Fort Hall
Edmo, Kesley
Thompson, Duane F.
Trahant, Mark N.
Kamiah
Moffett, Walter L.
Moses, Lily L.
Slickpoo, Allen P., Sr.
Lapwai
Moran, Ernest T.
Pinkham, Allen V.
Plummer
George, Osald C.
Lasarte, Bernard J.

ILLINOIS

Carbondale
MacLachlan, Bruce B.
Cary
David, Robert C.

Chicago
Crawford, Eugene
Tax, Sol
Taylor, Rhonda Harris
Collinsville
Schusky, Ernest L.
Evansville
Borman, Leonard D.
Hoxie, Frederick E.
Urbana
Bruner, Edward M.

INDIANA

Bloomington
Hurt, Wesley R.
Parks, Douglas R.
Fremont
Munger, Lynn
Indianapolis
Cummings, Vicki
Lafayette
Berthrong, Donald J.
West Lafayette
Parman, Donald L.

IOWA

Sioux City
Conley, Robert J.
Gordon, Patricia T.
Tama
Buffalo, George, Jr.
Mitchell, Louis

KANSAS

Council Grove
Milligan, Hariet
Hays
Wilson, Raymond
Horton
Thomas, Frederick R.
Lawrence
Ahshapanek Don C.
Gipp, Gerald
Homeratha, Phil
Lieb, Bertha K.
Lounsberry, Gary R.

Manhattan
May, Cheryl
O'Brien, Patricia J.
Powhattan
Kennedy, James H.
Surveyor, Virgil R.
Reserve
Keller, Nancy
Wichita
Jones, William M.
Rohn, Arthur H.

KENTUCKY

Lexington
Duffield, Lathel F.

LOUISIANA

Natchitoches
Medford, Claude, Jr.

MAINE

Houlton
Sabattis, Clair
Mt. Vernon
Hinkley, Edward C.
Old Town
Love, Timothy
Perry
Dana, Ralpha F.
Princeton
Sanborn, James H.
Sopiel, Sylvia
Washington County
Stevens, John W.

MARYLAND

Baltimore
Richardson, Barry
Cabin John
Price, B. Leigh
Mt. Ranier
Marks, Patricia Ann
Rockville
Bryan, Richard P.
Casebolt, Jack V.
Colombel, Pierce

Elrod, Sam
Emelio, John
Exendine, Joseph, M.D.
Exendine, Leah
Felsen, James, M.D.
Gashler, Dan
Henson, Richard A.
Kaufman, Steven, M.D.
McCloskey, Richard J.
Mecklenburg, Robert
Mitchell, Jimmy
Pearson, Billy
Reyes, Launa L.
Roach, Milburn H.
Roseleigh, Patricia F.
Sharlow, James
Shea, James
Shea, W. Timothy
Smith, James R.
Stout, Sadie
Swetter, Donald A.
Thomas, Arthur
Thurman, Robert
Todd, John, M.D.
Werito, Cecilia
Wilson, William
Wheaton
Reeser, Ralph R.

MASSACHUSETTS

Amherst
Salzmann, Zdenek
Boston
Gorman, Frederick J.E.
Falmouth
Mills, Earl H.
Gay Head
Gentry, Beatrice
Jamaica Plain
Sam, Jimmy L.
Lexington
Lester, Joan
Lowell
Burtt, J. Frederic
Middleboro
Moore, Daisy P.
Monterey
McAllester, David P.
Newton Centre
Manners, Robert A.

Northampton
Salisbury, Neal
West Peabody
Johns, Joseph F.
West Yarmouth
Edmunds, Judith A.

MICHIGAN

Ann Arbor
Ford, Richard I.
Kurath, Gertrude P.
Tanner, Helen H.
Baroga
Tolonen, Myrtle
Brimley
Teeple, Wade
Coldwater
Brauker, Shirley M.
Detroit
Boyd, Rose Marie
Hillman, James
Lowry, Irene
Kalamazoo
Bank, Theodore P., III
Ludington
Powell, Dick & Donna
Marquette
Hirst, Stephen M.
Pleasant
Sowmick, Arnold
Saulte Ste. Marie
Lumsden, Joseph K.
Picotta, Alvin
Suttons Bay
Raphael, Joseph
Wilson
Miller, Thomas G.
Philemon, Henry, Sr.

MINNESOTA

Cass Lake
Mayotta, Raymond
Wadena, Darrell
White, Hartley
Golden Valley
Spotted Eagle, Chris
Grand Portage
Hendrickson, James

Granite Falls
Howell, Irene
Hatfield
Walking Elk, Mitch
Matawan
Hampton, Eber
Minneapolis
Buffalohead, W. Roger
Cornelius-Fenton, Karen
Fleming, Darrell
Heeley, Steven, J.W.
Hoebel, E. Adamson
Means, Russell
Mollenhoff, Lori
Smith, Noreen
Yellowhammer, Joyce
Morton
Prescott, Michael
Nett Lake
Donald, Gary
Ogema
Nimohoyah, Sekon
Onamia
Gahbow, Arthur
Kegg, Matthews M.
Prior Lake
Crooks, Norman
Jaeger, Robert
Red Lake
Jourdain, Roger
Whiteman, Dennis
St. Louis Park
Wittstock, Laura W.
St. Paul
Morrison, George
Spencer, Robert F.
Westermeyer, Joseph, M.D.
Welch
Wells, Vine
White Earth
Martin, Peter J.

MISSISSIPPI

Carthage
Bell, William F.
Benn, Robert C.
Philadelphia
Gibson, Clay
Isaac, Calvin J.
Mann, Robert C.
Martin, Phillip

Scott, James R.
York, Kenneth H.
Union
Brescia, William, Jr.
Walnut Grove
Francisco, Eldon

MISSOURI

St. Louis
Browman, David L.
University City
Wax, Murray L.

MONTANA

Billings
Gilliland, Hap
Lucas, Merle R.
Box Elder
Stump, Rocky, Sr.
Bozeman
Morris, C. Patrick
Old Coyote, Barney
Browning
Baker, Anson A.
Boy, Calvin J.
Fairbanks, Michael
Fisher, Joe
Old Person, Earl
Pepion, Donald D.
Butte
Taulbee, Daniel J.
Crow Agency
Pease-Windy Boy, Janine
Stewart, Donald, Sr.
East Glacier Park
Bigspring, William F., Sr.
Kuka, King D.
Elder
Pereau, John
Harlem
Main, Elmer
Perez, Franklin
Lame Deer
Beartusk, Keith L.
Hollowbreast, Donald
McDonald, Arthur L.
Rowland, Allen
Rowland, Darius

Pablo
Felsman, Joseph
McDonald, Joseph
Poplar
Charity Wing
Clincher, Bonnie M.
Hollow, Norman
Ridenhower, Marilyn
St. Ignatius
Allard, L. Doug
McDonald, Walter
Stevensville
Brown, Joseph Epes

NEBRASKA

Lincoln
Grobsmith, Elizabeth
Macy
Miller, Wallace W.
Niobrara
Kitto, Richard
Omaha
Tyndell, Wayne
Winnebago
Christie, Joe C.
Du Bray, Alfred W.
Snake, Reuben A., Jr.
Weatherly, John

NEVADA

Austin
Rosse, William, Sr.
Carson City
Belgrade, Harold
Duckwater
Millett, Jerry
Elko
Whitford, Thomas
Fallon
Moyle, Alvin
Gardnerville
Frank, Robert L.
Incline Village
Clark-Price, Margaret
Las Vegas
Collins, Adele V.
Frye, Billy J.
Surrett, Clifton R.

Nixon
Shaw, Wilfred
Winder, Nathan W.
Owyhee
McKiney, Whitney
Reno
Jacobsen, William H., Jr.
Mose, E.
Schurz
Aragon, Arnold
Willie, Elvin, Jr.
Stewart
Hunter, Robert L.
Winnemucca
Harney, Robert
Yerington
Richardson, Kenneth

NEW HAMPSHIRE

Hanover
Dorris, Michael A.

NEW JERSEY

Bergenfield
Carter, Edward R.
Elizabeth
Kraft, Herbert C.
Fort Lee
Boissevain, Ethel
Leonia
Jaffe, A.J.
New Milford
Thomas, David H.
Princeton
Rosen, Lawrence
Rockleigh
Force, Roland W.
Teaneck
Begay, Eugene A., Sr.
Woodcliff
Begay, D.Y.

NEW MEXICO

Acoma Pueblo
Juanico, Juan
Salvador, Lilly

Alamagordo
Hall, C.R.
Albuquerque
Benham, William J., Jr.
Bennett, Robert L.
Brody, J.J.
Chavers, Dean
Clarke, Frank, M.D.
Crow, John O.
Deloria, P.S.
Edmo, Lorraine P.
Elgin, Alfred G., Jr.
English, Samuel F.
Johnny, Ronald E.
Johnson, Robert
Jojola, Ted
Lewis, Dave
Little, Vincent
Montoya, Samuel
Pena, Gilbert M.
Robertson, Ellen
Shopteese, John T.
Toya, Ronald G.
Wilkinson, Gerald

Algodones
McBride, Mary
Aztec
Doerfort, Hans M.
Gorman, Clarence N.
Arroyo Hondo
Schaafsma, Polly Dix
Bernalillo
Chaves, Esquipula
Raton, Eli Seo, Sr.
Church Rock
Linford, Laurence D.
Corrales
Bennett, Noel K.
Crownpoint
Plummer, Edward O.
Dulce
Parton, Petry D.
Espanola
Singer, Lawrence
Farmington
Housh, Raymond E.
Gallup
Bennet, Kay C.
Woodard, Tom
Isleta
Lucerno, Alvino

Jemez Pueblo
Momaday, Al
Momaday, Natachee S.
Las Vegas
Orr, Howell M.
Los Alamos
Harlow, Francis, H.
Mescalero
Chino, Wendell
Mora
Naranjo, Tito E.
Navajo
Jones, David S.
Portales
Agogino, George A.
Ruidoso
Ball, Eve
San Felipe Pueblo
Tenorio, Frank
San Juan Pueblo
Garcia, Marcelino
Trujillo, Jose E.
San Ysidro
Pino, Augustin
Santa Fe
Aguilar, Alfred
Ballard, Louis W.
Boissiere, Robert
Bovis, Pierre G.
Calkin, Laurie A.
Carpio, Jose
Dailey, Charles
Haozous, Bob
Hinds, Patrick S.
Houser, Allan
Ladd, Edmund J.
Lang, Richard W.
Lomahaftewa, Linda
McGrath, James A.
McGreevy, Susan B.
Montoya, Geronima C.
New, Lloyd H.
Ortiz, Alfonso A.
Padilla, Joe A.
Parra, Donna C.
Parrish, Rain
Parsons, Neil
Perez, David
Polese, Richard
Popovi Da
Sanchez, Gilbert
Scholder, Fritz
Viarrial, Jacob

Wade, Jon C.
Whitman, Kathy
Santo Domingo Pueblo
Garcia, Alex
Shiprock
Dodge, Marjorie T.
McCabe, Edward, Jr.
Taos
Gorman, R.C.
Sandoval, Joseph C.
Tohatchi
Bitsie, Oscar
Zuni
Lewis, Robert E.
Montgomery, John
Simplico, Chauncey
Tsabetsaye, Roger J.

NEW YORK

Basom
Sundown, Chief Corbett
Webster, Emerson C.
Briarwood
Hines, Mifauney S.
Brooklyn
Beatty, John J.
Bush, Michael A.
Eastchester
Oestreicher, David M.
Geneseo
Judkins, Russell A.
Gowanda
Mohawk, John
Guilderland
Samuelson, Lillien T.

Hogansburg
Cook, John A.
Garrow, Leonard
Jacobs, Alex A.
Swamp, Chief Jake
Huntington
Owens, Roger C.
Irving
Nitsch, Twylah H.
Williams, Dean V.
Katonah
Shoumatoff, Nicholas A.

Lewiston
Hewitt, Arnold
Patterson, Elma
Lockport
Newman, Harrison
Mastic
Beller, Samuel W., Jr.
Mastic Beach
Reason, Jamie T.

New York
Barz, Sandra
Dockstader, Frederick J.
Eager, George B.
Highwater, Jamake
James, Walter S., Jr.
Kreipe, Matha
McCord, David
Means, William A.
Roubideaux, Nanette S.
Smith, James G.E.
Starchild, Adam A.
Unger, Steven
Weatherford, Elizabeth
Nedrow
Shenandoah, Leon
Niagara Falls
Green, Elwood
Miller, Huron
Wilson, Duffy
Onchiota
Fadden, John K.
Fadden, Ray
Oneida
Goff, David J.
Ossining
Brennan, Louis A.
Poughkeepsie
Merrell, James H.
Rochester
Bell, Amelia R.
Hayes, Charles F., III
Hill, Arleigh
Rooseveltown
Rokwaho (Dan Thompson)
Salamanca
Abrams, George H.J.
Heron, George D.
John, Calvin
Vanatta, Shirley P.
Slingerlands
Fenton, William N.

Staten Island
Summers-Fitzgerald, Diosa
Syracuse
Seneca, William
Valley Stream
Cooke, David C.
Warnerville
Jimmie, Luke
Johannsen, Christina B.

NORTH CAROLINA

Cherokee
Chiltoskey, Goingback
Crowe, Amanda
Hughes, Juanita
Muskrat, Jeff W.
Robinson, Nathan W.
Wilnotu, John J.
Youngdeer, Robert
Durham
La Barre, Weston
Gastonia
Stout, Richard A.
Watts, Steven M.
Hollister
Richardson, Patricia R.
Laurinburg
Wetmore, Ruth L.
Maxton
Chief Wise Owl
Mooresville
Bonney, Rachel A.
Pembroke
Chavis, Angela Y.
Locklear, Juanita O.

NORTH DAKOTA

Belcourt
Emgee, Sr. Judith
Kepkin, Debbie L.
Lafromboise, Richard
Monette, Gerald
Schindler, Duane E.
Fort Totten
Davis, Rose-Marie
White, Elmer, Sr.
Fort Yates
Chase the Bear, Lionel
Crowfeather, Isabelle

Murphy, Charles W.
Stein, Wayne
New Town
Spotted Bear, Alyce
Wahpeton
LeRoy Chief

OHIO

Centerville
Eid, Leroy V.
Cincinnati
Neely, Sharlotte
Cleveland Heights
Callender, Charles
Columbus
Zaharlick, Ann Marie
Pepper Pike
Mahan, Harold D.
Piqua
Griffith, Gladys G.
Portsmouth
Brown, Charles Asa
Tippecanoe
AmyLee
Worthington
Chapman, Jane

OKLAHOMA

Ada
Denton, Coye E.
Pettigrew. Jackson D.
Anadarko
French, Edgar L., Jr.
Johnson, Patricia L.
Lamar, Newton
Littlechief, Barthell
Poolaw, Linda S.
Ragsdale, William P.
Stephenson, Bonnie
Thompson, Rupert
Wickcliffe, Dennis L.
Apache
Cleghorn, Mildred
Ardmore
Beaver, Fred
Browning, Zane
Lofton, Gene T.
Binger
Shemayne, Henry

Broken Bow
Smith, LaMarr
Chouteau
Tyner, James W.
Claremore
Collins, Reba N.
Concho
Edwards, John
Flores, William V.
Duncan
Spivey, Towana
Durant
Roberts, Hollis
Edmond
Cannon, T.C.
Fairland
Baker, Arlene R.
Fairfax
Moore, Tracey Ann
Tall Chief, George Eves
Fort Gibson
West, W. Richard
Gracemont
Standing, Nettie L.
Kaw City
Chouteau, M.M.
Lawton
Kahrahrah, Bernard
Locust Valley
Stone, Willard
McCloud
Wahpehah, James
Miami
Daugherty, John, Jr.
Follis, William
Moore, Louis
Naylor, Jack
Olds, Forest D.
Muskogee
Edmondson, Ed.
Ellison, Thomas J.
Hansen, Joan L.
Harrington, Virgil N.
Horsechief, Mary A.
Moore, Paul V.
Watkins, Mary Beth
Newkirk
James, Willie
Norman
Barse, Harold G.
Johnston, Robert
Moore, John H.

Opler, Moris E.
Simpson, Dana
Siria, Larry
Okmulgee
Cox, Claude
Oklahoma City
Doering, Mavis
Doonkeen, Eula N.
Downing, Ernest V.
Giago, Millie
Giago, Robert
Hampton, Carol C.M.
Hampton, James W., M.D.
Hunter, Terry
James, Overton
Meredith, Howard L.
Ragan, Connie S.
Okmulgee
Little, Harley
Robinson, Gary
Pawhuska
Shoemata, Jack
Pawnee
Chapman, Robert L.
Perkins
Murray, Wallace C.
Ponca City
Castor, Delia F.
Littlecook, Oliver
Quapaw
McKibben, Jesse
Sasakwa
Brown, John
Shawnee
Barrett, John A.
Bruno, Robert L.
Levi, Jerry R.
Levier, Francis A.
Little Axe, Danny
Sulcer, Patrick K.
Walker, Joe B.
Stillwater
Goodbear, Pearl R.G.
Stroud
Falls, Alvin
Tahlequah
Hair, John
Mankiller, Wilma P.
Parker, Joe
Sumner, Delores T.
Tecumseh
Bowlán, Lori A.

Tishomingo
Hutchings, Evelyn K.
Tulsa
Canard, Curtis Lee
Echohawk, Brummet
Krepps, Ethel C.
McClelland, John
McCombs, Solomon
Walter
Riddles, Leonard
Washita
Bales, Jean E.M.
Wewoka
Milan, James
Norman, Margaret J.
Shipp, Cecil
Woodward
Patterson, Patrick
Wyandotte
Cotter, Leonard N.

OREGON

Albany
Taylor, Virginia
Bandon
Red She Bear
Burns
Shake Spear, Vernon
Eugene
Cochran, George M.
Grande Ronde
Harrison, Katherine
Klamath Falls
Norris, Leonard
Monmouth
Walking Bull, Charles
Walking Bull, Montana
Pendleton
Patawa, Elwood
Sandoval, William
Portland
Engelstad, Kurt
Gogol, John M.
Speaks, Stanley M.
Voget, Fred W.
Roseburg
Jackson, Charles
Salem
Gray, Gerald J.

Siletz
Pigsley, Delores
Topash, Bernard
Warm Springs
Cornett, James D.
Jackson, Zane, Sr.
Smith, Gerald L.
Welch, Kay
West Linn
Lampman, Evelyn S.

PENNSYLVANIA

Allentown
Messinger, Carla J.S.
Brookville
Parker, E.M.
Bryn Mawr
DeLaguna, Frederica
Chester
Wallace, Anthony F.C.
Davids
King, Mary E.
Drexel Hill
Smith, Louise
Gettysburg
Porter, Frank W., III
Philadelphia
Glazer, Suzy
Juancito, Charles H.
Oliviero, Melanie Beth
Pittsburgh
Simms, Russell
State College
Noley, Grayson
Turbotville
Fogelman, Gary L.

RHODE ISLAND

Barrington
Hail, Barbara A.
Bristol
Gentis, Thierry
Giddings, Ruth E.
Kenyon
Watson, George

SOUTH CAROLINA

Rock Hill
Beck, Samuel
George, Evans M., Jr.
Haire, Wenonah G.
Sanders, E. Fred

SOUTH DAKOTA

Agency Village
Hawkins, Russell
Crazy Horse
Ziolkowsky, Ruth
Custer
Nauman, Chalres W.
Nauman, H. Jane
Eagle Butte
Garreaux, Hazel
Miner, Marcella
Rave, Austin J.
Rudell, J. Preston, Jr.
Thunder Hawk, Madonna
Flandreau
Ross, Agnes Allen
Sorensen, Carolyn
Wakeman, Richard K.
Fort Thompson
Kannon, Clyde D.
Morgan, Donald I
Wells, Wallace
Whitener, Donald E.
Lower Brule
O'Connor, Leo
Spears, Patrick
Marty
Zephier, Alvin
Mission
Beauvais, Archie B.
Dyc, Gloria
Loudner, Godfrey, Jr.
Ortiz, Simon J.
Oglala
Nespor, Elsie P.
Pierre
Canaday, Dayton W.
Kingman, A. Gay
Skye, Clarence
Pine Ridge
Bettleyoun, Lulu F.
Keith, C. Hobart
Kurth, Rev. E.J.

Simon, Bro. C.M.
Rapid City
Shunk, Harold W.
Sneve, Virgina D.H.
Rosebud
Gipp, William C.
Two Hawk, Webster
St. Francis
Gill, Joseph C.
White Hat, Albert H.
Sisseton
Houser, Schuyler
Spencer, Hargle
Spearfish
Theisc, R.D.
Stephen
Ross, Donald
Sturgis
Lee, Robert H.
Vermillion
Evans, Wayne H.
Hoover, Herbert T.
Howe, Oscar
Wagner
Cournoyer, Frank
Hare, Herbert
Howell, George E.

TENNESSEE

Memphis
White, Lonnie J.
Moscow
Fogelman, Billye Y.S.
Murfreesboro
Rolator, Fred S.
Nashville
Evans, Rex
Ferguson, Robert B.
Signal Mountain
Steele, William O.
Strawberry Plains
Peshewa, Macaki

TEXAS

Alpine
Elam, Earl H.
Austin
Apodaca, Raymond D.
Newcomb, William W., Jr.

Dallas
Grispe, Larry
Hail, Raven
El Paso
Hiser, Johny R.
Ramiriz, Raymond
Trussell, Larry
Grand Prairie
Lucero, Richard, Jr.
Lockhart
Falley, Nanci
Ralls
Parker, Wayne
Redwater
Morgan, Ronald J.
San Antonio
Adams, Richard E.W.

UTAH

Blanding
Clah, Herbert, Jr.
Boulder
Hardy, Dee
Centerville
Parashonts, Travis N.
Fort Duchesne
Collier, Lavern
Dincan, Clifford
Wopsock, Frank
Ibapah
Steele, Chester
Salt Lake City
Chiago, Robert K.
Clemmer, Janice W.
Crampton, C. Gregory
Madsen, Brigham D.
McLean, Robert E.
Overfield, Theresa

VIRGINIA

Alexandria
Engles, William L.
Fox, Dennis R.
Fox, Sandra J.H.
Matte, Sara J.
Arlington
Bruce, Louis R.
Dalrymple, Katherine C.
Harrison, David C.
Oxendine. Thomas

Taylor, Peter S.
Vasquez, Joseph C.
Falls Church
McElvain, W. Lee
Pale Moon, Princess
Viola, Herman J.
McLean
Wilcox, U. Vincent
Oakton
Armagost, James G.
MacNabb, Alexander S.
Reston
Ducheneaux, Franklin D.
Springfield
Holmes, Beverly C.
Monsen, Marie A.
Zilka, Carol L.
Vienna
Kickingbird, K. Kirke

WASHINGTON

Anacortes
Jones, Joan M.
Ariel
Smith, Don Lelooska
Bellingham
Kinley, Larry
Bremerton
Dixon, Lawrence D.
Chehalis
McDonald, Miki
Cheney
Hendrickx, Leonard
Darrington
Grant, Morris
Moses, David -
Davenport
Cook-Lynn, Elizabeth
Deming
Cooper, harry E.
Inchelium
Bourgeau, Dean
Kingston
Charles, Ronald G.
La Push
Jackson, Walter
Marysville
Jones, Stanley, Sr.
Moses Lake
Ruby, Robert, M.D.

Nespelem
Davis, George
Owhi, Harry
Oakville
Youckton, Percy
Olympia
Wells, Richard
Omak
Marchand, Thelma
Nicholson, Narcisse, Jr.
Port Angeles
Charles, Alan
Mike, Lorna J.
Port Orchard
DeBoer, Roy J.
Pullman
Ackerman, Lillian A.
Ackerman, Robert E.
Goss, James A.
Seattle
Morris, Elizabeth
Paul, Blair F.
Price, Frank
Quimby, George I.
Taylor, Gerald W.
Whitebear, Bernie
Shelton
Peterson, Gary
Whittener, David
Spokane
Brown, Joseph
James, Wabun
Sun Bear
Tacoma
Soboleff, Sasha
Wright, Frank, Jr.
Taholah
Delacruz, Joseph
Tokeland
Whitish, Rachel
Tonasket
Nicholson, Mary E.
Toppenish
Hokansen, Sherry
Jim, Roger R., Sr.
Olney, Hiram
Usk
Nenema, Glen
Wellpinit
Hill, James W.
Reutlinger, Barbara N.

302

Wenatchee
Hollow, A.E.
Hollow, Maude C.

WISCONSIN

Appleton
Skenandore, Paul A.
Ashland
Corbine, Joseph
Bayfield
Grunde, Richard
Eau Claire
Satz, Ronald N.
Fairchild
Thunder, Faye E.
Green Bay
Clifton, James A.
Hayward
Baker, Odric
DeMain, Paul
Gross, Mike
Schlender, James
Kenosha
Shipek, Florence C.
Keshena
Skenedore, Lynn
Lac du Flambeau
Dodge, Gary
Wildcat, William
Madison
Baerreis, David A.
Beaudin, John A.
Williams, Floyd
Williams, Robert A., Jr.
Milwaukee
Horsman, Reginald
Kehoe, Alice Beck
Lurie, Nancy O.
Prucha, Francis P.
Oneida
Gollnick, William
Powless, Purcell
Skenadore, Frances
Smith, Robert
Oregon
Deer, Ada E.
Seymour
Smith, Sheila S.
Tomah
Funmaker, Kenneth, Sr.
Redcloud, Merlin

Wauwatosa
Chicks, Sheldon A.
Webster
Taylor, Gene

WYOMING

Cody
Horse, Billy Evans
Horse Capture, George P.
Fort Washakie
Harris, Robert N., Sr.
Moose
Laubin, Gladys W.
Laubin, Reginald K.
Rock Springs
Neaman, Kenneth L.
St, Stephens
Headley, Louis R.

CANADA

ALBERTA
Calgary
Dempsey, Hugh A.
Heinrich, Albert C.

BRITISH COLUMBIA
Delta
Jilek, Wolfgang, M.D.
Jilek-Aall, Louise, M.D.
Vancouver
Ames, Michael M.
Maracle, Brian
Ridington, Robin

MANITOBA
Winnipeg
Laviolette, Rev. G. Omi
Townsend, Joan B.

NEW BRUNSWICK
Fredericton
Erickson, Vincent O.

N.W.T.
Yellowknife
Erasmus, Georges H.

NOVA SCOTIA
Halifax
McGee, Harold F., Jr.
Tantallon
Whitehead, Ruth H.

ONTARIO
Burlington
Damas, David
Nepean
Whiteside, Don
Ottawa
Cox, Bruce
Lee, Thomas E.
Peacock, Kenneth
Richmond Hill
Johnston, Basil H.
Toronto
Mason, K. Goyle

QUEBEC
Cantley
MacDonald, George F.

SASKATCHEWAN
Saskatoon
Fritz, Linda
Purich, Don
Waldram, James B.

HONG KONG
Shatin
Chiao, Chien

JAPAN
Ehime
Ballard, W.L.